DATE DUE

The Continental Novel:
A Checklist of Criticism in English
1900–1966

E. I. Kearney

and

L. S. Fitzgerald

The Scarecrow Press, Inc.

Metuchen, N. J.   1968

Dedicated to
J. P. F. and M. L. K.

Preface

This checklist has been compiled as a reference guide to much of the twentieth century (1900-1966) English literary criticism of the continental novel (including the novelle). Although not a complete bibliography, the work contains many items not conveniently categorized elsewhere, and may serve as a particularly useful guide for the novels of those authors for whom no complete listing of critical materials is yet available.

All of the criticisms listed herein have been read by the compilers. The page numbers refer to specific major criticism of each cited novel; minor references may appear elsewhere in the same work. Selective judgment was used only in relation to the amount of critical comment, with very brief criticism sometimes included for novels that have few items of reference. The amount of material read in order to compile this checklist made it impossible, except in a few cases, to check duplicate entries that might be condensations, expansions, or reprints of the original criticism. Such items are therefore listed separately.

In all sections except The Spanish and Portuguese Novel, most of the novel titles have been given in English. Original titles have been retained, however, for (1) some untranslated novels; (2) some translated novels commonly referred to by their untranslated titles; and (3) some novels that have several English translations with varying nonliteral versions of the original titles. Following the common practice of literary critics, we have retained the original titles of Spanish novels, many of which have not as yet been translated. Frequently-used English translations appear in parentheses after some of the Spanish titles.

Works of short fiction, travel fiction, and autobiographical fiction have been included in this checklist if various critics have referred to them as novels or novelles. If a novel is one of a series, additional items of criticism will often be found listed under the collective title, e.g., <u>Human Comedy</u>.

We wish to express our appreciation to the library staffs at the University of California at Los Angeles, the University of Southern California, and the Los Angeles Central Library--particularly in the Literature and Foreign Language departments--for their willing cooperation in helping to locate materials and to check information. Special thanks are also extended to our colleague Rudy J. Fuentes for his advice and assistance.

E. I. K.
L. S. F.

Table of Contents

Periodical Titles with Abbreviations Used in this Work

Aatseel	Aatseel Bulletin
ABC	American Book Collector
Accent	
AGR	American-German Review
AI	American Imago
American Journal of Sociology	
American Journal of Theology	
American Law Review	
American Review on the Soviet Union	
Anales Cervantinos	
Approach	
AQ	American Quarterly
AR	Antioch Review
ArQ	Arizona Quarterly
ASch	American Scholar
ASLHM	American Society of Legion of Honor Magazine
ASR	American-Scandinavian Review
Atenea	
Atlantic	
AUMLA	Journal of the Australasian Universities Language and Literature Association
BA	Books Abroad
BHR	Bibliotheque d'Humanisme et Renaissance
BHS	Bulletin of Hispanic Studies
Blackwood's Mag	Blackwood's Magazine
Bookman	
BSS	Bulletin of Spanish Studies
BuR	Bucknell Review
BUS	Bucknell University Studies
CalSS	California Slavic Studies
CathW	Catholic World
CC	Cross Currents
CE	College English
Centennial Review	
Chimera	
ChiR	Chicago Review
Christendom	
Christian Cent	Christian Century
ChS	Christian Scholar
CHSQ	California Historical Society Quarterly
Cithara (St. Bonaventure University)	
CJ	Classical Journal

CJF	Chicago Jewish Forum
CJR	Contemporary Jewish Record
CL	Comparative Literature
CLAJ	College Language Association Journal (Morgan State College, Baltimore)
ClareQ	Claremont Quarterly (Claremont, California)
CLS	Comparative Literature Studies (University of Maryland)
CMLR	Canadian Modern Language Review
ColQ	Colorado Quarterly
Commentary	
Commonweal	
ConRev	Contemporary Review
Cornhill	
CQR	Church Quarterly Review
Crit	Critique: Studies in Modern Fiction
Criticism	
Critique (Paris)	
CritQ	Critical Quarterly
CSP	Canadian Slavonic Papers
CUASRLL	Catholic University of America Studies in Romance Languages and Literatures
CUF	Columbia University Forum
Culture	
Daedalus (Proc. American Academy of Arts and Sciences)	
DelN	Delaware Notes
Delta (Amsterdam)	
Diderot Studies (Geneve)	
DownR	Downside Review
DR	Dalhousie Review
DubR	Dublin Review (London)
DVLG	Deutsche Vjerteljahresschrift fur Literaturwissenschaft und Geistesgeschichte
Economica	
ECr	L'Esprit Createur (Minneapolis)
Edda	
EDH	Essays by Divers Hands
Edinburgh Review	
EE	East Europe
EIC	Essays in Criticism (Oxford)
EJ	English Journal
EM	English Miscellany
Encounter (London)	
ER	English Review
Essays in French Lit	Essays in French Literature
ESl	Etudes Slaves et Est-Europeennes
Ethics	
Euphorion (Heidelberg)	
EUQ	Emory University Quarterly

EWR	East-West Review (Doshisha University, Kyoto, Japan)
Expl	Explicator
FHS	French Historical Studies
FiR	Filologia Romanza
FMLS	Forum for Modern Language Studies (University of St. Andrews, Scotland)
Forum H	Forum (Houston)
FR	French Review
Free World	
FS	French Studies
GL&L	German Life and Letters
GQ	German Quarterly
GR	Germanic Review
Harpers	
Harvard Studies and Notes in Philology	
Hispania (University of Kansas)	
History Today	
HJ	Hibbert Journal
HMP	Homenaje a Menendez Pidal
Horizon	
HR	Hispanic Review
HSS	Harvard Slavic Studies
HTR	Harvard Theological Review
HudR	Hudson Review
HunQ	Hungarian Quarterly (New York)
IJSLP	International Journal of Slavic Linguistics and Poetics
ILA	International Literary Annual (London)
International Journal of Ethics	
IQ	Italian Quarterly
IS	Italian Studies
ISLL	Illinois Studies in Language and Literature
ISS	Indiana Slavic Studies
Italica	
JAAC	Journal of Aesthetics and Art Criticism
JAF	Journal of American Folklore
JEGP	Journal of English and Germanic Philology
JGLS	Journal of the Gypsy Lore Society
JHI	Journal of the History of Ideas
JJR	James Joyce Review
Journal of Criminal Law	
Journal of Politics	
JP	Journal of Philosophy
JR	Journal of Religion
Judaism	
KFLQ	Kentucky Foreign Language Quarterly
KR	Kenyon Review
Landfall	
L&P	Literature and Psychology (New York)

LB	Leuvense Bijdragen
LE&W	Literature East and West
Life and Letters Today	
Listener	
LitR	Literary Review
Lituanus: Lithuanian Quarterly (Chicago)	
Living Age	
LMerc	London Mercury
LonM	London Magazine
LQR	London Quarterly Review
Mainstream	
M&L	Music and Letters
MD	Modern Drama
Meanjin	Meanjin Quarterly (University of Melbourne)
Methodist Review	
MFS	Modern Fiction Studies
MidQ	Midwest Quarterly
MinnR	Minnesota Review
MJ	Menorah Journal
ML	Modern Languages
MLF	Modern Language Forum
MLJ	Modern Language Journal
MLN	Modern Language Notes
MLQ	Modern Language Quarterly
MLR	Modern Language Review
ModA	Modern Age (Chicago)
Monatshefte	
Month	The Month
MP	Modern Philology
MQR	Michigan Quarterly Review
MR	Massachusetts Review (University of Massachusetts)
Music Rev	Music Review
Names	
N&Q	Notes and Queries
Nation (London)	
Neophil	Neophilologus (Groningen)
NEQ	New England Quarterly
NewS	New Statesman
New S&N	New Statesman and Nation
NHQ	The New Hungarian Quarterly
Nineteenth Century	
NM	Neuphilologische Mitteilungen
NMQ	New Mexico Quarterly
NYTBR	New York Times Book Review
Odyssey Rev	Odyssey Review
Opera News	
Pac Spec	Pacific Spectator
PEGS	Publications of the English Goethe Society
Person	The Personalist

Perspectives USA
PhR   Philosophical Review
PMLA   Publications of the Modern Language
                                      Association of America
POC   Problems of Communism
Poet Lore
PolR   Polish Review (New York)
PopAs   Popular Astronomy
PQ   Philological Quarterly (Iowa City)
PR   Partisan Review
PsyR   Psychoanalytic Review
QQ   Queen's Quarterly
QRL   Quarterly Review of Literature
                                      (Bard College)
Religion in Life
Renascence
Reporter
RF   Romanische Forschungen
RH   Revue Hispanique
RJ   Romanistisches Jahrbuch
RLC   Revue de Litterature Comparee
RMS   Renaissance and Modern Studies
                                      (University of Nottingham)
RN   Renaissance News
RomN   Romance Notes (University of North
                                      Carolina)
RPh   Romance Philology
RPol   Review of Politics (Notre Dame)
RR   Romanic Review
RUS   Rice University Studies
RusR   Russian Review
Salmagundi (Flushing, New York)
SAQ   South Atlantic Quarterly
SatR   Saturday Review
Scan   Scandinavica
SEEJ   Slavic and East European Journal
SEER   Slavonic and East European Review
Seminar
Shenandoah
SIR   Studies in Romanticism (Boston
                                      University)
SlavR   Slavic Review (Seattle)
Sociology and Social Research
SoR   Southern Review

Southwest Rev   Southwest Review
Soviet Russia Today
Soviet Studies
SovR   Soviet Review
SP   Studies in Philology
Spec   Spectator
SpR   Spanish Review
SR   Sewanee Review

SRen	Studies in the Renaissance
SS	Scandinavian Studies
SSF	Studies in Short Fiction (Newberry College, Newberry, S. C.)
Studies (Dublin)	
Survey	
Symposium	
TC	Twentieth Century
TCL	Twentieth Century Literature
Thought	
TLS	(London) Times Literary Supplement
TMV	Todd Memorial Volumes
TQ	Texas Quarterly (University of Texas)
TSL	Tennessee Studies in Literature
TSLL	(University of Texas) Studies in Literature and Language
TWA	Transactions of the Wisconsin Academy of Sciences, Arts, and Letters
UCPMP	University of California Publications in Modern Philology
UKCR	University Review (Kansas City, Mo.)
UNCSRLL	University of North Carolina Studies in the Romance Languages and Literatures
University of Missouri Studies	
University of Nevada Studies	
UQ	Ukrainian Quarterly
UR	Ukrainian Review
UTQ	University of Toronto Quarterly
VQR	Virginia Quarterly Review
WelshHR	Welsh History Review
Western Rev	Western Review
WHR	Western Humanities Review
World Today	
WPQ	Western Political Quarterly
WSCL	Wisconsin Studies in Contemporary Literature
WVUPP	West Virginia University Philological Papers
XUS	Xavier University Studies
YFS	Yale French Studies
YR	Yale Review

About, Edmond
  GERMAINE
    Saintsbury, George. A History of the French Novel (To
    the Close of the 19th Century). London: Macmillan and
    Company, 1919. pp. 432-434.
  TOLLA
    Saintsbury, George. A History of the French Novel (To
    the Close of the 19th Century). London: Macmillan and
    Company, 1919. pp. 428-432.

Alain-Fournier
  COLOMBE BLANCHET
    Gibson, Robert. The Quest of Alain-Fournier. London:
    Hamish Hamilton, 1953. pp. 241-246.
  LA MAISON DANS LA FORET
    Gibson, Robert. The Quest of Alain-Fournier. London:
    Hamish Hamilton, 1953. pp. 247-252.
  MIRACLES
    Ullmann, Stephen. The Image in the Modern French Novel.
    Cambridge: Cambridge University Press, 1960. pp. 100-
    102.
  THE WANDERER
    Bird, Alan. "Alain-Fournier." ConRev   184:158-162.
    September 1953.

    Champigny, Robert. "Portrait of a Symbolist Hero." Indi-
    ana University Public Humanities Series. No. 32. 1954. pp.
    1-160.

    Gibson, Robert. The Quest of Alain-Fournier. London:
    Hamish Hamilton, 1953. pp. 211-236.

    Locke, Frederick W. "LE GRAND MEAULNES: The Desire
    and the Pursuit of the Whole." Renascence 11: 135-146.
    Spring 1959.

    March, Harold M. "The 'Other Landscape' of Alain-Fourn-
    ier." PMLA 56: 266-279. March 1941.

    Paul, David. "The Mysterious Landscape: A Study of Alain-
    Fournier." Cornhill 162: 442-448. Autumn 1947.

    Savage, Catharine H. "Nostalgia in Alain-Fournier and
    Proust." FR 38: 167-172. December 1964.

    Schier, Donald. "LE GRAND MEAULNES." MLJ 36:129-132.
    March 1952.

Stubbs, Marcia C. "The Pilgrim Spirit." Accent 18: 121-
133. Spring 1958.

Turnell, Martin. "Alain-Fournier and LE GRAND
MEAULNES." SoR n. s. 2: 477-498. July 1966.

Turnell, Martin. "The Legend of Alain-Fournier." Commonweal 59: 581-582. March 1954.

Ullmann, Stephen. The Image in the Modern French
Novel. Cambridge: University Press, 1960. pp. 99-123.

Aragon, Louis
    LES COMMUNISTES
        Bree, Germaine and Margaret Guiton. An Age of Fiction:
        The French Novel from Gide to Camus. New Brunswick:
        Rutgers University Press, 1957. pp. 87-88.

        Savage, Catharine. Malraux, Sartre and Aragon as Polit-
        ical Novelists. Gainesville: University of Florida Press,
        1964. pp. 43-60.
    HOLY WEEK
        Bieber, Konrad. "A Do-It-Yourself Novel?" YFS 24: 41-
        47. Summer 1959.
    THE PASSENGERS OF DESTINY
        Bree, Germaine and Margaret Guiton. An Age of Fiction:
        The French Novel from Gide to Camus. New Brunswick:
        Rutgers University Press, 1957. pp. 85-87.
    A PEASANT FROM PARIS
        Firchow, Peter Edgerly. "NADJA and LE PAYSAN DE
        PARIS: Two Surrealist 'Novels.' " WSCL 6:294-301. Autumn
        1965.

d'Aulnoy, Marie Catherine
    HISTOIRE D'HYPOLITE, COMTE DE DUGLAS
        Jones, Shirley. "Examples of Sensibility in the Late
        Seventeenth-Century Feminine Novel in France." MLR
        61:203-205. April 1966.

Ayme, Marcel
    THE BARKEEP OF BLEMONT
        Bree, Germaine and Margaret Guiton. An Age of Fiction:
        The French Novel from Gide to Camus. New Brunswick:
        Rutgers University Press, 1957. pp. 94-96.

        Loy, J. Robert. "The Reality of Marcel Ayme's World."
        FR 28:119-121. December 1954.

        Voorhees, Richard J. "Marcel Ayme and Moral Chaos."
        Person 39:50-58. Winter 1958.

THE GREEN MARE
  Bree, Germaine and Margaret Guiton. An Age of Fiction:
  The French Novel from Gide to Camus. New Brunswick:
  Rutgers University Press, 1957. pp. 89-92.

  Loy, J. Robert. "The Reality of Marcel Ayme's World."
  FR 28:121-123. December 1954.
MAISON BASSE
  Loy, J. Robert. "The Reality of Marcel Ayme's World."
  FR 28:117-118. December 1954.
THE MIRACULOUS BARBER
  Voorhees, Richard J. "Marcel Ayme and Moral Chaos."
  Person 39:49-50. Winter 1958.
THE SECOND FACE
  Voorhees, Richard J. "Marcel Ayme and Moral Chaos."
  Person 39:53-54. Winter 1958.
THE SECRET STREAM
  Loy, J. Robert. "The Reality of Marcel Ayme's World."
  FR 28:118-119. December 1954.
LE TABLE AUX CREVES
  Loy, J. Robert. "The Reality of Marcel Ayme's World."
  FR 28:115-116. December 1954.
THE TRANSIENT HOUR
  Voorhees, Richard J. "Marcel Ayme and Moral Chaos."
  Person 39:50-56. Winter 1958.

Balzac, Honore de
  ARGOW LE PIRATE
    Garnand, H. J. The Influence of Walter Scott on the Works
    of Balzac. New York: Carranza and Company, 1926. pp.
    70-73.
  THE BACHELOR'S HOUSE
    Beebe, Maurice. "The Lesson of Balzac's Artists."
    Criticism 2:235-236. Summer 1960.
  BEATRIX
    "Beatrix in Wonderland." TLS 3193:333-334. May 10,
    1963.

    Bowen, Ray P. The Dramatic Construction of Balzac's
    Novels. Eugene: University of Oregon, 1946. pp. 55-58;
    95-96.
  UNE BLONDE
    Tolley, Bruce. "Two Unknown Novels by Balzac: MARIE
    STUART and UNE BLONDE." Symposium 18:61-65. Spring
    1964.
  LE CENTENAIRE
    Garnand, H. J. The Influence of Walter Scott on the Works
    of Balzac. New York: Carranza and Company, 1926. pp.
    61-64.
  CESAR BIROTTEAU
    Bowen, Ray P. The Dramatic Construction of Balzac's
    Novels. Eugene: University of Oregon, 1946. pp. 45-48;
    88-90; 115-116.

Fess, G. M. "Balzac's First Thought of CESAR BIROT-
TEAU." MLN 49:516-519. December 1934.

Giraud, R. Unheroic Heroes. New Brunswick: Rutgers Uni-
versity Press, 1957. pp. 101-114; 119-123.
THE CHOUANS
Barnes, Helen E. A Study of the Variations Between the
Original and the Standard Edition of Balzac's LES
CHOUANS. Chicago: University of Chicago Press, 1923.

Bowen, Ray P. The Dramatic Construction of Balzac's
Novels. Eugene: University of Oregon, 1946. pp. 17-20;
77-79; 104-105.

Dargan, E. Preston. "Balzac and Cooper: LES CHOUANS."
MP 13:1-21. August 1915.

Fess, Gilbert M. "The Documentary Background of Balzac's LES CHOUANS." MLN 69:601-605. December 1954.

Ham, Edward B. "The Vimont CHOUANS." RomN 1:2-6.
November 1959.

Shepherd, James L., III. "Balzac's Debt to Cooper's SPY
in LES CHOUANS." FR 28:145-152. December 1954.
COLONEL CHABERT
Bowen, Ray P. The Dramatic Construction of Balzac's
Novels. Eugene: University of Oregon, 1946. pp. 23-24;
80-81; 105-106.

George, Albert J. Short Fiction in France: 1800-1850.
Syracuse: Syracuse University Press, 1964. pp. 93-95.
THE COUNTRY DOCTOR
Bowen, Ray P. The Dramatic Construction of Balzac's
Novels. Eugene: University of Oregon, 1946. p. 25.

Plomer, William. "Lenin's Favorite Novel." Spec 159:
248-249. August 6, 1937.
COUSINE BETTE
Bowen, Ray P. The Dramatic Construction of Balzac's
Novels. Eugene: University of Oregon, 1946. pp. 60-65;
96-98; 117.

Oliver, E. J. Honore de Balzac. New York: Macmillan
and Company, 1964. pp. 132-146.

Pritchett, V. S. "Books in General." New S&N 26:387.
December 11, 1943.

Turnell, Martin. The Novel in France. New York: New
Directions, 1951. pp. 241-245.
LE COUSIN PONS
Adamson, Donald. "LE COUSIN PONS: The 'Paragraphe

Compose.' " MLR 59:209-213. April 1964.

Bowen, Ray P. The Dramatic Construction of Balzac's
Novels. Eugene: University of Oregon, 1946. pp. 65-68;
98-99.

Pritchett, V. S. "Books in General." New S&N 26:387.
December 11, 1943.

Pritchett, V. S. The Living Novel and Later Appreciations.
New York: Random House, 1964. pp. 332-339.

Rosaire, Forrest. "A Slice of Somber Life: LE COUSIN
PONS." Studies in Balzac's Realism (by Dargan, Crain,
and others). Chicago: University of Chicago Press, 1932.
pp. 191-213.

CURE DE TOURS

Bowen, Ray P. The Dramatic Construction of Balzac's
Novels. Eugene: University of Oregon, 1946. pp. 24-25.

George, Albert J. Short Fiction in France: 1800-1850.
Syracuse: Syracuse University Press, 1964. pp. 95-97.

Marhofer, Esther. "LE CURE DE TOURS: A Study in Top-
ography." Studies in Balzac's Realism (by Dargan, Crain,
and others). Chicago: University of Chicago Press, 1932.
pp. 91-119.

Turnell, Martin. The Novel in France. New York: New
Directions, 1951. pp. 238-241.

LE DANGIER D'ESTRE TROP COCQUEBIN

Fess, G. M. "A New Source for Balzac's CONTES DRO-
LATIQUES." MLN 52:419-421. June 1937.

LA DERNIERE FEE

Garnand, H. J. The Influence of Walter Scott on the Works
of Balzac. New York: Carranza and Company, 1926. pp.
68-70.

LA DERNIERE INCARNATION DE VAUTRIN

Bowen, Ray P. The Dramatic Construction of Balzac's
Novels. Eugene: University of Oregon, 1946. pp. 51-53; 91-
92; 116.

DOM GIGADAS

Garnand, H. J. The Influence of Walter Scott on the Works
of Balzac. New York: Carranza and Company, 1926. pp.
83-86.

THE ELIXIR OF LONG LIFE

Rudwin, Maximilian. "Balzac and the Fantastic." SR 33:
13-14. January 1925.

Tolley, Bruce. "The Source of Balzac's ELIXIR DE
LONGUE VIE." RLC 37:91-97. January - March 1963.

THE EMPLOYEES

Fess, G. M. "LES EMPLOYES and SCENES DE LA VIE

BUREAUCRATIQUE. " MLN 43:236-242. April 1928.

Scott, Mary W. "Variations Between the First and the
Final Edition of Balzac's LES EMPLOYES. " MP 23:315-
336. February 1926.
EUGENIE GRANDET
Bowen, Ray P. The Dramatic Construction of Balzac's
Novels. Eugene: University of Oregon, 1946. pp. 26-31;
81-82; 106.

Lush, Adaline Lincoln. "The House of the Miser:
EUGENIE GRANDET. " Studies in Balzac's Realism (by
Dargan, Crain, and others). Chicago: University of Chicago
Press, 1932. pp. 121-135.

Saintsbury, George. A History of the French Novel (To
the Close of the 19th Century). London: Macmillan and
Company, 1919. pp. 163-164.

Sandwith, M. T. E. "JANE EYRE and EUGENIE GRANDET."
Nineteenth Century 92:235-240. August 1922.

Turnell, Martin. The Novel in France, New York: New
Directions, 1951. pp. 235-238.
L'EXCOMMUNIE
Garnand, H. J. The Influence of Walter Scott on the
Works of Balzac. New York: Carranza and Company, 1926.
pp. 77-83.
GAMBARA
Rudwin, Maximilian. "Balzac and the Fantastic. " SR 33:
21-24. January 1925.
GAUDISSART
George, Albert J. Short Fiction in France: 1800-1850.
Syracuse: Syracuse University Press, 1964. pp. 98-99.
GOBSECK
Dallmann, William P. "Sealsfield and Balzac Again. "
JEGP 39:346-354. 1940.

George, Albert J. Short Fiction in France: 1800-1850.
Syracuse: Syracuse University Press, 1964. pp. 83-85.
THE HISTORY OF THE THIRTEEN
Bowen, Ray P. The Dramatic Construction of Balzac's
Novels. Eugene: University of Oregon, 1946. p. 25.
HUMAN COMEDY
Ahnebrink, Lars. "Dreiser's SISTER CARRIE and Bal-
zac. " Symposium 7:306-320. November 1963.

Auerbach, Erich. "In the Hotel de la Mole. " PR 18:285-
293. May - June 1951.

"Balzac and the Role of Costume in the Novel. " ASLHM
21:158-166. Summer 1950.

Bays, Gwendolyn. "Balzac as Seer." YFS 13:83-92.
Spring-Summer 1954.

Beebe, Maurice. "The Lesson of Balzac's Artists."
Criticism 2:221-225. Summer 1960.

Bertault, Philippe. Balzac and THE HUMAN COMEDY.
New York: New York University Press, 1963.

Blackburn, Bonnie. "Master and Apprentice: A Realistic
Relationship." Studies in Balzac's Realism (by Dargan,
Crain, and others). Chicago: University of Chicago Press,
1932. pp. 151-189.

Bowen, Ray P. "Balzac's Interior Descriptions as an
Element in Characterization." PMLA 40:289-301. June
1925.

Bowen, Ray P. "The Composition of Balzac's OEUVRE
DE JEUNESSE and LA COMEDIE HUMAINE: A Comparison." PMLA 55:815-822. September 1940.

Brombert, Victor. "Balzac and the Caricature of the
Intellect." FR 34:3-12. October 1960.

Brunetiere, Ferdinand. Honore de Balzac. Philadelphia:
J. B. Lippincott Company, 1906. pp. 66-225.

Canfield, Arthur Graves. The Reappearing Characters in
Balzac's COMEDIE HUMAINE. Chapel Hill: University of
North Carolina Press, 1961.

Cerfben, Anatole and Jules Christophe. Repertory of the
COMEDIE HUMAINE. Philadelphia: The Avil Publishing
Company, 1902.

Cook, Albert. The Meaning of Fiction. Detroit: Wayne
State University Press, 1960. pp. 64-82.

Crain, William L. "An Introduction to a Critical Edition
of LE SECRET DES RUGGIERI." The Evolution of Balzac's COMEDIE HUMAINE. (ed.) E. Preston Dargan and
Bernard Weinberg. Chicago: University of Chicago Press,
1942. pp. 280-366.

Crampton, Hope. "Melmoth in LA COMEDIE HUMAINE."
MLR 61:42-50. January 1966.

Dargan, E. P. "Balzac's General Method: An Analysis of
His Realism." Studies in Balzac's Realism (by Dargan,
Crain, and others). Chicago: University of Chicago Press,
1932. pp. 1-31.

Dargan, E. P. and W. L. Crain. "The First Monument:
LES CHOUANS. " Studies in Balzac's Realism (by Dargan,
Crain, and others). Chicago: University of Chicago Press,
1932. pp. 33-65.

Dargan, Edwin Preston. Honore de Balzac: A Force of
Nature. Chicago: University of Chicago Press, 1932. pp.
42-75.

Dargan, E. Preston. "Introduction: Balzac's Method of
Revision. " The Evolution of Balzac's COMEDIE HUMAINE.
(ed.) E. Preston Dargan and Bernard Weinberg. Chicago:
University of Chicago Press, 1942. pp. 1-20.

Dedinsky, Brucia L. "Development of the Scheme of the
COMEDIE HUMAINE: Distribution of the Stories. " The
Evolution of Balzac's COMEDIE HUMAINE. (ed.) E.
Preston Dargan and Bernard Weinberg. Chicago: Univer-
sity of Chicago Press, 1942. pp. 22-181.

Evans, Arthur R. , Jr. "Balzac and Maitre Frenhofer: An
Iconographic Note. " RomN 5:32-36. Autumn 1963.

Fanger, Donald. Dostoevsky and Romantic Realism. Cambridge: Harvard University Press, 1965. pp. 29-38.

Fess, Gilbert Malcolm. The Correspondence of Physical
and Material Factors with Character in Balzac. Philadelphia: University of Pennsylvania, 1924. (Publication of
the University of Pennsylvania Series in Romanic Language
and Literature. No. 10.)

Freeman, David. "Balzac's Misers. " DubR 193:46-57. July
1933.

Furber, Donald. "The Fate and Freedom of Balzac's
Courtesans. " FR 39: 346-353. December 1965.

Galpin, Alfred. "A Balzac Centenary: The Avant-Propos
of the COMEDIE HUMAINE. " FR 16:213-222. January 1943.

Garnand, H. J. The Influence of Walter Scott on the Works
of Balzac. New York: Carranza and Company, 1926. pp.
90-134.

Gendzier, Stephen J. "Art Criticism and the Novel: Diderot
and Balzac. " FR 35:302-310. January 1962.

Gest, John Marshall. "The Law and Lawyers of Balzac. "
American Law Review 46:481-516. July-August 1912.

Giraud, R. Unheroic Heroes. New Brunswick: Rutgers University Press, 1957. pp. 115-119; 127-131.

Gordon, R. K. "Sir Walter Scott and the COMEDIE HU-
MAINE." MLR 23:51-55. January 1928.

Ham, Edward B. "Melodrama and Balzac Reappearers."
KFLQ 5:83-86. 1958.

Hunt, Hubert J. Balzac's COMEDIE HUMAINE. London:
University of London Athlone Press, 1959.

Hunt, H. J. " 'Portraits' in LA COMEDIE HUMAINE."
RR 49:112-124. April 1958.

Jackson, Joseph F. "Dating Balzac's Adoption of the
Title of LA COMEDIE HUMAINE." MLN 42:525-526.
December 1927.

Levin, Harry. The Gates of Horn: A Study of Five French
Realists. New York: Oxford University Press, 1963. pp.
156-213.

Lock, Peter W. "Hoarders and Spendthrifts in LA
COMEDIE HUMAINE." MLR 61:29-41. January 1966.

Lynes, Carlos, Jr. "Reappearing Characters in the
COMEDIE HUMAINE: Toward a Revaluation." RR 37:329-
335. December 1946.

McNair, Lilian. "Balzac and Huxley." FR 12:476-479.
May 1939.

McVicker, Cecil Don. "Balzac's Literary Cuisine: Food
as an Element of Realism." FR 28:44-48. October 1954.

Mille, Pierre. The French Novel. Philadelphia: J. P.
Lippincott, 1930. pp. 63-74.

Oliver, E. J. Balzac the European. London: Sheed and
Ward, 1959. pp. 47-204.

Oliver, E. J. Honore de Balzac. New York: Macmillan
and Company, 1964. pp. 147-160.

Pfeiffer, Charles Leonard. Taste and Smell in Balzac's
Novels. Tucson: University of Arizona Press. (University
of Arizona Bulletin. Vol. 20.) 1949. 120 pp.

Raine, Kathleen. "LA COMEDIE HUMAINE." DubR 217:
39-46. July 1945.

Rogers, Samuel. Balzac and the Novel. Madison: University of Wisconsin Press, 1953. pp. 43-187.

Turnell, Martin. The Novel in France. New York: New

Directions, 1951. pp. 216-227.

Weinberg, Bernard. "Summaries of Variants in Twenty-
Six Stories." The Evolution of Balzac's COMEDIE HU-
MAINE. (ed.) E. Preston Dargan and Bernard Weinberg.
Chicago: University of Chicago Press, 1942. pp. 368-421.

Wenger, Jared. "Speed as a Technique in the Novels of
Balzac." PMLA 55:241-252. March 1940.

Wilson, Rachel. "Variations in LE CURE DE TOURS."
The Evolution of Balzac's COMEDIE HUMAINE. (ed.) E.
Preston Dargan and Bernard Weinberg. Chicago: Univer-
sity of Chicago Press, 1942. pp. 188-277.

Zeek, C. F. "Balzac as a Business Man." FR 25:96-103.
December 1951.

Zulli, Floyd, Jr. "Dantean Allusions in LA COMEDIE
HUMAINE." Italica 35:177-187. September 1958.

Zulli, Floyd, Jr. "Italy and LA COMEDIE HUMAINE."
Italica 34:20-29. March 1957.

Zweig, Stefan. Master Builders: A Typology of the Spirit.
New York: Viking Press, 1939. pp. 10-24.

Zweig, Stefan. Three Masters. New York: Viking Press,
1930. pp. 10-12.
L'ISRAELITE
        Garnand, H. J. The Influence of Walter Scott on the
        Works of Balzac. New York: Carranza and Company,
        1926. pp. 52-61.
JANE LA PALE
        Garnand, H. J. The Influence of Walter Scott on the
        Works of Balzac. New York: Carranza and Company,
        1926. pp. 73-76.
JEAN LOUIS
        Fess, G. M. "The Pyrrhonist in Balzac's JEAN LOUIS."
        MLN 44:171-173. March 1929.

        Garnand, H. J. The Influence of Walter Scott on the
        Works of Balzac. New York: Carranza and Company,
        1926. pp. 44-52.
JESUS CHRIST IN FLANDRES
        Palfrey, Thomas R. "Cooper and Balzac: THE HEADS-
        MAN." MP 29:335-341. February 1932.
THE LILY OF THE VALLEY
        Bowen, Ray P. The Dramatic Construction of Balzac's
        Novels. Eugene: University of Oregon, 1946. pp. 42-45;
        86-88.

        Hunt, H. J. "Balzac and Lady Ellenborough." FS 12:247-
        258. July 1958.

La Fleur, Paul T. "Sainte-Beuve, Balzac, and Thackeray."
MLR 9:518-519. October 1914.
LOST ILLUSIONS
Bart, B. F. "Balzac and Flaubert: Energy Versus Art."
RR 42:198-204. October 1951.

Beebe, Maurice. "The Lesson of Balzac's Artists."
Criticism 2:231-232. Summer 1960.

Bowen, Ray P. The Dramatic Construction of Balzac's
Novels. Eugene: University of Oregon, 1946. pp. 48-51;
90-91.

Chaikin, Milton. "Maupassant's BEL-AMI and Balzac."
RomN 2:109-112. Spring 1960.

Pritchett, V. S. "Books in General." New S&N 42:383-
384. October 6, 1951.

Spitzer, Leo. "Balzac and Flaubert Again." MLN 68:583-
590. December 1953.

Tolley, Bruce. "The 'Cenacle' of Balzac's ILLUSIONS
PERDUES." FS 15:324-334. October 1961.

Warren, F. M. "Was Balzac's ILLUSIONS PERDUES In-
fluenced by Stendhal?" MLN 43:179-180. March 1928.
LOUIS LAMBERT
Benson, Carl. "Yeats and Balzac's LOUIS LAMBERT."
MP 49:242-247. May 1952.

Buck, Stratton. "The Uses of Madness." TSL 3:63-67.
1958.

Gargano, James W. "THE AMBASSADORS and LOUIS
LAMBERT." MLN 75:211-213. March 1960.

Symons, A. The Symbolist Movement in Literature. New
York: E. P. Dutton and Company, 1958. pp. 103-105.
MAITRE CORNELIUS
Morris, George D. "Balzac's Treatment of History in
MAITRE CORNELIUS." PQ 10:356-368. October 1931.
MARIE STUART
Tolley, Bruce. "Two Unknown Novels by Balzac: MARIE
STUART and UNE BLONDE." Symposium 18:57-61. Spring
1964.
MELMOTH CONVERTED
Rudwin, Maximilian. "Balzac and the Fantastic." SR 33:
20-21. January 1925.
OEUVRES DE JEUNESSE
Bowen, Ray P. "The Composition of Balzac's OEUVRES
DE JEUNESSE and LA COMEDIE HUMAINE: A Compar-
ison." PMLA 55:815-822. September 1940.

PERE GORIOT
Auerbach, Erich. "In the Hotel de la Mole." PR 18:280-
284. May-June 1951. (Also in Auerbach, Mimesis. New
York: Doubleday and Company, 1957. pp. 413-417.)

Bowen, Ray P. The Dramatic Construction of Balzac's
Novels. Eugene: University of Oregon, 1946. pp. 36-42;
85-86; 107-115.

Conner, J. Wayne. "On Balzac's GORIOT." Symposium
8:68-73. Summer 1954.

Downing, George E. "A Famous Boarding-House: LE
PERE GORIOT." Studies in Balzac's Realism (by Dargan,
Crain, and others). Chicago: University of Chicago Press,
1932. pp. 136-150.

Fanger, Donald. Dostoevsky and Romantic Realism. Cambridge: Harvard University Press, 1965. pp. 38-56.

Hunt, Joel. "Balzac and Dostoevskij: Ethics and Eschatology." SEEJ 16:307-323. Winter 1958.

Keates, Laurence W. "Mysterious Miraculous Mandarin:
Origins, Literary Paternity, Implication in Ethics." RLC
40:511-516. October-December 1966.

Maugham, W. Somerset. Great Novelists and Their Novels.
Philadelphia: Winston Company, 1948. pp. 41-58.

Oliver, E. J. Honore de Balzac. New York: Macmillan
and Company, 1964. pp. 53-68.

Pugh, A. R. "Recurring Characters in LE PERE GORIOT."
MLR 57:518-522. October 1962.

Savage, Catharine H. "The Romantic PERE GORIOT." SIR
5:104-112. Winter 1966.

Turnell, Martin. The Novel in France. New York: New
Directions, 1951. pp. 228-235.

Yarrow, P. J. "LE PERE GORIOT Re-considered." EIC
7:363-373. October 1957.
PIERRETTE
Kanes, Martin. "Zola, Balzac and LA FORTUNE DES
ROGRON." FS 18:204-207. July 1964.
THE QUEST OF THE ABSOLUTE
Bowen, Ray P. The Dramatic Construction of Balzac's
Novels. Eugene: University of Oregon, 1946. pp. 31-36;
82-85; 106-107.
LE REQUISITIONNAIRE
George, Albert J. Short Fiction in France: 1800-1850.

Syracuse: Syracuse University Press, 1964. pp. 88-89.
THE SECRETS OF THE PRINCESS OF CADIGNAN
    Beebe, Maurice. "The Lesson of Balzac's Artists."
    Criticism 2:236-237. Summer 1960.
THE SPLENDORS AND MISERIES OF COURTESANS
    Beebe, Maurice. "The Lesson of Balzac's Artists."
    Criticism 2:232-235. Summer 1960.

    Fanger, Donald. Dostoevsky and Romantic Realism. Cam-
    bridge: Harvard University Press, 1965. pp. 58-63.
THE UNKNOWN MASTERPIECE
    Beebe, Maurice. "The Lesson of Balzac's Artists."
    Criticism 2:226-227. Summer 1960.

    Conner, Wayne. "Balzac's Frenhofer." MLN 69:335-338.
    May 1954.

    Evans, Arthur R., Jr. "THE CHEF-D'OEUVRE INCONNU:
    Balzac's Myth of Pygmalion and Modern Painting." RR
    53:187-198. October 1962.

    Gilman, Margaret. "Balzac and Diderot: LE CHEF
    D'OEUVRE INCONNU." PMLA 65:644-648. June 1950.

    Niess, Robert. "Another View of Zola's L'OEUVRE."
    RR 39:289-300. December 1948.
URSULE MIROUET
    Bowen, Ray P. The Dramatic Construction of Balzac's
    Novels. Eugene: University of Oregon, 1946. pp. 58-60.
EL VERDUGO
    Conner, Wayne. "The Genesis of Balzac's EL VERDUGO."
    LB 46:135-139. 1956-1957.
LE VICAIRE DES ARDENNES
    Garnand, H. J. The Influence of Walter Scott on the Works
    of Balzac. New York: Carranza and Company, 1926. pp.
    64-68.
VIE ET MALHEURS D'HORACE DE SAINT-AUBIN
    Langley, Ernest F. "A Balzac-Sandeau Episode - VIE ET
    MALHEURS DE HORACE DE SAINT-AUBIN." Harvard
    Studies and Notes in Philology and Literature 19:151-165.
    1937.
THE VILLAGE PRIEST
    Bowen, Ray P. The Dramatic Construction of Balzac's
    Novels. Eugene: University of Oregon, 1946. pp. 53-55;
    92-95; 116-117.
THE WILD ASS'S SKIN
    Beebe, Maurice. "The Lesson of Balzac's Artists."
    Criticism 2:228-231. Summer 1960.

    Bowen, Ray P. The Dramatic Construction of Balzac's
    Novels. Eugene: University of Oregon, 1946. pp. 20-23;
    79-80.

Gregg, Richard A. "Balzac and Women in THE QUEEN
OF SPADES. " SEEJ 10:279-281. Fall 1966.

Hunt, H. J. "Balzac's Pressmen. " FS 11:230-244. July
1957.

Millott, H. H. "LA PEAU DE CHAGRIN: Method in Madness. " Studies in Balzac's Realism (by Dargan, Crain,
and others). Chicago: University of Chicago Press, 1932.
pp. 68-89.

Nozick, Martin. "Unamuno and LA PEAU DE CHAGRIN."
MLN 65:255-256. April 1950.

Nykl, Alois Richard. "The Talisman in Balzac's LA
PEAU DE CHAGRIN. " MLN 34:479-481. December 1919.

Rudwin, Maximilian. "Balzac and the Fantastic. " SR 33:
14-17. January 1925.

Barbey d'Aurevilly, Jules
UNE VIEILLE MAITRESSE
    Place, Edwin B. "Spanish Sources of the 'Diabolism' of
    Barbey D'Aurevilly. " RR 19:332-338. October-December
    1928.

Barbusse, Henri
UNDER FIRE
    Mille, Pierre. The French Novel. Philadelphia: J. P.
    Lippincott, 1930. pp. 188-190.

Barres, Maurice
AMORI ET DOLORI SACRUM
    Cheydleur, Frederic D. "Maurice Barres as a Roman-
    ticist. " PMLA 41:472-474. 1926.
LES BASTIONS DE L'EST
    Cheydleur, Frederic D. "Maurice Barres as a Roman-
    ticist. " PMLA 41:475-478. 1926.
CULTE DU MOI
    Cheydleur, Frederic D. "Maurice Barres as a Roman-
    ticist. " PMLA 41:463-466. 1926.
L'ENNEMI DES LOIS
    Cheydleur, Frederic D. "Maurice Barres as a Roman-
    ticist. " PMLA 41:466-467. 1926.
LE ROMAN DE L'ENERGIE NATIONALE
    Cheydleur, Frederic D. "Maurice Barres as a Roman-
    ticist. " PMLA 41:470-472. 1926.

Beauvoir, Simone de
ALL MEN ARE MORTAL
    Bays, Gwendolyn. "Simone de Beauvoir: Ethics and Art. "
    YFS 1:110-111. Spring - Summer 1948.

THE BLOOD OF THE OTHERS
Bays, Gwendolyn. "Simone de Beauvoir: Ethics and Art. "
YFS 1:109-110. Spring - Summer 1948.

Brombert, Victor. The Intellectual Hero: Studies in the
French Novel 1880-1955. Philadelphia: Lippincott, 1961.
pp. 232-238.
THE MANDARINS
Ehrmann, Jacques. "Simone de Beauvoir and the Related
Destinies of Woman and the Intellectual. " YFS 27:29-32.
Spring - Summer 1961.

Hatzfeld, Helmut. Trends and Styles in Twentieth Century
French Literature. Washington, D. C.: Catholic University
of America Press, 1957. pp. 155-156.

Reck, Rima Drell. "LES MANDARINS: Sensibility, Re-
sponsibility. " YFS 27:33-40. Spring - Summer 1961.
SHE CAME TO STAY
Bays, Gwendolyn. "Simone de Beauvoir: Ethics and Art."
YFS 1:106-109. Spring - Summer 1948.

Douglas, Kenneth. "Sartre and the Self-Inflicted Wound. "
YFS 9:127-128.

Peyre, Henri. The Contemporary French Novel. New
York: Oxford University Press, 1955. pp. 252-255.

Beckett, Samuel
THE EXPULSION
Federman, Raymond. Journey to Chaos. Berkeley: Univer-
sity of California Press, 1965. pp. 177-205.

Fletcher, John. The Novels of Samuel Beckett. London:
Chatto and Windus, 1964. pp. 101-102.
HOW IT IS
Coe, Richard N. Samuel Beckett. New York: Grove Press,
Inc., 1964. pp. 81-87.

Cohn, Ruby. Samuel Beckett: Comic Gamut. New Brunswick: Rutgers University Press, 1962. Chapter 8.

Federman, Raymond. " 'How It Is' with Beckett's Fiction."
FR 38:459-468. February 1965.

Federman, Raymond. Journey to Chaos. Berkeley: University of California Press, 1965. pp. 3-13.

Kenner, Hugh. Flaubert, Joyce and Beckett: The Stoic
Comedians. Boston: Beacon Press, 1962. pp. 86-87.

Leventhal, A. J. "The Beckett Hero. " Samuel Beckett: A
Collection of Critical Essays. (ed.) Martin Esslin. Engle-

wood Cliffs: Prentice-Hall, Inc., 1965. pp. 42-46.

Tindall, William York. Samuel Beckett. New York: Columbia University Press, 1964. pp. 7-8.
MALONE DIES
Chambers, Ross. "Beckett's Brinkmanship." AUMLA 19:
57-74. May 1963.

Chambers, Ross. "Samuel Beckett and the Padded Cell."
Meanjin 21:457-458. No. 4, 1962.

Cmarada, Geraldine. "MALONE DIES: A Round of Consciousness." Symposium 14:199-212. Fall 1960.

Coe, Richard N. Samuel Beckett. New York: Grove Press,
Inc., 1964. pp. 62-68.

Cohn, Ruby. Samuel Beckett: Comic Gamut. New Brunswick: Rutgers University Press, 1962. pp. 120-121; 125-
128.

Cohn, Ruby. "Still Novel." YFS 24:48-53. Summer 1959.

Fletcher, John. The Novels of Samuel Beckett. London:
Chatto and Windus, 1964. pp. 151-176.

Glicksberg, Charles I. "Samuel Beckett's World of Fiction." ArQ 18:39-41. Spring 1962.

Greenberg, Alvin. "The Novel of Disintegration: Paradoxical Impossibility in Contemporary Fiction." WSCL 7:
110-112. Winter - Spring 1966.

Hamilton, Carol. "Portrait in Old Age: The Image of Man
in Beckett's Trilogy." WHR 16:157-165. Spring 1962.

Hoffman, Frederick J. Samuel Beckett: The Language of
Self. Carbondale: Southern Illinois University Press, 1962.
pp. 127-132.

Kenner, Hugh. Flaubert, Joyce and Beckett: The Stoic
Comedians. Boston: Beacon Press, 1962. pp. 83-86.

Oates, J. C. "The Trilogy of Samuel Beckett." Renascence
14:160-165. Spring 1962.

Pritchett, V. S. The Living Novel and Later Appreciations.
New York: Random House, 1964. pp. 315-318.

Scott, Nathan A., Jr. "The Recent Journey into the Zone
of Zero." Centennial Review 6:173-174. Spring 1962.

Tindall, William York. Samuel Beckett. New York: Columbia

University Press, 1964. pp. 26-29.
MERCIER ET CAMIOR
   Cohn, Ruby. Samuel Beckett: Comic Gamut. New Bruns-
   wick: Rutgers University Press, 1962.

   Federman, Raymond. Journey to Chaos. Berkeley: University of California Press, 1965. pp. 141-176.

   Fletcher, John. The Novels of Samuel Beckett. London:
   Chatto and Windus, 1964. pp. 110-118.
MOLLOY
   Chambers, Ross. "Beckett's Brinkmanship." AUMLA 19:
   57-74. May 1963.

   Chambers, Ross. "Samuel Beckett and the Padded Cell."
   Meanjin 21:454-456. No. 4, 1962.

   Coe, Richard N. Samuel Beckett. New York: Grove Press,
   Inc. , 1964. pp. 54-62.

   Cohn, Ruby. Samuel Beckett: Comic Gamut. New Brunswick:
   Rutgers University Press, 1962. pp. 115-120; Chapter 6.

   Cohn, Ruby. "Still Novel. " YFS 24:48-53. Summer 1959.

   Fletcher, John. The Novels of Samuel Beckett. London:
   Chatto and Windus, 1964. Chapter 5; pp. 119-150.

   Glicksberg, Charles I. "Samuel Beckett's World of Fiction. " ArQ 18:35-38. Spring 1962.

   Greenberg, Alvin. "The Novel of Disintegration: Paradoxical
   Impossibility in Contemporary Fiction. " WSCL 7:110-112.
   Winter - Spring 1966.

   Hamilton, Carol. "Portrait in Old Age: The Image of Man
   in Beckett's Trilogy. " WHR 16:157-165. Spring 1962.

   Hoffman, Frederick J. Samuel Beckett: The Language of
   Self. Carbondale: Southern Illinois University Press, 1962.
   pp. 121-127.

   Kenner, Hugh. Samuel Beckett: A Critical Study. London:
   John Calder, 1962. pp. 60-61.

   Oates, J. C. "The Trilogy of Samuel Beckett. " Renascence
   14:160-165. Spring 1962.

   Pritchett, V. S. The Living Novel and Later Appreciations.
   New York: Random House, 1964. pp. 315-317.

   Scott, Nathan A. , Jr. "The Recent Journey into the Zone
   of Zero. " Centennial Review 6:171-173. Spring 1962.

32 The French Novel

Tindall, William York. Samuel Beckett. New York: Columbia University Press, 1964. pp. 21-26.
MURPHY
Chambers, Ross. "Beckett's Brinkmanship." AUMLA 19: 57-74. May 1963.

Coe, Richard N. Samuel Beckett. New York: Grove Press, Inc., 1964. pp. 20-34.

Cohn, Ruby. Samuel Beckett: Comic Gamut. New Brunswick: Rutgers University Press, 1962. pp. 45-64.

Federman, Raymond. Journey to Chaos. Berkeley: University of California Press, 1965. pp. 56-93.

Fletcher, John. The Novels of Samuel Beckett. London: Chatto and Windus, 1964. Chapter 2.

Friedman, Melvin J. "The Novels of Samuel Beckett: An Amalgam of Joyce and Proust." CL 12:51-52. Winter 1960.

Glicksberg, Charles I. "Samuel Beckett's World of Fiction." ArQ 18:32-34. Spring 1962.

Greenberg, Alvin. "The Novel of Disintegration: Paradoxical Impossibility in Contemporary Fiction." WSCL 7:109-112. Winter - Spring 1966.

Hoffman, Frederick J. Samuel Beckett: The Language of Self. Carbondale: Southern Illinois University Press, 1962. pp. 105-114.

Jacobsen, Josephine and William R. Mueller. The Testament of Samuel Beckett. New York: Hill and Wang, 1964. pp. 21-32; 67-72.

Kenner, Hugh. Samuel Beckett: A Critical Study. London: John Calder, 1962. pp. 49-58.

Morse, J. Mitchell. "The Contemplative Life According to Samuel Beckett." HudR 15:516-519. Winter 1962-1963.

Scott, Nathan A., Jr. "The Recent Journey into the Zone of Zero." Centennial Review 6:162-164. Spring 1962.

Tindall, William York. Samuel Beckett. New York: Columbia University Press, 1964. pp. 13-17.

Wellworth, G. E. "Life in a Void: Samuel Beckett." UKCR 28:27. October 1961.
THE UNNAMABLE
Bersani, Leo. "No Exit for Beckett." PR 33:264-267. Spring 1966.

Chambers, Ross. "Beckett's Brinkmanship." AUMLA 19: 57-74. May 1963.

Chambers, Ross. "Samuel Beckett and the Padded Cell." Meanjin 21:458-462. No. 4, 1962.

Coe, Richard N. Samuel Beckett. New York: Grove Press, Inc., 1964. pp. 69-80.

Cohn, Ruby. Samuel Beckett: Comic Gamut. New Brunswick: Rutgers University Press, 1962. Chapter 6; pp. 121-125.

Cohn, Ruby. "Still Novel." YFS 24:48-53. Summer 1959.

Fletcher, John. The Novels of Samuel Beckett. London: Chatto and Windus, 1964. Chapter 7; pp. 179-194.

Glicksberg, Charles I. "Samuel Beckett's World of Fiction." ArQ 18:41-47. Spring 1962.

Hamilton, Carol. "Portrait in Old Age: The Image of Man in Beckett's Trilogy." WHR 16:162-163. Spring 1962.

Hoffman, Frederick J. Samuel Beckett: The Language of Self. Carbondale: Southern Illinois University Press, 1962. pp. 132-137.

Oates, J. C. "The Trilogy of Samuel Beckett." Renascence 14:160-165. Spring 1962.

Tindall, William York. Samuel Beckett. New York: Columbia University Press, 1964. pp. 29-33.

WATT

Bree, Germaine. "Beckett's Abstractors of Quintessence." FR 36:567-576. May 1963.

Coe, Richard N. Samuel Beckett. New York: Grove Press, Inc., 1964. pp. 36-53.

Cohn, Ruby. Samuel Beckett: Comic Gamut. New Brunswick: Rutgers University Press, 1962. pp. 65-94.

Cohn, Ruby. "WATT in the Light of THE CASTLE." CL 13: 154-166. Spring 1961.

Federman, Raymond. Journey to Chaos. Berkeley: University of California Press, 1960. pp. 94-132.

Fletcher, John. The Novels of Samuel Beckett. London: Chatto and Windus, 1964. Chapter 5; pp. 59-89.

Friedman, Melvin J. "The Novels of Samuel Beckett: An

Amalgam of Joyce and Proust. '' CL 12:52-53. Winter 1960.

Greenberg, Alvin. ''The Death of the Psyche: A Way to
the Self in the Contemporary Novel. '' Criticism 8:1-15.
Winter 1966.

Hesla, David H. ''The Shape of Chaos: A Reading of
Beckett's WATT. '' Crit 6:85-105. Spring 1963.

Hoefer, Jacquelin. ''WATT. '' Samuel Beckett: A Collection
of Critical Essays. (ed.) Martin Esslin. Englewood Cliffs:
Prentice-Hall, Inc. , 1965. pp. 62-76.

Hoffman, Frederick J. Samuel Beckett: The Language of
Self. Carbondale: Southern Illinois University Press, 1962.
pp. 114-119.

Jacobsen, Josephine and William R. Mueller. The Testament of Samuel Beckett. New York: Hill and Wang, 1964.
pp. 73-77.

Kenner, Hugh. Flaubert, Joyce and Beckett: The Stoic
Comedians. Boston: Beacon Press, 1962. pp. 78-82.

Kenner, Hugh. Samuel Beckett: A Critical Study. London:
John Calder, 1962. pp. 58-60.

Scott, Nathan A. , Jr. ''The Recent Journey into the Zone
of Zero. '' Centennial Review 6:164-169. Spring 1962.

Tindall, William York. Samuel Beckett. New York: Columbia University Press, 1964. pp. 17-21.

Warhaft, Sidney. ''Threne and Theme in WATT. '' WSCL
4:261-278. Autumn 1963.

Wellworth, G. E. ''Life in a Void: Samuel Beckett. '' UKCR
28:27-28. October 1961.

Bernanos, Georges
    THE CRIME
        Reck, Rima Drell. ''A Crime: Dostoyevsky and Bernanos.''
        Forum H 4:10-13. Spring-Summer 1964.
    THE DIARY OF A COUNTRY PRIEST
        Bree, Germaine and Margaret Guiton. An Age of Fiction:
        The French Novel from Gide to Camus. New Brunswick:
        Rutgers University Press, 1957. pp. 125-129.

        Frohock, W. M. ''Georges Bernanos and His Priest-Hero.''
        YFS 12:58.

        Nettelbeck, C. W. ''The Obsessional Dream World of
        Georges Bernanos. '' AUMLA 26:242-253. November 1966.

L'IMPOSTURE
>Frohock, W. M. "Georges Bernanos and His Priest-Hero. " YFS 12:55-57.

>Hatzfeld, Helmut. Trends and Styles in Twentieth Century French Literature. Washington, D. C.: Catholic University of America Press, 1957. pp. 175-177.

JOY
>Avegno, Hamilton P. "Some Notes on Pasternak's DR. ZHIVAGO and Bernanos' JOY. " XUS 1:26-33. April 1961.

MONSIEUR OUINE
>Bree, Germaine and Margaret Guiton. An Age of Fiction: The French Novel from Gide to Camus. New Brunswick: Rutgers University Press, 1957. pp. 128-131.

>Nettelbeck, C. W. "The Obsessional Dream World of Georges Bernanos. " AUMLA 26:242-253. November 1966.

>Sonnenfeld, Albert. "The Hostile Phantoms of Georges Bernanos: SOUS LE SOLEIL DE SATAN and M. OUINE. " ECr 4:217-221. Winter 1964.

THE STAR OF SATAN
>Bree, Germaine and Margaret Guiton. An Age of Fiction: The French Novel from Gide to Camus. New Brunswick: Rutgers University Press, 1957. pp. 122-124; 127.

>Conley, John J. "A Possible Source of Bernanos' Saint-Marin Episode. " RomN 5:101-105. Spring 1964.

>Frohock, W. M. "Georges Bernanos and His Priest-Hero." YFS 12:54-55.

>Mille, Pierre. The French Novel. Philadelphia: J. P. Lippincott, 1930. pp. 226-227.

>Sonnenfeld, Albert. "The Hostile Phantoms of Georges Bernanos: SOUS LE SOLEIL DE SATAN and M. OUINE. " ECr 4:210-217. Winter 1964.

Bernard, Catherine
>ELEONOR D'YVREE
>>Jones, Shirley. "Examples of Sensibility in the Late Seventeenth-Century Feminine Novel in France. " MLR 61:201-203. April 1966.

Besus, Roger
>UN HOMME POUR RIEN
>>Pitou, Spire. "The Genesis of a Novelist: Roger Besus. " BA 37:157-158. Spring 1963.
>LOUIS BRANCOURT
>>Pitou, Spire. "The Genesis of a Novelist: Roger Besus. " BA 37:159. Spring 1963.

LE REFUS
    Pitou, Spire. "The Genesis of a Novelist: Roger Besus."
    BA 37:158. Spring 1963.
LE SCANDALE
    Pitou, Spire. "The Genesis of a Novelist: Roger Besus."
    BA 37:159-160. Spring 1963.

Binet-Valmer
    LES METEQUES
        Bennett, Jesse Lee. "Three New French Novelists, Far-
        rere, Harry, Binet-Valmer." Poet Lore 27:594-595.
        Autumn 1916.

Bloy, Leon
    LE DESEPERE
        Heppenstall, Rayner. The Double Image: Mutations of
        Christian Mythology in the Work of Four French Catholic
        Writers of Today and Yesterday. London: Secker and War-
        burg, 1947. pp. 16-20.
    THE WOMAN WHO WAS POOR
        Heppenstall, Rayner. The Double Image: Mutations of
        Christian Mythology in the Work of Four French Catholic
        Writers of Today and Yesterday. London: Secker and War-
        burg, 1947. pp. 20-22.

Bourget, Paul
    L'APOSTAT
        Secor, Walter Todd. Paul Bourget and the Nouvelle. New
        York: King's Crown Press, 1948. pp. 199-200.
    THE DISCIPLE
        Davidson, Hugh M. "The ESSAIS DE PSYCHOLOGIE CON-
        TEMPORAINE and the Character of Adrien Sixte." MP
        46:34-48. August 1948.

        Guerard, Albert Leon. Five Masters of French Romance.
        New York: Scribner's Sons. pp. 198-203.

        Mondelli, Dr. Rudolph J. "Paul Bourget and the Concept
        of Moral Responsibility." CMLR 20:20-26. Summer 1960.
    UN DIVORCE
        Mondelli, Rudolph J. "The Church, Society, and Paul
        Bourget." Renascence 10:81-82. Winter 1958.
    L'ECHEANCE
        Secor, Walter Todd. Paul Bourget and the Nouvelle. New
        York: King's Crown Press, 1948. pp. 181-182.
    L'EMIGRE
        Mondelli, Rudolph J. "The Church, Society, and Paul
        Bourget." Renascence 10:83. Winter 1958.
    L'ETAPE
        Mondelli, Rudolph J. "The Church, Society, and Paul
        Bourget." Renascence 10:78-81. Winter 1958.
    LE FILS
        Secor, Walter Todd. Paul Bourget and the Nouvelle. New

York: King's Crown Press, 1948. pp. 192-194.
LE GESTE DU FILS
    Secor, Walter Todd. Paul Bourget and the Nouvelle. New
    York: King's Crown Press, 1948. pp. 196-198.
L'IRREPARABLE
    Secor, Walter Todd. Paul Bourget and the Nouvelle. New
    York: King's Crown Press, 1948. pp. 179-180.
LE JUSTICIER
    Secor, Walter Todd. Paul Bourget and the Nouvelle. New
    York: King's Crown Press, 1948. pp. 177-179.
LE LUXE DES AUTRES
    Secor, Walter Todd. Paul Bourget and the Nouvelle. New
    York: King's Crown Press, 1948. pp. 175-177.

Breton, Andre
NADJA
    Firchow, Peter Edgerly. "NADJA and LE PAYSAN DE
    PARIS: Two Surrealist 'Novels.' " WSCL 6:302-307.
    Autumn 1965.

    Lynes, Carlos. "Surrealism and the Novel: Breton's
    NADJA." FS 20:366-385. October 1966.

Butor, Michael
A CHANGE OF HEART
    Ames, Van Meter. "Butor and the Book. " JAAC 23:161-
    162. Fall 1964.

    Frohock, W. M. "Introduction to Butor. " YFS 24:55-56.
    Summer 1959.

    Hubert, Renee Riese. "Patterns in the Anti-Novel. " Forum
    H 3:14. Fall 1962.

    Le Sage, Laurent. "Michael Butor: Techniques of the
    Marvelous. " ECr 6:38-43. Spring 1966.

    Simon, John K. "View from the Train: Butor, Gide, Lar-
    baud. " FR 36:161-166. December 1962.

    Wilson, Clotilde. "LA MODIFICATION or Variations on a
    Theme by Mme. De Stael. " RR 55:278-282. December 1964.
DEGREES
    Ames, Van Meter. "Butor and the Book. " JAAC 23:162.
    Fall 1964.

    Le Sage, Laurent. "Michael Butor: Techniques of the Mar-
    velous. " ECr 6:38-43. Spring 1966.
L'EMPLOI DU TEMPS
    Ames, Van Meter. "Butor and the Book. " JAAC 23:160-
    161. Fall 1964.

    Frohock, W. M. "Introduction to Butor. " YFS 24:55.

Summer 1959.

Le Sage, Laurent. "Michael Butor: Techniques of the Mar-
velous. " ECr 6:38-43. Spring 1966.
PASSAGE DE MILAN
Ames, Van Meter. "Butor and the Book. " JAAC 23:160.
Fall 1964.

Frohock, W. M. "Introduction to Butor. " YFS 24:54-55.
Summer 1959.

Le Sage, Laurent. "Michael Butor: Techniques of the Mar-
velous. " ECr 6:38-43. Spring 1966.

La Calprenede, Gautier
CASSANDRA
Hill, Herbert Wynford. "La Calprenede's Romances and the
Restoration Drama. " University of Nevada Studies 2:3-56.
No. 3, 1910.
CLEOPATRA
Hill, Herbert Wynford. "La Calprenede's Romances and the
Restoration Drama. " University of Nevada Studies 2:3-56.
No. 3, 1910.
FARAMOND
Pitou, Spire. "An Eighteenth-Century Abridgment of La
Calprenede's FARAMOND. " MLN 67:178-181. March 1952.

Pitou, Spire, Jr. La Calprenede's FARAMOND: A Study of
the Sources, Structure, and Reputation of the Novel. Baltimore: Johns Hopkins Press, 1938. (Johns Hopkins Studies
in Romance Literature. Vol. 31.)

Pitou, Spire, Jr. "A Portuguese Adaptation of La Calprenede's FARAMOND. " MLN 54:192-194. March 1939.

Camus, Albert
THE FALL
Ames, Sanford. "LA CHUTE: From Summitry to Speleology."
FR 39:559-566. February 1966.

Bailey, Anthony. "The Isolated Man. " Commonweal 67:92-
93. October 1957.

Batt, Jean. "Albert Camus: From THE MYTH to THE
FALL. " Meanjin 16:418-419. December 1957.

Batt, Jean C. "The Themes of the Novels and Plays of
Albert Camus. " AUMLA 6:55-56. May 1957.

Brearley, Katherine. "The Theme of Isolation in Camus. "
KFLQ 9:121-122. 1962.

Bree, Germaine and Margaret Guiton. An Age of Fiction:

The French Novel from Gide to Camus. New Brunswick:
Rutgers University Press, 1957. pp. 229-233.

Bree, Germaine. Camus. New Brunswick: Rutgers University Press, 1961. Chapter 15.

Brockmann, Charles B. "Metamorphoses of Hell: The
Spiritual Quandary in LA CHUTE. " FR 35:361-368. February 1962.

Burke, Edward L. "Camus and the Pursuit of Happiness."
Thought 37:406-408. Autumn 1962.

Champigny, Robert. "Camus' Fictional Works: The Plight
of Innocence. " ASLHM 28:179-182. Summer 1957.

Champigny, Robert. "The Comedy of Ethics. " YFS 25:72-
74. Spring 1960.

Cruickshank, John. Albert Camus and the Literature of
Revolt. New York: Oxford University Press, 1959. pp.
181-188.

Dennis, William D. "Jean - Baptiste Clamence - A Resurrected Meursault?" CLAJ 8:81-87. September 1964.

Fitch, Brian T. "Aesthetic Distance and Inner Space in
the Novels of Camus. " MFS 10:286-291. Autumn 1964.

Girard, Rene. "Camus' Stranger Retried. " PMLA 79:519-
533. December 1964.

Glicksberg, Charles I. "Camus's Quest for God. " Southwest Rev 44:244-247. Summer 1959.

Hanna, Thomas. The Thought and Art of Albert Camus.
Chicago: Henry Regnery· Company, 1958. pp. 213-237.

Hartsock, Mildred. "Camus' THE FALL: Dialogue of
One. " MFS 7:357-364. Winter 1961-1962.

Jones, Marian. "Camus' Rebels. " WHR 12:55-56. Winter
1958.

King, Adele. Albert Camus. New York: Grove Press, 1964.
pp. 81-94.

King, Adele. "Structure and Meaning in LA CHUTE. "
PMLA 77:660-667. December 1962.

Lauer, Quentin. "Albert Camus: The Revolt Against Absurdity. " Thought 35:53-56. Spring 1960.

Lehan, Richard. "Levels of Reality in the Novels of Albert Camus." MFS 10:240-244. Autumn 1964.

Lewis, R. W. B. The Picaresque Saint. New York: J. P. Lippincott, 1959. pp. 104-108.

Loose, John. "The Christian as Camus's Absurd Man." JR 42:210-211. July 1962.

Louria, Yvette. " 'Dedoublement' in Dostoevsky and Camus." MLR 56:82-83. January 1961.

Matthews, J. H. "From THE STRANGER to THE FALL: Confession and Complicity." MFS 10:265-273. Autumn 1964.

Moeller, Charles. "Albert Camus: The Question of Hope." CC 8:179-183. Spring 1958.

Mueller, W. R. Prophetic Voices in New Fiction. New York: Associated Press, 1959. pp. 56-82.

Redfern, W. D. "Camus and Confusion." Symposium 20: 328-337. Winter 1966.

Roudiez, Leon S. "L'ETRANGER, LA CHUTE and the Aesthetic Legacy of Gide." FR 32:300-310. February 1959.

Royce, Barbara C. "LA CHUTE and SAINT GENET: The Question of Guilt." FR 39:709-716. April 1966.

St. Aubyn, F. C. "Albert Camus and the Death of the Other: An Existentialist Interpretation." FS 16:138-140. April 1962.

St. Aubyn, F. C. "Albert Camus: Dialogue or Monologue." BA 31:123-125. Spring 1963.

Scott, Nathan A. Albert Camus. London: Bowes and Bowes, 1962. pp. 82-88.

Starratt, Robert J. "An Analysis of Albert Camus' THE FALL." Cithara 1:27-38. November 1961.

Stourzh, Gerald. "The Unforgivable Sin: An Interpretation of THE FALL." ChiR 15:45-57. Summer 1961.

Strauss, Walter. "Albert Camus, Stone-Mason." MLN 77: 273-274. May 1962.

Thody, P. "Albert Camus." ConRev 190:349-352. December 1956.

Toenes, Sara. "Public Confession in LA CHUTE. " WSCL
4:305-318. Autumn 1963.

Trahan, Elizabeth. "Clamence vs. Dostoevsky: An Approach
to LA CHUTE. " CL 18:337-350. Fall 1966.

Ullmann, Stephen. The Image in the Modern French Novel.
Cambridge: Cambridge University Press, 1960. pp. 274-
287.

Viggiani, Carl A. "Camus and the Fall from Innocence. "
YFS 25:65-71. Spring 1960.

Wardman, H. W. "Parody in Camus. " Essays in French
Lit   2:25-28. November 1965.

Yalom, Marilyn K. "Albert Camus and the Myth of the
Trial. " MLQ 25:440-450. December 1964.

Yalom, Marilyn Koenick. "LA CHUTE and A HERO OF OUR
TIME. " FR 36:138-145. December 1962.
THE PLAGUE
Batt, Jean. "Albert Camus: From THE MYTH to THE
FALL. " Meanjin 16:416-417. December 1957.

Batt, Jean C. "The Themes of the Novels and Plays of
Albert Camus. " AUMLA 6:53-54. May 1957.

Bertocci, Angelo P. "Camus' LA PESTE and the Absurd. "
RR 49:33-41. February 1958.

Bespaloff, Rachel. "The World of the Man Condemned to
Death. " Camus. (ed.) Germaine Bree. Englewood Cliffs:
Prentice Hall, 1962. pp. 98-101.

Brearley, Katherine. "The Theme of Isolation in Camus. "
KFLQ 9:120-121. 1962.

Bree, Germaine and Margaret Guiton. An Age of Fiction:
The French Novel from Gide to Camus. New Brunswick:
Rutgers University Press, 1957. pp. 222-225.

Bree, Germaine. "Albert Camus and THE PLAGUE. " YFS
8:93-100. Fall - Winter 1958.

Bree, Germaine. Camus. New Brunswick: Rutgers University Press, 1961. pp. 118-130.

Bree, Germaine. "Poetry and the Novel. " The Culture of
France in Our Time. (ed.) Julian Park. Ithaca: Cornell
University Press, 1954. pp. 34-35.

Burke, Edward L. "Camus and the Pursuit of Happiness. "

Thought 37:401-403. Autumn 1962.

Champigny, Robert. "Camus' Fictional Works: The Plight of Innocence." ASLHM 28:176-179. Summer 1957.

Champigny, Robert. "Existentialism and the Modern French Novel." Thought 31:369-371. Autumn 1956.

Clough, Wilson O. "Camus' THE PLAGUE." ColQ 7:394-404. Spring 1959.

Cruickshank, John. Albert Camus and the Literature of Revolt. New York: Oxford University Press, 1959. pp. 167-181.

Cruickshank, John. "The Art of Allegory in LA PESTE." Symposium 11:61-72. Spring 1957.

Fitch, Brian T. "Aesthetic Distance and Inner Space in the Novels of Camus." MFS 10:285-286. Autumn 1964.

Frohock, W. M. "Camus: Image, Influence and Sensibility." YFS 4:97-99. Fall-Winter 1949.

Garvin, Harry R. "Camus and the American Novel." CL 8:197-202. Summer 1956.

Glicksberg, Charles. "The Novel and the Plague." UKCR 21:57-58. Autumn 1954.

Grobe, Edwin P. "Tarrou's Confession: the Ethical Force of the Past Definite." FR 39:550-558. February 1966.

Haggis, D. R. Albert Camus: LA PESTE. London: Edward Arnold, 1962.

Hallie, Philip. "Camus and the Literature of Revolt." CE 16:28-31. October 1954.

Hanna, Thomas L. "Albert Camus and the Christian Faith." JR 36:226-228. October 1956.

Hanna, Thomas. The Thought and Art of Albert Camus. Chicago: Henry Regnery Company, 1958. pp. 195-206.

Hatzfeld, Helmut. Trends and Styles in Twentieth Century French Literature. Washington, D. C.: Catholic University of America Press, 1957. pp. 150-152.

John, S. Beynon. "Image and Symbolism in the Work of Albert Camus." Camus. (ed.) Germaine Bree. Englewood Cliffs: Prentice-Hall, 1962. pp. 141-142.

King, Adele. Albert Camus. New York: Grove Press, 1964. pp. 64-80.

Lauer, Quentin. "Albert Camus: The Revolt Against Absurdity." Thought 35:49-52. Spring 1960.

Lehan, Richard. "Levels of Reality in the Novels of Albert Camus." MFS 10:237-240. Autumn 1964.

Lewis, R. W. B. The Picaresque Saint. New York: J. P. Lippincott, 1959. pp. 90-104.

Murchland, Bernard G. "Albert Camus: Rebel." CathW 188:311-312. January 1959.

Nelson, Roy Jay. "Malraux and Camus: The Myth of the Beleaguered City." KFLQ 13:86-94. Second Quarter 1966.

Parker, Emmett. Albert Camus: The Artist in the Arena. Madison: University of Wisconsin, 1965. pp. 112-114.

Peyre, Henri. The Contemporary French Novel. New York: Oxford University Press, 1955. pp. 246-251.

Picon, Gaeton. "Notes on THE PLAGUE." Camus. (ed.) Germaine Bree. Englewood Cliffs: Prentice-Hall, 1962. pp. 145-151.

Politzer, Heinz. "Franz Kafka and Albert Camus: Parables for Our Time." ChiR 14:58-65. Spring 1960.

Redfern, W. D. "Camus and Confusion." Symposium 20: 337-342. Winter 1966.

Rolo, Charles. "Albert Camus: A Good Man." Atlantic 201:30-31. May 1958.

St. Aubyn, F. C. "Albert Camus and the Death of the Other: An Existentialist Interpretation." FS 16:134-136. April 1962.

Sargent, Lyman Tower. "Existentialism and Utopianism: A Reply to Frederick L. Polak." MinnR 6:73-74. No. 1, 1966.

Scott, Nathan A. Albert Camus. London: Bowes and Bowes, 1962. pp. 52-62.

Sorenson, M. Susan. "An Existential Utopia." MinnR 4: 356-364. Spring 1964.

Strem, George G. "The Theme of Rebellion in the Works of Camus and Dostoievsky." RLC 40:255-257. April-June

1966.

Thody, Philip. Albert Camus: 1918-1960. London: Hamish
Hamilton, 1961. pp. 93-115.

Thody, Philip. Albert Camus: A Study of His Works. London: Hamish Hamilton, 1957. pp. 29-40.

Thody, Philip. "A Note on Camus and the American
Novel. " CL 9:245-247. Summer 1957.

Ullmann, Stephen. The Image in the Modern French Novel.
Cambridge: Cambridge University Press, 1960. pp. 254-
274.

Wardman, H. W. "Parody in Camus. " Essays in French
Lit 2: 21-25. November 1965.

Willhoite, Fred H. , Jr. "Albert Camus' Politics of Rebellion. " WPQ 14:402-403. June 1961.

Williams, Raymond. "Tragic Despair and Revolt. " CritQ
5:109-110. Summer 1963.

Zants, Emily. "Relationship of Judge and Priest in LA
PESTE. " FR 37:419-425. February 1964.
THE STRANGER
Batt, Jean. "Albert Camus: From THE MYTH to THE
FALL. " Meanjin 16:412-415. December 1957.

Batt, Jean C. "The Themes of the Novels and Plays of
Albert Camus. " AUMLA 6:48-50. May 1957.

Bespaloff, Rachel. "The World of the Man Condemned to
Death. " Camus. (ed.) Germaine Bree. Englewood Cliffs:
Prentice-Hall, 1962. pp. 92-98.

Brearley, Katherine. "The Theme of Isolation in Camus. "
KFLQ 9:119-120. 1962.

Bree, Germaine and Margaret Guiton. An Age of Fiction:
The French Novel from Gide to Camus. New Brunswick:
Rutgers University Press, 1957. pp. 220-225.

Bree, Germaine. Camus. New Brunswick: Rutgers University Press, 1961. pp. 112-117.

Bree, Germaine. "The Genesis of THE STRANGER. "
Shenandoah 12:3-10. Spring 1961.

Busst, A. J. L. "A Note on the Eccentric Christology of
Camus. " FS 16:47-49. January 1962.

Champigny, Robert. "Camus' Fictional Works: The Plight of Innocence." ASLHM 28:174-176. Summer 1957.

Champigny, Robert. "The Comedy of Ethics." YFS 25:72. Spring 1960.

Champigny, Robert. "Ethics and Aesthetics in THE STRANGER." Camus. (ed.) Germaine Bree. Englewood Cliffs: Prentice-Hall, 1962. pp. 122-131.

Champigny, Robert. "Existentialism and the Modern French Novel." Thought 31:367-369. Autumn 1956.

Christensen, Naomi. "L'ETRANGER: The Unheroic Hero." CE 24:235-236. December 1962.

Cruickshank, John. Albert Camus and the Literature of Revolt. New York: Oxford University Press, 1959. pp. 151-164.

Cruickshank, John. "Camus's Technique in L'ETRANGER." FS 10:241-253. July 1956.

Dennis, William D. "Jean-Baptiste Clamence -- A Resurrected Meursault?" CLAJ 8:81-87. September 1964.

Dennis, William D. "Meursault -- Consistent or Non-Consistent?" CLAJ 6:23-27. September 1962.

Feuerlicht, Ignace. "Camus's L'ETRANGER Reconsidered." PMLA 78:606-621. December 1963.

Fitch, Brian T. "Aesthetic Distance and Inner Space in the Novels of Camus." MFS 10:279-285. Autumn 1964.

Frohock, W. M. "Camus: Image, Influence and Sensibility." YFS Fall - Winter 1949.

Garvin, Harry R. "Camus and the American Novel." CL 8:195-197. Summer 1956.

Gershman, Herbert S. "On L'ETRANGER." FR 29:299-305. February 1956.

Girard, Rene. "Camus' Stranger Retried." PMLA 79:519-533. December 1964.

Grubbs, Henry A. "Albert Camus and Graham Greene." MLQ 10:33-42. March 1949.

Hallie, Philip. "Camus and the Literature of Revolt." CE 16:26-28. October 1954.

Hanna, Thomas. The Thought and Art of Albert Camus.
Chicago: Henry Regnery Company, 1958. pp. 46-64.

Hatzfeld, Helmut. Trends and Styles in Twentieth Century
French Literature. Washington, D. C. : Catholic University
of America Press, 1957. pp. 149-150.

Holdheim, William W. "Gide's PALUDES: The Humor of
Falsity. " FR 32:405-409. April 1959.

Hudon, Louis. "THE STRANGER and the Critics. " YFS
25:59-64. Spring 1960.

John, S. Beynon. "Image and Symbolism in the Work of
Albert Camus. " Camus. (ed.) Germaine Bree. Englewood
Cliffs: Prentice-Hall, 1962. pp. 136-138.

Jones, Marian. "Camus' Rebels. " WHR 12:54-55. Winter
1958.

Kamber, Gerald. "The Allegory of Names in L'ETRANG-
ER. " MLQ 22:292-301. September 1961.

King, Adele. Albert Camus. New York: Grove Press, 1964.
pp. 46-63.

Krieger, Murray. The Tragic Vision. New York: Holt,
Rinehart and Winston, 1960. pp. 144-153.

Lang, B. Renee. "Two Books, Two Creeds. " BA 21:385-
386. Autumn 1947.

Lehan, Richard. "Camus' L'ETRANGER and American Neo-
Realism. " BA 38:233-238. Summer 1964.

Lehan, Richard. "Levels of Reality in the Novels of Albert
Camus. " MFS 10:232-237. Autumn 1964.

Lesage, Laurence. "Albert Camus and Stendhal. " FR 23:
474-477. May 1950.

Lewis, R. W. B. The Picaresque Saint. New York: Lippincott, 1959. pp. 65-79.

Loose, John. "The Christian as Camus's Absurd Man. "
JR 42:209-210. July 1962.

Manly, William M. "Journey to Consciousness: The Symbolic Pattern in Camus' L'ETRANGER. " PMLA 79:321-
328. June 1964.

Matthews, J. H. "From THE STRANGER to THE FALL:
Confession and Complicity. " MFS 10:265-273. Autumn 1964.

Moseley, Edwin M. Pseudonyms of Christ in the Modern Novel. Pittsburgh: University of Pittsburgh Press, 1962. pp. 195-204.

Murray, Jack. "Three Murders in the Contemporary French Novel. " TSLL 6:366-370. Autumn 1964.

Parker, Emmett. Albert Camus: The Artist in the Arena. Madison: University of Wisconsin Press, 1965. pp. 42-45.

Peyre, Henri. The Contemporary French Novel. New York: Oxford University Press, 1955. pp. 243-246.

Politzer, Heinz. "Franz Kafka and Albert Camus: Parables for Our Time. " ChiR 14:52-57. Spring 1960.

Rhein, Phillip H. The Urge to Live: A Comparative Study of Franz Kafka's DER PROZESS and Albert Camus' L'ETRANGER. Chapel Hill: University of North Carolina Press, 1964.

Rolo, Charles. "Albert Camus: A Good Man. " Atlantic 201:30. May 1958.

Rose, Marilyn Gaddis. "Meursault as Pharmakos: A Reading of L'ETRANGER. " MFS 10:258-264. Autumn 1964.

Rossi, Louis R. "Albert Camus: The Plague of Absurdity." KR 20:402-415. Summer 1958.

Roudiez, Leon S. "L'Etranger, La Chute, and the Aesthetic Legacy of Gide. " FR 32:300-310. February 1959.

Roudiez, Leon S. "Strangers in Melville and Camus. " FR 31:217-226. January 1958.

St. Aubyn, F. C. "Albert Camus and the Death of the Other: An Existentialist Interpretation. " FS 16:128-133. April 1962.

Sandstrom, Glenn. "The Outsiders of Stendhal and Camus." MFS 10:245-257. Autumn 1964.

Sartre, Jean Paul. "An Explication of The Stranger. " Camus. (ed.) Germaine Bree. Englewood Cliffs: Prentice-Hall, 1962. pp. 108-121.

Scott, Nathan A. Albert Camus. London: Bowes and Bowes, 1962. pp. 30-36.

Smith, Albert B. "Restriction and Consciousness in Camus' L'Etranger. " SSF 3:451-453. Summer 1966.

Strauss, Walter A. "Albert Camus, Stone-Mason. " MLN
77:271-272. May 1962.

Thody, Philip. "A Note on Camus and the American Novel."
CL 9:243-244. Summer 1957.

Ullmann, Stephen. The Image in the Modern French Novel.
Cambridge: Cambridge University Press, 1960. pp. 244-
254.

Viggiani, Carl A. "Camus' L'ETRANGER" PMLA 71:865-
887. December 1956.

Wardman, H. W. "Parody in Camus. " Essays in French
Lit 2:17-21. November 1965.

Weinberg, Kurt. "The Theme of Exile. " YFS 25:36-40.
Spring 1960.

Yalom, Marilyn K. "Albert Camus and the Myth of the
Trial. " MLQ 25:435-438. December 1964.

Cayrol, Jean
    JE VIVRAI L'AMOUR DES AUTRES
        Lynes, Carlos, Jr. "Jean Cayrol and 'Le Romanesque
        Lazareen.' " YFS 8:109-112. Fall - Winter 1958.
    LA NOIRE
        Lynes, Carlos, Jr. "Jean Cayrol and 'Le Romanesque
        Lazareen.' " YFS 8:114-117. Fall - Winter 1958.

Ceard, Henry
    UNE BELLE JOURNEE
        Sachs, Murray. "The Esthetics of Naturalism. " ECr 4:76-
        83. Summer 1964.

Celine, Louis
    DEATH ON THE INSTALLMENT PLAN
        Hayman, David. Louis Ferdinand Celine. New York: Colum-
        bia University Press, 1965. pp. 28-37.
    GUIGNOL'S BAND
        Reck, Rima Drell. "Celine and the Aural Novel. " BA 39:
        405-406. Autumn 1965.
    JOURNEY TO THE END OF NIGHT
        Bree, Germaine and Margaret Guiton. An Age of Fiction:
        The French Novel from Gide to Camus. New Brunswick:
        Rutgers University Press, 1957. pp. 164-168.

        Glicksberg, Charles. "The Novel and the Plague. " UKCR
        21:56. Autumn 1954.

        Greenberg, Alvin. "The Novel of Disintegration: Paradox-
        ical Impossibility in Contemporary Fiction. " WSCL 7:103-
        108. Winter - Spring 1966.

Hayman, David. Louis-Ferdinand Celine. New York: Columbia University Press, 1965. pp. 22-28.

Hindus, Milton. "Celine: A Reappraisal." SoR n. s. 1:76-93.
Winter 1965.

Howe, Irving. "Celine: The Sod Beneath the Skin-I." New
Republic 149:19-22. July 20, 1963.

Matthews, J. H. "Celine's JOURNEY TO THE END OF
NIGHT." ConRev 191:158-161. March 1957.

Reck, Rima Drell. "Celine and the Aural Novel." BA 39:
405-406. Autumn 1965.

Trotsky, Leon. "Novelist and Politician." Atlantic 156:
413-420. October 1935.

Chateaubriand, Francois
    ATALA

Bede, Jean-Albert. "Chateaubriand: or, The Love of Genius
and The Genius of Love." ASLH M 33:147-148. No. 3, 1962.

Brown, Donald F. "Chateaubriand and the Story of Felic-
iana in Jorge Isaac's MARIA." MLN 62:326-329. May 1947.

Chapman, Arnold. "ATALA and NIAGARA: Further Comment." MLN 68:150-154. March 1953.

Facteau, Bernard A. "Notes on Chateaubriand's ATALA."
MLN 48:492-497. December 1933.

Frank, John C. "A Note on the Natural Bridge in ATALA."
MLN 64:406-410. June 1949.

George, Albert J. Short Fiction in France: 1800-1850.
Syracuse: Syracuse University Press, 1964. pp. 23-28.

Kendris, Christopher. "Patterns in ATALA and LAURETTE
OU LE CACHET ROUGE." FR 31:149-152. December 1957.

Maurois, Andre. Chateaubriand. New York: Harper and
Brothers, 1938. pp. 92-101.

Naylor, Louis Hastings. Chateaubriand and Virgil. Baltimore: Johns Hopkins Press, 1930. Chapter IV.

Schwartz, William Leonard. "Caleb Bingham's Translation
of ATALA." MLN 45:7-12. January 1930.

Valette, Rebecca M. "Chateaubriand's Debt to LES INCAS."
SIR 2:177-183. Spring 1963.

Walker, Thomas Capell. Chateaubriand's Natural Scenery:
A Study of His Descriptive Art. Baltimore: Johns Hopkins
Press, 1946. (Johns Hopkins Studies in Romance Liter-
atures and Languages. Vol. 21.) pp. 151-160.

THE GENIUS OF CHRISTIANITY
Hart, Charles Randall. Chateaubriand and Homer. Baltimore: Johns Hopkins Press, 1928. pp. 87-101.

Maurois, Andre. Chateaubriand. New York: Harper and
Brothers, 1938. Chapter IV.

Naylor, Louis Hastings. Chateaubriand and Virgil. Baltimore: Johns Hopkins Press, 1930. Chapter IV.

THE MARTYRS
Clayton, Vista. "A Contemporary Source for the Descrip-
tion of Heaven in LES MARTYRS. " RR 25:136-140. April-
June 1934.

Hart, Charles Randall. Chateaubriand and Homer. Baltimore: Johns Hopkins Press, 1928. pp. 102-154.

Maurois, Andre. Chateaubriand. New York: Harper and
Brothers, 1938. pp. 163-171.

Naylor, Louis Hastings. Chateaubriand and Virgil. Baltimore: Johns Hopkins Press, 1930. Chapter IV.

THE NATCHEZ
Bede, Jean-Albert. "Chateaubriand: or, The Love of
Genius and The Genius of Love. " ASLHM 33:148-149. No.
3, 1962.

Hart, Charles Randall. Chateaubriand and Homer. Baltimore: Johns Hopkins Press, 1928. pp. 33-86.

Naylor, Louis Hastings. Chateaubriand and Virgil. Baltimore: Johns Hopkins Press, 1930. pp. 115-138.

Walker, Thomas Capell. Chateaubriand's Natural Scenery:
A Study of His Descriptive Art. Baltimore: Johns Hopkins
Press, 1946. (Johns Hopkins Studies in Romance Liter-
atures and Languages. Vol. 21.) pp. 162-163.

RENE
Boorsch, Jean. "Motion and Rest in RENE. " YFS 13:76-
82. Spring - Summer 1954.

George, Albert J. Short Fiction in France: 1800-1850. Syracuse: Syracuse University Press, 1964. pp. 26-29.

Grimsley, Ronald. "Romantic Melancholy in Chateaubriand
and Kierkegaard. " CL 8:227-244. Summer 1956.

Naylor, Louis Hastings. Chateaubriand and Virgil. Baltimore: Johns Hopkins Press, 1930. Chapter IV.

Ridge, George Ross. "Representative Ideas of the Deathwish in Nineteenth-Century French Literature." KFLQ 7:
146-147. 1960.

Zimmermann, Eleonore M. "Re-reading RENE." FR 32:
247-253. January 1959.

Chauffin, Yvonne
  LE COMBAT DE JACOB
    Pitou, Spire. "Yvonne Chauffin's Tetralogy: A Study in
    Christian Suffering." Renascence 16:36-38. Fall 1963.
  LA PORTE DES HEBREUX
    Pitou, Spire. "Yvonne Chauffin's Tetralogy: A Study in
    Christian Suffering." Renascence 16:39-40. Fall 1963.
  QUE VOTRE VOLONTE SOIT FAITE
    Pitou, Spire. "Yvonne Chauffin's Tetralogy: A Study in
    Christian Suffering." Renascence 16:35-36. Fall 1963.

Cocteau, Jean
  THE GRAND ECART
    Bree, Germaine and Margaret Guiton. An Age of Fiction:
    The French Novel from Gide to Camus. New Brunswick:
    Rutgers University Press, 1957. pp. 142-144.
  THE HOLY TERRORS
    Bree, Germaine and Margaret Guiton. An Age of Fiction:
    The French Novel from Gide to Camus. New Brunswick:
    Rutgers University Press, 1957. pp. 145-149.

    Holloway, Owen. "Jean Cocteau: Professional Amateur."
    Listener 61:670-671. April 16, 1959.
  THOMAS THE IMPOSTOR
    Bree, Germaine and Margaret Guiton. An Age of Fiction:
    The French Novel from Gide to Camus. New Brunswick:
    Rutgers University Press, 1957. p. 145.

Colette
  CHERI
    Lesser, Simon O. "The Wages of Adjustment: CHERI and
    THE LAST OF CHERI." MinnR 4:212-225. Winter 1964.

    Olken, I. T. "Aspects of Imagery in Colette: Color and
    Light." PMLA 77:140-148. March 1962.

    Olken, I. T. "Imagery in CHERI and LA FIN DE CHERI."
    FS 16:245-261. July 1962.

    Olken, I. T. "Imagery in CHERI and LA FIN DE CHERI."
    SP 60:96-115. January 1963.

    Pritchett, V. S. "Books in General." New S&N 42:158.
    August 11, 1951.
  THE LAST OF CHERI
    Lesser, Simon O. "The Wages of Adjustment: CHERI and

THE LAST OF CHERI. '' MinnR 4:212-225. Winter 1964.

Olken, I. T. ''Aspects of Imagery in Colette: Color and Light. '' PMLA 77:140-148. March 1962.

Olken, I. T. ''Imagery in CHERI and LA FIN DE CHERI.'' FS 16:245-261. July 1962.

Olken, I. T. ''Imagery in CHERI and LA FIN DE CHERI.'' SP 60:96-115. January 1963.

Pritchett, V. S. ''Books in General. '' New S&N 42:158. August 11, 1951.

Constant, Benjamin
   ADOLPHE
      Blanchot, Maurice. ''ADOLPHE, or, The Curse of Real Feelings. '' YFS 13:62-75. Spring - Summer 1954.

      Blanchot, Maurice. ''ADOLPHE; or, the Misfortunes of Sincerity. '' Horizon 20:94-110. August 1949.

      Fairlie, Alison. ''The Art of Constant's ADOLPHE: Creation of Character. '' FMLS 2:253-263. July 1966.

      Fairlie, Alison. ''The Art of Constant's ADOLPHE: Structure and Style. '' FS 20:226-240. July 1966.

      George, Albert J. Short Fiction in France: 1800-1850. Syracuse: Syracuse University Press, 1964. pp. 47-52.

      Greshoff, C. J. ''ADOLPHE and the Romantic Delusion. '' FMLS 1:30-36. January 1965.

      Holdheim, William W. Benjamin Constant. London: Bowes and Bowes, 1961. pp. 41-48.

      Murry, John Middleton. The Conquest of Death. London: Peter Nevill Limited, 1951. pp. 125-306.

      Nicolson, Harold. Benjamin Constant. Garden City: Doubleday and Company, 1949. pp. 201-207.

      Shapiro, Norman R. ''The Symmetry of Benjamin Constant's ADOLPHE. '' FR 34:186-188. December 1960.

      Sullivan, Edward D. ''Constraint and Expansion in Benjamin Constant's ADOLPHE. '' FR 32:293-299. February 1959.

      Turnell, Martin. The Novel in France. New York: New Directions, 1951. pp. 91-122.

CECILE
>   Fay, Eliot G. "The Man Who Hesitated for Fifteen Years."
>   FR 27:323-330. April 1954.

>   Holdheim, William W. Benjamin Constant. London: Bowes
>   and Bowes, 1961. pp. 36-41.

Crebillon, Claude de
  LES EGAREMENTS
>   Mylne, Vivienne. The Eighteenth-Century French Novel:
>   Techniques of Illusion. Manchester: Manchester University
>   Press, 1965. pp. 125-140.
  LETTRES DE LA MARQUISE DE M —
>   Mylne, Vivienne. The Eighteenth-Century French Novel:
>   Techniques of Illusion. Manchester: Manchester University
>   Press, 1965. pp. 156-162.
  THE SOFA
>   Day, D. A. "On the Dating of Three Novels by Crebillon
>   Fils." MLR 56:391-392. July 1961.

Daudet, Alphonse
  L'EVANGELISTE
>   Dobie, G. V. Alphonse Daudet. London: Thomas Nelson and
>   Sons, Ltd., 1949. pp. 228-231.

>   Sachs, Murray. The Career of Alphonse Daudet: A Critical
>   Study. Cambridge: Harvard University Press, 1965. pp.
>   127-130.
  FREMONT AND RISLER
>   Dobie, G. V. Alphonse Daudet. London: Thomas Nelson and
>   Sons, Ltd., 1949. pp. 181-187.

>   Sachs, Murray. The Career of Alphonse Daudet: A Critical
>   Study. Cambridge: Harvard University Press, 1965. pp. 83-
>   97.
  L'IMMORTEL
>   Carter, Boyd G. "Alphonse Daudet and Darwinism." MLQ
>   6:93-98. March 1945.

>   Sachs, Murray. The Career of Alphonse Daudet: A Critical
>   Study. Cambridge: Harvard University Press, 1965. pp. 141-
>   148.
  JACK
>   Sachs, Murray. The Career of Alphonse Daudet: A Critical
>   Study. Cambridge: Harvard University Press, 1965. pp. 98-
>   103.
  KINGS IN EXILE
>   Dobie, G. V. Alphonse Daudet. London: Thomas Nelson and
>   Sons, Ltd., 1949. pp. 199-203.

>   Sachs, Murray. The Career of Alphonse Daudet: A Critical
>   Study. Cambridge: Harvard University Press, 1965. pp.
>   111-118.

THE LITTLE GOOD-FOR-NOTHING
Dobie, G. V. Alphonse Daudet. London: Thomas Nelson
and Sons, Ltd., 1949. pp. 105-113.

Sachs, Murray. The Career of Alphonse Daudet: A Critical
Study. Cambridge: Harvard University Press, 1965. pp. 50-
58; 83-97.
THE NABAB
Dobie, G. V. Alphonse Daudet. London: Thomas Nelson
and Sons, Ltd., 1949. Chapter 24.

Sachs, Murray. The Career of Alphonse Daudet: A Critical
Study. Cambridge: Harvard University Press, 1965. pp.
104-111.
NUMA ROUMESTAN
Dobie, G. V. Alphonse Daudet. London: Thomas Nelson and
Sons, Ltd., 1949. pp. 209-210; 212-214.

Sachs, Murray. The Career of Alphonse Daudet: A Critical
Study. Cambridge: Harvard University Press, 1965. pp.
119-127.
LA PETITE PAROISSE
Sachs, Murray. The Career of Alphonse Daudet: A Critical
Study. Cambridge: Harvard University Press, 1965. pp.
160-164.
PORT TARASCON
Sachs, Murray. "Alphonse Daudet's Tartarin Trilogy. "
MLR 61:215-217. April 1966.

Sachs, Murray. The Career of Alphonse Daudet: A Critical
Study. Cambridge: Harvard University Press, 1965. pp.
148-151.
ROSE ET NINETTE
Sachs, Murray. The Career of Alphonse Daudet: A Critical
Study. Cambridge: Harvard University Press, 1965. pp.
157-159.
SAPHO
Dobie, G. V. Alphonse Daudet. London: Thomas Nelson and
Sons, Ltd., 1949. pp. 232-234.

Pritchett, V. S. Books in General. London: Chatto and
Windus, 1953. pp. 104-109.

Pritchett, V. S. "Books in General. " New S&N 42:313-314.
September 22, 1951.

Sachs, Murray. The Career of Alphonse Daudet: A Critical
Study. Cambridge: Harvard University Press, 1965. pp.
130-135.
TARTARIN OF TARASCON
Dobie, G. V. Alphonse Daudet. London: Thomas Nelson and
Sons, Ltd., 1949. pp. 117-121.

Favreau, Alphonse R. "The Background of TARTARIN OF
TARASCON." ASLHM 17:282-292. Spring 1946.

Sachs, Murray. "Alphonse Daudet's Tartarin Trilogy."
MLR 61:210-213. April 1966.

Sachs, Murray. The Career of Alphonse Daudet: A Critical
Study. Cambridge: Harvard University Press, 1965. pp. 65-
73.
TARTARIN OVER THE ALPS
Dobie, G. V. Alphonse Daudet. London: Thomas Nelson and
Sons, Ltd., 1949. pp. 235-236.

Rogers, Franklin R. "Mark Twain and Daudet: A TRAMP
ABROAD and TARTARIN SUR LES ALPES." CL 16:254-
263. Summer 1964.

Sachs, Murray. "Alphonse Daudet's Tartarin Trilogy."
MLR 61:213-215. April 1966.

Sachs, Murray. The Career of Alphonse Daudet: A Critical
Study. Cambridge: Harvard University Press, 1965. pp.
136-140.

Denon, Vivant
POINT DE LENDEMAIN
Loy, J. Robert. "Love/Vengeance in the Late Eighteenth-
Century French Novel." ECr 3:158-160. Winter 1963.

Diderot, Denis
LES DEUX AMIS DE BOURBONNE
Geary, Edward J. "The Composition and Publication of
LES DEUX AMIS DE BOURBONNE." Diderot Studies. (ed.)
Otis E. Fellows and Norman L. Torrey. Syracuse: Syra-
cuse University Press, 1949. pp. 27-45.
THE INDISCREET JEWELS
Ellrich, Robert J. "The Structure of Diderot's LES
BIJOUX INDISCRETS." RR 52:279-289. December 1961.

Leov, Nola M. "Literary Techniques in LES BIJOUX IN-
DISCRETS." AUMLA 19:93-105. May 1963.

Mylne, Vivienne. The Eighteenth Century French Novel:
Techniques of Illusion. Manchester: Manchester University Press, 1965. pp. 219-220.

Wilson, Arthur M. Diderot: The Testing Years, 1713-1759.
New York: Oxford University Press, 1957. pp. 83-87.
JACQUES THE FATALIST
Baldwin, Charles Sears. "The Literary Influence of Sterne
in France." PMLA 17:226-229. 1902.

Brereton, Geoffrey. A Short History of French Literature.

London: Cassell, 1954. pp. 101-102

Crocker, Lester G. Diderot: The Embattled Philosopher.
New York: The Free Press, 1954. pp. 387-393.

Crocker, Lester G. Two Diderot Studies: Ethics and
Esthetics. Baltimore: Johns Hopkins Press, 1952. pp. 40-
41.

Fredman, Alice Green. Diderot and Sterne. New York:
Columbia University Press, 1955. pp. 119-120; 130-131;
136-137; 141-142; 144-145; 152-153.

Green, Alice G. "Diderot's Fictional Worlds. " Diderot
Studies I. (ed.) Otis E. Fellows and Norman L. Torrey.
Syracuse: Syracuse University Press, 1949. pp. 1-22.

Grimsley, Ronald. "Morality and Imagination in JACQUES
LE FATALISTE. " MLQ 19:283-293. December 1958.

Loy, J. Robert. Diderot's Determined Fatalist: A Critical
Appreciation of JACQUES LE FATALISTE. New York:
King's Crown Press, 1950.

Mylne, Vivienne. The Eighteenth-Century French Novel:
Techniques of Illusion. Manchester: Manchester University
Press, 1965. pp. 214-219.

Smith, I. H. "Diderot's JACQUES LE FATALISTE: Art
and Necessity. " AUMLA 8:17-23. May 1958.

Smith, I. H. "The Mme. de la Pommeraye Tale and Its
Commentaries. " AUMLA 17:18-29. May 1963.

Undank, Jack. "A New Date for JACQUES LE FATALISTE."
MLN 74:433-437. May 1959.

THE NUN
Crocker, Lester G. Diderot: The Embattled Philosopher.
New York: The Free Press, 1954. pp. 258-262.

Dieckmann, Herbert. "The PREFACE-ANNEXE of LA
RELIGIEUSE. " Diderot Studies II. (ed.) Otis E. Fellows
and Norman L. Torrey. Syracuse: Syracuse University
Press, 1952. pp. 21-38.

Fredman, Alice Green. Diderot and Sterne. New York:
Columbia University Press, 1955. pp. 114-115.

Mylne, Vivienne. The Eighteenth-Century French Novel:
Techniques of Illusion. Manchester: Manchester University
Press, 1965. pp. 198-214.
RAMEAU'S NEPHEW
Barricelli, Jean-Pierre. "Music and the Structure of

Diderot's LE NEVEU DE RAMEAU. " Criticism 5:95-111.
Spring 1963.

Becker, Carl. "The Dilemma of Diderot. " PhR 24:64-67.
January 1915.

Crocker, Lester G. Diderot: The Embattled Philosopher.
New York: The Free Press, 1954. pp. 262-275.

Farmer, Henry George. "Diderot and Rameau. " Music
Rev 22:181-188. August 1961.

Fellows, Otis E. "The Theme of Genius in Diderot's
NEVEU DE RAMEAU. " Diderot Studies II. (ed.) Otis E.
Fellows and Norman L. Torrey. Syracuse: Syracuse Uni-
versity Press, 1952. pp. 168-197.

Fredman, Alice Green. Diderot and Sterne. New York:
Columbia University Press, 1955. pp. 64-65; 115-116; 132-
133.

Geary, Edward J. "The Composition and Publication of
LES DEUX AMIS DE BOURBONNE. " Diderot Studies I.
(ed.) Otis E. Fellows and Norman L. Torrey. Syracuse:
Syracuse University Press, 1949. pp. 143-191.

Geen, Renee. "Valery and Diderot. " RomN 7:5-8. Autumn
1965.

Grimsley, Ronald. "Psychological Aspects of LE NEVEU
DE RAMEAU. " MLQ 16:195-209. September 1955.

Meyer, Paul H. "The Unity and Structure of Diderot's
NEVEU DE RAMEAU. " Criticism 2:362-386. Fall 1960.

Sandomirsky, L. Natalie. "The Ethical Standard of the
Genius in Diderot's NEVEU DE RAMEAU. " Symposium
18:46-53. Spring 1964.

Seiden, Milton F. "Jean-Francois Rameau and Diderot's
Neveu. " Diderot Studies I. (ed.) Otis E. Fellows and
Norman L. Torrey. Syracuse: Syracuse University Press,
1949. pp. 143-183.

Spitzer, Leo. Linguistics and Literary History: Essays in
Stylistics. Princeton: Princeton University Press, 1948.
pp. 152-161.

Duhamel, Georges
    THE PASQUIER CHRONICLES
        Bree, Germaine and Margaret Guiton. An Age of Fiction:
        The French Novel from Gide to Camus. New Brunswick:
        Rutgers University Press, 1957. pp. 63-67.

Hatzfeld, Helmut. Trends and Styles in Twentieth Century French Literature. Washington, D. C.: Catholic University of America Press, 1957. pp. 31-32.
SALAVIN'S JOURNAL
Peyre, Henri. The Contemporary French Novel. New York: Oxford University Press, 1955. pp. 50-52.

Dujardin, Edouard
LES LAURIERS SONT COUPES
Bowling, Lawrence Edward. "What Is the Stream of Consciousness Technique?" PMLA 65:333-345. June 1950.

Friedman, M. J. Stream of Consciousness. New Haven: Yale University Press, 1955. pp. 142-159.

King, C. D. "Edouard Dujardin, Inner Monologue and the Stream of Consciousness. " FS 7:116-127. April 1953.

Dumas pere
THE BLACK TULIP
Bell, A. Craig. Alexandre Dumas: A Biography and Study. London: Cassell and Company, Ltd., 1950. pp. 247-248.
THE COUNT OF MONTE CRISTO
Bell, A. Craig. Alexandre Dumas: A Biography and Study. London: Cassell and Company, Ltd., 1950. pp. 158-165; 194-196.

Maurois, Andre. Alexandre Dumas: A Great Life in Brief. New York: Alfred A. Knopf, 1955. pp. 124-126.

Maurois, Andre. The Titans. New York: Harper and Brothers, 1957. pp. 219-227.

Vestal, Stanley. "An Oscar for Dumas Pere. " BA 22:238-239. Summer 1948.
THE THREE MUSKETEERS
Bell, A. Craig. Alexandre Dumas: A Biography and Study. London: Cassell and Company, Ltd., 1950. pp. 150-164.

Garnett, R. S. "The Genius and the Ghost. " Blackwood's Mag 226:129-142. July 1929.

Maurois, Andre. The Titans. New York: Harper and Brothers, 1957. pp. 176-181.

Parker, Richard. "Some Additional Sources of Dumas's LES TROIS MOUSQUETAIRES. " MP 42:34-39. August 1944.

Vestal, Stanley. "An Oscar for Dumas Pere. " BA 22:239-240. Summer 1948.

Dumas fils
  L'AFFAIRE CLEMENCEAU
      Dunbar, Viola. "A Source for RODERICK HUDSON."
      MLN 63:303-310. May 1948.
  CAMILLE
      Zucker, A. E. and P. de F. Henderson. "CAMILLE as the
      Translation of LA DAME AUX CAMELIAS." MLN 49:472-
      476. November 1934.

Duras, Marguerite
  MODERATO CANTABILE
      Kneller, John W. "Elective Empathies and Musical Af-
      finities." YFS 27:114-120. Spring - Summer 1961.

      Morse, J. Mitchell. "The Choreography of 'The New
      Novel.' " HudR 16:405-407. Autumn 1963.
  THE SQUARE
      Hoog, Armand. "The Itinerary of Marguerite Duras."
      YFS 24:72-73. Summer 1959.

      Morse, J. Mitchell. "The Choreography of 'The New
      Novel.' " HudR 16:404-405. Autumn 1963.

Estaunie, Edouard
  L'APPEL DE LA ROUTE
      Bowen, Ray P. "Edouard Estaunie: Novelist of Loneliness."
      SR 35:36-38. January 1927.
  LES CHOSES VOIENT
      Crane, Christina. "A Study of the Priest Type in the
      Novels of Edouard Estaunie." FR 27:263-264. February
      1954.
  L'EMPREINTE
      Crane, Christina. "A Study of the Priest Type in the
      Novels of Edouard Estaunie." FR 27:261-262. February
      1954.

      Ilsley, Marjorie H. "Edouard Estaunie's Message." FR
      16:464-466. May 1943.
  L'EPAVE
      Crane, Christina. "A Study of the Priest Type in the
      Novels of Edouard Estaunie." FR 27:262. February 1954.
  LE FERMENT
      Ilsley, Marjorie H. "Edouard Estaunie's Message." FR
      16:466. May 1943.
  LE LABYRINTHE
      Bowen, Ray P. "Edouard Estaunie: Novelist of Loneli-
      ness." SR 35:38-39. January 1927.
  SOLITUDES
      Herman, Abraham. "Maupassant as a Source of Estaunie's
      Conception of Solitude." FR 18:141-145. January 1945.
  LA VIE SECRETE
      Ilsley, Marjorie H. "Edouard Estaunie's Message." FR 16:
      466-471. May 1943.

Fabre, Ferdinand
  L'ABBE TIGRANE
      Saintsbury, George. A History of the French Novel (To the
      Close of the 19th Century). London: Macmillan and Com-
      pany, 1919. pp. 519-521.
  LUCIFER
      Saintsbury, George. A History of the French Novel (To the
      Close of the 19th Century). London: Macmillan and Com-
      pany, 1919. pp. 524-525.
  LE MARQUIS DE PIERRERUE
      Saintsbury, George, A History of the French Novel (To the
      Close of the 19th Century). London: Macmillan and Com-
      pany, 1919. pp. 522-523.
  MON ONCLE
      Saintsbury, George. A History of the French Novel (To the
      Close of the 19th Century). London: Macmillan and Com-
      pany, 1919. pp. 523-524.
  NORINE
      Saintsbury, George. A History of the French Novel (To the
      Close of the 19th Century). London: Macmillan and Com-
      pany, 1919. pp. 521-522.

Flaubert, Gustave
  BOUVARD AND PECUCHET
      Faguet, Emile. Flaubert. Boston: Houghton Mifflin Company,
      1914. Chapter VIII.

      Kenner, Hugh. Flaubert, Joyce and Beckett: The Stoic
      Comedians. Boston: Beacon Press, 1962. pp. 4-15; 23-29.

      Levin, Harry. The Gates of Horn: A Study of Five French
      Realists. New York: Oxford University Press, 1963. pp.
      292-301.

      Neumeyer, Eva Maria. "The Landscape Garden as a Sym-
      bol in Rousseau, Goethe and Flaubert." JHI 8:209-217.
      April 1947.

      Rossi, Louis. "The Structure of Flaubert's BOUVARD ET
      PECUCHET, Vol. I. " MLQ 14:102-111. March 1953.

      Saintsbury, George. A History of the French Novel (To the
      Close of the 19th Century). London: Macmillan and Com-
      pany, 1919. pp. 409-410.

      Stonier, G. W. "BOUVARD AND PECUCHET. " New S&N
      11:225-226. February 15, 1936.

      Thorlby, Anthony. Gustave Flaubert and the Art of Realism.
      New Haven: Yale University Press, 1957. Chapter IV.

      Tillett, Margaret G. On Reading Flaubert. London: Oxford
      University Press, 1961. Chapter VII.

Trilling, Lionel. The Opposing Self: Nine Essays in Criticism. New York: Viking Press, 1955. pp. 173-205.

West, C. B. "Flaubert and Baudelaire: An Echo of 'Une Charogne' in BOUVARD ET PECUCHET. " MLR 55:417-418. July 1960.
HERODIAS
Cannon, Joyce H. "Flaubert's Documentation for HEROD-IAS. " FS 14:325-338. October 1960.

Cannon, Joyce. "Flaubert's Search for a Form in HERODIAS. " MLR 57:195-203. April 1962.

Tillett, Margaret G. On Reading Flaubert. London: Oxford University Press, 1961. Chapter VI.
LA LEGENDE DE SAINT JULIEN L'HOSPITALIER
Bart, Benjamin F. "The Moral of Flaubert's SAINT-JULIEN. " RR 38:23-33. February 1947.

Brombert, Victor. "Flaubert's SAINT JULIEN: The Sin of Existing. " PMLA 81:297-302. June 1966.

Raitt, A. W. "The Composition of Flaubert's SAINT JULIEN L'HOSPITALIER. " FS 19:358-369. October 1965.

Tillett, Margaret G. On Reading Flaubert. London: Oxford University Press, 1961. Chapter VI.
MADAME BOVARY
Adams, Robert M. Strains of Discord: Studies in Literary Openness. Ithaca: Cornell University Press, 1958. pp. 85-90.

Auerbach, Erich. "In the Hotel de la Mole. " PR 18:293-301. May - June 1951. (Also in Auerbach. Mimesis. New York: Doubleday and Company, 1957. pp. 425-433.)

Auerbach, Erich. "MADAME BOVARY. " Flaubert. (ed.) Raymond Giraud. Englewood Cliffs: Prentice-Hall, 1964. pp. 132-140.

Bart, B. F. "Aesthetic Distance in MADAME BOVARY. " PMLA 69:1112-1126. December 1954.

Bart, B. F. "Balzac and Flaubert: Energy Versus Art. " RR 42:198-204. October 1951.

Bart, B. F. "Flaubert's Documentation Goes Awry or What Color Were Emma Bovary's Eyes?" RomN 5:138. Spring 1964.

Bart, Benjamin F. Flaubert's Landscape Descriptions. Ann Arbor: University of Michigan Press, 1956. pp. 32-39.

Bart, B. F. "MADAME BOVARY After a Century. " FR
31:203-210. January 1958.

Baudelaire, Charles. "MADAME BOVARY. " Flaubert.
(ed.) Raymond Giraud. Englewood Cliffs: Prentice-Hall,
1964. pp. 88-96.

Bersani, Leo. "The Narrator and the Bourgeois Community in MADAME BOVARY." FR 32:527-533. May 1959.

Blackmur, R. P. "Madame Bovary: Beauty Out of Place."
KR 13:475-503. Summer 1951.

Brandes, Georg. Creative Spirits of the Nineteenth Century. New York: Crowell Company, 1923. pp. 223-266.

Brereton, Geoffrey. A Short History of French Literature.
London: Cassell, 1954. pp. 222-224.

Buck, Stratton. "For Emma Bovary. " SR 65:551-564.
Autumn 1957.

Buck, Stratton. Gustave Flaubert. New York: Twayne
Publishers, Inc., 1966. Chapter 5.

Cook, Albert. "Flaubert: The Riches of Detachment. " FR
32:124-126. December 1958.

Cook, Albert. The Meaning of Fiction. Detroit: Wayne
State University Press, 1960. pp. 100-106.

Croce, Benedetto. "Flaubert. " L Merc 5:488-492. March
1922.

Dauner, Louise. "Poetic Symbolism in MADAME BOVARY."
SAQ 55:207-220. April 1956.

Engstrom, Alfred G. "Flaubert's Correspondence and the
Ironic and Symbolic Structure of MADAME BOVARY. " SP
46:470-495. July 1949.

Engstrom, Alfred G. "Vergil, Ovid and the Cry of Fate
in MADAME BOVARY. " PQ 37:123-128. January 1958.

Eoff, Sherman H. The Modern Spanish Novel. New York:
New York University Press, 1961. pp. 58-67.

Faguet, Emile. Flaubert. Boston: Houghton Mifflin Company, 1914. Chapter VI.

Ferguson, Walter D. The Influence of Flaubert on George
Moore. Philadelphia: University of Pennsylvania Press,
1934. Chapter 4.

Gibian, George. "Love by the Book: Pushkin, Stendhal, Flaubert. " CL 8:105-108. Spring 1956.

Gilman, Margaret. "Two Critics and an Author: MADAME BOVARY Judged by Sainte-Beuve and by Baudelaire. " FR 15:138-146. December 1941.

Giraud, R. Unheroic Heroes. New Brunswick: Rutgers University Press, 1957. pp. 140-152.

Grant, Richard B. "The Role of Minerva in MADAME BOVARY. " RomN 6:113-115. Spring 1965.

Gregor, Ian and Brian Nicholas. The Moral and the Story. London: Faber and Faber, 1962. pp. 33-62.

Harvey, Lawrence E. "The Ironic Triumph of Rodolphe. " FR 30:121-125. December 1956.

Jean-Aubry, G. "Gustave Flaubert and Music. " M&L 31: 18-21. January 1950.

Johnson, Irwin A. "Notes on MADAME BOVARY, LES FLEURS DU MAL and Modern Symbolism. " FR 7:93-107. December 1933.

Kenner, Hugh. Flaubert, Joyce, and Beckett: The Stoic Comedians. Boston: Beacon Press, 1962. pp. 15-18; 22.

Lapp, John C. "Art and Hallucination in Flaubert. " FS 10:322-333. October 1956.

Levin, Harry. The Gates of Horn: A Study of Five French Realists. New York: Oxford University Press, 1963. pp. 246-269.

Levin, Harry. "MADAME BOVARY: The Cathedral and the Hospital. " EIC 2:1-23. January 1952.

Levine, George. "Madame Bovary and the Disappearing Author. " MFS 9:103-119. Summer 1963.

Lytle, Andrew. "In Defense of a Passionate and Incorruptible Heart. " SR 73:593-615. Autumn 1965.

Maugham, W. Somerset. Great Novelists and Their Novels. Philadelphia: Winston Company, 1948. pp. 137-156.

Maurois, Andre. "A Preface to MADAME BOVARY. " A Book of Prefaces. New York: The Limited Editions Club, 1941. pp. 19-28.

McCarthy, Mary. "On MADAME BOVARY. " PR 31:174-

188. Spring 1964.

Mein, Margaret. "Flaubert, a Precursor of Proust. " FS
17:218-234. July 1963.

de Mendelssohn, Peter. "Books and Writers. " Spec 186:
527. April 20, 1951.

Murry, John Middleton. Countries of the Mind: Essays in
Literary Criticism. New York: Dutton and Company, 1922.
pp. 218-222.

Nelson, Robert J. "MADAME BOVARY as Tragedy. " MLQ
18:323-330. December 1957.

O'Connor, Frank. The Mirror in the Roadway: A Study of
the Modern Novel. New York: Alfred A. Knopf, 1956. pp.
189-194.

Peyre, Henri. "MADAME BOVARY. " Varieties of Literary
Experience: Eighteen Essays in World Literature. (ed.)
Stanley Burnshaw. New York: New York University Press,
1962. pp. 331-352.

Poulet, Georges. "The Circle and the Center: Reality and
Madame Bovary. " Western Rev 19:245-260. Summer 1955.

Rinehart, Keith. "The Structure of MADAME BOVARY. "
FR 31:300-306. February 1958.

Rousset, Jean. "MADAME BOVARY or the Book About
Nothing. " Flaubert. (ed.) Raymond Giraud. Englewood
Cliffs: Prentice-Hall, 1964. pp. 112-131.

Saintsbury, George. A History of the French Novel (To the
Close of the 19th Century). London: Macmillan and Company, 1919. pp. 400-401.

Sarraute, Nathalie. "Flaubert. " PR 33:202-208. Spring
1966.

Spencer, Philip. Flaubert: A Biography. New York: Grove
Press, 1953. Chapter 8.

Spitzer, Leo. "Balzac and Flaubert Again. " MLN 68:583-
590. December 1953.

Stallman, Robert Wooster. "Flaubert's MADAME BOVARY."
CE 10:195-203. January 1949.

Steegmuller, Francis. Flaubert and MADAME BOVARY: A
Double Portrait. New York: Farrar, Straus and Company,
1950. pp. 253-400.

Stein, William Bysshe. "MADAME BOVARY and Cupid Unmasked. " SR 73:197-209. Spring 1965.

Stern, J. P. M. "EFFI BRIEST: MADAME BOVARY: ANNA KARENINA. " MLR 52:363-375. July 1957.

Symons, A. Figures of Seven Centuries. London: Constable and Company, 1917. pp. 131-140.

Thorlby, Anthony. Gustave Flaubert and the Art of Realism. New Haven: Yale University Press, 1957. Chapter III.

Tillett, Margaret G. On Reading Flaubert. London: Oxford University Press, 1961. Chapter II.

Tindall, William York. The Literary Symbol. Bloomington: Indiana University Press, 1955. pp. 73-76.

Todd, Olivier. "No Orchids for Madame Bovary. " Listener 57:226-227. February 7, 1957.

Turnell, Martin. "MADAME BOVARY. " Flaubert. (ed.) Raymond Giraud. Englewood Cliffs: Prentice-Hall, 1964. pp. 97-111.

Turnell, Martin. "MADAME BOVARY. " SR 65:531-550. Autumn 1957.

Turnell, Martin. The Novel in France. New York: New Directions, 1951. pp. 258-279.

Van Ghent, Dorothy. "Clarissa and Emma as Phedre. " PR 17:827-833. November - December 1950.

West, Ray B. , Jr. and Robert Wooster Stallman. The Art of Modern Fiction. New York: Holt, Rinehart and Winston, 1960. pp. 569-581.

Wilson, Edmund. The Triple Thinkers: Twelve Essays on Literary Subjects. New York: Oxford University Press, 1963. pp. 76-77.

NOVEMBRE

Coleman, A. Flaubert's Literary Development in the Light of His MEMOIRES D'UN FOU, NOVEMBRE and EDUCATION SENTIMENTALE. New York: Kraus Reprint Corp. , 1965. pp. 22-51; Part II.

Giraud, R. Unheroic Heroes. New Brunswick: Rutgers University Press, 1957. pp. 153-156.

Shanks, Lewis Piaget. Flaubert's Youth. Baltimore: Johns Hopkins Press, 1927. Chapter V.

UNE NUIT DE DON JUAN
    Singer, Armand E. "Flaubert's UNE NUIT DE DON JUAN."
    MLN 55:516-520. November 1940.
SALAMMBO
    Bart, Benjamin F. Flaubert's Landscape Descriptions.
    Ann Arbor: University of Michigan Press, 1956. pp. 40-47.

    Bonwit, Marianne. "A Prefiguration of the 'Defile de la
    Hache' Episode in Flaubert's SALAMMBO: His Juvenile
    Tale RAGE ET IMPUISSANCE. " RR 38:340-347. Decem-
    ber 1947.

    Brombert, Victor. "An Epic of Immobility. " HudR 19:24-
    43. Spring 1966.

    Buck, Stratton. Gustave Flaubert. New York: Twayne Pub-
    lishers, Inc. , 1966. Chapter 6.

    Dillingham, Louise B. "A Source of SALAMMBO." MLN
    40:71-76. January 1925.

    Faguet, Emile. Flaubert. Boston: Houghton Mifflin Com-
    pany, 1914. Chapter IV.

    Fay, P. B. and A. Coleman. Sources and Structure of
    Flaubert's SALAMMBO. New York: Kraus Reprint Corp. ,
    1965.

    "Gustave Flaubert. " ASLHM 15:274-275. Autumn 1944.

    Hamilton, Arthur. Sources of the Religious Element in
    Flaubert's SALAMMBO. Baltimore: Johns Hopkins Press,
    1917. (Elliott Monographs. Vol. 4.)

    Levin, Harry. The Gates of Horn: A Study of Five French
    Realists. New York: Oxford University Press, 1963. pp.
    272-285.

    Lukacs, Georg. "SALAMMBO. " Flaubert. (ed.) Raymond
    Giraud. Englewood Cliffs: Prentice-Hall, 1964. pp. 141-
    153.

    Palache, John Garber. Gautier and the Romantics. New
    York: Viking Press, 1926. pp. 98-100.

    Saintsbury, George. A History of the French Novel (To the
    Close of the 19th Century). London: Macmillan and Com-
    pany, 1919. pp. 401-403.

    Steegmuller, Francis. Flaubert and MADAME BOVARY: A
    Double Portrait. New York: Farrar, Straus and Company,
    1950. pp. 402-404.

Stonier, G. W. "Books in General." New S&N 35:417. May 22, 1948.

Symons, A. Figures of Seven Centuries. London: Constable and Company, 1917. pp. 131-140.

Symons, A. The Symbolist Movement in Literature. New York: E. P. Dutton and Company, 1958. pp. 134-139.

Thorlby, Anthony. Gustave Flaubert and the Art of Realism. New Haven: Yale University Press, 1957. Chapter II.

Tillett, Margaret G. On Reading Flaubert. London: Oxford University Press, 1961. Chapter III.

A SENTIMENTAL EDUCATION

Bart, B. F. "An Unsuspected Adviser on Flaubert's EDUCATION SENTIMENTALE: Adele Husson." FR 36:37-43. October 1962.

Bogan, Louise. Selected Criticism. New York: Noonday Press, 1955. pp. 223-230.

Bonwit, Marianne. "The Significance of the Dog in Flaubert's EDUCATION SENTIMENTALE." PMLA 62:517-524. June 1947.

Buck, Stratton. "The Chronology of the EDUCATION SENTIMENTALE." MLN 67:86-92. February 1952.

Buck, Stratton. Gustave Flaubert. New York: Twayne Publishers, Inc., 1966. p. 49.

Coleman, A. Flaubert's Literary Development in the Light of His MEMOIRS D'UN FOU, NOVEMBRE and EDUCATION SENTIMENTALE. New York: Kraus Reprint Corp., 1965. pp. 52-87; Part II.

Cook, Albert. "Flaubert: The Riches of Detachment." FR 32:126-129. December 1958.

Cook, Albert. The Meaning of Fiction. Detroit: Wayne State University Press, 1960. pp. 98-99; 106-112.

Faguet, Emile. Flaubert. Boston: Houghton Mifflin Company, 1914. Chapter VII.

Ferguson, Walter D. The Influence of Flaubert on George Moore. Philadelphia: University of Pennsylvania Press, 1934. Chapter 3.

Furst, Norbert. "The Structure of L'EDUCATION SENTIMENTALE and DER GRUNE HEINRICH." PMLA 56:249-260. March 1941.

Giraud, R. Unheroic Heroes. New Brunswick: Rutgers
University Press, 1957. pp. 140-152; 157-170.

Goodman, Paul. The Structure of Literature. Chicago:
University of Chicago Press, 1954. pp. 128-162.

Grubbs, Henry A. "Fictional Time and Chronology in the
EDUCATION SENTIMENTALE." KFLQ 5:183-188. 1958.

"Gustave Flaubert." ASLHM 15:275-276. Autumn 1944.

Hemmings, F. W. J. "Zola and L'EDUCATION SENTI-
MENTALE." RR 50:35-40. February 1959.

Jean-Aubry, G. "Gustave Flaubert and Music." M&L 31:
21-26. January 1950.

Levin, Harry. The Gates of Horn: A Study of Five French
Realists. New York: Oxford University Press, 1963. pp.
223-231.

Mercier, Vivian. "The Limitations of Flaubert." KR 19:
401-405. Summer 1957.

Moon, H. Kay. "Description: Flaubert's 'External World'
in L'EDUCATION SENTIMENTALE." FR 39:501-512.
February 1966.

Murry, John Middleton. Countries of the Mind: Essays in
Literary Criticism. New York: Dutton and Company, 1922.
pp. 214-216.

Palache, John Garber. Gautier and the Romantics. New
York: Viking Press, 1926. pp. 92-94.

Quennell, Peter. "The Analysis of Sentiment." New S&N
20:568. December 7, 1940.

Saintsbury, George. A History of the French Novel (To
the Close of the 19th Century). London: Macmillan and
Company, 1919. pp. 403-405.

Sarraute, Nathalie. "Flaubert." PR 33:200-202. Spring
1966.

Shanks, Lewis Piaget. Flaubert's Youth. Baltimore: Johns
Hopkins Press, 1927.

Steegmuller, Francis. Flaubert and MADAME BOVARY: A
Double Portrait. New York: Farrar, Straus and Company,
1950. pp. 404-405.

Stoltzfus, Ben F. "The Neurotic Love of Frederic Moreau."

FR 31:509-511. May 1958.

Thorlby, Anthony. Gustave Flaubert and the Art of Realism. New Haven: Yale University Press, 1957. Chapter II.

Tillett, Margaret G. On Reading Flaubert. London: Oxford University Press, 1961. Chapter IV.

Turnell, Martin. The Novel in France. New York: New Directions, 1951. pp. 280-298.

Wilson, Edmund. The Triple Thinkers: Twelve Essays on Literary Subjects. New York: Oxford University Press, 1963. pp. 78-83.

SIMPLE HEART

Madsen, Borge Gedso. "Realism, Irony, and Compassion in Flaubert's UN COEUR SIMPLE. " FR 27:253-258. February 1954.

Mankin, Paul A. "Additional Irony in UN COEUR SIMPLE." FR 35:411. February 1962.

Murry, John Middleton. Countries of the Mind: Essays in Literary Criticism. New York: Dutton and Company, 1922. pp. 216-218.

Showalter, English, Jr. "UN COEUR SIMPLE as an Ironic Reply to Bernardin de Saint-Pierre. " FR 40:47-55. October 1966.

Stoltzfus, Ben. "Point of View in UN COEUR SIMPLE. " FR 35:19-25. October 1961.

Thorlby, Anthony. Gustave Flaubert and the Art of Realism. New Haven: Yale University Press, 1957. Chapter V.

Tillett, Margaret G. On Reading Flaubert. London: Oxford University Press, 1961. Chapter VI.

TEMPTATION OF ST. ANTHONY

Bart, Benjamin F. Flaubert's Landscape Descriptions. Ann Arbor: University of Michigan Press, 1956. pp. 48-51.

Buck, Stratton. Gustave Flaubert. New York: Twayne Publishers, Inc. , 1966. Chapter 4.

Carmody, Francis J. "Further Sources of LA TENTATION DE SAINT ANTOINE. " RR 49:278-292. December 1958.

Carmody, Francis J. "Rimbaud and LA TENTATION DE SAINT ANTOINE. " PMLA 79:594-603. December 1964.

Faguet, Emile. Flaubert. Boston: Houghton Mifflin Company, 1914. Chapter 5.

Jasper, Gertrude. "The Influence of Flaubert's Travels in the Orient on the Last Edition of ST. ANTOINE." MLN 48:162-165. March 1933.

Levin, Harry. The Gates of Horn: A Study of Five French Realists. New York: Oxford University Press, 1963. pp. 231-245.

Ridge, George Ross. "Representative Ideas of the Deathwish in Nineteenth-Century French Literature." KFLQ 7:153-154. 1960.

Saintsbury, George. A History of the French Novel (To the Close of the 19th Century). London: Macmillan and Company, 1919. pp. 405-407.

Steegmuller, Francis. Flaubert and MADAME BOVARY: A Double Portrait. New York: Farrar, Straus and Company, 1950. pp. 11-171.

Thorlby, Anthony. Gustave Flaubert and the Art of Realism. New Haven: Yale University Press, 1957. Chapter II.

Tillett, Margaret G. On Reading Flaubert. London: Oxford University Press, 1961. Chapter V.

la Force, Charlotte
   HISTOIRE SECRETE DE BOURGOGNE
      Jones, Shirley. "Examples of Sensibility in the Late Seventeenth-Century Feminine Novel in France." MLR 61:206-207. April 1966.

France, Anatole
   THE AMETHYST RING
      Guerard, Albert Leon. Five Masters of French Romance. New York: Scribner's Sons. pp. 114-118.
   AT THE SIGN OF THE REINE PEDAUQUE
      Dargan, Edwin Preston. Anatole France. New York: Oxford University Press, 1937. pp. 486-501.

      Guerard, Albert Leon. Five Masters of French Romance. New York: Scribner's Sons. pp. 71-74.

      Jefferson, Carter. Anatole France: The Politics of Skepticism. New Brunswick: Rutgers University Press, 1965. pp. 74-75.

      Rudwin, M. J. The Devil in Legend and Literature. Chicago: Open Court Publishers, 1931. pp. 227-228.

Smith, Helen B. The Skepticism of Anatole France. Paris:
Les Presses Universitaires de France, 1927. Chapter 3.
BALTHASAR
Dargan, Edwin Preston. Anatole France. New York: Ox-
ford University Press, 1937. pp. 435-438.
BOOK OF MY FRIEND
Axelrad, Jacob. Anatole France: A Life Without Illusions
1844-1924. New York: Harper and Brothers, 1944. pp.
153-155.

Guerard, Albert Leon. Five Masters of French Romance.
New York: Scribner's Sons. pp. 60-65.

Rudwin, M. J. The Devil in Legend and Literature. Chi-
cago: Open Court Publishers, 1931. pp. 117-119.
CRAINQUEBILLE
Smith, Helen B. The Skepticism of Anatole France. Paris:
Les Presses Universitaires de France, 1927. pp. 27-28.
THE CRIME OF SYLVESTER BONNARD
Axelrad, Jacob. Anatole France: A Life Without Illusions
1844-1924. New York: Harper and Brothers, 1944. pp.
135-138.

Guerard, Albert Leon. Five Masters of French Romance.
New York: Scribner's Sons. pp. 55-60.

Hafter, Monroe Z. "LE CRIME DE SYLVESTRE BONNARD,
a Possible Source for EL AMIGO MANSO." Symposium
17:123-128. Summer 1963.

Smith, Helen B. The Skepticism of Anatole France. Paris:
Les Presses Universitaires de France, 1927. pp. 40-41; 43.

Walton, Loring Baker. Anatole France and the Greek
World. Durham: Duke University Press, 1950. pp. 77; 80-
81; 261.

Waterhouse, Frances A. "Anatole France's Recipe." SAQ
25:373-376. October 1926.
THE DESIRES OF JEAN SERVIEN
Guerard, Albert Leon. Five Masters of French Romance.
New York: Scribner's Sons. p. 60.
THE DRESSMAKER'S FORM
Guerard, Albert Leon. Five Masters of French Romance.
New York: Scribner's Sons. pp. 111-114.
THE ELM ON THE MALL
Guerard, Albert Leon. Five Masters of French Romance.
New York: Scribner's Sons. pp. 102-111.

Hamilton, D. Lee. "Notes on Historical References in
Anatole France's L'ORME DU MAIL." MP 38:73-83.
August 1940.

THE GODS ARE ATHIRST
    Axelrad, Jacob. Anatole France: A Life Without Illusions
    1844-1924. New York: Harper and Brothers, 1944. pp.
    384-386.

    Baldick, Robert. "In Praise of Anatole France." EDH
    32:12-14. 1963.

    Havens, George R. "Anatole France and the French Revo-
    lution." ASLHM 26:233-239. Autumn 1955.

    Jefferson, Carter. Anatole France: The Politics of Skepti-
    cism. New Brunswick: Rutgers University Press, 1965.
    pp. 169-172.

    May, James Lewis. Anatole France: The Man and His
    Work. London: John Lane The Bodley Head Ltd., 1924.
    pp. 140-151.
M. BERGERET IN PARIS
    Guerard, Albert Leon. Five Masters of French Romance.
    New York: Scribner's Sons. pp. 119-122.
A MUMMER'S TALE
    May, James Lewis. Anatole France: The Man and His
    Work. London: John Lane The Bodley Head Ltd., 1924.
    pp. 158-163.
ON THE WHITE STONE
    Guerard, Albert Leon. Five Masters of French Romance.
    New York: Scribner's Sons. pp. 124-129.
THE OPINIONS OF JEROME COIGNARD
    Dargan, Edwin Preston. Anatole France. New York: Oxford
    University Press, 1937. pp. 502-513.

    Smith, Helen B. The Skepticism of Anatole France. Paris:
    Les Presses Universitaires de France, 1927. Chapter 3.
PENGUIN ISLAND
    Axelrad, Jacob. Anatole France: A Life Without Illusions
    1844-1924. New York: Harper and Brothers, 1944. pp.
    339-341.

    Baldick, Robert. "In Praise of Anatole France." EDH 32:
    10-12. 1963.

    Dargan, E. Preston. "PENGUIN ISLE." SR 18:380-384.
    July 1910.

    Eccles, F. Y. "The Mantle of Voltaire." DubR 144:357-
    367. April 1909.

    Fitch, Girdler. "Did Grandville Inspire the ILE DES
    PINGOUINS?" MLN 53:527-529. November 1938.

    Guerard, Albert Leon. Five Masters of French Romance.
    New York: Scribner's Sons. pp. 130-133.

Jefferson, Carter. Anatole France: The Politics of Skepticism. New Brunswick: Rutgers University Press, 1965. pp. 152-156.

Kennett, W. T. E. "The Theme of PENGUIN ISLAND." RR 33:275-289. October 1942.

May, James Lewis. Anatole France: The Man and His Work. London: John Lane The Bodley Head Ltd., 1924. pp. 151-153.

Smith, Helen B. The Skepticism of Anatole France. Paris: Les Presses Universitaires de France, 1927. pp. 24-25.

Walton, Loring Baker. Anatole France and the Greek World. Durham: Duke University Press, 1950. pp. 16; 206-209.

PROCURATOR OF JUDEA
Chevalier, Haakon M. The Ironic Temper. New York: Oxford University Press, 1932. pp. 35-37.

May, James Lewis. Anatole France: The Man and His Work. London: John Lane The Bodley Head Ltd., 1924. pp. 165-168.

LE PUITS DE SAINTE CLAIRE
Smith, Helen B. The Skepticism of Anatole France. Paris: Les Presses Universitaires de France, 1927. Chapter 3.

THE RED LILY
Dargan, Edwin Preston. Anatole France. New York: Oxford University Press, 1937. pp. 513-528.

Guerard, Albert Leon. Five Masters of French Romance. New York: Scribner's Sons. pp. 74-90.

Jefferson, Carter. Anatole France: The Politics of Skepticism. New Brunswick: Rutgers University Press, 1965. pp. 86-87.

Smith, Helen B. The Skepticism of Anatole France. Paris: Les Presses Universitaires de France, 1927. Chapter 3.

Walton, Loring Baker. Anatole France and the Greek World. Durham: Duke University Press, 1950. pp. 262-264.

THE REVOLT OF THE ANGELS
Baldick, Robert. "In Praise of Anatole France." EDH 32:15-17. 1963.

May, James Lewis. Anatole France: The Man and His Work. London: John Lane The Bodley Head Ltd., 1924. pp. 153-158.

Smith, Helen B. The Skepticism of Anatole France. Paris:

Les Presses Universitaires de France, 1927. pp. 44-45.

Walton, Loring Baker. Anatole France and the Greek World. Durham: Duke University Press, 1950. pp. 10; 44; 268-272.

THAIS

Axelrad, Jacob. Anatole France: A Life Without Illusions 1844-1924. New York: Harper and Brothers, 1944. pp. 190-194.

Baldick, Robert. "In Praise of Anatole France." EDH 32: 6-8. 1963.

Dargan, Edwin Preston. Anatole France. New York: Oxford University Press, 1937. pp. 445-453.

Guerard, Albert Leon. Five Masters of French Romance. New York: Scribner's Sons. pp. 68-71.

Rudwin, M. J. The Devil in Legend and Literature. Chicago: Open Court Publishers, 1931. pp. 252-253.

Smith, Helen B. The Skepticism of Anatole France. Paris: Les Presses Universitaires de France, 1927. pp. 23-24; 41-44; 46-47.

Walton, Loring Baker. Anatole France and the Greek World. Durham: Duke University Press, 1950. pp. 28-29; 90-91; 231-248; 277; 281.

Walton, Loring Baker. "A Manuscript Fragment of THAIS: Its Stylistic and Other Revelations." PMLA 71:910-921. December 1956.

Fromentin, Eugene
DOMINIQUE

Evans, Arthur R., Jr. "The Art of Narrative in Fromentin's DOMINIQUE." MLN 79:270-276. May 1964.

Evans, Arthur R., Jr. The Literary Art of Eugene Fromentin. Baltimore: Johns Hopkins Press, 1964. Chapter 2.

Greshoff, G. J. "Fromentin's DOMINIQUE--An Analysis." EIC 11:164-189. April 1961.

Magowan, Robin. "Fromentin and Jewett: Pastoral Narrative in the Nineteenth Century." CL 16:335-337. Fall 1964.

Morgan, Charles. "An Old Novel Re-Born." HJ 47:219-225. April 1949.

Phillimore, J. S. "Eugene Fromentin." DubR 144:97-101.

January 1909.

Rhodes, S. A. "Sources of Fromentin's DOMINIQUE."
PMLA 45:939-949. September 1930.

Saintsbury, George. A History of the French Novel (To the
Close of the 19th Century). London: Macmillan and Company, 1919. pp. 277-280.

Sells, A. Lytton. "A Disciple of 'Obermann': Eugene Fromentin." MLR 36:68-85. January 1941.

West, Edward Sackville. "Books in General." New S&N
21:486; 488. May 10, 1941.

Wright, Barbara. "Fromentin's Concept of Creative Vision
in the Manuscript of DOMINIQUE." FS 18:213-226. July
1964.

Wright, Barbara. "VALDIEU: A Forgotten Precursor of
Fromentin's DOMINIQUE." MLR 60:520-528. October
1965.

Furetiere, Antoine
   ROMAN BOURGEOIS
      Strickland, William Emile. "Social and Literary Satire in
      Furetiere's ROMAN BOURGEOIS." FR 27:182-192. Jan-
      uary 1954.

Gadenne, Paul
   L'AVENUE
      Sussex, R. T. "The Novels of Paul Gadenne." AUMLA 16:
      156-157. November 1961.
   L'INVITATION CHEZ LES STIRL
      Sussex, R. T. "The Novels of Paul Gadenne." AUMLA
      16:151-153. November 1961.
   LA PLAGE DE SCHEVENINGEN
      Sussex, R. T. "The Novels of Paul Gadenne." AUMLA
      16:150-151. November 1961.
   SILOE
      Sussex, R. T. "The Novels of Paul Gadenne." AUMLA
      16:153-154. November 1961.

Gascar, Pierre
   THE ANIMALS
      Radke, Judith J. "The Metamorphoses of Animals and
      Men in Gascar's LES BETES." FR 39:85-91. October
      1965.
   LES MOUTONS DE FEU
      Henrey, K. H. "The Priest in the French Novel." CQR
      165:86-87. January - March 1964.
   THE SEASON OF THE DEAD
      Obuchowski, Chester W. "The Concentrationary World of

Pierre Gascar. " FR 34:332-335. February 1961.

Gautier, Theophile
   THE AMOROUS CORPSE
      Saintsbury, George. A History of the French Novel (To
      the Close of the 19th Century). London: Macmillan and
      Company, 1919. pp. 222-226.
   LE CAPITAINE FRANCASSE
      Richardson, Joanna. Theophile Gautier: His Life and
      Times. London: Max Reinhardt, 1958. pp. 181-185.
   MADEMOISELLE DE MAUPIN
      Palache, John Garber. Gautier and the Romantics. New
      York: Viking Press, 1926. pp. 41-43.

      Richardson, Joanna. Theophile Gautier: His Life and Times.
      London: Max Reinhardt, 1958. pp. 26-31.

      Shanks, Lewis Piaget. "Theophile Gautier. " SR 20:168-
      170. April 1912.
   THE ROMANCE OF THE MUMMY
      Coleman, Algernon. "Some Sources of the ROMAN DE
      LA MOMIE. " MP 19:337-360. May 1922.

      Schaffer, Aaron. "Flaubert's Correspondence and Gautier's
      ROMAN DE LA MOMIE. " PQ 19:337-338. October 1941.

Gide, Andre
   CAHIERS D'ANDRE WALTER
      Ames, Van Meter. Andre Gide. Norfolk: New Directions
      Books, 1947. pp. 5-9; 178-180.

      Bree, Germaine. Gide. New Brunswick: Rutgers Univer-
      sity Press, 1963. pp. 20-23; 31-37.

      Delay, Jean. The Youth of Andre Gide. Chicago: Univer-
      sity of Chicago Press, 1956. pp. 202-203; 215-217; 223-
      225; 232-233; 239-240; 246-250; 454-455.

      Hytier, Jean. Andre Gide. Garden City: Anchor Books,
      1962. pp. 27-28.

      Ireland, G. W. Gide. Edinburgh: Oliver and Boyd, 1963.
      pp. 5-12.

      Kennedy, Ellen Conroy. "Gide, Laforgue and the Eternal
      Feminine. " FS 17:28-29. January 1963.

      March, Harold. Gide and the Hound of Heaven. Phila-
      delphia: University of Pennsylvania Press, 1952. pp. 42-
      49; 60-61; 163-164.

      O'Brien, Justin. The Novel of Adolescence in France: The
      Study of a Literary Theme. New York: Columbia Univer-

sity Press, 1937. pp. 80-82.

O'Brien, Justin. Portrait of Andre Gide. New York: Alfred
A. Knopf, 1953. Chapter III.

Savage, Catharine H. "The Ideology of Andre Walter."
ECr 1:14-20. Spring 1961.

Starkie, Enid. Andre Gide. Cambridge: Bowes and Bowes,
1953. pp. 16-17.

Thomas, Lawrence. Andre Gide: The Ethic of the Artist.
London: Secker and Warburg, 1950. pp. 44-49.

Ullmann, Stephen. The Image in the Modern French Novel.
Cambridge: Cambridge University Press, 1960. pp. 7-12.
THE CAVES OF THE VATICAN
Adams, Robert M. Strains of Discord: Studies in Literary
Openness. Ithaca: Cornell University Press, 1958. pp. 100-
102.

Ames, Van Meter. Andre Gide. Norfolk: New Directions
Books, 1947. pp. 66-72.

Brachfeld, Georges I. Andre Gide and the Communist
Temptation. Geneve: Librairie E. Droz, 1959. pp. 60-62.

Bree, Germaine and Margaret Guiton. An Age of Fiction:
The French Novel from Gide to Camus. New Brunswick:
Rutgers University Press, 1957. pp. 30-33.

Bree, Germaine. Gide. New Brunswick: Rutgers University Press, 1963. pp. 176-193.

Bree, Germaine. "Time Sequences and Consequences in
the Gidian World." YFS 7:57-59. 1951.

Brereton, Geoffrey. A Short History of French Literature.
London: Cassell, 1954. pp. 239-240.

Buck, Philo M., Jr. Directions in Contemporary Literature.
New York: Oxford University Press, 1942. pp. 74-75.

Cordle, Thomas. "Gide and the Novel of the Egoist."
YFS 7:95-96. 1951.

Fayer, Mischa Harry. Gide, Freedom and Dostoevsky.
Burlington, Vt.: The Lane Press, 1946. pp. 121-122.

Fowlie, Wallace. Andre Gide: His Life and Art. New York:
Macmillan Company, 1965. pp. 68-75.

Geracht, Maurice Aron. "A Guide Through the Vatican

Caves: A Study of the Structure of LES CAVES DU VAT-
ICAN. '' WSCL 6:330-345. Autumn 1965.

Guerard, Albert J. Andre Gide. Cambridge: Harvard University Press, 1951. pp. 128-138.

Holdheim, William W. "Gide's CAVES DU VATICAN and
the Illusionism of the Novel. '' MLN 77:292-304. May
1962.

Hooker, Kenneth Ward. "Dostoyevsky and Gide. '' BUS 3:
172-175. November 1952.

Hytier, Jean. Andre Gide. Garden City: Anchor Books,
1962. pp. 91-119.

Ireland, G. W. Gide. Edinburgh: Oliver and Boyd, 1963.
pp. 45-54.

Mann, Klaus. Andre Gide. New York: Creative Press, Inc.,
1943. pp. 144-152.

March, Harold. Gide and the Hound of Heaven. Philadelphia: University of Pennsylvania Press, 1952. pp. 189-
208.

Merchant, Norris. "The Spiritual Dilemma of Andre
Gide. '' ColQ 7:406-409. Spring 1959.

Niemeyer, Carl. "Raskolnikov and Lafcadio. '' MFS 4:253-
261. Autumn 1958.

O'Brien, Justin. Portrait of Andre Gide. New York: Alfred
A. Knopf, 1953. Chapter VII.

Simon, John K. "View from the Train: Butor, Gide, Larbaud. '' FR 36:161-166. December 1962.

Smith, I. H. "Gide's Narcissism. '' AUMLA 3:12-13. August
1955.

Starkie, Enid. Andre Gide. Cambridge: Bowes and Bowes,
1953. pp. 33-35.

Starkie, Enid. "Andre Gide. '' Three Studies in French
Literature. New Haven: Yale University Press, 1956. pp.
178-180.

Steel, D. A. "Gide and the Conception of the Bastard. ''
FS 17:240-244. July 1963.

Thomas, Lawrence. Andre Gide: The Ethic of the Artist.
London: Secker and Warburg, 1950. pp. 156-167.

Ullmann, Stephen. The Image in the Modern French Novel. Cambridge: Cambridge University Press, 1960. pp. 42-52.

CORYDON

Ames, Van Meter. Andre Gide. Norfolk: New Directions Books, 1947. pp. 72-76; 85-86.

Ireland, G. W. Gide. Edinburgh: Oliver and Boyd, 1963. pp. 55-61.

Mann, Klaus. Andre Gide. New York: Creative Press, Inc., 1943. pp. 162-165.

March, Harold. Gide and the Hound of Heaven. Philadelphia: University of Pennsylvania Press, 1952. pp. 169-184.

O'Brien, Justin. Portrait of Andre Gide. New York: Alfred A. Knopf, 1953. Chapter X.

Starkie, Enid. Andre Gide. Cambridge: Bowes and Bowes, 1953. pp. 40-42.

Starkie, Enid. "Andre Gide." Three Studies in French Literature. New Haven: Yale University Press, 1956. pp. 190-192.

THE COUNTERFEITERS

Ames, Van Meter. Andre Gide. Norfolk: New Directions Books, 1947. pp. 28-29; 71-72.

Bogan, Louise. Selected Criticism. New York: Noonday Press, 1955. pp. 330-331.

Bree, Germaine and Margaret Guiton. An Age of Fiction: The French Novel from Gide to Camus. New Brunswick: Rutgers University Press, 1957. pp. 34-39.

Bree, Germaine. "Form and Content in Gide." FR 30: 423-428. May 1957.

Bree, Germaine. Gide. New Brunswick: Rutgers University Press, 1963. pp. 207-250; 256-257.

Bree, Germaine. "Time Sequences and Consequences in the Gidian World." YFS 7:55-57. 1951.

Buck, Philo M., Jr. Directions in Contemporary Literature. New York: Oxford University Press, 1942. pp. 75-78.

Cook, Albert. The Meaning of Fiction. Detroit: Wayne State University Press, 1960. pp. 35-37.

Cook, Albert. "Reflexive Attitudes: Sterne, Gogol, Gide."

Criticism 2:164-174. Spring 1960.

Cordle, Thomas. "Gide and the Novel of the Egoist. "
YFS 7:96-97. 1951.

Delay, Jean. The Youth of Andre Gide. Chicago: University of Chicago Press, 1956. pp. 100-101; 118-119; 132-
133.

Fayer, Mischa Harry. Gide, Freedom and Dostoevsky.
Burlington, Vt.: The Lane Press, 1946. pp. 90-92.

Fowlie, Wallace. Andre Gide: His Life and Art. New York:
Macmillan Company, 1965. pp. 85-97.

Freedman, Ralph. The Lyrical Novel: Studies in Hermann
Hesse, Andre Gide, and Virginia Woolf. Princeton: Princeton University Press, 1963. pp. 165-182.

Glicksberg, Charles I. "The Literary Struggle for Self-
hood. " Person 42:59-60. Winter 1961.

Guerard, Albert J. Andre Gide. Cambridge: Harvard University Press, 1951. pp. 148-174.

Guerard, Albert. "The Leading French Novelists of the
Present Moment. " CE 12:364-365. April 1951.

Hatzfeld, Helmut. Trends and Styles in Twentieth Century
French Literature. Washington, D.C.: Catholic University
of America Press, 1957. pp. 105-106.

Hill, Charles G. "Andre Gide and Blake's MARRIAGE OF
HEAVEN AND HELL. " CLS 3:24-31. No. 1, 1966.

Hooker, Kenneth Ward. "Dostoyevsky and Gide. " BUS
3:178-181. November 1952.

Hytier, Jean. Andre Gide. Garden City: Anchor Books,
1962. pp. 180-236.

Ireland, G. W. Gide. Edinburgh: Oliver and Boyd, 1963.
pp. 62-70.

Jackson, Elizabeth R. "The Evanescent World of the
FAUX-MONNAYEURS. " Symposium 16:103-113. Summer
1962.

Lebowitz, Naomi. "THE COUNTERFEITERS and the Epic
Pretence. " UTQ 33:291-309. April 1964.

Lynes, Carlos, Jr. "Andre Gide and the Problem of Form
in the Novel. " SoR 7:161-173. No. 1, 1941.

Mann, Klaus. Andre Gide. New York: Creative Press, Inc., 1943. pp. 181-192; 201-202.

March, Harold. Gide and the Hound of Heaven. Philadelphia: University of Pennsylvania Press, 1952. pp. 270-294; 344-345.

O'Brien, Justin. The Novel of Adolescence in France: The Study of a Literary Theme. New York: Columbia University Press, 1937. pp. 84-86.

O'Brien, Justin. Portrait of Andre Gide. New York: Alfred A. Knopf, 1953. Chapter VII.

Painter, George D. Andre Gide. London: Arthur Barker, Ltd., 1951. pp. 129-143.

Peyre, Henri. The Contemporary French Novel. New York: Oxford University Press, 1955. pp. 87-98.

Pritchett, V. S. Books in General. London: Chatto and Windus, 1953. pp. 134-137.

Slochower, Harry. No Voice Is Wholly Lost. New York: Creative Age Press, 1945. pp. 60-61.

Smith, I. H. "Gide's Narcissism." AUMLA 3:7-11. August 1955.

Starkie, Enid. Andre Gide. Cambridge: Bowes and Bowes, 1953. pp. 42-44.

Starkie, Enid. "Andre Gide." Three Studies in French Literature. New Haven: Yale University Press, 1956. pp. 193-196.

Steel, D. A. "Gide and the Conception of the Bastard." FS 17:240-247. July 1963.

Stock, Irvin. "Andre Gide, William Hale White and the Protestant Tradition." Accent 12:206-212. Autumn 1952.

Stock, Irvin. "A View of LES FAUX MONNAYEURS." YFS 7:72-80. 1951.

Sypher, Wylie. "Gide's Cubist Novel." KR 11:291-309. Spring 1949.

Tashjian, Dickran L. "THE COUNTERFEITERS by Andre Gide: the Esthetic Ontology of Dada." MinnR 6:50-57. No. 1, 1966.

Thody, Philip. "LES FAUX MONNAYEURS: The Theme of

Responsibility. " MLR 55:351-358. July 1960.

Thomas, Lawrence. Andre Gide: The Ethic of the Artist.
London: Secker and Warburg, 1950. pp. 190-209.

Ullmann, Stephen. The Image in the Modern French Novel.
Cambridge: Cambridge University Press, 1960. pp. 62-81.
THE FRUITS OF THE EARTH
Ames, Van Meter. Andre Gide. Norfolk: New Directions
Books, 1947. pp. 14-17; 34-41; 46-47; 80-81; 124-125.

Brachfeld, Georges I. Andre Gide and the Communist
Temptation. Geneve: Librairie E. Droz, 1959. pp. 24-27.

Bree, Germaine. Gide. New Brunswick: Rutgers University Press, 1963. pp. 56-58; 66-80.

Delay, Jean. The Youth of Andre Gide. Chicago: University of Chicago Press, 1956. pp. 348-349; 395-396; 444-
445; 467-469; 481-482.

Fowlie, Wallace. Andre Gide: His Life and Art. New York:
Macmillan Company, 1965. pp. 34-45.

Fowlie, Wallace. "Gide's Earliest Quest: LES NOUR-
RITURES TERRESTRES. " EIC 7:285-294. July 1952.

Freedman, Ralph. "Andre Gide's LES NOURRITURES
TERRESTRES: A Novel of Lyrical Perspective. " Western
Rev 18:271-288. Summer 1954.

Freedman, Ralph. The Lyrical Novel: Studies in Hermann
Hesse, Andre Gide, and Virginia Woolf. Princeton: Princeton University Press, 1963. pp. 134-156.

Hytier, Jean. Andre Gide. Garden City: Anchor Books,
1962. pp. 14-16.

Ireland, G. W. Gide. Edinburgh: Oliver and Boyd, 1963.
pp. 13-21.

Loughnan, Edmund Lloyd. "The Thirteenth Apostle. " SR
39:295-297. 1931.

Lynes, Carlos, Jr. "Northern Africa in Andre Gide's
Writings. " PMLA 57:856-858. September 1942.

Mann, Klaus. Andre Gide. New York: Creative Press, Inc.,
1943. pp. 86-96.

March, Harold. Gide and the Hound of Heaven. Philadelphia:
University of Pennsylvania Press, 1952. pp. 98-104.

O'Brien, Justin. "Gide's NOURRITURES TERRESTRES and Vergil's BUCOLICS." RR 43:117-125. April 1952.

O'Brien, Justin. Portrait of Andre Gide. New York: Alfred A. Knopf, 1953. Chapter V.

Rhodes, S. A. "Marcel Schwob and Andre Gide: A Literary Affinity." RR 22:28-37. January - March 1931.

Savage, Catharine H. "Gide's Criticism of Symbolism." MLR 61:608-609. October 1966.

Starkie, Enid. Andre Gide. Cambridge: Bowes and Bowes, 1953. pp. 20-24.

Starkie, Enid. "Andre Gide." Three Studies in French Literature. New Haven: Yale University Press, 1956. pp. 156-160.

Thomas, Lawrence. Andre Gide: The Ethic of the Artist. London: Secker and Warburg, 1950. pp. 82-90.
GENEVIEVE
Guerard, Albert J. Andre Gide. Cambridge: Harvard University Press, 1951. pp. 144-148.

Painter, George D. Andre Gide. London: Arthur Barker, Ltd., 1951. pp. 153-156.

Ullmann, Stephen. The Image in the Modern French Novel. Cambridge: Cambridge University Press, 1960. pp. 85-88.
THE IMMORALIST
Ames, Van Meter. Andre Gide. Norfolk: New Directions Books, 1947. pp. 15-21; 47-56; 63-64.

Brachfeld, Georges I. Andre Gide and the Communist Temptation. Geneve: Librairie E. Droz, 1959. pp. 58-60.

Bree, Germaine and Margaret Guiton. An Age of Fiction: The French Novel from Gide to Camus. New Brunswick: Rutgers University Press, 1957. pp. 27-29.

Bree, Germaine. Gide. New Brunswick: Rutgers University Press, 1963. pp. 124-142; 144-149; 152-154.

Brereton, Geoffrey. A Short History of French Literature. London: Cassell, 1954. pp. 238-239.

Buck, Philo M., Jr. Directions in Contemporary Literature. New York: Oxford University Press, 1942. pp. 68-71

Cordle, Thomas. "Gide and the Novel of the Egoist." YFS 7:92-93. 1951.

Delay, Jean. The Youth of Andre Gide. Chicago: University of Chicago Press, 1956. pp. 443-447.

Fowlie, Wallace. Andre Gide: His Life and Art. New York: Macmillan Company, 1965. pp. 46-56.

Fowlie, Wallace. Clowns and Angels: Studies in Modern French Literature. New York: Sheed and Ward, 1943. pp. 33-41.

Freedman, Ralph. The Lyrical Novel: Studies in Hermann Hesse, Andre Gide, and Virginia Woolf. Princeton: Princeton University Press, 1963. pp. 144-156.

Goodhand, Robert. "The Religious Leitmotif in L'IMMORALISTE. " RR 57:263-276. December 1966.

Guerard, Albert J. Andre Gide. Cambridge: Harvard University Press, 1951. pp. 99-118.

Ireland, G. W. Gide. Edinburgh: Oliver and Boyd, 1963. pp. 22-32.

Krieger, Murray. The Tragic Vision. New York: Holt, Rinehart and Winston, 1960. pp. 22-37.

Loughnan, Edmund Lloyd. "The Thirteenth Apostle. " SR 39:297-299. 1931.

Lynes, Carlos, Jr. "Northern Africa in Andre Gide's Writings. " PMLA 57:858-861. September 1942.

Mann, Klaus. Andre Gide. New York: Creative Press, Inc., 1943. pp. 100-106.

March, Harold. Gide and the Hound of Heaven. Philadelphia: University of Pennsylvania Press, 1952. pp. 117-123.

Merchant, Norris. "The Spiritual Dilemma of Andre Gide. " ColQ 7:415-417. Spring 1959.

O'Brien, Justin. Portrait of Andre Gide. New York: Alfred A. Knopf, 1953. Chapter VI.

Peyre, Henri. The Contemporary French Novel. New York: Oxford University Press, 1955. pp. 87-98.

Roudiez, Leon S. "L'ETRANGER, LA CHUTE, and the Aesthetic Legacy of Gide. " FR 32:300-310. February 1959.

Starkie, Enid. Andre Gide. Cambridge: Bowes and Bowes,

1953. pp. 29-30.

Starkie, Enid. "Andre Gide." Three Studies in French Literature." New Haven: Yale University Press, 1956. pp. 170-172.

Thomas, Lawrence. Andre Gide: The Ethic of the Artist. London: Secker and Warburg, 1950. pp. 125-144.

Turnell, Martin. "Andre Gide and the Disintegration of the Protestant Cell." YFS 7:25-29. 1951.

Ullmann, Stephen. The Image in the Modern French Novel. Cambridge: Cambridge University Press, 1960. pp. 23-30.

Wilkins, Burleigh Taylor. "L'IMMORALISTE Revisited." RR 53:112-127. April 1962.

ISABELLE

Bree, Germaine. Gide. New Brunswick: Rutgers University Press, 1963. pp. 170-175.

Gosse, Edmund. Portraits and Sketches. London: Wm. Heinemann, 1913. pp. 283-287.

Guerard, Albert J. Andre Gide. Cambridge: Harvard University Press, 1951. pp. 124-128.

Mann, Klaus. Andre Gide. New York: Creative Press, Inc., 1943. pp. 143-144.

March, Harold. Gide and the Hound of Heaven. Philadelphia: University of Pennsylvania Press, 1952. pp. 188-189.

Starkie, Enid. Andre Gide. Cambridge: Bowes and Bowes, 1953. pp. 32-33.

Starkie, Enid. "Andre Gide." Three Studies in French Literature. New Haven: Yale University Press, 1956. pp. 176-177.

Steel, D. A. "Gide and the Conception of the Bastard." FS 17:240-247. July 1963.

Ullmann, Stephen. The Image in the Modern French Novel. Cambridge: Cambridge University Press, 1960. pp. 36-42.

MARSHLANDS

Ames, Van Meter. Andre Gide. Norfolk: New Directions Books, 1947. pp. 40-41; 196-197; 234-235.

Delay, Jean. The Youth of Andre Gide. Chicago: University of Chicago Press, 1956. pp. 363-367; 372-374; 377-384.

Fowlie, Wallace. Andre Gide: His Life and Art. New York: Macmillan Company, 1965. pp. 24-26.

Gosse, Edmund. Portraits and Sketches. London: Wm. Heinemann, 1913. pp. 272-273.

Holdheim, William W. "Gide's PALUDES: The Humor of Falsity." FR 32:401-409. April 1959.

Hytier, Jean. Andre Gide. Garden City: Anchor Books, 1962. pp. 69-90.

Kennedy, Ellen Conroy. "Gide, Laforgue and the Eternal Feminine." FS 17:36-38. January 1963.

O'Brien, Justin. Portrait of Andre Gide. New York: Alfred A. Knopf, 1953. Chapter V.

Savage, Catharine H. "Gide's Criticism of Symbolism." MLR 61:607-608. October 1966.

THE PASTORAL SYMPHONY
Cordle, Thomas. "Gide and the Novel of the Egoist." YFS 7:94-95. 1951.

Cruickshank, John. "Gide's Treatment of Time in LA SYMPHONIE PASTORALE." EIC 7:134-143. April 1957.

Cruickshank, John. "A Note on Gide's SYMPHONIE PASTORALE." MLR 49:475-478. October 1954.

Fowlie, Wallace. Andre Gide: His Life and Art. New York: Macmillan Company, 1965. pp. 76-84.

Freedman, Ralph. "Imagination and Form in Andre Gide." Accent 17:219-228. Autumn 1957.

Freedman, Ralph. The Lyrical Novel: Studies in Hermann Hesse, Andre Gide, and Virginia Woolf. Princeton: Princeton University Press, 1963. pp. 156-164.

Guerard, Albert J. Andre Gide. Cambridge: Harvard University Press, 1951. pp. 139-144.

Harvey, Lawrence E. "The Utopia of Blindness in Gide's SYMPHONIE PASTORALE." MP 55:188-197. February 1958.

Mann, Klaus. Andre Gide. New York: Creative Press, Inc., 1943. pp. 152-156.

March, Harold. Gide and the Hound of Heaven. Philadelphia: University of Pennsylvania Press, 1952. pp. 253-257.

Moore, W. G. "Andre Gide's SYMPHONIE PASTORALE."

FS 4:16-26. January 1950.

O'Brien, Justin. Portrait of Andre Gide. New York: Alfred A. Knopf, 1953. Chapter VIII.

Parnell, Charles. "Andre Gide and His SYMPHONIE PASTORALE." YFS 7:60-71. 1951.

Peyre, Henri. The Contemporary French Novel. New York: Oxford University Press, 1955. pp. 87-98.

Starkie, Enid. Andre Gide. Cambridge: Bowes and Bowes, 1953. pp. 37-38.

Thomas, Lawrence. Andre Gide: The Ethic of the Artist. London: Secker and Warburg, 1950. pp. 102-104.

Turnell, Martin. "Andre Gide and the Disintegration of the Protestant Cell." YFS 7:29-31. 1951.

Ullmann, Stephen. The Image in the Modern French Novel. Cambridge: Cambridge University Press, 1960. pp. 52-61.
PROMETHEUS MISBOUND
Ames, Van Meter. Andre Gide. Norfolk: New Directions Books, 1947. pp. 43-46.

Bree, Germaine. Gide. New Brunswick: Rutgers University Press, 1963. pp. 86-97.

Holdheim, William W. "The Dual Structure of the PROMETHEE MAL ENCHAINE." MLN 74:714-720. December 1959.

Hytier, Jean. Andre Gide. Garden City: Anchor Books, 1962. pp. 82-90.

Loy, J. Robert. "Prometheus, Theseus, the Uncommon Man and an Eagle." YFS 7:32-36. 1951.

March, Harold. Gide and the Hound of Heaven. Philadelphia: University of Pennsylvania Press, 1952. pp. 108-115.

O'Brien, Justin. Portrait of Andre Gide. New York: Alfred A. Knopf, 1953. Chapter VI and Chapter IX.

Starkie, Enid. Andre Gide. Cambridge: Bowes and Bowes, 1953. pp. 24-26.

Starkie, Enid. "Andre Gide." Three Studies in French Literature. New Haven: Yale University Press, 1956. pp. 161-168.

Thomas, Lawrence. Andre Gide: The Ethic of the Artist.
London: Secker and Warburg, 1950. pp. 110-120.
RETURN OF THE PRODIGAL
Bree, Germaine. Gide. New Brunswick: Rutgers University
Press, 1963. pp. 143-146; 149-152.

Fowlie, Wallace. Andre Gide: His Life and Art. New York:
Macmillan Company, 1965. pp. 57-61.

Mann, Klaus. Andre Gide. New York: Creative Press, Inc.,
1943. pp. 107-110.
ROBERT
Bree, Germaine. Gide. New Brunswick: Rutgers University
Press, 1963. pp. 258-259.

Guerard, Albert J. Andre Gide. Cambridge: Harvard University Press, 1951. pp. 144-148.

Painter, George D. Andre Gide. London: Arthur Barker,
Ltd., 1951. pp. 151-153.

Thomas, Lawrence. Andre Gide: The Ethic of the Artist.
London: Secker and Warburg, 1950. pp. 214-217.

Ullmann, Stephen. The Image in the Modern French Novel.
Cambridge: Cambridge University Press, 1960. pp. 83-85.
THE SCHOOL FOR WIVES
Ames, Van Meter. Andre Gide. Norfolk: New Directions
Books, 1947. pp. 108-110.

Bree, Germaine. Gide. New Brunswick: Rutgers University
Press, 1963. pp. 256-259.

Guerard, Albert J. Andre Gide. Cambridge: Harvard University Press, 1951. pp. 144-148.

Painter, George D. Andre Gide. London: Arthur Barker,
Ltd., 1951. pp. 149-151.

Ullmann, Stephen. The Image in the Modern French Novel.
Cambridge: Cambridge University Press, 1960. pp. 81-83.
STRAIT IS THE GATE
Ames, Van Meter. Andre Gide. Norfolk: New Directions
Books, 1947. pp. 18-21; 55-64; 225-228.

Bonheim, Jean and Helmut. "Structure and Symbolism in
Gide's LA PORTE ETROITE." FR 31:487-497. May 1958.

Boyd, Ernest. Studies from Ten Literatures. New York:
Charles Scribner's Sons, 1925. pp. 38-40.

Brachfeld, Georges I. Andre Gide and the Communist
Temptation. Geneve: Librairie E. Droz, 1959. pp. 55-58.

Bree, Germaine. Gide. New Brunswick: Rutgers University Press, 1963. pp. 145-147; 152-162; 174-177.

Buck, Philo M., Jr. Directions in Contemporary Literature. New York: Oxford University Press, 1942. pp. 72-74.

Cordle, Thomas. "Gide and the Novel of the Egoist." YFS 7:93-94. 1951.

Delay, Jean. The Youth of Andre Gide. Chicago: University of Chicago Press, 1956. pp. 52-53; 85-86; 218-219.

Fowlie, Wallace. Andre Gide: His Life and Art. New York: Macmillan Company, 1965. pp. 61-67.

Freedman, Ralph. "Imagination and Form in Andre Gide." Accent 17:219-228. Autumn 1957.

Freedman, Ralph. The Lyrical Novel: Studies in Hermann Hesse, Andre Gide, and Virginia Woolf. Princeton: Princeton University Press, 1963. pp. 156-164.

Gosse, Edmund. Portraits and Sketches. London: Wm. Heinemann, 1913. pp. 273-283.

Guerard, Albert J. Andre Gide. Cambridge: Harvard University Press, 1951. pp. 118-124.

Ireland, G. W. Gide. Edinburgh: Oliver and Boyd, 1963. pp. 32-44.

Mann, Klaus. Andre Gide. New York: Creative Press, Inc., 1943. pp. 117-125.

March, Harold. Gide and the Hound of Heaven. Philadelphia: University of Pennsylvania Press, 1952. pp. 28-29; 166-168.

O'Brien, Justin. Portrait of Andre Gide. New York: Alfred A. Knopf, 1953. Chapter VIII.

Roudiez, Leon S. "L'ETRANGER, LA CHUTE and the Aesthetic Legacy of Gide." FR 32:300-310. February 1959.

Starkie, Enid. Andre Gide. Cambridge: Bowes and Bowes, 1953. pp. 30-32.

Starkie, Enid. "Andre Gide." Three Studies in French Literature. New Haven: Yale University Press, 1956. pp. 172-175.

Thomas, Lawrence. Andre Gide: The Ethic of the Artist. London: Secker and Warburg, 1950. pp. 145-155.

Turnell, Martin. "Andre Gide and the Disintegration of the Protestant Cell." YFS 7:21-25. 1951.

Ullmann, Stephen. The Image in the Modern French Novel. Cambridge: Cambridge University Press, 1960. pp. 30-36.

LA TENTATIVE AMOUREUSE

Delay, Jean. The Youth of Andre Gide. Chicago: University of Chicago Press, 1956. pp. 314-320.

O'Brien, Justin. Portrait of Andre Gide. New York: Alfred A. Knopf, 1953. Chapter IV.

Thomas, Lawrence. Andre Gide: The Ethic of the Artist. London: Secker and Warburg, 1950. pp. 54-62.

THESEUS

Ames, Van Meter. Andre Gide. Norfolk: New Directions Books, 1947. pp. 116-117.

Bree, Germaine. Gide. New Brunswick: Rutgers University Press, 1963. pp. 265-270.

Fowlie, Wallace. Andre Gide: His Life and Art. New York: Macmillan Company, 1965. pp. 111-120.

Lang, B. Renee. "Two Books, Two Creeds." BA 21:383-384. Autumn 1947.

Loy, J. Robert. "Prometheus, Theseus, the Uncommon Man and an Eagle." YFS 7:36-43. 1951.

Painter, George D. Andre Gide. London: Arthur Barker, Ltd., 1951. pp. 179-183.

Ullmann, Stephen. The Image in the Modern French Novel. Cambridge: Cambridge University Press, 1960. pp. 88-94.

URIEN'S VOYAGE

Bree, Germaine. Gide. New Brunswick: Rutgers University Press, 1963. pp. 45-49.

Delay, Jean. The Youth of Andre Gide. Chicago: University of Chicago Press, 1956. pp. 302-311.

Freedman, Ralph. The Lyrical Novel: Studies in Hermann Hesse, Andre Gide, and Virginia Woolf. Princeton: Princeton University Press, 1963. pp. 130-134.

Kennedy, Ellen Conroy. "Gide, Laforgue, and the Eternal Feminine." FS 17:32-35. January 1963.

March, Harold. Gide and the Hound of Heaven. Philadelphia: University of Pennsylvania Press, 1952. pp. 59-62.

O'Brien, Justin. Portrait of Andre Gide. New York: Alfred
A. Knopf, 1953. Chapter IV.

Savage, Catharine H. "Gide's Criticism of Symbolism."
MLR 61:606-607. October 1966.

Starkie, Enid. Andre Gide. Cambridge: Bowes and Bowes,
1953. p. 18.

Ullmann, Stephen. The Image in the Modern French Novel.
Cambridge: Cambridge University Press, 1960. pp. 12-16.

Giono, Jean
  LES AMES FORTES
      Smith, Maxwell A. Jean Giono. New York: Twayne Pub-
      lishers, Inc., 1966. pp. 136-139.
  ANGELO
      Smith, Maxwell A. Jean Giono. New York: Twayne Pub-
      lishers, Inc., 1966. pp. 147-149.
  BATTLES IN THE MOUNTAIN
      Smith, Maxwell A. Jean Giono. New York: Twayne Pub-
      lishers, Inc., 1966. pp. 84-87.
  BLUE BOY
      Peyre, Henri. The Contemporary French Novel. New York:
      Oxford University Press, 1955. pp. 129-131; 134-136.

      Smith, Maxwell A. Jean Giono. New York: Twayne Pub-
      lishers, Inc., 1966. pp. 65-67.
  DEUX CAVALIERS DE L'ORAGE
      de Pomerai, Odile. "An Unknown Giono: DEUX CAVALIERS
      DE L'ORAGE." FR 39:78-84. October 1965.
  LE GRAND TROUPEAU
      Peyre, Henri. The Contemporary French Novel. New York:
      Oxford University Press, 1955. pp. 134-135.

      Smith, Maxwell A. "Giono as a Pacifist." RomN 1:7-9.
      November 1959.

      Smith, Maxwell A. Jean Giono. New York: Twayne Pub-
      lishers, Inc., 1966. pp. 63-65.
  LES GRANDS CHEMINS
      Smith, Maxwell A. Jean Giono. New York: Twayne Pub-
      lishers, Inc., 1966. pp. 139-141.
  HARVEST
      Smith, Maxwell A. "Giono's Trilogy of Pan." TSL 2:77-
      79. 1957.
  HILL OF DESTINY
      Smith, Maxwell A. "Giono's Trilogy of Pan." TSL 2:73-
      75. 1957.
  THE HORSEMAN ON THE ROOF
      Smith, Maxwell A. "Giono's Cycle of the Hussard Novels."
      FR 35:288-291. January 1962.

Smith, Maxwell A. Jean Giono. New York: Twayne Pub-
lishers, Inc., 1966. pp. 149-152.
JOY OF MAN'S DESIRING
Smith, Maxwell A. Jean Giono. New York: Twayne Pub-
lishers, Inc., 1966. pp. 80-84.
LOVERS ARE NEVER LOSERS
Smith, Maxwell A. "Giono's Trilogy of Pan." TSL 2:75-
77. 1957.
THE MALEDICTION
Goodrich, Norma Lorre. "LE MOULIN DE POLOGNE and
its Narrator." FR 40:65-76. October 1966.

Smith, Maxwell A. Jean Giono. New York: Twayne Pub-
lishers, Inc., 1966. pp. 141-143.
MORT D'UN PERSONNAGE
Smith, Maxwell A. "Giono's Cycle of the Hussard Novels."
FR 35:294. January 1962.
NAISSANCE DE L'ODYSSEE
Smith, Maxwell A. "Giono's Use of the Ulysses Concept."
FR 31:42-46. October 1957.

Stanford, W. B. The Ulysses Theme. Oxford: Basil Black-
well, 1963. pp. 199-200.
NOE
Smith, Maxwell A. Jean Giono. New York: Twayne Pub-
lishers, Inc., 1966. pp. 134-136.
PAULINE
Smith, Maxwell A. Jean Giono. New York: Twayne Pub-
lishers, Inc., 1966. pp. 155-156.
UN ROI SANS DIVERTISSEMENT
De Pomerai, Odile. "A Novelist Turns to Films: Jean
Giono and the Cinema." TCL 12:61-65. July 1966.

Smith, Maxwell A. Jean Giono. New York: Twayne Pub-
lishers, Inc., 1966. pp. 131-134.
THE SONG OF THE WORLD
Bree, Germaine and Margaret Guiton. An Age of Fiction:
The French Novel from Gide to Camus. New Brunswick:
Rutgers University Press, 1957. pp. 111-112.

Peyre, Henri. The Contemporary French Novel. New York:
Oxford University Press, 1955. pp. 137-140.

Smith, Maxwell A. Jean Giono. New York: Twayne Publishers, Inc., 1966. pp. 76-80.

Walker, Hallam. "Myth in Giono's LE CHANT DU MONDE."
Symposium 15:139-146. Summer 1961.
THE STRAW MAN
Smith, Maxwell A. "Giono's Cycle of the Hussard Novels."
FR 35:291-293. January 1962.

Smith, Maxwell A. Jean Giono. New York: Twayne Pub-

lishers, Inc., 1966. pp. 152-155.
THE TRILOGY OF PAN
    Peyre, Henri. The Contemporary French Novel. New York:
    Oxford University Press, 1955. pp. 133-134.
LES VRAIES RICHESSES
    Smith, Maxwell A. Jean Giono. New York: Twayne Pub-
    lishers, Inc., 1966. pp. 94-97.

Giraudoux, Jean
    THE ADVENTURES OF JEROME BARDINI
        LeSage, Laurent. Jean Giraudoux, His Life and Works.
        State College: Pennsylvania State University Press, 1959.
        pp. 59-60.

        McLendon, Will L. "Giraudoux and the Split Personality."
        PMLA 73:575; 581. December 1958.
    THE CHOSEN ONE
        McLendon, Will L. "Giraudoux and the Split Personality."
        PMLA 73:580. December 1958.
    LE DERNIER REVE
        LeSage, L. "Jean Giraudoux, Hoffmann, and LE DERNIER
        REVE D'EDMOND ABOUT." RLC 24:103-107. January -
        March 1950.
    EGLANTINE
        Goodhand, Robert. "Psychological Development in Jean
        Giraudoux's EGLANTINE." FR 38:173-179. December
        1964.
    JULIETTE VISITS THE LAND OF MAN
        McLendon, Will L. "Giraudoux and the Split Personality."
        PMLA 73:580-581. December 1958.
    MY FRIEND FROM LIMOUSIN
        LeSage, Laurent. Jean Giraudoux, His Life and Works.
        State College: Pennsylvania State University Press, 1959.
        pp. 49-52.
    THE SCHOOL FOR INDIFFERENCE
        McLendon, Will L. "Giraudoux and the Split Personality."
        PMLA 73:575-577. December 1958.
    SIMON THE PATHETIC
        LeSage, Laurent. Jean Giraudoux, His Life and Works.
        State College: Pennsylvania State University Press, 1959.
        pp. 40-41.

        Stuart, Eleanor. "More About SIMON LE PATHETIQUE."
        FR 31:554-557. May 1958.

Gobineau, Joseph Arthur de
    LES PLEIADES
        Tenenbaum, Louis. "Love in the Prose Fiction of
        Gobineau." MLQ 18:107-112. June 1957.

Goncourt, Edmond de
    CHERIE
        Billy, Andre. The Goncourt Brothers. London: Andre

Deutsch, Ltd. , 1960. pp. 231-234.
ELISA
   Billy, Andre. The Goncourt Brothers. London: Andre
   Deutsch, Ltd. , 1960. pp. 221-225.
LA FAUSTIN
   Billy, Andre. The Goncourt Brothers. London: Andre
   Deutsch, Ltd. , 1960. pp. 229-231.
THE ZEMGANNO BROTHERS
   Billy, Andre. The Goncourt Brothers. London: Andre
   Deutsch, Ltd. , 1960. pp. 225-229.

Goncourt, Edmond and Jules de
   CHARLES DEMAILLY
      Baldick, Robert. The Goncourts. London: Bowes and Bowes,
      1960. pp. 18-22.

      Billy, Andre. The Goncourt Brothers. London: Andre
      Deutsch, Ltd. , 1960. pp. 77-78.
   EN 18
      Baldick, Robert. The Goncourts. London: Bowes and Bowes,
      1960. pp. 15-16.
   GERMINIE LACERTEUX
      Auerbach, Erich. Mimesis. New York: Doubleday and Com-
      pany, 1957. pp. 434-445.

      Baldick, Robert. The Goncourts. London: Bowes and Bowes,
      1960. pp. 31-39.

      Billy, Andre. The Goncourt Brothers. London: Andre
      Deutsch, Ltd. , 1960. pp. 135-139.
   MADAME GERVAISIS
      Billy, Andre. The Goncourt Brothers. London: Andre
      Deutsch, Ltd. , 1960. pp. 158-166.
   MANETTE SALOMON
      Baldick, Robert. The Goncourts. London: Bowes and Bowes,
      1960. pp. 41-46.

      Billy, Andre. The Goncourt Brothers. London: Andre
      Deutsch, Ltd. , 1960. pp. 154-158.
   RENEE MAUPERIN
      Baldick, Robert. The Goncourts. London: Bowes and Bowes,
      1960. pp. 26-30.

      Billy, Andre. The Goncourt Brothers. London: Andre
      Deutsch, Ltd. , 1960. pp. 131-135.
   SOEUR PHILOMENE
      Baldick, Robert. The Goncourts. London: Bowes and Bowes,
      1960. pp. 22-26.

      Billy, Andre. The Goncourt Brothers. London: Andre
      Deutsch, Ltd. , 1960. pp. 80-82.

Gourmont, Remy de
   THE HORSES OF DIOMEDE
      Burne, Glenn S. Remy de Gourmont: His Ideas and Influ-
      ence in England and America. Carbondale: Southern Illinois
      University Press, 1963. pp. 17; 31-33; 112.
   SIXTINE
      Burne, Glenn S. Remy de Gourmont: His Ideas and Influ-
      ence in England and America. Carbondale: Southern Illinois
      University Press, 1963. pp. 33-34.

Grainville, Cousin de
   LE DERNIER HOMME
      Majewski, Henry F. "Grainville's LE DERNIER HOMME."
      Symposium 17:114-122. Summer 1963.

Green[e], Julian [Julien]
   AVARICE HOUSE
      Keating, L. Clark. "Julien Green and Nathaniel Haw-
      thorne. " FR 28:485-492. May 1955.

      Kohler, Dayton. "Julian Green: Modern Gothic. " SR 40:
      145. 1932.

      Stokes, Samuel. Julian Green and the Thorn of Puritanism.
      New York: King's Crown Press, 1955. pp. 20-21; 25-26.
   BRIGHTON ROCKS
      Stratford, Phillip. Faith and Fiction. Notre Dame: Univer-
      sity of Notre Dame Press, 1964. pp. 166-170; 192-197;
      217-218.
   THE CLOSED GARDEN
      Kohler, Dayton. "Julian Green: Modern Gothic. " SR 40:
      145-146. 1932.

      "Paris and Savannah. " TLS 2577:381-382. June 22, 1951.

      Stokes, Samuel. Julian Green and the Thorn of Puritanism.
      New York: King's Crown Press, 1955. pp. 37-38.
   THE CONFIDENTIAL AGENT
      Stratford, Phillip. Faith and Fiction. Notre Dame: Univer-
      sity of Notre Dame Press, 1964. pp. 232-235.
   THE DARK JOURNEY
      Kohler, Dayton. "Julian Green: Modern Gothic. " SR 40:
      146-147. 1932.

      "Paris and Savannah. " TLS 2577:382. June 22, 1951.

      Stokes, Samuel. Julian Green and the Thorn of Puritanism.
      New York: King's Crown Press, 1955. pp. 21; 38-39; 119.
   THE DREAMER
      Hatzfeld, Helmut. Trends and Styles in Twentieth Century
      French Literature. Washington, D. C.: Catholic University
      of America Press, 1957. pp. 88-89.

Stokes, Samuel. Julian Green and the Thorn of Puritanism. New York: King's Crown Press, 1955. pp. 23; 27-29; 44-45; 48-49.

END OF THE AFFAIR
Stratford, Phillip. Faith and Fiction. Notre Dame: University of Notre Dame Press, 1964. pp. 196-198; 205-206; 306-308.

ENGLAND MADE ME
Stratford, Phillip. Faith and Fiction. Notre Dame: University of Notre Dame Press, 1964. pp. 132-137.

GUN FOR SALE
Stratford, Phillip. Faith and Fiction. Notre Dame: University of Notre Dame Press, 1964. pp. 188-192; 214-216.

THE HEART OF THE MATTER
Stratford, Phillip. Faith and Fiction. Notre Dame: University of Notre Dame Press, 1964. pp. 232-237.

IT'S A BATTLEFIELD
Stratford, Phillip. Faith and Fiction. Notre Dame: University of Notre Dame Press, 1964. pp. 120-122; 132-133.

THE MAN WITHIN
Stratford, Phillip. Faith and Fiction. Notre Dame: University of Notre Dame Press, 1964. pp. 91-108; 178-181.

MIDNIGHT
Bree, Germaine and Margaret Guiton. An Age of Fiction: The French Novel from Gide to Camus. New Brunswick: Rutgers University Press, 1957. pp. 103-104.

Hatzfeld, Helmut. Trends and Styles in Twentieth Century French Literature. Washington, D. C.: Catholic University of America Press, 1957. pp. 89-90.

Rose, Marilyn Gaddis." 'Usher' as Myth in Green's MINUIT. " RomN 5:110-114. Spring 1964.

Stokes, Samuel. Julian Green and the Thorn of Puritanism. New York: King's Crown Press, 1955. pp. 54-61; 66-67.

THE MINISTRY OF FEAR
Stratford, Phillip. Faith and Fiction. Notre Dame: University of Notre Dame Press, 1964. pp. 106-109; 232-235.

MOIRA
Bree, Germaine and Margaret Guiton. An Age of Fiction: The French Novel from Gide to Camus. New Brunswick: Rutgers University Press, 1957. pp. 104-105.

"Paris and Savannah. " TLS 2577:382-383. June 22, 1951.

Stokes, Samuel. Julian Green and the Thorn of Puritanism. New York: King's Crown Press, 1955. pp. 100; 103-104; 112; 114-115.

THE NAME OF ACTION
Stratford, Phillip. Faith and Fiction. Notre Dame: University of Notre Dame Press, 1964. pp. 98-108.

THE PILGRIM ON THE EARTH
>   Kohler, Dayton. "Julian Green: Modern Gothic. " SR 40:
>   144-145. 1932.
THE QUIET AMERICAN
>   Stratford, Phillip. Faith and Fiction. Notre Dame: Univer-
>   sity of Notre Dame Press, 1964. pp. 306-320.
RUMOUR AT NIGHTFALL
>   Stratford, Phillip. Faith and Fiction. Notre Dame: Univer-
>   sity of Notre Dame Press, 1964. pp. 102-108; 118-120;
>   170-173.
STAMBOUL TRAIN
>   Stratford, Phillip. Faith and Fiction. Notre Dame: Univer-
>   sity of Notre Dame Press, 1964. pp. 111-116; 119-123.
THEN SHALL THE DUST RETURN
>   Stokes, Samuel. Julian Green and the Thorn of Puritanism.
>   New York: King's Crown Press, 1955. pp. 68-75.
LE VOYAGEUR SUR LA TERRE
>   Stokes, Samuel. Julian Green and the Thorn of Puritanism.
>   New York: King's Crown Press, 1955. pp. 15-16; 19; 24.

Harry, Myriam
>   L'ILE DE VOLUPTE
>   Bennett, Jesse Lee. "Three New French Novelists, Far-
>   rere, Harry, Binet-Valmer. " Poet Lore 27:593-594.
>   Autumn 1916.

Hugo, Victor
>   HAN OF ICELAND
>   Moore, Olin H. "Victor Hugo as a Humorist Before 1840."
>   PMLA 65:135-137. March 1950.

>   Seth-Smith, Beatrice C. "Mallet's HISTOIRE DE DANNE-
>   MARC as a Source of HAN D'ISLANDE. " MLR 13:297-311.
>   July 1918.
THE HUNCHBACK OF NOTRE DAME
>   Bach, Max. "First Reactions to Victor Hugo's NOTRE-
>   DAME DE PARIS. " KFLQ 3:59-65. 1956.

>   Chesterton, G. K. A Handful of Authors. London: Sheed
>   and Ward, 1953. pp. 38; 40.

>   Davidson, A. F. Victor Hugo: His Life and Character. Lon-
>   don: Eveleigh Nash, 1912. pp. 93-96.

>   Duclaux, Mme. Victor Hugo. London: Constable and Com-
>   pany, Ltd., 1921. Chapter 12.

>   Guyer, Foster Erwin. The Titan: Victor Hugo. New York:
>   S. F. Vanni, 1955. pp. 77-101.

>   Hooker, Kenneth Ward. The Fortunes of Victor Hugo in
>   England. New York: Columbia University Press, 1938. pp.
>   27-42.

Moore, Olin H. "How Victor Hugo Created the Characters of NOTRE-DAME DE PARIS. " PMLA 57:255-274. March 1942.

Pritchett, V. S. The Living Novel and Later Appreciations. New York: Random House, 1964. pp. 353-358.

THE MAN WHO LAUGHS

Davidson, A. F. Victor Hugo: His Life and Character. London: Eveleigh Nash, 1912. pp. 273-274.

Duclaux, Mme. Victor Hugo. London: Constable and Company, Ltd. , 1921. pp. 210-211.

Grant, Elliott M. The Career of Victor Hugo. Cambridge: Harvard University Press, 1945. pp. 285-291.

Hooker, Kenneth Ward. The Fortunes of Victor Hugo in England. New York: Columbia University Press, 1938. pp. 171-185.

Kaiser, John Boynton. "The Comprachicos. " Journal of Criminal Law 4:247-264. July 1913.

LES MISERABLES

Carriere, J.-M. "A Seventeenth Century Precursor of Mgr Myriel. " FR 10:285-292. February 1937.

Chesterton, G. K. A Handful of Authors. London: Sheed and Ward, 1953. pp. 36-44.

Davidson, A. F. Victor Hugo: His Life and Character. London: Eveleigh Nash, 1912. pp. 250-255.

Duclaux, Mme. Victor Hugo. London: Constable and Company, Ltd. , 1921. pp. 203-209.

Grant, Elliott M. The Career of Victor Hugo. Cambridge: Harvard University Press, 1945. Chapter 13.

Guyer, Foster Erwin. The Titan: Victor Hugo. New York: S. F. Vanni, 1955. pp. 101-113.

Hooker, Kenneth Ward. The Fortunes of Victor Hugo in England. New York: Columbia University Press, 1938. pp. 143-158.

Josephson, Matthew. Victor Hugo: A Realistic Biography of the Great Romantic. New York: Doubleday, Doran and Company, Inc. , 1942. Chapter 18.

"A Literary Curiosity. " Spec 112:732-733. May 2, 1914.

Maurois, Andre. Olympio: The Life of Victor Hugo. New York: Harper Brothers, 1956. pp. 352-358.

Maurois, Andre. Victor Hugo. London: Thames and Hudson, 1966. pp. 95-99.

Moore, Olin H. "Realism in LES MISERABLES. " PMLA 61:211-228. March 1946.

Moore, Olin H. "Some Translations of LES MISERABLES." MLN 74:240-246. March 1959.

Pritchett, V. S. The Living Novel and Later Appreciations. New York: Random House, 1964. pp. 353-358.

Rosselet, Jeanne. "First Reactions to LES MISERABLES in the United States. " MLN 67:39-43. January 1952.

Spencer, Philip. "A Note on Paul Meurice and LES MISERABLES. " MLR 51:566-568. October 1956.

NINETY-THREE
Davidson, A. F. Victor Hugo: His Life and Character. London: Eveleigh Nash, 1912. pp. 299-300.

Duclaux, Mme. Victor Hugo. London: Constable and Company, Ltd. , 1921. pp. 244-245.

Grant, Elliott M. The Career of Victor Hugo. Cambridge: Harvard University Press, 1945. Chapter 17.

Guyer, Foster Erwin. The Titan: Victor Hugo. New York: S. F. Vanni, 1955. pp. 119-120.

Maurois, Andre. Victor Hugo. London: Thames and Hudson, 1966. pp. 114-117.

Moore, Olin H. "Further Sources of Victor Hugo's QUATREVINGT-TREIZE. " PMLA 41:452-461. March 1926.

Moore, Olin H. "The Sources of Hugo's QUATREVINGT-TREIZE. " PMLA 39:368-405. June 1924.

THE TOILERS OF THE SEA
Davidson, A. F. Victor Hugo: His Life and Character. London: Eveleigh Nash, 1912. pp. 262-263.

Duclaux, Mme. Victor Hugo. London: Constable and Company, Ltd. , 1921. pp. 209-211.

Grant, Elliott M. The Career of Victor Hugo. Cambridge: Harvard University Press, 1945. pp. 277-285.

Guyer, Foster Erwin. The Titan: Victor Hugo. New York: S. F. Vanni, 1955. pp. 113-119.

Hooker, Kenneth Ward. The Fortunes of Victor Hugo in England. New York: Columbia University Press, 1938. pp.

159-170.

Maurois, Andre. Olympio: The Life of Victor Hugo. New York: Harper and Brothers, 1956. pp. 363-370.

Maurois, Andre. Victor Hugo. London: Thames and Hudson, 1966. pp. 99-100.

Huysmans, Joris Karl
   AGAINST THE GRAIN
      Baldick, Robert. The Life of J.-K. Huysmans. Oxford: Clarendon Press, 1955. pp. 77-98; 329-330.

      Brandreth, Henry R. T. Huysmans. New York: Hillary House Publishers, Ltd., 1963. pp. 41-43; 54-68.

      D'Entremont, Elaine. "The Influence of Joris Karl Huysmans' A REBOURS on Ruben Dario." RomN 5:37-39. Autumn 1963.

      Ellis, Havelock. Affirmations. Boston: Houghton Mifflin and Company, 1922. pp. 172-187; 196-199.

      Fixler, Michael. "The Affinities Between J.-K. Huysmans and the 'Rosicrucian' Stories of W. B. Yeats." PMLA 74:464-467. September 1959.

      Freedman, Ralph. The Lyrical Novel: Studies in Hermann Hesse, Andre Gide, and Virginia Woolf. Princeton: Princeton University Press, 1963. pp. 35-38.

      Laver, James. The First Decadent. London: Faber and Faber, Ltd., 1954. Chapter 5.

      Stewart, S. M. "J.-K. Huysmans and George Moore." RR 25:197-206. July - September 1934.

      Thomas, W. E. "J.-K. Huysmans and A REBOURS." ML 38:56-60. June 1957.
   THE CATHEDRAL
      Baldick, Robert. The Life of J.-K. Huysmans. Oxford: Clarendon Press, 1955. pp. 228-241; 253-254; 260-261.

      Brandreth, Henry R. T. Huysmans. New York: Hillary House Publishers, Ltd., 1963. Chapter VI.
   DOWN THERE
      Baldick, Robert. The Life of J.-K. Huysmans. Oxford: Clarendon Press, 1955. pp. 142-168.

      Brandreth, Henry R. T. Huysmans. New York: Hillary House Publishers, Ltd., 1963. Chapter IV.

      Ellis, Havelock. Affirmations. Boston: Houghton Mifflin

and Company, 1922. pp. 193-195.

Fixler, Michael. "The Affinities Between J. -K. Huysmans and the 'Rosicrucian' Stories of W. B. Yeats." PMLA 74:467-468. September 1959.

Laver, James. The First Decadent. London: Faber and Faber, Ltd., 1954. Chapter 7.

DOWNSTREAM

Brandreth, Henry R. T. Huysmans. New York: Hillary House Publishers, Ltd., 1963. pp. 38-41.

EN MENAGE

Baldick, Robert. The Life of J. -K. Huysmans. Oxford: Clarendon Press, 1955. pp. 58-63.

Brandreth, Henry R. T. Huysmans. New York: Hillary House Publishers, Ltd., 1963. pp. 33-38.

Ellis, Havelock. Affirmations. Boston: Houghton Mifflin and Company, 1922. pp. 168-169.

EN RADE

Baldick, Robert. The Life of J. -K. Huysmans. Oxford: Clarendon Press, 1955. pp. 101-105.

Brandreth, Henry R. T. Huysmans. New York: Hillary House Publishers, Ltd., 1963. pp. 41-43.

Ellis, Havelock. Affirmations. Boston: Houghton Mifflin and Company, 1922. pp. 187-190.

Matthews, J. H. "EN RADE and Huysmans' Departure from Naturalism." ECr 4:84-93. Summer 1964.

EN ROUTE

Baldick, Robert. The Life of J. -K. Huysmans. Oxford: Clarendon Press, 1955. pp. 205-208; 223-228.

Brandreth, Henry R. T. Huysmans. New York: Hillary House Publishers, Ltd., 1963. Chapter V.

Ellis, Havelock. Affirmations. Boston: Houghton Mifflin and Company, 1922. pp. 196-203.

Laver, James. The First Decadent. London: Faber and Faber, Ltd., 1954. Chapter 9.

MARTHE

Baldick, Robert. The Life of J. -K. Huysmans. Oxford: Clarendon Press, 1955. pp. 29-36; 48-49.

Brandreth, Henry R. T. Huysmans. New York: Hillary House Publishers, Ltd., 1963. pp. 19-26.

Ellis, Havelock. Affirmations. Boston: Houghton Mifflin and Company, 1922. pp. 165-166.

THE OBLATE
    Baldick, Robert. The Life of J.-K. Huysmans. Oxford:
    Clarendon Press, 1955. pp. 315-322.

    Brandreth, Henry R. T. Huysmans. New York: Hillary
    House Publishers, Ltd., 1963. pp. 108-115.
ST. LYDWINE
    Baldick, Robert. The Life of J.-K. Huysmans. Oxford:
    Clarendon Press, 1955. pp. 290-293.

    Brandreth, Henry R. T. Huysmans. New York: Hillary
    House Publishers, Ltd., 1963. pp. 104-108.
LES SOEURS VATARD
    Brandreth, Henry R. T. Huysmans. New York: Hillary
    House Publishers, Ltd., 1963. pp. 31-33.

Laclos, Pierre de
    LES LIAISONS DANGEREUSES
        Cherpack, Clifton. "A New Look at LES LIAISONS DAN-
        GEREUSES." MLN 74:513-521. June 1959.

        Gay, Peter. "Three Stages on Love's Way." Encounter
        9:13-16. August 1957.

        Greshoff, C. J. "The Moral Structure of LES LIAISONS
        DANGEREUSES." FR 37:383-399. February 1964.

        Grimsley, Ronald. "Don Juanism in LES LIAISONS DAN-
        GEREUSES." FS 14:1-17. January 1960.

        Guy, Basil. "The Prince de Ligne, Laclos, and the
        LIAISONS DANGEREUSES: Two Notes." RR 55:260-267.
        December 1964.

        Hudon, E. Sculley. "Love and Myth in LES LIAISONS
        DANGEREUSES." YFS 11:25-38. 1951.

        Kohn, Renee J. "Four Centuries of French Novel: Evolu-
        tion of the Hero." ASLHM 29:78-82. No. 2. 1958.

        Loy, J. Robert. "Love/Vengeance in the Late Eighteenth-
        Century French Novel." ECr 3:160-163. Winter 1963.

        May, Georges. "The Witticisms of Monsieur de Valmont."
        ECr 3:181-187. Winter 1963.

        Mead, William. "LES LIAISONS DANGEREUSES and Moral
        'Usefulness.'" PMLA 75:563-570. December 1960.

        Mylne, Vivienne. The Eighteenth-Century French Novel:
        Techniques of Illusion. Manchester: Manchester University
        Press, 1965. pp. 233-244.

Thelander, Dorothy. Laclos and the Epistolary Novel. Geneve: Librairie Droz, 1963.

Turnell, Martin. The Novel in France. New York: New Directions, 1951. pp. 49-77.

Vartanian, Aram. "The Marquise de Merteuil: A Case of Mistaken Identity. " ECr 3:172-180. Winter 1963.

"The War of the Sexes. " TLS 3133:177-178. March 16, 1962.

Lafayette, Madame de
     LA COMTESSE DE TENDE
          Scott, J. W. "Criticism and LA COMTESSE DE TENDE. " MLR 50:15-24. January 1955.
     LA PRINCESSE DE CLEVES
          Ashton, H. "The Confession of the Princess of Cleves. " MLN 34:134-139. March 1919.

          Brereton, Geoffrey. A Short History of French Literature. London: Cassell, 1954. pp. 117-118.

          Hyman, Richard J. "The Virtuous PRINCESSE DE CLEVES. " FR 38:15-22. October 1964.

          Jones, Shirley. "Examples of Sensibility in the Late Seventeenth-Century Feminine Novel in France. " MLR 61:199-201. April 1966.

          Kaplan, David. "The Lover's Test Theme in Cervantes and Madame de Lafayette. " FR 26:285-290. February 1953.

          Kohn, Renee J. "Four Centuries of French Novel: Evolution of the Hero. " ASLHM 29:76-78. No. 2. 1958.

          Mille, Pierre. The French Novel. Philadelphia: J. P. Lippincott, 1930. pp. 29-35.

          Morrissette, Bruce A. "Marcel Langlois' Untenable Attribution of LA PRINCESSE DE CLEVES to Fontenelle. " MLN 61:267-270. April 1946.

          Morrissette, Bruce A. "Richard Aldington's Proposed 'Source' for LA PRINCESSE DE CLEVES. " MLN 63:164-167. March 1948.

          Rountree, Benjamin C. James's MADAME DE MAUVES and Madame de LaFayette's PRINCESSE DE CLEVES. " SSF 1:264-271. Summer 1964.

          Scott, J. W. "The 'Digressions' of the PRINCESSE DE CLEVES. " FS 11:315-321. October 1957.

Scott, J. W. "Le 'Prince' de Cleves." MLR 52:339-346.
July 1957.

Simon, John Kenneth. "A Study of Classical Gesture: Henry
James and Madame de Lafayette." CLS 3:273-282. No. 3,
1966.

Taubman, Robert. "LA PRINCESSE DE CLEVES." New
S&N 65:81-82. January 18, 1963.

Turnell, Martin. The Novel in France. New York: New Directions, 1951. pp. 25-47.

Woodbridge, Benjamin M. "Mme. de Montespan and LA
PRINCESSE DE CLEVES." MLN 33:79-85. February 1918.

Woodbridge, Benj. M. "LA PRINCESSE DE CLEVES."
MLN 35:279-282. May 1920.
ZAIDE
Grise, Sister Magdala. "Madame de Lafayette's Presenta-
tion of Love in ZAIDE." FR 36:359-364. February 1963.

Larbaud, Valery
A. O. BARNABOOTH
Friedman, Melvin. "Valery Larbaud: The Two Traditions
of Eros." YFS 11:95-96.
FERMINA MARQUEZ
Friedman, M. J. Stream of Consciousness. New Haven:
Yale University Press, 1955. p. 164.

Friedman, Melvin. "Valery Larbaud: The Two Traditions
of Eros." YFS 11:94-95.

La Salle, Antoine de
RECONFORT DE MADAME DE FRESNE
Ferrier, Janet. "Antoine de La Salle and the Beginning
of Naturalism in French Prose." FS 10:216-223. 1956.

Leautaud, Paul
LE PETIT AMI
Weiner, Seymour S. "Sincerity and Variants: Paul Leau-
taud's PETIT AMI." Symposium 14:165-185. Fall 1960.

Le Sage, Alain Rene
GIL BLAS
Cordasco, Francesco. "Llorente and the Originality of the
GIL BLAS." PQ 26:206-218. July 1947.

Cordasco, Francesco. "Smollett and the Translation of
the GIL BLAS." MLQ 10:68-71. March 1949.

Green, F. C. French Novelists, Manners and Ideas: From
the Renaissance to the Revolution. New York: D. Appleton

and Company, 1930. pp. 74-80.

Iknayon, Marguerite. "The Fortunes of GIL BLAS During the Romantic Period." FR 31:370-377. April 1958.

Kurrelmeyer, W. "GIL BLAS and DON SYLVIO." MLN 34:78-81. February 1919.

Mylne, Vivienne. The Eighteenth-Century French Novel: Techniques of Illusion. Manchester: Manchester University Press, 1965. pp. 49-72.

Mylne, Vivienne. "Structure and Symbolism in GIL BLAS." FS 15:134-145. April 1961.

Levi-Strauss, Claude
    TRISTES TROPIQUES
        Donato, Eugenio. "TRISTES TROPIQUES: The Endless Journey." MLN 81:270-287. May 1966.

Loti, Pierre
    A COMMON SAILOR
        Guerard, Albert Leon. Five Masters of French Romance. New York: Scribner's Sons. pp. 156-157.
    THE DISENCHANTED
        Guerard, Albert Leon. Five Masters of French Romance. New York: Scribner's Sons. pp. 159-161.
    ICELANDIC FISHERMAN
        Baird, James. Ishmael. Baltimore: Johns Hopkins Press, 1956. pp. 135-136; 347-348.

        Guerard, Albert Leon. Five Masters of French Romance. New York: Scribner's Sons. pp. 151-154.
    MADAME CHRYSANTHEMUM
        Guerard, Albert Leon. Five Masters of French Romance. New York: Scribner's Sons. pp. 154-155.
    MY BROTHER YVES
        Guerard, Albert Leon. Five Masters of French Romance. New York: Scribner's Sons. pp. 149-151.
    RAMUNTCHO
        Guerard, Albert Leon. Five Masters of French Romance. New York: Scribner's Sons. pp. 157-159.
    ROMAN D'UN SPAHI
        Bussom, Thomas W. "Pierre Loti and THE ROMAN D'UN SPAHI." SAQ 26:40-49. January 1927.

Malegue, Joseph
    AUGUSTIN OU LE MAITRE EST LA
        Brombert, Victor. The Intellectual Hero: Studies in the French Novel, 1880-1955. Philadelphia: Lippincott, 1961. pp. 223-226.

Mallet-Joris, Francoise
  THE HOUSE OF LIES
      Reck, Rima Drell. "Francoise Mallet-Joris and the
      Anatomy of the Will. " YFS 24:75-77. Summer 1959.
  THE RED ROOM
      Reck, Rima Drell. "Francoise Mallet-Joris and the
      Anatomy of the Will. " YFS 24:74-75. Summer 1959.

Malraux, Andre
  THE CONQUERORS
      Blend, Charles D. Andre Malraux: Tragic Humanist. Colum-
      bus: Ohio State University Press, 1963. pp. 21-29; 82-88.

      Blumenthal, Gerda. Andre Malraux. Baltimore: Johns Hop-
      kins Press, 1960.   pp. 3-9.

      Bree, Germaine and Margaret Guiton. An Age of Fiction:
      The French Novel from Gide to Camus. New Brunswick:
      Rutgers University Press, 1957. pp. 182-186.

      Chiaromonte, Nicola. "Malraux and the Demons of Ac-
      tion. " PR 15:783-784. July 1948.

      Frohock, W. M. Andre Malraux and the Tragic Imagina-
      tion. Stanford: Stanford University Press, 1952. pp. 36-
      46.

      Gannon, Edward. The Honor of Being a Man. Chicago:
      Loyola University Press, 1957. pp. 7-8; 29-30; 40-44; 60-
      61; 70-76.

      Hatzfeld, Helmut. Trends and Styles in Twentieth Century
      French Literature. Washington, D. C. : Catholic University
      of America Press, 1957. pp. 33-35.

      Howe, Irving. Politics and the Novel. New York: Meridan
      Books, 1957. pp. 207-210.

      Langlois, Walter G. Andre Malraux: The Indo-China Adven-
      tures. New York: Fredrich A. Praeger Publishers, 1966.
      pp. 224-228.

      Peyre, Henri. The Contemporary French Novel. New York:
      Oxford University Press, 1955. pp. 193-195.

      Reck, Rima Drell. "Malraux's Heroes: Activists and
      Aesthetes. " UKCR 28:40-44. October 1961.

      Saisselin, Remy G. "Malraux: From the Hero to the
      Artist. " JAAC 16:256-257. December 1957.
  DAYS OF WRATH
      Blend, Charles D. Andre Malraux: Tragic Humanist.
      Columbus: Ohio State University Press, 1963. pp. 31-32;

103-106.

Blumenthal, Gerda. Andre Malraux. Baltimore: Johns Hopkins Press, 1960. pp. 59-62.

Frohock, W. M. Andre Malraux and the Tragic Imagination. Stanford: Stanford University Press, 1952. pp. 93-104.

Frohock, W. M. "LE TEMPS DU MEPRIS: A Note on Malraux as Man of Letters." RR 39:130-139. April 1948.

Gannon, Edward. The Honor of Being a Man. Chicago: Loyola University Press, 1957. pp. 78-84.

Hartman, Geoffrey H. Andre Malraux. London: Bowes and Bowes, 1960. pp. 53-59.

Herz, Micheline. "Woman's Fate." YFS 18:17-18. Winter 1957.

Slochower, Harry. No Voice Is Wholly Lost. New York: Creative Age Press, 1945. pp. 324-327.

Sonnenfeld, Albert. "Malraux and the Tyranny of Time: The Circle and the Gesture." RR 54:204-208. October 1963.

LUNES EN PAPIER
Lewis, R. W. B. The Picaresque Saint. New York: Lippincott, 1959. pp. 277-295.

MAN'S FATE
Blend, Charles D. Andre Malraux: Tragic Humanist. Columbus: Ohio State University Press, 1963. pp. 25-30; 90-103.

Blotner, Joseph L. The Political Novel. Garden City: Doubleday and Company, 1955. pp. 24-25; 44-45.

Blumenthal, Gerda. Andre Malraux. Baltimore: Johns Hopkins Press, 1960. pp. 25-40; 48-56; 62-69.

Chiaromonte, Nicola. "Malraux and the Demons of Action." PR 15:784-787. July 1948.

Cook, Albert. The Meaning of Fiction. Detroit: Wayne State University Press, 1960. pp. 175-177.

Cordle, Thomas H. "Malraux and Nietzsche's BIRTH OF TRAGEDY." BuR 8:95-102. February 1959.

Frohock, W. M. Andre Malraux and the Tragic Imagination. Stanford: Stanford University Press, 1952. pp. 16-18; 141-144.

Frohock, W. M. "Notes for a Malraux Bibliography."
MLN 65:392-395. June 1950.

Frohock, W. M. "Notes on Malraux's Symbols." RR 42:
276-281. December 1951.

Gannon, Edward. The Honor of Being a Man. Chicago:
Loyola University Press, 1957. pp. 54-69; 83-86.

Glicksberg, Charles I. The Tragic Vision in Twentieth-
Century Literature. Carbondale: Southern Illinois University
Press, 1963. pp. 141-146.

Hartman, Geoffrey H. Andre Malraux. London: Bowes and
Bowes, 1960. pp. 9-18; 42-52.

Herz, Micheline. "Woman's Fate." YFS 18:12-17. Winter
1957.

Howe, Irving. Politics and the Novel. New York: Meridan
Books, 1957. pp. 210-217.

Krieger, Murray. The Tragic Vision. New York: Holt,
Rinehart and Winston, 1960. pp. 50-72.

Langlois, Walter G. Andre Malraux: The Indo-China Adventure. New York: Fredrich A. Praeger Publisher, 1966. pp.
228-229.

Leefmans, Bert M-P. "Malraux and Tragedy: The Structure of LA CONDITION HUMAINE." RR 44:208-214. October
1953.

Mathewson, Rufus W., Jr. "Dostoevskij and Malraux."
American Contributions to the Fourth International Congress of Slavicists. The Hague: Mouton and Company, 1958.
pp. 220-221.

Moseley, Edwin M. Pseudonyms of Christ in the Modern
Novel. Pittsburgh: University of Pittsburgh Press, 1962.
pp. 183-189.

Nelson, Roy Jay. "Malraux and Camus: The Myth of the
Beleaguered City." KFLQ 13:86-94. Second Quarter 1966.

Peyre, Henri. The Contemporary French Novel. New York:
Oxford University Press, 1955. pp. 197-201.

Reck, Rima Drell. "The Heroes in the Novels of Malraux." UKCR 28:151-156. December 1961.

Reck, Rima Drell. "Malraux's Heroes: Activists and
Aesthetes." UKCR 28:39-45. October 1961.

Rees, G. O. "Sound and Silence in Malraux's Novels. "
FR 32:223-230. January 1959.

Rice, Philip Blair. "Malraux and the Individual Will. "
International Journal of Ethics 48:184-188. January 1938.

Righter, William. The Rhetorical Hero. London: Routledge
and Kegan Paul, 1964. pp. 68-69.

Roedig, Charles F. "Andre Malraux in Asia. " ASLHM
32:159-163, No. 3, 1961.

St. Aubyn, F. C. "Andre Malraux: The Syntax of Great-
ness. " FR 34:140-145. December 1960.

Savage, Catharine. Malraux, Sartre, and Aragon as Political Novelists. Gainesville: University of Florida Press,
1964. p. 7.

Slochower, Harry. "Freud and Marx in Contemporary
Literature. " SR 49:320-321. July - September 1941.

Slochower, Harry. No Voice Is Wholly Lost. New York:
Creative Age Press, 1945. pp. 320-324.
MAN'S HOPE
Baumgartner, Paul. "Solitude and Involvement: Two
Aspects of Tragedy in Malraux's Novels. " FR 38:767-772.
May 1965.

Blend, Charles D. Andre Malraux: Tragic Humanist.
Columbus: Ohio State University Press, 1963. pp. 33-35;
106-126.

Blumenthal, Gerta. Andre Malraux. Baltimore: Johns Hopkins Press, 1960. pp. 69-95.

Bree, Germaine and Margaret Guiton. An Age of Fiction:
The French Novel from Gide to Camus. New Brunswick:
Rutgers University Press, 1957. pp. 186-192.

Brombert, Victor. "Malraux: Passion and Intellect. " YFS
18:71-73. Winter 1957.

Cordle, Thomas H. "Malraux and Nietzsche's BIRTH OF
TRAGEDY. " BuR 8:95-102. February 1959.

Frohock, W. M. Andre Malraux and the Tragic Imagination. Stanford: Stanford University Press, 1952. pp. 104-
125; 141-143.

Gannon, Edward. The Honor of Being a Man. Chicago:
Loyola University Press, 1957. pp. 84-90.

Harrington, Michael. "Andre Malraux: Metamorphosis of the Hero." PR 21:658-659. November - December 1954.

Hartman, Geoffrey H. Andre Malraux. London: Bowes and Bowes, 1960. pp. 59-66.

Picon, Gaetan. "MAN'S HOPE." YFS 18:3-6. Winter 1957.

Reck, Rima Drell. "The Heroes in the Novels of Malraux." UKCR 28:153-157. December 1961.

Reck, Rima Drell. "Malraux's Heroes: Activists and Aesthetes." UKCR 28:45-46. October 1961.

Rees, G. O. "Sound and Silence in Malraux's Novels." FR 32:224-230. January 1959.

Slochower, Harry. "Freud and Marx in Contemporary Literature." SR 49:322. July-September 1941.

Slochower, Harry. No Voice Is Wholly Lost. New York: Creative Age Press, 1945. pp. 327-330.

Sonnenfeld, Albert. "Malraux and the Tyranny of Time: The Circle and the Gesture." RR 54:205-212. October 1963.

THE ROYAL WAY

Ball, Bertrand Logan, Jr. "Nature, Symbol of Death in LA VOIE ROYALE." FR 35:390-395. February 1962.

Blend, Charles D. Andre Malraux: Tragic Humanist. Columbus: Ohio State University Press, 1963. pp. 22-29; 88-90.

Blumenthal, Gerda. Andre Malraux. Baltimore: Johns Hopkins Press, 1960. pp. 9-22.

Boak, Denis. "Malraux's LA VOIE ROYALE." FS 19:42-50. January 1965.

Casey, Bill. "Andre Malraux's Heart of Darkness." TCL 5:21-26. April 1959.

Chiaromonte, Nicola. "Malraux and the Demons of Action." PR 15:781-782. July 1948.

Cordle, Thomas. "The Royal Way." YFS 18:20-26. Winter 1957.

Frohock, W. M. Andre Malraux and the Tragic Imagination. Stanford: Stanford University Press, 1952. pp. 47-57; 92-94.

Frohock, W. M. "Notes on Malraux's Symbols." RR 42: 274-276. December 1951.

Gannon, Edward. The Honor of Being a Man. Chicago: Loyola University Press, 1957. pp. 30-33; 43-49; 60-61.

Hartman, Geoffrey H. Andre Malraux. London: Bowes and Bowes, 1960. pp. 38-42.

Herz, Micheline. "Woman's Fate." YFS 18:11-12. Winter 1957.

Lewis, R. W. B. The Picaresque Saint. New York: Lippincott, 1959. pp. 279-295.

Peyre, Henri. The Contemporary French Novel. New York: Oxford University Press, 1955. pp. 195-197.

Rice, Philip Blair. "Malraux and the Individual Will." International Journal of Ethics 48:184. January 1938.

Turnell, Martin. "Malraux's Fate." Commonweal 82:411-412. June 1965.

THE WALNUT TREES OF ALTENBURG
Blend, Charles D. Andre Malraux: Tragic Humanist. Columbus: Ohio State University Press, 1963. pp. 39-41; 126-133.

Bree, Germaine and Margaret Guiton. An Age of Fiction: The French Novel from Gide to Camus. New Brunswick: Rutgers University Press, 1957. pp. 192-193.

Bree, Germaine. "Poetry of the Novel." The Culture of France in Our Time. (ed.) Julian Park. Ithaca: Cornell University Press, 1954. pp. 23-25.

Frank, Joseph. "Andre Malraux: The Image of Man." HudR 14:50-67. Spring 1961.

Frank, Joseph. "Malraux and the Image of Man." New Republic 131:18-19. August 30, 1954.

Frohock, W. M. Andre Malraux and the Tragic Imagination. Stanford: Stanford University Press, 1952. pp. 126-148.

Gannon, Edward. The Honor of Being a Man. Chicago: Loyola University Press, 1957. pp. 14-15; 91-92; 106-115.

Hartman, Geoffrey H. Andre Malraux. London: Bowes and Bowes, 1960. pp. 66-72.

Lewis, R. W. B. The Picaresque Saint. New York: Lippincott, 1959. pp. 276-277.

Mathewson, Rufus W., Jr. "Dostoevskij and Malraux."
American Contributions to the Fourth International Congress of Slavicists. The Hague: Mouton and Company,
1958. pp. 221-223.

Peyre, Henri. The Contemporary French Novel. New
York: Oxford University Press, 1955. pp. 209-212.

Reck, Rima Drell. "Malraux's Transitional Novel: LES
NOYERS DE L'ALTENBURG." FR 34:537-544. May 1961.

Righter, William. The Rhetorical Hero. London: Routledge and Kegan Paul, 1964. pp. 11-20; 25-27; 30-31.

Marivaux, Pierre de
  MARIANNE
      Baldwin, Edward Chauncey. "Marivaux's Place in the
      Development of Character Portrayal." PMLA 27:181-
      185. 1912.

      Cismaru, Alfred. "Marivaux's Religious Characters."
      Cithara 4:49-50. November 1964.

      Green, F. C. French Novelists, Manners and Ideas:
      From the Renaissance to the Revolution. New York: D.
      Appleton and Company, 1930. pp. 99-104.

      Haac, Oscar A. "Marivaux and the Human Heart."
      EUQ 12:41-42. March 1956.

      Hughes, Helen Sard. "Translations of the VIE DE
      MARIANNE and Their Relation to Contemporary English
      Fiction." MP 15:107-128. December 1917.

      Mylne, Vivienne. The Eighteenth-Century French Novel:
      Techniques of Illusion. Manchester: Manchester University Press, 1965. pp. 104-115.
  THE UPSTART PEASANT
      Green, F. C. French Novelists, Manners and Ideas:
      From the Renaissance to the Revolution. New York: D.
      Appleton and Company, 1930. pp. 104-110.

      Koch, Philip. "A Source of LE PAYSAN PARVENU."
      MLN 75:44-49. January 1960.

      Mylne, Vivienne. The Eighteenth-Century French Novel:
      Techniques of Illusion. Manchester: Manchester University Press, 1965. pp. 115-124.

Marmontel
  THE INCAS

Valette, Rebecca M. "Chateaubriand's Debt to LES INCAS." SIR 2:177-183. Spring 1963.

Martin du Gard, Roger
 DEVENIR

Boak, Denis. Roger Martin du Gard. Oxford: Clarendon Press, 1963. Chapter 2.

Bree, Germaine and Margaret Guiton. An Age of Fiction: The French Novel from Gide to Camus. New Brunswick: Rutgers University Press, 1957. pp. 76-78.
 ETE 1914

Boak, Denis. Roger Martin du Gard. Oxford: Clarendon Press, 1963. Chapter 7.
 JEAN BAROIS

Boak, Denis. Roger Martin du Gard. Oxford: Clarendon Press, 1963. Chapter 4.

Bree, Germaine and Margaret Guiton. An Age of Fiction: The French Novel from Gide to Camus. New Brunswick: Rutgers University Press, 1957. pp. 76-78.

Brombert, Victor. The Intellectual Hero: Studies in the French Novel 1880-1955. Philadelphia: Lippincott, 1961. Chapter 6; pp. 223-226.

Gibson, Robert. Roger Martin du Gard. London: Bowes and Bowes, 1961. Chapter II.

Hatzfeld, Helmut. Trends and Styles in Twentieth Century French Literature. Washington, D.C.: Catholic University of America Press, 1957. pp. 30-31.

Kaiser, Grant E. "Roger Martin du Gard's JEAN BAROIS: An Experiment in Novelistic Form." Symposium 14:135-141. Summer 1960.

Peyre, Henri. The Contemporary French Novel. New York: Oxford University Press, 1955. pp. 42-44.

Roudiez, Leon S. "The Function of Irony in Roger Martin du Gard." RR 48:277-280. December 1957.

Wood, John S. "Roger Martin du Gard." FS 14:130-133. April 1960.
 LES THIBAULT

Boak, Denis. Roger Martin du Gard. Oxford: Clarendon Press, 1963. Chapter 5.

Bree, Germaine and Margaret Guiton. An Age of Fiction: The French Novel from Gide to Camus. New Brunswick: Rutgers University Press, 1957. pp. 79-84.

Gibson, Robert. Roger Martin du Gard. London: Bowes and Bowes, 1961. Chapter III.

Guerard, Albert. "The Leading French Novelists of the Present Moment. " CE 12:365. April 1951.

Hall, Thomas White. "A Note on the So-called 'Change in Technique' in LES THIBAULT of Roger Martin du Gard. " FR 27:108-113. December 1953.

Hatzfeld, Helmut. Trends and Styles in Twentieth Century French Literature. Washington, D. C.: Catholic Univeristy of America Press, 1957. pp. 28-30.

Moore-Rinvolucri, Mina J. "Les Thibault and Their Creator. " ML 33:85-89. September 1952.

Peyre, Henri. The Contemporary French Novel. New York: Oxford University Press, 1955. pp. 39-42.

Roudiez, Leon S. "The Function of Irony in Roger Martin du Gard. " RR 48:280-284. December 1957.

Wood, John S. "Roger Martin du Gard. " FS 14:134-140. April 1960.

L'UNE DE NOUS
Boak, C. D. "An Early Work by Roger Martin du Gard." AUMLA 20:318-330. November 1963.

Boak, Denis. Roger Martin du Gard. Oxford: Clarendon Press, 1963. Chapter 3.

Maupassant, Guy de
FINE FRIEND
Boyd, Ernest. Guy de Maupassant. New York: Alfred A. Knopf, 1926. pp. 178-181.

Chaikin, Milton. "Maupassant's BEL-AMI and Balzac. " RomN 2:109-112. Spring 1960.

Grant, Richard B. "The Function of the First Chapter of Maupassant's BEL-AMI. " MLN 76:748-752. December 1961.

Smith, Maxwell A. "Maupassant as a Novelist. " TSL 1:44. 1956.

Steegmuller, Francis. Maupassant: A Lion in the Path. New York: Random House, 1949. pp. 211-228.

Sullivan, Edward D. Maupassant the Novelist. Princeton: Princeton University Press, 1954. pp. 72-93.

Weisstein, Ulrich. "Maupassant's BEL AMI and Heinrich
Mann's IM SCHLARAFFENLAND. " RomN 2:124-128.
Spring 1961.
THE MASTER PASSION
Boyd, Ernest. Guy de Maupassant. New York: Alfred A.
Knopf, 1926. pp. 215-216.

Saintsbury, George. A History of the French Novel (To
the Close of the 19th Century). London: Macmillan and
Company, 1919. pp. 491-493.

Smith, Maxwell A. "Maupassant as a Novelist. " TSL
1:46. 1956.

Sullivan, Edward D. Maupassant the Novelist. Princeton:
Princeton University Press, 1954. pp. 120-141.
MONT-ORIOL
Boyd, Ernest. Guy de Maupassant. New York: Alfred A.
Knopf, 1926. pp. 191-195.

Saintsbury, George. A History of the French Novel (To
the Close of the 19th Century). London: Macmillan and
Company, 1919. pp. 490-491.

Smith, Maxwell A. "Maupassant as a Novelist. " TSL
1:44-45. 1956.

Sullivan, Edward D. Maupassant the Novelist. Princeton:
Princeton University Press, 1954. pp. 94-101.
ONE LIFE
Boyd, Ernest. Guy de Maupassant. New York: Alfred A.
Knopf, 1926. pp. 132-135.

Grant, Richard B. "Imagery as a Means of Psychological Revelation in Maupassant's UNE VIE. " SP 60:669-
684. October 1963.

Pritchett, V. S. Books in General. London: Chatto and
Windus, 1953. pp. 95-99.

Saintsbury, George. A History of the French Novel (To
the Close of the 19th Century). London: Macmillan and
Company, 1919. pp. 489-490.

Smith, Maxwell A. "Maupassant as a Novelist. " TSL
1:43-44. 1956.

Steegmuller, Francis. Maupassant: A Lion in the Path.
New York: Random House, 1949. pp. 165-172.

Sullivan, Edward D. Maupassant the Novelist. Princeton:
Princeton University Press, 1954. pp. 57-71.

OUR HEART
Boyd, Ernest. Guy de Maupassant. New York: Alfred A. Knopf, 1926. pp. 218-219; 224-225.

Niess, Robert J. "Autobiographical Symbolism in Maupassant's Last Works." Symposium 14:218-220. Fall 1960.

Sullivan, Edward D. Maupassant the Novelist. Princeton: Princeton University Press, 1954. pp. 141-156.

Sullivan, Edward D. "Portrait of the Artist: Maupassant and NOTRE COEUR." FR 22:136-141. December 1948.
LE PAPA DE SIMON
Artinian, Artine. "First Publication of Maupassant's PAPA DE SIMON." MLN 63:469-470. November 1948.
PIERRE AND JEAN
Freimanis, Dzintars. "More on the Meaning of PIERRE ET JEAN." FR 38:326-331. January 1965.

Grant, Elliott M. "On the Meaning of Maupassant's PIERRE ET JEAN." FR 36:469-473. April 1963.

Niess, Robert J. "PIERRE ET JEAN: Some Symbols." FR 32:511-519. May 1959.

Sachs, Murray. "The Meaning of Maupassant's PIERRE ET JEAN." FR 34:244-250. January 1961.

Saintsbury, George. A History of the French Novel (To the Close of the 19th Century). London: Macmillan and Company, 1919. pp. 493-495.

Simon, Ernest. "Descriptive and Analytical Techniques in Maupassant's PIERRE ET JEAN." RR 51:45-52. February 1960.

Smith, Maxwell A. "Maupassant as a Novelist." TSL 1:45-46. 1956.

Steegmuller, Francis. Maupassant: A Lion in the Path. New York: Random House, 1949. pp. 260-271.

Sullivan, Edward D. Maupassant the Novelist. Princeton: Princeton University Press, 1954. pp. 102-119.
PIERROT
Matthews, J. H. "Oblique Narration in Maupassant's PIERROT." ML 42:48-54. June 1961.
UNE VENDETTA
Lancaster, H. Carrington. "A Chinese Source for Maupassant." MLN 63:405-406. June 1948.

Mauriac, Claude
ALL WOMEN ARE FATAL

Johnston, Stuart L. "Structure in the Novels of Claude
Mauriac. " FR 38:451-452. February 1965.
DINNER PARTY
Johnston, Stuart L. "Structure in the Novels of Claude
Mauriac. " FR 38:452-455. February 1965.
THE MARQUISE WENT OUT AT FIVE
Johnston, Stuart L. "Structure in the Novels of Claude
Mauriac. " FR 38:453-457. February 1965.

Mauriac, Francois
THE DARK ANGELS
Heppenstall, Raynor. The Double Image; Mutations of
Christian Mythology in the Work of Four French Catholic
Writers of Today and Yesterday. London: Secker and War-
burg, 1947. pp. 50-51.

Iyengar, K. R. Sprinivasa. Francois Mauriac. New York:
Asia Publishing House, 1963. pp. 63-67.

Jenkins, Cecil. Mauriac. New York: Barnes and Noble,
Inc. , 1965. pp. 96-97.
DESERT OF LOVE
Fowlie, Wallace. "Mauriac's Dark Hero. " SR 56:51-55.
Winter 1948.

Humiliata, Sister Mary. "The Theme of Isolation in
Mauriac's THE DESERT OF LOVE. " TCL 7:107-112.
October 1961.

Iyengar, K. R. Sprinivasa. Francois Mauriac. New York:
Asia Publishing House, 1963. pp. 32-35.

Jerome, Sister M. "Human and Divine Love in Dante
and Mauriac. " Renascence 18:178-179. Summer 1966.

Peyre, Henri. The Contemporary French Novel. New
York: Oxford University Press, 1955. pp. 111-113.

Rubin, Louis D. , Jr. "Francois Mauriac and the Free-
dom of the Religious Novelist." SoR n. s. 2:38. January
1966.
THE END OF THE NIGHT
Iyengar, K. R. Sprinivasa. Francois Mauriac. New York:
Asia Publishing House, 1963. pp. 47-53.

Jenkins, Cecil. Mauriac. New York: Barnes and Noble,
Inc. , 1965. pp. 92-95.

Stratford, Phillip. Faith and Fiction. Notre Dame: Uni-
versity of Notre Dame Press, 1964. pp. 223-226.
THE ENEMY
Iyengar, K. R. Sprinivasa. Francois Mauriac. New York:
Asia Publishing House, 1963. pp. 82-87.

FLESH AND BLOOD
Iyengar, K. R. Sprinivasa. Francois Mauriac. New York:
Asia Publishing House, 1963. pp. 12-16.

Jenkins, Cecil. Mauriac. New York: Barnes and Noble,
Inc., 1965. pp. 44-46.

Stratford, Phillip. Faith and Fiction. Notre Dame: Univer-
sity of Notre Dame Press, 1964. pp. 80-81.
THE FRONTENAC MYSTERY
Iyengar, K. R. Sprinivasa. Francois Mauriac. New York:
Asia Publishing House, 1963. pp. 77-81.

Jenkins, Cecil. Mauriac. New York: Barnes and Noble,
Inc. , 1965. pp. 88-89.

Stratford, Phillip. Faith and Fiction. Notre Dame: Univer-
sity of Notre Dame Press, 1964. pp. 244-245.
GENITRIX
Bree, Germaine and Margaret Guiton. An Age of Fiction:
The French Novel from Gide to Camus. New Brunswick:
Rutgers University Press, 1957. pp. 117-118.

Fowlie, Wallace. "Mauriac's Dark Hero. " SR 56:47-51.
Winter 1948.

Iyengar, K. R. Sprinivasa. Francois Mauriac. New York:
Asia Publishing House, 1963. pp. 24-26.

Jenkins, Cecil. Mauriac. New York: Barnes and Noble,
Inc. , 1965. pp. 57-61.

Murphy, Eugene F. "Mauriac's GENITRIX. " Expl 13:
Item 37. April 1955.

Peyre, Henri. The Contemporary French Novel. New
York: Oxford University Press, 1955. pp. 110-111.

Rubin, Louis D. , Jr. "Francois Mauriac and the Freedom of the Religious Novelist. " SoR n. s. 2:29-30. January 1966.

Stratford, Phillip. Faith and Fiction. Notre Dame: Uni-
versity of Notre Dame Press, 1964. pp. 157-160.
A KISS FOR THE LEPER
Bree, Germaine and Margaret Guiton. An Age of Fic-
tion: The French Novel from Gide to Camus. New
Brunswick: Rutgers University Press, 1957. pp. 116-117.

Iyengar, K. R. Sprinivasa. Francois Mauriac. New York:
Asia Publishing House, 1963. pp. 21-23.

Jenkins, Cecil. Mauriac. New York: Barnes and Noble,

Inc. , 1965. pp. 47-49; 55-56.

Peyre, Henri. The Contemporary French Novel. New
York: Oxford University Press, 1955. pp. 108-110.

Rubin, Louis D. , Jr. "Francois Mauriac and the Freedom of the Religious Novelist." SoR n. s. 2:27-29. January
1966.

Stoker, J. T. "The Question of Grace in Mauriac's
Novels. " Culture 26:292-294. September 1965.

Stratford, Phillip. Faith and Fiction. Notre Dame: University of Notre Dame Press, 1964. pp. 1-30.

THE LAMB
Bree, Germaine and Margaret Guiton. An Age of Fiction:
The French Novel from Gide to Camus. New Brunswick:
Rutgers University Press, 1957. pp. 114-115.

Dillistone, F. W. The Novelist and the Passion Story.
New York: Sheed and Ward, 1960. pp. 27-44.

Iyengar, K. R. Sprinivasa. Francois Mauriac. New York:
Asia Publishing House, 1963. pp. 112-116.

Klibbe, Lawrence H. "Mauriac's Incredible 'Priest.' "
CathW 182:116-119. November 1955.

LINES OF LIFE
Iyengar, K. R. Sprinivasa. Francois Mauriac. New York:
Asia Publishing House, 1963. pp. 54-57.

Rubin, Louis D. , Jr. "Francois Mauriac and the Freedom of the Religious Novelist. " SoR n. s. 2:21. January
1966.

Stratford, Phillip. Faith and Fiction. Notre Dame: University of Notre Dame Press, 1964. pp. 145-149

THE LITTLE MISERY
Iyengar, K. R. Sprinivasa. Francois Mauriac. New York:
Asia Publishing House, 1963. pp. 103-107.

THE LOVED AND THE UNLOVED
Iyengar, K. R. Sprinivasa. Francois Mauriac. New York:
Asia Publishing House, 1963. pp. 108-111.

Stratford, Phillip. Faith and Fiction. Notre Dame: University of Notre Dame Press, 1964. pp. 301-306.

QUESTIONS OF PRECEDENCE
Iyengar, K. R. Sprinivasa. Francois Mauriac. New York:
Asia Publishing House, 1963. pp. 17-20.

Jenkins, Cecil. Mauriac. New York: Barnes and Noble,
Inc. , 1965. pp. 46-47.

Stratford, Phillip. Faith and Fiction. Notre Dame: University of Notre Dame Press, 1964. pp. 79-85.

THE RIVER OF FIRE

Iyengar, K. R. Sprinivasa. Francois Mauriac. New York: Asia Publishing House, 1963. pp. 27-31.

Jenkins, Cecil. Mauriac. New York: Barnes and Noble, Inc., 1965. pp. 56-57.

Stratford, Phillip. Faith and Fiction. Notre Dame: University of Notre Dame Press, 1964. pp. 143-149.

THE STUFF OF YOUTH

Iyengar, K. R. Sprinivasa. Francois Mauriac. New York: Asia Publishing House, 1963. pp. 7-11.

Jenkins, Cecil. Mauriac. New York: Barnes and Noble, Inc., 1965. pp. 43-44.

Stratford, Phillip. Faith and Fiction. Notre Dame: University of Notre Dame Press, 1964. pp. 33-41.

THAT WHICH WAS LOST

Iyengar, K. R. Sprinivasa. Francois Mauriac. New York: Asia Publishing House, 1963. pp. 58-62.

THERESE

Bree, Germaine and Margaret Guiton. An Age of Fiction: The French Novel from Gide to Camus. New Brunswick: Rutgers University Press, 1957. pp. 118-120.

Gregor, Ian and Brian Nicholas. The Moral and the Story. London: Faber and Faber, 1962. pp. 207-216.

Iyengar, K. R. Sprinivasa. Francois Mauriac. New York: Asia Publishing House, 1963. pp. 36-40; 41-46.

Jenkins, Cecil. Mauriac. New York: Barnes and Noble, Inc., 1965. pp. 95-96.

Murray, Jack. "Three Murders in the Contemporary French Novel." TSLL 6:363-366. Autumn 1964.

Rubin, Louis D., Jr. "Francois Mauriac and the Freedom of the Religious Novelist." SoR n. s. 2:32-38. January 1966.

Stratford, Phillip. Faith and Fiction. Notre Dame: University of Notre Dame Press, 1964. pp. 154-160; 216-217.

THE UNKNOWN SEA

Heppenstall, Raynor. The Double Image; Mutations of Christian Mythology in the Work of Four French Catholic Writers of Today and Yesterday. London: Secker and Warburg, 1947. pp. 51-52.

Iyengar, K. R. Sprinivasa. Francois Mauriac. New York:
Asia Publishing House, 1963. pp. 88-94.

THE VIPERS' TANGLE

Bree, Germaine and Margaret Guiton. An Age of Fiction:
The French Novel from Gide to Camus. New Brunswick:
Rutgers University Press, 1957. pp. 120-122.

Iyengar, K. R. Sprinivasa. Francois Mauriac. New York:
Asia Publishing House, 1963. pp. 68-76.

Jenkins, Cecil. Mauriac. New York: Barnes and Noble,
Inc., 1965. pp. 81-88.

Jerome, Sister M. "Human and Divine Love in Dante and
Mauriac." Renascence 18:179-181. Summer 1966.

Peyre, Henri. The Contemporary French Novel. New York:
Oxford University Press, 1955. pp. 105-106; 113-115.

Stoker, J. T. "The Question of Grace in Mauriac's
Novels." Culture 26:295-302. September 1965.

Stratford, Phillip. Faith and Fiction. Notre Dame: University of Notre Dame Press, 1964. pp. 193-198.

Tartella, Vincent P. "Thematic Imagery in Mauriac's
VIPERS' TANGLE." Renascence 17:195-200. Summer
1965.

A WOMAN OF THE PHARISEES

Heppenstall, Raynor. The Double Image; Mutations of
Christian Mythology in the Work of Four French Catholic
Writers of Today and Yesterday. London: Secker and War-
burg, 1947. pp. 52-54.

Iyengars, K. R. Sprinivasa. Francois Mauriac. New York:
Asia Publishing House, 1963. pp. 95-102.

Jenkins, Cecil. Mauriac. New York: Barnes and Noble,
Inc., 1965. pp. 97-99.

Jerome, Sister M. "Human and Divine Love in Dante and
Mauriac." Renascence 18:181-184. Summer 1966.

Peyre, Henri. The Contemporary French Novel. New
York: Oxford University Press, 1955. pp. 115-119.

Stratford, Phillip. Faith and Fiction. Notre Dame: University of Notre Dame Press, 1964. pp. 290-299.

YOUNG MAN IN CHAINS

Iyengar, K. R. Sprinivasa. Francois Mauriac. New York:
Asia Publishing House, 1963. p. 7.

Jenkins, Cecil. Mauriac. New York: Barnes and Noble,

Inc., 1965. pp. 42-43.

Stratford, Phillip. Faith and Fiction. Notre Dame: University of Notre Dame Press, 1964. pp. 69-74.

Maurois, Andre
ATMOSPHERE OF LOVE
Haxo, Henry E. "Andre Maurois, Novelist and Essayist." FR 6:217. February 1933.
THE FAMILY CIRCLE
Haxo, Henry E. "Andre Maurois, Novelist and Essayist." FR 6:218-220. February 1933.
TERRE PROMISE
Bentley, Charles A. "Rilke and Andre Maurois." MLN 69:340-343. May 1954.
THE WEIGHER OF SOULS
Haxo, Henry E. "Andre Maurois, Novelist and Essayist." FR 6:218. February 1933.

Merimee, Prosper
CARMEN
George, Albert J. Short Fiction in France: 1800-1850. Syracuse: Syracuse University Press, 1964. pp. 128-131.

Northup, George T. "The Influence of George Borrow upon Prosper Merimee." MP 13:15-28. July 1915.
COLOMBA
George, Albert J. Short Fiction in France: 1800-1850. Syracuse: Syracuse University Press, 1964. pp. 125-128.
THE DOUBLE MISTAKE
George, Albert J. Short Fiction in France: 1800-1850. Syracuse: Syracuse University Press, 1964. pp. 122-125.
L'ENLEVEMENT DE LA REDOUTE
George, Albert J. Short Fiction in France: 1800-1850. Syracuse: Syracuse University Press, 1964. pp. 109-111.
MATEO FALCONE
George, Albert J. Short Fiction in France: 1800-1850. Syracuse: Syracuse University Press, 1964. pp. 107-109.
LE VASE ETRUSQUE
George, Albert J. Short Fiction in France: 1800-1850. Syracuse: Syracuse University Press, 1964. pp. 117-120.
THE VENUS OF ILLE
Bowman, Frank Paul. "Narrator and Myth in Merimee's VENUS D'ILLE." FR 33:475-482. April 1960.

Mesnil, Armand du
VALDIEU
Wright, Barbara. "VALDIEU: A Forgotten Precursor of Fromentin's DOMINIQUE." MLR 60:520-528. October 1965.

Meurice, Paul
LA FAMILLE AUBRY

Spencer, Philip. "A Note on Paul Meurice and LES
MISERABLES. " MLR 51:566-568. October 1956.

Mirbeau, Octave
THE TORTURE GARDEN
Burns, Wayne. "IN THE PENAL COLONY: Variations on
a Theme by Octave Mirbeau. " Accent 17:45-51. Winter
1957.

Montaurier, Jean
COMME A TRAVERS LE FEU
Henrey, K. H. "The Priest in the French Novel. " CQR
165:82-85. January-March 1964.

Montherlant, Henry de
THE BACHELORS
Baro, Gene. "Montherlant and the Morals of Adjustment."
SR 69:707-708. Autumn 1961.

Enright, D. J. "The Passion of Indifference. " NewS 68:
215-216. August 14, 1964.

Pritchett, V. S. The Living Novel and Later Appreciations.
New York: Random House, 1964. pp. 366-370.
THE BULLFIGHTERS
Frohock, W. M. "The Climax of Montherlant's BESTI-
AIRES. " RR 43:266-271. December 1952.

Pitou, Spire. "Henry de Montherlant: The First Decade."
Renascence 5:122-123. Spring 1953.
CHAOS AND NIGHT
Enright, D. J. "The Passion of Indifference. " NewS 68:
215. August 14, 1964.
DESERT LOVE
Pritchett, V. S. "Henri de Montherlant. " New S&N 53:
842-843. June 29, 1957.
THE DREAM
Pitou, Spire. "Henry de Montherlant: The First Decade."
Renascence 5:120-122. Spring 1953.
THE LEPERS
Enright, D. J. "The Passion of Indifference. " NewS 68:
215. August 14, 1964.
MASTER OF SANTIAGO
Enright, D. J. "The Passion of Indifference. " NewS 68:
215-216. August 14, 1964.
LES OLYMPIQUES
Pitou, Spire. "Henry de Montherlant: The First Decade."
Renascence 5:124. Spring 1953.

Nerval, Gerard de
AURELIA
Radcliff-Umstead, Douglas. "Cainism and Gerard de Ner-
val. " PQ 45:406-408. April 1966.

Rinsler, Norma. "Gerard de Nerval's Celestial City and the Chain of Souls." SIR 2:87-106. Winter 1963.

"World of a Visionary." TLS, May 16, 1958, p. 262.
LE MARQUIS DE FAYOLLE
 Rhodes, S. A. "Gerard de Nerval's Unfinished Novel." RR 35:299-306. December 1944.
OCTAVIE
 Rhodes, S. A. "Note on Gerard de Nerval's OCTAVIE." MLN 60:172-176. March 1945.
VOYAGE EN ORIENT
 Cargo, Robert T. "Gerard de Nerval's Benoni." RomN 7:12-15. Autumn 1965.

Nimier, Richard
 THE BLUE HUSSAR
  Magny, Claude-Edmonde. "Richard Nimier." YFS 8:56-76. Fall - Winter 1958.
 LES EPEES
  Magny, Claude-Edmonde. "Richard Nimier." YFS 8:56-76. Fall - Winter 1958.

Nodier, Charles
 LA FEE AUX MIETTES
  George, Albert J. Short Fiction in France: 1800-1850. Syracuse: Syracuse University Press, 1964. pp. 37-40.
 TRILBY
  George, Albert J. Short Fiction in France: 1800-1850. Syracuse: Syracuse University Press, 1964. pp. 36-37.

Pinget, Robert
 GRAAL FLIBUSTE
  Morse, J. Mitchell. "The Choreography of 'The New Novel.' " HudR 16:417-419. Autumn 1963.
 L'INQUISITOIRE
  Steisel, Marie-Georgette. "Pinget's Method in L'IN-QUISITOIRE." BA 40:267-271. Summer 1966.

Prevost, Antoine Francois
 CLEVELAND, OU LE PHILOSOPHE ANGLAIS
  Cooper, Berenice. "The Abbe Prevost and the Jesuits." TWA 43:125-132. 1954.

  Woodbridge, Benj. M. "Romantic Tendencies in the Novels of the Abbe Prevost." PMLA 26:324-328. June 1911.
 THE DEAN OF COLERAINE
  Beaumont, Ernest. "Abbe Prevost and the Art Ambiguity." DubR 229:166-170. Second Quarter 1955.

  Mylne, Vivienne. The Eighteenth-Century French Novel: Techniques of Illusion. Manchester: Manchester University Press, 1965. pp. 83-90.

HISTORY OF A MODERN GREEK LADY
    Beaumont, Ernest. "Abbe Prevost and the Art of Am-
    biguity. " DubR 229:170-174. Second Quarter 1955.

    Turnell, Martin. "The Novels of the Abbe Prevost. "
    SR 61:596-598. Autumn 1953.
MANON LESCAUT (See also MEMOIRS AND ADVENTURES OF
A MAN OF QUALITY)
    Auerbach, Erich. Mimesis. New York: Doubleday and
    Company, 1957. pp. 347-352.

    Beaumont, Ernest. "Abbe Prevost and the Art of Am-
    biguity. " DubR 229:165-166. Second Quarter 1955.

    Burdett, Osbert. "MANON LESCAUT. " LMerc 24:344-350.
    August 1931.

    Frautschi, R. L. "MANON LESCAUT: The Exemplary
    Attitude. " FR 37:288-295. January 1964.

    Green, F. C. "Is MANON LESCAUT a Jansenist Novel?"
    MLR 33:528-539. October 1938.

    Hammer, Carl, Jr. "Goethe, Prevost, and Louisiana. "
    MLQ 16:332-338. December 1955.

    Havens, George R. "The Date of Composition of MANON
    LESCAUT. " MLN 33:150-154. March 1918.

    Kurz, Harry. "MANON LESCAUT (A Study in Unchanging
    Critics). " TMV 1:221-226. 1930.

    Mead, William. "Manon Lescaut, c'est moi?" ECr 6:85-
    96. Summer 1966.

    Mylne, Vivienne. The Eighteenth-Century French Novel:
    Techniques of Illusion. Manchester: Manchester Univer-
    sity Press, 1965. pp. 90-103.

    Nichols, Stephen G. , Jr. "The Double Register of Time
    and Character in MANON LESCAUT. " RomN 7:149-154.
    Spring 1966.

    Rodway, A. E. "MOLL FLANDERS and MANON LES-
    CAUT. " EIC 3:303-320. July 1953.

    Turnell, Martin. "The Novels   of the Abbe Prevost. "
    SR 61:582-594. Autumn 1953.
MEMOIRES D'UN HONNETE HOMME
    Turnell, Martin. "The Novels of the Abbe Prevost. "
    SR 61:598-600. Autumn 1953.
MEMOIRS AND ADVENTURES OF A MAN OF QUALITY
    Anderson, Paul Bunyan. "English Drama Transferred to

Prevost's Fiction. " <u>MLN</u> 49:178-180. March 1934.

Mylne, Vivienne. <u>The Eighteenth-Century French Novel:</u>
<u>Techniques of Illusion.</u> Manchester: Manchester Univer-
sity Press, 1965. pp. 73-74.

Proust, Marcel
   THE CAPTIVE
       Barker, Richard H. <u>Marcel Proust: A Biography.</u> New
       York: Criterion Books, 1958. pp. 302-308.

       Fowlie, Wallace. <u>A Reading of Proust.</u> Garden City:
       Doubleday and Company, 1964. Chapters 12 and 13.

       Green, F. C. <u>The Mind of Proust.</u> Cambridge University
       Press, 1949. Chapter VII; pp. 273-352.

       Hindus, Milton. <u>A Reader's Guide to Marcel Proust.</u> New
       York: The Noonday Press, 1962. pp. 125-145.

       Leon, Derrick. <u>Introduction to Proust: His Life, His</u>
       <u>Circle and His Work.</u> London: Routledge and Kegan Paul,
       Ltd., 1951. pp. 169-170.

       March, Harold. "The Imprisoned. " <u>YFS</u> 34:44-54. June
       1965.

       March, Harold. <u>The Two Worlds of Marcel Proust.</u>
       Philadelphia: University of Pennsylvania Press, 1948.
       pp. 132-136; 146-149.

       Mein, Margaret. <u>Proust's Challenge to Time.</u> Manches-
       ter: Manchester University Press, 1962. pp. 101-102;
       107-109.

       Miller, Milton L. <u>Nostalgia: A Psychoanalytic Study of</u>
       <u>Marcel Proust.</u> Boston: Houghton Mifflin Company, 1956.
       pp. 65-82.
   CITIES OF THE PLAIN
       Barker, Richard H. <u>Marcel Proust: A Biography.</u> New
       York: Criterion Books, 1958. pp. 295-302; 327-333; 341-
       349.

       Fowlie, Wallace. <u>A Reading of Proust.</u> Garden City:
       Doubleday and Company, 1964. Chapters 10-11.

       Green, F. C. <u>The Mind of Proust.</u> Cambridge Univer-
       sity Press, 1949. Chapters V-VI; pp. 184-272.

       Hindus, Milton. <u>A Reader's Guide to Marcel Proust.</u>
       New York: The Noonday Press, 1962. pp. 107-124.

       Leon, Derrick. <u>Introduction to Proust: His Life, His</u>

Circle and His Work. London: Routledge and Kegan Paul, Ltd., 1951. pp. 160-163.

March, Harold. The Two Worlds of Marcel Proust. Philadelphia: University of Pennsylvania Press, 1948. pp. 130-133; 143-147.

Miller, Milton L. Nostalgia: A Psychoanalytic Study of Marcel Proust. Boston: Houghton Mifflin Company, 1956. pp. 55-64.

GUERMANTES' WAY

Barker, Richard H. Marcel Proust: A Biography. New York: Criterion Books, 1958. pp. 289-295; 321-326; 331-333.

Buck, Philo M., Jr. Directions in Contemporary Literature. New York: Oxford University Press, 1942. pp. 115-116.

Fowlie, Wallace. A Reading of Proust. Garden City: Doubleday and Company, 1964. Chapters 8-9.

Green, F. C. The Mind of Proust. Cambridge University Press, 1949. pp. 115-183; Chapters III-IV.

Hindus, Milton. A Reader's Guide to Marcel Proust. New York: The Noonday Press, 1962. pp. 83-106.

Leon, Derrick. Introduction to Proust: His Life, His Circle and His Work. London: Routledge and Kegan Paul, Ltd., 1951. pp. 156-157.

March, Harold. The Two Worlds of Marcel Proust. Philadelphia: University of Pennsylvania Press, 1948. pp. 146-148.

Miller, Milton L. Nostalgia: A Psychoanalytic Study of Marcel Proust. Boston: Houghton Mifflin Company, 1956. pp. 45-54.

JEAN SANTEUIL

Alderman, Sidney S. "Young Proust's Search for Lost Time." SAQ 57:42-49. Winter 1958.

Barker, Richard H. Marcel Proust: A Biography. New York: Criterion Books, 1958. pp. 82-84; 93-103.

Bell, William Stewart. "The Prototype for Proust's Jean Santeuil." MLN 73:46-50. January 1958.

Bree, Germaine. "JEAN SANTEUIL: An Appraisal." ECr 5:14-25. Spring 1965.

Cocking, J. M. "Marcel Proust." Three Studies in Mod-

ern French Literature. (ed.) Erich Heller. New Haven:
Yale University Press, 1956. pp. 18-79; 88-127.

Cook, Gladys E. "Marcel Proust: From Analysis to Creation. " BuR 8:17-37. November 1958.

Duthie, E. L. "The Family Circle in Proust's JEAN
SANTEUIL. " ConRev 184:224-228. October 1953.

Edel, Leon. The Modern Psychological Novel. New York:
Grosset and Dunlap, 1955. pp. 109-112.

Girard, Rene. "Introduction. " Proust: A Collection of
Critical Essays. (ed.) Rene Girard. Englewood Cliffs,
N. J.: Prentice-Hall, 1962. pp. 8-10.

Hindus, Milton. The Proustian Vision. New York: Columbia University Press, 1954. pp. 29-32.

Hindus, Milton. A Reader's Guide to Marcel Proust. New
York: Noonday Press, 1962. pp. 196-220.

Hodson, W. L. "Proust's Methods of Character Presentation in LES PLAISIRS ET LES JOURS and JEAN
SANTEUIL. " MLR 57:44-46. January 1962.

Jackson, Elizabeth R. "The Genesis of the Involuntary
Memory in Proust's Early Works. " PMLA 76:588-591.
December 1961.

Lean, Tangye. "A Proust Gap Bridged. " Spec 190:207-
208. February 20, 1953.

Mein, Margaret. Proust's Challenge to Time. Manchester: Manchester University Press, 1962. pp. 66-69.

Miller, Milton L. Nostalgia: A Psychoanalytic Study of
Marcel Proust. Boston: Houghton Mifflin Company, 1956.
pp. 114-115; 272-286.

O'Brien, Justin. "The Wisdom of the Young Proust. "
RR 45:121-124. April 1954.

Paul, David. "Time and the Novelist. " PR 21:645-646.
November-December 1954.

Rogers, B. G. Proust's Narrative Techniques. Geneve:
Librairie Droz, 1965. Part I, Chapter III.

Strauss, Walter A. "Criticism and Creation. " Proust:
A Collection of Critical Essays. (ed.) Rene Girard. Englewood Cliffs, N. J.: Prentice-Hall, 1962. pp. 57-58.

PLEASURES AND DAYS
Adelson, Dorothy. "Proust's Earlier and Later Styles:
A Textual Comparison." RR 34:127-138. April 1943.

Hindus, Milton. A Reader's Guide to Marcel Proust.
New York: The Noonday Press, 1962. pp. 181-185.

Jackson, Elizabeth R. "The Genesis of the Involuntary
Memory in Proust's Early Works." PMLA 76:586-588.
December 1961.

Rogers, B. G. Proust's Narrative Techniques. Geneve:
Librairie Droz, 1965. Part I, Chapter I.

Smith, Logan Pearsall. "The 'Little Proust.'" Marcel
Proust: Reviews and Estimates. (ed.) Gladys Dudley
Lindner. Stanford: Stanford University Press, 1942. pp.
22-25.
REMEMBRANCE OF THINGS PAST
Agar, Herbert. "Proust and the Modern Dilemma." ER
55:372-379. October 1932.

Alden, Douglas W. "Origins of the Unconscious and Sub-
conscious in Proust." MLQ 4:343-357. September 1943.

Alderman, Sidney S. "Young Proust's Search for Lost
Time." SAQ 57:39-54. Winter 1958.

Auchincloss, Louis. "Proust's Picture of Society." PR
27:690-701. Fall 1960.

Baker, Joseph E. "Ivory Tower as Laboratory: Pater
and Proust." Accent 19:206-216. Autumn 1959.

Barker, Richard H. Marcel Proust: A Biography. New
York: Criterion Books, 1958. pp. 167-170.

Bell, Clive. "Proust." Marcel Proust: Reviews and Estimates. (ed.) Gladys Dudley Lindner. Stanford: Stanford
University Press, 1942. pp. 118-127.

Bell, William Stewart. Proust's Nocturnal Muse. New
York: Columbia University Press, 1962. Chapters II, III,
IV.

Bettman, Dane. "Marcel Proust Explains Himself." SR
40:229-240. 1932.

Birn, Randi Marie. "Love and Communication: An Interpretation of Proust's Albertine." FR 40:221-228. November 1966.

Bisson, L. A. "Marcel Proust and Madame Leon Daudet:

A Source and an Example of 'Affective Memory.' '' MLR 36:473-479. October 1941.

Bisson, L. A. "Proust, Bergson, and George Eliot. " MLR 40:104-114. April 1945.

Black, Carl John, Jr. "Albertine as an Allegorical Figure of Time. " RR 54:171-186. October 1963.

Borton, Samuel. "A Tentative Essay on Dante and Proust." DelN 31:33-42. 1958.

Bourke, L. H. "Jealousy. " Culture 19:5-87. March 1958.

Bree, Germaine and Margaret Guiton. An Age of Fiction: The French Novel from Gide to Camus. New Brunswick: Rutgers University Press, 1957. pp. 39-42.

Bree, Germaine. "The Enchanted World of Marcel Proust. " ASLHM 33:9-27. No. 1, 1962.

Bree, Germaine. "From JEAN SANTEUIL to TIME REGAINED. " BuR 6:16-21. December 1956.

Brereton, Geoffrey. A Short History of French Literature. London: Cassell, 1954. pp. 242-244.

Bussom, Thomas W. "Marcel Proust and Painting. " RR 34:54-70. February 1943.

Champigny, Robert. "Proust, Beyson and Other Philosophers. " Proust: A Collection of Critical Essays. (ed.) Rene Girard. Englewood Cliffs, N. J.: Prentice-Hall, 1962.

Clark, Charles N. "Love and Time: The Erotic Imagery of Marcel Proust. " YFS 11:80-90.

Cocking, J. M. "Marcel Proust. " Three Studies in Modern French Literature. (ed.) Erich Heller. New Haven: Yale University Press, 1956. pp. 18-79; 88-127.

Cohn, Robert Greer. "Sartre Versus Proust. " PR 28: 633-645. 1961.

Cook, Albert. The Meaning of Fiction. Detroit: Wayne State University Press, 1960. pp. 282-297.

Cook, Albert. "Proust: The Invisible Stilts of Time. " MFS 4:118-126. Summer 1958.

Cordle, Thomas H. "The Role of Dreams in A LA RECHERCHE DU TEMPS PERDU. " RR 42:261-273. December 1951.

Cruickshank, John. "The Shifting World of Proust."
Crit Q 8:220-228. Autumn 1966.

Deakin, William. "D. H. Lawrence's Attacks on Proust
and Joyce." EIC 7:383-395. October 1957.

Dickman, Adolphe J. "Time and Memory in Marcel
Proust's Novels." MLF 23:12-17. February 1938.

Drake, William. Contemporary European Writers. New
York: John Day Company, 1928. pp. 1-12.

Dupee, F. W. "Marcel Proust and the Imagination of
Duchesses." Society and Self in the Novel. (ed.) Mark
Schorer. New York: Columbia University Press, 1956.
pp. 51-59.

Garrett, Helen T. "Marcel Proust's Vision of the French
Social Hierarchy." MLF 40:95-103. December 1955.

Girard, Rene. "Introduction." Proust: A Collection of
Critical Essays. (ed.) Rene Girard. Englewood Cliffs,
N. J.: Prentice-Hall, 1962. pp. 7-12.

Glicksberg, Charles I. "The Literary Struggle for Self-
hood." Person 42:54-55. Winter 1961.

Graham, Victor E. "Proust's Alchemy." MLR 60:197-206.
April 1965.

Graham, Victor E. "Water Imagery and Symbolism in
Proust." RR 50:118-128. April 1959.

Green, Federick C. "French Novel from Revolution to
Proust." Marcel Proust: Reviews and Estimates. (ed.)
Gladys Dudley Lindner. Stanford: Stanford University Press,
1942. pp. 148-153.

Gross, Beverly. "Narrative Time and the Open-ended
Novel." Criticism 8:364-367. Fall 1966.

Grubbs, Henry A. "Sartre's Recapturing of Lost Time."
MLN 73:515-522. November 1958.

Guedalla, Philip. "A Gallery." Marcel Proust: Reviews
and Estimates. (ed.) Gladys Dudley Lindner. Stanford:
Stanford University Press, 1942. pp. 72-74.

Gutwirth, Marcel. "Swann and the Duchess." FR 38:143-
151. December 1964.

Haldane, Charlotte. Marcel Proust. London: Arthur Barker, Ltd., 1951. pp. 23-26.

Harper, Ralph. "Remembering Eternity: St. Augustine and Proust." Thought 34:592-606. Winter 1959-1960.

Hartley, Anthony. "Proust's Way." Spec 200:51. January 10, 1958.

Hatzfeld, Helmut. Trends and Styles in Twentieth Century French Literature. Washington, D. C.: Catholic University of America Press, 1957. pp. 68-80.

Heiney, Donald. "Illiers and Combray: A Study in Literary Geography." TCL 1:17-25. April 1955.

Heppenstall, Rayner. "Morel." TC 165:482-492. May 1959.

Hogan, John Arthur. "The Past Recaptured: Marcel Proust's Aesthetic Theory." Ethics 49:187-203. January 1939.

Hoog, Armand. "Time, Fate and Photography in the World of Marcel Proust." ASLHM 32:49-60. No. 1, 1961.

Houston, John Porter. "The Grandparents of Proust's Narrator: A Conflation." PQ 42:134-137. January 1963.

Houston, John Porter. "Literature and Psychology: The Case of Proust." ECr 5:3-13. Spring 1965.

Houston, J. P. "Temporal Patterns in A LA RECHERCHE DU TEMPS PERDU." FS 16:33-44. January 1962.

Hyde, John K. "Proust, His Jews and His Jewishness." FR 39:837-848. May 1966.

Jackson, Elizabeth R. "The Crystallization of A LA RECHERCHE DU TEMPS PERDU 1908-1909." FR 38:157-166. December 1964.

Jefferson, Louise M. "Proust and Racine." YFS 34:99-105. June 1965.

Johnson, J. Theodore, Jr. "From Artistic Celibacy to Artistic Contemplation." YFS 34:81-89. June 1965.

Johnson, Pamela Hansford. "Marcel Proust: Illusion and Reality." EDH 32:58-71. 1963.

Jones, David L. "DOLORES DISPARUE." Symposium 20: 135-140. Summer 1966.

Kohn, Renee J. "Four Centuries of French Novel: Evolution of the Hero. " ASLHM 29:84-85. No. 2, 1958.

Kolb, Philip. "Inadvertent Repetitions of Material in A LA RECHERCHE DU TEMPS PERDU. " PMLA 51:249-262. March 1936.

Kolb, Philip. "Proust's Protagonist as a 'Beacon.' " ECr 5:38-47. Spring 1965.

Krutch, Joseph Wood. Five Masters. New York: Jonathan Cape and Harrison Smith, 1930. pp. 284-328.

Lalou, Rene. "The Ego and the Universe. " Marcel Proust: Reviews and Estimates. (ed.) Gladys Dudley Lindner. Stanford: Stanford University Press, 1942. pp. 64-67.

Lavrin, Janko. "Dostoyevsky and Proust. " SEER 5:609-627. March 1927.

Leon, Derrick. "Introduction to Proust. " Marcel Proust: Reviews and Estimates. (ed.) Gladys Dudley Lindner. Stanford: Stanford University Press, 1942. pp. 278-285.

Leon, Derrick. Introduction to Proust: His Life, His Circle and His Work. London: Routledge and Kegan Paul, Ltd., 1951. pp. 213-215.

Levin, Harry. The Gates of Horn: A Study of Five French Realists. New York: Oxford University Press, 1963. pp. 391-444.

Levin, Harry. "Proust, Gide, and the Sexes. " PMLA 65: 648-652. June 1950.

Levy, Sylvia Narins. "Proust's Realistic Treatment of Illness. " FR 15:233-238. January 1942. (Continued in FR 15:324-329. February 1942; FR 15:421-424. March 1942.)

Lewis, Philip E. "Idealism and Reality. " YFS 34:24-28. June 1965.

Linn, John Gaywood. "Notes on Proust's Manipulation of Chronology. " RR 52:210-225. October 1961.

Linn, John Gaywood. "Proust's Theatre Metaphors. " RR 49:179-190. October 1958.

Lynes, Carlos, Jr. "Proust and Albertine: On the Limits of Autobiography and of Psychological Truth in the Novel." JAAC 10:328-337. June 1952.

Macksey, Richard. "The Architecture of Time: Dialectics

and Structure. " Proust: A Collection of Critical Essays.
(ed.) Rene Girard. Englewood Cliffs, N.J.: Prentice-Hall,
1962. pp. 104-121.

March, Harold. "The Proustian Manner. " RR 35:52-72.
February 1944.

Marks, Jonathan E. "The Verdurins and Their Cult. " YFS
34:73-80. June 1965.

Martin-Chauffier, Louis. "Proust and the Double 'I' of Two
Characters. " PR 16:1011-1026. October 1949.

Maurois, Andre. Proust: Portrait of a Genius. New York:
Harper and Brothers Publishers, 1950. Chapters VI, VII,
VIII.

Mayne, Ethel Colburn. "The Spell of Proust. " Marcel
Proust: Reviews and Estimates. (ed.) Gladys Dudley Lindner. Stanford: Stanford University Press, 1942. pp. 31-33.

Morrow, John H. "The Comic Element in A LA RE-
CHERCHE DU TEMPS PERDU. " FR 27:114-121. December
1953.

Moss, Howard. The Magic Lantern of Marcel Proust. New
York: Macmillan Company, 1962.

Moss, Howard. "The Two Ways. " SR 70:451-463. Summer
1962.

Murray, Jack. "Dinners at Rivebelle: A Study in Proust's
Search for the 'Moi Profond. ' " MLQ 24:263-273. September 1963.

Murray, Jack. "The Esthetic Dilemma in Marcel Proust."
FR 36:125-132. December 1962.

Murray, Jack. "The Mystery of Others. " YFS 34:65-72.
June 1965.

Murray, Jack. "Proust's Robert de Saint-Loup and the
Diagnostic Eye. " TSLL 6:68-75. Spring 1964.

Murry, John Middleton. Discoveries: Essays in Literary
Criticism. London: Collins Sons and Company, Ltd. , 1924.
pp. 118-127.

Murry, J. Middleton. "Marcel Proust: A New Sensibility. "
Marcel Proust: Reviews and Estimates. (ed.) Gladys Dudley Lindner. Stanford: Stanford University Press, 1942. pp.
4-8.

Nitzberg, Howard. "A LA RECHERCHE DU TEMPS PERDU:
Mirror-Image as a Level of Extratemporal Existence. "
FR 34:440-444. April 1961.

O'Brien, Justin. "Albertine the Ambiguous: Notes on
Proust's Transposition of Sexes. " PMLA 64:933-952.
December 1949.

O'Brien, Justin. "An Aspect of Proust's Baron de Char-
lus. " RR 55:38-41. February 1964.

O'Brien, Justin. "Marcel Proust as a 'Moraliste.' " RR
39:50-57. February 1948.

O'Brien, Justin. "Marcel Proust's Maxims Again. " MLN
64:410-412. June 1949.

O'Brien, Justin. "Proust's Use of Syllepsis. " PMLA 69:
741-752. September 1954.

O'Connor, Frank. The Mirror in the Roadway: A Study of
the Modern Novel. New York: Alfred A. Knopf, 1956. pp.
280-294.

Ortega y Gasset, Jose. "Time, Distance, and Form in
Proust. " HudR 11:504-513. Winter 1958-1959.

Paul, David. "Time and the Novelist. " PR 21:646-649.
November - December 1954.

Philip, Michel. "The Hidden Onlooker. " YFS 34:37-42.
June 1965.

Pierre-Quint, Leon. "Marcel Proust: His Life and Work. "
Marcel Proust: Reviews and Estimates. (ed.) Gladys Dudley Lindner. Stanford: Stanford University Press, 1942. pp.
99-106.

Poulet, Georges. "Proust. " CC 5:236-256. Summer 1955.

Rhodes, S. A. "Marcel Proust and His Jewish Characters."
SR 39:144-157. April - June 1931.

Riva, Raymond T. "Death and Immortality in the Works
of Marcel Proust. " FR 35:463-471. April 1962.

Riva, Raymond T. "A Probable Model for Proust's Elstir."
MLN 78:307-313. May 1963.

Rogers, Brian G. "Narrative Tones and Perspectives in
Proust's Novel. " MLR 60:207-211. April 1965.

Rogers, B. G. Proust's Narrative Techniques. Geneve:

Librairie Droz, 1965. Part II, Chapters II - IV; Part III.

Rosenfeld, Paul. "Men Seen." Marcel Proust: Reviews
and Estimates. (ed.) Gladys Dudley Lindner. Stanford:
Stanford University Press, 1942. pp. 82-84.

Rubin, Louis D., Jr. "The Self Recaptured." KR 25:398-
404. Summer 1963.

Ryan, James. "Descriptions of Music by Proust and
Gustavo Adolfo Becquer." Hispania 46:274-278. May 1963.

Samuel, Maurice. "The Concealments of Marcel: Proust's
Jewishness." Commentary 29:8-22. January 1960.

Saurat, Denis. "France." Contemporary Movements in
European Literature. (ed.) William Rose and J. Isaacs.
London: George Routledge and Sons, Ltd., 1928. pp. 31-52.

Savage, Catherine [sic] H. "Death in A LA RECHERCHE DU
TEMPS PERDU." Forum H 4:7-11. Spring - Summer 1963.

Savage, Catharine H. "Nostalgia in Alain-Fournier and
Proust." FR 38:167-172. December 1964.

Shattuck, Roger. "Making Time: A Study of Stravinsky,
Proust, and Sartre." KR 25:250-252. Spring 1963.

Shattuck, Roger. "Proust's Stilts." YFS 34:91-98. June
1965.

Slochower, Harry. "Marcel Proust: Revolt Against the
Tyranny of Time." SR 51:370-381. 1943.

Spagnoli, John J. "The Social Attitude of Marcel Proust."
Marcel Proust: Reviews and Estimates. (ed.) Gladys Dudley
Lindner. Stanford: Stanford University Press, 1942. pp.
213-227.

Sticca, Sandro. "Anticipation as a Literary Technique in
Proust's A LA RECHERCHE DU TEMPS PERDU." Symposium 20:254-261. Fall 1966.

Strauss, Walter A. "Criticism and Creation." Proust: A
Collection of Critical Essays. (ed.) Rene Girard. Englewood Cliffs, N. J.: Prentice-Hall, 1962. pp. 53-68.

Switzer, Richard. "The Madeleine and the Biscotte." FR
30:303-308. February 1957.

Thibaudeau, Barbara. "Condemned to Die." YFS 34:55-
63. June 1965.

Tindall, William York. The Literary Symbol. Bloomington: Indiana University Press, 1955. pp. 119-121; 209-211.

Tolmachev, M. V. "Impressionist-Classicist Tensions." YFS 34:29-35. June 1965.

Turnell, Martin. The Novel in France. New York: New Directions, 1951. pp. 336-393.

Vance, Vera Lindholm. "Proust's Guermantes as Birds." FR 35:3-10. October 1961.

Virtanen, Reino. "Proust's Metaphors from the Natural and the Exact Sciences." PMLA 69:1038-1059. December 1954.

Waters, Harold A. "The Narrator, Not Marcel." FR 33: 389-392. February 1960.

Wilson, Clothilde. "Proust's Color Vision." FR 16:411-415. March 1943.

Wilson, Edmund. "Axel's Castle." Marcel Proust: Reviews and Estimates. (ed.) Gladys Dudley Lindner. Stanford: Stanford University Press, 1942. pp. 140-148.

SWANN IN LOVE

Bell, William S. "Proust's UN AMOUR DE SWANN: A Voyage to Cytherea." ECr 5:26-37. Spring 1965.

Cocking, J. M. "Marcel Proust." Three Studies in Modern French Literature. (ed.) Erich Heller. New Haven: Yale University Press, 1956. pp. 80-84; 88-127.

Hicks, Eric C. "Swann's Dream and the World of Sleep." YFS 34:106-116. June 1965.

Kneller, John W. "The Musical Structure of Proust's UN AMOUR DE SWANN." YFS 4:55-62.

SWANN'S WAY

Adelson, Dorothy. "Proust's Earlier and Later Styles: A Textual Comparison." RR 34:127-138. April 1943.

Alden, Douglas W. Marcel Proust and His French Critics. Los Angeles: Lymanhouse, 1940. Chapter II.

Barker, Richard H. Marcel Proust: A Biography. New York: Criterion Books, 1958. pp. 202-225.

Bennett, Arnold. "The Last Word." Marcel Proust: Reviews and Estimates. (ed.) Gladys Dudley Lindner. Stanford: Stanford University Press, 1942. pp. 49-51.

Bree, Germaine and Margaret Guiton. An Age of Fiction:

The French Novel from Gide to Camus. New Brunswick: Rutgers University Press, 1957. pp. 49-53.

Buck, Philo M., Jr. Directions in Contemporary Literature. New York: Oxford University Press, 1942. pp. 114-115.

Cocking, J. M. Proust. New Haven: Yale University Press, 1956. pp. 52-55.

Cook, Gladys E. "Marcel Proust: From Analysis to Creation." BuR 8:17-37. November 1958.

Edel, Leon. The Modern Psychological Novel. New York: Grosset and Dunlap, 1955. pp. 105-109; 116-117.

Fowlie, Wallace. A Reading of Proust. Garden City: Doubleday and Company, 1964. Chapters 4-5.

Galantiere, Lewis. "Introduction to SWANN'S WAY." Marcel Proust: Reviews and Estimates. Stanford: Stanford University Press, 1942. pp. 112-114.

Green, F. C. The Mind of Proust. Cambridge University Press, 1949. pp. 6-60; Chapter I.

Hatzfeld, Helmut. Trends and Styles in Twentieth Century French Literature. Washington, D. C.: Catholic University of America Press, 1957. pp. 68-69.

Hindus, Milton. A Reader's Guide to Marcel Proust. New York: The Noonday Press, 1962. pp. 16-62.

Kolb, Philip. "An Enigmatic Proustian Metaphor." RR 54: 187-197. October 1963.

Leon, Derrick. Introduction to Proust: His Life, His Circle and His Work. London: Routledge and Kegan Paul, Ltd., 1951. pp. 136-138; 149-150.

March, Harold. The Two Worlds of Marcel Proust. Philadelphia: University of Pennsylvania Press, 1948. pp. 106-112; 135-142; 150-154.

Miller, Milton L. Nostalgia: A Psychoanalytic Study of Marcel Proust. Boston: Houghton Mifflin Company, 1956. pp. 24-31.

Murry, John Middleton. Discoveries: Essays in Literary Criticism. London: Collins Sons and Company, Ltd., 1924. pp. 108-118.

Murry, J. Middleton. "Proust and the Modern Consciousness." Marcel Proust: Reviews and Estimates. (ed.) Gladys

Dudley Lindner. Stanford: Stanford University Press, 1942. pp. 35-38.

Turner, W. J. "The Little Phrase." Marcel Proust: Reviews and Estimates. (ed.) Gladys Dudley Lindner. Stanford: Stanford University Press, 1942. pp. 40-41.
THE SWEET CHEAT GONE
Barker, Richard H. Marcel Proust: A Biography. New York: Criterion Books, 1958. pp. 305-307.

Fowlie, Wallace. A Reading of Proust. Garden City: Doubleday and Company, 1964. Chapters 14-15.

Green, F. C. The Mind of Proust. Cambridge University Press, 1949. Chapters VIII, IX; pp. 353-441.

Hatzfeld, Helmut. Trends and Styles in Twentieth Century French Literature. Washington, D. C.: Catholic University of America Press, 1957. pp. 73-74.

Hindus, Milton. A Reader's Guide to Marcel Proust. New York: The Noonday Press, 1962. pp. 146-160.

Leon, Derrick. Introduction to Proust: His Life, His Circle and His Work. London: Routledge and Kegan Paul, Ltd., 1951. pp. 196-210; 271-279; 300-301.

McMahon, Joseph H. "From Things to Themes." YFS 34: 5-17. June 1965.

March, Harold. The Two Worlds of Marcel Proust. Philadelphia: University of Pennsylvania Press, 1948. pp. 116-122.

Miller, Milton L. Nostalgia: A Psychoanalytic Study of Marcel Proust. Boston: Houghton Mifflin Company, 1956. pp. 83-96.
TIME RECAPTURED
Barker, Richard H. Marcel Proust: A Biography. New York: Criterion Books, 1958. pp. 307-318.

Bree, Germaine and Margaret Guiton. An Age of Fiction: The French Novel from Gide to Camus. New Brunswick: Rutgers University Press, 1957. pp. 42-49.

Buck, Philo M., Jr. Directions in Contemporary Literature. New York: Oxford University Press, 1942. pp. 116-122.

Cocking, J. M. "Marcel Proust." Three Studies in Modern French Literature. (ed.) Erich Heller. New Haven: Yale University Press, 1956. pp. 44-79; 88-127.

Edel, Leon. The Modern Psychological Novel. New York:
Grosset and Dunlap, 1955. pp. 114-115.

Fowlie, Wallace. A Reading of Proust. Garden City: Doubleday and Company, 1964. Chapters 16-17.

Green, F. C. The Mind of Proust. Cambridge University
Press, 1949. Chapters X-XI; pp. 442-546.

Hindus, Milton. A Reader's Guide to Marcel Proust. New
York: The Noonday Press, 1962. pp. 161-180.

Leon, Derrick. Introduction to Proust: His Life, His Circle
and His Work. London: Routledge and Kegan Paul, Ltd.,
1951. pp. 295-298; Part 2, Chapter 7.

March, Harold. The Two Worlds of Marcel Proust. Philadelphia: University of Pennsylvania Press, 1948. pp. 147-
148.

Mein, Margaret. Proust's Challenge to Time. Manchester:
Manchester University Press, 1962. pp. 23-27; 31-32; 56-
62.

O'Brien, Justin. "Fall and Redemption in Proust." MLN
79:281-283. May 1964.

Rhodes, S. A. "The 'Guermantes Fete' in LE TEMPS
RETROUVE." PQ 17:144-148. April 1938.

WITHIN A BUDDING GROVE

Barker, Richard H. Marcel Proust: A Biography. New York:
Criterion Books, 1958. pp. 263-288.

Fowlie, Wallace. A Reading of Proust. Garden City: Doubleday and Company, 1964. Chapters 6-7.

Green, F. C. The Mind of Proust. Cambridge University
Press, 1949. Chapter II; pp. 61-114.

Hatzfeld, Helmut. Trends and Styles in Twentieth Century
French Literature. Washington, D.C.: Catholic University
of America Press, 1957. pp. 69-70.

Hindus, Milton. A Reader's Guide to Marcel Proust. New
York: The Noonday Press, 1962. pp. 63-82.

Leon, Derrick. Introduction to Proust: His Life, His Circle
and His Work. London: Routledge and Kegan Paul, Ltd.,
1951. pp. 163-164.

March, Harold. The Two Worlds of Marcel Proust. Philadelphia: University of Pennsylvania Press, 1948. pp. 141-
143.

Miller, Milton L. Nostalgia: A Psychoanalytic Study of
Marcel Proust. Boston: Houghton Mifflin Company, 1956.
pp. 32-44.

Queneau, Raymond
     FLY IN THE OINTMENT
          Bree, Germaine and Margaret Guiton. An Age of Fiction:
          The French Novel from Gide to Camus. New Brunswick:
          Rutgers University Press, 1957. pp. 169-170.
     SAINT GLINGLIN
          Bree, Germaine and Margaret Guiton. An Age of Fiction:
          The French Novel from Gide to Camus. New Brunswick:
          Rutgers University Press, 1957. pp. 174-176.
     THE SUNDAY OF LIFE
          Bree, Germaine and Margaret Guiton. An Age of Fiction:
          The French Novel from Gide to Camus. New Brunswick:
          Rutgers University Press, 1957. pp. 172-173.

Rabelais, Francois
     GARGANTUA AND PANTAGRUEL
          Armitage, R. H. "Is GARGANTUA a Reworking of
          PANTAGRUEL I?" PMLA 59:944-951. 1944.

          Auerbach, Erich. "The World in Pantagruel's Mouth. "
          PR 17:672-692. September - October 1950. (Also in Auer-
          bach, Mimesis. New York: Doubleday and Company, 1957.
          pp. 229-249.)

          Bart, B. F. "Aspects of the Comic in Pulci and Rabelais."
          MLQ 11:156-163. June 1950.

          Brereton, Geoffrey. A Short History of French Literature.
          London: Cassell, 1954. pp. 58-60.

          Brown, Harcourt. "Ideas and Rablais [sic]. " BuR 9:177-
          186. December 1960.

          Carpenter, Nan Cooke. "The Authenticity of Rabelais'
          FIFTH BOOK: Musical Criteria. " MLQ 13:299-304. Sep-
          tember 1952.

          Carpenter, Nan Cooke. "Rabelais and the Androgyne. "
          MLN 68:452-457. November 1953.

          Carpenter, Nan Cooke. "Rabelais and the Chanson. "
          PMLA 65:1212-1232. December 1950.

          Carpenter, Nan Cooke. "Rabelais and the Greek Dances. "
          MLN 64:251-255. April 1949.

          Carpenter, Nan Cooke. Rabelais and Music. Chapel Hill:
          University of North Carolina Press, 1954.

Carpenter, Nan Cooke. "Rabelais and Musical Ideas. " RR 41:14-25. February 1950.

Carpenter, Nan Cooke. "Rabelais and Musical Symbols. " RR 40:3-17. February 1949.

Chappell, A. F. The Enigma of Rabelais. Cambridge University Press, 1924. pp. 45-90; 120-191.

Chappell, A. F. "Rabelais and the Authority of the Ancients. " MLR 18:29-36. January 1923.

Clement, N. H. "The Eclecticism of Rabelais. " PMLA 42:339-384. June 1927.

Darby, George O. S. "The Pilgrims in Gargantua's Salad. " MP 33:125-128. November 1935.

Derrett, J. Duncan M. "Rabelais' Legal Learning and the Trial of Bridoye. " BHR 25:111-171. January 1963.

Eddy, William A. "Rabelais, --A Source for GULLIVER'S TRAVELS. " MLN 37:416-418. November 1922.

Eskin, Stanley G. "Mythic Unity in Rabelais. " PMLA 79: 548-553. December 1964.

Eskin, Stanley G. " Physis and Antiphysie: The Idea of Nature in Rabelais and Calcagnini. " CL 14:167-173. Spring 1962.

Francis, K. H. "The Mechanism of the Magnetic Doors in Rabelais, Book V, Chapter 37. " FS 13:293-302. October 1959.

Francis, K. H. "Rabelais and Mathematics. " BHR 21:85-97. January 1959.

Francon, Marcel. "Francesco Colonna's 'Poliphili Hypnerotomachia' and Rabelais. " MLR 50:52-55. January 1955.

Francon, Marcel. "A Note on the Word 'Symbolisation' in the TIERS LIVRE. " MLR 55:84-85. January 1960.

Francon, Marcel. "Two Notes on GARGANTUA AND PANTAGRUEL. " MLR 59:371-374. July 1964.

Frautschi, R. L. "The 'Enigme en Prophetie' (GARGANTUA LVIII) and the Question of Authorship. " FS 17:331-339. October 1963.

Frautschi, R. L. "Nicolas de Troyes and the Presumed

Borrowings from PANTAGRUEL. " MLQ 22:345-350. December 1961.

Frohock, W. M. "Panurge as Comic Character. " YFS 23: 71-76. Summer 1959.

Gest, John Marshall. "The Trial of Judge Bridlegoose, as Reported by Francois Rabelais. " America Law Review 58:402-421. May - June 1924.

Gifford, G. H. "A Note on Rabelais I, 1. " MLN 42:83-84. February 1927.

Gray, Floyd. "Ambiguity and Point of View in the Prologue to GARGANTUA. " RR 56:12-21. February 1965.

Gray, Floyd. "Structure and Meaning in the Prologue to the TIERS LIVRE. " ECr 3:57-62. Summer 1963.

Griffin, Robert. "Rabelais' 'humanisme devot. ' " ECr 3:75-79. Summer 1963.

Gruber, Vivian M. "Rabelais: The Didactics of Moderation." ECr 3:80-86. Summer 1963.

Hartley, K. H. "Rabelais and Pulci. " AUMLA 9:71-77. November 1958.

Hornstein, Lillian Herlands. " 'Marie Toy... Marie Poinct': An Anglo-Latin Parallel. " MLR 52:569-570. October 1957.

Keller, Abraham C. "The Books and Stories of Rabelais. " RR 53:241-259. December 1963.

Keller, Abraham C. "The Idea of Progress in Rabelais. " PMLA 66:235-243. March 1951.

Keller, Abraham C. "Pace and Timing in Rabelais's Stories. " SRen 10:108-125. 1963.

Krailsheimer, A. J. Rabelais and the Franciscans. Oxford: Clarendon Press, 1963.

Krailsheimer, A. J. "The Significance of the Pan Legend in Rabelais' Thought. " MLR 56:13-23. January 1961.

Lapp, John C. "Three Attitudes toward Astrology. " PMLA 64:531-534. June 1949.

Lewis, D. B. Wyndham. Doctor Rabelais. New York: Sheed and Ward, 1957. pp. 116-129; 136-147; 174-190; 211-227.

Mallam, Duncan. "Joyce and Rabelais. " UKCR 23:99-110.

144 The French Novel

Winter 1956.

Michaud, G. L. "Luis Vives and Rabelais' Pedagogy. "
PMLA 38:419-424. June 1923.

Misrahi, Jean. "Rabelais: GARGANTUA AND PANTAGRUEL,
BOOKS I AND II. " The Great Books: A Christian Appraisal.
Vol. 4. (ed.) Harold C. Gardiner. New York: The Devin-
Adair Company, 1953. pp. 85-93.

Nock, Albert Jay. Francis Rabelais. New York: Harper and
Brothers Publishers, 1929. Chapters 4-5.

Pitou, Spire. "Rabelais, La Fontaine, Richelet, and 'La
Touselle. ' " MLN 65: 399-403. June 1950.

Plattard, Jean. The Life of Francois Rabelais. London:
George Routledge and Sons, 1930. Chapters 9; 11; 14; 16, 17.

Powys, John Cowper. Rabelais. London: The Bodley Head,
1948. Part 2, pp. 93-129; Part 4, pp. 283-416.

Powys, John Cowper. Visions and Revisions. New York: G.
Arnold Shaw, 1915. pp. 25-34.

Salomon, Richard. "A Trace of Durer in Rabelais. " MLN
58:498-501. November 1943.

Schutz, A. H. "Why Did Rabelais Satirize the Library of
Saint-Victor?" MLN 70:39-41. January 1955.

Screech, M. A. "The Death of Pan and the Death of
Heroes in the Fourth Book of Rabelais. " BHR 17:36-55.
January 1955.

Screech, M. A. "Girolamo Cardano's DE SAPIENTIA and
the TIERS LIVRE DE PANTAGRUEL. " BHR 25:97-110.
January 1963.

Screech, M. A. "Rabelais and the Sarabaites. " BHR 21:
451-452. April 1959.

Screech, M. A. "Rabelais, DeBillon and Erasmus (A Reexamination of Rabelais's Attitude to Women). " BHR 13:
253-265. September 1951.

Screech, M. A. The Rabelaisian Marriage. London: Edward
Arnold (Publishers) Ltd. , 1958. Chapters 2-8.

Screech, M. A. "The Sense of Rabelais's 'Enigme en
Prophetie' (GARGANTUA LVIII). " BHR 18:392-404. September 1956.

Seiver, George O. "Cicero's DE ORATORE and Rabelais. "
PMLA 59:655-671. September 1944.

Smith, Grace P. "Rabelais and the Figure of Man as In-
verted Tree. " PQ 17:218-219. April 1938.

Smith, W. F. "Rabelais' Lists of Fowls, Fishes, Serpents
and Wild Beasts. " MLR 13:431-438. October 1918.

Stevens, Linton C. "Rabelais and Aristophanes. " SP 55:24-
30. January 1958.

Stewart, Herbert L. "Rabelais the Humanist. " Person 24:
402-414. October 1943.

Tetel, Marcel. "Rabelais and Folengo. " CL 15:357-364.
Fall 1963.

Tetel, Marcel. "Trends in Italian Criticism of Rabelais. "
RLC 40:541-551. October - December 1966.

Thompson, C. R. "Rabelais and IVLIVS EXCLVSUS. " PQ
22:80-82. January 1943.

Tilley, A. "The Fifth Book of Rabelais. " MLR 22:409-
420. October 1927.

Tilley, Arthur. Francois Rabelais. Philadelphia: Lippincott,
1907. Chapters 5-10.

Turner, Robert E. "Rabelais and the Bridge of Mantrible."
MLN 47:505-508. December 1932.

Wadsworth, James B. "LES ALIBANTES of Rabelais. "
MLN 71:584-587. December 1956.

Watson, Francis. Laughter for Pluto. London: Lovat Dickson,
Ltd. , 1933. Chapters 5; 7.

Weinberg, Bernard. "Rabelais as an Artist. " TQ 3:175-
188. Autumn 1960.

Wells, Whitney Hastings. "MOBY DICK and Rabelais. "
MLN 38:123. February 1923.

Whitaker, Thomas R. "The Drinkers and History: Rabelais,
Balzac, and Joyce. " CL 11:157-161. Spring 1959.

Willcocks, M. P. The Laughing Philosopher. London:
George Allen and Unwin, Ltd. , 1950. pp. 107-127.

Williams, Edward B. "The Observations of Epistemon and
Condign Punishment. " ECr 3:63-67. Summer 1963.

Winter, John F. "Visual Variety and Spatial Grandeur in
Rabelais. " RR 56:81-91. April 1965.

Zeldin, Jesse. "The Abbey and the Bottle. " ECr 3:68-74.
Summer 1963.

Radiguet, Raymond
    THE DEVIL IN THE FLESH
        Peyre, Henri. The Contemporary French Novel. New York:
        Oxford University Press, 1955. pp. 62-65.

Reybaud, Louis
    JEROME PATUROT A LA RECHERCHE D'UNE POSITION SOCIALE
        Scales, D. P. "French Manners Under the July Monarchy:
        Louis Reybaud's Humorous Novel. " AUMLA 2:21-30. August
        1954.

Robbe-Grillet, Alain
    THE GUM ERASERS
        Barnes, Hazel E. "The Ins and Outs of Alain Robbe-Gril-
        let. " ChiR 15:39-40. Winter - Spring 1962.

        Champigny, Robert. "In Search of the Pure 'Recit.' "
        ASLHM 27:331-335. Winter 1956-1957.

        Fontenilles, Alfred. "Reflections on the New Novel. " ColQ
        12:171-173. Autumn 1963.

        Morrissette, Bruce. Alain Robbe-Grillet. New York: Colum-
        bia University Press, 1965. pp. 12-18.

        Morrissette, Bruce. "Oedipus and Existentialism: LES
        GOMMES of Robbe-Grillet. " WSCL 1:43-70. Fall 1960.

        Stoltzfus, Ben F. Alain Robbe-Grillet. Carbondale: Southern
        Illinois University Press, 1964. Chapter 4.

        Weightman, J. G. "Alain Robbe-Grillet. " Encounter 18:34-
        35. March 1962.
    IN THE LABYRINTH
        Barnes, Hazel E. "The Ins and Outs of Alain Robbe-Grillet."
        ChiR 15:36-39. Winter - Spring 1962.

        Brooke-Rose, Christine. "The Baroque Imagination of
        Robbe-Grillet. " MFS 11:410-423. Winter 1965-1966.

        Cortland, Peter. "The Landscapes of Robbe-Grillet. " Crit
        6:91-98. Winter 1963-1964.

        Morrissette, Bruce. Alain Robbe-Grillet. New York: Colum-
        bia University Press, 1965. pp. 29-33.

        Stoltzfus, Ben F. Alain Robbe-Grillet. Carbondale: Southern

Illinois University Press, 1964. Chapter 4.

Weightman, J. G. "Alain Robbe-Grillet. " Encounter 18:
38-39. March 1962.
JEALOUSY
Alter, Jean V. "The Treatment of Time in Alain Robbe-
Grillet's LA JALOUSIE. " CLAJ 3:46-55. September 1959.

Barnes, Hazel E. "The Ins and Outs of Alain Robbe-Grillet. " ChiR 15:34-36. Winter - Spring 1962.

Bree, Germaine. "JALOUSIE: New Blinds or Old?" YFS
24:87-90. Summer 1959.

Cortland, Peter. "The Landscapes of Robbe-Grillet. " Crit
6: 87-91. Winter 1963-1964.

Evans, Calvin. "Cinematography and Robbe-Grillet's
JEALOUSY. " Nine Essays in Modern Literature. (ed.)
Donald E. Stanford. Baton Rouge: Louisiana State Univer-
sity Press, 1965. pp. 117-128.

Gibian, George. "Soviet Russian and French Avant-garde
Fiction: Contrasts in Attitudes towards Emotion. " CLS
Special Advance Number: 62-63. 1963.

Morrissette, Bruce. Alain Robbe-Grillet. New York: Columbia University Press, 1965. pp. 24-29.

Penot, Dominique. "Psychology of the Characters in Robbe-
Grillet's LA JALOUSIE. " BA 40:5-15. Winter 1966.

Stoltzfus, Ben F. Alain Robbe-Grillet. Carbondale: Southern
Illinois University Press, 1964. Chapter 2.

Stoltzfus, Ben. "Alain Robbe-Grillet and Surrealism. "
MLN 78:271-275. May 1963.

Weightman, J. G. "Alain Robbe-Grillet. " Encounter 18:37.
March 1962.
LAST YEAR AT MARIENBAD
Alter, Jean V. "Alain Robbe-Grillet and the 'Cinemato-
graphic Style. ' " MLJ 48:363-366. October 1964.

Morrissette, Bruce. Alain Robbe-Grillet. New York: Columbia University Press, 1965. pp. 33-37.

Stoltzfus, Ben F. Alain Robbe-Grillet. Carbondale: Southern
Illinois University Press, 1964. Chapter 6.
THE VOYEUR
Barnes, Hazel E. "The Ins and Outs of Alain Robbe-Grillet."
ChiR 15:27-34. Winter - Spring 1962.

Champigny, Robert. "In Search of the Pure 'Recit.' "
ASLHM 27:335-343. Winter 1956-1957.

Hubert, Renee Riese. "Patterns in the Anti-Novel." Forum
H 3:14-15. Fall 1962.

Morrissette, Bruce. Alain Robbe-Grillet. New York: Columbia University Press, 1965. pp. 18-23.

Morrissette, Bruce. "The New Novel in France." ChiR 15:
16-17. Winter - Spring 1962.

Morse, J. Mitchell. "The Choreography of 'The New
Novel.' " HudR 16:409-413. Autumn 1963.

Murray, Jack. "Three Murders in the Contemporary French
Novel." TSLL 6:370-373. Autumn 1964.

Stoltzfus, Ben F. Alain Robbe-Grillet. Carbondale: Southern
Illinois University Press, 1964. Chapters 2-3.

Stoltzfus, Ben. "Alain Robbe-Grillet and Surrealism."
MLN 78:271-277. May 1963.

Stoltzfus, Ben F. "A Novel of Objective Subjectivity: LE
VOYEUR by Alain Robbe-Grillet." PMLA 77:499-507. September 1962.

Weightman, J. G. "Alain Robbe-Grillet." Encounter 18:
35-37. March 1962.

Weiner, Seymour S. "A Look at Techniques and Meaning
in Robbe-Grillet's VOYEUR." MLQ 23:217-224. September
1962.

Rochefort, Christiane
    WARRIOR'S REST
        McMahon, Joseph H. "What Rest for the Weary?" YFS 37:
        131-139. Spring - Summer 1961.

Rod, Edouard
    LA COURSE A LA MORT
        Saintsbury, George. A History of the French Novel (To the
        Close of the 19th Century). London: Macmillan and Com-
        pany, 1919. pp. 548-550.
    LA-HAUT
        Saintsbury, George. A History of the French Novel (To the
        Close of the 19th Century). London: Macmillan and Com-
        pany, 1919. pp. 547-548.
    LA SACRIFIEE
        Saintsbury, George. A History of the French Novel (To the
        Close of the 19th Century). London: Macmillan and Com-
        pany, 1919. pp. 544-545.

LE SILENCE
    Saintsbury, George. A History of the French Novel (To the
    Close of the 19th Century). London: Macmillan and Com-
    pany, 1919. pp. 546-547.
LA VIE PRIVEE DE MICHEL TEISSIER
    Saintsbury, George. A History of the French Novel (To the
    Close of the 19th Century). London: Macmillan and Com-
    pany, 1919. pp. 543-544.

Rolland, Romain
    CLERAMBAULT
        Zweig, Stefan. Romain Roland. New York: Thomas Seltzer,
        1921. pp. 339-347.
    COLAS BREUGNON
        Zweig, Stefan. Romain Rolland. New York: Thomas Seltzer,
        1921. pp. 241-253.
    JEAN-CHRISTOPHE
        Aron, Albert W. "Romain Rolland and Goethe." Monat-
        shefte 30:102-105. March - April 1938.

        Beiswanger, George W. "Artist, Philosopher, and the Ideal
        Society." JP 28:577-579. October 8, 1931.

        Church, Henry Ward. "Some New Comments on JEAN-
        CHRISTOPHE by Its Author." MP 27:345-357. February
        1930.

        Drake, William A. "Romain Rolland." SR 32:386-404. Octo-
        ber 1924.

        Sice, David. "JEAN-CHRISTOPHE as a 'Musical' Novel."
        FR 39:862-874. May 1966.

        Watson, G. "Socialism and Revolution in JEAN-
        CHRISTOPHE." Essays in French Literature 2:30-41. Nov-
        ember 1965.

        Zweig, Stefan. Romain Rolland. New York: Thomas Seltzer,
        1921. pp. 172-175; 184-194; 200-210; 229-236.

Romains, Jules
    THE BODY'S RAPTURE
        Buck, Philo M., Jr. Directions in Contemporary Liter-
        ature. New York: Oxford University Press, 1942. pp. 206-
        208.
    THE DEATH OF A NOBODY
        Bree, Germaine and Margaret Guiton. An Age of Fiction:
        The French Novel from Gide to Camus. New Brunswick:
        Rutgers University Press, 1957. pp. 68-69.

        Buck, Philo M., Jr. Directions in Contemporary Liter-
        ature. New York: Oxford University Press, 1942. pp. 205-
        206.

Hatzfeld, Helmut. Trends and Styles in Twentieth Century
French Literature. Washington, D. C. : Catholic University
of America Press, 1957. pp. 15-16.

Wilson, Clotilde. "Sartre's Graveyard of Chimeras: LA
NAUSEE and MORT DE QUELQU'UN. " FR 38:744-753.
May 1965.
MEN OF GOOD WILL
Bergholz, Harry. "Jules Romains and His MEN OF GOOD
WILL. " MLJ 35:303-309. April 1951.

Bree, Germaine and Margaret Guiton. An Age of Fiction:
The French Novel from Gide to Camus. New Brunswick:
Rugers University Press, 1957. pp. 70-76.

Buck, Philo M. , Jr. Directions in Contemporary Literature. New York: Oxford University Press, 1942. pp. 209-
212.

Fowlie, Wallace. Clowns and Angels: Studies in Modern
French Literature. New York: Sheed and Ward, 1943. pp.
62-78.

Fowlie, Wallace. "The Novel of Jules Romains. " SoR
7:880-892. Spring 1942.

Hatzfeld, Helmut. Trends and Styles in Twentieth Century
French Literature. Washington, D. C. : Catholic University
of America Press, 1957. pp. 16-19.

Parks, Edd Winfield. "The Mosaic Technique in the Novel."
South Atlantic Studies for Sturgis E. Leavitt. (ed.) Thomas
B. Stroup and Sterling A. Stoudemire. Washington, D. C. :
The Scarecrow Press, 1953. pp. 208-210.

Peyre, Henri. The Contemporary French Novel. New
York: Oxford University Press, 1955. pp. 52-55.
THE PROUD AND THE MEEK
Buck, Philo M. , Jr. Directions in Contemporary Liter-
ature. New York: Oxford University Press, 1942. pp. 212-
217.
PSYCHE
Bree, Germaine and Margaret Guiton. An Age of Fiction:
The French Novel from Gide to Camus. New Brunswick:
Rutgers University Press, 1957. pp. 69-70.
VERDUN
Peyre, Henri. The Contemporary French Novel. New
York: Oxford University Press, 1955. pp. 58-60.
WHEN THE SHIP
Buck, Philo M. , Jr. Directions in Contemporary Liter-
ature. New York: Oxford University Press, 1942. pp. 206-
209.

Rousseau, Jean Jacques
    EMILE
        Brereton, Geoffrey. A Short History of French Literature.
        London: Cassell, 1954. pp. 104-107.

        Broome, J. H. Rousseau: A Study of His Thought. New
        York: Barnes and Noble, 1963. Chapter 5.

        Burgelin, Pierre. "The Secondary Education of Emile."
        YFS 28:106-111. Fall - Winter 1961.

        Eliassen, R. H. "Rousseau Under the Searchlights of
        Modern Education." ABC 12:10-14. Summer 1962.

        Hudson, William Henry. Rousseau and Naturalism in Life
        and Thought. New York: Charles Scribner's Sons, 1903.
        pp. 180-206.

        McConnell, Allen. "Rousseau and Radiscev." SEEJ n. s.
        8:263-267. Fall 1964.

        Meyer, Paul H. "The Individual and Society in Rous-
        seau's EMILE." MLQ 19:99-114. June 1958.

        Politzer, Robert L. "Rousseau on Language Education."
        MLF 41:23-34. June 1956.

        Shanks, Lewis Piaget. "A Possible Source for Rousseau's
        Name 'Emile.' " MLN 42:243-244. April 1927.

        Warner, James H. "Emile in Eighteenth-Century England."
        PMLA 59:773-791. September 1944.

        Winwar, Frances. Jean-Jacques Rousseau: Conscience of
        an Era. New York: Random House, 1961. pp. 263-265.
    JULIE (THE NEW HELOISE)
        Broome, J. H. Rousseau: A Study of His Thought. New
        York: Barnes and Noble, 1963. Chapter 7.

        Brown, F. Andrew. "Rousseau's Bomston and Muralt."
        MLF 39:126-129. December 1954.

        Cherpack, Clifton. "Space, Time, and Memory in LA
        NOUVELLE HELOISE." ECr 3:167-171. Winter 1963.

        Cook, T. I. "The Influence of the Protestant Atmosphere
        of Geneva on the Character and Writings of Rousseau."
        Economica 8:203-204. June 1928.

        Gay, Peter. "Three Stages on Love's Way." Encounter
        9:10-13. August 1957.

        Green, F. C. French Novelists, Manners and Ideas: From

the Renaissance to the Revolution. New York: D. Appleton
and Company, 1930. pp. 192-207.

Green, F. C. "Medieval and Modern Sensibility." MLR
32:553-570. October 1937.

Grimsley, Ronald. "The Human Problem in LA NOUVELLE
HELOISE." MLR 53:171-184. April 1958.

Grimsley, Ronald. Jean-Jacques Rousseau: A Study in Self-
Awareness. Cardiff: University of Wales Press, 1961. pp.
116-151.

Hall, H. Gaston. "The Concept of Virtue in LA NOUVELLE
HELOISE." YFS 28:20-33. Fall - Winter 1961.

Havens, George R. "The Sources of Rousseau's Edouard
Bomston." MP 17:13-27. July 1919.

Havens, George R. "The Theory of 'Natural Goodness' in
Rousseau's NOUVELLE HELOISE." MLN 36:385-394.
November 1921.

Hoffding, Harald. Jean Jacques Rousseau and His Philosophy. New Haven: Yale University Press, 1930. pp. 83-89.

Hudson, William Henry. Rousseau and Naturalism in Life
and Thought. New York: Charles Scribner's Sons, 1903. pp.
153-179.

Kneller, John W. "Nerval and Rousseau." PMLA 68:150-
155. March 1953.

Lowe, L. F. H. "Saint-Preux's Trip to Sion in the
NOUVELLE HELOISE." RR 18:134-141. April - June 1927.

Macklem, Michael. "Rousseau and the Romantic Ethic."
FS 4:325-332. October 1950.

Mead, William. "LA NOUVELLE HELOISE and the Public
of 1761." YFS 28:13-19. Fall - Winter 1961.

Mille, Pierre. The French Novel. Philadelphia: J. P. Lippincott, 1930. pp. 49-55.

Mylne, Vivienne. The Eighteenth-Century French Novel:
Techniques of Illusion. Manchester: Manchester University
Press, 1965. pp. 167-191.

Neumeyer, Eva Maria. "The Landscape Garden as a Symbol in Rousseau, Goethe and Flaubert." JHI 8:187-197.
April 1947.

Starobinski, Jean. "Rousseau and the Longing for Trans-
parence. " ASLHM 27:154-158. Summer 1956.

Vartanian, Aram. "The Death of Julie: A Psychological
Post-mortem." ECr 6:77-84. Summer 1966.

Vermeil, Edmond. "Goethe and the West. " MLR 44:507-
510. October 1949.

Warner, James H. "Eighteenth-Century English Reactions
to the NOUVELLE HELOISE. " PMLA 52:803-819. September 1937.

Winwar, Frances. Jean-Jacques Rousseau: Conscience of
an Era. New York: Random House, 1961. pp. 248-254.

Wolpe, Hans. "Psychological Ambiguity in LA NOUVELLE
HELOISE. " UTQ 28:279-290. April 1959.

Sade, Marquis de
   JULIETTE
      Taylor, Robert E. "The Sexpressive 'S' in Sade and Sartre."
      YFS 11:20-21.
   JUSTINE
      Giraud, Raymond. "The First JUSTINE. " YFS 35:39-47.
      December 1965.

      Taylor, Robert E. "The Sexpressive 'S' in Sade and Sartre."
      YFS 11:20-21.

Sagan, Francoise
   AIMEZ-VOUS BRAHMS?
      Guggenheim, Michel. "AIMEZ-VOUS BRAHMS: Solitude
      and the Quest for Happiness. " YFS 24:91-95. Summer 1959.
   A CERTAIN SMILE
      Hatzfeld, Helmut. Trends and Styles in Twentieth Century
      French Literature. Washington, D. C.: Catholic University
      of America Press, 1957. pp. 129-130.
   THOSE WITHOUT SHADOWS
      Bloch-Michel, Jean. "Francs and Rubles. " PR 25:117-121.
      Winter 1958.

Sainte-Beuve, Charles
   VOLUPTE
      Giese, William Frederick. Sainte-Beuve: A Literary Por-
      trait. Madison: University of Wisconsin, 1931. (University
      of Wisconsin Studies in Language and Literature. No. 31.)
      pp. 113-126.

      Lafleur, Paul T. "Sainte-Beuve, Balzac, and Thackeray. "
      MLR 9:517-518. October 1914.

      Smith, Horatio. "Sainte-Beuve; Montaigne; Human Nature."

Saint-Exupery, Antoine de
    CITADELLE
        Mitchell, Bonner. "Mystical Imagery in Saint-Exupery's
        First and Last Works. " KFLQ 6:166-167. 1959.

        Mitchell, Bonner. "LE PETIT PRINCE and CITADELLE:
        Two Experiments in the Didactic Style. " FR 33:454-461.
        April 1960.

        Price, Robert H. "Saint Exupery's Conception of God. "
        FR 33:563-567. May 1960.

        Smith, Maxwell A. "Saint Exupery's CITADELLE. " FR 25:
        16-22. October 1951.

        Wadsworth, Philip A. "Saint Exupery, Artist and Human-
        ist. " MLQ 12:96-99. March 1951.
    THE LITTLE PRINCE
        Mitchell, Bonner. "LE PETIT PRINCE and CITADELLE:
        Two Experiments in the Didactic Style. " FR 33:454-461.
        April 1960.
    NIGHT FLIGHT
        Bree, Germaine and Margaret Guiton. An Age of Fiction:
        The French Novel from Gide to Camus. New Brunswick:
        Rutgers University Press, 1957. pp. 195-197.

        Fay, Eliot G. "The Philosophy of Saint Exupery. " MLJ
        31:92-93. February 1947.

        Peyre, Henri. The Contemporary French Novel. New York:
        Oxford University Press, 1955. pp. 167-169.
    SOUTHERN MAIL
        Bree, Germaine and Margaret Guiton. An Age of Fiction:
        The French Novel from Gide to Camus. New Brunswick:
        Rutgers University Press, 1957. pp. 194-195.

        Mitchell, Bonner. "Mystical Imagery in Saint-Exupery's
        First and Last Works. " KFLQ 6:164-166. 1959.

        Wadsworth, Philip A. "Saint Exupery, Artist and Human-
        ist. " MLQ 12:100-101. March 1951.
    WIND, SAND AND STARS
        Peyre, Henri. The Contemporary French Novel. New York:
        Oxford University Press, 1955. pp. 169-173.

Saint-Pierre, Bernardin
    PAUL AND VIRGINIA
        Green, F. C. French Novelists, Manners and Ideas: From
        the Renaissance to the Revolution. New York: D. Apple-
        ton and Company, 1930. pp. 211-215.

Mylne, Vivienne. The Eighteenth-Century French Novel.
Manchester: Manchester University Press, 1965. pp. 245-
262.

Snow, Sinclair. "The Similarity of Poe's ELEONORA to
Bernardin de Saint-Pierre's PAUL ET VIRGINIE. " Rom N
5:40-44. Autumn 1963.

Sand, George
   THE ACTRESS AND THE NUN
      Doumic, Rene. George Sand: Some Aspects of Her Life and
      Work. New York: G. P. Putnam's Sons, 1910. pp. 72-76.

      Grebanier, Frances Winwar. The Life of the Heart: George
      Sand and Her Times. New York: Harper and Brothers Pub-
      lishers, 1945. pp. 105-106.

      Howe, Marie Jenney. George Sand: The Search for Love.
      New York: John Day Company, 1927. pp. 94-100.
   LES BEAUX MESSIEURS DE BOIS-DORE
      Saintsbury, George. A History of the French Novel (To the
      Close of the 19th Century). London: Macmillan and Com-
      pany, 1919. pp. 201-203.
   CONSUELO
      Saintsbury, George. A History of the French Novel (To the
      Close of the 19th Century). London: Macmillan and Com-
      pany, 1919. pp. 185-191.
   ELLE ET LUI
      Howe, Marie Jenney. George Sand: The Search for Love.
      New York: John Day Company, 1927. pp. 305-307.
   INDIANA
      Doumic, Rene. George Sand: Some Aspects of Her Life
      and Work. New York: G. P. Putnam's Sons, 1910. pp. 76-
      83.

      Grebanier, Frances Winwar. The Life of the Heart: George
      Sand and Her Times. New York: Harper and Brothers Pub-
      lishers, 1945. pp. 106-108.

      Howe, Marie Jenney. George Sand: The Search for Love.
      New York: John Day Company, 1927. pp. 96-103.

      Seyd, Felizia. Romantic Rebel: The Life and Times of
      George Sand. New York: Viking Press, 1940. pp. 61-66.
   JACQUES
      Doumic, Rene. George Sand: Some Aspects of Her Life and
      Work. New York: G. P. Putnam's Sons, 1910. pp. 86-93.

      Howe, Marie Jenney. George Sand: The Search for Love.
      New York: John Day Company, 1927. pp. 171-172.
   LELIA
      Grebanier, Frances Winwar. The Life of the Heart: George
      Sand and Her Times. New York: Harper and Brothers

Publishers, 1945. pp. 128-132.

Howe, Marie Jenney. George Sand: The Search for Love.
New York: John Day Company, 1927. pp. 110-116.

Saintsbury, George. A History of the French Novel (To the
Close of the 19th Century). London: Macmillan and Company, 1919. pp. 181-183.

Seyd, Felizia. Romantic Rebel: The Life and Times of
George Sand. New York: Viking Press, 1940. pp. 71-74.
LUCREZIA FLORIANI
Grebanier, Frances Winwar. The Life of the Heart: George
Sand and Her Times. New York: Harper and Brothers Pub-
lishers, 1945. pp. 264-266.

Howe, Marie Jenney. George Sand: The Search for Love.
New York: John Day Company, 1927. pp. 263-266.

Saintsbury, George. A History of the French Novel (To the
Close of the 19th Century). London: Macmillan and Com-
pany, 1919. pp. 191-196.
LA PETITE FADETTE
Saintsbury, George. A History of the French Novel (To the
Close of the 19th Century). London: Macmillan and Com-
pany, 1919. pp. 196-199.
VALENTINE
Doumic, Rene. George Sand: Some Aspects of Her Life
and Work. New York: G. P. Putnam's Sons, 1910. pp. 83-
86.

Sarraute, Nathalie
THE GOLDEN FRUITS
Cismaru, Alfred. "The Reader as Co-Creater [sic] in
Nathalie Sarrute's [sic] Novels." Renascence 16:206-207.
Summer 1964.
MARTEREAU
Cismaru, Alfred. "The Reader as Co-Creater [sic] in
Nathalie Sarrute's [sic] Novels." Renascence 16:203-204.
Summer 1964.

Cohn, Ruby. "A Diminishing Difference." YFS 27:102-104.
Spring - Summer 1961.

Cohn, Ruby. "Nathalie Sarraute's Sub-Conciousversations
[sic]." MLN 78:265-267. May 1963.

Grobe, Edwin P. "Symbolic Sound Patterns in Nathalie
Sarraute's MARTEREAU." FR 40:84-91. October 1966.

Pritchett, V. S. "They." NewS 68:539, 542. October 9,
1964.

THE PLANETARIUM
>Cismaru, Alfred. "The Reader as Co-Creater [sic] in Nathalie Sarrute's [sic] Novels. " Renascence 16:205-206. Summer 1964.

>Cohn, Ruby. "A Diminishing Difference." YFS 27:104-105. Spring - Summer 1961.

>Cohn, Ruby. "Nathalie Sarraute's Sub-Conciousversations [sic]. " MLN 78:267-270. May 1963.

>Minor, Anne. "Nathalie Sarraute and LA PLANETARIUM. " YFS 24:96-100. Summer 1959.

PORTRAIT OF AN UNKNOWN
>Cismaru, Alfred. "The Reader as Co-Creater [sic] in Nathalie Sarrute's [sic] Novels. " Renascence 16:204-205. Summer 1964.

>Cohn, Ruby. "A Diminishing Difference. " YFS 27:101-102. Spring - Summer 1961.

>Cohn, Ruby. "Nathalie Sarraute's Sub-Conciousversations [sic]. " MLN 78:262-265. May 1963.

>Hubert, Renee Riese. "Patterns in the Anti-Novel. " Forum H 3:12-13. Fall 1962.

>Sartre, Jean Paul. "The Anti-Novel of Nathalie Sarraute. " YFS 16:40-41. Winter 1955.

>Wood, Margery. "Norman Mailer and Nathalie Sarraute: A Comparison of Existential Novels. " MinnR 6:67-72. No. 1, 1966.

TROPISMS
>Cismaru, Alfred. "The Reader as Co-Creater [sic] in Nathalie Sarrute's [sic] Novels. " Renascence 16:202-203. Summer 1964.

>Cohn, Ruby. "A Diminishing Difference. " YFS 27:100-101. Spring - Summer 1961.

>Sartre, Jean Paul. "The Anti-Novel of Nathalie Sarraute. " YFS 16:41-44. Winter 1955.

Sartre, Jean Paul
>AGE OF REASON
>>Bree, Germaine and Margaret Guiton. An Age of Fiction: The French Novel from Gide to Camus. New Brunswick: Rutgers University Press, 1957. pp. 211-213.

>>Church, Margaret. Time and Reality. Chapel Hill: University of North Carolina Press, 1962. pp. 263-268.

Douglas, Kenneth. "Sartre and the Self-Inflicted Wound. " YFS 9:125-126.

Edinborough, Arnold. "Sartre and the Existentialist Novel." QQ 56:105-112. Spring 1949.

Eoff, Sherman H. The Modern Spanish Novel. New York: New York University Press, 1961. pp. 222-233.

Fowlie, Wallace. "Existentialist Hero: A Study of L'AGE DE RAISON. " YFS 1:53-61. Spring - Summer 1948.

Glicksberg, Charles I. "Literary Existentialism. " ArQ 9:32-34. Spring 1953.

Glicksberg, Charles I. "The Literary Struggle for Self-hood. " Person 42:58. Winter 1961.

Harvey, W. J. Character and the Novel. Ithaca: Cornell University Press, 1965. pp. 165-181.

Savage, Catharine. Malraux, Sartre and, Aragon as Political Novelists. Gainesville: University of Florida Press, 1964. pp. 22-29.

Thody, Philip. Jean-Paul Sartre: A Literary and Political Study. London: Hamish Hamilton, 1960. pp. 44-52.

NAUSEA
Abrams, Fred. "Sartre, Unamuno, and the 'Hole Theory.' " RomN 5:6-11. Autumn 1963.

Arnold, A. James. "LA NAUSEE Revisited. " FR 39:199-213. November 1965.

Bree, Germaine and Margaret Guiton. An Age of Fiction: The French Novel from Gide to Camus. New Brunswick: Rutgers University Press, 1957. pp. 205-210.

Bree, Germaine. "Poetry of the Novel. " The Culture of France in Our Time. (ed.) Julian Park. Ithaca: Cornell University Press, 1954. pp. 30-32.

Champigny, Robert. "Existentialism and the Modern French Novel. " Thought 31:371; 377. Autumn 1956.

Champigny, Robert. Stages on Sartre's Way. Bloomington: Indiana University Press, 1959. (Indiana University Publications: Humanities Series. Number 42.) pp. 23-45.

Church, Margaret. Time and Reality. Chapel Hill: University of North Carolina Press, 1962. pp. 257-263.

Cohn, Robert G. "Sartre's First Novel: LA NAUSEE. "

YFS 1:62-65. Spring - Summer 1948.

Cranston, Maurice. Jean-Paul Sartre. New York: Grove Press, Inc. , 1962. pp. 13-21.

Cranston, Maurice. "Jean-Paul Sartre. " Encounter 18:34-36. April 1962.

Douglas, Kenneth. "Sartre and the Self-Inflicted Wound. " YFS 9:123-124.

Grubbs, Henry A. "Sartre's Recapturing of Lost Time. " MLN 73:515-522. November 1958.

Harvey, W. J. Character and the Novel. Ithaca: Cornell University Press, 1965. pp. 155-158; 170-171.

Hatzfeld, Helmut. Trends and Styles in Twentieth Century French Literature. Washington, D. C. : Catholic University of America Press, 1957. pp. 138-140.

Jameson, Fred. "The Laughter of Nausea. " YFS 23:26-32. Summer 1959.

Kohn, Renee J. "Four Centuries of French Novel: Evolution of the Hero. " ASLHM 29:85-86. No. 2, 1958.

Magny, Claude-Edmonde. "The Duplicity of Being. " Sartre: A Collection of Critical Essays. (ed.) Edith Kern. Englewood Cliffs: Prentice-Hall, Inc. , 1062. pp. 21-30.

Mendel, Sydney. "From Solitude to Salvation: A Study in Development. " YFS 30:47-55.

Murdoch, Iris. Sartre: Romantic Rationalist. New Haven: Yale University Press, 1953. pp. 1-14.

Oxenhandler, Neal. "The Metaphor of Metaphor in LA NAUSEE. " ChiR 15:47-54. Summer - Autumn 1962.

Peyre, Henri. The Contemporary French Novel. New York: Oxford University Press, 1955. pp. 225-227.

Shattuck, Roger. "Making Time: A Study of Stravinsky, Proust, and Sartre. " KR 25:252-254. Spring 1963.

Simon, John K. "Faulkner and Sartre: Metamorphosis and the Obscene. " CL 15:216-225. Summer 1963.

Will, Frederic. "Sartre and the Question of Character in Literature. " PMLA 76:457-459. September 1961.

Wilson, Clotilde. "Sartre's Graveyard of Chimeras: LA

NAUSEE and MORT DE QUELQU'UN. " FR 38:744-753.
May 1965.
PATHS OF LIBERTY
Bree, Germaine. "Poetry and the Novel. " The Culture of
France in Our Time. (ed.) Julian Park. Ithaca: Cornell
University Press, 1954. pp. 32-33.

Champigny, Robert. "Existentialism and the Modern French
Novel. " Thought 31:378-382. Autumn 1956.

Cranston, Maurice. Jean-Paul Sartre. New York: Grove
Press, Inc. , 1962. pp. 67-78.

Murdoch, Iris. Sartre: Romantic Rationalist. New Haven:
Yale University Press, 1953. pp. 15-26; 48-53.

Peyre, Henri. The Contemporary French Novel. New York:
Oxford University Press, 1955. pp. 228-230.

Thody, Philip. Jean-Paul Sartre: A Literary and Political
Study. London: Hamish Hamilton, 1960. pp. 59-68.
THE REPRIEVE
Blotner, Joseph L. The Political Novel. Garden City: Double-
day and Company, 1955. p. 45.

Church, Margaret. Time and Reality. Chapel Hill: University of North Carolina Press, 1962. pp. 268-270.

Glicksberg, Charles I. "Literary Existentialism. " ArQ
9:34-36. Spring 1953.

Glicksberg, Charles I. "The Literary Struggle for Self-
hood. " Person 42:58. Winter 1961.

Savage, Catharine. Malraux, Sartre, and Aragon as Political
Novelists. Gainesville: University of Florida Press, 1964.
pp. 29-31.

Thody, Philip. Jean-Paul Sartre: A Literary and Political
Study. London: Hamish Hamilton, 1960. pp. 52-57.
TROUBLED SLEEP
Bree, Germaine and Margaret Guiton. An Age of Fiction:
The French Novel from Gide to Camus. New Brunswick:
Rutgers University Press, 1957. pp. 213-216.

Savage, Catharine. Malraux, Sartre, and Aragon as Political
Novelists. Gainesville: University of Florida Press, 1964.
pp. 31-35.

Thody, Philip. Jean-Paul Sartre: A Literary and Political
Study. London: Hamish Hamilton, 1960. pp. 57-59.

Scarron, Paul
  L'ADULTERE INNOCENT
    Phelps, Naomi Forsythe. The Queen's Invalid. Baltimore:
    Johns Hopkins Press, 1951. pp. 237-239.
  LE CHATIMENT DE L'AVARICE
    Phelps, Naomi Forsythe. The Queen's Invalid. Baltimore.
    Johns Hopkins Press, 1951. pp. 241-242.
  LES HYPOCRITES
    Phelps, Naomi Forsythe. The Queen's Invalid. Baltimore:
    Johns Hopkins Press, 1951. pp. 239-241.
  LA PRECAUTION INUTILE
    Phelps, Naomi Forsythe. The Queen's Invalid. Baltimore:
    Johns Hopkins Press, 1951. pp. 237-239.
  ROMAN COMIQUE
    Phelps, Naomi Forsythe. The Queen's Invalid. Baltimore:
    Johns Hopkins Press, 1951. pp. 151-167.

    Secord, Arthur W. ROBERT DRURY'S JOURNAL and Other
    Studies. Urbana: University of Illinois, 1961. pp. 134-158.

    Simon, Ernest. "The Function of the Spanish Stories in
    Scarron's ROMAN COMIQUE. " ECr 3:130-136. Fall 1963.

    Stein, Harold. "Goldsmith's Translation of the ROMAN
    COMIQUE. " MLN 49:171-178. March 1934.

De Scudery, Mlle.
  CLELIE, HISTOIRE ROMAINE
    Van Eerde, John. "The Olympic Games in Mlle De Scudery
    and Fontenelle. " CLAJ 4:49-51. September 1960.
  GRAND CYRUS
    Barton, Francis B. "The Sources of the Story of SESOS-
    TRIS ET TIMARETE ın LE GRAND CYRUS. " MP 19:257-
    268. February 1922.
  IBRAHIM OU L'ILLUSTRE BASSA
    Coleman, Algernon. "A Source of IBRAHIM OU L'IL-
    LUSTRE BASSA. " RR 29:129-140. April 1938.
  LE PRINCE DEGUISE
    Matulka, Barbara. "The Main Source of Scudery's LE
    PRINCE DEGUISE: The PRIMALEON. " RR 25:1-14. Jan-
    uary - March 1934.

Simenon, George
  THE BOTTOM OF THE BOTTLE
    Tremblay, N. J. "Simenon's Psychological 'Westerns. ' "
    ArQ 10:223-226. Autumn 1954.
  THE LOST MARE RANCH
    Tremblay, N. J. "Simenon's Psychological 'Westerns. ' "
    ArQ 10:219-223. Autumn 1954.

Simon, Claude
  THE WIND
    Guicharnaud, Jacques. "Remembrance of Things Passing:

Claude Simon. '' YFS 24:101-108. Summer 1959.

Stael, Madame de
    CORINNE
        Andrews, Wayne. Germaine: A Portrait of Madame de Stael.
        New York: Atheneum, 1963. pp. 157-159.

        Baker, George M. ''Madame de Stael's Attitude toward
        Nature. '' SR 20:54-64. January 1912.

        Goldsmith, Margaret. Madame de Stael: Portrait of a Lib-
        beral in the Revolutionary Age. London: Longman, Green
        and Company, 1938. pp. 210-213.

        Gutwirth, Madelyn. ''Mme de Stael's Debt to PHEDRE:
        CORINNE. '' SIR 3:161-176. Spring 1964.

        Herold, Christopher. Mistress to an Age: A Life of Ma-
        dame de Stael. Indianapolis: Bobbs-Merrill Company,
        Inc., 1958. Chapter 15.

        Weintraub, Wiktor. ''The Problem of Improvisation in
        Romantic Literature. '' CL 16:121-122. Spring 1964.

        Wilson, Clotilde. ''LA MODIFICATION or Variations on a
        Theme by Mme. De Stael. '' RR 55:278-282. December
        1964.
    DELPHINE
        Baker, George M. ''Madame de Stael's Attitude toward
        Nature. '' SR 20:50-54. January 1912.

        Goldsmith, Margaret. Madame de Stael: Portrait of a Lib-
        eral in the Revolutionary Age. London: Longmans, Green
        and Company, 1938. pp. 188-190.

Stendhal
    L'ABBESSE DE CASTRO
        George, Albert J. Short Fiction in France: 1800-1850.
        Syracuse: Syracuse University Press, 1964. pp. 74-76.
    ARMANCE
        Adams, Robert M. Stendhal: Notes on a Novelist. New York:
        Noonday Press, 1959. pp. 146-151.

        Atherton, John. Stendhal. London: Bowes and Bowes, 1965.
        pp. 24-26.

        Caraccio, Armand. Stendhal. New York: New York Univer-
        sity Press, 1965. pp. 136-147.

        Clewes, Howard. Stendhal: An Introduction to a Novelist.
        London: Arthur Barker, Ltd. , 1950. pp. 66-71.

        Green, F. C. Stendhal. Cambridge: The University Press,

1939. pp. 188-198.

Hemmings, F. W. J. "Stendhal, Self Plagiarist. " ECr 2:
19-25. Spring 1962.

Hemmings, F. W. J. Stendhal: A Study of His Novels. Oxford: Clarendon Press, 1964. Chapter III.

Josephson, Matthew. Stendhal or Pursuit of Happiness.
New York: Doubleday and Company, Inc. , 1946. pp. 307-
328.

Saintsbury, George. A History of the French Novel (To the
Close of the 19th Century). London: Macmillan and Company, 1919. pp. 135-137.

Turnell, Martin. "The Key and the Purse. " TC 157:257-
272. March 1955.
LES CENCI
Gay, Lucy M. "Two Notes on LES CENCI of Stendhal. "
RR 21:137-141. April - June 1930.

George, Albert J. Short Fiction in France: 1800-1850.
Syracuse: Syracuse University Press, 1964. pp. 72-73.
THE CHARTERHOUSE OF PARMA
Adams, Robert M. Stendhal: Notes on a Novelist. New York:
Noonday Press, 1959. Chapter 4.

Atherton, John. Stendhal. London: Bowes and Bowes, 1965.
pp. 30-35.

Blackmur, R. P. "THE CHARTERHOUSE OF PARMA. "
KR 26:211-231. Winter 1964.

Blotner, Joseph L. The Political Novelists. Garden City:
Doubleday and Company, 1955. p. 44.

Brussaly, Manuel. The Political Ideas of Stendhal. New
York: Columbia University Press, 1933. pp. 70-74.

Caraccio, Armand. Stendhal. New York: New York University Press, 1965. pp. 173-186.

Clewes, Howard. Stendhal: An Introduction to a Novelist.
London: Arthur Barker, Ltd. , 1950. pp. 100-112.

Cook, Albert. The Meaning of Fiction. Detroit: Wayne
State University Press, 1960. pp. 49-61.

Cook, Albert. "Stendhal's Irony. " EIC 8:355-369. October
1958.

Goodheart, Eugene. "Style and Energy in the CHARTER-

HOUSE OF PARMA. '' Symposium 20:117-132. Summer 1966.

Green, F. C. Stendhal. Cambridge: The University Press, 1939. pp. 288-304.

Hemmings, F. W. J. ''A Note on the Origins of LA CHAR- TREUSE DE PARME. '' MLR 58:392-395. July 1963.

Hemmings, F. W. J. Stendhal: A Study of His Novels. Ox- ford: Clarendon Press, 1964. pp. 21-22; 49-50; 94-95; Chapter VI.

Howe, Irving. Politics and the Novel. New York: Meridan Books, 1957. pp. 39-50.

Josephson, Matthew. Stendhal or Pursuit of Happiness. New York: Doubleday and Company, Inc., 1946. pp. 418-441.

Kronenberger, Louis. ''Stendhal's CHARTERHOUSE: Su- preme Study of Worldliness.'' MQR 5:163-171. Summer 1966.

Levin, Harry. The Gates of Horn: A Study of Five French Realists. New York: Oxford University Press, 1963. pp. 130-149.

Saintsbury, George. A History of the French Novel (To the Close of the 19th Century). London: Macmillan and Com- pany, 1919. pp. 137-140.

Sells, A. Lytton. ''LA CHARTREUSE DE PARME: The Prob- lem of Composition. '' MLQ 12:204-215. June 1951.

Sells, A. Lytton. ''LA CHARTREUSE DE PARME: The Prob- lem of Style. '' MLQ 11:486-491. December 1950.

Stephan, Philip. ''Count Mosca's Role in LA CHARTREUSE DE PARME. '' ECr 2:38-42. Spring 1962.

Strachey, Lytton. Books and Characters. New York: Har- court, Brace and Company, 1922. pp. 269-293.

Temmer, Mark. ''Comedy in THE CHARTERHOUSE OF PARMA. '' YFS 23:92-99. Summer 1959.

Turnell, Martin. The Novel in France. New York: New Directions, 1951. pp. 184-206.

Wardman, H. W. ''LA CHARTREUSE DE PARME: Ironical Ambiguity. '' KR 17:449-471. Summer 1955.
LE COFFRE ET LE REVENANT
    George, Albert J. Short Fiction in France: 1800-1850. Syracuse: Syracuse University Press, 1964. pp. 67-69.

LAMIEL
> Green, F. C. Stendhal. Cambridge: The University Press,
> 1939. pp. 308-311.

LUCIEN LEUWEN
> Adams, Robert M. Stendhal: Notes on a Novelist. New York:
> Noonday Press, 1959. pp. 144-146; 152-158.
>
> Atherton, John. Stendhal. London: Bowes and Bowes, 1965.
> pp. 45-46.
>
> Brombert, Victor. "Stendhal: Creation and Self-Knowledge."
> RR 43:191-197. October 1952.
>
> Caraccio, Armand. Stendhal. New York: New York Univer-
> sity Press, 1965. pp. 163-166.
>
> Dombey, Paul. "Books in General." New S&N 31:303.
> April 27, 1946.
>
> Giraud, R. Unheroic Heroes. New Brunswick: Rutgers Uni-
> versity Press, 1957. pp. 59-87.
>
> Green, F. C. Stendhal. Cambridge: The University Press,
> 1939. pp. 255-269.
>
> Hemmings, F. W. J. Stendhal: A Study of His Novels. Ox-
> ford: Clarendon Press, 1964. Chapter V.
>
> Pritchett, V. S. Books in General. London: Chatto and
> Windus, 1953. pp. 123-129.
>
> Pritchett, V. S. "Books in General." New S&N 41:371-
> 372. March 31, 1951.
>
> Turnell, Martin. The Novel in France. New York: New
> Directions, 1951. pp. 161-183.

THE RED AND THE BLACK
> Adams, Robert Martin. "Metilde: or a Lesson in Logic."
> HudR 11:41-45. Spring 1958.
>
> Adams, Robert M. Stendhal: Notes on a Novelist. New York:
> Noonday Press, 1959. pp. 151-152.
>
> Adams, Robert M. Strains of Discord: Studies in Literary
> Openness. Ithaca: Cornell University Press, 1958. pp. 93-
> 97.
>
> Atherton, John. Stendhal. London: Bowes and Bowes, 1965.
> pp. 26-30.
>
> Auerbach, Erich. "In the Hotel de la Mole." PR 18:265-
> 269. May - June 1951. (Also in Auerbach, Mimesis. New
> York: Doubleday and Company, 1957. pp. 400-403.)

Borgerhoff, E. B. O. "The Anagram in LE ROUGE ET LE NOIR. " MLN 68:383-386. June 1953.

Caraccio, Armand. Stendhal. New York: New York University Press, 1965. pp. 148-161.

Clewes, Howard. Stendhal: An Introduction to a Novelist. London: Arthur Barker, Ltd. , 1950. pp. 73-84.

Cook, Albert. "Stendhal's Irony. " EIC 8:355-369. October 1958.

Friedman, Melvin J. "The Cracked Vase. " RomN 7:127-129. Spring 1966.

Gibian, George. "Love by the Book: Pushkin, Stendhal, Flaubert. " CL 8:103-105. Spring 1956.

Grant, Richard B. "The Death of Julien Sorel. " ECr 2:26-30. Spring 1962.

Green, F. C. Stendhal. Cambridge: The University Press, 1939. pp. 214-238.

Hemmings, F. W. J. "Julien Sorel and Julian the Apostate." FS 16:229-242. July 1962.

Hemmings, F. W. J. Stendhal: A Study of His Novels. Oxford: Clarendon Press, 1964. pp. 20-21; 56-57; 65-67; 71-73.

Howe, Irving. Politics and the Novel. New York: Meridan Books, 1957. pp. 36-39.

Hugo, Howard E. "Two Strange Interviews: Rousseau's CONFESSIONS and Stendhal's LE ROUGE ET LE NOIR. " FR 25:164-172. January 1952.

Josephson, Matthew. Stendhal or Pursuit of Happiness. New York: Doubleday and Company, Inc. , 1946. pp. 329-353.

Kohn, Renee J. "Four Centuries of French Novel: Evolution of the Hero. " ASLHM 29:82-84. No. 2, 1958.

Maugham, W. Somerset. Great Novelists and Their Novels. Philadelphia: Winston Company, 1948. pp. 95-112.

Merrill, Francis E. "Stendhal and the Self: A Study in the Sociology of Literature. " American Journal of Sociology 66:448-453. March 1961.

O'Connor, Frank. The Mirror in the Roadway: A Study of

the Modern Novel. New York: Alfred A. Knopf, 1956. pp. 51-54.

Pronger, Lester J. "Marmontel as a Source of Stendhal." MLN 56:433-435. June 1941.

Saintsbury, George. A History of the French Novel (To the Close of the 19th Century). London: Macmillan and Company, 1919. pp. 141-146.

Sandstrom, Glenn. "The Outsiders of Stendhal and Camus." MFS 10:245-257. Autumn 1964.

Strachey, Lytton. Books and Characters. New York: Harcourt, Brace and Company, 1922. pp. 269-293.

Turnell, Martin. The Novel in France. New York: New Directions, 1951. pp. 141-160.

Warren, F. M. "Was Balzac's ILLUSIONS PERDUES an Influence on Stendhal?" MLN 43:179-180. March 1928.

Tallemant, Paul
    VOYAGE TO THE ISLE OF LOVE
        Karlinsky, Simon. "Tallemant and the Beginning of the Novel in Russia." CL 15:226-230. Summer 1963.

Theuriet, M. Andre
    LE FILS MAUGARS
        Saintsbury, George. A History of the French Novel (To the Close of the 19th Century). London: Macmillan and Company, 1919. pp. 531-532.
    SAUVAGEONNE
        Saintsbury, George. A History of the French Novel (To the Close of the 19th Century). London: Macmillan and Company, 1919. pp. 530-531.

TSONNONTHOUAN
        Foster, James R. "A Forgotten Noble Savage, Tsonnonthouan." MLQ 14:348-359. December 1953.

Valery, Paul
    MONSIEUR TESTE
        Grubbs, Henry A. "The Date of Composition of Valery's LA SOIREE AVEC MONSIEUR TESTE." MLN 75:585-589. November 1960.

        Ince, W. N. "Composition in Valery's Writings on Monsieur Teste." ECr 41:19-27. Spring 1964.

        LeSage, Laurence. "Three Translations from the French." SR 56:531-533. Summer 1948.

        Mackay, Agnes Ethel. The Universal Self: A Study of Paul

Valery. London: Routledge and Kegan Paul, 1961. pp. 82-92.

Waldrop, Rosmarie. "MONSIEUR TESTE and DER PTOLEMAER: Abstractness in the Fiction of Valery and Benn. " EWR 1:317-327. Winter 1965.

Veiras, Denis
    HISTORY OF THE SEVARITES
        Aldridge, A. Owen. "Polygamy in Early Fiction: Henry Neville and Denis Veiras. " PMLA 65:464-472. June 1950.

Verne, Jules
    AROUND THE MOON
        Lafleur, Laurence J. "Marvelous Voyages--IV: Jules Verne, AROUND THE MOON. " Pop As 50:377-379. August 1942. (Continued in October 1942. pp. 431-433.)
    AROUND THE WORLD IN EIGHTY DAYS
        Allott, Kenneth. Jules Verne. New York: Macmillan Company, 1941. pp. 168-174.

        Auden, W. H. "Balaam and the Ass: The Master-Servant Relationship in Literature. " Thought 29:265-269. Summer 1954.

        Waltz, George H., Jr. Jules Verne: The Biography of an Imagination. New York: Henry Holt and Company, 1943. pp. 144-146.
    CASTLE IN THE CARPATHIANS
        Allott, Kenneth. Jules Verne. New York: Macmillan Company, 1941. pp. 228-229.
    CHILD OF THE CAVERN
        Allott, Kenneth. Jules Verne. New York: Macmillan Company, 1941. pp. 112-114.
    THE CHILDREN OF CAPTAIN GRANT
        Allott, Kenneth. Jules Verne. New York: Macmillan Company, 1941. pp. 112-114.
    CLIPPER OF THE CLOUDS
        Allott, Kenneth. Jules Verne. New York: Macmillan Company, 1941. pp. 201-207.
    FROM THE EARTH TO THE MOON
        Lafleur, Laurence J. "Marvelous Voyages--III: Jules Verne's FROM THE EARTH TO THE MOON. " Pop As 50: 196-198. April 1942. (Continued in June 1942. pp. 315-317.)

        Waltz, George H., Jr. Jules Verne: The Biography of an Imagination. New York: Henry Holt and Company, 1943. pp. 109-111; 190-191; 201-202.
    JOURNEY TO THE CENTER OF THE EARTH
        Allott, Kenneth. Jules Verne. New York: Macmillan Company, 1941. pp. 96-103.

        Lafleur, Laurence J. "Marvelous Voyages--I: Jules Verne's

JOURNEY TO THE CENTER OF THE EARTH. '' Pop As 50:
16-21. January 1942.

Waltz, George H. , Jr. Jules Verne: The Biography of an
Imagination. New York: Henry Holt and Company, 1943. pp.
102-108.
TWENTY THOUSAND LEAGUES UNDER THE SEA
Allott, Kenneth. Jules Verne. New York: Macmillan Com-
pany, 1941. pp. 113-120.

Waltz, George H. , Jr. Jules Verne: The Biography of an
Imagination. New York: Henry Holt and Company, 1943. pp.
124-131.

De Vigny, Alfred
CINQ MARS
Smith, Maxwell. "Alfred de Vigny, Founder of the French
Historical Novel. '' FR 13:6-10. October 1939.
DAPHNE
Gillies, Camilla Hay. "Julian the Apostate in Montaigne
and Vigny. '' MLR 55:578-579. October 1960.
LAURETTE OU LE CACHET ROUGE
Kendris, Christopher. '' Patterns in ATALA and LAURETTE
OU LE CACHET ROUGE. '' FR 31:149-152. December 1957.
SERVITUDE ET GRANDEUR MILITAIRES
London, Philip W. "The Military Necessity: BILLY BUDD
and Vigny. '' CL 14:176-186. Spring 1962.

Smith, Maxwell. "Alfred de Vigny, Founder of the French
Historical Novel. '' FR 13:11 13. October 1939.
STELLO
Smith, Maxwell. "Alfred de Vigny, Founder of the French
Historical Novel. '' FR 13:10-11. October 1939.

Voltaire
CANDIDE
Barber, W. H. Voltaire: Candide. London: Edward Arnold
(Publishers) Inc. , 1960.

Bottiglia, William F. "Candide's Garden. '' PMLA 66:718-
733. September 1951.

Bottiglia, William F. "The Eldorado Episode in CANDIDE.''
PMLA 73:339-347. September 1958.

Brandes, Georg. Voltaire. New York: Albert and Charles
Boni, 1930. pp. 143-146.

Brightman, Edgar S. "The Lisbon Earthquake: A Study in
Religious Valuation. '' American Journal of Theology 23:
506-508. October 1919.

Broome, J. H. "Voltaire and Fougeret de Moubron: A

CANDIDE Problem Reconsidered. " MLR 55:509-518. October 1960.

Brown, James L. "Reference to Cunegonde in 1756." MLN 68:490-491. November 1953.

Fitch, Robert Elliot. "A Tale of Two Pilgrims: A Comparison of Bunyan's PILGRIM'S PROGRESS and Voltaire's CANDIDE. " HJ 48:388-393. July 1950.

Havens, George R. "The Composition of Voltaire's CANDIDE. " MLN 47:225-234. April 1932.

Hazard, Paul. European Thought in the Eighteenth Century. New Haven: Yale University Press, 1954. Chapter III, Part 3.

Kahn, Ludwig W. "Voltaire's CANDIDE and the Problem of Secularization. " PMLA 67:886-888. September 1952.

Krappe, Alexander H. "The Subterraneous Voyage. " PQ 20:119-130. April 1941.

McGhee, Dorothy M. "Voltaire's CANDIDE and Gracian's EL CRITICON. " PMLA 52:778-784. September 1937.

Marsland, Amy L. "Voltaire: Satire and Sedition. " RR 57:37-40. February 1966.

Maurois, Andre. Voltaire. Edinburgh: University Press, 1932. pp. 109-113.

Meyer, Adolph. Voltaire: Man of Justice. U. S. A.: Howell, Sokin Publishers, 1945. pp. 312-316.

Pappas, John N. "Voltaire and the Problem of Evil. " ECr 3:199-206. Winter 1963.

Price, William Raleigh. The Symbolism of Voltaire's Novels. New York: AMS Press, 1966. pp. 1-21; 198-229.

Shaw, E. P. "A Note on the Publication of CANDIDE. " MLN 71:430-431. June 1956.

Thaddeus, Victor. Voltaire: Genius of Mockery. New York: Brentano's Publishers, 1928. pp. 198-203.

Torrey, Norman L. "The Date of Composition of CANDIDE and Voltaire's Corrections. " MLN 44:445-447. November 1929.

Torrey, Norman L. The Spirit of Voltaire. New York: Columbia University Press, 1938. pp. 49-51.

Triebel, L. A. "The Bicentenary of CANDIDE. " Con Rev 195: 181-183. March 1959.

Wade, Ira O. "The La Valliere MS of CANDIDE. " FR 30: 3-4. October 1956.

Wade, Ira O. Voltaire and CANDIDE: A Study in the Fusion of History, Art, and Philosophy. Princeton: Princeton University Press, 1959.

Wade, Ira O. "Voltaire's Quarrel with Science. " BuR 8: 287-298. December 1959.

L'INGENU

Wade, Ira O. Studies on Voltaire: With Some Unpublished Papers of Mme. du Chatelet. Princeton: Princeton University Press, 1947. pp. 12-21.

MICROMEGAS

Barber, W. H. "The Genesis of Voltaire's MICROMEGAS. " FS 11:1-14. January 1957.

ZADIG

Foulet, Alfred. "Zadig and Job. " MLN 75:421-423. May 1960.

Lichtenstein, Julius. "The Title of Voltaire's ZADIG. " FR 33:65-67. October 1959.

Loss, H. "An Analogue of 'L'Ermite' in ZADIG. " MLN 61:115-118. February 1946.

Loss, H. "A Prototype of the Story in ZADIG (Ch. III): LE CHIEN ET LE CHEVAL. " MLN 52:576-577. December 1937.

Meyer, Adolph. Voltaire: Man of Justice. U. S. A.: Howell, Sokin Publishers, 1945. pp. 245-246.

Meyerson, Harold. "Note on the Etymology of Names in Voltaire's ZADIG. " MLN 54:597-598. December 1939.

Price, William Raleigh. The Symbolism of Voltaire's Novels. New York: A. M. S. Press, 1966. pp. 39-86.

van Roosbroeck, G. L. "A Neglected Source of ZADIG. " NM 33:224-226. 1932.

Siegel, June Sigler. "Voltaire, ZADIG, and the Problem of Evil. " RR 50:25-34. February 1959.

Yourcenar, Marguerite

THE MEMOIRS OF HADRIAN

Houstan, John. "THE MEMOIRS OF HADRIAN by Marguerite Yourcenar. " YFS 27:140-141. Spring - Summer 1961.

Zoe-Oldenbourg, Madame
    DESTINY OF FIRE
        Hoffmann, Leon-Francois. "Notes on Madame Zoe-Olden-
        bourg's DESTINY OF FIRE. " YFS 27:127-130. Spring -
        Summer 1961.

Zola, Emile
    L'ARGENT
        Grant, Richard B. "The Jewish Question in Zola's L'-
        ARGENT. " PMLA 70:955-967. December 1955.

        Grant, Richard B. "The Problem of Zola's Character Cre-
        ation in L'ARGENT. " KFLQ 8:58-65. 1961.

        Hemmings, F. W. J. Emile Zola. Oxford: Clarendon Press,
        1953. pp. 225-227; 268-270.
    L'ASSOMMOIR
        Gregor, Ian and Brian Nicholas. The Moral and the Story.
        London: Faber and Faber, 1962. pp. 63-97.

        Hemmings, F. W. J. Emile Zola. Oxford: Clarendon Press,
        1953. pp. 71-72; 91-106; 145-146; 212-213.

        Pritchett, V. S. Books in General. London: Chatto and
        Windus, 1953. pp. 116-122.

        Pritchett, V. S. "Books in General. " New S&N 43:128-
        129. February 2, 1952.

        Symons, A. The Symbolist Movement in Literature. New
        York: E. P. Dutton and Company, 1958. pp. 154-164.
    ATTACK ON THE MILL
        Jones, Malcolm Bancroft. "L'ATTAQUE DU MOULIN in
        American Translation. " MLN 57:207-208. March 1942.
    AU BONHEUR DES DAMES
        Hemmings, F. W. J. Emile Zola. Oxford: Clarendon Press,
        1953. pp. 160-161.
    LA BETE HUMAINE
        Gauthier, E. Paul. "New Light on Zola and Physiognomy. "
        PMLA 75:300-302. June 1960.

        Hemmings, F. W. J. Emile Zola. Oxford: Clarendon Press,
        1953. pp. 141-142; 160-161; 215-219; 222-224.

        Kanes, Martin. " 'Il Faudrait Creuser L'Histoire': Notes on
        the Composition of LA BETE HUMAINE. " RR 52:17-26.
        February 1961.

        Kanes, Martin. Zola's LA BETE HUMAINE. Berkeley: Uni-
        versity of California Press, 1962.

        Matthews, J. H. "The Railway in Zola's LA BETE HU-
        MAINE. " Symposium 14:53-58. Spring 1960.

LA CONFESSION DE CLAUDE
Hemmings, F. W. J. Emile Zola. Oxford: Clarendon Press, 1953. pp. 7-12.

Lapp, John. "The Critical Reception of Zola's CONFESSION DE CLAUDE. " MLN 68:457-462. November 1953.

Lapp, John C. Zola Before ROUGON MACQUART. Toronto: University of Toronto Press, 1964. pp. 48-66.

Weinstein, Sophie R. "The Genesis of Zola's LA CONFESSION DE CLAUDE. " MLN 53:196-198. March 1938.
LA CONQUETE DE PLASSANS
Hemmings, F. W. J. Emile Zola. Oxford: Clarendon Press, 1953. pp. 45-46; 78-80.
LA CUREE
Grant, Elliott M. "The Composition of LA CUREE. " RR 45: 29-44. February 1954.

Hemmings, F. W. J. Emile Zola. Oxford: Clarendon Press, 1953. pp. 76-80; 88-89.

Josephson, Matthew. Zola and His Time. Garden City: Garden City Publishing Company, Inc. , 1928. pp. 174-177.
LA DEBACLE
Colvert, James B. "THE RED BADGE OF COURAGE and a Review of Zola's LA DEBACLE. " MLN 71:98-100. February 1956.

Hemmings, F. W. J. Emile Zola. Oxford: Clarendon Press, 1953. pp. 230-234.

Josephson, Matthew. Zola and His Time. Garden City: Garden City Publishing Company, Inc. , 1928. pp. 336-340.

Rhodes, S. A. "The Source of Zola's Medical References in LA DEBACLE. " MLN 45:109-111. February 1930.

Rufener, Helen La Rue. Biography of a War Novel: Zola's LA DEBACLE. Morningside Heights: King's Crown Press, 1946.

West, Edward Sackville. "Books in General. " New S&N 22:331. October 4, 1941.
LE DOCTEUR PASCAL
Hemmings, F. W. J. Emile Zola. Oxford: Clarendon Press, 1953. pp. 173-174; 234-239.

Josephson, Matthew. Zola and His Time. Garden City: Garden City Publishing Company, Inc. , 1928. pp. 350-353.
LA FAUTE DE L'ABBE MOURET
Brown, Calvin S. "Parallel Incidents in Emile Zola and Tomasi di Lampedusa. " CL 15:193-202. Summer 1963.

Brown, Donald F. "A Naturalistic Version of Genesis:
Zola and Aluizio Azevedo. " HR 12:344-351. October 1944.

Brown, Donald F. "Two Naturalistic Versions of Genesis:
Zola and Pardo Bazan. " MLN 52:243-248. April 1937.

Chaikin, Milton. "A French Source for George Moore's A
MERE ACCIDENT. " MLN 71:28-30. January 1956.

Hemmings, F. W. J. Emile Zola. Oxford: Clarendon Press,
1953. pp. 84-89; 205-206.

Hemmings, F. W. J. "The Secret Sources of LA FAUTE
DE L'ABBE MOURET. " FS 13:226-239. July 1959.

Josephson, Matthew. Zola and His Time. Garden City:
Garden City Publishing Company, Inc. , 1928. pp. 209-212.

Walker, Philip. "Prophetic Myths in Zola. " PMLA 74:444-
447. September 1959.
FECONDITE
Josephson, Matthew. Zola and His Time. Garden City:
Garden City Publishing Company, Inc. , 1928. pp. 490-492.
LA FORTUNE DES ROUGON
Gauthier, E. Paul. "New Light on Zola and Physiognomy. "
PMLA 75:297-298. June 1960.

Hemmings, F. W. J. Emile Zola. Oxford: Clarendon Press,
1953. pp. 57-62; 73-74; 79-80.

Kanes, Martin. "Zola, Balzac and LA FORTUNE DES
ROGRON. " FS 18:203-212. July 1964.
GERMINAL
Bennetton, Norman A. "Social Thought in Emile Zola."
Sociology and Social Research 13:375-376. 1928-1929.

Blankenagel, John C. "The Mob in Zola's GERMINAL and
in Hauptmann's WEAVERS. " PMLA 39:705-721. September
1924.

Brown, Donald F. "A Chilean GERMINAL: Zola and Bal-
domero Lillo. " MLN 65:47-52. January 1950.

Eoff, Sherman H. The Modern Spanish Novel. New York:
New York University Press, 1961. pp. 96-109.

Grant, Elliott M. "Concerning the Sources of GERMINAL. "
RR 49:168-178. October 1958.

Grant, Elliott M. "Marriage or Murder: Zola's Hesitations
Concerning Cecile Gregoire. " FS 15:41-45. January 1961.

Grant, Elliott M. "The Newspapers of GERMINAL: Their

Identity and Significance." MLR 55:87-89. January 1960.

Grant, Elliott M. Zola's GERMINAL: A Critical and Historical Study. Leicester: Leicester University Press, 1962.

Grant, Richard B. "Zola's Germinal." Expl 18:Item 37.
March 1960.

Hemmings, F. W. J. Emile Zola. Oxford: Clarendon Press,
1953. pp. 175-199; 201-202; 283-284.

Levin, Harry. The Gates of Horn: A Study of Five French
Realists. New York: Oxford University Press, 1963. pp.
326-331.

Moore, Charles H. "A Hearing on GERMINAL and DIE
WEBER." GR 33:30-40. February 1958.

Pritchett, V. S. "Books in General." New S&N 21:188-189.
February 22, 1941.

Walker, Philip. "The 'Ebauche' of GERMINAL." PMLA 80:
571-583. December 1965.

Walker, Philip. "Prophetic Myths in Zola." PMLA 74:447-
451. September 1959.

Walker, Philip. "Zola's Art of Characterization in GERM-
INAL." ECr 4:60-67. Summer 1964.

Walker, Philip. "Zola's Use of Color Imagery in GERM-
INAL." PMLA 77:442-449. September 1962. (Replies in
PMLA 79:348-354. June 1964)
LA JOIE DE VIVRE
Hemmings, F. W. J. Emile Zola. Oxford: Clarendon Press,
1953. pp. 170-175.

Niess, Robert J. "Autobiographical Elements in Zola's LA
JOIE DE VIVRE." PMLA 56:1133-1149. December 1941.

Niess, Robert J. "Zola's Final Revisions of LA JOIE DE
VIVRE." MLN 58:537-539. November 1943.

Niess, Robert J. "Zola's LA JOIE DE VIVRE and LA MORT
D'OLIVIER BECAILLE." MLN 57:205-207. March 1942.

Niess, Robert J. "Zola's LA JOIE DE VIVRE and the Opera
LAZARE." RR 34:223-227. October 1943.
LOURDES
Hemmings, F. W. J. Emile Zola. Oxford: Clarendon Press,
1953. pp. 255-259.

McCrossen, Vincent A. "Zola, Werfel, and the Song of

Bernadette. " Renascence 14:34-38. Autumn 1961.
MADELEINE FERAT
    Hemmings, F. W. J. Emile Zola. Oxford: Clarendon Press,
    1953. pp. 23-32.

    Josephson, Matthew. Zola and His Time. Garden City:
    Garden City Publishing Company, Inc., 1928. pp. 130-132.

    Lapp, John C. "The Watcher Betrayed and the Fatal Woman:
    Some Recurring Patterns in Zola. " PMLA 74:276-280. June
    1959.

    Lapp, John C. Zola Before ROUGON MACQUART. Toronto:
    University of Toronto Press, 1964. pp. 121-158.
NANA
    Duncan, Phillip A. "Genesis of the Longchamp Scene in
    Zola's NANA. " MLN 75:684-689. December 1960.

    Hemmings, F. W. J. Emile Zola. Oxford: Clarendon Press,
    1953. pp. 145-146; 150-155; 161-162; 192-193.

    Josephson, Matthew. Zola and His Time. Garden City:
    Garden City Publishing Company, Inc., 1928. pp. 256-265.

    Lapp, John C. "The Watcher Betrayed and the Fatal Woman:
    Some Recurring Patterns in Zola. " PMLA 74:280-281. June
    1959.

    Leonard, Frances McNeely. "NANA: Symbol and Action. "
    MFS 9:149-158. Summer 1963.
L'OEUVRE
    Brown, Calvin S. "Music in Zola's Fiction. " PMLA 71:86-
    91. March 1956.

    Hemmings, F. W. J. Emile Zola. Oxford: Clarendon Press,
    1953. pp. 202-204.

    Josephson, Matthew. Zola and His Time. Garden City:
    Garden City Publishing Company, Inc., 1928. pp. 299-300.

    Niess, Robert J. "Another View of Zola's L'OEUVRE. "
    RR 39:282-300. December 1948.

    Niess, Robert J. "Antithesis and 'Reprise' in Zola's L'-
    OEUVRE. " ECr 4:68-75. Summer 1964.

    Niess, Robert J. "George Moore and Emile Zola Again. "
    Symposium 20:43-48. Spring 1966.

    Niess, Robert J. "Henry James and Zola: A Parallel. "
    RLC 30:93-98. 1956.

    Niess, Robert J. "Zola's L'OEUVRE and RECONQUISTA of

Gamboa. " PMLA 61:577-583. June 1946.

Pritchett, V. S. Books in General. London: Chatto and
Windus, 1953. pp. 110-116.

Pritchett, V. S. "Books in General. " New S&N 39:578-
579. May 20, 1950.
PARIS
Grant, Elliott M. "Zola and the Sacre-Coeur. " FS 20:246-
252. July 1966.

Hemmings, F. W. J. Emile Zola. Oxford: Clarendon Press,
1953. pp. 268-273.
POT-BOUILLE
Bennetton, Norman A. "Social Thought in Emile Zola. "
Sociology and Social Research 13:371-372. 1928-1929.

Grant, Elliott M. "The Political Scene in Zola's POT-
BOUILLE. " FS 8:342-347. October 1954.

Hemmings, F. W. J. Emile Zola. Oxford: Clarendon Press,
1953. pp. 155-160; 212-213.
LE REVE
Grant, Elliott M. "The Bishop's Role in Zola's LE REVE. "
RR 53:105-111. April 1962.

Hemmings, F. W. J. Emile Zola. Oxford: Clarendon Press,
1953. pp. 221-223.

Matthews, J. H. "Zola's LE REVE as an Experimental
Novel. " MLR 52:187-194. April 1957.
ROME
Hemmings, F. W. J. Emile Zola. Oxford: Clarendon Press,
1953. pp. 259-265.
ROUGON-MACQUART
Hemmings, F. W. J. "The Elaboration of Character in the
'Ebauches' of Zola's ROUGON-MACQUART Novels. " PMLA
81:286-296. June 1966.

Wenger, Jared. "The Art of the Flashlight: Violent Tech-
nique in LES ROUGON-MACQUART. " PMLA 57:1137-1159.
December 1942.
SON EXCELLENCE EUGENE ROUGON
Grant, Elliott. "Studies on Zola's SON EXCELLENCE EU-
GENE ROUGON. " RR 44:24-39. February 1953.

Grant, Richard B. Zola's SON EXCELLENCE EUGENE
ROUGON. Durham: Duke, 1960.

Hemmings, F. W. J. Emile Zola. Oxford: Clarendon Press,
1953. pp. 57-58; 69-71; 89-90.
LA TERRE
Harvey, Lawrence E. "The Cycle Myth in LA TERRE of

Zola. " PQ 38:89-95. January 1959.

Hemmings, F. W. J. Emile Zola. Oxford: Clarendon Press, 1953. pp. 204-215.

Pritchett, V. S. "Books in General. " New S&N 48:134-135. July 31, 1954.
THERESE RAQUIN
Atkins, Stuart. "A Possible Dickens' Influence in Zola. " MLQ 8:303-308. September 1947.

Hemmings, F. W. J. Emile Zola. Oxford: Clarendon Press, 1953. pp. 23-34; 145-146.

Josephson, Matthew. Zola and His Time. Garden City: Garden City Publishing Company, Inc., 1928. pp. 117-121.

Lapp, John C. Zola Before ROUGON MACQUART. Toronto: University of Toronto Press, 1964. pp. 88-120.

Niess, Robert J. "Hawthorne and Zola--An Influence?" RLC 27:446-452. 1953.
TRAVAIL
Hemmings, F. W. J. Emile Zola. Oxford: Clarendon Press, 1953. pp. 282-286.
LE VENTRE DE PARIS
Hemmings, F. W. J. Emile Zola. Oxford: Clarendon Press, 1953. pp. 81-84; 89-90.
VERITE
Hemmings, F. W. J. Emile Zola. Oxford: Clarendon Press, 1953. pp. 286-289.

Agusti, Ignacio
MARIONA REBULL
Wade, Gerald E. "A New Spanish Novelist. " MLJ 31:426-429. November 1947.
EL VIUDO RIUS
Wade, Gerald E. "A New Spanish Novelist. " MLJ 31:426-430. November 1947.

Alarcon, Pedro Antonio de
EL CAPITAN VENENO (CAPTAIN POISON)
Winslow, Richard W. "The Distinction of Structure in Alarcon's EL SOMBRERO DE TRES PICOS and EL CAPITAN VENENO. " Hispania 46:715-720. December 1963.
EL ESCANDALO
Warren, L. A. Modern Spanish Literature. Vol. I. London: Brentano's, Ltd., 1929. pp. 116-117.
EL EXTRANJERO
Krappe, Alexander H. "The Source of Pedro Antonio de Alarcon's EL EXTRANJERO. " HR 11:72-76. January 1943.
EL NINO DE LA BOLA (THE INFANT WITH THE GLOBE)
Warren, L. A. Modern Spanish Literature. Vol. I. London: Brentano's, Ltd., 1929. pp. 114-116.
LA PRODIGA
Warren, L. A. Modern Spanish Literature. Vol. I. London: Brentano's, Ltd., 1929. pp. 117-118.
EL SOMBRERO DE TRES PICOS (THE THREE-CORNERED HAT)
Hodge, H. S. Vere. "THE THREE-CORNERED HAT. " SatR 156:104. July 22, 1933.

Place, Edwin B. "The Antecedents of EL SOMBRERO DE TRES PICOS. " PQ 8:39-42. January 1929.

Warren, L. A. Modern Spanish Literature. Vol. I. London: Brentano's, Ltd., 1929. pp. 113-114.

Winslow, Richard W. "The Distinction of Structure in Alarcon's EL SOMBRERO DE TRES PICOS and EL CAPITAN VENENO. " Hispania 46:715-720. December 1963.

Alas, Leopoldo (Clarin)
LA REGENTA
Avrett, Robert. "The Treatment of Satire in the Novels of Leopoldo Alas (Clarin). " Hispania 24:223-230. May 1941.

Brent, Albert. "Leopoldo Alas and LA REGENTA. " University of Missouri Studies 24:11-131. No. 2, 1951.

Bull, William E. " 'Clarin' and His Critics. " MLF 35:107-
109. September - December 1950.

Bull, William E. "The Liberalism of Leopoldo Alas. " HR
10:330-331. October 1942.

Bull, William E. "The Naturalistic Theories of Leopoldo
Alas. " PMLA 57:536-547. June 1942.

Chandler, Richard E. and Kessel Schwartz. A New History
of Spanish Literature. Baton Rouge: Louisiana State University Press, 1961. pp. 220-221.

Durand, Frank. "Characterization in LA REGENTA: Point
of View and Theme. " BHS 41:86-100. April 1964.

Durand, Frank. "Structural Unity in Leopoldo Alas' LA
REGENTA. " HR 31:324-335. October 1963.

Eoff, Sherman H. The Modern Spanish Novel. New York:
New York University Press, 1961. pp. 71-84.

Warren, L. A. Modern Spanish Literature. Vol. I. London:
Brentano's, Ltd., 1929. pp. 172-179.

Weber, Frances. "The Dynamics of Motif in Leopoldo
Alas's LA REGENTA. " RR 57:188-199. October 1966.

Weber, Frances Wyers. "Ideology and Religious Parody in
the Novels of Leopoldo Alas. " BHS 43:197-203. July 1966.
SU UNICO HIJO
    Owen, Arthur L. "Psychological Aspects of Spanish Real-
    ism. " Hispania 14:6-7. February 1931.

    Weber, Frances Wyers. "Ideology and Religious Parody in
    the Novels of Leopoldo Alas. " BHS 43:203-208. July 1966.

Alcala Yanez y Rivera, Jeronimo de
    EL DONADO HABLADOR
    Childers, J. Wesley. "Sources of the 'Magic Twig' Story
    from EL DONADO HABLADOR. " Hispania 49:729-732. De-
    cember 1966.

Aleman, Mateo
    DORIDO AND CLORINIA
    McGrady, Donald. "DORIDO AND CLORINIA: An Italianate
    Novella by Mateo Aleman. " RomN 8:91-95. Autumn 1966.
    GUZMAN DE ALFARACHE
    Beberfall, Lester. "The 'Picaro' in Context. " Hispania 37:
    289-292. September 1954.

    Chandler, Richard E. and Kessel Schwartz. A New History

of Spanish Literature. Baton Rouge: Louisiana State University Press, 1961. pp. 183-184.

Del Piero, R. A. "The Picaresque Philosophy in GUZMAN DE ALFARACHE. " MLF 42:152-156. December 1957.

Eoff, Sherman. "A Galdosian Version of Picaresque Psychology. " MLF 38:5-9. March - June 1953.

Eoff, Sherman. "The Picaresque Psychology of Guzman de Alfarache. " HR 21:107-119. April 1953.

Glaser, Edward. "Two Anti-Semitic Word Plays in the GUZMAN DE ALFARACHE. " MLN 69:343-348. May 1954.

Grass, Roland. "Morality in the Picaresque Novel. " Hispania 42:194-196. May 1959.

Gray, Malcolm Jerome. An Index to GUZMAN DE ALFARACHE. New Brunswick: Rutgers University Press, 1948. 90 pp.

McGrady, Donald. "Heliodorus' Influence on Mateo Aleman." HR 34:49-53. January 1966.

McGrady, Donald. "Masuccio and Aleman: Italian Renaissance and Spanish Baroque. " CL 18:203-210. Summer 1966.

McGrady, Donald. "A Pirated Edition of GUZMAN DE ALFARACHE: More Light on Mateo Aleman's Life. " HR 34:326-328. October 1966.

McGrady, Donald. "Was Mateo Aleman in Italy?" HR 31: 148-152. April 1963.

Merimee, Ernest. A History of Spanish Literature. New York: Holt and Company, 1930. pp. 314-316.

Randall, Dale B. J. The Golden Tapestry. Durham: Duke University Press, 1963. pp. 132-134; 174-184.

Rotunda, D. P. "The GUZMAN DE ALFARACHE and Italian 'Novellistica.' " RR 24:129-133. April - June 1933.

Stamm, James R. "The Uses and Types of Humor in the Picaresque Novel. " Hispania 42:482-485. December 1959.

Williams, Robert H. "Satirical Rules of Etiquette in the 'Siglo de Oro.' " Hispania 13:293-300. October 1930.

Altamira, Raphael
    REPOSO
        Fagg, John E. "An Autobiographical Novel by Raphael

Altamira. " Hispania 37:295-301. September 1954.

Azorin, Gabriel
EL CABALLERO INACTUAL
Lott, Robert E. "Azorin's Experimental Period and Sur-
realism. " PMLA 79:312. June 1964.
DIARIO DE UN ENFERMO
Livingstone, Leon. "The 'Esthetic of Repose' in Azorin's
DIARIO DE UN ENFERMO. " Symposium 20:241-251. Fall
1966.
EL LIBRO DE LEVANTE
Lott, Robert E. "Azorin's Experimental Period and Sur-
realism. " PMLA 79:312-313. June 1964.
NEUSTRO PADRE SAN DANIEL
Madariaga, Salvador de. The Genius of Spain and Other
Essays. Oxford: Clarendon Press, 1923. pp. 163-164.
PUEBLO
Lott, Robert E. "Azorin's Experimental Period and Sur-
realism. " PMLA 79:313-315. June 1964.

Baroja, Pio
AGONIAS DE NUESTRO TIEMPO
Shaw, D. L. "The Concept of 'Ataraxia' in the Later Novels
of Baroja. " BHS 34:33-34. January 1957.
EL ARBOL DE LA CIENCIA (THE TREE OF KNOWLEDGE)
Eoff, Sherman H. The Modern Spanish Novel. New York:
New York University Press, 1961. pp. 167-172.

Fox, E. Inman. "Baroja and Schopenhauer. " RLC 37:355-
359. July - September 1963.

Reid, John T. Modern Spain and Liberalism: A Study in Lit-
erary Contrasts. Stanford University Press, 1937. pp. 68-
70.
AURORA ROJA
Reid, John T. Modern Spain and Liberalism: A Study in Lit-
erary Contrasts. Stanford University Press, 1937. pp. 102-
104.
CESAR O NADA (CAESAR OR NOTHING)
Shaw, D. L. "Two Novels of Baroja: An Illustration of His
Technique. " BHS 40:155-156. July 1963.
LA DAMA ERRANTE (THE WANDERING LADY)
Nicholson, Helen S. The Novel of Protest and the Spanish
Republic. Tucson: University of Arizona, 1939. pp. 9-10.
EL GRAN TORBELLINO DEL MUNDO
Shaw, D. L. "Two Novels of Baroja: An Illustration of His
Technique. " BHS 40:156-158. July 1963.
LAS INQUIETUDES DE SHANTI ANDIA (THE RESTLESSNESS OF
SHANTI ANDIA)
Pritchett, V. S. "Pio Baroja: An Independent Temper. "
NewS 58:396-397. September 26, 1959.
EL MAYORAZZO DE LABRAZ (LORD OF LABRAZ)
Knox, Robert B. "The Structure of EL MAYORAZZO DE

LABRAZ. " Hispania 38:285-290. September 1955.
LAS TRAGEDIAS GROTESCAS
    Borenstein, Walter. "Baroja's Uncomplimentary Stereotype
    of the Latin American. " Symposium 11:50-52. Spring 1957.
ZALACAIN, EL AVENTURERO
    Eoff, Sherman H. The Modern Spanish Novel. New York:
    New York University Press, 1961. pp. 172-185.

    Jones, R. J. "Urbia and Zaro: Birth and Burial of Zala-
    cain. " CMLR 22:29-35. March 1966.

    Jones, R. L. "Laguardia. " CMLR 22:25-26. March 1966.

Blasco Ibanez, Vicente
    A LOS PIES DE VENUS
    Devlin, John. Spanish-Anticlericalism: A Study in Modern
    Alienation. New York: Los Americas Publishing Company,
    1966. pp. 109-110.
    ARROZ Y TARTANA (RICE AND CANOE)
    Warren, L. A. Modern Spanish Literature. Vol. I. London:
    Brentano's, Ltd. , 1929. pp. 183-186.
    LA BARRACA (THE HUT)
    Devlin, John. Spanish-Anticlericalism: A Study in Modern
    Alienation. New York: Los Americas Publishing Company,
    1966. pp. 97-98.
    LA BODEGA
    Devlin, John. Spanish-Anticlericalism: A Study in Modern
    Alienation. New York: Los Americas Publishing Company,
    1966. pp. 107-108.

    Nicholson, Helen S. The Novel of Protest and the Spanish
    Republic. Tucson: University of Arizona, 1939. pp. 6-7.
    CANAS Y BARRO (REEDS AND MUD)
    Devlin, John. Spanish-Anticlericalism: A Study in Modern
    Alienation. New York: Los Americas Publishing Company,
    1966. pp. 98-99.

    Eoff, Sherman H. The Modern Spanish Novel. New York:
    New York University Press, 1961. pp. 115-119.

    Warren, L. A. Modern Spanish Literature. Vol. I. London:
    Brentano's, Ltd. , 1929. pp. 186-188.
    LA CATEDRAL (SHADOW OF THE CATHEDRAL)
    Devlin, John. Spanish-Anticlericalism: A Study in Modern
    Alienation. New York: Los Americas Publishing Company,
    1966. pp. 97-104.

    Kercheville, F. M. and Raymond Hale. "Ibanez and Spanish
    Republicanism. " MLJ 17:344-347. February 1933.

    Nicholson, Helen S. The Novel of Protest and the Spanish
    Republic. Tucson: University of Arizona, 1939. pp. 5-6.

Warren, L. A. Modern Spanish Literature. Vol. I. London:
Brentano's, Ltd., 1929. pp. 189-193.
LOS CUATRO JINETES DEL APOCALIPSIS (FOUR HORSEMEN
OF THE APOCALYPSE)
Zweig, Stefan. "Hartrott and Hitler." Free World 4:234-
235. December 1942.
ENTRE NARANJOS
Warren, L. A. Modern Spanish Literature. Vol. I. London:
Brentano's, Ltd., 1929. pp. 188-189.
FLOR DE MAYO
Warren, L. A. Modern Spanish Literature. Vol. I. London:
Brentano's, Ltd., 1929. pp. 181-183.
LA HORDA
Devlin, John. Spanish-Anticlericalism: A Study in Modern
Alienation. New York: Los Americas Publishing Company,
1966. p. 108.

Warren, L. A. Modern Spanish Literature. Vol. I. London:
Brentano's, Ltd., 1929. p. 193.
EL INTRUSO
Devlin, John. Spanish-Anticlericalism: A Study in Modern
Alienation. New York: Los Americas Publishing Company,
1966. pp. 104-107.
LOS MUERTOS MANDAN
Lundeberg, Olav K. "The Sand-Chopin Episode in LOS
MUERTOS MANDAN." Hispania 15:135-140. March 1932.
EL PAPA DEL MAR
Devlin, John. Spanish-Anticlericalism: A Study in Modern
Alienation. New York: Los Americas Publishing Company,
1966. p. 109.
SONNICA LA CORTESANA
Warren, L. A. Modern Spanish Literature. Vol. I. London:
Brentano's, Ltd., 1929. p. 189.
LA TIERRA DE TODOS
Warren, L. A. Modern Spanish Literature. Vol. I. London:
Brentano's, Ltd., 1929. pp. 194-195.

Caballero, Fernan
CLEMENCIA
Warren, L. A. Modern Spanish Literature. Vol. I. London:
Brentano's, Ltd., 1929. pp. 83-86.
ELIA O LA ESPAÑA TREINTA AÑOS HA
Hespelt, E. Herman and Stanley T. Williams. "Washington
Irving's Notes on Fernan Caballero's Stories." PMLA 49:
1135-1136. December 1934.
LA FAMILIA DE ALVAREDA (ALVAREDA FAMILY)
Hespelt, E. Herman. "The Genesis of LA FAMILIA DE
ALVAREDA." HR 2:179-201. July 1934.

Hespelt, E. Herman and Stanley T. Williams. "Washington
Irving's Notes on Fernan Cabellero's Stories." PMLA 49:
1131-1139. December 1934.

LA GAVIOTA (THE SEA GULL)
Ford, J. D. M. Main Currents of Spanish Literature. New York: Holt and Company, 1919. pp. 222-223.

Owen, Arthur L. "Psychological Aspects of Spanish Realism. " Hispania 14:1-2. February 1931.

Qualia, Charles B. "LA GAVIOTA One Hundred Years After. " Hispania 34:63-67. February 1951.

Walton, L. B. Perez Galdos and the Spanish Novel of the Nineteenth Century. London: J. M. Dent and Sons, 1927. pp. 20-23.

Warren, L. A. Modern Spanish Literature. Vol. I. London: Brentano's, Ltd., 1929. pp. 74-80.

Camba, Francisco
EL PECADO DE SAN JESUSITO
Warren, L. A. Modern Spanish Literature. Vol. I. London: Brentano's, Ltd., 1929. pp. 317-318.
LA REVOLUCION DE LAINO
Warren, L. A. Modern Spanish Literature. Vol. I. London: Brentano's, Ltd., 1929. p. 318.

Carcano, Francisco
LA HIJA DE MARTE
Douglas, Frances. "Contemporary Spanish Literature. " Hispania 14:148-149. March 1931.

Cela, Camilo Jose
LA CATIRA
Kirsner, Robert. The Novels and Travels of Camilo Jose Cela. Chapel Hill: University of North Carolina Press, 1963. pp. 93-99.
LA COLMENA
Flasher, John J. "Aspects of Novelistic Technique in Cela's LA COLMENA. " WVUPP 12:30-43. November 1959.

Kirsner, Robert. The Novels and Travels of Camilo Jose Cela. Chapel Hill: University of North Carolina Press, 1963. pp. 57-84.
LA FAMILIA DE PASCUAL DUARTE (THE FAMILY OF PASCUAL DUARTE)
Donahue, Francis. "Cela and Spanish 'Tremendismo.' " WHR 20:301-306. Autumn 1966.

Eoff, Sherman. "Tragedy of the Unwanted Person, in Three Versions: Pablos de Segovia, Pito Perez, Pascual Duarte. " Hispania 39:193-195. May 1956.

Feldman, David M. "Camilo Jose Cela and LA FAMILIA DE PASCUAL DUARTE. " Hispania 44:656-659. December

1961.

Kirsner, Robert. The Novels and Travels of Camilo Jose Cela. Chapel Hill: University of North Carolina Press, 1963. pp. 21-34.

Wade, Gerald E. "The Cult of Violence in the Contemporary Spanish Novel." TSL 1:51-53. 1956.
MRS. CALDWELL HABLA CON SU HIJO
Kirsner, Robert. The Novels and Travels of Camilo Jose Cela. Chapel Hill: University of North Carolina Press, 1963. pp. 85-92.
NEUVAS ANDANZAS Y DESVENTURAS DE LAZARILLO DE TORMES
Kirsner, Robert. The Novels and Travels of Camilo Jose Cela. Chapel Hill: University of North Carolina Press, 1963. pp. 47-56.

Rand, Marguerite C. "Lazarillo de Tormes, Classic and Contemporary." Hispania 44:222-229. May 1961.
PABELLON DE REPOSO
Kirsner, Robert. The Novels and Travels of Camilo Jose Cela. Chapel Hill: University of North Carolina Press, 1963. pp. 35-46.
LA CELESTINA
Ayllon, Candido. "Death in LA CELESTINA." Hispania 41: 160-163. May 1958.

Ayllon, Candido. "Negativism and Dramatic Structure in LA CELESTINA." Hispania 46:290-294. May 1963.

Ayllon, Candido. "Petrarch and Fernando de Rojas." RR 54:81-94. April 1963.

Barbera, Raymond E. "Calisto: The Paradoxical Hero." Hispania 47:256-257. May 1964.

Barbera, Raymond E. "A Harlot, a Heroine." Hispania 48: 790-797. December 1965.

Barbera, Raymond E. "Sempronio." Hispania 45:441-442. September 1962.

Basdekis, Demetrius. "Romantic Elements in LA CELESTINA." Hispania 44:52-54. March 1961.

Bell, Aubrey F. G. Castilian Literature. Oxford: Clarendon Press, 1938. pp. 41-54.

Brault, Gerard J. "English Translations of the CELESTINA in the Sixteenth Century." HR 28:301-312. October 1960.

Chandler, Richard E. and Kessel Schwartz. A New History

of Spanish Literature. Baton Rouge: Louisiana State University Press, 1961. pp. 172-175.

Clarke, Butler. Spanish Literature: An Elementary Handbook. London: George Allen and Unwin Ltd., 1921. pp. 81-86.

Deyermond, A. D. The Petrarchan Sources of LA CELESTINA. London: Oxford University Press, 1961.

Deyermond, A. D. "The Text-Book Mishandled: Andreas Capellanus and the Opening Scene of LA CELESTINA." Neophil 45:218-221. July 1961.

Earle, Peter G. "Four Stage Adaptations of LA CELESTINA." Hispania 38:46-51. March 1955.

Earle, Peter G. "Love Concepts in LA CARCEL DE AMOR and LA CELESTINA." Hispania 39:92-95. March 1956.

Flightner, James A. "Pleberio." Hispania 47:79-81. March 1964.

Foster, David William. "Some Attitudes towards Love in the CELESTINA." Hispania 48:484-491. September 1965.

Frank, Rachel. "Four Paradoxes in THE CELESTINA." RR 38:53-68. February 1947.

Gillet, Joseph E. " 'Comedor de huevos' (?) (CELESTINA, Aucto I)." HR 24:144-147. April 1956.

Gilman, Stephen. "A Propos of 'El Tiempo en LA CELESTINA' by Manuel J. Asensio." HR 21:42-45. January 1953.

Gilman, Stephen. "The 'Argumentos' to LA CELESTINA." RPh 8:71-78. November 1954.

Gilman, Stephen. The Art of LA CELESTINA. Madison: University of Wisconsin Press, 1956.

Gilman, Stephen. "The Case of Alvaro de Montalban." MLN 78:113-125. March 1963.

Gilman, Stephen. "The Fall of Fortune: From Allegory to Fiction." FiR 4:337-354. October-December 1957.

Gilman, Stephen. "Fortune and Space in LA CELESTINA." RF 66:342-360. 1955.

Gilman, Stephen. "Rebirth of a Classic: CELESTINA." Varieties of Literary Experience: Eighteen Essays in World Literature. (ed.) Stanley Burnshaw. New York: New York

University Press, 1962. pp. 283-305.

Gilman, Stephen and Michael J. Ruggerio. "Rodrigo de Reinosa and LA CELESTINA. " RF 73:255-284. 1961.

Green, Otis H. "Additional Note on the CELESTINA and the Inquisition. " HR 16:70-71. January 1948.

Green, Otis H. "The CELESTINA and the Inquisition. " HR 15:211-216. January 1947.

Green, Otis H. " 'Lo de tu abuela con el ximio' (CELESTINA, auto I). " HR 24:1-12. January 1956.

Green, Otis H. "On Rojas' Description of Melibea. " HR 14: 254-256. July 1946.

Heller, J. L. and R. L. Grismer. "Seneca in the Celestinesque Novel. " HR 12:29-48. January 1944.

Herriott, J. Homer. "The Authorship of Act I of LA CELESTINA. " HR 31:153-159. April 1963.

Herriott, J. Homer. Towards a Critical Edition of the CELESTINA: A Filiation of Early Editions. Madison and Milwaukee: University of Wisconsin Press, 1964. 293 pp.

Houck, Helen Phipps. "Mabbe's Paganization of the CELESTINA. " PMLA 54:422-431. June 1939.

House, Ralph E. , Margaret Mulroney, and Ilse G. Probst. "Notes on the Authorship of the CELESTINA. " PQ 3:81-91. April 1924.

House, Ralph E. "The Present Status of the Problem of Authorship of the CELESTINA. " PQ 2:38-47. January 1923.

Krause, Anna. "Deciphering the Epistle-Preface to the COMEDIA DE CALISTO Y MELIBEA. " RR 44:89-101. April 1953.

LaGrone, Gregory G. "Salas Barbadillo and the CELESTINA. " HR 9:440-458. October 1941.

Lida de Malkiel, Maria Rosa. "Two Spanish Masterpieces: THE BOOK OF GOOD LOVE and THE CELESTINA. " ISLL 49:51-98. 1961.

Loehlin, Marian R. "Celestina of the Twenty Hands. " Hispania 42:309-316. September 1959.

Macdonald, Inez. "Some Observations on the CELESTINA." HR 22:264-281. October 1954.

McPheeters, D. W. "The Corrector Alonso de Proaza and the CELESTINA. " HR 24:13-25. January 1956.

McPheeters, D. W. "The Element of Fatality in the TRAGI-COMEDIA DE CALISTO Y MELIBEA. " Symposium 8:331-334. Winter 1954.

Martin, John W. "Some Uses of the Old Spanish Past Subjunctives (With Reference to the Authorship of LA CELESTINA). " RPh 12:52-67. August 1958.

Mendeloff, Henry. "The Passive Voice in LA CELESTINA." RPh 18:41-46. August 1964.

Moore, John A. "Ambivalence of Will in LA CELESTINA. " Hispania 47:251-255. May 1964.

Morby, Edwin S. "LA CELESTINA Viewed as a Morality Play. " RPh 16:323-331. February 1963.

Northrup, George Tyler. An Introduction to Spanish Literature. Chicago: University of Chicago Press, 1925. pp. 162-169.

Olson, Paul R. "An Ovidian Conceit in Petrarch and Rojas." MLN 81:217-221. March 1966.

Penney, Clara Louisa. The Book Called CELESTINA. New York: Hispanic Society of America, 1954. 157 pp.

Perrier, J. L. A Short History of Spanish Literature. Williamsport: Bayard Press, 1924. pp. 23-25.

Poston, Lawrence Sanford, Jr. An Etymological Vocabulary to THE CELESTINA, A-E. Chicago: University of Chicago Libraries, 1940.

Randall, Dale B. J. The Golden Tapestry. Durham: Duke University Press, 1963. pp. 164-173.

Reynolds, John J. " 'La Moca Esperaua al Ministro. ' " RomN 5:200-202. Spring 1964.

Russell, P. E. "Ambiguity in LA CELESTINA. " BHS 40:35-40. January 1963.

Russell, P. E. "The Art of Fernando de Rojas. " BHS 34:160-167. July 1957.

Russell, P. E. "Literary Tradition and Social Reality in LA CELESTINA. " BHS 41:230-237. October 1964.

Schevill, Rudolph. Cervantes. London: John Murray, 1919.

pp. 177-181.

Sisto, David T. "The String in the Conjurations of LA
CELESTINA and DONA BARBARA. " RomN 1:50-52. November 1959.

Spitzer, Leo. "A New Book on the Art of THE CELESTINA."
HR 25:1-25. January 1957. (Rejoinder by Stephen Gilman:
HR 25:112-121. April 1957.)

"Star-Crossed Lovers. " TLS, June 19, 1959, p. 368.

Vollmer, Sylvia M. "The Position of Woman in Spain as
Seen in Spanish Literature. " Hispania 8:230-232. October
1925.

Wardropper, Bruce W. "Pleberio's Lament for Melibea
and the Medieval Elegiac Tradition. " MLN 79:140-152.
March 1964.

Webber, Edwin J. "The CELESTINA as an 'Arte de
Amores. ' " MP 55:145-153. February 1958.

Webber, Edwin J. "Tragedy and Comedy in the CELES-
TINA. " Hispania 35:318-320. August 1952.

Cervantes, Miguel de
   EL AMANTE LIBERAL (THE LIBERAL LOVER)
      de Sismonde, J. C. L. Simonde. Historical View of the
      Literature of the South of Europe. London: Henry G. Bohn,
      1902. pp. 258-260.
   EL CASAMIENTO ENGANOSO
      Grant, R. Patricia. "Cervantes' EL CASAMIENTO EN-
      GANOSO and Fletcher's RULE A WIFE AND HAVE A
      WIFE. " HR 12:330-338. October 1944.

      Montgomery, Lois. "Confided Property. " RR 18:30-31.
      January - March 1927.

      Waley, Pamela. "The Unity of the CASAMIENTO EN-
      GANOSO and the COLOQUIO DE LOS PERROS. " BHS 34:
      201-212. October 1957.
   CELOSO EXTREMENO (THE JEALOUS ESTREMADURAN)
      Atkinson, William C. "Cervantes, El Pinciano, and the
      NOVELAS EJEMPLARES. " HR 16:203-204. July 1948.

      Lewis, D. B. Wyndham. The Shadow of Cervantes. New
      York: Sheed and Ward, 1962. pp. 156-157.
   COLOQUIO DE LOS PERROS (THE COLLOQUY OF THE DOGS)
      Hansen, Terrence L. "Folk Narrative Motifs, Beliefs, and
      Proverbs in Cervantes' EXEMPLARY NOVELS. " JAF 72:
      25-28. January - March 1959.

Murillo, L. A. "Cervantes' COLOQUIO DE LOS PERROS, a Novel-Dialogue. " MP 58:174-185. February 1961.

Selig, Karl Ludwig. "Cervantes and the Jesuits. " MLN 73: 514-515. November 1958.

Waley, Pamela. "The Unity of the CASAMIENTO EN-GANOSO and the COLOQUIO DE LOS PERROS. " BHS 34: 201-212. October 1957.

DON QUIXOTE

Abrams, Fred. "A Possible Italian Source of Sancho Panza's First Judgment at Barataria. " Italica 41:438-441. December 1964.

Adams, Robert M. Strains of Discord: Studies in Literary Openness. Ithaca: Cornell University Press, 1958. pp. 73-85.

Arnold, H. H. "The Most Difficult Passage of DON QUIJOTE. " MLN 50:182-185. March 1935.

Atkinson, William C. "Cervantes, El Pinciano, and the NOVELAS EJEMPLARES. " HR 16:202-203. July 1948.

Auden, W. H. "Balaam and the Ass: The Master-Servant Relationship in Literature. " Thought 29:261-265. Summer 1954.

Auden, W. H. "The Ironic Hero. " Horizon 20:86-94. July 1949.

Auerbach, Erich. Mimesis. New York: Doubleday and Company, 1957. pp. 293-315.

Barrick, Mac E. "Sancho's Trip to El Toboso: A Possible Source. " MLN 81:222-225. March 1966.

Barto, Philip Stephan. "The Subterranean Grail Paradise of Cervantes. " PMLA 38:401-411. June 1923.

Bates, Margaret. "Cervantes' Criticism of TIRANT LO BLANCH. " HR 21:142-144. April 1953.

Bell, Aubrey F. G. Castilian Literature. Oxford: Clarendon Press, 1938. pp. 141-157.

Bell, Aubrey F. G. Cervantes. Norman: University of Oklahoma Press, 1947. pp. 201-222.

Bell, Aubrey F. G. "The Character of Cervantes. " RH 80: 713-716. December 1930.

Bell, Aubrey F. G. "The Unknown Cervantes. " BSS 24:238-

241. October 1947.

Bell, Aubrey F. G. "The Wisdom of Don Quixote. " BA 21:
259-263. Summer 1947.

Bleznick, Donald W. "Don Quijote's Advice to Governor
Sancho Panza. " Hispania 40:62-64. March 1957.

Boynton, Mary Fuertes. "An Oxford Don Quixote. " Hispania
47:738-749. December 1964.

Brenan, Gerald. The Literature of the Spanish People. Cambridge: Cambridge University Press, 1951. pp. 178-198.

Brenan, Gerald. "Novelists-Philosophers: Cervantes. "
Horizon 18:25-46. July 1948.

Brenes, Dalai. "The Orthodoxy of Cervantes. " Hispania 40:
312-316. September 1957.

Broderick, James H. and Hubert L. Dreyfus. "Curds and
Lions in DON QUIJOTE: A Study of Chapter 17, Book II. "
MLQ 18:100-106. June 1957.

Browne, James R. "Cervantes and the 'Galeotes' Episode. "
Hispania 41:460-463. December 1958.

Browne, James R. "Recognition and the 'Galeotes' Episode."
Hispania 42:42-43. March 1959.

Cameron, Edith. "Women in DON QUIJOTE. " Hispania 9:
137-157. May 1926.

Cary-Elwes, Columba and Edward Sarmiento. "A Note to
Don Quixote's Adventure with the Men in White. " BHS 32:
125-129. July 1955.

Casaldvero, Joaquin. "The Composition of DON QUIXOTE."
Cervantes Across the Centuries. (ed.) Angel Flores and M.
J. Bernardete. New York: Dryden Press, 1947. pp. 56-93.

Casella, Mario. "Critical Realism." Cervantes Across the
Centuries. (ed.) Angel Flores and M. J. Bernardete. New
York: Dryden Press, 1947. pp. 195-214.

Castro, Americo. "Incarnation in DON QUIXOTE. " Cervantes Across the Centuries. (ed.) Angel Flores and M. J.
Bernardete. New York: Dryden Press, 1947. pp. 136-178.

Castro, Americo. "The Prefaces to DON QUIXOTE. " PQ
21:65-96. January 1942.

Chandler, Richard E. and Kessel Schwartz. A New History

of Spanish Literature. Baton Rouge: Louisiana State University Press, 1961. pp. 192-198.

Chesterton, G. K. "The Return of Don Quixote." Living Age 274:631-633. September 7, 1912.

Ciruti, Joan E. "Cervantes and the Words He Says Are Arabic." Hispania 40:70-72. March 1957.

Clarke, Butler. Spanish Literature: An Elementary Handbook. London: George Allen and Unwin, Ltd., 1921. pp. 149-152.

Cook, Albert. The Meaning of Fiction. Detroit: Wayne State University Press, 1960. pp. 7-23.

Croce, Benedetto. "The 'Simpatia' of DON QUIXOTE." Cervantes Across the Centuries. (ed.) Angel Flores and M. J. Bernardete. New York: Dryden Press, 1947. pp. 179-182.

Crocker, Lester G. "DON QUIJOTE, Epic of Frustration." RR 42:178-188. October 1951.

Crocker, Lester G. "HAMLET, DON QUIJOTE, LA VIDA ES SUENO: The Quest for Values." PMLA 69:278-313. March 1954.

Dale, George Irving. "The Chronology of DON QUIJOTE, Part I." Hispania 21:179-186. October 1938.

Engelbert, Jo Anne. "A Sancho for Saint Francis." Hispania 46:287-289. May 1963.

Entwistle, William J. Cervantes. Oxford: Clarendon Press, 1940. pp. 150-158.

Entwistle, William J. "Experience and Doctrine in Spanish Literature." BSS 21:128-130. July 1944.

Fitzmaurice-Kelly, James. Chapters on Spanish Literature. London: Archibald Constable and Company, 1908. pp. 151-159; 160-162.

Ford, J. D. M. Main Currents of Spanish Literature. New York: Holt and Company, 1919. pp. 94-101.

Frank, Waldo. "The Career of a Hero." Cervantes Across the Centuries. (ed.) Angel Flores and M. J. Bernardete. New York: Dryden Press, 1947. pp. 183-194.

Frank, Waldo. "DON QUIXOTE: A Modern Scripture." VQR 2:94-111. January 1926.

Fry, Gloria M. "Symbolic Action in the Episode of the Cave of Montesinos from DON QUIJOTE. " Hispania 48: 468-473. September 1965.

Fucilla, Joseph G. "The Cave of Montesinos. " Italica 29: 170-173. September 1952.

Fucilla, Joseph G. "The Role of the 'Cortegiano' in the Second Part of DON QUIJOTE. " Hispania 33:291-295. November 1950.

Gillespie, Ruth C. "Don Quijote and the 'Pecados Mortales. ' " Hispania 42:40-41. March 1959.

Gilman, Stephen. "Alonso Fernandez de Avellaneda, a Reconsideration and a Bibliography. " HR 14:304-321. October 1946. [QUIJOTE APOCRIFO]

Glaser, Edward. "The Literary Fame of Cervantes in Seventeenth-Century Portugal. " HR 23:203-211. July 1955.

Goggio, Emilio. "The Dual Role of Dulcinea in Cervantes' DON QUIJOTE DE LA MANCHA. " MLQ 13:285-291. September 1952.

Green, Otis H. "El 'Ingenioso' Hidalgo. " HR 25:175-190. July 1957.

Green, Otis H. Spain and the Western Tradition: The Castilian Mind in Literature from EL CID to Calderon. Vol. IV. Madison: University of Wisconsin Press, 1966. pp. 60-73.

Haley, George. "The Narrator in DON QUIJOTE: Maese Pedro's Puppet Show. " MLN 80:145-165. March 1965.

Hall, Robert A. , Jr. "A Possible Italian Model for Don Quixote. " Italica 24:233-234. September 1947.

Harden, Robert. "The Coins in DON QUIXOTE. " SP 59:524-538. July 1962.

Hatzfeld, Helmut. "Results from QUIJOTE Criticism Since 1947. " Anales Cervantinos 2:131-157. 1952.

Hatzfeld, Helmut A. "Thirty Years of Cervantes Criticism." Hispania 30:321-328. August 1947.

Haywood, Charles. "Cervantes and Music. " Hispania 31:132-149. May 1948.

Heiser, M. F. "Cervantes in the United States. " HR 15:409-435. October 1947.

Hendrix, W. S. "Sancho Panza and the Comic Types of
the Sixteenth Century. " HMP 2:485-494. 1925.

Herman, Ernest F. "Why Cervantes Holds Such an Im-
portant Place in Spanish Literature. " Hispania 7:317-320.
November 1924.

Herman, J. Chalmers. "Galdos' Expressed Appreciation
for DON QUIJOTE. " MLJ 36:31-34. January 1952.

Hilton, Ronald. "Four Centuries of Cervantes: The Historical Anatomy of a Best-Selling Masterpiece. " Hispania
30:310-320. August 1947.

Hinz, John. "Alice Meets the Don. " SAQ 52:253-266. April
1953.

Hoffman, E. Lewis. "Cloth and Clothing in the QUIJOTE. "
KFLQ 10:82-89. Second Quarter 1963.

Houck, Helen Phipps. "Substantive Address Used Between
Don Quijote and Sancho Panza. " HR 5:60-72. January 1937.

Immerwahr, Raymond. "Structural Symmetry in the Epi-
sodic Narratives of DON QUIJOTE, Part One. " CL 10:121-
135. Spring 1958.

Kaplan, David. "The Lover's Test Theme in Cervantes and
Madame de Lafayette. " FR 26:285-290. February 1953.

Knowles, Edwin B. , Jr. "Allusions to DON QUIXOTE Before 1660. " PQ 20:573-586. October 1941.

Knowles, Edwin B. , Jr. "DON QUIXOTE Through English
Eyes." Hispania 23:103-115. May 1940.

Knowles, Edwin B. , Jr. "The First and Second Editions of
Shelton's DON QUIXOTE Part I: A Collation and Dating. "
HR 9:252-265. April 1941.

Krutch, Joseph Wood. Five Masters. New York: Jonathan
Cape and Harrison Smith, 1930. pp. 86-101.

Levi, Albert William. "The Three Masks. " KR 18:178-182.
Spring 1956.

Levin, Harry. "DON QUIXOTE and MOBY DICK. " Cervantes
Across the Centuries. (ed.) Angel Flores and M. J. Bernardete. New York: Dryden Press, 1947. pp. 217-226.

Levin, Harry. "The Example of Cervantes. " Perspectives
USA 16:15-31. Summer 1956.

Levin, Harry. "The Example of Cervantes." Society and Self in the Novel. (ed.) Mark Schorer. New York: Columbia University Press, 1956. pp. 3-25.

Lewis, D. B. Wyndham. The Shadow of Cervantes. New York: Sheed and Ward, 1962. pp. 119-133.

Livermore, Ann. "Cervantes and St. Augustine." Month 26: 261-277. November 1961.

Lott, Robert E. "PEPITA JIMENEZ and DON QUIXOTE: A Structural Comparison." Hispania 45:395-400. September 1962.

Lussky, Alfred Edwin. "Cervantes and Tieck's Idealism." PMLA 43:1082-1097. December 1928.

McCready, Warren T. "Cervantes and the 'Cabellero Fonseca.'" MLN 73:33-35. January 1958.

McDonald, W. U., Jr. "Hazlitt's Use of DON QUIXOTE Allusions." RomN 2:27-30. Fall 1960.

McDonald, W. U., Jr. "Inglis' RAMBLES: A Romantic Tribute to DON QUIXOTE." CL 12:33-41. Winter 1960.

MacEoin, Gary. Cervantes. Milwaukee: The Bruce Publishing Company, 1950. pp. 155-179.

Madariaga, Salvador de. "Cervantes and His Time." VQR 37:234-248. Spring 1961.

Madariaga, Salvador de. DON QUIXOTE: An Introductory Essay in Psychology. Oxford University Press, 1935.

Madariaga, Salvador de. "Our Don Quixote." Hispania 11: 91-118. March 1928.

Mandel, Oscar. "The Function of the Norm in DON QUIXOTE." MP 55:154-163. February 1958.

Mann, Thomas. Essays of Three Decades. New York: Alfred A. Knopf, 1947. pp. 429-464.

Menendez-Pidal, Ramon. "The Genesis of DON QUIXOTE." Cervantes Across the Centuries. (ed.) Angel Flores and M. J. Bernardete. New York: Dryden Press, 1947. pp. 32-55.

Merimee, Ernest. A History of Spanish Literature. New York: Holt and Company, 1930. pp. 306-313.

Monas, Sidney. "The Lion in the Cage: The Quixote of

Reality. " MR 1:156-175. Fall 1959.

Moore, John A. "The Idealism of Sancho Panza. " Hispania 41:73-76. March 1958.

Moore, John A. "Is Truth Relative for Cervantes?" Hispania 44:660-662. December 1961.

Morel-Futro, A. "Social and Historical Background. " Cervantes Across the Centuries. (ed.) Angel Flores and M. J. Bernardete. New York: Dryden Press, 1947. pp. 101-127.

Northrup, George Tyler. An Introduction to Spanish Literature. Chicago: University of Chicago Press, 1925. pp. 252-261.

Novitsky, Pavel I. "Thematic Design. " Cervantes Across the Centuries. (ed.) Angel Flores and M. J. Bernardete. New York: Dryden Press, 1947. pp. 239-245.

Oelschlager, Victor R. B. "Sancho's Zest for the Quest. " Hispania 35:18-24. February 1952.

Ortega, Joaquin. "Rethinking Cervantes. " NMQ 17:405-418. Winter 1947.

Ortega y Gasset, Jose. "The Nature of the Novel. " HudR 10:24-42. Spring 1957.

Parker, A. A. "Fielding and the Structure of DON QUIXOTE." BHS 33:1-14. January 1956.

Peery, William. "THE CURIOUS IMPERTINENT in AMENDS FOR LADIES. " HR 14:344-353. October 1946.

Perrier, J. L. A Short History of Spanish Literature. Williamsport: Bayard Press, 1924. pp. 56-57.

Place, Edwin B. "Cervantes and the AMADIS. " Hispanic Studies in Honor of Nicholson B. Adams. (ed.) John Esten Keller and Karl-Ludwig Selig. Chapel Hill: University of North Carolina Press, 1966. pp. 131-140.

Predmore, Michael P. "Madariaga's Debt to Unamuno's VIDA DE DON QUIJOTE Y SANCHO. " Hispania 47:288-294. May 1964.

Predmore, Richard L. An Index to DON QUIJOTE. New Brunswick: Rutgers University Press, 1938. 102 pp.

Predmore, Richard L. "On Rereading DON QUIXOTE. " SAQ 49:498-506. October 1950.

Pritchett, V. S. "Books in General." New S&N 34:333. October 25, 1947.

Pritchett, V. S. "Books in General." New S&N 45:372-373. March 28, 1953.

Pritchett, V. S. The Living Novel and Later Appreciations. New York: Random House, 1964. pp. 439-445.

Ramirez, Alejandro. "The Concept of Ignorance in DON QUIXOTE." PQ 45:474-479. April 1966.

Randall, Dale B. J. The Golden Tapestry. Durham: Duke University Press, 1963. pp. 83-94; 134-136.

Riley, E. C. Cervantes's Theory of the Novel. Oxford: Clarendon Press, 1962.

Riley, Edward C. "Don Quixote and the Imitation of Models." BHS 31:3-16. January 1954.

Riley, Edward C. " 'El alba bella que las perlas cria': Dawn-Description in the Novels of Cervantes." BHS 33:132-137. July 1956.

Riley, E. C. "Who's Who in DON QUIXOTE? or an Approach to the Problem of Identity." MLN 81:113-130. March 1966.

Rio, Angel del. "The Equivoco of DON QUIXOTE." Varieties of Literary Experience: Eighteen Essays in World Literature. (ed.) Stanley Burnshaw. New York: New York University Press, 1962. pp. 215-240.

Rivers, Elias L. "On the Prefatory Pages of DON QUIXOTE, Part II." MLN 75:214-221. March 1960.

Roades, Sister Mary Teresa. "DON QUIXOTE and MODERN CHIVALRY." Hispania 32:320-325. August 1949.

Rogers, James Frederick. "Cervantes as Health Teacher." SR 24:282-286. July 1916.

Salingar, L. G. "DON QUIXOTE as a Prose Epic." FMLS 2:53-68. January 1966.

Sanchez, Joseph. "A Note on the Date of Composition of DON QUIJOTE." HR 4:375-378. October 1936.

Sarmiento, Edward. "On the Interpretation of DON QUIXOTE." BHS 37:146-153. July 1960.

Sarmiento, Edward. "Wordsworth and Don Quijote." BHS

38:113-119. January 1961.

Schevill, Rudolph. Cervantes. London: John Murray, 1919. pp. 40-43; 204-291; 368-369.

Schuster, Edward James. "Schizophrenia and the Flight from Reality in Golden Age Spanish Literature." KFLQ 13:107-108. Second Quarter 1966.

Schweitzer, Christoph E. "Harsdorffer and DON QUIXOTE." PQ 37:87-94. January 1958.

Smith, Paul C. "Cervantes and Galdos: The Duques and Ido del Sagrario." RomN 8:47-50. Autumn 1966.

Soons, C. A. "Cide Hamete Benengeli: His Significance for DON QUIJOTE." MLR 54:351-357. July 1959.

Soons, C. A. "A Speculation of Giordano Bruno and DON QUIJOTE." RF 71:92-102. 1959.

Spitzer, Leo. Linguistics and Literary History: Essays in Stylistics. Princeton: Princeton University Press, 1948. pp. 41-73.

Spitzer, Leo. "On the Significance of DON QUIJOTE." MLN 77:113-129. March 1962.

Stagg, Geoffrey. " 'El Sabio Cide Hamete Venengeli.' " BHS 33:218-225. October 1956.

Swanson, Roy Arthur. "The 'Humor' of Don Quixote." RR 54:161-170. October 1963.

Templin, E. H. " 'Labradores' in the QUIJOTE." HR 30: 21-51. January 1962.

Tharpe, Dorothy. "The 'Education' of Sancho as Seen in His Personal References." MLJ 45:244-248. October 1961.

Thomas, H. "What Cervantes Meant by 'Gothic Letters.' " MLR 33:412-416. July 1938.

Thomas, Sister Marie. "Extraneous Episodes in DON QUIJOTE." Hispania 36:305-308. August 1953.

Trend, J. B. "Books and Writers." Spec 186:18. January 5, 1951.

Turgenev, Ivan. HAMLET and DON QUIXOTE. London: Hendersons, 1930.

Vollmer, Sylvia M. "The Position of Woman in Spain as

Seen in Spanish Literature. " Hispania 8:313-319. November 1925.

Wardropper, Bruce W. "The Pertinence of EL CURIOSO IMPERTINENTE. " PMLA 72:587-600. September 1957.

Willis, Raymond S. , Jr. The Phantom Chapters of the QUIJOTE. New York: Hispanic Institute in the United States, 1953. 128 pp.

Wilson, Edward M. "Edmund Gayton on Don Quixote, Andres, and Juan Haldudo. " CL 2:64-72. Winter 1950.
LAS DOS DONCELLAS (LOVE'S PILGRIMAGE)
Frank, Rachel. "Deceit in Cervantes' NOVELAS EJEMPLARES. " HR 13:246-249. July 1945.

Thompson, Jennifer. "The Structure of Cervantes' LAS DOS DONCELLAS. " BHS 40:144-150. July 1963.

Vollmer, Sylvia M. "The Position of Woman in Spain as Seen in Spanish Literature. " Hispania 8:310-312. November 1925.
LA ESPANOLA INGLESA (THE SPANISH LADY OF ENGLAND)
Singleton, Mack. "The Date of LA ESPANOLA INGLESA. " Hispania 30:329-335. August 1947.
LA GALATEA
Chandler, Richard E. and Kessel Schwartz. A New History of Spanish Literature. Baton Rouge: Louisiana State University Press, 1961. p. 189.

Ford, J. D. M. Main Currents of Spanish Literature. New York: Holt and Company, 1919. pp. 89-90.

Lewis, D. B. Wyndham. The Shadow of Cervantes. New York: Sheed and Ward, 1962. pp. 95-98.

Lowe, Jennifer. "The 'Cuestion de Amor' and the Structure of Cervantes' GALATEA. " BHS 43:101-108. April 1966.

Schevill, Rudolph. Cervantes. London: John Murray, 1919. pp. 93-125.

de Sismonde, J. C. L. Simonde. Historical View of the Literature of the South of Europe. London: Henry G. Bohn, 1902. pp. 270-271.

Stagg, Geoffrey. "Plagiarism in LA GALATEA. " FiR 6: 255-276. 1959.
LA GITANILLA (THE SPANISH GYPSY)
Atkinson, William C. "Cervantes, El Pinciano, and the NOVELAS EJEMPLARES. " HR 16:200-202. July 1948.

Selig, Karl-Ludwig. "Concerning the Structure of Cervantes' LA GITANILLA. " RJ 13:273-276. 1962.

de Sismonde, J. C. L. Simonde. Historical View of the Literature of the South of Europe. London: Henry G. Bohn, 1902. pp. 255-258.

Starkie, Walter. "Cervantes and the Gypsies. " JGLS 39: 145-151. July - October 1960.

LA ILUSTRE FREGONA (THE ILLUSTRIOUS KITCHENMAID)
Lewis, D. B. Wyndham. The Shadow of Cervantes. New York: Sheed and Ward, 1962. pp. 157-158.

EL LICENCIADO VIDRIERA (DR. GLASS CASE)
Casa, Frank P. "The Structural Unity of EL LICENCIADO VIDRIERA. " BHS 41:242-246. October 1964.

King, Edmund L. "A Note on EL LICENCIADO VIDRIERA." MLN 69:99-102. February 1954.

Lewis, D. B. Wyndham. The Shadow of Cervantes. New York: Sheed and Ward, 1962. pp. 153-156.

Rand, Marguerite C. "EL LICENCIADO VIDRIERA, Created by Cervantes, Re-Created by Azorin. " Hispania 37: 141-151. May 1954.

Singer, Armand E. "Cervantes' LICENCIADO VIDRIERA: Its Form and Substance. " WVUPP 8:13-31. October 1951.

Singer, Armand E. "The Literary Progeny of Cervantes's EL LICENCIADO VIDRIERA. " WVUPP 5:59-72. May 1947.

Singer, Armand E. "The Sources, Meaning, and Use of the Madness Theme in Cervantes' LICENCIADO VIDRIERA. " WVUPP 6:31-53. June 1949.

NOVELAS EJEMPLARES (EXEMPLARY NOVELS)
Lewis, D. B. Wyndham. The Shadow of Cervantes.   New York: Sheed and Ward, 1962. pp. 150-160.

Merimee, Ernest. A History of Spanish Literature. New York: Holt and Company, 1930. pp. 304-306.

Pierce, Frank. "Reality and Realism in the EXEMPLARY NOVELS. " BHS 30:134-142. July - September 1953.

Schevill, Rudolph. Cervantes. London: John Murray, 1919. pp. 292-329.

PERSILES Y SIGISMUNDA
Chandler, Richard E. and Kessel Schwartz. A New History of Spanish Literature. Baton Rouge: Louisiana State University Press, 1961. pp. 190-192.

Ford, J. D. M. Main Currents of Spanish Literature. New York: Holt and Company, 1919. pp. 101-102.

Howarth, W. D. "Cervantes and Fletcher: A Theme with
Variations. " MLR 56:563-566. October 1961.

Lewis, D. B. Wyndham. The Shadow of Cervantes. New
York: Sheed and Ward, 1962. pp. 187-188.

Merimee, Ernest. A History of Spanish Literature. New
York: Holt and Company, 1930. pp. 302-304.

Randall, Dale B. J. The Golden Tapestry. Durham: Duke
University Press, 1963. pp. 94-102.

Riley, E. C. Cervantes's Theory of the Novel.   Oxford:
Clarendon Press, 1962.

Singleton, Mack. "The PERSILES Mystery. " Cervantes
Across the Centuries. (ed.) Angel Flores and M. J. Bernardete. New York: Dryden Press, 1947. pp. 227-238.

de Sismonde, J. C. L. Simonde. Historical View of the
Literature of the South of Europe. London: Henry G. Bohn,
1902. pp. 262-270.

RINCONETE Y CORTADILLO
Atkinson, William C. "Cervantes, El Pinciano, and the
NOVELAS EJEMPLARES. " HR 16:201-202. July 1948.

de Sismonde, J. C. L. Simonde. Historical View of the
Literature of the South of Europe. London: Henry G. Bohn,
1902. pp. 260-261.

Chagas, Manuel Pinheiro
    NOVELAS HISTORICAS
        Parker, J. H. "Henry the Navigator in Modern Portuguese
        Literature. " KFLQ 10:27-29. First Quarter 1963.

Clarin (See Alas)

Conde, Carmen
    EL MANOS DEL SILENCIO
        Cardona, Rodolfo. "Carmen Conde and the Generation of
        1936. " Hispania 46:39-43. March 1963.

Cortada, J.
    LORENZO
        Brown, Reginald F. "The Romantic Novel in Catalonia. "
        HR 13:318-322. October 1945.
    EL TEMPLARIO Y LA VILLANA
        Brown, Reginald F. "The Romantic Novel in Catalonia. "
        HR 13:314-318. October 1945.

Cosca Vayo, E. de
    LOS TERREMOTOS DE ORIHUELA
        Brown, Reginald F. "The Romantic Novel in Catalonia. "

HR 13:309-313. October 1945.

Delibes, Miguel
EL CAMINO
Johnson, Ernest A., Jr. "Miguel Delibes, EL CAMINO--
A Way of Life." Hispania 46:748-752. December 1963.

Diaz-Caneja, Guillermo
EL SOBRE EN BLANCO (THE UNADDRESSED ENVELOPE)
Douglas, Frances. "Guillermo Diaz-Caneja." Hispania 5:
29-30. February 1922.

Enriquez Gomez, Antonio
EL SIGLO PITAGORICO Y VIDA DE DON GREGORIO GUADANA
Atkinson, Wm. "Studies in Literary Decadence: I. The
Picaresque Novel." BSS 4:24-26. January 1927.

Espina, Concha
LA ESFINGE MARAGATA (MARIFLOR)
Douglas, Frances. "Concha Espina: A New Star Ascendant."
Hispania 7:115-116. March 1924.

Rosenberg, S. L. Millard. "Concha Espina, Poet Novelist
of the Montana." MLF 18:77-78. April 1933.

Warren, L. A. Modern Spanish Literature. Vol. I. London:
Brentano's, Ltd., 1929. pp. 300-303.
LA ROSA DE LOS VIENTOS
Warren, L. A. Modern Spanish Literature. Vol. I. London:
Brentano's, Ltd., 1929. pp. 303-311.

Escudero, Pamplona
LOS PUEBLOS DORMIDOS
Warren, L. A. Modern Spanish Literature. Vol. I. London:
Brentano's, Ltd., 1929. pp. 353-354.

Espronceda, Jose de
SANCHO SALDANA
Adams, Nicholson B. "Notes on Espronceda's SANCHO
SALDANA." HR 5:304-308. October 1937.
ESTEBANILLO GONZALEZ
Bates, Arthur S. "Historical Characters in ESTEBANILLO
GONZALEZ." HR 8:63-66. January 1940.

de Flores, Juan
GRIMALTE Y GRADISSA
Matulka, Barbara. The Novels of Juan de Flores and
Their European Diffusion. New York: Institute of French
Studies, 1931. pp. 246-327.

Waley, Pamela. "Love and Honour in the NOVELAS
SENTIMENTALES of Diego de San Pedro and Juan de Flores."
BHS 43:267-275. October 1966.

GRISEL Y MIRABELLA
    Matulka, Barbara. The Novels of Juan de Flores and
    Their European Diffusion. New York: Institute of French
    Studies, 1931. pp. 5-237.

    Waley, Pamela. "Love and Honour in the NOVELAS
    SENTIMENTALES of Diego de San Pedro and Juan de Flores."
    BHS 43:263-267. October 1966.

Florez, Fernandez
    VOLVORETA
        Warren, L. A. Modern Spanish Literature. Vol. I. London:
        Brentano's, Ltd., 1929. pp. 312-316.

Forrellat, Luisa
    SIEMPRE EN CAPILLA
        McMahon, Dorothy. "Humor in Nadal-Award Spanish
        Novels." KFLQ 8:75-76. Second Quarter 1961.

Ganivet, Angel
    LA CONQUISTA DEL REINO DE MAYA
        Osborne, Robert E. "Angel Ganivet and Henry Stanley."
        HR 23:29-32. January 1955.
    LOS TRABAJOS DE PIO CID
        Warren, L. A. Modern Spanish Literature. Vol. I. London:
        Brentano's, Ltd., 1929. pp. 207-210.

Gironella, Jose Maria
    LOS CIPRESES CREEN EN DIOS (THE CYPRESSES BELIEVE IN
    GOD)
        Devlin, John. "Arturo Barea and Jose Maria Gironella--
        Two Interpreters of the Spanish Labyrinth." Hispania 41:
        145-147. May 1958.

        Grupp, William J. "Jose Maria Gironella, Spanish Novelist."
        KFLQ 4:131-135. Third Quarter 1957.

        Urbanski, Edmund Stephen. "Revolutionary Novels of
        Gironella and Pasternak." Hispania 43:191-197. May 1960.

        Wade, Gerald E. "The Cult of Violence in the Contempor-
        ary Spanish Novel." TSL 1:55-56. 1956.
    UN HOMBRE
        Grupp, William J. "Jose Maria Gironella, Spanish Novelist."
        KFLQ 4:129-130. Third Quarter 1957.

        Klibbe, Lawrence H. "Gironella's WHERE THE SOIL WAS
        SHALLOW." CathW 188:399-402. February 1959.
    LA MAREA
        Grupp, William J. "Jose Maria Gironella, Spanish Novelist."
        KFLQ 4:131. Third Quarter 1957.

Goytisolo, Juan
  EL CIRCO
      Schwartz, Kessel. "The Novels of Juan Goytisolo." His-
      pania 47:303. May 1964.
  DUELO EN EL PARAISO
      Schwartz, Kessel. "The Novels of Juan Goytisolo." His-
      pania 47:303. May 1964.
  FIESTAS
      Schwartz, Kessel. "The Novels of Juan Goytisolo." His-
      pania 47:304-305. May 1964.
  LA ISLA
      Schwartz, Kessel. "The Novels of Juan Goytisolo." His-
      pania 47:305-306. May 1964.
  JUEGOS DE MANOS
      Schwartz, Kessel. "The Novels of Juan Goytisolo." His-
      pania 47:302-303. May 1964.
  LA RESACA
      Schwartz, Kessel. "The Novels of Juan Goytisolo." His-
      pania 47:303-304. May 1964.

Gracian, Baltasar
  EL CRITICON
      Iventosch, Herman. "Moral-Allegorical Names in Gracian's
      CRITICON." Names 9:215-233. December 1961.

      McGhee, Dorothy M. "Voltaire's CANDIDE and Gracian's
      EL CRITICON." PMLA 52:778-784. September 1937.

      Sarmiento, E. "A Preliminary Survey of Gracian's
      CRITICON." PQ 12:235-254. July 1033.

      Waley, P. J. "Giambattista Marino and Gracian's Falsirena."
      BHS 34:169-171. July 1957.

      Walton, L. B. "Two Allegorical Journeys: A Comparison
      Between Bunyan's PILGRIM'S PROGRESS and Gracian's EL
      CRITICON." BHS 36:28-36. January 1959.

LA HISTORIA DEL ABENCERRAJE Y DE LA HERMOSA JARIFA
      Chandler, Richard E. and Kessel Schwartz. A New History
      of Spanish Literature. Baton Rouge: Louisiana State Univer-
      sity Press, 1961. pp. 177-178.

      Glenn, Richard F. "The Moral Implications of EL ABEN-
      CERRAJE." MLN 80:202-209. March 1965.

      Matulka, Barbara. "On the European Diffusion of the LAST
      OF THE ABENCERRAJES Story in the Sixteenth Century."
      Hispania 16:369-388. November - December 1933.

Isla y Rojo, Jose Francisco
  FRAY GERUNDIO
      Helman, Edith F. "Padre Isla and Goya." Hispania 38:150-
      157. May 1955.

Sebold, Russell P. "Naturalistic Tendencies and the Descent of the Hero in Isla's FRAY GERUNDIO. " Hispania 41:308-314. September 1958.

Jarnes, Benjamin
   LOCURA Y MUERTE DE NADIE
      Ilie, Paul. "Benjamin Jarnes: Aspects of the Dehumanized Novel. " PMLA 76:247-253. June 1961.
   TEORIA DEL ZUMBEL
      Douglas, Frances. "Contemporary Spanish Literature. " Hispania 14:151. March 1931.

Laforet, Carmen
   LA ISLA Y LOS DEMONIOS
      DeCoster, Cyrus C. "Carmen Laforet: A Tentative Evaluation. " Hispania 40:188-189. May 1957.

      Zamora, Rafael Vasquez. "Appearance of Carmen Laforet on the Spanish Literary Scene. " BA 30:396. Autumn 1956.
   LA MUJER NUEVA
      DeCoster, Cyrus C. "Carmen Laforet: A Tentative Evaluation. " Hispania 40:190-191. May 1957.
   NADA
      DeCoster, Cyrus C. "Carmen Laforet: A Tentative Evaluation. " Hispania 40:187-188. May 1957.

      Eoff, Sherman. "NADA by Carmen Laforet: A Venture in Mechanistic Dynamics. " Hispania 35:207-211. May 1952.

      Wade, Gerald E. "The Cult of Violence in the Contemporary Spanish Novel. " TSL 1:53-54. 1956.

      Zamora, Rafael Vasquez. "Appearance of Carmen Laforet on the Spanish Literary Scene. " BA 30:394-396. Autumn 1956.

Larra, Mariano Jose
   EL DONCEL DE DON ENRIQUE EL DOLIENTE
      Adams, Nicholson B. "A Note on Larra's EL DONCEL. " HR 9:218-221. January 1941.

      Warren, L. A. Modern Spanish Literature. Vol. I. London: Brentano's, Ltd., 1929. pp. 63-64.

LAZARILLO DE TORMES
      Atkinson, Wm. "Studies in Literary Decadence: I. The Picaresque Novel. " BSS 4:21-23. January 1927.

      Beberfall, Lester. "The 'Picaro' in Context. " Hispania 37:288-291. September 1954.

      Chandler, Richard E. and Kessel Schwartz. A New History of Spanish Literature. Baton Rouge: Louisiana State University Press, 1961. pp. 181-183.

Chapman, K. P. "LAZARILLO DE TORMES, a Jest-Book and Benedik. " MLR 55:565-567. October 1960.

Clarke, Butler. Spanish Literature: An Elementary Handbook. London: George Allen and Unwin, Ltd., 1921. pp. 88-90.

Deyermond, A. D. "The Corrupted Vision: Further Thoughts on LAZARILLO DE TORMES. " FMLS 1:246-249. July 1965.

Deyermond, A. D. "Lazarus and Lazarillo. " SSF 2:351-357. Summer 1965.

Gillet, Joseph E. "A Note on the LAZARILLO DE TORMES." MLN 55:130-134. February 1940.

Gilman, Stephen. "The Death of Lazarillo de Tormes. " PMLA 81:149-166. June 1966.

Grass, Roland. "Morality in the Picaresque Novel. " Hispania 42:196-198. May 1959.

Hespelt, E. Herman. "The First German Translation of LAZARILLO DE TORMES. " HR 4:170-175. April 1936.

Hollmann, Werner. "Thomas Mann's FELIX KRULL and LAZARILLO. " MLN 66:445-451. November 1951.

Hutman, Norma Louise. "Universality and Unity in the LAZARILLO DE TORMES. " PMLA 76:469-473. December 1961.

Keller, Daniel S. "A Curious Latin Version of LAZARILLO DE TORMES. " PQ 37:105-110. January 1958.

Lovett, Gabriel H. "LAZARILLO DE TORMES in Russia. " MLJ 36:166-174. April 1952.

Merimee, Ernest. A History of Spanish Literature. New York: Holt and Company, 1930. pp. 205-206.

Morris, C. B. "Lazaro and the Squire: 'Hombres de Bien.' " BHS 41:238-241. October 1964.

Perez, Louis C. "On Laughter in the LAZARILLO DE TORMES. " Hispania 43:529-532. December 1960.

Perrier, J. L. A Short History of Spanish Literature. Williamsport: Bayard Press, 1924. pp. 45-46.

Piper, Anson C. "The 'Breadly Paradise' of Lazarillo de Tormes. " Hispania 44:269-271. May 1961.

Rand, Marguerite C. "Lazarillo de Tormes, Classic and
Contemporary. " Hispania 44:222-229. May 1961.

Randall, Dale B. J. The Golden Tapestry. Durham: Duke
University Press, 1963. pp. 57-64.

Selig, Karl Ludwig. "Concerning Gogol's DEAD SOULS and
LAZARILLO DE TORMES. " Symposium 8:138-139. Summer
1954.

Sims, E. R. "Four Seventeenth Century Translations of
LAZARILLO DE TORMES. " HR 5:316-332. October 1937.

Sims, E. R. "An Italian Translation of LAZARILLO DE
TORMES. " HR 3:331-337. October 1935.

Sloan, Arthur St. Clair. "Juan de Luna's LAZARILLO and
the French Translation of 1660. " MLN 36:141-143. March
1921.

Stamm, James R. "The Uses and Types of Humor in the
Picaresque Novel. " Hispania 42:482-485. December 1959.

Tarr, F. Courtney. "Literary and Artistic Unity in the
LAZARILLO DE TORMES. " PMLA 42:404-421. June 1927.

Willis, Raymond S. "Lazarillo and the Pardoner: The
Artistic Necessity of the Fifth 'Tractado.' " HR 27:267-
279. July 1959.

Woodward, L. J. "Author-Reader Relationship in the
LAZARILLO DEL TORMES. " FMLS 1:43-53. January 1965.

Leon, Ricardo
    EL AMOR DE LOS AMORES
        Rosenberg, S. L. Millard. "Ricardo Leon, Artist and
        Patriot. " Hispania 13:189-194. May 1930.
    LA CASTA DE HIDALGOS
        Warren, L. A. Modern Spanish Literature. Vol. I. London:
        Brentano's, Ltd. , 1929. p. 222.
    LOS CENTAUROS
        Warren, L. A. Modern Spanish Literature. Vol. I. London:
        Brentano's, Ltd. , 1929. pp. 223-238.
    EL HOMBRE NUEVO
        Reid, John T. Modern Spain and Liberalism: A Study in
        Literary Contrasts. Stanford University Press, 1937. pp.
        148-151.
    ROJO Y GUALDA
        Reid, John T. Modern Spain and Liberalism: A Study in
        Literary Contrasts. Stanford University Press, 1937. pp.
        169-179.

LOS TRABAJADORES DE LA MUERTE
> Reid, John T. Modern Spain and Liberalism: A Study in Literary Contrasts. Stanford University Press, 1937. pp. 192-193.

LIBRO DEL CABALLERO CIFAR
> Scholberg, Kenneth R. "The Structure of the CABALLERO CIFAR." MLN 79:113-124. March 1964.

Lopez de Ubeda, Francisco
> PICARA JUSTINA
>> Merimee, Ernest. A History of Spanish Literature. New York: Holt and Company, 1930. p. 316.

Macias Picavea, Ricardo
> LA TIERRA DE CAMPOS
>> Warren, L. A. Modern Spanish Literature. Vol. I. London: Brentano's, Ltd., 1929. pp. 142-151.

Madariaga, Salvador de
> EL ENEMIGO DE DIOS
>> Sedwick, Frank. "Madariaga, EL ENEMIGO DE DIOS, and the Nature of Charity." Hispania 43:169-172. May 1960.

Martin Descalzo, Jose Luis
> LA FRONTERA DE DIOS
>> McMahon, Dorothy. "Humor in Nadal-Award Spanish Novels." KFLQ 8:80-83. Second Quarter 1961.

Martinez Sierra, Gregorio
> LA HUMILDE VERDAD
>> Douglas, Frances. "Gregorio Martinez Sierra." Hispania 5:259-260. November 1922.
> SOL DE LA TARDE
>> Douglas, Frances. "Gregorio Martinez Sierra." Hispania 5:261-263. November 1922.
> TU ERES LA PAZ
>> Douglas, Frances. "Gregorio Martinez Sierra." Hispania 6:12-13. February 1923.

Mata, Pedro
> UN GRITO EN LA NOCHE
>> Warren, L. A. Modern Spanish Literature. Vol. I. London: Brentano's, Ltd., 1929. pp. 338-339.

Matute, Ana Maria
> LOS ABEL
>> Winecoff, Janet. "Style and Solitude in the Works of Ana Maria Matute." Hispania 49:65-66. March 1966.
> EN ESTA TIERRA
>> Winecoff, Janet. "Style and Solitude in the Works of Ana Maria Matute." Hispania 49:66-67. March 1966.
> FIESTA AL NOROESTE
>> Winecoff, Janet. "Style and Solitude in the Works of Ana

Maria Matute. " Hispania 49:62-65. March 1966.
LOS HIJOS MUERTOS
    Winecoff, Janet. "Style and Solitude in the Works of Ana
    Maria Matute. " Hispania 49:66-67. March 1966.

    Wythe, George. "The World of Ana Maria Matute. " BA
    40:22-23. Winter 1966.
PRIMERA MEMORIA
    Wythe, George. "The World of Ana Maria Matute. " BA
    40:25-27. Winter 1966.
LOS SOLDADOS LLORAN DE NOCHE
    Wythe, George. "The World of Ana Maria Matute." BA
    40:26-27. Winter 1966.

Montalvo, Garci O.
    AMADIS DE GAULA
        Chandler, Richard E. and Kessel Schwartz. A New History
        of Spanish Literature. Baton Rouge: Louisiana State Univer-
        sity Press, 1961. pp. 167-169.

        Place, Edwin B. "Fictional Evolution: The Old French
        Romances and the Primitive AMADIS Reworked by Mon-
        talvo. " PMLA 71:521-529. June 1956.

Montemayor, Jorge
    DIANA
        Atkinson, Wm. "Studies in Literary Decadence: III. The
        Pastoral Novel. " BSS 4:120-126. July 1927.

        Avalle-Arce, Juan Bautista. "The DIANA of Montemayor:
        Tradition and Innovation. " PMLA 74:1-6. March 1959.

        Chandler, Richard E. and Kessel Schwartz. A New History
        of Spanish Literature. Baton Rouge: Louisiana State Univer-
        sity Press, 1961. pp. 176-177.

        Harrison, T. P., Jr. "THE FAERIE QUEENE and the
        DIANA. " PQ 9:51-56. January 1930.

        Lowe, Jennifer. "The 'Cuestion de Amor' and the Structure
        of Cervantes' GALATEA. " BHS 43:100-101. April 1966.

        Randall, Dale B. J. The Golden Tapestry. Durham: Duke
        University Press, 1963. pp. 69-83.

        Sole-Leris, A. "The Theory of Love in the Two DIANAS:
        A Contrast. " BHS 36:65-79. April 1959.

        Wardropper, Bruce W. "The DIANA of Montemayor: Reval-
        uation and Interpretation. " SP 48:126-144. April 1951.

Nombela y Tabares, Julio
LA FIEBRE DE RIQUEZAS; SIETE ANOS EN CALIFORNIA (THE
LUST FOR RICHES; SEVEN YEARS IN CALIFORNIA)
Monguio, Luis. "LUST FOR RICHES: A Spanish Nineteenth
Century Novel of the Gold Rush and Its Sources. " CHSQ 27:
237-247. September 1948.

de Ocharan Mazas, Don Luis
MARICHU
Warren, L. A. Modern Spanish Literature. Vol. I. London:
Brentano's, Ltd., 1929. pp. 238-251.

Oviedo y Valdes, Gonzalo Fernandez de
CLARIBALTE
Turner, Daymond. "Oviedo's CLARIBALTE: The First
American Novel. " RomN 7:65-68. Autumn 1964.

Palacio Valdes, Armando
LA ALDEA PERDIDA (THE RUINED VILLAGE)
Glascock, C. C. Two Modern Spanish Novelists. Austin:
University of Texas Bulletin No. 2625, July 1, 1926. pp.
70-72.
LA ALEGRIA DEL CAPITAN RIBOT (CAPTAIN RIBOT'S JOY)
Glascock, C. C. Two Modern Spanish Novelists. Austin:
University of Texas Bulletin No. 2625, July 1, 1926. pp.
68-70.
EL CUARTO PODER (THE FOURTH POWER)
Glascock, C. C. Two Modern Spanish Novelists. Austin:
University of Texas Bulletin No. 2625, July 1, 1926. pp.
58-59.
LA ESPUMA (THE FROTH)
Glascock, C. C. Two Modern Spanish Novelists. Austin:
University of Texas Bulletin No. 2625, July 1, 1926. pp.
63-64.
LA FE (FAITH)
Beardsley, Wilfred A. "Certain Considerations Inviting
Reappraisal of LA FE, by Armando Palacio Valdes. "
Hispania 17:127-138. May 1934.

Beardsley, Wilfred A. "Priesthood and Religion in the
Novels of Armando Palacio Valdes. " TMV 1:59-68. 1930.

Glascock, C. C. Two Modern Spanish Novelists. Austin:
University of Texas Bulletin No. 2625, July 1, 1926. pp.
64-65.

Warren, L. A. Modern Spanish Literature. Vol. I. London:
Brentano's, Ltd., 1929. pp. 170-171.
LA HERMANA SAN SULPICIO (SISTER SAINT SULPICE)
Glascock, C. C. Two Modern Spanish Novelists. Austin:
University of Texas Bulletin No. 2625, July 1, 1926. pp.
59-63.

Showerman, Grant. "A Spanish Novelist." SR 22:395-397.
October 1914.

EL IDILIO DE UN ENFERMO (THE INVALID'S IDYL)

Glascock, C. C. Two Modern Spanish Novelists. Austin:
University of Texas Bulletin No. 2625, July 1, 1926. p.
55.

JOSE

Glascock, C. C. Two Modern Spanish Novelists. Austin:
University of Texas Bulletin No. 2625, July 1, 1926. pp.
55-57.

LOS MAJOS DE CADIZ (POPULAR DANDIES OF CADIZ)

Glascock, C. C. Two Modern Spanish Novelists. Austin:
University of Texas Bulletin No. 2625, July 1, 1926. pp.
66-68.

MARTA Y MARIA (THE MARQUIS OF PENALTA)

Ford, J. D. M. Main Currents of Spanish Literature. New
York: Holt and Company, 1919. pp. 235-236.

Glascock, C. C. Two Modern Spanish Novelists. Austin:
University of Texas Bulletin No. 2625, July 1, 1926. pp.
50-55.

Owen, Arthur L. "Psychological Aspects of Spanish Realism." Hispania 14:3-4. February 1931.

Showerman, Grant. "A Spanish Novelist." SR 22:392-394.
October 1914.

Warren, L. A. Modern Spanish Literature. Vol. I. London:
Brentano's, Ltd., 1929. pp. 166-168.

MAXIMINA

Glascock, C. C. Two Modern Spanish Novelists. Austin:
University of Texas Bulletin No. 2625, July 1, 1926. pp.
57-58.

RIVERITA

Glascock, C. C. Two Modern Spanish Novelists. Austin:
University of Texas Bulletin No. 2625, July 1, 1926. pp.
57-58.

EL SENORITO OCTAVIO

Glascock, C. C. Two Modern Spanish Novelists. Austin:
University of Texas Bulletin No. 2625, July 1, 1926. pp.
49-50.

Showerman, Grant. "A Spanish Novelist." SR 22:390-391.
October 1914.

TRISTAN O EL PESIMISMO

Glascock, C. C. Two Modern Spanish Novelists. Austin:
University of Texas Bulletin No. 2625, July 1, 1926. p. 72.

Warren, L. A. Modern Spanish Literature. Vol. I. London:
Brentano's, Ltd., 1929. pp. 171-172.

THE PALMERIN CYCLE

Chandler, Richard E. and Kessel Schwartz. A New History

of Spanish Literature. Baton Rouge: Louisiana State University Press, 1961. pp. 169-170.

Pardo Bazan, Emilia
   EL CISNE DE VILAMORTA (THE SWAN OF VILAMORTA)
     Glascock, C. C. Two Modern Spanish Novelists. Austin:
     University of Texas Bulletin No. 2625, July 1, 1926. pp.
     21-23.
   UNA CRISTIANA (A CHRISTIAN WOMAN)
     Glascock, C. C. Two Modern Spanish Novelists. Austin:
     University of Texas Bulletin No. 2625, July 1, 1926. pp.
     27-29.
   INSOLACION (SUNSTROKE)
     Brown, Donald Fowler. The Catholic Naturalism of Pardo
     Bazan. UNCSRLL 28: 107-113. 1957.

     Glascock, C. C. Two Modern Spanish Novelists. Austin:
     University of Texas Bulletin No. 2625 July 1, 1926. p. 26.
   LA MADRE NATURALEZA (MOTHER NATURE)
     Brown, Donald Fowler. The Catholic Naturalism of Pardo
     Bazan. UNCSRLL 28:99-107. 1957.

     Brown, Donald F. "Two Naturalistic Versions of Genesis:
     Zola and Pardo Bazan." MLN 52:243-248. April 1937.

     Giles, Mary E. "Impressionist Techniques in Descriptions
     by Emilia Pardo Bazan." HR 30:309-311. October 1962.

     Glascock, C. C. Two Modern Spanish Novelists. Austin:
     University of Texas Bulletin No. 2625, July 1, 1926 pp.
     24-26.

     Kirby, Harry L., Jr. "Pardo Bazan, Darwinism and LA
     MADRE NATURALEZA." Hispania 47:733-737. December
     1964.

     Knox, Robert B. "Artistry and Balance in LA MADRE
     NATURALEZA." Hispania 41:64-70. March 1958.
   MORRINA (HOMESICKNESS)
     Brown, Donald Fowler. The Catholic Naturalism of Pardo
     Bazan. UNCSRLL 28:113-122. 1957.

     Glascock, C. C. Two Modern Spanish Novelists. Austin:
     University of Texas Bulletin No. 2625, July 1, 1926. pp.
     26-27.
   PASCUAL LOPEZ
     Glascock, C. C. Two Modern Spanish Novelists. Austin:
     University of Texas Bulletin No. 2625, July 1, 1926. p. 7.
   LOS PAZOS DE ULLOA (THE PALACE OF ULLOA)
     Brown, Donald Fowler. The Catholic Naturalism of Pardo
     Bazan. UNCSRLL 28:83-99. 1957.

     Eoff, Sherman H. The Modern Spanish Novel. New York:

New York University Press, 1961. pp. 109-115.

Glascock, C. C. Two Modern Spanish Novelists. Austin:
University of Texas Bulletin No. 2625, July 1, 1926. pp.
23-24.

Warren, L. A. Modern Spanish Literature. Vol. I. London:
Brentano's, Ltd., 1929. pp. 155-165.
LA PIEDRA ANGULAR
Brown, Donald Fowler. The Catholic Naturalism of Pardo
Bazan. UNCSRLL 28:122-129. 1957.

Warren, L. A. Modern Spanish Literature. Vol. I. London:
Brentano's, Ltd., 1929. pp. 165-166.
LA QUIMERA (THE CHIMERA)
Glascock, C. C. "LA QUIMERA, by Emilia Pardo Bazan. "
Hispania 9:86-94. March 1926.

Glascock, C. C. Two Modern Spanish Novelists. Austin:
University of Texas Bulletin No. 2625, July 1, 1926. pp.
32-36.

Owen, Arthur L. "Psychological Aspects of Spanish Real-
ism. " Hispania 14:5-6. February 1931.
EL SALUDO DE LAS BRUJAS (THE SORCERESSES' GREETING)
Glascock, C. C. Two Modern Spanish Novelists. Austin:
University of Texas Bulletin No. 2625, July 1, 1926. pp.
31-32.
EL TESORO DE GASTON
Hilton, Ronald. "Dona Emilia Pardo-Bazan and the
'Europeanization' of Spain. " Symposium 6:304-305. Novem-
ber 1952.
LA TRIBUNA (THE TRIBUNE)
Brown, Donald Fowler. The Catholic Naturalism of Pardo
Bazan. UNCSRLL 28:73-83. 1957.

Giles, Mary E. "Impressionist Techniques in Descriptions by Emilia Pardo Bazan. " HR 30:307-309. October
1962.

Glascock, C. C. Two Modern Spanish Novelists. Austin:
University of Texas Bulletin No. 2625, July 1, 1926. pp.
20-21.
UN VIAJE DE NOVIOS (A WEDDING JOURNEY)
Davis, Gifford. "The Critical Reception of Naturalism in
Spain Before LA CUESTION PALPITANTE. " HR 22:105-
107. April 1954.

Glascock, C. C. Two Modern Spanish Novelists. Austin:
University of Texas Bulletin No. 2625, July 1, 1926. pp.
7-8; 19-20.

Pereda, Jose Maria de
  DE TAL PALO, TAL ASTILLA
    Davis, Gifford. "The Critical Reception of Naturalism in
    Spain Before LA CUESTION PALPITANTE. " HR 22:101-
    102. April 1954.
  DON GONZALO GONZALEZ DE LA GONZALERA
    Warren, L. A. Modern Spanish Literature. Vol. I. London:
    Brentano's, Ltd., 1929. pp. 120-124.
  PEDRO SANCHEZ
    Eddy, Nelson W. "Pardo Bazan, Menendez y Pelayo, and
    Pereda Criticism. " RR 37:336-345. December 1946.
  PENAS ARRIBA
    Warren, L. A. Modern Spanish Literature. Vol. I. London:
    Brentano's, Ltd., 1929. pp. 124-133.
  LA PUCHERA
    Lincoln, J. N. "A Note on the Indebtedness of Pereda's
    LA PUCHERA to Breton's LA INDEPENDENCIA. " HR 11:
    260-263. July 1943.
  SOTILEZA
    Eoff, Sherman H. The Modern Spanish Novel. New York:
    New York University Press, 1961. pp. 40-50.

    Eoff, Sherman. "Pereda's Realism: His Style. " Studies in
    Honor of Frederick W. Shipley. St. Louis: Washington Uni-
    versity Studies No. 14, 1942. pp. 152-156.

    Qualia, Charles B. "Pereda's Naturalism in SOTILEZA. "
    Hispania 37:409-413. December 1954.

    Warren, L. A. Modern Spanish Literature. Vol. I. London:
    Brentano's, Ltd., 1929. p. 120.

Perez de Ayala, Ramon
  A. M. D. G.
    Devlin, John. Spanish Anticlericalism: A Study in Modern
    Alienation. New York: Los Americas Publishing Company,
    1966. pp. 154-159.

    Nicholson, Helen S. The Novel of Protest and the Spanish
    Republic. Tucson: University of Arizona, 1939. pp. 11-13.
  BELARMINO Y APOLONIO (DON GUILLEN AND LA PINTA)
    Lamb, Norman J. "The Art of BELARMINO Y APOLONIO."
    BSS 17:127-138. July 1940.

    Leighton, Charles H. "The Structure of BELARMINO Y
    APOLONIO. " BHS 37:237-243. October 1960.

    Levy, Bernard. "Perez de Ayala's BELARMINO Y APOL-
    ONIO. " SpR 3:74-81. November 1936.

    Livingstone, Leon. "The Theme of the 'Paradoxe sur le
    Comedien' in the Novels of Perez de Ayala. " HR 22:217-
    218. July 1954.

Madariaga, Salvador de. The Genius of Spain and Other
Essays. Oxford: Clarendon Press, 1923. pp. 83-86.

Weber, Frances Wyers. The Literary Perspectivism of
Ramon Perez de Ayala. Chapel Hill: University of North
Carolina Press, 1966. pp. 50-77.

Weber, Frances. "Relativity and the Novel: Perez De
Ayala's BELARMINO Y APOLONIO. " PQ 43:253-271. April
1964.
LA CAIDA DE LOS LIMONES (THE FALL OF THE HOUSE OF
LIMON)
Noble, Beth. "The Descriptive Genius of Perez de Ayala
in LA CAIDA DE LOS LIMONES. " Hispania 40:171-175.
May 1957.

Weber, Frances Wyers. The Literary Perspectivism of
Ramon Perez de Ayala. Chapel Hill: University of North
Carolina Press, 1966. pp. 43-46.
LUNA DE MIEL, LUNA DE HIEL (HONEY MOON, VINEGAR
MOON)
Devlin, John. Spanish-Anticlericalism: A Study in Modern
Alienation. New York: Los Americas Publishing Company,
1966. pp. 149-154.
LUZ DE DOMINGO
Hartsook, John H. "Literary Tradition as Form in Perez
de Ayala. " RomN 7:21-25. Autumn 1964.
NOVELAS POEMÁTICAS
Madariaga, Salvador de. The Genius of Spain and Other
Essays. Oxford: Clarendon Press, 1923. pp. 82-83.
LA PATA DE LA RAPOSA (THE FOX'S PAW)
Shaw, D. L. "On the Ideology of Perez de Ayala. " MLQ 22:
160-163. June 1961.

Warren, L. A. Modern Spanish Literature. Vol. I. London:
Brentano's, Ltd., 1929. pp. 288-293.
PROMETEO (PROMETHEUS)
Fabian, Donald L. "Action and Idea in AMOR Y PEDA-
GOGIA and PROMETEO. " Hispania 41:30-34. March 1958.

Madariaga, Salvador de. The Genius of Spain and Other Essays. Oxford: Clarendon Press, 1923. pp. 82-83.

Weber, Frances Wyers. The Literary Perspectivism of
Ramon Perez de Ayala. Chapel Hill: University of North
Carolina Press, 1966. pp. 41-42.
TIGRE JUAN (TIGER JOHN)
Livingstone, Leon. "The Theme of the 'Paradoxe sur le
Comedien' in the Novels of Perez de Ayala. " HR 22:218-
220. July 1954.

Weber, Frances Wyers. The Literary Perspectivism of
Ramon Perez de Ayala. Chapel Hill: University of North

Carolina Press, 1966. pp. 79-87.
TINIEBLAS EN LAS CUMBRES
Weber, Frances Wyers. The Literary Perspectivism of
Ramon Perez de Ayala. Chapel Hill: University of North
Carolina Press, 1966. pp. 39-40.
TROTERAS Y DANZADERAS
Fabian, Donald L. "The Progress of the Artist: A Major
Theme in the Early Novels of Perez de Ayala. " HR 26:109-
116. April 1958.

Perez Galdos, Benito
EL ABUELO (THE GRANDFATHER)
Alfieri, J. J. "The Double Image of Avarice in Galdos'
Novels. " Hispania 46:727. December 1963.

Berkowitz, H. Chonon. Perez Galdos: Spanish Liberal Crusader. Madison: University of Wisconsin Press, 1948. pp.
329-333.

Walton, L. B. Perez Galdos and the Spanish Novel of the
Nineteenth Century. London: J. M. Dent and Sons, 1927.
pp. 210-213.
AITA TETTAUEN
Chamberlin, Vernon A. "Galdos' Sephardic Types. " Sym-
posium 17:85-97. Summer 1963.
EL AMIGO MANSO
Berkowitz, H. Chonon. Perez Galdos: Spanish Liberal Cru-
sader. Madison: University of Wisconsin Press, 1948. pp.
157-159.

Brenan, Gerald. The Literature of the Spanish People. Cambridge: Cambridge University Press, 1951. pp. 393-394.

Davies, G. A. "Galdos' EL AMIGO MANSO: An Experiment
in Didactic Method. " BHS 39:16-30. January 1962.

Hafter, Monroe Z. "LE CRIME DE SYLVESTRE BONNARD,
a Possible Source for EL AMIGO MANSO. " Symposium 17:
123-128. Summer 1963.

Hafter, Monroe Z. "Ironic Reprise in Galdos' Novels. "
PMLA 76:234-235. June 1961.

Livingstone, Leon. "Interior Duplication and the Problem
of Form in the Modern Spanish Novel. " PMLA 73:399-400.
September 1958.

Russell, Robert H. "EL AMIGO MANSO: Galdos with a
Mirror. " MLN 78:161-168. March 1963.

Steele, Charles W. "The Krausist Educator as Depicted by
Galdos. " KFLQ 5:138-140. Third Quarter 1958.

Walton, L. B. Perez Galdos and the Spanish Novel of the
Nineteenth Century. London: J. M. Dent and Sons, 1927. pp.
151-154.

ANGEL GUERRA

Berkowitz, H. Chonon. Perez Galdos: Spanish Liberal Crusader. Madison: University of Wisconsin Press, 1948. pp.
312-314.

Brenan, Gerald. The Literature of the Spanish People. Cambridge: Cambridge University Press, 1951. pp. 400-403.

Chandler, Richard E. and Kessel Schwartz. A New History
of Spanish Literature. Baton Rouge: Louisiana State University Press, 1961. pp. 217-218.

Elliott, Leota W. and F. M. Kercheville. "Galdos and Abnormal Psychology." Hispania 23:33-34. February 1940.

Eoff, Sherman H. The Novels of Perez Galdos. St. Louis:
Washington University Studies, November 1954. pp. 73-83;
140-141.

Walton, L. B. Perez Galdos and the Spanish Novel of the
Nineteenth Century. London: J. M. Dent and Sons, 1927.
pp. 185-195.

EL AUDAZ

Eoff, Sherman. "The Formative Period of Galdos' Social-
Psychological Perspective." RR 41:36-37. February 1950.

Erickson, Effie L. "The Influence of Charles Dickens on
the Novels of Benito Perez Galdos." Hispania 19:424-425.
December 1936.

Walton, L. B. Perez Galdos and the Spanish Novel of the
Nineteenth Century. London: J. M. Dent and Sons, 1927.
pp. 49-55.

CADIZ

Brown, Donald F. "More Light on the Mother of Galdos."
Hispania 39:402-407. December 1956.

CARLOS VI, EN LA RAPITA

Chamberlin, Vernon A. "Galdos' Sephardic Types." Symposium 17:85-97. Summer 1963.

CASANDRA

Chamberlin, Vernon A. "Galdos' Use of Yellow in Character Delineation." PMLA 79:161-162. March 1964.

Walton, L. B. Perez Galdos and the Spanish Novel of the
Nineteenth Century. London: J. M. Dent and Sons, 1927.
pp. 213-215.

LA CORTE DE CARLOS IV

Rogers, Paul Patrick. "Galdos and Tamayo's Letter-Substi-
tution Devia." RR 45:117-120. April 1954.

LA DE BRINGAS (THE SPENDTHRIFTS)
Brenan, Gerald. The Literature of the Spanish People. Cambridge: Cambridge University Press, 1951. pp. 394-396.

Pritchett, V. S. "Books in General." New S&N 42:710-711. December 15, 1951.

Shoemaker, William H. "Galdos' Classical Scene in LA DE BRINGAS." HR 27:423-434. October 1959.

Walton, L. B. Perez Galdos and the Spanish Novel of the Nineteenth Century. London: J. M. Dent and Sons, 1927. pp. 161-163.

LA DE LOS TRISTES DESTINOS
Shoemaker, William H. "Galdos' LA DE LOS TRISTES DESTINOS and Its Shakespearean Connections." MLN 71: 114-119. February 1956.

LA DESHEREDADA (THE DISINHERITED LADY)
Brenan, Gerald. The Literature of the Spanish People. Cambridge: Cambridge University Press, 1951. pp. 392-393.

Hafter, Monroe Z. "Galdos' Presentation of Isidora in LA DESHEREDADA." MP 60:22-30. August 1962.

Park, Dorothy G. and Hilario Saenz. "Galdos's Ideas on Education." Hispania 27:139-147. May 1944.

Russell, Robert H. "The Structure of LA DESHEREDADA." MLN 76:794-800. December 1961.

Walton, L. B. Perez Galdos and the Spanish Novel of the Nineteenth Century. London: J. M. Dent and Sons, 1927. pp. 130-150.

EL 19 DE MARZO Y EL 2 DE MAYO
Alfieri, J. J. "The Double Image of Avarice in Galdos' Novels." Hispania 46:722-723. December 1963.

EL DOCTOR CENTENO
Park, Dorothy G. and Hilario Saenz. "Galdos's Ideas on Education." Hispania 27:141-147. May 1944.

Walton, L. B. Perez Galdos and the Spanish Novel of the Nineteenth Century. London: J. M. Dent and Sons, 1927. pp. 154-158.

DONA PERFECTA
Berkowitz, H. Chonon. Perez Galdos: Spanish Liberal Crusader. Madison: University of Wisconsin Press, 1948. pp. 134-135; 151-152; 277-278; 292-293.

Brown, Donald F. "An Argentine DONA PERFECTA: Galdos and Manuel Galvez." Hispania 47:282-287. May 1964.

Devlin, John. Spanish-Anticlericalism: A Study in Modern Alienation. New York: Los Americas Publishing Company,

1966. pp. 87-90.

Eoff, Sherman. "The Formative Period of Galdos' Social-
Psychological Perspective." RR 41:40. February 1950.

Eoff, Sherman H. The Novels of Perez Galdos. St. Louis:
Washington University Studies, November 1954. pp. 7-8;
65-67.

Ford, J. D. M. Main Currents of Spanish Literature. New
York: Holt and Company, 1919. pp. 240-241.

Jones, C. A. "Galdos's Second Thoughts on DONA PER-
FECTA." MLR 54:570-573. October 1959.

Krappe, Alexander Haggerty. "The Sources of B. Perez
Galdos, DONA PERFECTA, Cap. VI." PQ 7:303-306. July
1928.

Mazzara, Richard A. "Some Fresh 'Perspectivas' on Galdos' DONA PERFECTA." Hispania 40:49-56. March 1957.

Sisto, David T. "Dona Perfecta and Dona Barbara." Hispania 37:167-170. May 1954.

Sisto, David T. "Perez Galdos' DONA PERFECTA and
Louis Bromfield's A GOOD WOMAN." Symposium 11:273-
279. Fall 1957.

Walton, L. B. Perez Galdos and the Spanish Novel of the
Nineteenth Century. London: J. M. Dent and Sons, 1927.
pp. 66-81.

EPISODIOS NACIONALES
Madariaga, Salvador de. The Genius of Spain and Other
Essays. Oxford: Clarendon Press, 1923. pp. 49-51.

Perrier, J. L. A Short History of Spanish Literature.
Williamsport: Bayard Press, 1924. pp. 128-129.

Walton, L. B. Perez Galdos and the Spanish Novel of the
Nineteenth Century. London: J. M. Dent and Sons, 1927.
pp. 56-65.

LA FAMILIA DE LEON ROCH (THE FAMILY OF LEON ROCH)
Berkowitz, H. Chonon. Perez Galdos: Spanish Liberal Crusader. Madison: University of Wisconsin Press, 1948. pp.
106-107; 145-146; 152-157.

Devlin, John. Spanish-Anticlericalism: A Study in Modern
Alienation. New York: Los Americas Publishing Company,
1966. pp. 90-92.

Steele, Charles W. "The Krausist Educator as Depicted by
Galdos." KFLQ 5:136-138. Third Quarter 1958.

Walton, L. B. Perez Galdos and the Spanish Novel of the Nineteenth Century. London: J. M. Dent and Sons, 1927. pp. 100-120.

LA FONTANA DE ORO

Berkowitz, H. Chonon. Perez Galdos: Spanish Liberal Crusader. Madison: University of Wisconsin Press, 1948. pp. 80-81; 84-88; 97-98; 133-134.

Elliott, Leota W. and F. M. Kercheville. "Galdos and Abnormal Psychology. " Hispania 23:30-31. February 1940.

Eoff, Sherman. "The Formative Period of Galdos' Social-Psychological Perspective. " RR 41:34-36. February 1950.

Erickson, Effie L. "The Influence of Charles Dickens on the Novels of Benito Perez Galdos. " Hispania 19:423-424. December 1936.

Hafter, Monroe Z. "The Hero in Galdos' LA FONTANA DE ORO. " MP 57:37-43. August 1959.

Hafter, Monroe Z. "Ironic Reprise in Galdos' Novels. " PMLA 76:233-234. June 1961.

Smieja, Florian. "An Alternative Ending of LA FONTANA DE ORO. " MLR 61:426-433. July 1966.

Walton, L. B. Perez Galdos and the Spanish Novel of the Nineteenth Century. London: J. M. Dent and Sons, 1927. pp. 38-49.

FORTUNATA Y JACINTA

Armistead, S. G. "The Canarian Background of Perez Galdos' 'echar los tiempos. ' " RPh 7:190-192. November 1953-February 1954.

Berkowitz, H. Chonon. Perez Galdos: Spanish Liberal Crusader. Madison: University of Wisconsin Press, 1948. pp. 105-107; 185-187; 219-221.

Brenan, Gerald. The Literature of the Spanish People. Cambridge: Cambridge University Press, 1951. pp. 396-400.

Brooks, J. L. "The Character of Dona Guillermina Pacheco in Galdos' Novel, FORTUNATA Y JACINTA. " BHS 38:86-94. January 1961.

Calley, Louise Nelson. "Galdos's Concept of Primitivism: A Romantic View of the Character of Fortunata. " Hispania 44:663-665. December 1961.

Chandler, Richard E. and Kessel Schwartz. A New History of Spanish Literature. Baton Rouge: Louisiana State University Press, 1961. p. 217.

Elliott, Leota W. and F. M. Kercheville. "Galdos and Abnormal Psychology. " Hispania 23:32-33. February 1940.

Eoff, Sherman H. The Modern Spanish Novel. New York: New York University Press, 1961. pp. 127-147.

Eoff, Sherman H. The Novels of Perez Galdos. St. Louis: Washington University Studies, November 1954. pp. 119-120.

Eoff, Sherman. "The Treatment of Individual Personality in FORTUNATA Y JACINTA. " HR 17:269-289. October 1949.

Hafter, Monroe Z. "Ironic Reprise in Galdos' Novels. " PMLA 76:235-237. June 1961.

Kirsner, Robert. "Galdos' Attitude Towards Spain as Seen in the Characters of FORTUNATA Y JACINTA. " PMLA 66:124-137. March 1951.

Madariaga, Salvador de. The Genius of Spain and Other Essays. Oxford: Clarendon Press, 1923. pp. 55-56.

Smith, Paul C. "Cervantes and Galdos: The Duques and Ido del Sagrario. " RomN 8:47-50. Autumn 1966.

Walton, L. B. Perez Galdos and the Spanish Novel of the Nineteenth Century. London: J. M. Dent and Sons, 1927. pp. 165-179.
GLORIA
Alfieri, J. J. "The Double Image of Avarice in Galdos' Novels. " Hispania 46:723-724. December 1963.

Berkowitz, H. Chonon. Perez Galdos: Spanish Liberal Crusader. Madison: University of Wisconsin Press, 1948. pp. 104-105; 137-141; 151-152; 292-293.

Devlin, John. Spanish-Anticlericalism: A Study in Modern Alienation. New York: Los Americas Publishing Company, 1966. pp. 82-87.

Eoff, Sherman H. The Novels of Perez Galdos. St. Louis: Washington University Studies, November 1954. pp. 8-10.

Eoff, Sherman H. "The Spanish Novel of 'Ideas': Critical Opinion (1836-1880). " PMLA 55:548-550. June 1940.

Erickson, Effie L. "The Influence of Charles Dickens on the Novels of Benito Perez Galdos. " Hispania 19:425-426. December 1936.

Pattison, Walter T. Benito Perez Galdos and the Creative Process. Minneapolis: University of Minnesota Press, 1954.

pp. 18-113.

Walton, L. B. Perez Galdos and the Spanish Novel of the
Nineteenth Century. London: J. M. Dent and Sons, 1927.
pp. 81-100.

Warren, L. A. Modern Spanish Literature. Vol. I. London:
Brentano's, Ltd., 1929. pp. 139-142.
HALMA
Alfieri, J. J. "The Double Image of Avarice in Galdos'
Novels." Hispania 46:726-727. December 1963.

Walton, L. B. Perez Galdos and the Spanish Novel of the
Nineteenth Century. London: J. M. Dent and Sons, 1927.
pp. 206-208.
LA INCOGNITA
Hafter, Monroe Z. "Ironic Reprise in Galdos' Novels."
PMLA 76:237-239. June 1961.

Walton, L. B. Perez Galdos and the Spanish Novel of the
Nineteenth Century. London: J. M. Dent and Sons, 1927.
pp. 181-182.
MARIANELA
Alfieri, J. J. "The Double Image of Avarice in Galdos'
Novels." Hispania 46:724-725. December 1963.

Berkowitz, H. Chonon. Perez Galdos: Spanish Liberal Crusader. Madison: University of Wisconsin Press, 1948. pp.
143-145.

Blanco, Louise S. "Origin and History of the Plot of
MARIANELA." Hispania 48:463-467. September 1965.

Chandler, Richard E. and Kessel Schwartz. A New History
of Spanish Literature. Baton Rouge: Louisiana State University Press, 1961. pp. 216-217.

Eoff, Sherman H. The Novels of Perez Galdos. St. Louis:
Washington University Studies, November 1954. pp. 10-11;
132-133.

Jones, C. A. "Galdos' MARIANELA and the Approach to
Reality." MLR 56:515-519. October 1961.

Lister, John Thomas. "Symbolism in MARIANELA." Hispania 14:347-350. November 1931.

Pattison, Walter T. Benito Perez Galdos and the Creative
Process. Minneapolis: University of Minnesota Press, 1954.
pp. 114-136.

Walton, L. B. Perez Galdos and the Spanish Novel of the
Nineteenth Century. London: J. M. Dent and Sons, 1927.

pp. 121-129.

Warren, L. A. Modern Spanish Literature. Vol. I. London:
Brentano's, Ltd., 1929. pp. 137-138.
MIAU
Brenan, Gerald. The Literature of the Spanish People. Cam-
bridge: Cambridge University Press, 1951. pp. 400-401.

Eoff, Sherman H. The Novels of Perez Galdos. St. Louis:
Washington University Studies, November 1954. pp. 29-30.

Walton, L. B. Perez Galdos and the Spanish Novel of the
Nineteenth Century. London: J. M. Dent and Sons, 1927.
pp. 180-181.

Weber, Robert J. The MIAU Manuscript of Benito Perez
Galdos: A Critical Study. Berkeley: University of California
Press, 1964.
MISERICORDIA (COMPASSION)
Berkowitz, H. Chonon. Perez Galdos: Spanish Liberal Cru-
sader. Madison: University of Wisconsin Press, 1948. pp.
329-330.

Chamberlin, Vernon A. "The Significance of the Name
Almudena in Galdos' MISERICORDIA. " Hispania 47:491-494.
September 1964.

Eoff, Sherman H. The Novels of Perez Galdos. St. Louis:
Washington University Studies, November 1954. pp. 16-23;
92-96.

Walton, L. B. Perez Galdos and the Spanish Novel of the
Nineteenth Century. London: J. M. Dent and Sons, 1927.
pp. 208-210.
NAZARIN
Eoff, Sherman H. The Novels of Perez Galdos. St. Louis:
Washington University Studies, November 1954. pp. 69-72;
121-126.

Walton, L. B. Perez Galdos and the Spanish Novel of the
Nineteenth Century. London: J. M. Dent and Sons, 1927.
pp. 205-206.
LO PROHIBIDO
Chamberlin, Vernon A. "Galdos' Chromatic Symbolism Key
in LO PROHIBIDO. " HR 32:109-117. April 1964.

Elliott, Leota W. and F. M. Kercheville. "Galdos and Abnormal Psychology." Hispania 23:34. February 1940.

Eoff, Sherman. "A Galdosian Version of Picaresque Psychology. " MLF 38:1-12. March - June 1953.

Walton, L. B. Perez Galdos and the Spanish Novel of the

Nineteenth Century. London: J. M. Dent and Sons, 1927.
pp. 163-165.
REALIDAD
    Berkowitz, H. Chonon. Perez Galdos: Spanish Liberal Cru-
    sader. Madison: University of Wisconsin Press, 1948. pp.
    224-225.

    Eoff, Sherman H. The Novels of Perez Galdos. St. Louis:
    Washington University Studies, November 1954. pp. 15-16;
    142-147.

    Hafter, Monroe Z. "Ironic Reprise in Galdos' Novels. "
    PMLA 76:237-239. June 1961.

    Portnoff, George. "The Influence of Tolstoy's ANA
    KARENINA on Galdos' REALIDAD. " Hispania 15:208-214.
    May 1932.

    Walton, L. B. Perez Galdos and the Spanish Novel of the
    Nineteenth Century. London: J. M. Dent and Sons, 1927.
    pp. 182-184.
LA SOMBRA
    Berkowitz, H. Chonon. Perez Galdos: Spanish Liberal Cru-
    sader. Madison: University of Wisconsin Press, 1948. pp.
    79-80.
TORMENTO
    Durand, Frank. "Two Problems in Galdos's TORMENTO. "
    MLN 79:513-525. December 1964.

    Eoff, Sherman H. The Novels of Perez Galdos. St. Louis:
    Washington University Studies, November 1954. pp. 118-
    120.

    Walton, L. B. Perez Galdos and the Spanish Novel of the
    Nineteenth Century. London: J. M. Dent and Sons, 1927.
    pp. 158-161.
TORQUEMADA EN LA CRUZ
    Berkowitz, H. Chonon. Perez Galdos: Spanish Liberal Cru-
    sader. Madison: University of Wisconsin Press, 1948. pp.
    315-316.

    Owen, Arthur L. "The TORQUEMADA of Galdos. " Hispania
    7:167-168. May 1924.

    Walton, L. B. Perez Galdos and the Spanish Novel of the
    Nineteenth Century. London: J. M. Dent and Sons, 1927.
    pp. 200-205.
TORQUEMADA EN LA HOGUERA
    Alfieri, J. J. "The Double Image of Avarice in Galdos'
    Novels. " Hispania 46:725-726. December 1963.

    Eoff, Sherman H. The Novels of Perez Galdos. St. Louis:
    Washington University Studies, November 1954. pp. 105-106.

Kirsner, Robert. "Perez Galdos' Vision of Spain in TORQUEMADA EN LA HOGUERA. " BHS 27:229-235. October - December 1950.

Owen, Arthur L. "The TORQUEMADA of Galdos. " Hispania 7:165-167. May 1924.

Ullman, Pierre L. "The Exordium of TORQUEMADA EN LA HOGUERA. " MLN 80:258-260. March 1965.

Walton, L. B. Perez Galdos and the Spanish Novel of the Nineteenth Century. London: J. M. Dent and Sons, 1927. pp. 200-205.

TORQUEMADA EN EL PURGATORIO

Owen, Arthur L. "The TORQUEMADA of Galdos. " Hispania 7:168-169. May 1924.

Walton, L. B. Perez Galdos and the Spanish Novel of the Nineteenth Century. London: J. M. Dent and Sons, 1927. pp. 200-205.

TORQUEMADA Y SAN PEDRO

Owen, Arthur L. "The TORQUEMADA of Galdos. " Hispania 7:169-170. May 1924.

Walton, L. B. Perez Galdos and the Spanish Novel of the Nineteenth Century. London: J. M. Dent and Sons, 1927. pp. 200-205.

TRISTANA

Eoff, Sherman H. The Novels of Perez Galdos. St. Louis: Washington University Studies, November 1954. pp. 50-53.

Walton, L. B. Perez Galdos and the Spanish Novel of the Nineteenth Century. London: J. M. Dent and Sons, 1927. pp. 195-199.

ZARAGOZA

Gilman, Stephen. "Realism and the Epic in Galdos' ZARAGOZA. " Estudios Hispanicos, Homenaje a Archer M. Huntington. Wellesley: Wellesley College, 1952. pp. 171-192.

Rodriguez, Alfred. "Galdos' Use of the Classics in ZARAGOZA. " MLN 79:211-213. March 1964.

Perez de Hita, Gines

HISTORIA DE LOS BANDOS DE LOS ZEGRIES Y ABENCERRAJES

Chandler, Richard E. and Kessel Schwartz. A New History of Spanish Literature. Baton Rouge: Louisiana State University Press, 1961. pp. 178-179.

Merimee, Ernest. A History of Spanish Literature. New York: Holt and Company, 1930. pp. 294-295.

Perez Lugin, Alejandro

LA CASA DE LA TROYA

Warren, L. A. Modern Spanish Literature. Vol. I. London:

Brentano's, Ltd., 1929. p. 317.

Picon, Jacinto Octavio
  JUANITA TENORIO
      Warren, L. A. Modern Spanish Literature. Vol. I. London:
      Brentano's, Ltd., 1929. pp. 321-323.

Polo, Gil
  DIANA
      Jones, R. O. "Bembo, Gil Polo, Garcilaso: Three Accounts
      of Love." RLC 40:526-540. October - December 1966.

      Sole-Leris, A. "Psychological Realism in the Pastoral
      Novel: Gil Polo's DIANA ENAMORADA." BHS 39:43-47.
      January 1962.

      Sole-Leris, A. "The Theory of Love in the Two DIANAS:
      A Contrast." BHS 36:65-79. April 1959.

de Queiroz, Eca
  A CIDADE E AS SERRAS (THE CITY AND THE MOUNTAIN)
      Warren, L. A. Modern Spanish Literature. Vol. I. London:
      Brentano's, Ltd., 1929. p. 253.
  O CRIME DO PADRE AMARO (THE SIN OF FATHER AMARO)
      Loos, Dorothy S. "Eca de Queiroz' Influence on the Natur-
      alistic Novel of Brazil (1880-1903)." Symposium 9:141-
      145. Spring 1955.

      Warren, L. A. Modern Spanish Literature. Vol. I. London:
      Brentano's, Ltd., 1929. p. 252.
  OS MAIAS
      Warren, L. A. Modern Spanish Literature. Vol. I. London:
      Brentano's, Ltd., 1929. pp. 253-254.
  O MANDARIM
      Keates, Laurence W. "Mysterious Miraculous Mandarin:
      Origins, Literary Paternity, Implication in Ethics." RLC
      40:520-523. October - December 1966.
  O PRIMO BAZILIO
      Loos, Dorothy S. "Eca de Queiroz' Influence on the Natur-
      alistic Novel of Brazil (1880-1903)." Symposium 9:141-145.
      Spring 1955.
  A RELIQUIA
      Boyd, Ernest. Studies from Ten Literatures. New York:
      Charles Scribner's Sons, 1925. pp. 191-193.

Quevedo, Francisco de
  EL BUSCON (THE SCAVENGER)
      Eoff, Sherman. "Tragedy of the Unwanted Person, in
      Three Versions: Pablos de Segovia, Pito Perez, Pascual
      Duarte." Hispania 39:191-192. May 1956.

      Fitzmaurice-Kelly, James. "LA VIDA DEL BUSCON." RH
      43:1-9. June 1918.

Grass, Roland. "Morality in the Picaresque Novel. " Hispania 42:193-194. May 1959.

Harter, Hugh A. "Language and Mask: The Problem of Reality in Quevedo's BUSCON. " KFLQ 9:205-208. Fourth Quarter 1962.

Iventosch, Herman. "Onomastic Invention in the BUSCON. " HR 29:15-32. January 1961.

May, T. E. "Good and Evil in the BUSCON: A Survey. " MLR 45:319-335. July 1950.

Merimee, Ernest. A History of Spanish Literature. New York: Holt and Company, 1930. p. 317.

Parker, A. A. "The Psychology of the 'Picaro' in EL BUSCON. " MLR 42:58-69. January 1947.

Randall, Dale B. J. "The Classical Ending of Quevedo's BUSCON. " HR 32:101-108. April 1964.

Randall, Dale B. J. The Golden Tapestry. Durham: Duke University Press, 1963. pp. 206-214.

Stamm, James R. "The Uses and Types of Humor in the Picaresque Novel. " Hispania 42:484-485. December 1959.

Quiroga, Elena
   ALGO PASA EN LA CALLE
      Brent, Albert. "The Novels of Elena Quiroga. " Hispania 42: 211-212. May 1959.
   LA CARETA
      Brent, Albert. "The Novels of Elena Quiroga. " Hispania 42:212-213. May 1959.
   LA ENFERMA
      Brent, Albert. "The Novels of Elena Quiroga. " Hispania 42:212. May 1959.
   LA SANGRE
      Brent, Albert. "The Novels of Elena Quiroga. " Hispania 42:211. May 1959.
   VIENTO DEL NORTE
      Brent, Albert. "The Novels of Elena Quiroga. " Hispania 42:210-211. May 1959.

Remiro de Navarra, Baptista
   LOS PELIGROS DE MADRID
      Iventosch, Herman. "Spanish Baroque Parody in Mock Titles and Fictional Names. " RPh 15:29-39. August 1961.

Rojas, Fernando de (See CELESTINA)

Romero, Luis
    CASTA DE AYER
        Grupp, William John. "Two Novels by Luis Romero." His-
        pania 39:203-205. May 1956.
    LA NORIA
        Grupp, William John. "Two Novels by Luis Romero." His-
        pania 39:201-203. May 1956.

Salas Barbadillo, Alonso Jeronimo de
    DON DIEGO DE NOCHE
        Peyton, Myron A. "Salas Barbadillo's DON DIEGO DE
        NOCHE." PMLA 64:484-506. June 1949.
    LA INGENIOSA ELENA
        LaGrone, Gregory G. "Salas Barbadillo and the CELES-
        TINA." HR 9:440-448. October 1941.
    EL SAGAZ ESTACIO
        LaGrone, Gregory G. "Quevedo and Salas Barbadillo."
        HR 10:224-230. July 1942.

        LaGrone, Gregory G. "Salas Barbadillo and the CELES-
        TINA." HR 9:452-457. October 1941.

Salvador, Tomas
    LOS ATRACADORES
        Shoemaker, Theodore H. "The Novels of Tomas Salvador."
        Hispania 44:68. March 1961.
    CABO DE VARA
        Shoemaker, Theodore H. "The Novels of Tomas Salvador."
        Hispania 44:68-69. March 1961.
    CUERDA DE PRESOS
        Shoemaker, Theodore H. "The Novels of Tomas Salvador."
        Hispania 44:67. March 1961.
    DIALOGOS EN LA OSCURIDAD
        Shoemaker, Theodore H. "The Novels of Tomas Salvador."
        Hispania 44:70-71. March 1961.
    DIVISION 250
        Shoemaker, Theodore H. "The Novels of Tomas Salvador."
        Hispania 44:70. March 1961.
    EL HARAGAN
        Shoemaker, Theodore H. "The Novels of Tomas Salvador."
        Hispania 44:71. March 1961.
    HISTORIAS DE VALCANILLO
        Shoemaker, Theodore H. "The Novels of Tomas Salvador."
        Hispania 44:69. March 1961.

San Pedro, Diego de
    CARCEL DE AMOR
        Chandler, Richard E. and Kessel Schwartz. A New History
        of Spanish Literature. Baton Rouge: Louisiana State Univer-
        sity Press, 1961. p. 171.

        Earle, Peter G. "Love Concepts in LA CARCEL DE AMOR
        and LA CELESTINA." Hispania 39:92-95. March 1956.

Flightner, James A. "The Popularity of the CARCEL DE
AMOR. " Hispania 47:475-478. September 1964.

Waley, Pamela. "Love and Honour in the NOVELAS
SENTIMENTALES of Diego de San Pedro and Juan de Flores."
BHS 43:259-263. October 1966.

Wardropper, Bruce W. "Allegory and the Role of 'El
Autor' in the CARCEL DE AMOR. " PQ 31:39-44. January
1952.

Whinnom, Keith. "Diego de San Pedro's Stylistic Reform."
BHS 37:1-15. January 1960.
TRACTADO DE AMORES
    Waley, Pamela. "Love and Honour in the NOVELAS SEN-
    TIMENTALES of Diego de San Pedro and Juan de Flores."
    BHS 43:253-259. October 1966.

Segura, Juan de
    PROCESSO DE CARTAS DE AMORES
        Place, Edwin B. "The First Novel of Letters: The PRO-
        CESSO DE CARTAS DE AMORES of Juan de Segura. " SpR
        2:36-40. March 1935.

Sender, Ramon
    IMAN
        Douglas, Frances. "Contemporary Spanish Literature. "
        Hispania 14:149-150. March 1931.
    EL LUGAR DEL HOMBRE
        Eoff, Sherman H. The Modern Spanish Novel. New York:
        New York University Press, 1961. pp. 247-254.

        Olstad, Charles. "The Rebel in Sender's EL LUGAR DEL
        HOMBRE. " Hispania 47:95-99. March 1964.
    MR. WITT EN EL CANTON
        Brown, Reginald F. "A Reader's Notes on the Contemporary
        Spanish Novel. " BSS 14:193-196. October 1937.
    LA NOCHE DE LAS CIEN CABEZAS
        Brown, Reginald F. "A Reader's Notes on the Contempor-
        ary Spanish Novel. " BSS 14:190-193. October 1937.
    PROVERBIO DE LA MUERTE (THE SPHERE)
        Eoff, Sherman H. The Modern Spanish Novel. New York:
        New York University Press, 1961. pp. 238-247.

        King, Charles L. "Sender: Aragonese in New Mexico. "
        MLJ 36:244. May 1952.

        King, Charles L. "Sender's 'Spherical' Philosophy. "
        PMLA 69:993-999. December 1954.
    EL VERDUGO AFABLE (THE AFFABLE HANGMAN)
        Wade, Gerald E. "The Cult of Violence in the Contempor-
        ary Spanish Novel. " TSL 1:54-55. 1956.

Sola, Jaime
   EL ALMA DE LA ALDEA
      Warren, L. A. Modern Spanish Literature. Vol. I. London:
      Brentano's, Ltd., 1929. p. 320.

Soriano, Elena
   ESPEJISMOS
      Winecoff, Janet. "Existentialism in the Novels of Elena
      Soriano." Hispania 47:312-313. May 1964.
   MEDEA
      Winecoff, Janet. "Existentialism in the Novels of Elena
      Soriano." Hispania 47:313-314. May 1964.
   LA PLAYA DE LOS LOCOS
      Winecoff, Janet. "Existentialism in the Novels of Elena
      Soriano." Hispania 47:310-312. May 1964.

Tapia, Eugenio de
   EL VIAGE DE UN CURIOSO POR MADRID
      Porter, M. E. "Eugenio de Tapia: A Forerunner of Meso-
      nero Romanos." HR 8:145-155. April 1940.

Tirso de Molina
   EL BANDOLERO
      Soons, C. A. "Poetic Elements in the Plots of Tirso's
      Novels." BHS 32:196-202. October 1955.

Torrente Ballester, Gonzalo
   DON JUAN
      Winecoff, Janet. "The Theater and Novels of Gonzalo Tor-
      rente Ballester." Hispania 48:426-427. September 1965.
   LOS GOZOS Y LAS SOMBRAS
      Winecoff, Janet. "The Theater and Novels of Gonzalo Tor-
      rente Ballester." Hispania 48:425-426. September 1965.

Trigo, Felipe
   LOS ABISMOS
      Watkins, Alma Taylor. Eroticism in the Novels of Filipe
      [sic] Trigo. New York: Bookman Associates, 1954. pp.
      132-134.
   ALMA EN LOS LABIOS
      Watkins, Alma Taylor. Eroticism in the Novels of Filipe
      [sic] Trigo. New York: Bookman Associates, 1954. pp.
      95-98.
   LA ALTISIMA
      Watkins, Alma Taylor. Eroticism in the Novels of Filipe
      [sic] Trigo. New York: Bookman Associates, 1954. pp.
      98-102.
   LA BRUTA
      Watkins, Alma Taylor. Eroticism in the Novels of Filipe
      [sic] Trigo. New York: Bookman Associates, 1954. pp.
      87-90.
   LA CLAVE
      Watkins, Alma Taylor. Eroticism in the Novels of Filipe

[sic] Trigo. New York: Bookman Associates, 1954. pp. 90-93.

DEL FRIO AL FUEGO
    Watkins, Alma Taylor. Eroticism in the Novels of Filipe [sic] Trigo. New York: Bookman Associates, 1954. pp. 82-84.

EN LA CARRERA
    Watkins, Alma Taylor. Eroticism in the Novels of Filipe [sic] Trigo. New York: Bookman Associates, 1954. pp. 102-105.

LAS EVAS DEL PARAISO
    Watkins, Alma Taylor. Eroticism in the Novels of Filipe [sic] Trigo. New York: Bookman Associates, 1954. pp. 93-95.

LAS INGENUAS
    Watkins, Alma Taylor. Eroticism in the Novels of Filipe [sic] Trigo. New York: Bookman Associates, 1954. pp. 70-73.

JARRAPELLEJOS
    Watkins, Alma Taylor. Eroticism in the Novels of Filipe [sic] Trigo. New York: Bookman Associates, 1954. pp. 128-132.

EL MEDICO RURAL
    Watkins, Alma Taylor. Eroticism in the Novels of Filipe [sic] Trigo. New York: Bookman Associates, 1954. pp. 105-108.

MURIO DE UN BESO
    Watkins, Alma Taylor. Eroticism in the Novels of Filipe [sic] Trigo. New York: Bookman Associates, 1954. pp. 126-128.

LA SED DE AMAR
    Watkins, Alma Taylor. Eroticism in the Novels of Filipe [sic] Trigo. New York: Bookman Associates, 1954. pp. 73-82.

SI SI PORQUE
    Warren, L. A. Modern Spanish Literature. Vol. I. London: Brentano's, Ltd., 1929. pp. 326-327.

    Watkins, Alma Taylor. Eroticism in the Novels of Filipe [sic] Trigo. New York: Bookman Associates, 1954. pp. 134-138.

SOR DEMONIO
    Watkins, Alma Taylor. Eroticism in the Novels of Filipe [sic] Trigo. New York: Bookman Associates, 1954. pp. 84-87.

Unamuno, Miguel de
    ABEL SANCHEZ
        Eoff, Sherman H. The Modern Spanish Novel. New York: New York University Press, 1961. pp. 194-197.

        Ilie, Paul. "Unamuno, Gorky, and the Cain Myth: Toward a Theory of Personality." HR 29:314-323. October 1961.

Kinney, Arthur F. "The Multiple Heroes of ABEL SAN-
CHEZ. " SSF 1:251-257. Summer 1964.

Kronik, John W. "Unamuno's ABEL SANCHEZ and Alas's
BENEDICTINO: A Thematic Parallel. " Spanish Thought and
Letters in the Twentieth Century. (ed.) German Bleiberg
and E. Inman Fox. Nashville: Vanderbilt University Press,
1966. pp. 287-297.

Marias, Julian. Miguel de Unamuno. Cambridge: Harvard
University Press, 1966. pp. 94-101.

Valdes, Mario J. Death in the Literature of Unamuno. Ur-
bana: University of Illinois Press, 1964. (ISLL 54) pp. 92-
95.
AMOR Y PEDAGOGIA (LOVE AND PEDAGOGY)
Fabian, Donald L. "Action and Idea in AMOR Y PEDA-
GOGIA and PROMETEO. " Hispania 41:30-34. March 1958.

Marias, Julian. Miguel de Unamuno. Cambridge: Harvard
University Press, 1966. pp. 85-88.

Valdes, Mario J. Death in the Literature of Unamuno. Ur-
bana: University of Illinois Press, 1964. (ISLL 54) pp. 76-
81; 129.
EL CANTO DE LAS AGUAS ETERNAS
Valdes, Mario J. Death in the Literature of Unamuno. Ur-
bana: University of Illinois Press, 1964. (ISLL 54) pp. 81-
83.
COMO SE HACE UNA NOVELA
Sarmiento, E. "Considerations Towards a Revaluation of
Unamuno. " BSS 20:91-101. April - July 1943.

Valdes, Mario J. Death in the Literature of Unamuno. Ur-
bana: University of Illinois Press, 1964. (ISLL 54) pp. 134-
137.
DON SANDALIO
Marias, Julian. Miguel de Unamuno. Cambridge: Harvard
University Press, 1966. pp. 101-104.

Valdes, Mario J. Death in the Literature of Unamuno. Ur-
bana: University of Illinois Press, 1964. (ISLL 54) pp. 137-
139.
NADA MENOS QUE TODO UN HOMBRE
Valdes, Mario J. Death in the Literature of Unamuno. Ur-
bana: University of Illinois Press, 1964. (ISLL 54) pp. 90-
92.
NIEBLA
Abrams, Fred. "Sartre, Unamuno, and the 'Hole Theory.' "
RomN 5:6-11. Autumn 1963.

Blanco Aguinaga, Carlos. "Unamuno's NIEBLA: Existence
and the Game of Fiction. " MLN 79:188-205. March 1964.

Eoff, Sherman H. The Modern Spanish Novel. New York:
New York University Press, 1961. pp. 191-194.

Foster, David William. "The Novel as Metaphor in NIEBLA. "
Renascence 18:201-208. Summer 1966.

Livingstone, Leon. "Interior Duplication and the Problem of
Form in the Modern Spanish Novel. " PMLA 73:399-400.
September 1958.

Madariaga, Salvador de. The Genius of Spain and Other Essays. Oxford: Clarendon Press, 1923. pp. 106-107.

Marias, Julian. Miguel de Unamuno. Cambridge: Harvard
University Press, 1966. pp. 88-94.

Ribbans, Geoffrey. "The Structure of Unamuno's NIEBLA. "
Spanish Thought and Letters in the Twentieth Century. (ed.)
German Bleiberg and E. Inman Fox. Nashville: Vanderbilt
University Press, 1966. pp. 395-406.

Valdes, Mario J. Death in the Literature of Unamuno. Ur-
bana: University of Illinois Press, 1964. (ISLL 54) pp. 87-
90.

Warren, L. A. Modern Spanish Literature. Vol. I. London:
Brentano's, Ltd. , 1929. pp. 202-203.

Webber, Ruth House. "Kierkegaard and the Elaboration of
Unamuno's NIEBLA. " HR 32:118-134. April 1964.
PAZ EN LA GUERRA
Livingstone, L. "Unamuno and the Aesthetic of the Novel. "
Hispania 24:442-445. December 1941.

Marias, Julian. Miguel de Unamuno. Cambridge: Harvard
University Press, 1966. pp. 78-85.

Valdes, Mario J. Death in the Literature of Unamuno. Ur-
bana: University of Illinois Press, 1964. (ISLL 54) pp. 42-
44; 70-76.
SAN MANUEL BUENO, MARTIR
Eoff, Sherman H. The Modern Spanish Novel. New York:
New York University Press, 1961. pp. 197-212.

Falconieri, John V. "The Sources of Unamuno's SAN
MANUEL BUENO, MARTIR. " RomN 5:18-22. Autumn 1963.

Marias, Julian. Miguel de Unamuno. Cambridge: Harvard
University Press, 1966. pp. 113-119.

Paucker, Eleanor K. "SAN MANUEL BUENO, MARTIR: A
Possible Source in Spanish American Literature. " Hispania
37:414-416. December 1954.

Valdes, Mario J. Death in the Literature of Unamuno. Ur-
bana: University of Illinois Press, 1964. (ISLL 54) pp. 95-
98.

Valdes, Mario J. "Faith and Despair: A Comparative Study
of a Narrative Theme. " Hispania 49:373-379. September
1966.
LA TIA TULA
Marias, Julian. Miguel de Unamuno. Cambridge: Harvard
University Press. 1966. pp. 104-113.

Valdes, Mario J. Death in the Literature of Unamuno. Ur-
bana: University of Illinois Press, 1964. (ISLL 54) pp. 130-
133.

Valera, Don Juan
  EL COMENDADOR MENDOZA
    Warren, L. A. Modern Spanish Literature. Vol. I. London:
    Brentano's, Ltd., 1929. p. 111.
  DONA LUZ
    Brenan, Gerald. The Literature of the Spanish People. Cam-
    bridge: Cambridge University Press, 1951. p. 385.

    Warren, L. A. Modern Spanish Literature. Vol. I. London:
    Brentano's, Ltd., 1929. pp. 105-107.
  PEPITA JIMENEZ
    Ford, J. D. M. Main Currents of Spanish Literature. New
    York: Holt and Company, 1919. pp. 224-226.

    Lott, Robert E. "PEPITA JIMENEZ and DON QUIXOTE: A
    Structural Comparison. " Hispania 45:395-400. September
    1962.

    Northrup, George Tyler. An Introduction to Spanish Liter-
    ature. Chicago: University of Chicago Press, 1925. pp.
    370-371.

    Owen, Arthur L. "Psychological Aspects of Spanish Real-
    ism. " Hispania 14:2-3. February 1931.

    Warren, L. A. Modern Spanish Literature. Vol. I. London:
    Brentano's, Ltd., 1929. p. 105.

Valle-Inclan, Ramon del
  COMEDIAS BARBARAS
    Madariaga, Salvador de. The Genius of Spain and Other Es-
    says. Oxford: Clarendon Press, 1923. pp. 142-144.
  FLOR DE SANTIDAD
    Madariaga, Salvador de. The Genius of Spain and Other Es-
    says. Oxford: Clarendon Press, 1923. pp. 139-140.
  EL RUEDO IBERICO
    Franco, Jean. "The Concept of Time in EL RUEDO IBER-
    ICO. " BHS 39:177-187. July 1962.

SONATA DE ESTIO
    Warren, L. A. Modern Spanish Literature. Vol. I. London:
    Brentano's, Ltd., 1929. p. 258.
SONATA DE OTONO
    Warren, L. A. Modern Spanish Literature. Vol. I. London:
    Brentano's, Ltd., 1929. pp. 258-260.
SONATA DE PRIMAVERA
    Warren, L. A. Modern Spanish Literature. Vol. I. London:
    Brentano's, Ltd., 1929. pp. 257-258.

Vilallonga, Jose
  L'HOMME DE SANG (THE MAN OF BLOOD)
    Eyster, Warren. "Two Spanish Novels." SR 69:701-704.
    Autumn 1961.

Villalonga, Llorenc
  BEARN O LA SALA DE LAS MUNECAS
    DeBoer, Josephine. "Four Mallorcan Satirists." Symposium
    14:195-196. Fall 1960.
  DESENLACE EN MONTLLEO
    DeBoer, Josephine. "Four Mallorcan Satirists." Symposium
    14:197-198. Fall 1960.
  MORT DE DAMA
    DeBoer, Josephine. "Four Mallorcan Satirists." Symposium
    14:188-190. Fall 1960.
  LA NOVELLA DE PALMIRA
    DeBoer, Josephine. "Four Mallorcan Satirists." Symposium
    14:194. Fall 1960.

Villegas, Antonio de
  EL ABENCERRAJE
    Perrier, J. L. A Short History of Spanish Literature.
    Williamsport: Bayard Press, 1924. pp. 43-44.

Zunzunegui, Juan Antonio
  LA VIDA COMO ES
    Winecoff, Janet. "The Twentieth Century Picaresque Novel
    and Zunzunegui's LA VIDA COMO ES." RomN 7:108-112.
    Spring 1966.

d'Angouleme, Marguerite
HEPTAMERON
Hartley, K. H. Bandello and the Heptameron. London:
Cambridge University Press, 1960. 37 pp.

d'Annunzio, Gabriele
THE CHILD OF PLEASURE
Harding, Bertita. Age Cannot Wither: The Story of Duse
and d'Annunzio. Philadelphia: J. B. Lippincott Company,
1947. pp. 116-118.

Kennard, Joseph Spencer. Italian Romance Writers. New
York: Brentano's, 1906. pp. 397-405.

Rhodes, Anthony. The Poet as Superman: A Life of Gabriele
D'Annunzio. London: Weidenfeld and Nicolson, 1959. pp.
43-45.

Traversi, D. A. "D'Annunzio and Modern Italy." DubR
209:142-145. October 1941.

Winwar, Frances. Wingless Victory: A Biography of Gab-
riele D'Annunzio and Eleonora Duse. New York: Harper
and Brothers, 1956. pp. 84-85.
EPISCOPO AND COMPANY
Kennard, Joseph Spencer. Italian Romance Writers. New
York: Brentano's, 1906. pp. 390-396.
THE FLAME OF LIFE
Blissett, William. "D. H. Lawrence, D'Annunzio, Wagner."
WSCL 7:29-32. Winter - Spring 1966.

Brown, Calvin S. "James Thompson and d'Annunzio on
Durer's 'Melencolia.' " JAAC 19:32-33. Fall 1960.

Harding, Bertita. Age Cannot Wither: The Story of Duse
and d'Annunzio. Philadelphia: J. B. Lippincott Company,
1947. pp. 141-146.

Kennard, Joseph Spencer. Italian Romance Writers. New
York: Brentano's, 1906. pp. 430-436.

Rhodes, Anthony. The Poet as Superman: A Life of Gabriele D'Annunzio. London: Weidenfeld and Nicolson, 1959.
pp. 100-103.

Winwar, Frances. Wingless Victory: A Biography of

Gabriele D'Annunzio and Eleonora Duse. New York: Harper and Brothers, 1956. pp. 185-189.

THE INTRUDER

Kennard, Joseph Spencer. Italian Romance Writers. New York: Brentano's, 1906. pp. 417-422.

Rhodes, Anthony. The Poet as Superman: A Life of Gabriele D'Annunzio. London: Weidenfeld and Nicolson, 1959. pp. 43-45.

Traversi, D. A. "D'Annunzio and Modern Italy." DubR 209:145-149. October 1941.

Winwar, Frances. Wingless Victory: A Biography of Gabriele D'Annunzio and Eleonora Duse. New York: Harper and Brothers, 1956. pp. 86-90.

THE TRIUMPH OF DEATH

Blissett, William. "D. H. Lawrence, D'Annunzio, Wagner." WSCL 7:28-29. Winter - Spring 1966.

Kennard, Joseph Spencer. Italian Romance Writers. New York: Brentano's, 1906. pp. 405-417.

Rhodes, Anthony. The Poet as Superman: A Life of Gabriele D'Annunzio. London: Weidenfeld and Nicolson, 1959. pp. 44-46.

Winwar, Frances. Wingless Victory: A Biography of Gabriele D'Annunzio and Eleonora Duse. New York: Harper and Brothers, 1956. pp. 85-86.

VIRGIN OF THE HILLS

Kennard, Joseph Spencer. Italian Romance Writers. New York: Brentano's, 1906. pp. 422-430.

d'Azeglio, Massimo

ETTORE FIERAMOSCA

Kennard, Joseph Spencer. Italian Romance Writers. New York: Brentano's, 1906. pp. 123-124.

NICCOLO DE'LAPI

Kennard, Joseph Spencer. Italian Romance Writers. New York: Brentano's, 1906. pp. 124-131.

Boccaccio, Giovanni

CORBACCIO

Jeffery, V. M. "Boccaccio's Titles and the Meaning of CORBACCIO." MLR 28:194-204. April 1933.

DECAMERON

Auerbach, Erich. Mimesis. New York: Doubleday and Company, 1957. pp. 177-203.

Carswell, Catherene. The Tranquil Heart. New York: Harcourt, Brace and Company, 1937. pp. 275-288.

Cate, Wirt Armistead. "The Problem of the Origin of the

Griselda Story. " SP 29:389-405. July 1932.

Chandler, S. Bernard. "Man, Emotion and Intellect in the
DECAMERON. " PQ 39:400-412. October 1960.

Chubb, Thomas Caldecot. The Life of Giovanni Boccaccio.
New York: Albert and Charles Boni, 1930. Chapter 17.

Cioffari, Vincenzo. "The Conception of Fortune in the
DECAMERON. " Italica 17:129-137. December 1940.

Clubb, Louise George. "Boccaccio and the Boundaries of
Love. " Italica 37:188-195. September 1960.

Coulter, Cornelia C. "The Road to Alagna. " PQ 18:332-336.
October 1939.

De Sanctis, Francesco. History of Italian Literature, Vol-
ume I. New York: Harcourt, Brace and Company, 1931. pp.
290-359.

Dick, Hugh G. "The Lover in a Cask: A Tale of a Tub. "
Italica 18:12-13. March 1941.

Farnham, Willard. "England's Discovery of the DECAM-
ERON. " PMLA 39:123-139. March 1924.

Ferrante, Joan M. "The Frame Characters of the DECAM-
ERON: A Progression of Virtues. " RPh 19:212-226. November 1965.

Green, Richard H. "Nature and Love in the Late Middle
Ages. " MLN 79:58-70. January 1964.

Hall, Robert A. , Jr. A Short History of Italian Literature.
Ithaca: Linguistica, 1951. pp. 111-118.

Hutton, Edward. Giovanni Boccaccio: A Biographical Study.
London: John Lane, 1910. pp. 174-179; 292-296; 311-316.

Jones, Florence N. Boccaccio and His Imitators. Chicago:
University of Chicago Press, 1910.

Kern, Edith G. "The Gardens in the DECAMERON Cornice."
PMLA 66:505-523. June 1951.

Krutch, Joseph Wood. "Boccaccio and His DECAMERON. "
Atlantic 145:656-660. May 1930.

Krutch, Joseph Wood. Five Masters. New York: Jonathan
Cape and Harrison Smith, 1930. pp. 41-52.

Lee, A. C. The DECAMERON: Its Sources and Analogues.

New York: D. Nutt, 1909.

Lipari, Angelo. "On 'Meaning' in the DECAMERON. " Italica 22:101-108. September 1945.

Lipari, Angelo. "The Structure and Real Significance of the DECAMERON. " Essays in Honor of Albert Feuillerat. (Yale Romanic Studies 22, 1943.) pp. 43-83.

Matenko, Percy. "The Prototype of Cipolla in MARIO UND DER ZAUBERER. " Italica 31:133-135. September 1954.

Mathes, Hamilton A. "DECAMERON, III, 3, and a 'Canzone a Ballo' of Lorenzo de' Medici. " MP 48:82-85. November 1950.

Montgomery, Lois. "Confided Property. " RR 18:27-29. January - March 1927.

de' Negri, Enrico. "The Legendary Style of the DECAMERON. " RR 43:166-189. October 1952.

Raleigh, Walter. "Boccaccio. " ER 14:210-229. May 1913.

Scaglione, Aldo D. Nature and Love in the Late Middle Ages. Berkeley: University of California Press, 1963. pp. 48-125.

Singleton, Charles S. and Leo Spitzer. "DECAMERON VIII, 9: 'Carapignare. ' " MLN 59:88-92. February 1944.

Singleton, Charles S. "On 'Meaning' in the DECAMERON. " Italica 21:117-124. September 1944.

Singleton, Charles S. "The Uses of the DECAMERON. " MLN 79:71-76. January 1964.

Symonds, John Addington. Renaissance in Italy. Vol. IV. Scribner, 1900. Chapter 2.

Tucker, T. G. The Foreign Debt of English Literature. London: George Bell and Sons, 1907. pp. 194-197.
FILOCOLO
Moore, Olin H. "Boccaccio's FILOCOLO and the Annunciation. " MLN 33:438-440. November 1918.

Perella, Nicolas J. "The World of Boccaccio's FILOCOLO." PMLA 76:330-339. September 1961.

Borgese, G. A.
RUBE
Boyd, Ernest. Studies from Ten Literatures. New York: Charles Scribner's Sons, 1925. pp. 182-185.

Brancati, Vitoliano
IL BELL ANTONIO
    Tenenbaum, Louis. "Vitoliano Brancati and Sicilian Erot-
    icism. " BA 31:234-235. Summer 1957.

Bresciani, Antonio
THE JEW OF VERONA
    White, Alex S. "THE JEW OF VERONA. " CJF 15:120-123.
    Winter 1956.

Butti, Enrico
AUTOMATON
    Kennard, Joseph Spencer. Italian Romance Writers. New
    York: Brentano's, 1906. pp. 375-377.
ENCHANTMENT
    Kennard, Joseph Spencer. Italian Romance Writers. New
    York: Brentano's, 1906. pp. 377-383.
L'IMMORALE
    Kennard, Joseph Spencer. Italian Romance Writers. New
    York: Brentano's, 1906. pp. 372-375.

Buzzati, Dino
THE DESERT OF THE TARTARS
    Biasin, Gian-Paolo. "The Secret Fears of Men: Dino Buz-
    zati. " IQ 6:80-82. Summer 1962.
THE GREAT PORTRAIT
    Biasin, Gian-Paolo. "The Secret Fears of Men: Dino Buz-
    zati. " IQ 6:86-89. Summer 1962.

Capuana, Luigi
GIACINTA
    Walker, E. A. "Structural Techniques in Luigi Capuana's
    Novels. " Italica 42:265-270. September 1965.
IL MARCHESE DI ROCCAVERDINA
    Walker, E. A. "Structural Techniques in Luigi Capuana's
    Novels. " Italica 42:272-274. September 1965.
PROFUMO
    Walker, E. A. "Structural Techniques in Luigi Capuana's
    Novels. " Italica 42:270-272. September 1965.

Cassola, Carlo
BEBO'S GIRL
    Sampoli, Furio. "The Italian Novel of Recent Years. " IQ
    7:26-27. Summer 1963.

    Scrivano, Riccardo. "Carlo Cassola and New Italian Fic-
    tion. " IQ 6:60-61. Fall - Winter 1962.
UN CUORE ARIDO
    Sampoli, Furio. "The Italian Novel of Recent Years. " IQ
    7:27-28. Summer 1963.

Deledda, Grazia
ANIME ONESTE

Kennard, Joseph Spencer. Italian Romance Writers. New
York: Brentano's, 1906. pp. 352-354.
ASHES
Kennard, Joseph Spencer. Italian Romance Writers. New
York: Brentano's, 1906. pp. 363-365.

Mifaud, John. "The Latest Nobel Prize Winner." NewS 30:
623. February 25, 1928.
ELIAS PORTOLU
Kennard, Joseph Spencer. Italian Romance Writers. New
York: Brentano's, 1906. pp. 354-363.
VECCHIO DELLA MONTAGNA
Kennard, Joseph Spencer. Italian Romance Writers. New
York: Brentano's, 1906. pp. 365-367.

Fogazzaro, Antonio
DANIELE CORTIS
Beaumont, Ernest. "Antonio Fogazzaro, 1842-1911." Month
26:291-292. November 1961.

Kennard, Joseph Spencer. Italian Romance Writers. New
York: Brentano's, 1906. pp. 218-220.
LEILA
Beaumont, Ernest. "Antonio Fogazzaro, 1842-1911." Month
26:294-295. November 1961.

Corrigan, Beatrice. "Antonio Fogazzaro and Wilkie Collins." CL 13:50-51. Winter 1961.

Hall, Robert A., Jr. "Fogazzaro's Maironi Tetralogy."
Italica 42:255-258. June 1965.
LITTLE WORLD OF THE PAST
Hall, Robert A., Jr. "Fogazzaro's Maironi Tetralogy."
Italica 42:249-251. June 1965.

Kennard, Joseph Spencer. Italian Romance Writers. New
York: Brentano's, 1906. pp. 220-238.

Pasinetti, P. M. "Fogazzaro's Little World of the Past:
Program Notes for an Italian 'Classic.' " IQ 7:3-14. Fall -
Winter 1963.

Wilkins, Ernest Hatch. A History of Italian Literature. Cambridge: Harvard University Press, 1954. pp. 471-472.
THE MAN OF THE WORLD
Beaumont, Ernest. "Antonio Fogazzaro, 1842-1911." Month
26:293-294. November 1961.

Corrigan, Beatrice. "Antonio Fogazzaro and Wilkie Collins." CL 13:47-50. Winter 1961.

Hall, Robert A., Jr. "Fogazzaro's Maironi Tetralogy."
Italica 42:251-253. June 1965.

Kennard, Joseph Spencer. Italian Romance Writers. New
York: Brentano's, 1906. pp. 238-241.
THE MYSTERY OF THE POET
Beaumont, Ernest. "Antonio Fogazzaro, 1842-1911." Month
26:291-293. November 1961.
THE SAINT
Hall, Robert A., Jr. "Fogazzaro's Maironi Tetralogy."
Italica 42:253-255. June 1965.

Hall, Robert A., Jr. "Fogazzaro's IL SANTO and Hoch-
huth's DER STELLVERTRETER." IQ 10:22-32. Winter -
Spring 1966.
THE WOMAN
Corrigan, Beatrice. "Antonio Fogazzaro and Wilkie Col-
lins." CL 13:39-46. Winter 1961.

Kennard, Joseph Spencer. Italian Romance Writers. New
York: Brentano's, 1906. pp. 216-218.

Foscolo, Ugo
IACOPO ORTIS
McCormick, C. A. "Ugo Foscolo and IACOPO ORTIS: Cre-
ator and Character." AUMLA 9:22-33. November 1958.

Gadda, Carlo Emilio
QUER PASTICCIACCIO BRUTTO DE VIA MERULANA
Varnai, Ugo. "Italian Letters in 1957." ILA 1:190-191.
1958.

Grossi, Tommaso
MARCO VISCONTI
Collison-Morby, Lacy. Modern Italian Literature. London:
Sir Isaac Pitman and Sons, 1911. pp. 241-243.

Kennard, Joseph Spencer. Italian Romance Writers. New
York: Brentano's, 1906. pp. 152-154.

Guerrazzi, Francesco
THE SEIGE OF FLORENCE
Kennard, Joseph Spencer. Italian Romance Writers. New
York: Brentano's, 1906. pp. 137-138.

Luciani, Vincent. "Guicciardini and the 'Risorgimento.'"
Italica 18:188. December 1941.

La Capria, Raffaele
FERITO A MORTE
Sampoli, Furio. "The Italian Novel of Recent Years." IQ
7:28-32. Summer 1963.

Levi, Carlo
CHRIST STOPPED AT EBOLI
Chiaromonte, Nicola. "Realism and Neorealism in Contem-

porary Italian Literature. " CE 14:437-438. May 1953.

Golino, Carlo L. "Some Aspects of Contemporary Italian
Fiction. " MLF 37:9-10. March - June 1952.
THE WATCH
Chiaromonte, Nicola. "Realism and Neorealism in Contem-
porary Italian Literature. " CE 14:438. May 1953.

Lorenzini, Carlo
PINOCCHIO
Gilbert, Allan. "The Sea-Monster in Ariosto's CINQUE
CANTI and in PINOCCHIO. " Italica 33:260-263. December
1956.

Malaparte, Curzio
THE SKIN
Goldstone, Herbert. "Malaparte and Moravia: Concerning
Failure and Estimate. " Western Rev 17:229-230. Spring
1953.

Manzoni, Alessandro
THE BETROTHED
Chandler, S. Bernard. "The Innominato's Perception of
Time in I PROMESSI SPOSI. " PQ 42:548-557. October 1963.

Chandler, S. B. "Point of View in the Descriptions of I
PROMESSI SPOSI. " Italica 43:386-400. December 1966.

Chase, Richard. "Notes on Manzoni's I PROMESSI SPOSI
and the English and European Traditions. " EM 8:109-123.
1957.

Collison-Morby, Lacy. Modern Italian Literature. London:
Sir Isaac Pitman and Sons, 1911. pp. 199-205.

Collison-Morby. "The PROMESSI SPOSI. " Nation (Lond)
33:742-743. September 15, 1923.

Colquhoun, Archibald. Manzoni and His Times. New York:
Dutton, 1954. pp. 165-197.

De Simone, Joseph Francis. Alessandro Manzoni: Esthetics
and Literary Criticism. New York: S. F. Vanni, 1946. pp.
67-86.

De Simone, Joseph F. "Manzoni and the Fine Arts. " Italica
28:271-278. December 1951.

Feuchtwanger, Lion. The House of Desdemona or The
Laurels and Limitations of Historical Fiction. Detroit:
Wayne State University Press, 1963. pp. 61-64.

Freidson, Marion Facinger. "The Meaning of Gertrude in I

PROMESSI SPOSI. " Italica 28:27-32. March 1951.

Hall, Robert A. , Jr. A Short History of Italian Literature.
Ithaca: Linguistica, 1951. pp. 365-366; 367-369.

Kennard, Joseph Spencer. Italian Romance Writers. New
York: Brentano's, 1906. pp. 89-115.

Meiklejohn, M. F. M. "Sir Walter Scott and Alessandro
Manzoni. " IS 12:91-98. 1957.

Norman, Hilda L. "Renzo's Garden. " Italica 16:120-122.
December 1939.

Orne, Jerrold. "The Sources of I PROMESSI SPOSI. " MP
38:405-420. May 1941.

Pritchett, V. S. Books in General. London: Chatto and
Windus, 1953. pp. 13-18.

Pritchett, V. S. "Books in General. " New S&N 42:208-209.
August 25, 1951.

Ragusa, Olga. "The Latest Manzoni. " IQ 5:107-116. Winter
1961.

Wall, Bernard. Alessandro Manzoni. New Haven: Yale University Press, 1954. pp. 23-56.

Wall, Bernard. "Manzoni's Novel and His Ideas. " DubR
226:28-40. Second Quarter 1952.

Wilkins, Ernest Hatch. A History of Italian Literature.
Cambridge: Harvard University Press, 1954. pp. 393-396.

Zimmermann, Eleonore M. "Structural Patterns in I
PROMESSI SPOSI. " Italica 39:159-172. September 1962.

Mastronardi, Lucio
    IL MAESTRO DI VIGEVANO
        Pacifici, Sergio. "From Engagement to Alienation: A View
        of Contemporary Italian Literature. " Italica 40:253-255.
        September 1963.

Masuccio, Salernitano
    NOVELLA 33
        Moore, Olin H. "The Sources of Masuccio's Thirty-Third
        Novella. " Italica 15:156-159. September 1938.

Morante, Elsa
    ARTURO'S ISLAND
        Ferrucci, Franco. "Elsa Morante's Limbo Without Elysium."
        IQ 7:34-50. Fall - Winter 1963.

McCormick, E. Allen. "Utopia and Point of View: Narrative
Method in Morante's L'ISOLA DI ARTURO and Keyserling's
SCHWULE TAGE. " Symposium 15:114-129. Summer 1961.

Varnai, Ugo. "Italian Letters in 1957. " ILA 1:188-189.
1958.

THE HOUSE OF LIARS
Ferrucci, Franco. "Elsa Morante's Limbo Without Elysium."
IQ 7:30-42. Fall - Winter 1963.

Moravia, Alberto
THE CONFORMIST
Baldanza, Frank. "The Classicism of Alberto Moravia. "
MFS 3:314-316. Winter 1957-1958.

Golino, Carlo L. "Alberto Moravia. " MLJ 36:338. Novem-
ber 1952.
CONJUGAL LOVE
Baldanza, Frank. "The Classicism of Alberto Moravia. "
MFS 3:316-317. Winter 1957-1958.

Golino, Carlo L. "Alberto Moravia. " MLJ 36:338. Novem-
ber 1952.
THE EMPTY CANVAS
Sampoli, Furio. "The Italian Novel of Recent Years. " IQ 7:
20-23. Summer 1963.
THE FANCY DRESS PARTY
Chiaromonte, Nicola. "Moravia and the Theater. " PR 26:
643-646. Fall 1959.

Goldstone, Herbert. "Malaparte and Moravia: Concerning
Failure and Estimate. " Western Rev 17:230-232. Spring
1953.

Golino, Carlo L. "Some Aspects of Contemporary Italian
Fiction. " MLF 37:7. March - June 1952.
A GHOST AT NOON
Baldanza, Frank. "The Classicism of Alberto Moravia. "
MFS 3:316-318. Winter 1957-1958.

Goldstone, Herbert. "The Ghost of Moravia. " SR 63:665-
667. October - December 1956.

Parris, Robert. "She Loves Me, She Loves Me Not. " New
Republic 132:21. May 30, 1955.
THE INDIFFERENT
Bontempo, O. A. "Italian Literature in 1929. " RR 21:83.
January - March 1930.

Chiaromonte, Nicola. "Realism and Neorealism in Contemporary Italian Literature. " CE 14:433-434. May 1953.

Goldstone, Herbert. "The Ghost of Moravia. " SR 63:667-

668. October - December 1956.

Golino, Carlo L. "Alberto Moravia. " MLJ 36:335-336.
November 1952.

Golino, Carlo L. "Some Aspects of Contemporary Italian
Fiction. " MLF 37:6. March - June 1952.

Moravia, Alberto. "About My Novels. " TC 164:530-532.
December 1958.

Pacifici, Sergio J. "Alberto Moravia and THE AGE OF IN-
DIFFERENCE. " Symposium 8:321-326. Winter 1954.
TWO ADOLESCENTS
Baldanza, Frank. "The Classicism of Alberto Moravia. "
MFS 3:313. Winter 1957-1958.

Waldhorn, Hilda K. "Two Adolescents. " L&P 12:43-51.
Spring 1962.
TWO WOMEN
Heiney, Donald. "Moravia's America. " WHR 18:323-329.
Autumn 1964.

Varnai, Ugo. "Italian Letters in 1957. " ILA 1:186-187.
1958.
THE WOMAN OF ROME
Baldanza, Frank. "The Classicism of Alberto Moravia. "
MFS 3:314. Winter 1957-1958.

Golino, Carlo L. "Alberto Moravia. " MLJ 36:337-338.
November 1952.

Mitchell, Bonner. "Moravia's Proletarian Roman Intellect-
uals. " MLJ 44:303. November 1960.

Rolo, Charles J. "Alberto Moravia. " Atlantic 195:71. February 1955.

Neera, Anna
SENIO
Kennard, Joseph Spencer. Italian Romance Writers. New
York: Brentano's, 1906. pp. 344-346.

Nievo, Ippolito
CONFESSIONS OF AN ITALIAN
Alberico, Alfred F. "Nievo's Disquieting Pisana. " Italica
37:13-21. March 1960.

Iliescu, Nicolae. "The Position of Ippolito Nievo in the
Nineteenth-Century Italian Novel. " PMLA 75:275-282. June
1960.

Ragusa, Olga. "Nievo, the Writer: Tendencies in Criticism."

IQ 2:20-34. Summer 1958.

Pasinetti, P. M.
    LA CONFUSIONE
        Della Terza, Dante. "Contemporary Italian Novelists:
        Language and Style in P. M. Pasinetti's LA CONFUSIONE."
        IQ 8:64-76. Spring 1964.

        Houston, M. T. and S. N. Rosenberg. "The Onomastics of
        Pasinetti. " IQ 10:41-43. Fall 1966.
    ROSSO VENEZIANO
        Della Terza, Dante. "Italian Fiction from Pavese to Prat-
        olini: 1950-1960. " IQ 3:38. Fall 1959.

        Houston, M. T. and S. N. Rosenberg. "The Onomastics of
        Pasinetti. " IQ 10:33-41. Fall 1966.

Pavese, Cesare
    FUOCO GRANDE
        Della Terza, Dante. "Italian Fiction from Pavese to Prat-
        olini: 1950-1960. " IQ 3:30-31. Fall 1959.
    THE MOON AND THE BONFIRES
        Fiedler, Leslie A. "Introducing Cesare Pavese. " KR 16:
        548-553. Autumn 1954.

        Freccero, John. "Mythos and Logos: THE MOON AND THE
        BONFIRES. " IQ 4:3-16. Winter 1961.

        Norton, Peter M. "Cesare Pavese and the American Night-
        mare. " MLN 77:24-36. January 1962.

        Taubman, Robert. "Cesare Pavese. " NewS 68:119. July
        24, 1964.

        Tenenbaum, Louis. "Character Treatment in Pavese's Fic-
        tion. " Symposium 15:136-138. Summer 1961.

Pea, Enrico
    MOSCARDINO
        Norman, Hilda L. "A Curious Trilogy. " Italica 11:52-53.
        June 1934.
    IL SERVITORE DEL DIAVOLO
        Norman, Hilda L. "A Curious Trilogy. " Italica 11:53-54.
        June 1934.
    IL VOLTO SANTO
        Norman, Hilda L. "A Curious Trilogy. " Italica 11:53.
        June 1934.

Pirandello, Luigi
    THE DIARY OF SERAFINO GUBBIO, CINEMA OPERATOR
        Starkie, Walter. Luigi Pirandello. London: J. M. Dent and
        Sons, 1926. pp. 112-117.

GIUSTINO RONCELLA NATO BOGGIOLO (SUO MARITO)
    Golino, Carlo L. "Pirandello's Least Known Novel. " Italica
    26:263-268. December 1949.

    Sedwick, Frank. "Unamuno and Pirandello Revisited. "
    Italica 33:48-49. March 1956.
THE LATE MATTIA PASCAL
    Del, Arundell. "Italy. " Contemporary Movements in Euro-
    pean Literature. London: George Routledge and Son, Ltd. ,
    1928. pp. 147-148.

    Fiskin, A. M. I. "Luigi Pirandello: The Tragedy of the
    Man Who Thinks. " Italica 25:47-48. March 1948.

    Hughes, Merritt Y. "Pirandello's Humor. " SR 35:177-178.
    April 1927.

    Poggioli, Renato. "Pirandello in Retrospect. " IQ 1:29-31.
    Winter 1958.

    Starkie, Walter. Luigi Pirandello. London: J. M. Dent and
    Sons, 1926. pp. 104-112.

    Williams, Orlo. "Luigi Pirandello. " Cornhill 55:276-278.
    September 1923.
ONE, NONE AND A HUNDRED THOUSAND
    Livingston, Arthur. Essays on Modern Italian Literature.
    New York: S. F. Vanni, 1950. pp. 91-94.

Pratolini, Vasco
A HERO OF OUR TIMES
    Golino, Carlo L. "Some Aspects of Contemporary Italian
    Fiction. " MLF 37:14-15. March - June 1952.
METELLO (See also UNA STORIA ITALIANA)
    Della Terza, Dante. "Italian Fiction from Pavese to Prat-
    olini: 1950-1960. " IQ 3:34-35. Fall 1959.
A TALE OF POOR LOVERS
    Golino, Carlo L. "Some Aspects of Contemporary Italian
    Fiction. " MLF 37:14. March - June 1952.

    Rosengarten, Frank. Vasco Pratolini: The Development of
    a Social Novelist. Carbondale: Southern Illinois University
    Press, 1965. pp. 64-75.
UNA STORIA ITALIANA
    Rosengarten, Frank. Vasco Pratolini: The Development of
    a Social Novelist. Carbondale: Southern Illinois University
    Press, 1965. pp. 88-95.

    Rosengarten, Frank. "Vasco Pratolini's UNA STORIA
    ITALIANA and the Question of Literary Realism. " Italica
    40:62-71. March 1963.

Ranieri, Antonio
    GINEVRA
        Corrigan, Beatrice. "Neopolitan Romanticism and the So-
        cial Conscience." SIR 5:113-118. Winter 1966.

Rimanelli, Giose
    THE DAY OF THE LION
        Ricciardelli, Michael. "Development of Giose Rimanelli's
        Fiction." BA 40:386-387. Autumn 1966.
    ORIGINAL SIN
        Ricciardelli, Michael. "Development of Giose Rimanelli's
        Fiction." BA 40:387-388. Autumn 1966.
    UNA POSIZIONE SOCIALE
        Ricciardelli, Michael. "Development of Giose Rimanelli's
        Fiction." BA 40:388-390. Autumn 1966.

de Roberto, Frederigo
    ILLUSIONE
        Kennard, Joseph Spencer. Italian Romance Writers. New
        York: Brentano's, 1906. pp. 321-323.
    VICERE
        Kennard, Joseph Spencer. Italian Romance Writers. New
        York: Brentano's, 1906. pp. 313-321.

Rosini, Giovanni
    LUISA STROZZI
        Luciani, Vincent. "Guicciardini and the 'Risorgimento.'"
        Italica 18:187-188. December 1941.

Serao, Matilde
    LA CONQUISTA DI ROMA
        Gisolfi, Anthony M. "Matilde Serao's Conquest of Rome."
        Italica 37:28-35. March 1960.
    VITA E AVENTURE DI RICCARDO JOANNA
        Gisolfi, Anthony M. "Matilde Serao's Conquest of Rome."
        Italica 37:35-40. March 1960.

Silone, Ignazio
    BREAD AND WINE
        Allen, Walter. "Ignazio Silone." LonM 2:61-63. January
        1955.

        Chiaromonte, Nicola. "Realism and Neorealism in Contem-
        porary Italian Literature." CE 14:436. May 1953.

        Farrell, James T. "Ignazio Silone." SoR 4:771-777. 1938-
        39.

        Hope, Francis. "Ignazio Silone." NewS 68:120-121. July
        24, 1964.

        Howe, Irving. Politics and the Novel. New York: Meridan
        Books, 1957. pp. 219-224.

Johnson, Elaine Hoesington. "The Political Novels of
Ignazio Silone. " Person 34:45. Summer 1953.

Krieger, Murray. The Tragic Vision. New York: Holt, Rinehart and Winston, 1960. pp. 72-85.

Lewis, R. W. B. The Picaresque Saint. New York: Lippincott, 1959. pp. 109-178.

Mitgang, Herbert. "A Talk with Ignazio Silone About
BREAD AND WINE. " NYTBR, October 21, 1962. pp. 4, 48.

Moseley, Edwin M. Pseudonyms of Christ in the Modern
Novel. Pittsburgh: University of Pittsburgh Press, 1962.
pp. 177-183.

Roland, Albert. "Christian Implications in Anti-Stalinist
Novels. " Religion in Life 22:409-410. Summer 1953.

Scott, Nathan A. , Jr. Rehearsals of Discomposure. New
York: Columbia University Press, 1952. pp. 78-80; 88-98.

Slochower, Harry. No Voice Is Wholly Lost. New York:
Creative Age Press, 1945. pp. 63-69.

Weatherhead, A. Kingsley. "Ignazio Silone: Community and
the Failure of Language. " MFS 7:158-168. Summer 1961.
FONTAMARA
Allen, Walter. "Ignazio Silone. " LonM 2:60-61. January
1955.

Blotner, Joseph L. The Political Novel. Garden City:
Doubleday and Company, 1955. p. 25.

Chiaromonte, Nicola. "Realism and Neorealism in Contemporary Italian Literature. " CE 14:435. May 1953.

Farrell, James T. "Ignazio Silone. " SoR 4:773-777. 1938-
39.

Howe, Irving. Politics and the Novel. New York: Meridan
Books, 1957. pp. 217-219.

Lewis, R. W. B. The Picaresque Saint. New York: Lippincott, 1959. pp. 109-178.

Scott, Nathan A. , Jr. Rehearsals of Discomposure. New
York: Columbia University Press, 1952. pp. 80-88.

Slochower, Harry. No Voice Is Wholly Lost. New York:
Creative Age Press, 1945. pp. 62-63.
THE FOX AND THE CAMELLIAS
"Moralist with a Cause. " TLS, August 18, 1961. p. 548.

A HANDFUL OF BLACKBERRIES
Bergin, Thomas G. "From Revolution to Freedom. " SatR,
October 24, 1953. p. 64.

Chiaromonte, Nicola. "Realism and Neorealism in Contemporary Italian Literature. " CE 14:436-437. May 1953.

Chiaromonte, Nicola. "Return to Fontamara. " PR 21:310-
311. May - June 1954.

Howe, Irving. Politics and the Novel. New York: Meridan
Books, 1957. pp. 224-226.

Mueller, W. R. Prophetic Voices in New Fiction. New York:
Association Press, 1959. pp. 158-183.

Warner, Rex. "Party and Church. " Spec 192:655-656. May
28, 1954.
THE SECRET OF LUCA
Weatherhead, A. Kingsley. "Ignazio Silone: Community and
the Failure of Language. " MFS 7:164-168. Summer 1961.
THE SEED BENEATH THE SNOW
Allen, Walter. "Ignazio Silone. " LonM 2:63-67. January
1955.

Glicksberg, Charles I. "Anti-Communism in Fiction. "
SAQ 53:489-490. October 1954.

Hope, Francis. "Ignazio Silone. " NewS 68:120-121. July
24, 1964.

Roland, Albert. "Christian Implications in Anti-Stalinist
Novels. " Religion in Life 22:411-412. Summer 1953.

Scott, Nathan A. , Jr. Rehearsals of Discomposure. New
York: Columbia University Press, 1952. pp. 99-107.

Svevo, Italo
THE CONFESSIONS OF ZENO
Freccero, John. "Zeno's Last Cigarette. " MLN 77:3-23.
January 1962.

"A Man Grows Older. " TLS, March 30, 1962. p. 210.

Nelson, Lowry, Jr. "A Survey of Svevo. " IQ 3:17-24.
Summer 1959.
A LIFE
"A Man Grows Older. " TLS, March 30, 1962. p. 210.

Nelson, Lowry, Jr. "A Survey of Svevo. " IQ 3:8-12. Sum-
mer 1959.
SENILITA
"A Man Grows Older. " TLS, March 30, 1962. p. 210.

Nelson, Lowry, Jr. "A Survey of Svevo. " IQ 3:12-17. Summer 1959.

Pfohl, Russell. "Imagery as Disease in SENILITA. " MLN 76:143-150. February 1961.

Tomasi di Lampedusa, Giuseppe
THE LEOPARD
Biasin, Gian-Paolo. "The Prince and the Siren. " MLN 78: 31-50. January 1963.

Brown, Calvin S. "Parallel Incidents in Emile Zola and Tomasi di Lampedusa. " CL 15:193-202. Summer 1963.

Colquhoun, Archibald. "Lampedusa in Sicily: The Lair of the Leopard. " Atlantic 211:91-110. February 1963.

Eskin, Stanley G. "Animal Imagery in IL GATTOPARDO. " Italica 39:189-194. September 1962.

Evans, Arthur and Catherine. " 'Salina E Svelto': The Symbolism of Change in IL GATTOPARDO. " WSCL 4:298-304. Autumn 1963.

Forster, E. M. "The Prince's Tale. " Spec 204:702. May 13, 1960.

Gilbert, John. "The Metamorphosis of the Gods in IL GATTOPARDO. " MLN 81:22-32. January 1966.

Meyers, Jeffrey. "Symbol and Structure in THE LEOPARD." IQ 9:50-70. Summer - Fall 1965.

Nolan, David. "Lampedusa's THE LEOPARD. " Studies 55: 403-414. Winter 1966.

Pallotta, A. "IL GATTOPARDO: A Theme-Structure Analysis. " Italica 43:57-65. March 1966.

Speight, Kathleen. "Italian Novels of Today (II). " ML 41: 93-94. September 1960.

Verga, Giovanni
HELENA'S HUSBAND
Bergin, Thomas Goddard. Giovanni Verga. New Haven: Yale University Press, 1931. pp. 66-71.
THE HOUSE BY THE MEDLAR TREE
Bergin, Thomas Goddard. Giovanni Verga. New Haven: Yale University Press, 1931. pp. 46-63.

Biasin, Gian-Paolo. "The Sicily of Verga and Sciascia. " IQ 9:7-10. Summer - Fall 1965.

Chandler, S. B. "The Movement of Life in Verga." Italica
35:91-99. June 1958.

DeVito, Anthony J. "The Struggle for Existence in the Work
of Giovanni Verga." Italica 18:179-185. December 1941.

Hartley, K. H. "Giovanni Verga and Zola." AUMLA 17:72-
75. May 1962.

Kennard, Joseph Spencer. Italian Romance Writers. New
York: Brentano's, 1906. pp. 258-262.

Pritchett, V. S. Books in General. London: Chatto and
Windus, 1953. pp. 20-23.

Pritchett, V. S. "Books in General." New S&N 40:176-177.
August 12, 1950.

Wilkins, Ernest Hatch. A History of Italian Literature.
Cambridge: Harvard University Press, 1954. pp. 454-455.
MASTRO-DON GESUALDO
   Bates, Ralph. "Verga Reconsidered." New Republic 113:
   526. October 8, 1945.

   Biasin, Gian-Paolo. "The Sicily of Verga and Sciascia."
   IQ 9:10-12. Summer - Fall 1965.

   Kennard, Joseph Spencer. Italian Romance Writers. New
   York: Brentano's, 1906. pp. 262-269.

   Pritchett, V. S. Books in General. London: Chatto and
   Windus, 1953. pp. 23-24.

   Pritchett, V. S. "Books in General." New S&N 26:139-140.
   August 28, 1943.

   Wilkins, Ernest Hatch. A History of Italian Literature.
   Cambridge: Harvard University Press, 1954. pp. 456-457.
NEDDA
   Bergin, Thomas Goddard. Giovanni Verga. New Haven: Yale
   University Press, 1931. pp. 38-45.

Vittorini, Elio
   CONVERSATION IN SICILY
      Lewis, R. W. B. "Elio Vittorini." IQ 4:60. Fall 1960.

      Pacifici, Sergio J. "Elio Vittorini." BA 29:402-403. Autumn
      1955.

      Polletta, Nicholas V. "CONVERSAZIONE IN SICILIA: Liter-
      ature of Nostalgia." Italica 41:415-429. December 1964.
   THE RED CARNATION
      Lewis, R. W. B. "Elio Vittorini." IQ 4:59-60. Fall 1960.

Vittorini, Elio. "Truth and Censorship: The Story of THE
RED CARNATION. " WHR 9:197-208. Summer 1955.
THE TWILIGHT OF THE ELEPHANT
Lewis, R. W. B. "Elio Vittorini. " IQ 4:60-61. Fall 1960.

Volponi, Paolo
MEMORIALE
Pacifici, Sergio. "From Engagement to Alienation: A View
of Contemporary Italian Literature. " Italica 40:252-253.
September 1963.

Alexis, Willibald
    SCHLOSS AVALON (WALLADMOR)
        Thomas, Lionel. "SCHLOSS AVALON -- A German Histor-
        ical Novel with an English Setting." GL&L 10:97-105. Jan-
        uary 1957.

        Thomas, L. H. C. "WALLADMOR: A Pseudo-Translation
        of Sir Walter Scott." MLR 46:218-231. April 1951.
    THE WEREWOLF
        Thomas, L. H. C. "DER WERWOLF by Willibald Alexis."
        MLR 51:378-389. July 1956.

Arnim, Achim von
    DER TOLLE INVALIDE
        Silz, Walter. Realism and Reality. Chapel Hill: University
        of North Carolina Press, 1954. pp. 29-35.

        Washington, Lawrence M. and Ida H. "The Several Aspects
        of Fire in Achim von Arnim's DER TOLLE INVALIDE." GQ
        37:498-505. November 1964.

Beer, Johann
    SIMPLIZIANISCHER WELTKUCKER
        Knight, K. G. "The Novels of Johann Beer (1655-1700)."
        MLR 56:200-203. April 1961.
    SOMMERTAGE
        Knight, K. G. "The Novels of Johann Beer (1655-1700)."
        MLR 56:203-211. April 1961.
    WINTERNACHTE
        Knight, K. G. "The Novels of Johann Beer (1655-1700)."
        MLR 56:203-211. April 1961.

Beer-Hofmann, Richard
    DER TOD GEORGS
        Liptzin, Solomon. Richard Beer-Hofmann. New York: Bloch
        Publishing Company, 1936. pp. 16-19.

Benn, Gottfried
    DER PTOLEMAER
        Waldrop, Rosmarie. "MONSIEUR TESTE and DER PTOLE-
        MAER: Abstractness in the Fiction of Valery and Benn."
        EWR 1:317-327. Winter 1965.

Bergengruen, Werner
    DIE FEUERPROBE
        Hofacker, Erich. "Justice and Grace as Presented in Ber-

gengruen's Fiction. " GR 31:100. April 1956.
THE FIRE SIGNAL
    Hofacker, Erich. "Bergengruen's DAS FEUERZEICHEN
    and Kleist's MICHAEL KOHLHAAS. " Monatshefte 47:349-
    357. November 1955.

    Hofacker, Erich. "Justice and Grace as Presented in Bergen-
    gruen's Fiction. " GR 31:99-100. April 1956.
DAS HORNUNGER HEIMWEH
    Guder, G. "Bergengruen's DAS HORNUNGER HEIMWEH. "
    ML 37:64-68. March 1956.
IN HEAVEN AS ON EARTH
    Kirchberger, Lida. "Bergengruen's Novel of the Berlin
    Panic. " Monatshefte 46:199-206. April - May 1954.
JUNGFRAULICHKEIT
    Willibrand, W. A. "On Interpreting Bergengruen's Short
    Story JUNGFRAULICHKEIT. " Monatshefte 44:65-78. Feb-
    ruary 1952.
A MATTER OF CONSCIENCE
    Hofacker, Erich. "Justice and Grace as Presented in Bergen-
    gruen's Fiction. " GR 31:102-103. April 1956.
DER TOD VON REVAL
    Ritchie, J. M. "Allegory and Mannerism in Werner Bergen-
    gruen and his DER TOD VON REVAL. " GL&L 13:248-254.
    July 1960.

Boll, Heinrich
    ACQUAINTED WITH THE NIGHT
    Coupe, W. A. "Heinrich Boll's UND SAGTE KEIN EIN-
    ZIGES WORT--An Analysis. "   GL&L 17:238-249. April
    1964.

    Waidson, H. M. "The Novels and Stories of Heinrich Boll. "
    GL&L 12:267-270. July 1959.

    Ziolkowski, Theodore. "Heinrich Boll: Conscience and
    Craft. " BA 34:218-219. Summer 1960.
HOUSE WITHOUT KEEPER
    Waidson, H. M. "The Novels and Stories of Heinrich Boll."
    GL&L 12:269-270. July 1959.

    Ziolkowski, Theodore. "Heinrich Boll: Conscience and
    Craft. " BA 34:219-220. Summer 1960.
THE TRAIN WAS ON TIME
    Ziolkowski, Theodore. "Heinrich Boll: Conscience and
    Craft. " BA 34:216-218. Summer 1960.
WHERE ART THOU, ADAM?
    Ziolkowski, Theodore. "Heinrich Boll: Conscience and
    Craft. " BA 34:217-218. Summer 1960.

Brecht, Bertold
    THREEPENNY NOVEL
    Pritchett, V. S. "THREEPENNY NOVEL. " NewS 55:606-

607. May 10, 1958.

Bredel, Willi
   VERWANDTE UND BEKANNTE
      Andrews, R. C. "The Novel as a Political Vade-mecum:
      Willi Bredel's VERWANDTE UND BEKANNTE. " GL&L 10:
      131-138. January 1957.

Brentano, Clemens
   GODWI
      Fitzell, John. The Hermit in German Literature. Chapel
      Hill: University of North Carolina Press, 1961. pp. 66-71.

      Reed, Eugene E. "The Union of the Arts in Brentano's
      GODWI. " GR 29:102-118. April 1954.
   THE STORY OF JUST CASPER AND FAIR ANNIE
      Jones, George F. Honor in German Literature. Chapel Hill:
      University of North Carolina Press, 1959. pp. 170-172.

      Silz, Walter. Realism and Reality. Chapel Hill: University
      of North Carolina Press, 1954. pp. 17-28.

Broch, Hermann
   THE BEWITCHMENT
      Ziolkowski, Theodore. Hermann Broch. New York: Colum-
      bia University Press, 1964. pp. 24-30.
   THE DEATH OF VIRGIL
      Arendt, Hannah. "The Achievement of Hermann Broch. "
      KR 11:480-483. Summer 1949.

      Breuer, Robert. "Hermann Broch: Poet and Philosopher. "
      ILA 2:164-166. 1959.

      Herd, E. W. "Hermann Broch and the Legitimacy of the
      Novel. " GL&L 13:262-277. July 1960.

      Rosenfeld, Paul. "THE DEATH OF VIRGIL. " Chimera 3:
      47-55. Spring 1945.

      Weigand, Hermann J. "Broch's DEATH OF VERGIL [sic]:
      Program Notes. " PMLA 62:525-554. June 1947.

      White, John J. "Broch, Virgil, and the Cycle of History. "
      GR 41:104-110. March 1966.

      Ziolkowski, Theodore. Hermann Broch. New York: Colum-
      bia University Press, 1964. pp. 30-39.
   THE INNOCENT ONES
      Weigand, Hermann J. "Hermann Broch's DIE SCHULD-
      LOSEN: An Approach. " PMLA 68:323-334. June 1953.

      White, John J. "Broch, Virgil, and the Cycle of History. "
      GR 41:104-110. March 1966.

Ziolkowski, Theodore. Hermann Broch. New York: Columbia University Press, 1964. pp. 39-44.

THE SLEEPWALKERS
Arendt, Hannah. "The Achievement of Hermann Broch. "
KR 11:477-480. Summer 1949.

Herd, Eric. "The Guilt of the Hero in the Novels of Hermann Broch. " GL&L 18:30-39. October 1964.

Herd, E. W. "Hermann Broch and the Legitimacy of the
Novel. " GL&L 13:262-277. July 1960.

Muir, Edwin. "Hermann Broch. " Bookman 75:664-668.
November 1932.

Schoolfield, G. C. "Broch's Sleepwalkers: Aeneas and the
Apostles. " JJR 2:i-ii; 21-37. Spring - Summer 1958.

Ziolkowski, Theodore. Hermann Broch. New York: Columbia University Press, 1964. pp. 10-22.

THE TEMPTER
Breuer, Robert. "Hermann Broch: Poet and Philosopher. "
ILA 2:162-163. 1959.

Hardin, James N. , Jr. "DER VERSUCHER and Hermann
Broch's Attitude Toward Positivism. " GQ 39:29-41. January 1966.

Herd, Eric. "The Guilt of the Hero in the Novels of Hermann Broch. " GL&L 18:30-39. October 1964.

Schoolfield, George C. "Notes on Broch's DER VERSUCHER."
Monatshefte 48:1-16. January 1956.

Buchner, Georg
    LENZ
        Stern, J. P. Re-Interpretations. London: Thames and Hud-
        son, 1964. pp. 86-93; 125-155.

Canetti, Elias
    THE TOWER OF BABEL
        Parry, Idris. "Elias Canetti's Novel: DIE BLENDUNG. "
        Essays in German Literature - I. (ed.) F. Norman. London:
        University of London Institute of German Studies, 1965. pp.
        145-166.

Conradi, Hermann
    ADAM MAN
        Boulby, M. "Neo-Romanticism in German Naturalist Liter-
        ature: The Theme of the 'Übergangsmensch' in Hermann
        Conradi's Novel ADAM MENSCH. " GL&L 6:306-310. July
        1953.

Doblin, Alfred
  ALEXANDER SQUARE, BERLIN
      Slochower, Harry. "Franz Werfel and Alfred Doblin: The
      Problem of Individualism versus Collectivism in BAR-
      BARA and BERLIN ALEXANDERPLATZ. " JEGP 33:107-112.
      January 1934.
  WALLENSTEIN
      Feuchtwanger, Lion. The House of Desdemona or The
      Laurels and Limitations of Historical Fiction. Detroit:
      Wayne State University Press, 1963. pp. 189-193.

Doderer, Heimito von
  THE DEMONS
      Swales, M. W. "The Narrator in the Novels of Heimito von
      Doderer. " MLR 61:87-93. January 1966.
  EIN MORD, DEN JEDER BEGEHT
      Hayward-Jones, Sylvia. "Fate, Guilt and Freedom in Hei-
      mito von Doderer's EIN MORD, DEN JEDER BEGEHT and
      EIN UMWEG. " GL&L 14:160-164. April 1961.
  THE STRUDLHOF STEPS
      Swales, M. W. "The Narrator in the Novels of Heimito von
      Doderer. " MLR 61:86-90. January 1966.
  EIN UMWEG
      Hayward-Jones, Sylvia. "Fate, Guilt and Freedom in Hei-
      mito von Doderer's EIN MORD, DEN JEDER BEGEHT and
      EIN UMWEG. " GL&L 14:160-164. April 1961.

Droste-Hulshoff, Annette von
  THE JEW'S BEECH TREE
      Jones, George F. Honor in German Literature. Chapel Hill:
      University of North Carolina Press, 1959. pp. 172-174.

      Schatzky, Brigette E. "Annette von Droste-Hulshoff. " Ger-
      man Men of Letters. Vol. 1. (ed.) Alex Natan. Philadelphia:
      Dufour Ed. , 1962. pp. 85-87.

      Silz, Walter. Realism and Reality. Chapel Hill: University
      of North Carolina Press, 1954. pp. 36-51.

Durrenmatt, Friedrich
  THE DEADLY GAME
      Gontrum, Peter B. "Ritter, Tod und Teufel: Protagonist
      and Antagonist in Prose Works of Friedrich Durrenmatt. "
      Seminar 1:88-98. Fall 1965.
  THE JUDGE AND HIS HANGMAN
      Gillis, William. "Durrenmatt and the Detectives. " GQ 35:
      71-74. January 1962.

      Gontrum, Peter B. "Ritter, Tod und Teufel: Protagonist
      and Antagonist in Prose Works of Friedrich Durrenmatt. "
      Seminar 1:88-98. Fall 1965.
  THE PLEDGE
      Heilman, Robert B. "The Lure of the Demonic: James and

Durrenmatt. " CL 13:348-357. Fall 1961.

Eichendorff, Joseph
FROM THE LIFE OF A GOOD-FOR-NOTHING
Gould, Chester Nathan. "Literary Satire in Eichendorff's
AUS DEM LEBEN EINES TAUGENICHTS. " JEGP 33:167-
177. April 1934.

Osthaus, Carl. "A Reply to 'Note on the Interpretation of
"Pensionsanstalt" in TAUGENICHTS' by Wayland D. Hand,
University of California at Los Angeles. " Monatshefte 31:
186-188. April 1939.

Schumann, Detlev W. "Eichendorff's TAUGENICHTS and
Romanticism. " GQ 9:141-153. November 1936.
PRESENTIMENT AND THE PRESENT
Riley, Thomas A. "Eichendorff and Schiller: The Interpre-
tation of a Paragraph in AHNUNG UND GEGENWART. "
Monatshefte 50:119-128. March 1958.

Ernst, Paul
WIE DIE FLUGEL BRECHEN
McFarlane, J. W. "An Unpublished Novel by Paul Ernst. "
PMLA 66:96-106. March 1951.

Fallada, Hans
LITTLE MAN, WHAT NOW?
Liptzin, Sol. Historical Survey of German Literature. New
York: Prentice Hall, 1936. p. 248.

Slochower, Harry. No Voice Is Wholly Lost. New York:
Creative Age Press, 1945. p. 217.
ONCE WE HAD A CHILD
Slochower, Harry. No Voice Is Wholly Lost. New York:
Creative Age Press, 1945. pp. 218-219.
SPARROW FARM
Slochower, Harry. No Voice Is Wholly Lost. New York:
Creative Age Press, 1945. pp. 219-221.

Feuchtwanger, Lion
JOSEPHUS
Yuill, W. E. "Lion Feuchtwanger. " German Men of Letters. Vol. 3. (ed.) Alex Natan. London: Oswald Wolff, 1964.
pp. 191-194.
THE OPPERMANNS
Yuill, W. E. "Lion Feuchtwanger. " German Men of Letters. Vol. 3. (ed.) Alex Natan. London: Oswald Wolff,
1964. pp. 189-190.
PARIS GAZETTE
Yuill, W. E. "Lion Feuchtwanger. " German Men of Letters. Vol. 3. (ed.) Alex Natan. London: Oswald Wolff, 1964.
pp. 190-191.

POWER
> Burkhard, Arthur. "Thomas Becket and Josef Susz Oppen-
> heimer as Fathers." GR 6:144-153. April 1931.

> Yuill, W. E. "Lion Feuchtwanger." German Men of Letters.
> Vol. 3 (ed.) Alex Natan. London: Oswald Wolff, 1964. pp.
> 183-186.

SUCCESS
> Yuill, W. E. "Lion Feuchtwanger." German Men of Letters.
> Vol. 3 (ed.) Alex Natan. London: Oswald Wolff, 1964. pp.
> 187-189.

Flex, Walter
WANDERER BETWEEN TWO WORLDS
> Pfeiler, William K. War and the German Mind. New York:
> Columbia University Press, 1941. pp. 82-87.

Fontane, Theodor
BEFORE THE STORM
> Frye, Lawrence O. "The Unreal in Fontane's Novels."
> GR 37:106-108. March 1962.

CECILE
> Garland, H. B. "Theodor Fontane." German Men of Letters.
> Vol. 1 (ed.) Alex Natan. Philadelphia: Dufour Ed., 1962.
> pp. 226-227.

> Koester, Rudolf. "Death by Miscalculation: Some Notes on
> Suicide in Fontane's Prose." GL&L 20:35-36. October 1966.

> Park, Rosemary. "Theodor Fontane's Unheroic Heroes."
> GR 14:37-38. February 1939.

EFFI BRIEST
> Carter, T. E. "A Leitmotif in Fontane's EFFI BRIEST."
> GL&L 10:38-42. October 1956.

> Eickhorst, William. Decadence in German Fiction. Denver:
> Swallow, 1953. pp. 31-33.

> Frye, Lawrence O. "The Unreal in Fontane's Novels." GR
> 37:110-114. March 1962.

> Garland, H. B. "Theodor Fontane." German Men of Letters.
> Vol. 1 (ed.) Alex Natan. Philadelphia: Dufour Ed., 1962.
> pp. 228-229.

> Hewett-Thayer, Harvey. The Modern German Novel. Boston:
> Marshall Jones, 1924. pp. 36-40.

> Park, Rosemary. "Theodor Fontane's Unheroic Heroes."
> GR 14:39-41. February 1939.

> Pascal, Roy. The German Novel. Manchester: Manchester
> University Press, 1956. pp. 198-206.

Robertson, John G. History of German Literature. New York: Putnam, 1902. p. 610.

Rose, Ernst. "Theodor Fontane's Novels and the Spirit of Old Age. " GR 23:259-260. December 1948.

Stern, J. P. M. "EFFI BRIEST: MADAME BOVARY: ANNA KARENINA. " MLR 52:363-375. July 1957.

Stern, J. P. Re-Interpretations. London: Thames and Hudson, 1964. pp. 316-339.

Thanner, Josef. "Symbol and Function of the Symbol in Theodor Fontane's EFFI BRIEST. " Monatshefte 57:187-192. April - May 1965.

ELLERNKLIPP

Frye, Lawrence O. "The Unreal in Fontane's Novels. " GR 37:108-113. March 1962.

FRAU JENNY TREIBEL

Garland, H. B. "Theodor Fontane. " German Men of Letters. Vol. 1 (ed.) Alex Natan. Philadelphia: Dufour Ed. , 1962. pp. 229-230.

Hewett-Thayer, Harvey. The Modern German Novel. Boston: Marshall Jones, 1924. pp. 47-51.

Park, Rosemary. "Theodor Fontane's Unheroic Heroes. " GR 14:35-36. February 1939.

Rowley, Brian A. "Theodor Fontane: A German Novelist in the European Tradition?" GL&L 15:82-84. October 1961.

Shears, Lambert A. "Thackeray's PENDENNIS as a Source of Fontane's FRAU JENNY TREIBEL. " PMLA 40:211-216. March 1925.

GRETE MINDE

Delp, W. E. "Around Fontane's GRETE MINDE. " ML 40: 18-19. March 1959.

QUITT

Davis, Arthur L. "Theodor Fontane's Interest in America as Revealed by His Novel QUITT. " AGR 19:28-29. February 1953.

SCHACH VON WUTHENOW

Hewett-Thayer, Harvey. The Modern German Novel. Boston: Marshall Jones, 1924. pp. 40-43.

Koester, Rudolf. "Death by Miscalculation: Some Notes on Suicide in Fontane's Prose. " GL&L 20:37. October 1966.

DER STECHLIN

Barlow, D. "Symbolism in Fontane's DER STECHLIN. " GL&L 12:282-286. July 1959.

Garland, H. B. "Theodor Fontane. " German Men of Letters.

(ed.) Alex Natan. London: Oswald Wolff, 1961. p. 230.

Genschmer, Fred. "Theodor Fontane: A Study in Restraint." Monatshefte 33:270-271. October 1941.

Rose, Ernst. "Theodor Fontane's Novels and the Spirit of
Old Age." GR 23:260-261. December 1948.
STINE
  Hewett-Thayer, Harvey. The Modern German Novel. Bos-
  ton: Marshall Jones, 1924. pp. 46-47.
TRIALS AND TRIBULATIONS
  Garland, H. B. "Theodor Fontane." German Men of Letters.
  (ed.) Alex Natan. London: Oswald Wolff, 1961. pp. 226-
  228.

  Hewett-Thayer, Harvey. The Modern German Novel. Boston: Marshall Jones, 1924. pp. 44-46.
UNWIEDERBRINGLICH
  Hewett-Thayer, Harvey. The Modern German Novel. Boston: Marshall Jones, 1924. p. 43.

  Park, Rosemary. "Theodor Fontane's Unheroic Heroes."
  GR 14:36-37. February 1939.

Frenssen, Gustav
  OTTO BABENDIEK
    Church, Howard W. "Otto Babendiek and David Copperfield."
    GR 11:44-49. January 1936.

Freytag, Gustave
  THE ANCESTORS
    Warner Library. Vol. 10. (ed.) John W. Cunliffe and Ash-
    by H. Thorndike. New York: Knickerbocker Press, 1916.
    pp. 6014-6015.
  DEBIT AND CREDIT
    Liptzin, Sol. Historical Survey of German Literature. New
    York: Prentice-Hall, 1936. pp. 149-150.

    Robertson, John G. History of German Literature. New
    York: Putnam, 1902. pp. 574-575.

    Silz, Walter. "Freytag's SOLL UND HABEN and Raabe's
    DER HUNGERPASTOR." MLN 39:10-18. January 1924.

    Warner Library. Vol. 10. (ed.) John W. Cunliffe and Ashby
    H. Thorndike. New York: Knickerbocker Press, 1917. pp.
    6011-6013.
  THE LOST MANUSCRIPT
    Warner Library. Vol. 10. (ed.) John W. Cunliffe and Ashby
    H. Thorndike. New York: Knickerbocker Press, 1917. pp.
    6013-6014.

Frisch, Max
    HOMO FABER
        Bradley, Brigitte L. "Max Frisch's HOMO FABER: Theme
        and Structural Devices. " GR 41:279-290. November 1966.
    STILLER
        Esslin, Martin. "Max Frisch. " German Men of Letters.
        Vol. 3. (ed.) Alex Natan. London: Oswald Wolff, 1964. pp.
        314-315.

Gerstacker, Friedrich
    GERMELSHAUSEN
        Evans, Clarence. "A Cultural Link Between Nineteenth-
        Century Germany and the Arkansas Ozarks. " MLJ 35:523-
        530. November 1951.

        Krumpelmann, John T. "Gerstacker's GERMELSHAUSEN
        and Lerner's BRIGADOON. " Monatshefte 40:396-400. Novem-
        ber 1948.

        Thomas, J. Wesley. "William Gilmore Simms' HELEN
        HALSEY as the Source for Friedrich Gerstacker's GER-
        MELSHAUSEN. " Monatshefte 45:141-144. March 1953.

        Vowles, Guy R. "Gerstaecker's GERMELSHAUSEN and
        Lie's FINNEBLOD. " Monatshefte 41:293-294. October 1949.

Goes, Albrecht
    THE BURNT OFFERING
        Trainer, J. "Two Prose Works of Albrecht Goes. " ML 42:
        137-139. December 1961.
    RESTLESS NIGHT
        Trainer, J. "Two Prose Works of Albrecht Goes. " ML 42:
        137-139. December 1961.

Goethe, Johann von
    ELECTIVE AFFINITIES
        Bielschowsky, Albert. The Life of Goethe. Vol. II. New
        York: Putnam, 1905. pp. 347-387.

        Blankenagel, John C. "An Early American Review of DIE
        WAHLVERWANDTSCHAFTEN. " JEGP 35:383-388. July
        1936.

        Brown, P. Hume. Life of Goethe. Vol. II. New York: Henry
        Holt and Company, 1920. Chapter 30.

        Clark, Robert T. , Jr. "The Metamorphosis of Character in
        DIE WAHLVERWANDTSCHAFTEN. " GR 29:243-253. De-
        cember 1954.

        Croce, Douglas. Goethe. London: Methuen and Company,
        1923. pp. 157-167.

Dickson, Keith. "Spatial Concentration and Themes in DIE WAHLVERWANDTSCHAFTEN. " FMLS 1:159-174. April 1965.

Dickson, Keith. "The Temporal Structure of DIE WAHLVER-WANDTSCHAFTEN. " GR 41:170-185. May 1966.

Dieckmann, Liselotte. "Repeated Mirror Reflections: The Technique of Goethe's Novels. " SIR 1:167-174. Spring 1962.

Ellis, J. M. "Names in FAUST and DIE WAHLVERWANDT-SCHAFTEN. " Seminar 1:25-30. Spring 1965.

Friedenthal, Richard. Goethe, His Life and Times. New York: World Publishing Company, 1965. pp. 415-418.

Hatfield, Henry. Goethe: A Critical Introduction. Norfolk: New Directions Books, 1963. pp. 101-106.

Hatfield, Henry C. "Towards the Interpretation of DIE WAHLVERWANDTSCHAFTEN. " GR 23:104-114. April 1948.

Hochwald, Ilse E. "Eliot's COCKTAIL PARTY and Goethe's WAHLVERWANDTSCHAFTEN. " GR 29:254-259. December 1954.

Jaeger, Hans. "Goethe's 'Novelle' DIE WAHLVERWANDT-SCHAFTEN?" GR 34:14-38. February 1959.

Mann, Thomas. Past Masters. New York: Alfred A. Knopf, 1933. pp. 103-114.

Maurer, K. W. "Goethe's ELECTIVE AFFINITIES. " MLR 42:342-352. July 1947.

Mulloy, W. J. "The German Catholic Estimate of Goethe. " UCPMP 24:373-374. July 1944.

Neumeyer, Eva Maria. "The Landscape Garden as a Symbol in Rousseau, Goethe and Flaubert. " JHI 8:197-207. April 1947.

Robertson, J. G. The Life and Work of Goethe. New York: Dutton and Company, 1932. pp. 237-247.

Thomas, Calvin. Goethe. New York: Knopf, Inc. , 1929. pp. 297-300.

Thomas, R. Hinton. "DIE WAHLVERWANDTSCHAFTEN and Mann's DER TOD IN VENEDIG. " PEGS, 1954-1955, pp. 101-130.

HERMANN AND DOROTHEA

Bielschowsky, Albert. The Life of Goethe. Vol. II. New York: Putnam, 1905. pp. 269-310.

Clayton, Vista. "The Relation of JOSEPH by Bitaube to Goethe's HERMANN AND DOROTHEA. " RR 28:146-150. April 1937.

Croce, Douglas. Goethe. London: Methuen and Company, 1923. pp. 129-140.

Holland, Bernard. "HERMANN AND DOROTHEA. " DubR 173:112-127. July - December 1923.

Mulloy, William J. "The German Catholic Estimate of Goethe. " UCPMP 24:394. July 1944.

Robertson, J. G. The Life and Work of Goethe. New York: Dutton and Company, 1932. pp. 197-202.

MAERCHEN

Hiebel, Frederick. "Goethe's MAERCHEN in the Light of Novalis. " PMLA 63:918-934. September 1948.

WERTHER

Atkins, Stuart Pratt. "J. C. Lavater and Goethe: Problems of Psychology and Theology in DIE LIEDEN DES JUNGEN WERTHERS. " PMLA 63:520-576. June 1948.

Atkins, Stuart. The Testament of Werther. Cambridge: Harvard University Press, 1949. 322 pp.

Atkins, Stuart. "Werther's 'Misfallen an uns selbst, das immer mit einem Neide verknupft ist. ' " MLR 43:96-98. January 1948. (Reply: Wilkinson, Elizabeth M. "A further Note on the Meaning of 'Neid' in Werther's Letter of 1 July 1771. " MLR 44:243-246. April 1949; Atkins, Stuart. "Werther's 'Neid'--A Reply. " MLR 44:385-386. July 1949.)

Bielschowsky, Albert. The Life of Goethe. Vol. I. New York: Putnam and Sons, 1905. pp. 189-202.

Brandes, Georg. Main Currents in Nineteenth Century Literature. New York: Boni and Liverwright, 1924. pp. 20-28.

Brown, P. Hume. Life of Goethe. Vol. I. New York: Henry Holt and Company, 1920. Chapter 10.

Butler, E. M. "The Element of Time in Goethe's WERTHER and Kafka's PROZESS. " GL&L 12:248-258. July 1959.

Clark, Robert T. , Jr. "The Psychological Framework of Goethe's WERTHER. " JEGP 46:273-278. July 1947.

Dieckmann, Liselotte. "Repeated Mirror Reflections: The Techniques of Goethe's Novels. " SIR 1:158-160. Spring 1962.

Diez, Max. "The Principle of the Dominant Metaphor in Goethe's WERTHER. " PMLA 51:830-841. September 1936;

985-1006. December 1936.

Dvoretzky, Edward. "Goethe's WERTHER and Lessing's EMILIA GALOTTI. " GL&L 16:23-26. October 1962.

Ferguson, Robert. "Goldsmith and the Notions 'Grille' and 'Wandrer' in WERTHERS LEIDEN. " MLN 17:346-355. June 1902. (Continued in MLN 17:411-418. November 1902.)

Friedenthal, Richard. Goethe, His Life and Times. New York: World Publishing Company, 1965. pp. 128-132.

Graham, Ilse Appelbaum. "Minds Without Medium: Reflections on EMILIA GALOTTI and WERTHERS LEIDEN. " Euphorion 56:3-24. 1962.

Hatfield, Henry. Goethe: A Critical Introduction. Norfolk: New Directions Books, 1963. pp. 36-41.

Hegeman, Daniel Van Brunt. "Boswell and the Abt Jerusalem: A Note on the Background of WERTHER. " JEGP 44: 367-369. October 1945.

Ittner, Robert T. "Werther and EMILIA GALOTTI. " JEGP 41:418-426. October 1942.

Lange, Victor. Great German Short Novels and Stories. New York: Modern Library, 1952. pp. xi-xii.

Liptzin, Sol. Historical Survey of German Literature. New York: Prentice-Hall, 1936. pp. 41-43.

Long, Orie William. "The Attitude of Eminent Englishmen and Americans toward WERTER. " MP 14:455-466. December 1916.

Long, Orie William. "English and American Imitations of Goethe's WERTER. " MP 14:193-216. August 1916.

McIlvenna, Estelle. "The 'Philistine' in Sturm und Drang." MLR 33:33-34. 1938.

Mulloy, William J. "The German Catholic Estimate of Goethe. " UCPMP 24:371-372. July 1944.

Nevinson, Henry W. Goethe: Man and Poet. New York: Harcourt, Brace and Company, 1932. pp. 38-49.

Parry, Idris. "Werther and Lord Chandos. " PEGS 33:75-98. 1962-1963.

Pascal, Roy. The German Sturm und Drang. Manchester: Manchester University Press, 1952. pp. 65-66; 68-69; 73-

74; 112-113; 141-143; 150-153; 202-203; 291-293.

Reiss, Hans. "DIE LEIDEN DES JUNGEN WERTHERS: A Reconsideration." MLQ 20:81-96. March 1959.

Robertson, J. G. The Life and Works of Goethe. New York: Dutton and Company, 1932. pp. 50-60.

Rose, William. Men, Myths, and Movements in German Literature. London: Allen and Unwin Ltd., 1931. pp. 125-155.

Ryder, Frank G. "George Ticknor's SORROWS OF YOUNG WERTER." CL 1:360-372. Fall 1949.

Ryder, Frank G. "Season, Day, and Hour--Time as Metaphor in Goethe's WERTHER." JEGP 63:389-407. July 1964.

Schumann, Detlev W. "Some Notes on WERTHER." JEGP 55:533-549. October 1956.

Stahl, E. L. "The Genesis of Symbolist Theories in Germany." MLR 41:308-309. July 1946.

Thomas, Calvin. Goethe. New York: Knopf, Inc., 1929. pp. 281; 285-291.

Tucker, T. G. The Foreign Debt of English Literature. London: Geo. Bell and Sons, 1907. pp. 242-243.
WILHELM MEISTER
Arndt, Karl J. R. "The Harmony Society and WILHELM MEISTERS WANDERJAHRE." CL 10:193-202. Summer 1958.

Bergstraesser, Arnold. Goethe's Image of Man and Society. Chicago: Henry Regnery Company, 1949. pp. 235-318.

Bielschowsky, Albert. The Life of Goethe. Vol. III. New York: Putnam, 1905. pp. 189-268.

Blackall, Eric A. "Wilhelm Meister's Pious Pilgrimage." GL&L 18:246-251. July 1965.

Brandes, Georg. Wolfgang Goethe. New York: Nicholas L. Brown, 1924. pp. 301-314.

Brown, P. Hume. Life of Goethe. Vol. II. New York: Henry Holt and Company, 1920. Chapters 35-36.

Cawley, F. Stanton. "An Ovidian Prototype of a Character in WILHELM MEISTER." MLN 40:288-292. May 1925.

Clark, Robert T., Jr. "Personality and Society in WIL-

HELM MEISTERS LEHRJAHRE. '' Southwest Goethe Festival. (ed.) Gilbert J. Jordan. Dallas: Southern Methodist University, 1949. pp. 85-98.

Croce, Douglas. Goethe. London: Methuen and Company, 1923. pp. 168-177.

Diamond, William. "Wilhelm Meister's Interpretation of Hamlet. '' MP 23:89-101. August 1925.

Dieckmann, Liselotte. "The Conception of Freedom in Goethe's Works. '' PEGS 32:42-45. 1961-1962.

Dieckmann, Liselotte. "Repeated Mirror Reflections: The Techniques of Goethe's Novels. '' SIR 1:160-167. Spring 1962.

Francke, Kuno. Social Forces in German Literature. New York: Henry Holt and Company, 1901. pp. 355-359; 532-533.

Friedenthal, Richard. Goethe, His Life and Times. New York: World Publishing Company, 1965. pp. 357-363.

Halpert, Inge D. "Wilhelm Meister and Josef Knecht. '' GQ 34:11-20. January 1961.

Hammer, Carl. "WILHELM MEISTERS WANDERJAHRE and Rousseau. '' Southwest Goethe Festival. (ed.) Gilbert J. Jordan. Dallas: Southern Methodist University, 1949. pp. 34-50.

Hatch, Mary Gies. "The Development of Goethe's Concept of the Calling in WILHELM MEISTERS LEHRJAHRE and the WANDERJAHRE. '' GQ 32:217-226. May 1959.

Hatfield, Henry. Goethe: A Critical Introduction. Cambridge: Harvard University Press, 1964. pp. 84-91; 121-129.

Hatfield, Henry. "WILHELM MEISTERS LEHRJAHRE and 'Progressive Universalpoesie. ' '' GR 36:221-229. October 1961.

Hellersberg-Wendriner, Anna. "America in the World View of the Aged Goethe. '' GR 14:270-276. December 1939.

Hohlfeld, A. R. "The Poems in Carlyle's Translation of WILHELM MEISTER. '' MLN 36:205-211. April 1921.

Howe, Susanne. Wilhelm Meister and His English Kinsmen: Apprentices to Life. New York: Columbia University Press, 1930.

Immerwahr, Raymond. "Friedrich Schlegel's Essay 'On Goethe's MEISTER. ' '' Monatshefte 49:1-21. January 1957.

Ittner, Robert T. "Novalis' Attitudes Toward WILHELM MEISTER with Reference to the Conception of His HEINRICH VON OFTERDINGEN. " JEGP 37:542-554. October 1938.

Kornbluth, Martin L. "The Reception of WILHELM MEISTER in America. " Symposium 13:128-133. Spring 1959.

Krehbiel, August R. "Herder as Jarno in WILHELM MEISTER, Book III. " MP 17:325-329. October 1919.

Liptzin, Sol. Historical Survey of German Literature. New York: Prentice-Hall, 1936. pp. 54; 138.

Mulloy, William J. "The German Catholic Estimate of Goethe. " UCPMP 24:372-373; 393-394. July 1944.

Pascal, Roy. The German Novel. Manchester: Manchester University Press, 1956. pp. 3-29.

Pfund, Harry W. "Goethe and the Quakers. " GR 14:267-269. No. 4, 1939.

Plath, O. E. "Schiller's Influence on WILHELM MEISTER." MLN 31:257-267. May 1916.

Porterfield, Allen W. "WILHELM MEISTERS LEHRJAHRE and IMMENSEE. " MLN 41:513-516. December 1926.

Robertson, J. G. Goethe and the Twentieth Century. New York: G. P. Putnam's Sons, 1912. pp. 56-62.

Robertson, J. G. The Life and Work of Goethe. New York: Dutton and Company, 1932. pp. 185-197; 263-273.

Rose, Ernst. History of German Literature. New York: New York University Press, 1960. pp. 182-184.

Stock, Irvin. "A View of WILHELM MEISTER'S APPRENTICESHIP. " PMLA 72:84-103. March 1957.

Thomas, Calvin. Goethe. New York: Knopf, Inc. , 1929. pp. 291-297.

Waidson, H. M. "Death by Water: Or, The Childhood of Wilhelm Meister. " MLR 56:44-53. January 1961.

Gotthelf, Jeremias
        THE BLACK SPIDER
            Keller, R. E. "Language and Style in Jeremias Gotthelf's DIE SCHWARZE SPINNE. " GL&L 10:2-13. October 1956.

Grass, Gunter
        CAT AND MOUSE

Bruce, James C. "The Equivocating Narrator in Gunter Grass's KATZ UND MAUS. " Monatshefte 58:139-149. Summer 1966.

Cunliffe, W. G. "Gunter Grass: KATZ UND MAUS. " SSF 3: 174-185. Winter 1966.

Ruhleder, Karl H. "A Pattern of Messianic Thought in Gunter Grass' CAT AND MOUSE. " GQ 39:599-612. November 1966.

DOG YEARS

Cunliffe, W. G. "Aspects of the Absurd in Gunter Grass. " WSCL 7:314-326. Autumn 1966.

Steiner, George. "The Nerve of Gunter Grass. " Commentary 37:77-80. May 1964.

THE TIN DRUM

Cunliffe, W. G. "Aspects of the Absurd in Gunter Grass. " WSCL 7:311-325. Autumn 1966.

Hanson, William P. "Oskar, Rasputin and Goethe. " CMLR 20:29-32. Fall 1963.

Ivey, Frederick. "THE TIN DRUM; or Retreat to the Word." Wichita State University Bulletin 42. February 1966. 16 pp.

Jerde, C. D. "A Corridor of Pathos: Notes on the Fiction of Guenter Grass. " MinnR 4:558-560. Summer 1964.

Pike, Burton. "Objects vs. People in the Recent German Novel. " WSCL 7:307. Autumn 1966.

Sharfman, William L. "The Organization of Experience in THE TIN DRUM." MinnR 6:59-65. No. 1, 1966.

Willson, A. Leslie. "The Grotesque Everyman in Gunter Grass's DIE BLECHTROMMEL. " Monatshefte 58:131-138. Summer 1966.

Grillparzer, Franz

THE ANCESTRESS

Arlt, Gustave O. "A Source of Grillparzer's AHNFRAU. " MP 29:91-100. August 1931.

THE POOR MINSTREL

Drake, Patricia. Grillparzer and Biedermeier. Waco: Baylor University Press, 1953. pp. 177-183.

Nolte, Fred O. Grillparzer, Lessing, and Goethe. Lancaster: Lancaster Press, 1938. pp. 84-89.

Silz, Walter. Realism and Reality. Chapel Hill: University of North Carolina Press, 1954. pp. 67-78.

Stern, J. P. Re-Interpretations. London: Thames and Hudson, 1964. pp. 61-77.

Grimmelshausen, Franz
THE FEMALE VAGRANT
Hayens, Kenneth. Grimmelshausen. London: Humphrey Milford Oxford University Press, 1932. (St. Andrews University Publication No. 34.) pp. 156-187.

Hiller, Robert L. "The Sutler's Cart and The Lump of Gold." GR 39:137-144. March 1964.
SIMPLICISSIMUS
Feuchtwanger, Lion. The House of Desdemona or The Laurels and Limitations of Historical Fiction. Detroit: Wayne State University Press, 1963. p. 186.

Fitzell, John. The Hermit in German Literature. Chapel Hill: University of North Carolina Press, 1961. pp. 4-9.

Gilbert, Mary E. "Simplex and the Battle of Wittstock." GL&L 18:264-269. July 1965.

Gudde, Erwin G. "Grimmelshausen's SIMPLICIUS SIMPLICISSIMUS and DeFoe's ROBINSON CRUSOE." PQ 4:110-120. April 1925.

Hammer, Carl, Jr. "SIMPLICISSIMUS and the Literary Historians." Monatshefte 40:457-464. December 1948.

Hayens, Kenneth. Grimmelshausen. London: Humphrey Milford Oxford University Press, 1932. (St. Andrews University Publications No. 34.) pp. 80-155.

Hennig, John. "Simplicius Simplicissimus's British Relations." MLR 40:37-45. January 1945.

Jacobson, John W. "The Culpable Male: Grimmelshausen on Women." GQ 39:153-154. March 1966.

Jones, George F. Honor in German Literature. Chapel Hill: University of North Carolina Press, 1959. p. 145.

Robertson, John G. History of German Literature. New York: Putnam, 1902. pp. 227-230.

Weil, H. H. "The Conception of the Adventurer in German Baroque Literature." GL&L 6:285-291. July 1953.

Weil, Hans Hartmut. "The Conception of Friendship in German Baroque Literature." GL&L 13:106-115. January 1960.

VOGELNEST
Hayens, Kenneth. Grimmelshausen. London: Humphrey Milford Oxford University Press, 1932. (St. Andrews University Publication No. 34.) pp. 188-222.

Jacobson, John W. "The Culpable Male: Grimmelshausen on Women. " GQ 39:155-161. March 1966.

Gutzkow, Karl
BLASEDOW UND SEINE SOHNE
Rathje, George G. "Literary and Social Significance of the Satire in Karl Gutzkow's BLASEDOW UND SEINE SOHNE. " GR 16:177-184. October 1941.
DOUBTING GIRL
Morse, J. Mitchell. "Karl Gutzkow and the Modern Novel. " Journal of General Education 15:175-189. October 1963.

Hauff, Wilhelm
LICHTENSTEIN
Thompson, Garrett W. "Wilhelm Hauff's Specific Relation to Walter Scott. " PMLA 26:549-592. December 1911.

Hauptmann, Gerhart
ATLANTIS
Holl, Karl. Gerhart Hauptmann: His Life and His Work 1862-1902. London: Gay and Hancock, Ltd. , 1913. pp. 86-90.

Wahr, Fred B. "INDIPOHDI in Hauptmann's Development. " GR 11:92-93. April 1936.
FLAGMAN THIEL
Heller, Otto. Studies in Modern German Literature. Boston: Ginn and Company, 1905. pp. 158-161.

Ordon, Marianne. "Unconscious Contents in BAHNWARTER THIEL. " GR 26:223-229. October 1951.

Remak, Henry H. H. "Vinegar and Water: Allegory and Symbolism. " Literary Symbolism. (ed.) Helmut Rehder. Austin: University of Texas Press, 1965. pp. 55-57.

Silz, Walter. Realism and Reality. Chapel Hill: University of North Carolina Press, 1954. pp. 137-152.
THE FOOL IN CHRIST
Buck, Philo M. , Jr. Directions in Contemporary Literature. New York: Oxford University Press, 1942. pp. 50-54.

Campbell, T. M. "Gerhart Hauptmann--Christian or Pagan?" MLJ 8:357-361. March 1924.

Heuser, Frederick W. J. "The Mystical Hauptmann. " GR 7:39-42. January 1932.

Holl, Karl. Gerhart Hauptmann: His Life and His Work 1862-1902. London: Gay and Hancock, Ltd., 1913. pp. 83-86.

Lessing, Otto E. Masters in Modern German Literature. Dresden: Verlag, 1912. pp. 131-134.

Sinden, Margaret. "Hauptmann's EMANUEL QUINT. " GR 29:269-281. December 1954.

Steinhauer, H. "Hauptmann's Vision of Christ: An Interpretive Study of DER NARR IN CHRISTO EMANUEL QUINT. " Monatshefte 29:331-340. November 1937.

Wahr, Fred B. "INDIPOHDI in Hauptmann's Development. " GR 11:91-92. April 1936.

Weimar, Karl S. "Another Look at Gerhart Hauptmann's DER NARR IN CHRISTO EMANUEL QUINT. " GR 34:209-222. October 1959.
IN THE CONFUSION OF VOCATION
   Ellis, Frances H. "Literary Symbolism in Hauptmann's Novel IM WIRBEL DER BERUFUNG. " Monatshefte 34:326-332. October 1942.
THE ISLAND OF THE GREAT MOTHER
   Steinhauer, H. "Hauptmann's Utopian Fantasy, DIE INSEL DER GROSSEN MUTTER. " MLN 53:516-521. November 1938.
DAS MEERWUNDER
   Steinhauer, Harry. "Hauptmann's DAS MEERWUNDER: An Analysis. " JEGP 51:49-60. January 1952.

Heinse, Wilhelm
   ARDINGHELLO
      Hofe, Harold von. "Heinse, America, and Utopianism. " PMLA 72:390-402. June 1957.

      Reed, Eugene E. "The Transitional Significance of Heinse's ARDINGHELLO. " MLQ 16:268-273. September 1955.

      Rose, William. From Goethe to Byron. London: Routledge and Sons, 1924. pp. 147-151.
   LAIDION
      Hofe, Harold von. "Heinse, America, and Utopianism. " PMLA 72:390-402. June 1957.

Hesse, Hermann
   DEATH AND THE LOVER
      Rose, Ernst. Faith from the Abyss. New York: New York University Press, 1965. pp. 98-109.

      Taylor, Harley U. "The Death Wish and Suicide in the Novels of Hermann Hesse. " WVUPP 13:60-62. December

1961.

Ziolkowski, Theodore. The Novels of Hermann Hesse: A Study in Theme and Structure. Princeton: Princeton University Press, 1965. pp. 229-252.

DEMIAN

Fickert, Kurt J. "The Development of the Outsider Concept in Hesse's Novels." Monatshefte 52:173-175. April - May 1960.

Freedman, Ralph. The Lyrical Novel: Studies in Hermann Hesse, Andre Gide, and Virginia Woolf. Princeton: Princeton University Press, 1963. pp. 58-72.

Ziolkowski, Theodore. The Novels of Hermann Hesse: A Study in Theme and Structure. Princeton: Princeton University Press, 1965. pp. 87-145.

JOURNEY TO THE EAST

Engel, Eva J. "Hermann Hesse." German Men of Letters. Vol. 2. (ed.) Alex Natan. London: Oswald Wolff, 1963. pp. 266-267.

Farquharson, R. H. "The Identity and Significance of Leo in Hesse's MORGENLANDFAHRT." Monatshefte 53:122-128. February 1921.

Middleton, J. C. "Hermann Hesse's MORGENLANDFAHRT." GR 32:299-310. December 1957.

Peppard, Murray B. "Hermann Hesse: From Eastern Journey to Castalia." Monatshefte 50:247-255. October 1958.

Rose, Ernst. Faith from the Abyss. New York: New York University Press, 1965. pp. 110-111.

Willson, A. Leslie. "Hesse's Veil of Isis." Monatshefte 55:317-318. November 1963.

Ziolkowski, Theodore. The Novels of Hermann Hesse: A Study in Theme and Structure. Princeton: Princeton University Press, 1965. pp. 253-282.

KLEIN AND WAGNER

Bennett, E. K. History of the German Novelle. Cambridge: Cambridge University Press, 1961. p. 263.

Taylor, Harley U. "The Death Wish and Suicide in the Novels of Hermann Hesse." WVUPP 13:56-57. December 1961.

MAGISTER LUDI

Boulby, Mark. " 'Der Vierte Lebenslauf' as a Key to DAS GLASPERLENSPIEL." MLR 61:635-646. October 1966.

Cohn, Hilde D. "The Symbolic End of Hermann Hesse's

GLASPERLENSPIEL. " MLQ 11:347-357. September 1950.

Engel, Eva J. "Hermann Hesse. " German Men of Letters.
Vol. 2. (ed.) Alex Natan. London: Oswald Wolff, 1963. pp.
255-264.

Field, G. W. "Music and Morality in Thomas Mann and
Hermann Hesse. " UTQ 24:182-189. January 1955.

Freedman, Ralph. The Lyrical Novel: Studies in Hermann
Hesse, Andre Gide, and Virginia Woolf. Princeton: Princeton University Press, 1963. pp. 96-114.

Freedman, Ralph. "Romantic Imagination: Hermann Hesse
as a Modern Novelist. " PMLA 73:275-284. June 1958.

Halpert, Inge D. "Wilhelm Meister and Josef Knecht. " GQ
34:11-20. January 1931.

Jehle, Mimi. "The 'Garden' in the Works of Hermann
Hesse. " GQ 24:46-47. January 1951.

Johnson, Sidney M. "The Autobiographies in Hermann
Hesse's GLASPERLENSPIEL. " GQ 29:160-171. May 1956.

Koester, Rudolf. "The Portrayal of Age in Hesse's Narrative Prose. " GR 41:113-116. March 1966.

Middleton, J. C. "An Enigma Transfigured in Hermann
Hesse's GLASPERLENSPIEL. " GL&L 10:298-302. July
1957.

Mileck, Joseph. "Hermann Hesse's GLASPERLENSPIEL. "
UCPMP 36:243-270. October 1952.

Naumann, Walter. "The Individual and Society in the Work
of Hermann Hesse. " Monatshefte 41:33-42. January 1949.

Negus, Kenneth. "On the Death of Josef Knecht in Hermann
Hesse's GLASPERLENSPIEL. " Monatshefte 53:181-189.
February 1961.

Peppard, Murray B. "Hermann Hesse: From Eastern Journey to Castalia. " Monatshefte 50:247-255. October 1958.

Peppard, Murray B. "Hermann Hesse's Ladder of Learning. " KFLQ 3:13-20. No. 1, 1956.

Taylor, Harley U. "The Death Wish and Suicide in the
Novels of Hermann Hesse. " WVUPP 13:62-64. December
1961.

Willson, A. Leslic. "Hesse's Veil of Isis. " Monatshefte

55:318-321. November 1963.

Ziolkowski, Theodore. The Novels of Hermann Hesse: A Study in Theme and Structure. Princeton: Princeton University Press, 1965. pp. 283-338.

ROSSHALDE

Jehle, Mimi. "The 'Garden' in the Works of Hermann Hesse." GQ 24:47-48. January 1951.

SIDDHARTHA

Baird, James. Ishmael. Baltimore: Johns Hopkins Press, 1956. pp. 424-425.

Beerman, Hans. "Hermann Hesse and the Bhagavad-Gita." MidQ 1:27-40. October 1959.

Koester, Rudolf. "The Portrayal of Age in Hesse's Narrative Prose." GR 41:114-115. March 1966.

Malthaner, Johannes. "Hermann Hesse--SIDDHARTHA." GQ 25:103-109. March 1952.

Rose, Ernst. Faith from the Abyss. New York: New York University Press, 1965. pp. 68-77.

Shaw, Leroy R. "Time and the Structure of Hermann Hesse's SIDDHARTHA." Symposium 11:204-224. Fall 1957.

Taylor, Harley U. "The Death Wish and Suicide in the Novels of Hermann Hesse." WVUPP 13:57-59. December 1961.

Ziolkowski, Theodore. The Novels of Hermann Hesse: A Study in Theme and Structure. Princeton: Princeton University Press, 1965. pp. 146-177.

STEPPENWOLF

Domino, Ruth. "The Hunchback and the Wings." Approach 2:20-28. Summer 1947.

Fickert, Kurt J. "The Development of the Outsider Concept in Hesse's Novels." Monatshefte 52:175-178. April - May 1960.

Field, G. W. "Music and Morality in Thomas Mann and Hermann Hesse." UTQ 24:179-181. January 1955.

Flaxman, Seymour L. "DER STEPPENWOLF: Hesse's Portrait of the Intellectual." MLQ 15:349-358. December 1954.

Freedman, Ralph. The Lyrical Novel: Studies in Hermann Hesse, Andre Gide, and Virginia Woolf. Princeton: Princeton University Press, 1963. pp. 73-94.

Freedman, Ralph. "Romantic Imagination: Hermann Hesse

as a Modern Novelist. " PMLA 73:275-284. June 1958.

Rose, Ernst. Faith from the Abyss. New York: New York
University Press, 1965. pp. 87-97.

Taylor, Harley U. "The Death Wish and Suicide in the
Novels of Hermann Hesse. " WVUPP 13:59-60. December
1961.

Townsend, Stanley R. "The German Humanist Hermann
Hesse. " MLF 32:1-12. March - June 1947.

Ziolkowski, Theodore. "Hermann Hesse's STEPPENWOLF:
A Sonata in Prose. " MLQ 19:115-133. June 1958.

Ziolkowski, Theodore. The Novels of Hermann Hesse: A
Study in Theme and Structure. Princeton: Princeton Uni-
versity Press, 1965. pp. 178-228.
UNDER THE WHEEL
Fickert, Kurt J. "The Development of the Outsider Con-
cept in Hesse's Novels. " Monatshefte 52:172-173. April -
May 1960.

Taylor, Harley U. "The Death Wish and Suicide in the
Novels of Hermann Hesse." WVUPP 13:52-55. December
1961.

Willecke, Frederick H. "Style and Form of Hermann
Hesse's UNTERM RAD. " KFLQ 8:147-156. No. 3, 1961.

Hoffmann, E. T. A.
THE COOPER OF NUREMBERG
Neumann, Alfred. "Cooper to Goldsmith: A Literary Pre-
cursor to Wagner's Meistersinger. " Opera News 16:11-13.
March 17, 1952.
THE DEVIL'S ELIXIR
Hewett-Thayer, Harvey W. "E. T. A. Hoffmann and Religious
Faith. " GR 13:278-280. October 1938.

Hewett-Thayer, Harvey W. Hoffmann: Author of the Tales.
Princeton: Princeton University Press, 1948. pp. 250-274.

Mollenauer, Robert. "The Three Periods of E. T. A. Hoffmann's Romanticism: An Attempt at a Definition. " SIR 2:
227-229. Summer 1963.

Negus, Kenneth. E. T. A. Hoffmann's Other World. Philadelphia: University of Pennsylvania Press, 1965. pp. 82-86.

Negus, Kenneth G. "The Family Tree in E. T. A. Hoffmann's DIE ELIXIERE DES TEUFELS. " PMLA 73:516-520.
December 1958.

Schoolfield, George C. "Peter Schonfeld and Johann Stich." MLN 67:465-468. November 1952.

Wain, Marianne. "The Double in Romantic Narrative: A Preliminary Study. " GR 36:265-266. December 1961.
THE ENTAIL
    Hewett-Thayer, Harvey W. Hoffmann: Author of the Tales. Princeton: Princeton University Press, 1948. pp. 313-319.

    Negus, Kenneth. "The Allusions to Schiller's DER GEIS-TERSEHER in E. T. A. Hoffmann's DAS MAJORAT: Meaning and Background. " GQ 32:341-355. November 1959.

    Negus, Kenneth. E. T. A. Hoffmann's Other World. Phila-delphia: University of Pennsylvania Press, 1965. pp. 100-103.
THE GOLDEN POT
    Bruning, Peter. "E. T. A. Hoffmann and the Philistine. " GQ 28:113-116. March 1955.

    Hewett-Thayer, Harvey W. Hoffmann: Author of the Tales. Princeton: Princeton University Press, 1948. pp. 218-227.

    McGlathery, James M. "The Suicide Motif in E. T. A. Hoff-mann's DER GOLDNE TOPF. " Monatshefte 58:115-123. Summer 1966.

    Mollenauer, Robert. "The Three Periods of E. T. A. Hoff-mann's Romanticism: An Attempt at a Definition. " SIR 2: 222-225. Summer 1963.

    Negus, Kenneth. "E. T. A. Hoffmann's DER GOLDNE TOPF: Its Romantic Myth. " GR 34:262-275. December 1959.

    Negus, Kenneth. E. T. A. Hoffmann's Other World. Phila-delphia: University of Pennsylvania Press, 1965. pp. 53-66.

    Taylor, Robert. Hoffmann. New York: Hillary House Pub-lishers, 1963. pp. 12-15.

    Thalmann, Marianne. The Romantic Fairy Tale. Ann Arbor: University of Michigan Press, 1964. pp. 96-100.
DER KAMPF DER SANGER
    Hewett-Thayer, Harvey W. "A Source of Hoffmann's DER KAMPF DER SANGER. " MLN 63:526-527. December 1948.
THE KING'S BETROTHED
    Hewett-Thayer, Harvey W. Hoffmann: Author of the Tales. Princeton: Princeton University Press, 1948. pp. 237-240.
LITTLE ZACK
    Hewett-Thayer, Harvey W. Hoffmann: Author of the Tales. Princeton: Princeton University Press, 1948. pp. 227-233.

Negus, Kenneth. E. T. A. Hoffmann's Other World. Philadelphia: University of Pennsylvania Press, 1965. pp. 128-136.

MLLE. DE SCUDERI
Hewett-Thayer, Harvey W. Hoffmann: Author of the Tales. Princeton: Princeton University Press, 1948. pp. 319-323.

Negus, Kenneth. E. T. A. Hoffmann's Other World. Philadelphia: University of Pennsylvania Press, 1965. pp. 104-109.

DER MAGNETISEUR
Mollenauer, Robert. "The Three Periods of E. T. A. Hoffmann's Romanticism: An Attempt at a Definition." SIR 2: 225-227. Summer 1963.

Porterfield, Allen W. "Where Literary Enthusiasm Failed." GQ 11:173-177. November 1938.

MASTER FLEA
Hewett-Thayer, Harvey W. Hoffmann: Author of the Tales. Princeton: Princeton University Press, 1948. pp. 243-249.

McClain, William H. "E. T. A. Hoffmann as Psychological Realist: A Study of MEISTER FLOH." Monatshefte 47:65-80. February 1955.

Mollenauer, Robert. "The Three Periods of E. T. A. Hoffmann's Romanticism: An Attempt at a Definition." SIR 2: 237-238. Summer 1963.

Negus, Kenneth. E. T. A. Hoffmann's Other World. Philadelphia: University of Pennsylvania Press, 1965. pp. 149-157.

THE MINES OF FALUN
Negus, Kenneth. E. T. A. Hoffmann's Other World. Philadelphia: University of Pennsylvania Press, 1965. pp. 109-113.

NUTCRACKER AND MOUSE KING
Negus, Kenneth. E. T. A. Hoffmann's Other World. Philadelphia: University of Pennsylvania Press, 1965. pp. 120-123.

PRINZESSIN BRAMBILLA
Hewett-Thayer, Harvey W. Hoffmann: Author of the Tales. Princeton: Princeton University Press, 1948. pp. 233-237.

Negus, Kenneth. E. T. A. Hoffmann's Other World. Philadelphia: University of Pennsylvania Press, 1965. pp. 139-149.

THE SANDMAN
Prawer, S. S. "Hoffmann's Uncanny Guest: A Reading of DER SANDMANN." GL&L 18:297-308. July 1965.

SERAPION
Fitzell, John. The Hermit in German Literature. Chapel Hill: University of North Carolina Press, 1961. pp. 83-86.

THE STRANGE CHILD
> Negus, Kenneth. E. T. A. Hoffmann's Other World. Phila-
> delphia: University of Pennsylvania Press, 1965. pp. 123-
> 128.

TOMCAT MURR
> Bruning, Peter. "E. T. A. Hoffmann and the Philistine."
> GQ 28:117-119. March 1955.

> Hewett-Thayer, Harvey W. "E. T. A. Hoffmann and Religious
> Faith." GR 13:277-278. October 1938.

> Hewett-Thayer, Harvey W. Hoffmann: Author of the Tales.
> Princeton: Princeton University Press, 1948. pp. 287-312.

> Mollenauer, Robert. "The Three Periods of E. T. A. Hoff-
> mann's Romanticism: An Attempt at a Definition." SIR 2:
> 231-232. Summer 1963.

> Morgan, Estelle. "E. T. A. Hoffmann and the Philistine."
> ML 42:141-143. December 1961.

> Negus, Kenneth. E. T. A. Hoffmann's Other World. Phila-
> delphia: University of Pennsylvania Press, 1965. pp. 158-
> 167.

> Nock, Francis J. "E. T. A. Hoffmann and Nonsense." GQ
> 35:65-68. January 1962.

THE VOW
> Pierce, Frederick E. "Scott and Hoffmann." MLN 45:457-
> 460. November 1930.

Hofmannsthal, Hugo von
> DAS ERLEBNIS DES MARSCHALLS VON BASSOMPIERRE
>> Gilbert, Mary E. "Some Observations on Hofmannsthal's
>> Two Novellen REITERGESCHICHTE and DAS ERLEBNIS
>> DES MARSCHALLS VON BASSOMPIERRE." GL&L 11:102-
>> 111. January 1958.
> REITERGESCHICHTE
>> Gilbert, Mary E. "Some Observations on Hofmannsthal's
>> Two Novellen REITERGESCHICHTE and DAS ERLEBNIS
>> DES MARSCHALLS VON BASSOMPIERRE." GL&L 11:102-
>> 111. January 1958.

Holderlin, Johann
> HYPERION
>> Fitzell, John. The Hermit in German Literature. Chapel
>> Hill: University of North Carolina Press, 1961. pp. 95-
>> 101.

>> Fuerst, Norbert. "Three Great German Novels of Educa-
>> tion." Monatshefte 38:340-347. October 1946.

Huch, Ricarda
  DER GROSSE KRIEG
      Feuchtwanger, Lion. The House of Desdemona or the
      Laurels and Limitations of Historical Fiction. Detroit:
      Wayne State University Press, 1963. pp. 183-186.

Immermann, Karl
  THE EPIGONES
      Francke, Kuno. Social Forces in German Literature. New
      York: Henry Holt and Company, 1901. pp. 511-512.

      Jennings, Lee Byron. The Ludicrous Demon. Berkeley: Uni-
      versity of California Press, 1963. Chapter III.

      Liptzin, Sol. Historical Survey of German Literature. New
      York: Prentice Hall, 1936. pp. 139-140.
  MUNCHHAUSEN
      Francke, Kuno. Social Forces in German Literature. New
      York: Henry Holt and Company, 1901. pp. 512-514.

      Jennings, Lee B. "Immermann's MUNCHHAUSEN and the
      Post-Romantic Predicament. " KFLQ 10:145-148. No. 3,
      1963.

Jacobi
  EDWARD ALLWILL
      Geissendoerfer, Theodore. "Jacobi's ALLWILL and Jean
      Paul's TITAN. " JEGP 27:361-365. 1928.

      Rose, William. From Goethe to Byron. London: Routledge
      and Sons, 1924. pp. 119-130.

Johnson, Uwe
  SPECULATIONS ABOUT JAKOB
      Detweiler, Robert. "SPECULATIONS ABOUT JAKOB: The
      Truth of Ambiguity. " Monatshefte 58:25-31. Spring 1966.

      Pike, Burton. "Objects vs. People in the Recent German
      Novel. " WSCL 7:309. Autumn 1966.

Junger, Ernst
  HELIOPOLIS
      Peppard, M. B. "Ernst Junger's HELIOPOLIS. " Symposium
      7:250-261. November 1953.

      Rey, W. H. "The Destiny of Man in the Modern Utopian
      Novel. " Symposium 6:140-156. May 1952.

      Stern, J. P. Ernst Junger. New Haven: Yale University
      Press, 1953. pp. 16-17.
  ON THE MARBLE CLIFFS
      Stern, J. P. Ernst Junger. New Haven: Yale University
      Press, 1953. pp. 13-14.

THE STORM OF STEEL
  Hoffman, Frederick J. "The Moment of Violence: Ernst
  Junger and the Literary Problem of Fact. " EIC 10:405-
  421. October 1960.

  Stern, J. P. Ernst Junger. New Haven: Yale University
  Press, 1953. pp. 28-30.
VISIT TO GODENHOLM
  Peppard, Murray B. "Ernst Junger: Norse Myths and Nihil-
  ism. " Monatshefte 46:1-10. January 1954.
THE WORKINGMAN
  Peppard, M. B. "Ernst Junger's HELIOPOLIS. " Symposium
  7:250-261. November 1953.

Kafka, Franz
  AMERIKA
    Bergel, Lienhard. "AMERIKA: Its Meaning. " Franz Kafka
    Today. (ed.) Angel Flores. Madison: University of Wiscon-
    sin, 1958. pp. 117-126.

    Church, Margaret. Time and Reality. Chapel Hill: Univer-
    sity of North Carolina Press, 1962. pp. 190-192.

    Collins, H. Platzer. "Kafka's 'Double Figure' as a Literary
    Device. " Monatshefte 55:7-12. January 1963.

    Goodman, Paul. Kafka's Prayer. New York: Vanguard Press,
    1947. pp. 188-193.

    Gunvaldsen, K. M. "Franz Kafka and Psychoanalysis. "
    UTQ 32:273-275. April 1963.

    Levi, P. Margot. "K., an Exploration of the Names of
    Kafka's Central Characters. " Names 14:3-4. March 1966.

    Macklem, Michael. "Kafka and the Myth of Tristan. " DR
    30:335-337. January 1951.

    Mahoney, John L. "Symbolism and Calvinism in the Novels
    of Kafka. " Renascence 15:200-207. Summer 1963.

    Neider, Charles. The Frozen Sea. New York: Russell and
    Russell, 1962. Chapter V.

    Pascal, Roy. The German Novel. Manchester: Manchester
    University Press, 1956. pp. 219-226.

    Politzer, Heinz. Franz Kafka: Parable and Paradox. New
    York: Cornell University Press, 1962. pp. 116-162.

    Ruland, Richard E. "A View from Back Home: Kafka's
    AMERIKA. " AQ 13:33-42. Spring 1961.

Russell, Francis. Three Studies in Twentieth Century
Obscurity. Aldington: Hand and Flower Press, 1954. pp.
58-59.

Spilka, Mark. "AMERIKA: Its Genesis. " Franz Kafka Today. (ed.) Angel Flores. Madison: University of Wisconsin,
1958. pp. 95-116.

Spilka, Mark. "Kafka and Dickens: The Country Sweet-
heart. " AI 16:367-377. Winter 1959.

Tedlock, E. W., Jr. "Kafka's Imitation of DAVID COP-
PERFIELD. " CL 7:52-62. Winter 1955.

Tilton, John W. "Kafka's AMERIKA as a Novel of Salvation. " Criticism 3:321-332. Fall 1961.

Turner, Alison. "Kafka's Two Worlds of Music. " Monatshefte 55:272-274. October 1963.

Tyler, Parker. "Kafka's and Chaplin's AMERIKA. " SR 58:
299-311. Spring 1950.

Vasata, Rudolf. "AMERIKA and Charles Dickens. " The
Kafka Problem. (ed.) Angel Flores. New York: New Directions Books, 1946. pp. 134-139.

THE BURROW

Goodman, Paul. Kafka's Prayer. New York: Vanguard
Press, 1947. pp. 222-227.

Politzer, Heinz. Franz Kafka: Parable and Paradox. New
York: Cornell University Press, 1962. pp. 318-333.

Walker, Augusta. "Allegory: A Light Conceit. " PR 22:484-
490. Fall 1955.

THE CASTLE

Baker, James R. "THE CASTLE: A Problem in Structure. "
TCL 3:74-77. July 1957.

Braybrooke, Neville. "Celestial Castles: An Approach to
Saint Teresa and Franz Kafka. " DubR 229:437-445. 1955.

Braybrooke, Neville. "The Geography of the Soul: St.
Teresa and Kafka. " DR 38:324-330. Autumn 1958.

Brod, Max. "THE CASTLE: Its Genesis. " Franz Kafka Today. (ed.) Angel Flores. Madison: University of Wisconsin,
1958. pp. 161-164.

Brod, Max. "The Homeless Stranger. " The Kafka Problem.
(ed.) Angel Flores. New York: New Directions Books, 1946.
pp. 179-180.

Camus, Albert. "Hope and the Absurd in the Work of Franz Kafka. " Kafka: A Collection of Critical Essays. (ed.) Ronald Gray. New York: Prentice Hall, 1962. pp. 148-155.

Church, Margaret. "Kafka and Proust: A Contrast in Time." BuR 7:110-112. December 1957.

Church, Margaret. Time and Reality. Chapel Hill: University of North Carolina Press, 1962. pp. 197-201.

Church, Margaret. "Time and Reality in Kafka's THE TRIAL and THE CASTLE. " TCL 2:65-68. July 1956.

Cohn, Ruby. "WATT in the Light of THE CASTLE. " CL 13: 154-166. Spring 1961.

Collignon, Jean. "Kafka's Humor. " YFS 16:55-62. Winter 1955-1956.

Collins, H. Platzer. "Kafka's 'Double Figure' as a Literary Device. " Monatshefte 55:7-12. January 1963.

Cook, Albert. The Meaning of Fiction. Detroit: Wayne State University Press, 1960. pp. 250-258.

Daniel-rops. "The Castle of Despair. " The Kafka Problem. (ed.) Angel Flores. New York: New Directions Books, 1946. pp. 184-191.

Goodman, Paul. Kafka's Prayer. New York: Vanguard Press, 1947. pp. 188-222.

Goodman, Paul. The Structure of Literature. Chicago: University of Chicago Press, 1954. pp. 173-183.

Gray, Ronald. Kafka's Castle. Cambridge: Cambridge University Press, 1956. pp. 1-82.

Heller, Erich. "The World of Franz Kafka. " Kafka: A Collection of Critical Essays. (ed.) Ronald Gray. New York: Prentice-Hall, 1962. pp. 101-122.

Macklem, Michael. "Kafka and the Myth of Tristan. " DR 30:340-341. January 1951.

Mahoney, John L. "Symbolism and Calvinism in the Novels of Kafka. " Renascence 15:200-207. Summer 1963.

Muir, Edwin. "Franz Kafka. " Kafka: A Collection of Critical Essays. (ed.) Ronald Gray. New York: Prentice-Hall, 1962. pp. 33-44.

Muir, Edwin. "A Note on Franz Kafka. " Bookman 72:238-

239. November 1930.

Neider, Charles. The Frozen Sea. New York: Russell and Russell, 1962. pp. 122-152.

Olafson, Frederick A. "Kafka and the Primacy of the Ethical. " HudR 13:60-73. Spring 1960.

Pascal, Roy. The German Novel. Manchester: Manchester University Press, 1956. pp. 233-244.

Pearce, Donald. "THE CASTLE: Kafka's Divine Comedy. " Franz Kafka Today. (ed.) Angel Flores. Madison: University of Wisconsin, 1958. pp. 165-172.

Pike, Burton. "Objects vs. People in the Recent German Novel. " WSCL 7:306. Autumn 1966.

Politzer, Heinz. Franz Kafka: Parable and Paradox. New York: Cornell University Press, 1962. pp. 218-281.

Reed, Eugene E. "Franz Kafka: Possession and Being. " Monatshefte 50:359-366. December 1958.

Reed, Eugene E. "Moral Polarity in Kafka's DER PROZESS and DAS SCHLOSS. " Monatshefte 46:317-324. November 1954.

Reiss, H. S. "Franz Kafka's Conception of Humour. " MLR 44:535-540. October 1949.

Russell, Francis. Three Studies in Twentieth Century Obscurity. Aldington: Hand and Flower Press, 1954. pp. 59-65.

Saurat, Denis. "A Note on THE CASTLE. " The Kafka Problem. (ed.) Angel Flores. New York: New Directions Books, 1946. pp. 181-183.

Savage, D. S. "Franz Kafka: Faith and Vocation. " SR 54: 222-240. Spring 1946.

Scott, N. A. Rehearsals of Discomposure. New York: Columbia University Press, 1952. pp. 47-56.

Slochower, Harry. No Voice Is Wholly Lost. New York: Creative Age Press, 1945. pp. 114-125.

Steinberg, Erwin R. "K. of THE CASTLE: Ostensible Land-Surveyor. " CE 27:185-189. December 1965.

Steinberg, M. W. "Franz Kafka: The Achievement of Certitude. " QQ 68:97-103. Spring 1961.

Swander, Homer. "THE CASTLE: Kafka's Village." Franz
Kafka Today. (ed.) Angel Flores. Madison: University of
Wisconsin, 1958. pp. 173-192.

Tindall, William York. The Literary Symbol. Bloomington:
Indiana University Press, 1955. pp. 139-141.

Vivas, Eliseo. "Kafka's Distorted Mask." Kafka: A Collection of Critical Essays. (ed.) Ronald Gray. New York: Prentice-Hall, 1962. pp. 137-142.

Warren, Austin. "Franz Kafka." Kafka: A Collection of
Critical Essays. (ed.) Ronald Gray. New York: Prentice-
Hall, 1962. pp. 125-132.

Warren, Austin. "Kosmos Kafka." SoR 7:350-363. Autumn
1941.

Weinstein, Leo. "Kafka's Ape: Heel or Hero?" MFS 8:76-
79. Spring 1962.
A COUNTRY DOCTOR
Busacca, Basil. "A COUNTRY DOCTOR." Franz Kafka Today. (ed.) Angel Flores. Madison: University of Wisconsin,
1958. pp. 45-54.

Cooperman, Stanley. "Kafka's A COUNTRY DOCTOR:
Microcosm of Symbolism." UKCR 24:75-80. Autumn 1957.

Goldstein, Bluma. "A Study of the Wound in Stories by
Franz Kafka." GR 41:214-217. May 1966.

Guth, Hans P. "Symbol and Contextual Restraint in Kafka's
COUNTRY DOCTOR." PMLA 80:427-431. 1965.

Hopkins, Gerard Manley. "Kafka's A COUNTRY DOCTOR."
Expl 16: Item 45. May 1958.

Lainoff, Seymour. "The Country Doctors of Kafka and
Turgenev." Symposium 16:130-135. Summer 1962.

Lange, Victor. Great German Short Novels and Stories. New
York: Modern Library, 1952. pp. xix-xxi.

Lawson, Richard H. "Kafka's DER LANDARZT." Monatshefte 49:265-271. October 1957.

Leiter, Louis H. "A Problem in Analysis: Franz Kafka's
A COUNTRY DOCTOR." JAAC 16:337-347. March 1958.

Levi, P. Margot. "K., An Exploration of the Names of
Kafka's Central Characters." Names 14:5. March 1966.

Marson, Eric and Keith Leopold. "Kafka, Freud, and EIN

LANDARZT. " GQ 37:146-160. March 1964.

Politzer, Heinz. Franz Kafka: Parable and Paradox. New York: Cornell University Press, 1962. pp. 87-98.

Salinger, Herman. "More Light on Kafka's LANDARZT. " Monatshefte 53:97-104. March 1961.

White, William M. "A Reexamination of Kafka's THE COUNTRY DOCTOR as Moral Allegory. " SSF 3:345-347. Spring 1966.

EIN BESUCH IM BERGWERK
Pasley, J. M. S. "Franz Kafka: EIN BESUCH IM BERGWERK. " GL&L 18:40-46. October 1964.

THE GREAT WALL OF CHINA
Church, Margaret. Time and Reality. Chapel Hill: University of North Carolina Press, 1962. pp. 185-190.

Collignon, Jean. "Kafka's Humor. " YFS 16:54-58. Winter 1955.

Wood, Frank. "Hofmannsthal and Kafka: Two Motifs. " GQ 31:110-112. March 1958.

THE HUNGER ARTIST
Moyer, Patricia. "Time and the Artist in Kafka and Hawthorne. " MFS 4:295-306. Winter 1958-1959.

Politzer, Heinz. Franz Kafka: Parable and Paradox. New York: Cornell University Press, 1962. pp. 303-308.

Spann, Meno. "Franz Kafka's Leopard. " GR 34:85-104. April 1959.

Waidson, H. M. "The Starvation-Artist and the Leopard. " GR 35:262-269. December 1960.

West, Ray B. , Jr. and Robert Wooster Stollman. The Art of Modern Fiction. New York: Holt, Rinehart and Winston, 1960. pp. 366-372.

Wood, Cecil. "On the Tendency of Nature to Intimate Art. " MinnR 6:140-148. No. 2, 1966.

HUNTER GRACCHUS
Knieger, Bernard. "Kafka's THE HUNTER GRACCHUS. " Expl 17: Item 39. March 1959.

IN THE PENAL COLONY
Adams, Robert M. Strains of Discord: Studies in Literary Openness. Ithaca: Cornell University Press, 1958. pp. 169-171.

Burns, Wayne. "IN THE PENAL COLONY: Variations on a Theme by Octave Mirbeau. " Accent 17:45-51. Winter 1957.

Burns, Wayne. "Kafka and Alex Comfort: The Penal Colony Revisited. " ArQ 8:101-120. Summer 1952.

Church, Margaret. Time and Reality. Chapel Hill: University of North Carolina Press, 1962. pp. 185-190.

Fickert, Kurt J. "Kafka's IN THE PENAL COLONY. " Expl 24: Item 11. September 1965.

Globus, Gordon G. and Richard C. Pillard. "Tausk's IN-FLUENCING MACHINE and Kafka's IN THE PENAL COL-ONY. " AI 23:191-207. Fall 1966.

Goldstein, Bluma. "A Study of the Wound in Stories by Franz Kafka. " GR 41:206-207. May 1966.

Gunvaldsen, K. M. "Franz Kafka and Psychoanalysis. " UTQ 32:275-281. April 1963.

Neider, Charles. The Frozen Sea. New York: Russell and Russell, 1962. pp. 78-80.

Politzer, Heinz. Franz Kafka: Parable and Paradox. New York: Cornell University Press, 1962. pp. 98-115.

Thomas, J. D. "The Dark at the End of the Tunnel: Kafka's IN THE PENAL COLONY. " SSF 4:12-18. Fall 1966.

Warren, Austin. "Kosmos Kafka. " SoR 7:363-365. Autumn 1941.

Warren, Austin. "THE PENAL COLONY. " The Kafka Problem. (ed.) Angel Flores. New York: New Directions Books, 1946. pp. 140-142.
INVESTIGATIONS OF A DOG
Turner, Alison. "Kafka's Two Worlds of Music. " Monatshefte 55:269-279. October 1963.
THE JUDGMENT
Flores, Kate. "Franz Kafka and the Nameless Guilt. " QRL 3:382-405. 1947.

Flores, Kate. "THE JUDGMENT. " Franz Kafka Today. (ed.) Angel Flores. Madison: University of Wisconsin, 1958. pp. 5-24.

Foulkes, A. P. "Dream Pictures in Kafka's Writing. " GR 40:17-18. January 1965.

Greenberg, Martin. "The Literature of Truth. " Salmagundi 1:5-22. Fall 1965.

Levi, P. Margot. "K. , an Exploration of the Names of Kafka's Central Characters. " Names 14:2-3. March 1966.

Macklem, Michael. "Kafka and the Myth of Tristan." DR 30:337-340. January 1951.

Marson, E. L. "Franz Kafka's DAS URTEIL." AUMLA 16: 167-178. November 1961.

Politzer, Heinz. Franz Kafka: Parable and Paradox. New York: Cornell University Press, 1962. pp. 53-65.

Ruhleder, Karl. "Franz Kafka's DAS URTEIL: An Interpretation." Monatshefte 55:13-21. January 1963.

Russell, Francis. Three Studies in Twentieth Century Obscurity. Aldington: Hand and Flower Press, 1954. pp. 55-58.

Steinberg, Erwin R. "Franz Kafka and the God of Israel." Judaism 12:144-149. Spring 1963.

Steinberg, Erwin R. "The Judgment in Kafka's THE JUDGMENT." MFS 8:23-30. Spring 1962.

Von White, John J. "Franz Kafka's DAS URTEIL--an Interpretation." DVLG 38:208-229. July 1964.

METAMORPHOSIS

Adams, Robert M. Strains of Discord: Studies in Literary Openness. Ithaca: Cornell University Press, 1958. pp. 171-177.

Angus, Douglas. "Kafka's METAMORPHOSIS and THE BEAUTY AND THE BEAST Tale." JEGP 53:69-71. January 1954.

Erlich, Victor. "Gogol and Kafka: Note on 'Realism' and 'Surrealism.' " For Roman Jakobson. The Hague: Mouton and Company, 1956. pp. 102-104.

Freedman, Ralph. "Kafka's Obscurity: The Illusion of Logic in Narrative." MFS 8:65-70. Spring 1962.

Goldstein, Bluma. "A Study of the Wound in Stories by Franz Kafka." GR 41:208-214. May 1966.

Holland, Norman N. "Realism and Unrealism: Kafka's METAMORPHOSIS." MFS 4:143-150. Summer 1958.

Landsberg, Paul L. "THE METAMORPHOSIS." The Kafka Problem. (ed.) Angel Flores. New York: New Directions Books, 1946. pp. 122-133.

Luke, F. D. "Kafka's DIE VERWANDLUNG." MLR 46:232-245. April 1951.

Luke, F. D. "THE METAMORPHOSIS." Franz Kafka Today. (ed.) Angel Flores. Madison: University of Wisconsin, 1958. pp. 25-44.

Madden, William A. "A Myth of Meditation: Kafka's META-MORPHOSIS." Thought 26:246-266. Summer 1951.

Martin, Peter A. "The Cockroach as an Identification; With Reference to Kafka's METAMORPHOSIS." AI 16:65-71. Spring 1959.

Neider, Charles. The Frozen Sea. New York: Russell and Russell, 1962. pp. 77-78; Chapter V.

Pfeiffer, Johannes. "The Metamorphosis." Kafka: A Collection of Critical Essays. (ed.) Ronald Gray. New York: Prentice-Hall, 1962. pp. 53-59.

Politzer, Heinz. Franz Kafka: Parable and Paradox. New York: Cornell University Press, 1962. pp. 65-82.

Russell, Francis. Three Studies in Twentieth Century Obscurity. Aldington: Hand and Flower Press, 1954. pp. 52-55.

Scott, Nathan A., Jr. Rehearsals of Discomposure. New York: Columbia University Press, 1952. pp. 37-39.

Seyppel, Joachim H. "The Animal Theme and Totemism in Franz Kafka." AI 13:82-86. Spring 1956.

Sokel, Walter H. "Kafka's METAMORPHOSIS: Rebellion and Punishment." Monatshefte 48:203-214. April - May 1956.

Spilka, Mark. "Dickens and Kafka: 'The Technique of the Grotesque.'" MinnR 1:452-455. Summer 1961.

Spilka, Mark. "Kafka's Sources for THE METAMORPHOSIS." CL 11:289-307. Fall 1959.

Taylor, Alexander. "The Waking: The Theme of Kafka's METAMORPHOSIS." SSF 2:337-342. Summer 1965.

Webster, Peter Dow. "Franz Kafka's METAMORPHOSIS as Death and Resurrection Fantasy." AI 16:349-365. Winter 1959.

THE MOUSE FOLK

Levi, P. Margot. "K., an Exploration of the Names of Kafka's Central Characters." Names 14:7-8. March 1966.

Politzer, Heinz. Franz Kafka: Parable and Paradox. New York: Cornell University Press, 1962. pp. 308-318.

A REPORT TO AN ACADEMY
>Weinstein, Leo. "Kafka's Ape: Heel or Hero?" MFS 8:75-
>79. Spring 1962.

DAS SCHWEIGEN DER SIRENEN
>Foulkes, A. P. "An Interpretation of Kafka's DAS SCHWEI-
>GEN DER SIRENEN. " JEGP 64:98-104. January 1965.

THE TRIAL
>Adolf, Helen. "From EVERYMAN and ELCKERLIJC to Hof-
>mannsthal and Kafka. " CL 9:212-214. Summer 1957.

>Butler, E. M. "The Element of Time in Goethe's WERTHER
>and Kafka's PROZESS. " GL&L 12:248-258. July 1959.

>Camus, Albert. "Hope and the Absurd in the Work of Franz
>Kafka. " Kafka: A Collection of Critical Essays. (ed.) Ronald
>Gray. New York: Prentice-Hall, 1962. pp. 147-155.

>Church, Margaret. "Kafka and Proust: A Contrast in Time."
>BuR 7:110-112. December 1957.

>Church, Margaret. Time and Reality. Chapel Hill: Univer-
>sity of North Carolina Press, 1962. pp. 192-197.

>Church, Margaret. "Time and Reality in Kafka's THE
>TRIAL and THE CASTLE. " TCL 2:62-65. July 1956.

>Dauvin, Rene. "THE TRIAL: Its Meaning. " Franz Kafka
>Today. (ed.) Angel Flores. Madison: University of Wiscon-
>sin, 1958. pp. 145-160.

>Deinert, Herbert. "Kafka's Parable BEFORE THE LAW. "
>GR 39:192-200. May 1964.

>Dyson, A. E. "Trial by Enigma. " TC 160:49-64. July -
>December 1956.

>Feuerlicht, Ignace. "Kafka's Chaplain. " GQ 39:208-220.
>March 1966.

>Fickert, Kurt J. "The Window Metaphor in Kafka's TRIAL."
>Monatshefte 58:345-351. Winter 1966.

>Goodman, Paul. Kafka's Prayer. New York: Vanguard
>Press, 1947. pp. ix-xii; 147-182.

>Gunvaldsen, Kaare. "The Plot of Kafka's TRIAL. " Monat-
>shefte 56:1-14. January 1964.

>Hoffman, Frederick J. "Kafka's THE TRIAL: The Assailant
>as Landscape. " BuR 9:89-105. May 1960.

>Kartiganer, Donald M. "Job and Joseph K.: Myth in Kafka's
>THE TRIAL. " MFS 8:31-43. Spring 1962.

294   The German Novel

Kelly, John. "Franz Kafka's TRIAL and the Theology of Crisis." SoR 5:748-766. Spring 1940.

Krieger, Murray. The Tragic Vision. New York: Holt, Rinehart and Winston, 1960. pp. 114-144.

Leopold, Keith. "Breaks in Perspective in Franz Kafka's DER PROZESS." GQ 36:31-38. January 1963.

Lesser, Simon O. "The Source of Guilt and the Sense of Guilt--Kafka's THE TRIAL." MFS 8:44-60. Spring 1962.

Levi, P. Margot. "K., An Exploration of the Names of Kafka's Central Characters." Names 14:6-7. March 1966.

Macklem, Michael. "Kafka and the Myth of Tristan." DR 30:337-340. January 1951.

Mahoney, John L. "Symbolism and Calvinism in the Novels of Kafka." Renascence 15:200-207. Summer 1963.

Mueller, W. R. Prophetic Voices in New Fiction. New York: Association Press, 1959. pp. 83-109.

Muir, Edwin. "A Note on Franz Kafka." Bookman 72:239. November 1930.

Neider, Charles. The Frozen Sea. New York: Russell and Russell, 1962. pp. 153-181.

Pascal, Roy. The German Novel. Manchester: Manchester University Press, 1956. pp. 226-233.

Politzer, Heinz. "Franz Kafka and Albert Camus: Parables for Our Time." ChiR 14:52-57. Spring 1960.

Politzer, Heinz. Franz Kafka: Parable and Paradox. New York: Cornell University Press, 1962. pp. 163-217.

Politzer, Heinz. "The Puzzle of Kafka's Prosecuting Attorney." PMLA 75:432-438. September 1960.

Rahv, Philip. "THE DEATH OF IVAN ILYICH and Joseph K." SoR 5:174-185. Summer 1939.

Rahv, Philip. "Franz Kafka: The Hero as Lonely Man." KR 1:68-74. Winter 1939.

Rahv, Philip. Image and Idea. Norfolk: Laughlin, 1949. pp. 111-127.

Reed, Eugene E. "Franz Kafka: Possession and Being." Monatshefte 50:359-366. December 1958.

Reed, Eugene E. "Moral Polarity in Kafka's DER PROZESS and DAS SCHLOSS. " Monatshefte 46:317-324. November 1954.

Reiss, H. S. "Franz Kafka's Conception of Humour. " MLR 44:535-540. October 1949.

Rhein, Phillip H. The Urge to Live: A Comparative Study of Franz Kafka's DER PROZESS and Albert Camus' L' ETRANGER. Chapel Hill: University of North Carolina Press, 1964.

Russell, Francis. Three Studies in Twentieth Century Obscurity. Aldington: Hand and Flower Press, 1954. pp. 59-65.

St. Leon, R. "Religious Motives in Kafka's DER PROZESS." AUMLA 19:21-38. May 1963.

Scott, N. A. Rehearsals of Discomposure. New York: Columbia University Press, 1952. pp. 56-63.

Slochower, Harry. No Voice Is Wholly Lost. New York: Creative Age Press, 1945. pp. 109-114.

Spaini, Alberto. "THE TRIAL. " The Kafka Problem. (ed.) Angel Flores. New York: New Directions Books, 1946. pp. 143-150.

Steinberg, M. W. "Franz Kafka: The Achievement of Certitude. " QQ 68:95-97. Spring 1961.

Uyttersprot, Herman. "THE TRIAL: Its Structure. " Franz Kafka Today. (ed.) Angel Flores. Madison: University of Wisconsin, 1958. pp. 127-144.

Vivas, Eliseo. Creation and Discovery. New York: The Noonday Press, 1955. pp. 35-40.

Vivas, Eliseo. "Kafka's Distorted Mask. " Kafka: A Collection of Critical Essays. (ed.) Ronald Gray. New York: Prentice-Hall, 1962. pp. 137-142.

Waldmeir, Joseph J. "Anti-Semitism as an Issue in the Trial of Kafka's Joseph K. " BA 35:10-15. Winter 1961.

Warren, Austin. "Franz Kafka. " Kafka: A Collection of Critical Essays. (ed.) Ronald Gray. New York: Prentice-Hall, 1962. pp. 126-132.

Warren, Austin. "Kosmos Kafka. " SoR 7:350-363. Autumn 1941.

Webster, Peter. " 'Dies Irae' in the Unconscious. " CE
12:10. October 1950.

Weinstein, Leo. "Kafka's Ape: Heel or Hero?" MFS 8:76-
79. Spring 1962.

Wilson, A. K. "Null and Void. " GL&L 14:165-169. April
1961.

Kastner, Erich
     EMIL AND THE DETECTIVE
          Wiley, Raymond A. "The Role of Mother in Five Pre-
          War School Editions of Erich Kastner's Works. " GQ 28:
          22-24. January 1955.
     EMIL AND THE TRIPLETS
          Wiley, Raymond. "The Role of Mother in Five Pre-War
          School Editions of Erich Kastner's Works. " GQ 28:30-33.
          January 1955.
     FABIAN
          Winkelman, John. "Social Criticism in the Early Works of
          Erich Kastner. " University of Missouri Studies 25:27-135.
          No. 4, 1953.
     DAS FLIEGENDE KLASSENZIMMER
          Wiley, Raymond A. "The Role of Mother in Five Pre-War
          School Editions of Erich Kastner's Works. " GQ 28:26-28.
          January 1955.
     PUNKTCHEN UND ANTON
          Wiley, Raymond A. "The Role of Mother in Five Pre-War
          School Editions of Erich Kastner's Works. " GQ 28:24-26.
          January 1955.
     THREE MEN IN THE SNOW
          Wiley, Raymond A. "The Role of Mother in Five Pre-War
          School Editions of Erich Kastner's Works. " GQ 28:28-30.
          January 1955.

Kaufmann, Richard
     HEAVEN PAYS NO DIVIDENDS
          Blotner, Joseph L. The Political Novel. Garden City: Double-
          day and Company, 1955. p. 47.

Keller, Gottfried
     THE ABUSED LOVE LETTERS
          Lob, Ladislaus. "DIE MISSBRAUCHTEN LIEBESBRIEFE:
          A Story of Human Vocation. " GL&L 20:13-24. October
          1966.
     THE BANNER OF THE UPRIGHT SEVEN
          Hauch, Edward Franklin. Gottfried Keller as a Democratic
          Idealist. New York: Columbia University Press, 1916. pp.
          27-33.
     CLOTHES MAKE THE MAN
          Atkins, Stuart. "Vestis Virum Reddit (Gottfried Keller's
          KLEIDER MACHEN LEUTE). " Monatshefte 36:95-102. Feb-
          ruary 1944.

GREEN HENRY
Bennett, E. K. History of the German Novelle. Cambridge:
Cambridge University Press, 1961. p. 177.

Furst, Norbert. "The Conclusion of Keller's GRUNER
HEINRICH. " MLN 55:285-289. April 1940.

Furst, Norbert. "The Structure of L'EDUCATION SENTI-
MENTALE and DER GRUNE HEINRICH. " PMLA 56:249-260.
March 1941.

Hahn, Walther. "The Motif of Light in Gottfried Keller's
Prose Works. " KFLQ 11:97-98. No. 2, 1964.

Hauch, Edward Franklin. Gottfried Keller as a Democratic
Idealist. New York: Columbia University Press, 1916. pp.
40-42; 57-66.

Klenze, Camillo von. From Goethe to Hauptmann. New York:
Viking Press, 1926. pp. 126-128.

Lindsay, F. M. "Gottfried Keller. " German Men of Letters. Vol. I. (ed.) Alex Natan. London: Oswald Wolff, 1961.
pp. 176-179.

Pascal, Roy. The German Novel. Manchester: Manchester
University Press, 1956. pp. 30-51.

Reichert, Herbert W. "Caricature in Keller's DER GRUNE
HEINRICH. " Monatshefte 48:371-379. December 1956.

Robertson, John G. History of German Literature. New
York: Putnam, 1902. pp. 580-581.

Schreiber, William I. "Gottfried Keller's Use of Proverbs
and Proverbial Expressions. " JEGP 53:514-523. October
1954.

Stern, J. P. Re-Interpretations. London: Thames and Hud-
son, 1964. pp. 302-308.
MARTIN SALANDER
Hahn, Walther. "The Motif of Light in Gottfried Keller's
Prose Works. " KFLQ 11:98-99. No. 2, 1964.

Hauch, Edward Franklin. Gottfried Keller as a Democratic
Idealist. New York: Columbia University Press, 1916. pp.
33-39.

von Hofe, Harold. "Gottfried Keller's Conception of the
Unique Character of Swiss Democracy. " Monatshefte 35:
78-80. February 1943.

Lindsay, F. M. "Gottfried Keller. " German Men of Letters.

Vol. I. (ed.) Alex Natan. London: Oswald Wolff, 1961. pp.
189-190.

Ritchie, J. M. "The Place of MARTIN SALANDER in Gottfried Keller's Evolution as a Prose Writer. " MLR 52:214-
222. April 1957.

Schreiber, William I. "Gottfried Keller's Use of Proverbs
and Proverbial Expressions. " JEGP 53:517-523. October
1954.
SEVEN LEGENDS
Hahn, Walther. "The Motif of Light in Gottfried Keller's
Prose Works. " KFLQ 11:95-97. No. 2, 1964.

Hauch, Edward Franklin. Gottfried Keller as a Democratic
Idealist. New York: Columbia University Press, 1916. pp.
55-59.

Lindsay, F. M. "Gottfried Keller. " German Men of Letters.
Vol. I. (ed.) Alex Natan. London: Oswald Wolff, 1961. pp.
182-184.

Liptzin, Sol. Historical Survey of German Literature. New
York: Prentice-Hall, 1936. pp. 146-147.
SHORT NOVELS OF ZURICH
Lindsay, F. M. "Gottfried Keller. " German Men of Letters.
Vol. I. (ed.) Alex Natan. London: Oswald Wolff, 1961. pp.
184-187.
DAS SINNGEDICHT
Leckie, R. William, Jr. "Gottfried Keller's DAS SINNGE-
DICHT as a Novella Cycle. " GR 40:96-115. March 1965.

Lindsay, F. M. "Gottfried Keller. " German Men of Letters.
Vol. I. (ed.) Alex Natan. London: Oswald Wolff, 1961. pp.
187-189.
THREE DECENT COMB MAKERS
Jennings, Lee B. "Gottfried Keller and the Grotesque. "
Monatshefte 50:12-13. January 1958.
URSULA
Hahn, Walther. "The Motif of Light in Gottfried Keller's
Prose Works. " KFLQ 11:93-95. No. 2, 1964.
A VILLAGE ROMEO AND JULIET
Casson, Allan. "THE MILL ON THE FLOSS and Keller's
ROMEO UND JULIA AUF DEM DORFE. " MLN 71:20-22.
January 1960.

Fife, Hildegarde Wichert. "Keller's Dark Fiddler in Nineteenth-Century Symbolism of Evil. " GL&L 16:117-127.
January 1963.

Hahn, Walther. "The Motif of Light in Gottfried Keller's
Prose Works. " KFLQ 11:88-89. No. 2, 1964.

Jennings, Lee B. "Gottfried Keller and the Grotesque. "
Monatshefte 50:9-12. January 1958.

Jones, George F. Honor in German Literature. Chapel Hill:
University of North Carolina Press, 1959. pp. 176-180.

Liptzin, Sol. Historical Survey of German Literature. New
York: Prentice Hall, 1936. pp. 142-146.

Phelps, Reginald H. "Keller's Technique of Composition
in ROMEO UND JULIA AUF DEM DORFE. " GR 24:34-51.
February 1949.

Rehder, Helmut. "ROMEO UND JULIA AUF DEM DORFE--
An Analysis. " Monatshefte 35:416-434. December 1943.

Remak, Henry H. H. "Vinegar and Water: Allegory and
Symbolism. " Literary Symbolism. (ed.) Helmut Rehder.
Austin: University of Texas, 1965. pp. 49-54.

Silz, Walter. "Motivation in Keller's ROMEO UND JULIA."
GQ 8:1-11. January 1935.

Silz, Walter. Realism and Reality. Chapel Hill: University
of North Carolina Press, 1954. pp. 79-93.
DAS VERLORENE LACHEN
    Hauch, Edward Franklin. Gottfried Keller as a Democratic
    Idealist. New York: Columbia University Press, 1916. pp.
    53-55.

    Jennings, Lee B. "Gottfried Keller and the Grotesque. "
    Monatshefte 50:13-14. January 1958.

Keyserling, Eduard von
    SULTRY DAYS
        McCormick, E. Allen. "Utopia and Point of View: Narrative
        Method in Morante's L'ISOLA DI ARTURO and Keyserling's
        SCHWULE TAGE. " Symposium 15:114-129. Summer 1961.

Kleist, Heinrich von
    THE EARTHQUAKE IN CHILE
        Blankenagel, John C. "Heinrich von Kleist: DAS ERDBEBEN
        IN CHILI. " GR 8:30-39. January 1933.

        Ellis, J. M. "Kleist's DAS ERDBEBEN IN CHILE. " PEGS
        33:10-55. 1962-1963.

        Silz, Walter. Heinrich von Kleist. Philadelphia: University
        of Pennsylvania Press, 1961. pp. 13-27.

MICHAEL KOHLHAAS
> Hofacker, Erich. "Bergengruen's DAS FEUERZEICHEN and
> Kleist's MICHAEL KOHLHAAS. " Monatshefte 47:349-357.
> November 1955.

> Jones, George F. Honor in German Literature. Chapel Hill:
> University of North Carolina Press, 1959. pp. 169-170.

> King, Rolf. "The Figure of Luther in Kleist's MICHAEL
> KOHLHAAS. " GR 9:18-25. January 1934.

> Mason, G. R. From Gottsched to Hebbel.   London: Harrap
> and Company, 1961. pp. 206-208.

> Passage, Charles E. "MICHAEL KOHLHAAS: Form Analy-
> sis. " GR 30:181-197. October 1955.

> Silz, Walter. Heinrich von Kleist. Philadelphia: University
> of Pennsylvania Press, 1961. pp. 173-198.

Klinger, Friedrich von
> FAUSTS LEBEN, THATEN UND HOLLENFAHRT
>> Fitzell, John. The Hermit in German Literature. Chapel
>> Hill: University of North Carolina Press, 1961. pp. 80-82.
> GESCHICHTE GIAFARS DES BARMECIDEN
>> Rose, William. From Goethe to Byron. London: Routledge
>> and Sons, 1924. pp. 158-160.

Koestler, Arthur
> AGE OF LONGING
>> Glicksberg, Charles I. "Anti-Communism in Fiction. " SAQ
>> 53:488-489. October 1954.

>> Glicksberg, Charles I. "Anti-Utopianism in Modern Liter-
>> ature. " Southwest Review 37:226-227. Summer 1952.
> ARRIVAL AND DEPARTURE
>> Atkins, John. Arthur Koestler. London: Neville Spearman,
>> Ltd. , 1956. pp. 81-90.

>> Davis, Robert Gorham. "The Sharp Horns of Koestler's
>> Dilemmas. " AR 4:513-515. Winter 1944-1945.

>> Nedava, J. Arthur Koestler. London: Robert Anscombe and
>> Company, Ltd. , 1948. pp. 44-45.

>> Pritchett, V. S. Books in General. London: Chatto and
>> Windus, 1953. pp. 166-167.

>> Roland, Albert. "Christian Implications in Anti-Stalinist
>> Novels. " Religion in Life 22:407-408. Summer 1953.
> DARKNESS AT NOON
>> Atkins, John. Arthur Koestler. London: Neville Spearman,
>> Ltd. , 1956. pp. 177-184.

Blotner, Joseph L. The Political Novel. Garden City:
Doubleday and Company, 1955. pp. 26, 77.

Davis, Robert Gorham. "The Sharp Horns of Koestler's
Dilemma. " AR 4:510-513. Winter 1944-1945.

Howe, Irving. Politics and the Novel. New York: Meridan
Books, 1957. pp. 227-232.

Martin, Kingsley. "Bourgeois Ethics. " New S&N 21:130-
131. February 8, 1941.

Moseley, Edwin M. Pseudonyms of Christ in the Modern
Novel. Pittsburgh: University of Pittsburgh Press, 1962.
pp. 189-194.

Nedava, J. Arthur Koestler. London: Robert Anscombe and
Company, Ltd., 1948. pp. 32-34; 40.

Pritchett, V. S. Books in General. London: Chatto and
Windus, 1953. pp. 164-166.

Roland, Albert. "Christian Implications in Anti-Stalinist
Novels. " Religion in Life 22:406-408. Summer 1953.
THE GLADIATORS
Atkins, John. Arthur Koestler. London: Neville Spearman,
Ltd. , 1956. pp. 117-121.

Davis, Robert Gorham. "The Sharp Horns of Koestler's
Dilemma. " AR 4:505-508. Winter 1944-1945.

Nedava, J. Arthur Koestler. London: Robert Anscombe and
Company, Ltd. , 1948. pp. 35-36.

Pritchett, V. S. Books in General. London: Chatto and
Windus, 1953. pp. 160-164.
SCUM OF THE EARTH
Martin, Kingsley. "SCUM OF THE EARTH. " New S&N 22:
339-340. October 11, 1941.
THIEVES IN THE NIGHT
Glazer, Nathan. "The Parlor Terrorists: Koestler's Fellow-
Travelers and their Politics. " Commentary 3:55-58. January
1947. (Discussion: Commentary 3:285-287. March 1947.)

Mortimer, Raymond. "Arthur Koestler. " Cornhill 162:216-
222. Winter 1946.

Nedava, J. Arthur Koestler. London: Robert Anscombe and
Company, Ltd. , 1948. pp. 49-59.

Pritchett, V. S. Books in General. London: Chatto and
Windus, 1953. pp. 167-172.

Rahv, Philip. "Jews of the Ice Age. " Commentary 2:591-
593. December 1946.

Kramp
    DIE JUNGLINGE
        Boeschenstein, H. The German Novel, 1939-1944. Toronto:
        University of Toronto Press, 1949. pp. 73-77.

Langgasser, Elisabeth
    THE INDELIBLE SEAL
        Politzer, Heinz. "THE INDELIBLE SEAL of Elisabeth Lang-
        gasser. " GR 27:200-209. October 1952.

        Reid, J. C. "The Novels of Elisabeth Langgasser. " DownR
        78:118-125. Spring 1960.
    THE QUEST
        Reid, J. C. "The Novels of Elisabeth Langgasser. " DownR
        78:120-127. Spring 1960.
    UNTERGETAUCHT
        Steinhauer, Harry. "Submerged Heroism: Elisabeth Lang-
        gasser's Story UNTERGETAUCHT. " MLN 74:153-159. Feb-
        ruary 1959.

La Roche, Sophie von
    ERSCHEINUNGEN AM SEE ONEIDA
        Lange, Victor. "Visitors to Lake Oneida: An Account of the
        Background of Sophie von La Roche's Novel ERSCHEINUN-
        GEN AM SEE ONEIDA. " Symposium 2:48-78. May 1948.

Le Fort, Gertrud von
    AM TORE DES HIMMELS
        Wood, Frank. "Gertrud von Le Fort and Bertolt Brecht:
        Counter Reformation and Atomic Bomb. " Studies in Ger-
        man Literature. (ed.) Carl Hammer, Jr. Baton Rouge:
        Louisiana State University Press, 1963. pp. 137-141.
    THE LAST ON THE SCAFFOLD
        O'Boyle, Ita. Gertrud von le Fort: An Introduction to the
        Prose Work. Fordham University Press, 1964. pp. 43-62.

        O'Boyle, Ita. "Gertrud von le Fort's DIE LETZTE AM
        SCHAFOTT. " GL&L 16:98-104. January 1963.

        O'Sharkey, Eithne M. "Bernanos and the Carmelite Mar-
        tyrs. " DubR, Summer 1966, pp. 183-184.
    THE POPE FROM THE GHETTO
        Hilton, I. "Gertrud von Le Fort--A Christian Writer. "
        GL&L 15:300-308. July 1962.

        Klieneberger, H. R. "The Work of Gertrud von le Fort. "
        Studies 50:438-439. Winter 1961.
    THE VEIL OF VERONICA
        Hilton, I. "Gertrud von Le Fort--A Christian Writer. "
        GL&L 15:300-308. July 1962.

Klieneberger, H. R. "The Work of Gertrud von le Fort. "
Studies 50:441-443. Winter 1961.

O'Boyle, Ita. Gertrud von le Fort: An Introduction to the
Prose Work. Fordham University Press, 1964. pp. 3-23.
THE WEDDING OF MAGDEBURG
Klieneberger, H. R. "The Work of Gertrud von le Fort. "
Studies 50:437-438. Winter 1961.
THE WREATH OF ANGELS
O'Boyle, Ita. Gertud von le Fort: An Introduction to the
Prose Work. Fordham University Press, 1964. pp. 24-42.

Wunderlich, Eva C. "Gertrud von le Fort's Fight for the
Living Spirit. " GR 27:300-303. No. 4, 1952.

Lenz
DER WALDBRUDER
Fitzell, John. The Hermit in German Literature. Chapel
Hill: University of North Carolina Press, 1961. pp. 59-64.

Ludwig, Otto
AUS DEM REGEN IN DIE TRAUFE
McClain, William H. Between Real and Ideal: The Course
of Otto Ludwig's Development as a Narrative Writer. Chapel
Hill: University of North Carolina Press, 1963. pp. 52-56.
BETWEEN HEAVEN AND EARTH
Atkins, Stuart. "A Note on Fritz Nettenmair. " Monatshefte
31:349-352. November 1939.

McClain, William H. Between Real and Ideal: The Course
of Otto Ludwig's Development as a Narrative Writer. Chapel
Hill: University of North Carolina Press, 1963. pp. 57-68.
DIE BUSCHNOVELLE
McClain, William H. Between Real and Ideal: The Course
of Otto Ludwig's Development as a Narrative Writer. Chapel
Hill: University of North Carolina Press, 1963. pp. 38-39.

Silz, Walter. "Nature in the Tales of Otto Ludwig. " MLN
41:10-11. January 1926.
DIE EMANZIPATION DER DOMESTIKEN
McClain, William H. Between Real and Ideal: The Course
of Otto Ludwig's Development as a Narrative Writer. Chapel
Hill: University of North Carolina Press, 1963. pp. 13-20.
DAS HAUSGESINDE
McClain, William H. Between Real and Ideal: The Course
of Otto Ludwig's Development as a Narrative Writer. Chapel
Hill: University of North Carolina Press, 1963. pp. 8-12.
DIE HEITERETEI
McClain, William H. Between Real and Ideal: The Course
of Otto Ludwig's Development as a Narrative Writer. Chapel
Hill: University of North Carolina Press, 1963. pp. 45-52.

Silz, Walter. "Nature in the Tales of Otto Ludwig. " MLN

41:11-12. January 1926.
MARIA
    McClain, William H. Between Real and Ideal: The Course
    of Otto Ludwig's Development as a Narrative Writer. Chapel
    Hill: University of North Carolina Press, 1963. pp. 30-37.

    Silz, Walter. "Nature in the Tales of Otto Ludwig." MLN
    41:9-10. January 1926.
DIE WAHRHAFTIGE GESCHICHTE VON DEN DREI WUNSCHEN
    McClain, William H. Between Real and Ideal: The Course
    of Otto Ludwig's Development as a Narrative Writer. Chapel
    Hill: University of North Carolina Press, 1963. pp. 21-29.

Mackay, John Henry
    THE ANARCHISTS
        Riley, Thomas A. "New England Anarchism in Germany."
        NEQ 18:32-33. March 1945.
    DER FREIHEITSUCHER
        Riley, Thomas A. "New England Anarchism in Germany."
        NEQ 18:33-36. March 1945.

Mann, Heinrich
    DIE ARMEN
        Hardaway, R. Travis. "Mann's 'Kaiserreich' Trilogy and
        the Democratic Spirit." JEGP 53:319-333. July 1954.
    AUFERSTEHUNG
        Linn, Rolf N. "Portrait of Two Despots by Heinrich Mann."
        GR 30:125-134. April 1955.
    DIE BRANZILLA
        Linn, Rolf N. "Heinrich Mann's DIE BRANZILLA." Monat-
        shefte 50:75-85. February 1958.
    DIE GÖTTINNEN
        Nicholls, Roger A. "Heinrich Mann and Nietzsche." MLQ
        21:165-178. June 1960.
    THE HEAD
        Hardaway, R. Travis. "Mann's 'Kaiserreich' Trilogy and
        the Democratic Spirit." JEGP 53:319-333. July 1954.
    HENRY IV
        Weisstein, Ulrich. "Heinrich Mann, Montaigne and HENRI
        QUATRE." RLC 36:71-83. January - March 1962.

        Weisstein, Ulrich. "Humanism and the Novel: An Introduc-
        tion to Heinrich Mann's HENRI QUATRE." Monatshefte 51:
        13-24. January 1959.

        Yuill, W. E. "Heinrich Mann." German Men of Letters.
        Vol. 2. (ed.) Alex Natan. London: Oswald Wolff, 1963. pp.
        214-218.
    IM SCHLARAFFENLAND
        Weisstein, Ulrich. "Maupassant's BEL AMI and Heinrich
        Mann's IM SCHLARAFFENLAND." RomN 2:124-128. Spring
        1961.

KOBES
> Linn, Rolf N. "Heinrich Mann and the German Inflation. "
> MLQ 23:80-83. March 1962.

THE LITTLE SUPERMAN
> Bertaux, Felix. Panorama of German Literature. New York:
> McGraw Hill, 1935. p. 132.

> Hardaway, R. Travis. "Mann's 'Kaiserreich' Trilogy and
> the Democratic Spirit. " JEGP 53:319-333. July 1954.

> Yuill, W. E. "Heinrich Mann. " German Men of Letters.
> Vol. 2. (ed.) Alex Natan. London: Oswald Wolff, 1963. pp.
> 206-210.

PIPPO SPANO
> Linn, Rolf N. "The Place of PIPPO SPANO in the Work of
> Heinrich Mann. " MLF 37:130-143. March - June 1952.

THE SMALL TOWN
> Lessing, Otto E. Masters in Modern German Literature.
> Dresden: Verlag, 1912. pp. 175-179.

> Weisstein, Ulrich. "DIE KLEINE STADT: Art, Life and
> Politics in Heinrich Mann's Novel. " GL&L 13:255-261. July
> 1960.

DER TYRANN
> Linn, Rolf N. "Portrait of Two Despots by Heinrich Mann."
> GR 30:125-134. April 1955.

Mann, Thomas
> THE BELOVED RETURNS
> > Braak, Menno ter. "THE BELOVED RETURNS. " The
> > Stature of Thomas Mann. New York: New Directions, 1947.
> > pp. 181-187.

> > Crick, Joyce. "Psycho-analytical Elements in Thomas
> > Mann's Novel LOTTE IN WEIMAR. " L&P 10:69-75. Summer
> > 1960.

> > Dickson, Keith. "The Technique of a 'Musikalisch-Ideeller
> > Beziehungskomplex' in LOTTE IN WEIMAR." MLR 59:413-
> > 424. August 1964.

> > Glebe, William. "The Diseased Artist Achieves a New
> > Health: Thomas Mann's LOTTE IN WEIMAR. " MLQ 22:55-
> > 62. March 1961.

> > Hatfield, Henry. Thomas Mann. Norfolk: New Directions
> > Books, 1951. pp. 121-126.

> > Hughes, William N. "Thomas Mann and the Platonic Adulter-
> > er. " Monatshefte 51:77-80. February 1959.

> > Mueller, Gustav E. "On Thomas Mann's LOTTE IN WEIMAR."
> > BA 19:231-236. Summer 1945.

Slochower, Harry, "Mann's Latest Novels." Accent 4:4-6.
Autumn 1943.

Slochower, Harry. No Voice Is Wholly Lost. New York:
Creative Age Press, Inc., 1945. pp. 355-358.
BLACK SWAN
    Hirschbach, Frank Donald. The Arrow and the Lyre: A
    Study of the Role of Love in the Works of Thomas Mann.
    The Hague: Martinus Nijhoff, 1955. pp. 24-26.

    McWilliams, James R. "Thomas Mann's DIE BETROGENE -
    A Study in Ambivalence." CLAJ 10:56-63. September 1966.

    Mileck, Joseph. "A Comparative Study of DIE BETROGENE
    and DEATH IN VENICE." MLF 42:124-129. December 1957.

    Parry, Idris. "Thomas Mann's Latest Phase." GL&L 8:
    241-246. July 1955.
THE BLOOD OF THE WALSUNGS
    Blissett, William. "Thomas Mann: The Last Wagnerite."
    GR 35:55-57. February 1960.

    Hirschbach, Frank Donald. The Arrow and the Lyre: A Study
    of the Role of Love in the Works of Thomas Mann. The
    Hague: Martinus Nijhoff, 1955. pp. 9-10.
THE BUDDENBROOKS
    Brennan, Joseph G. Thomas Mann's World. New York:
    Columbia University Press, 1942. pp. 1-9; 41-44; 68-69.

    Burgum, Edwin Berry. "The Sense of the Present in Thomas
    Mann." AR 2:389-394. Fall 1942.

    Burkhard, Arthur. "The Genealogical Novel in Scandinavia."
    PMLA 44:310-313. March 1929.

    Burkhard, Arthur. "Mann's Treatment of the Marked Man."
    PMLA 43:563-564. June 1928.

    Church, Margaret. Time and Reality. Chapel Hill: Univer-
    sity of North Carolina Press, 1963. pp. 134-137.

    Clark, A. F. B. "The Dialectical Humanism of Thomas
    Mann." UTQ 8:90-93. October 1938.

    Cleugh, James. Thomas Mann. London: Martin Secker, 1933.
    pp. 79-97.

    Eickhorst, William. Decadence in German Fiction. Denver:
    Swallow, 1953. pp. 48-50.

    Gray, Ronald. The German Tradition in Literature 1871-
    1945. Cambridge: University Press, 1965. pp. 105-136.

Hatfield, Henry. Thomas Mann. Norfolk: New Directions
Books, 1951. pp. 31-50.

Hatfield, Henry C. "Thomas Mann's BUDDENBROOKS: The
World of the Father. " UTQ 20:33-44. October 1950.

Heller, Erich. The Ironic German. Boston: Little, Brown
and Company, 1958. pp. 27-67.

Hirschbach, Frank Donald. The Arrow and the Lyre: A
Study of the Role of Love in the Works of Thomas Mann.
The Hague: Martinus Nijhoff, 1955. pp. 33-42.

Hughes, William N. "Thomas Mann and the Platonic Adulter-
er. " Monatshefte 51:76-80. February 1959.

Kaufmann, Fritz. Thomas Mann: The World as Will and
Representation. Boston: Beacon Press, 1957. pp. 85-94.

Liptzin, Sol. Historical Survey of German Literature. Prentice-Hall, 1936. pp. 216-218.

Lovett, Robert M. "BUDDENBROOKS. " The Stature of
Thomas Mann. (ed.) Charles Neider. New York: New Directions, 1947. pp. 111-118.

March, George. "Thomas Mann and the Novel of Decadence."
SR 37:496-497. October 1929.

Root, John G. "Stylistic Irony in Thomas Mann. " GR 35:
97-99. April 1960.

Schneck, Erna H. "Women in the Works of Thomas Mann. "
Monatshefte 32:145-164. April 1940.

Thomas, R. Hinton. Thomas Mann. Oxford: Clarendon
Press, 1956. pp. 35-58.

Zucker, A. E. "The Genealogical Novel Again. " PMLA 44:
925-927. September 1929.
CONFESSIONS OF FELIX KRULL
Church, Margaret. Time and Reality. Chapel Hill: University of North Carolina Press, 1962. pp. 168-170.

Eichner, Hans. "Aspects of Parody in the Works of Thomas Mann. " MLR 47:33-34. January 1952.

Heilman, Robert B. "Variations on Picaresque. " SR 66:
547-577. October - December 1958.

Heller, Erich. The Ironic German. Boston: Little, Brown
and Company, 1958. pp. 279-285.

Heller, Erich. "Parody, Tragic and Comic: Mann's DOCTOR FAUSTUS and FELIX KRULL. " SR 66:539-546. October - December 1958.

Hollmann, Werner. "Thomas Mann's FELIX KRULL and LAZARILLO. " MLN 66:445-451. November 1951.

Hunt, Joel A. "The Stylistics of a Foreign Language: Thomas Mann's Use of French. " GR 32:24-25. February 1957.

Kleine, Don W. "Felix Krull as a Fairy Tale Hero. " Accent 19:131-141. Summer 1959.

Parry, Idris. "Thomas Mann's Latest Phase. " GL&L 8:246-251. July 1955.

Riley, Anthony W. "Three Cryptic Quotations in Thomas Mann's FELIX KRULL. " JEGP 65:99-106. January 1966.

Sands, Donald B. "The Light and Shadow of Thomas Mann's FELIX KRULL. " Renascence 13:119-124. Spring 1961.

Schiffer, Eva. "Changes in an Episode: A Note on FELIX KRULL. " MLQ 24:257-262. September 1963.

Schiffer, Eva. "Manolescu's Memoirs: The Beginning of FELIX KRULL. " Monatshefte 41:283-292. November 1960.

Seidlin, Oskar. "Picaresque Elements in Thomas Mann's Works. " MLQ 12:184-200. June 1951.

Smeed, J. W. "The Role of Professor Kuckuck in FELIX KRULL. " MLR 59:411-412. July 1964.

Stilwell, Robert L. "Mann's CONFESSIONS OF FELIX KRULL, CONFIDENCE MAN. " Expl 20: Item 24. November 1961.
DEATH IN VENICE
Amory, Frederic. "The Classical Style of DER TOD IN VENEDIG. " MLR 59:399-409. July 1964.

Brennan, Joseph G. Thomas Mann's World. New York: Columbia University Press, 1942. pp. 63-65; 129-130.

Buck, Philo M. , Jr. Directions in Contemporary Literature. New York: Oxford University Press, 1942. pp. 298-304.

Burgum, Edwin Berry. "The Sense of the Present in Thomas Mann. " AR 2:400-401. Fall 1942.

Church, Margaret. "DEATH IN VENICE: A Study of Creativity. " CE 23:648-651. May 1962.

Church, Margaret. Time and Reality. Chapel Hill: University of North Carolina Press, 1962. pp. 143-146.

Clark, A. F. B. "The Dialectical Humanism of Thomas Mann. " UTQ 8:97. October 1938.

Cleugh, James. Thomas Mann. London: Martin Secker, 1933. pp. 136-145.

Daemmrich, Horst S. "Mann's Portrait of the Artist: Archetypal Patterns. " BuR 14:36-37. December 1966.

Eichner, Hans. "Aspects of Parody in the Works of Thomas Mann. " MLR 47:34. January 1952.

Frank, Bruno. "DEATH IN VENICE. " The Stature of Thomas Mann. (ed.) Charles Neider. New York: New Directions, 1947. pp. 119-123.

Gray, Ronald. The German Tradition in Literature 1871-1945. Cambridge: Cambridge University Press, 1965. pp. 145-156.

Gronicka, Andre von. "Myth Plus Psychology: A Style Analysis of DEATH IN VENICE. " GR 31:191-205. October 1956.

Gustafson, Lorraine. "Xenophon and DER TOD IN VENE-DIG. " GR 21:209-214. October 1946.

Hatfield, Henry. Thomas Mann. Norfolk: New Directions Books, 1951. pp. 61-63.

Heller, Erich. The Ironic German. Boston: Little, Brown and Company, 1958. pp. 97-115.

Hepworth, James B. "Tadzio--Sabazios: Notes on DEATH IN VENICE. " WHR 17:172-175. Spring 1963.

Hirschbach, Frank Donald. The Arrow and the Lyre: A Study of the Role of Love in the Works of Thomas Mann. The Hague: Martinus Nijhoff, 1955. pp. 17-21.

Kirchberger, Lida. "DEATH IN VENICE and the Eighteenth Century. " Monatshefte 58:321-333. Winter 1966.

Lehnert, Herbert. "Note on Mann's DER TOD IN VENEDIG and the ODYSSEY. " PMLA 80:306. June 1965.

Lewisohn, Ludwig. "DEATH IN VENICE. " The Stature of Thomas Mann. (ed.) Charles Neider. New York: New Directions, 1947. pp. 124-128.

Liptzin, Sol. Historical Survey of German Literature. New

York: Prentice-Hall, 1936. pp. 219-221.

McClain, William H. "Wagnerian Overtones in DER TOD IN VENEDIG. " MLN 79:481-495. December 1964.

MacIver, R. M. Great Moral Dilemmas. New York: Harper and Brothers, 1956. pp. 25-36.

McNamara, Eugene. "DEATH IN VENICE: The Disguised Self. " CE 24:233-234. December 1962.

March, George. "Thomas Mann and the Novel of Decadence." SR 37:497-499. October 1929.

Martin, John S. "Circean Seduction in Three Works by Thomas Mann. " MLN 78:346-352. October 1963.

Mileck, Joseph. "A Comparative Study of DIE BETROGENE and DEATH IN VENICE. " MLF 42:124-129. December 1957.

Pearson, Gabriel. "The Heroism of Thomas Mann. " ILA 1:127-128. 1958.

Root, John G. "Stylistic Irony in Thomas Mann. " GR 35:94-102. April 1960.

Seyppel, Joachim H. "Two Variations on a Theme: Dying in Venice. " L&P 7:8-12. February 1957.

Stavenhagen, Lee. "The Name Tadzio in DER TOD IN VENEDIG. " GQ 35:20-23. January 1963.

Stelzmann, Rainulf A. "Thomas Mann's DEATH IN VENICE: 'Res et Imago. ' " XUS 3:160-167. December 1964.

Thomas, R. Hinton. Thomas Mann. Oxford: Clarendon Press, 1956. pp. 59-84.

Thomas, R. Hinton. "DIE WAHLVERWANDTSCHAFTEN and Mann's DER TOD IN VENEDIG. " PEGS, 1954-1955, pp. 101-130.

Traschen, Isadore. "The Uses of Myth in DEATH IN VENICE. " MFS 11:165-179. Summer 1965.

Urdang, Constance. "Faust in Venice: The Artist and the Legend in DEATH IN VENICE. " Accent 18:253-267. Autumn 1958.

Venable, Vernon. "DEATH IN VENICE. " The Stature of Thomas Mann. (ed.) Charles Neider. New York: New Directions, 1947. pp. 129-141.

Venable, Vernon. "Poetic Reason in Thomas Mann." VQR 14:64-76. Winter 1938.

THE DILETTANTE

Hirschbach, Frank Donald. The Arrow and the Lyre: A Study of the Role of Love in the Works of Thomas Mann. The Hague: Martinus Nijhoff, 1955. pp. 8-9.

Zerner, Marianne. "Thomas Mann's DER BAJAZZO, a Parody of Dostoevski's NOTES FROM UNDERGROUND." Monatshefte 56:286-290. November 1964.

DOCTOR FAUSTUS

Ames, Van Meter. "The Humanism of Thomas Mann." JAAC 10:253-257. March 1952.

Blackmur, R. P. "Parody and Critique: Notes on Thomas Mann's DOCTOR FAUSTUS." KR 12:20-40. Winter 1950.

Blankenagel, John C. "A Nietzsche Episode in Thomas Mann's DOKTOR FAUSTUS." MLN 63:387-390. June 1948.

Blissett, William. "Thomas Mann: The Last Wagnerite." GR 35:70-74. February 1960.

Blomster, W. V. "Textual Variations in DOKTOR FAUSTUS." GR 39:183-191. May 1964.

Boeninger, H. R. "Zeitblom, Spiritual Descendant of Goethe's Wagner and Wagner's Beckmesser." GL&L 13:38-43. October 1959.

Bonwit, Marianne. "Babel in Modern Fiction." CL 2:243-246. Summer 1950.

Brown, Calvin S. "The Entomological Sources of Mann's Poisonous Butterfly." GR 37:116-120. March 1962.

Charney, Hanna and Maurice. "DOCTOR FAUSTUS and MON FAUST: An Excursus in Dualism." Symposium 16:45-53. Spring 1962.

Church, Margaret. Time and Reality. Chapel Hill: University of North Carolina Press, 1962. pp. 162-166.

Daemmrich, Horst S. "Mann's Portrait of the Artist: Archetypal Patterns." BuR 14:37-40. December 1966.

Eichner, Hans. "Aspects of Parody in the Works of Thomas Mann." MLR 47:30-33. June 1952.

Eichner, Hans. "The Place of DOKTOR FAUSTUS in the Work of Thomas Mann." GL&L 1:289-302. July 1948.

Engelberg, Edward. "Thomas Mann's Faust and Beethoven."

Monatshefte 47:112-116. February 1955.

Field, G. W. "Music and Morality in Thomas Mann and
Hermann Hesse. " UTQ 24:176-178. January 1955.

Frank, Joseph. "Reaction as Progress: or, The Devil's
Domain. " HudR 2:38-53. Spring 1949.

Frank, Joseph. "Reaction as Progress: Thomas Mann's DR.
FAUSTUS. " ChiR 15:19-39. Autumn 1961.

Gray, Ronald. The German Tradition in Literature 1871-
1945. Cambridge: University Press, 1965. pp.
208-223.

Gronicka, Andre. "Thomas Mann's DOKTOR FAUSTUS, "
GR 23:206-218. October 1948.

Hatfield, Henry C. "Two Notes on Thomas Mann's DOKTOR
FAUSTUS. " MLF 34:11-17. March - June 1949.

Heller, Erich. The Ironic German. Boston: Little, Brown
and Company, 1958. pp. 259-279.

Heller, Erich. "Parody, Tragic and Comic: Mann's DOCTOR
FAUSTUS and FELIX KRULL. " SR 66:519-546. October -
December 1958.

Heller, Erich. "Thomas Mann and the 'Domestic Perver-
sity. ' " Encounter 12:54-56. March 1959.

Hirschbach, Frank Donald. The Arrow and the Lyre: A
Study of the Role of Love in the Works of Thomas Mann.
The Hague: Martinus Nijhoff, 1955. pp. 115-148.

Hunt, Joel. "The Stylistics of a Foreign Language: Thomas
Mann's Use of French. " GR 32:19-20. February 1957.

Kahler, Erich. "Thomas Mann's DOCTOR FAUSTUS. "
Commentary 7:348-357. April 1949.

Kaufmann, Fritz. Thomas Mann: The World as Will and
Representation. Boston: Beacon Press, 1957. pp. 197-238.

Kaye, Julian B. "Conrad's UNDER WESTERN EYES and
Mann's DOCTOR FAUSTUS. " CL 9:60-65. Winter 1957.

Krieger, Murray. The Tragic Vision. New York: Holt,
Rinehart and Winston, 1960. pp. 87-102.

Lindsay, J. M. Thomas Mann. Oxford: Blackwell, 1954.
pp. 113-124.

Lyon, James K. "Words and Music: Thomas Mann's Tone-Poem DOCTOR FAUSTUS. " WHR 13:99-102. Winter 1959.

Mann, Michael. "The Musical Symbolism in Thomas Mann's DOCTOR FAUSTUS. " Music Rev 17:314-322. November 1956.

Mann, Thomas. The Story of a Novel. New York: Alfred A. Knopf, 1961. 233 pp.

Orton, G. "The Archaic Language in Thomas Mann's DOKTOR FAUSTUS. " MLR 45:70-75. January 1950.

Oswald, Victor A. , Jr. "Full Fathom Five: Notes on Some Devices in Thomas Mann's DOKTOR FAUSTUS. " GR 24:274-278. December 1949.

Oswald, Victor A. , Jr. "Thomas Mann and the Mermaid: A Note on Constructivistic Music. " MLN 65:171-175. March 1950.

Oswald, Victor A., Jr. "Thomas Mann's DOKTOR FAUSTUS: The Enigma of Frau von Tolna. " GR 23:249-253. December 1948.

Raleigh, John Henry. "Mann's Double Vision: DOCTOR FAUSTUS and THE HOLY SINNER. " Pac Spec 7:380-392. Autumn 1953.

Reed, Carroll E. "Thomas Mann and the Faust Tradition. " JEGP 51:17-34. January 1952.

Reichert, Herbert W. "Goethe's Faust in Two Novels of Thomas Mann. " GQ 22:209-214. November 1949.

Rey, W. H. "Return to Health? 'Disease' in Mann's DOCTOR FAUSTUS. " PMLA 65:21-26. March 1950.

Rice, Philip Blair. "The Merging Parallels: Mann's DOCTOR FAUSTUS. " KR 11:199-217. Spring 1949.

Rolo, Charles J. "Mann and His Mephistopheles. " Atlantic 182:92-94. November 1948.

Sender, Ramon J. "Faustian Germany and Thomas Mann. " NMQ 19:193-206. Summer 1949.

Stein, Jack M. "Adrian Leverkuhn As a Composer. " GR 25:257-274. December 1950.

Stern, J. P. "Thomas Mann's Last Period. " CritQ 8:249-253. Autumn 1966.

Stewart, John L. "On the Making of DOCTOR FAUSTUS."
SR 59:329-342. April - June 1951.

Taubes, Jacob. "From Cult to Culture." PR 21:387-400.
July - August 1954.

Thomas, R. Hinton. Thomas Mann. Oxford: Clarendon
Press, 1956. pp. 137-167.

Tuska, Jon. "The Vision of Doktor Faustus." GR 40:
277-309. November 4, 1965.

White, James F. "Echo's Prayers in Thomas Mann's DOK-
TOR FAUSTUS." Monatshefte 42:385-394. December 1950.

Wiemann, H. "Thomas Mann and DOKTOR FAUSTUS."
AUMLA 4:39-45. May 1956.

Williams, W. D. "Thomas Mann's DOCTOR FAUSTUS."
GL&L 12:273-281. July 1959.

Wirtz, Erika A. "Thomas Mann, Humorist and Educator."
ML 47:149-150. December 1966.

Yourcenar, Marguerite. "Humanism in Thomas Mann." PR
23:153-170. Spring 1956.
FALLEN
Hirschbach, Frank Donald. The Arrow and the Lyre: A Study
of the Role of Love in the Works of Thomas Mann. The
Hague: Martinus Nijhoff, 1955. pp. 3-5.
FIORENZA
Clark, A. F. B. "The Dialectical Humanism of Thomas
Mann." UTQ 8:94-95. October 1938.
THE HOLY SINNER
Bercovitch, Sacvan. "Thomas Mann's 'Heavenly Alchemy':
The Politics of THE HOLY SINNER." Symposium 20:293-
304. Winter 1966.

Brandt, Thomas O. "Narcissism in Thomas Mann's DER
ERWAHLTE." GL&L 7:233-241. July 1954.

Church, Margaret. Time and Reality. Chapel Hill: University of North Carolina Press, 1962. pp. 166-167.

Fraiberg, Selma. "Two Modern Incest Heroes." PR 28:651-
661. No. 5-6, 1961.

Furstenheim, E. G. "The Place of DER ERWAHLTE in the
Work of Thomas Mann." MLR 51:55-70. January 1956.

McClain, William H. "Irony and Belief in Thomas Mann's
DER ERWAHLTE." Monatshefte 43:319-323. November
1951.

Raleigh, John Henry. "Mann's Double Vision: DOCTOR FAUSTUS and THE HOLY SINNER. " PacSpec 7:380-392. Autumn 1953.

Schoolfield, George C. "Thomas Mann and the Honest Pagans. " PQ 36:280-285. April 1957.

Stock, Irvin. "Mann's Christian Parable: A View of THE HOLY SINNER. " Accent 14:98-114. Spring 1954.

West, Ray B. , Jr. "Thomas Mann: Moral Precept as Psychological Truth. " SR 60:310-317. 1952.

Weigand, Hermann J. "Thomas Mann's GREGORIUS I-III. " GR 27:10-30. February 1952.

Weigand, Hermann J. "Thomas Mann's GREGORIUS IV-V. " GR 27:83-95. April 1952.

JOSEPH AND HIS BROTHERS

Ackermann, Paul Kurt. "Comments on JOSEPH UND SEINE BRUDER in Some Unpublished Letters from Thomas Mann to Rene Schickele. " Monatshefte 54:197-200. April - May 1962.

Ames, Van Meter. "The Humanism of Thomas Mann. " JAAC 10:248-253. March 1952.

Bab, Julius. "JOSEPH AND HIS BROTHERS. " The Stature of Thomas Mann. (ed.) Charles Neider. New York: New Directions, 1947. pp. 195-210.

Bennett, E. K. History of the German Novelle. Cambridge: University Press, 1961. p. 259.

Blissett, William. "Thomas Mann: The Last Wagnerite. " GR 35:65-70. February 1960.

Bloch, Adele. "The Archetypal Influence in Thomas Mann's JOSEPH AND HIS BROTHERS. " GR 38:151-156. March 1963.

Brennan, Joseph G. Thomas Mann's World. New York: Columbia University Press, 1942. pp. 66-67.

Buck, Philo M. , Jr. Directions in Contemporary Literature. New York: Oxford University Press, 1942. pp. 305-310; 312-313.

Cather, Willa. Not Under Forty. New York: Knopf, 1936. pp. 96-122.

Church, Margaret. Time and Reality. Chapel Hill: University of North Carolina Press, 1962. pp. 154-162.

Clark, A. F. B. "The Dialectical Humanism of Thomas Mann." UTQ 8:101-105. October 1938.

Follett, Wilson. "Time and Thomas Mann." Atlantic 161: 792-794. June 1938.

Frederick, John. "Thomas Mann and JOSEPH THE PROVIDER." CE 6:1-5. October 1944.

Gray, Ronald. The German Tradition in Literature 1871-1945. Cambridge: University Press, 1965. pp. 185-207.

Hatfield, Henry. Thomas Mann. Norfolk: New Directions Books, 1951. pp. 95-120.

Heller, Erich. The Ironic German. Boston: Little, Brown and Company, 1958. pp. 219-258.

Heller, Peter. "Some Functions of the Leitmotiv in Thomas Mann's Joseph Tetralogy." GR 22:126-141. April 1947.

Hirschbach, Frank Donald. The Arrow and the Lyre: A Study of the Role of Love in the Works of Thomas Mann. The Hague: Martinus Nijhoff, 1955. pp. 85-114.

Kaufmann, Fritz. Thomas Mann: The World as Will and Representation. Boston: Beacon Press, 1957. pp. 129-168.

Levin, Harry. "JOSEPH THE PROVIDER." The Stature of Thomas Mann (ed.) Charles Neider. New York: New Directions, 1947. pp. 211-217.

Lindsay, J. M. Thomas Mann. Oxford: Blackwell Press, 1954. pp. 100-112.

Liptzin, Sol. Historical Survey of German Literature. New York: Prentice-Hall, 1936. pp. 223-224.

Mann, Thomas. "The Joseph Novels." The Stature of Thomas Mann. (ed.) Charles Neider. New York: New Directions, 1947. pp. 218-232.

Mann, Thomas. The Theme of the Joseph Novels. Washington: Library of Congress, 1942. 24 pp.

Ordon, Edmund. "Thomas Mann's 'Joseph'--Cycle and the American Critic." Monatshefte 35:286-296. May 1943. (Continued, 318-330. October 1943.)

Politzer, Heinz. "America in the Later Writings of Thomas Mann." MLF 37:91-100. September - December 1952.

Rice, Philip Blair. "Thomas Mann and the Religious Revival. " KR 7:366-373. Summer 1945.

Rosenberg, Harold. "Thomas Mann's JOSEPH: A Humanist Myth. " CJR 8:154-162. April 1945.

Seidenspinner, Clarence. "How to Read Thomas Mann. " Religion in Life 14:126-129. Winter 1944-1945.

Seidlin, Oskar. "Laurence Sterne's TRISTRAM SHANDY and Thomas Mann's JOSEPH THE PROVIDER. " MLQ 8:101-118. March 1947.

Sell, Friedrich Carl. "Thomas Mann and the Problem of Anti-Intellectualism. " GR 15:289-291. December 1940.

Slochower, Harry. No Voice Is Wholly Lost. New York: Creative Age Press, 1945. pp. 338-355.

Slochower, Harry. Thomas Mann's Joseph Story. New York: Knopf, 1938.

Stern, J. P. "Thomas Mann's Last Period. " CritQ 8:245-249. Autumn 1966.

Stockhammer, Morris. "Thomas Mann's Job-Jacob. " Judaism 8:242-246. Summer 1959.

Thomas, R. Hinton. Thomas Mann. Oxford: Clarendon Press, 1956. pp. 112-136.

Van Doren, Mark. "JOSEPH AND HIS BROTHERS: A Comedy in Four Parts. " ASch 26:289-302. Summer 1957.

Watts, Harold H. "Thomas Mann and the Opposites. " SAQ 45:102-114. 1946.

Watts, Harold H. "The Thrice-Told Tale: Thomas Mann's Myth for His Times. " QRL 4:299-310. No. 3, 1949.

LITTLE HERR FRIEDEMANN

Hirschbach, Frank Donald. The Arrow and the Lyre: A Study of the Role of Love in the Works of Thomas Mann. The Hague: Martinus Nijhoff, 1955. pp. 5-8.

Thomas, R. Hinton. Thomas Mann: The Mediation of Art. Oxford: Clarendon Press, 1956. pp. 21-26.

West, Ray B. , Jr. and Robert Wooster Stallman. The Art of Modern Fiction. New York: Holt, Rinehart and Winston, 1960. pp. 316-319.

West, Ray B. , Jr. "Three Methods of Modern Fiction. " CE 12:196-198. January 1951.

MAGIC MOUNTAIN

Ames, Van Meter. "The Humanism of Thomas Mann."
JAAC 10:247-248. March 1952.

Beach, Joseph W. "THE MAGIC MOUNTAIN." The Stature
of Thomas Mann. (ed.) Charles Neider. New York: New
Directions, 1947. pp. 142-149.

Blackmur, R. P. "Hans Castorp, Small Lord of Counterpo-
sitions." HudR 1:318-339. Autumn 1948.

Blissett, William. "Thomas Mann: The Last Wagnerite."
GR 35:57-65. February 1960.

Bohning, Elizabeth E. "The 'Hintergrundsgestalten' in THE
MAGIC MOUNTAIN." GQ 18:189-202. November 1945.

Braun, Frank X. "A Lesson in Articulation in Thomas
Mann's ZAUBERBERG." Monatshefte 58:124-130. Summer
1966.

Brennan, Joseph G. Thomas Mann's World. New York:
Columbia University Press, 1942. pp. 48-69; 97-108; 120-
123; 144-147.

Buck, Philo M., Jr. Directions in Contemporary Literature. New York: Oxford University Press, 1942. pp. 295-
298.

Burgum, Edwin Berry. "The Sense of the Present in Thomas Mann." AR 2:394-400. Fall 1942.

Church, Margaret. Time and Reality. Chapel Hill: University of North Carolina Press, 1962. pp. 146-154.

Clark, A. F. B. "The Dialectical Humanism of Thomas
Mann." UTQ 8:98-101. October 1938.

Cleugh, James. Thomas Mann. London: Martin Secker,
1933. pp. 181-197.

Gaertner, Johannes A. "Dialectic Thought in Thomas
Mann's THE MAGIC MOUNTAIN." GQ 38:605-618. November 1965.

Gray, Ronald. The German Tradition in Literature 1871-
1945. Cambridge: University Press, 1965. pp.
157-172.

Harvey, W. J. Character and the Novel. Ithaca: Cornell
University Press, 1965. pp. 100-108.

Hatfield, Henry. Thomas Mann. Norfolk: New Directions

Books, 1951. pp. 66-87.

Heller, Erich. The Ironic German. Boston: Little, Brown and Company, 1958. pp. 169-214.

Hindus, Milton. "The Duels in Mann and Turgenev. " CL 11:308-312. Fall 1959.

Hirschbach, Frank Donald. The Arrow and the Lyre: A Study of the Role of Love in the Works of Thomas Mann. The Hague: Martinus Nijhoff, 1955. pp. 53-84.

Hunt, Joel A. "Mann and Whitman: Humaniores Litterae. " CL 14:266-271. Summer 1962.

Hunt, Joel A. "The Stylistics of a Foreign Language: Thomas Mann's Use of French. " GR 32:22-23; 27-28. February 1957.

Kaufmann, Fritz. Thomas Mann: The World as Will and Representation. Boston: Beacon Press, 1957. pp. 95-118; 125-129.

Kratz, Henry. "A Methodological Critique of W. R. Maurer's 'Names from THE MAGIC MOUNTAIN. ' " Names 11: 20-25. March 1963.

Krieger, Murray. The Tragic Vision. New York: Holt, Rinehart and Winston, 1960. pp. 102-113.

Lesser, J. "Of Thomas Mann's Renunciation. " GR 25:245-256. December 1950.

Liptzin, Sol. Historical Survey of German Literature. New York: Prentice-Hall, 1936. pp. 221-223.

March, George. "Thomas Mann and the Novel of Decadence." SR 37:499-503. 1929.

Martin, John S. "Circean Seduction in Three Works by Thomas Mann. " MLN 78:346-352. October 1963.

Maurer, Warren R. "Names from THE MAGIC MOUNTAIN." Names 9:248-259. December 1961.

Miller, R. D. The Two Faces of Hermes. Harrogate: Duchy Press, 1962. 124 pp.

Mumford, Lewis. "THE MAGIC MOUNTAIN. " The Stature of Thomas Mann. (ed.) Charles Neider. New York: New Directions, 1947. pp. 150-155.

Pascal, Roy. The German Novel. Manchester: Manchester

University Press, 1956. pp. 76-98.

Passage, Charles E. "Hans Castorp's Musical Incantation. "
GR 38:238-256. May 1963.

Pearson, Gabriel. "The Heroism of Thomas Mann. " ILA 1:
128-129. 1958.

Rebelsky, Freda Gould. "Coming of Age in Davos: An Analysis of the Maturation of Hans Castorp in Thomas Mann's
THE MAGIC MOUNTAIN. " AI 18:413-421. Winter 1961.

Reichert, Herbert W. "Goethe's Faust in Two Novels of
Thomas Mann. " GQ 22:209-214. November 1949.

Roth, Maria C. "Mynheer Peeperkorn in the Light of
Schopenhauer's Philosophy. " Monatshefte 58:335-343. Winter 1966.

Schneck, Erna H. "Women in the Works of Thomas Mann. "
Monatshefte 32:145-164. April 1940.

Schultz, H. Stefan. "On the Interpretation of Thomas Mann's
DER ZAUBERBERG. " MP 52:110-122. November 1954.

Seidenspinner, Clarence. "How to Read Thomas Mann. "
Religion in Life 14:123-126. Winter 1944-1945.

Slochower, Harry. No Voice Is Wholly Lost. New York:
Creative Age Press, 1945. pp. 336-337.

Slochower, Harry. Three Ways of Modern Man. New York:
International Publishers, 1937. pp. 50-104.

Struc, Roman R. "The Threat of Chaos: Stifter's BERG-
KRISTALL and Thomas Mann's 'Schnee. ' " MLQ 24:323-
332. December 1963.

Thirlwall, John C. "Orphic Influence in MAGIC MOUNTAIN."
GR 25:290-298. February 1950.

Thomas, R. Hinton. Thomas Mann. Oxford: Clarendon
Press, 1956. pp. 85-111.

Tindall, William York. The Literary Symbol. Bloomington:
Indiana University Press, 1955. pp. 171-174.

Weigand, Hermann J. "THE MAGIC MOUNTAIN. " The Stature of Thomas Mann. (ed.) Charles Neider. New York:
New Directions, 1947. pp. 156-164.

Weigand, Hermann J. A Study of THE MAGIC MOUNTAIN:
Thomas Mann's Novel DER ZAUBERBERG. New York:

D. Appleton-Century, 1933.

Young, Frederic. "The Conflict of Nature and Spirit. "
Christendom 13:59-68. Winter 1948.

Yourcenar, Marguerite. "Humanism in Thomas Mann. "
PR 23:153-170. Spring 1956.

Zinberg, Dorothy S. and Norman E. Zinberg. "Hans Castorp: Identity Crisis Without Resolution. " AI 20:393-402.
Winter 1963.

A MAN AND HIS DOG
Braun, Frank X. "Thomas Mann's Canine Idyl. " Monatshefte 49:207-211. April - May 1957.

MARIO AND THE MAGICIAN
Brennan, Joseph G. Thomas Mann's World. New York:
Columbia University Press, 1942. pp. 150-152.

Gray, Ronald. The German Tradition in Literature 1871-
1945. Cambridge: Cambridge University Press, 1965. pp.
173-184.

Hatfield, Henry C. "MARIO AND THE MAGICIAN. " The
Stature of Thomas Mann. (ed.) Charles Neider. New York:
New Directions, 1947. pp. 168-173.

Hatfield, Henry. Thomas Mann. Norfolk: New Directions
Books, 1951. pp. 90-94.

Hatfield, Henry C. "Thomas Mann's MARIO UND DER
ZAUBERER: An Interpretation. " GR 21:306-312. December
1946.

Martin, John S. "Circean Seduction in Three Works by
Thomas Mann. " MLN 78:346-352. October 1963.

Matenko, Percy. "The Prototype of Cipolla in MARIO UND
DER ZAUBERER. " Italica 31:133-135. September 1954.

Slochower, Harry. Three Ways of Modern Man. New York:
International Publishers, 1945. pp. 100-101.

ROYAL HIGHNESS
Brennan, Joseph G. Thomas Mann's World. New York:
Columbia University Press, 1942. pp. 18-19.

Burgum, Edwin Berry. "The Sense of the Present in
Thomas Mann. " AR 2:388-389. Fall 1942.

Burkhard, Arthur. "Thomas Mann's Appraisal of the Poet."
PMLA 46:897. 1931.

Clark, A. F. B. "The Dialectical Humanism of Thomas
Mann. " UTQ 8:95-97. October 1938.

Frey, Erich A. "An American Prototype in Thomas Mann's KONIGLICHE HOHEIT." KFLQ 13:125-129. Third Quarter 1966.

Hatfield, Henry. Thomas Mann. Norfolk: New Directions Books, 1951. pp. 57-60.

Heller, Erich. The Ironic German. Boston: Little, Brown and Company, 1958. pp. 96-97.

Hirschbach, Frank Donald. The Arrow and the Lyre: A Study of the Role of Love in the Works of Thomas Mann. The Hague: Martinus Nijhoff, 1955. pp. 42-52.

Vordtriede, Werner. "A Case of Transposed Heads in Thomas Mann's KONIGLICHE HOHEIT." MLN 74:49-51. January 1959.

TONIO KROGER

Basilius, H. A. "Thomas Mann's Use of Musical Structure and Techniques in TONIO KROGER." GR 19:284-308. December 1944.

Bennett, E. K. History of the German Novelle. Cambridge: University Press, 1961. pp. 254-255.

Brennan, Joseph G. Thomas Mann's World. New York: Columbia University Press, 1942. pp. 11-13; 19-22; 115-117.

Burkhard, Arthur. "Mann's Treatment of the Marked Man." PMLA 43:562-563. June 1928.

Burkhard, Arthur. "Thomas Mann's Appraisal of the Poet." PMLA 46:887-893. 1931.

Church, Margaret. Time and Reality. Chapel Hill: University of North Carolina Press, 1962. pp. 137-143.

Clark, A. F. B. "The Dialectical Humanism of Thomas Mann." UTQ 8:93-94. October 1938.

Cleugh, James. Thomas Mann: A Study. London: Martin Secker, 1933. pp. 97-101.

Gray, Ronald. The German Tradition 1871-1945. Cambridge: University Press, 1965. pp. 137-145.

Hatfield, Henry. Thomas Mann. Norfolk: New Directions Books, 1951. pp. 52-56.

Heller, Erich. The Ironic German. Boston: Little, Brown and Company, 1958. pp. 68-85.

Hirschbach, Frank Donald. The Arrow and the Lyre: A
Study of the Role of Love in the Works of Thomas Mann.
The Hague: Martinus Nijhoff, 1955. pp. 14-17.

Hunt, Joel A. "The Stylistics of a Foreign Language: Thomas Mann's Use of French. " GR 32:21-22. February 1957.

March, George. "Thomas Mann and the Novel of Decadence."
SR 37:493-496. October 1929.

Maurer, K. W. "TONIO KROGER and HAMLET. " MLR 43:
520. October 1948.

Morgan, B. Q. "On Translating TONIO KROGER. " GQ 19:
220-225. May 1946.

Pearson, Gabriel. "The Heroism of Thomas Mann. " ILA
1:126-127. 1958.

Root, Winthrop H. "Grillparzer's SAPPHO and Thomas
Mann's TONIO KROGER. " Monatshefte 29:59-64. February
1937.

Wilson, Kenneth. "The Dance as Symbol and Leitmotiv in
Thomas Mann's TONIO KROGER. " GR 29:282-287. Decem-
ber 1954.
TRANSPOSED HEADS
Brennan, Joseph G. Thomas Mann's World. New York:
Columbia University Press, 1942. pp. 184-187.

Campbell, Joseph. "Heinrich Zimmer. " PR 20:444-451.
July - August 1953.

Church, Margaret. Time and Reality. Chapel Hill: University of North Carolina Press, 1962. p. 162.

Fleissner, Else M. "Stylistic Confusion in Thomas Mann's
Indian Legend, THE TRANSPOSED HEADS. " GR 18:209-
212. October 1943.

Hirschbach, Frank Donald. The Arrow and the Lyre: A
Study of the Role of Love in the Works of Thomas Mann.
The Hague: Martinus Nijhoff, 1955. pp. 21-24.

Slochower, Harry. "Mann's Latest Novels. " Accent 4:6-8.
Autumn 1943.

Willson, A. Leslie. "Thomas Mann's DIE VERTAUSCHTEN
KOPFE: The Catalyst of Creation. " Monatshefte 49:313-
321. November 1957.
TRISTAN
Bennett, E. K. History of the German Novelle. Cambridge:
University Press, 1961. p. 253.

Burkhard, Arthur. "Thomas Mann's Appraisal of the Poet."
PMLA 46:894-896. 1931.

Cleugh, James. Thomas Mann. London: Martin Secker,
1933. pp. 101-105.

Hatfield, Henry. Thomas Mann. Norfolk: New Directions
Books, 1951. pp. 24-26.

Hirschbach, Frank Donald. The Arrow and the Lyre: A
Study of the Role of Love in the Works of Thomas Mann.
The Hague: Martinus Nijhoff, 1955. pp. 10-14.

Hughes, William N. "Thomas Mann and the Platonic Adulter-
er. " Monatshefte 51:76-80. February 1959.

Kirchberger, Lida. "Thomas Mann's TRISTAN. " GR 36:
282-297. December 1961.
THE WARDROBE
Hatfield, Henry C. "Charon and DER KLEIDERSCHRANK. "
MLN 65:100-102. February 1950.

Meyer, Conrad Ferdinand
DAS AMULETT
Blankenagel, John C. "Conrad Ferdinand Meyer: DAS
AMULETT. " JEGP 33:270-279. April 1934.

Park, Rosemary. "Concrete Objects in Conrad Ferdinand
Meyer's Novellen. " GR 18:252. December 1943.
ANGELA BORGIA
Park, Rosemary. "Concrete Objects in Conrad Ferdinand
Meyer's Novellen." GR 18:263-264. December 1943.
JURG JENATSCH
Park, Rosemary. "Concrete Objects in Conrad Ferdinand
Meyer's Novellen. " GR 18:259-260. December 1943.
THE MONK'S WEDDING
Park, Rosemary. "Concrete Objects in Conrad Ferdinand
Meyer's Novellen. " GR 18:256-257. December 1943.
THE PAGE OF GUSTAVUS ADOLPHUS
Burkhard, Arthur and Henry H. Stevens. "Conrad Ferdinand
Meyer Reveals Himself: A Critical Examination of GUSTAV
ADOLFS PAGE. " GR 15:191-212. October 1940.

Park, Rosemary. "Concrete Objects in Conrad Ferdinand
Meyer's Novellen. " GR 18:254-255. December 1943.
PLAUTUS IN THE CONVENT
Park, Rosemary. "Concrete Objects in Conrad Ferdinand
Meyer's Novellen. " GR 18:253-254. December 1943.
THE SAINT
Burkhard, Arthur. "Thomas Becket and Josef Susz Oppen-
heimer as Fathers. " GR 6:144-153. April 1931.

Hardaway, R. Travis. "C. F. Meyer's DER HEILIGE in

Relation to Its Sources. " PMLA 58:245-263. March 1943.

Park, Rosemary. "Concrete Objects in Conrad Ferdinand
Meyer's Novellen. " GR 18:260-261. December 1943.

Silz, Walter. Realism and Reality. Chapel Hill: University
of North Carolina Press, 1954. pp. 94-116.
THE SHOT FROM THE PULPIT
        Park, Rosemary. "Concrete Objects in Conrad Ferdinand
        Meyer's Novellen. " GR 18:252-253. December 1943.
THE SUFFERINGS OF A BOY
        Park, Rosemary. "Concrete Objects in Conrad Ferdinand
        Meyer's Novellen. " GR 18:255-256. December 1943.
THE TEMPTATION OF PESCARA
        Park, Rosemary. "Concrete Objects in Conrad Ferdinand
        Meyer's Novellen. " GR 18:261-262. December 1943.
THE WOMAN JUDGE
        Park, Rosemary. "Concrete Objects in Conrad Ferdinand
        Meyer's Novellen. " GR 18:257-259. December 1943.

Morike, Eduard
    PAINTER NOLTEN
        Hewett-Thayer, Harvey W. "Morike's Occultism and the
        Revision of MALER NOLTEN. " PMLA 71:386-413. June
        1956.

        Hewett-Thayer, Harvey W. "Traditional Technique in
        Morike's MALER NOLTEN. " GR 32:259-266. December
        1957.

        Immerwahr, Raymond. "The Inception of 'Mozart auf der
        Reise nach Prag. ' " PMLA 70:390-407. June 1955.

        Jennings, Leo B. "Morike's Grotesquery: A Post-Romantic
        Phenomenon. " JEGP 59:600-616. October 1960.

        Prawer, S. S. "Morike's Second Thoughts. " MP 57:24-36.
        August 1959.

Moritz, Karl
    ANTON REISER
        Kurrelmeyer, W. "A Fragment of an Earlier Version of
        ANTON REISER. " MLN 33:1-7. January 1918.

        Rose, William. From Goethe to Byron. London: Routledge
        and Sons, 1924. pp. 91-107.

        Zeydel, Edwin H. "The Relation of K. P. Moritz's ANTON
        REISER to Romanticism. " GR 3:304-327. October 1928.

Moscherosch, Johann Michael
    SOLDATEN - LEBEN
        Knight, K. G. "Moscherosch's Novel SOLDATEN-LEBEN."

GL&L 7:48-55. October 1953.

Musaus, Johann Karl August von
GRANDISON DER ZWEITE
Stern, Guy. "A German Imitation of Fielding: Musaus'
GRANDISON DER ZWEITE. " CL 10:335-343. Fall 1958.

Musil, Robert
GRIGIA
McCormick, E. Allen. "Ambivalence in Musil's DREI
FRAUEN: Notes on Meaning and Method. " Monatshefte 54:
183-195. April - May 1962.
MAN WITHOUT QUALITIES
Boeninger, Helmut R. "The Rediscovery of Robert Musil. "
MLF 37:115-119. September - December 1952.

Braun, Wilhelm. "Moosbrugger Dances. " GR 35:214-230.
October 1960.

Braun, W. "Musil and the Pendulum of the Intellect. "
Monatshefte 49:109-119. March 1957.

Braun, W. "Musil's 'Erdensekretariat der Genauigkeit und
Seele, ' A Clue to the Philosophy of the Hero of DER MANN
OHNE EIGENSCHAFTEN. " Monatshefte 46:305-316. Novem-
ber 1954.

Braun, Wilhelm. "Musil's Musicians. " Monatshefte 52:9-
17. January 1960.

Braun, W. "Musil's Siamese Twins. " GR 33:41-52. February 1958.

Braun, W. "The Temptation of Ulrich: The Problem of
True and False Unity in Musil's DER MANN OHNE EIGEN-
SCHAFTEN. " GQ 29:29-37. January 1956.

Isitt, Yvonne. "Robert Musil. " German Men of Letters.
Vol. 3. (ed.) Alex Natan. London: Oswald Wolff, 1964. pp.
252-260.

Kermode, Frank. "Robert Musil. " KR 28:225-226. March
1966.

Meyerhoff, Hans. "The Writer as Intellectual. " PR 21:98-
108. January - February 1954.

Reichert, Herbert W. "Nietzschean Influence in Musil's
DER MANN OHNE EIGENSCHAFTEN. " GQ 39:12-28. Jan-
uary 1966.
DIE PORTUGIESIN
McCormick, E. Allen. "Ambivalence in Musil's DREI
FRAUEN: Notes on Meaning and Method. " Monatshefte 54:

183-195. April - May 1962.
DIE SCHWARMER
>Isitt, Yvonne. "Robert Musil. " German Men of Letters.
>Vol. 3. (ed.) Alex Natan. London: Oswald Wolff, 1964. pp.
>242-244.
TONKA
>Braun, Wilhelm. "An Interpretation of Musil's Novelle
>TONKA. " Monatshefte 53:73-85. February 1961.

>McCormick, E. Allen. "Ambivalence in Musil's DREI
>FRAUEN: Notes on Meaning and Method. " Monatshefte 54:
>183-195. April - May 1962.
YOUNG TORLESS
>Goldgar, Harry. "The Square Root of Minus One: Freud
>and Robert Musil's TORLESS. " CL 17:118-132. Spring 1965.

>Isitt, Yvonne. "Robert Musil. " German Men of Letters.
>Vol. 3. (ed.) Alex Natan. London: Oswald Wolff, 1964. pp.
>239-241.

>White, John J. "Mathematical Imagery In Musil's YOUNG
>TORLESS and Zamyatin's WE. " CL 18:71-78. Winter 1966.

Novalis (F. von Hardenberg)
>HEINRICH VON OFTERDINGEN
>>Fitzell, John. The Hermit in German Literature. Chapel
>>Hill: University of North Carolina Press, 1961. pp. 101-
>>105.

>>Freedman, Ralph. The Lyrical Novel: Studies in Hermann
>>Hesse, Andre Gide, and Virginia Woolf. Princeton: Prince-
>>ton University Press, 1963. pp. 25-27.

>>Reed, Eugene E. "Novalis' HEINRICH VON OFTERDINGEN
>>as GESAMTKUNSTWERK. " PQ 33:200-211. April 1954.

>>Rose, William. Men, Myths and Movements in German
>>Literature. London: Allen and Unwin, Ltd. , 1931. pp. 194-
>>199.

>>Willoughby, L. A. The Romantic Movement in Germany.
>>Oxford: University Press, 1930. pp. 99-100.

>>Willson, A. Leslie. "The Blane Blume: A New Dimension. "
>>GR 34:50-58. February 1959.

>>Zimmermann, Eleonore M. "HEINRICH VON OFTERDINGEN:
>>A Striving Towards Unity. " GR 31:269-275. December 1956.

Paul, Jean (Richter)
>HESPERUS
>>Rose, William. From Goethe to Byron. London: Routledge
>>and Sons, 1924. pp. 171-173.

THE INVISIBLE LODGE
>   Brewer, Edward V. "Jean Paul's UNSICHTBARE LOGE
>   and Early German Romanticism. " GR 8:165-177. July
>   1933.

TITAN
>   Geissendoerfer, Theodore. "Jacobi's ALLWILL and Jean
>   Paul's TITAN. " JEGP 27:365-370. 1928.

>   Rose, Ernst. History of German Literature. New York:
>   New York University Press, 1960. p. 208.

>   Rose, William. From Goethe to Byron. London: Routledge
>   and Sons, 1924. pp. 173-180.

Ponten, Josef
>   DIE BOCKREITER
>>   Shears, Lambert A. "The Novellen of Josef Ponten. " GR
>>   11:52-53. January 1936.
>   DIE INSEL
>>   Shears, Lambert A. "The Novellen of Josef Ponten. " GR
>>   11:51-52. January 1936.
>   DIE MEISTER
>>   Shears, Lambert A. "The Novellen of Josef Ponten. " GR
>>   11:53-54. January 1936.

Raabe, Wilhelm
>   ABU TELFAN
>>   Baer, Lydia. "Raabe's and Wiechert's Novel Trilogies. "
>>   Monatshefte 46:20-21. January 1954.

>>   Eckelman, E. O. "Wilhelm Raabe's Trilogy: DER HUNGER-
>>   PASTOR, ABU TELFAN, DER SCHUDDERUMP. " MP 16:
>>   525-541. January 1919.

>>   Fairley, Barker. Wilhelm Raabe: An Introduction to His
>>   Novels. Oxford: Clarendon Press, 1961. pp. 161-181.

>>   Silz, Walter. "Pessimism in Raabe's Stuttgart Trilogy. "
>>   PMLA 39:692-697. September 1924.
>   THE BURIAL CART
>>   Eckelman, E. O. "Wilhelm Raabe's Trilogy: DER HUNGER-
>>   PASTOR, ABU TELFAN, DER SCHUDDERUMP. " MP 16:
>>   525-541. January 1919.

>>   Fairley, Barker. Wilhelm Raabe: An Introduction to His
>>   Novels. Oxford: Clarendon Press, 1961. pp. 161-181.

>>   Silz, Walter. "Pessimism in Raabe's Stuttgart Trilogy. "
>>   PMLA 39:697-704. September 1924.
>   THE CAKE EATER
>>   Fairley, Barker. Wilhelm Raabe: An Introduction to His
>>   Novels. Oxford: Clarendon Press, 1961. pp. 1-18.

DIE CHRONIK DER SPERLINGSGASSE
    Fairley, Barker. Wilhelm Raabe: An Introduction to His
    Novels. Oxford: Clarendon Press, 1961. pp. 182-195.
HASTENBECK
    Fairley, Barker. "A Misinterpretation of Raabe's HASTEN-
    BECK." MLR 57:575-578. October 1962.

    Fairley, Barker. Wilhelm Raabe: An Introduction to His
    Novels. Oxford: Clarendon Press, 1961. pp. 72-90.
HORACKER
    Fairley, Barker. Wilhelm Raabe: An Introduction to His
    Novels. Oxford: Clarendon Press, 1961. pp. 91-107.
DAS HORN VON WANZA
    Fairley, Barker. Wilhelm Raabe: An Introduction to His
    Novels. Oxford: Clarendon Press, 1961. pp. 54-71.
THE HUNGER-PASTOR
    Baer, Lydia. "Raabe's and Wiechert's Novel Trilogies."
    Monatshefte 46:11-24. January 1954.

    Eckelman, E. O. "Wilhelm Raabe's Trilogy: DER HUNGER-
    PASTOR, ABU TELFAN, DER SCHUDDERUMP." MP 16:
    525-541. January 1919.

    Fairley, Barker. Wilhelm Raabe: An Introduction to His
    Novels. Oxford: Clarendon Press, 1961. pp. 161-181.

    Silz, Walter. "Freytag's SOLL UND HABEN and Raabe's
    DER HUNGERPASTOR." MLN 39:10-18. January 1924.

    Silz, Walter. "Pessimism in Raabe's Stuttgart Trilogy."
    PMLA 39:688-692. September 1924.
IM ALTEN EISEN
    Fairley, Barker. Wilhelm Raabe: An Introduction to His
    Novels. Oxford: Clarendon Press, 1961. pp. 126-142.
DAS ODFERD
    Fairley, Barker. Wilhelm Raabe: An Introduction to His
    Novels. Oxford: Clarendon Press, 1961. pp. 108-125.

PFISTERS MUHLE
    Fairley, Barker. Wilhelm Raabe: An Introduction to His
    Novels. Oxford: Clarendon Press, 1961. pp. 37-53.
PRINZESSIN FISCH
    Fairley, Barker. Wilhelm Raabe: An Introduction to His
    Novels. Oxford: Clarendon Press, 1961. pp. 19-36.
UNRUHIGE GASTE
    Fairley, Barker. Wilhelm Raabe: An Introduction to His
    Novels. Oxford: Clarendon Press, 1961. pp. 143-160.

Remarque, Erich
    ALL QUIET ON THE WESTERN FRONT
        Bostock, J. Knight. Some Well-known German War Novels.
        Oxford: B. H. Blackwell, 1931. pp. 3-10.

Moseley, Edwin M. Pseudonyms of Christ in the Modern Novel. Pittsburgh: University of Pittsburgh Press, 1962. pp. 89-104.

Pfeiler, William K. War and the German Mind. New York: Columbia University Press, 1941. pp. 141-144.

Wolle, Francis. "Novels of Two World Wars." WHR 5:285-287. Summer 1951.

Rilke, Rainer Maria
  THE NOTEBOOKS OF MALTE LAURIDS BRIGGE
    Fuerst, Norbert. "Three German Novels of Education." Monatshefte 38:463-478. December 1946.

    Gray, Ronald. The German Tradition in Literature 1871-1945. Cambridge: University Press, 1965. pp. 263-277.

    Madsen, Borge Gedso. "Influences from J. P. Jacobsen and Sigbjorn Obstfelder on Rainer Maria Rilke's DIE AUF-ZEICHNUNGEN DES MALTE LAURIDS BRIGGE." SS 26: 105-114. August 1954.

    Pike, Burton. "Objects vs. People in the Recent German Novel." WSCL 7:304-305. Autumn 1966.

Roth, Joseph
  BALLAD OF A HUNDRED DAYS
    Powell, Ward H. "Joseph Roth, Ironic Primitivist." Monatshefte 53:117-118. March 1961.
  THE RADETSKY MARCH
    Powell, Ward H. "Joseph Roth, Ironic Primitivist." Monatshefte 53:119-121. March 1961.

Schlegel, Dorothea
  FLORENTIN
    Thornton, Karin Stuebben. "Enlightenment and Romanticism in the Work of Dorothea Schlegel." GQ 39:163-172. March 1966.

Schnitzler, Arthur
  CASANOVA'S HOMECOMING
    Slochower, Harry. No Voice Is Wholly Lost. New York: Creative Age Press, 1945. p. 28.
  FLIGHT INTO DARKNESS
    Weiss, Robert O. "A Study of the Psychiatric Elements in Schnitzler's FLUCHT IN DIE FINSTERNIS." GR 33:251-275. December 1958.
  FRAULEIN ELSE
    Oswald, Victor and Veronica Pinter Mindes. "Schnitzler's FRAULEIN ELSE and the Psychoanalytic Theory of Neuroses." GR 26:279-288. October 1951.

    Slochower, Harry. No Voice Is Wholly Lost. New York:

Creative Age Press, 1945. pp. 28-29.
DIE HIRTENFLOTE
Liptzin, Sol. Arthur Schnitzler. New York: Prentice-Hall, 1932. pp. 73-78.
KOMODIE DER VERFUHRUNG
Liptzin, Sol. Arthur Schnitzler. New York: Prentice-Hall, 1932. pp. 227-243.
THE PROPHECY
Lawson, Richard H. "An Interpretation of DIE WEISSAG-UNG. " Studies in Arthur Schnitzler. (ed.) Herbert W. Reichert and Herman Salinger. Chapel Hill: University of North Carolina Press, 1963. pp. 71-78.
REDEGONDA'S DIARY
Lawson, Richard H. "Schnitzler's DAS TAGEBUCH DER REDEGONDA. " GR 35:202-213. October 1960.
THE ROAD TO THE OPEN
Garland, H. B. "Arthur Schnitzler. " German Men of Letters. Vol. 2. (ed.) Alex Natan. London: Oswald Wolff, 1963. pp. 71-74.

Ilmer, Frida. "Schnitzler's Attitudes with Regard to the Transcendental. " GR 10:115-116. April 1935.

Kann, Robert A. "The Image of the Austrian in Arthur Schnitzler's Writings. " Studies in Arthur Schnitzler. (ed.) Herbert W. Reichert and Herman Salinger. Chapel Hill: University of North Carolina Press, 1963. pp. 60-64.

Liptzin, Sol. Arthur Schnitzler. New York: Prentice-Hall, 1932. pp. 108-209; 210-223.

Liptzin, Solomon. Germany's Stepchildren. Philadelphia: The Jewish Publication Society of America, 1944. pp. 127-132.

Reichert, Herbert W. "Nietzsche and Schnitzler. " Studies in Arthur Schnitzler. (ed.) Herbert W. Reichert and Herman Salinger. Chapel Hill: University of North Carolina Press, 1963. pp. 99-105.
THERESA
Slochower, Harry. No Voice Is Wholly Lost. New York: Creative Age Press, 1945. pp. 29-31.

Sealsfield, Charles
THE CABIN LOG
Krumpelmann, John T. "A Source for Local Color in Seals-field's CAJUTENBUCH. " JEGP 43:427-433. October 1944.
PFLANZERLEBEN UND DIE FARBIGEN
Shears, L. A. "Storm and Sealsfield. " GR 8:178-182. July 1933.

Seghers, Anna
AUF DEM WEGE ZUR AMERIKANISCHEN BOTSCHAFT

Triesch, Manfred. "Martyrdom and Everlasting Life: Two
Stories by Anna Seghers. " SSF 3:241-242. Winter 1966.

THE DECISION

Andrews, R. C. "Anna Seghers' DIE ENTSCHEIDUNG. "
GL&L 15:259-262. July 1962.

REVOLT OF THE FISHERMEN

Triesch, Manfred. "Martyrdom and Everlasting Life: Two
Stories by Anna Seghers. " SSF 3:238-241. Winter 1966.

Seidel, Ina

BROMSESHOF

McKittrick, Mary. " 'Weltinnigkeit': An Introductory Study
of Ina Seidel. " Monatshefte 30:87-88. February 1938.

DAS HAUS ZUM MONDE

McKittrick, Mary. " 'Weltinnigkeit': An Introductory Study
of Ina Seidel. " Monatshefte 30:85-86. February 1938.

DAS LABYRINTH

McKittrick, Mary. " 'Weltinnigkeit': An Introductory Study
of Ina Seidel. " Monatshefte 30:86-87. February 1938.

RENEE AND RAINER

McKittrick, Mary. " 'Weltinnigkeit': An Introductory Study
of Ina Seidel. " Monatshefte 30:88. February 1938.

DER WEG OHNE WAHL

McKittrick, Mary. " 'Weltinnigkeit': An Introductory Study
of Ina Seidel. " Monatshefte 30:90. February 1938.

THE WISH CHILD

McKittrick, Mary. " 'Weltinnigkeit': An Introductory Study
of Ina Seidel. " Monatshefte 30:88-90. February 1938.

Spielhagen, F.

THE HOHENSTEINS

Hewett-Thayer, Harvey W. "Ferdinand Lassalle in the
Novels of Spielhagen and Meredith. " GR 19:186-196. October
1944.

IN RANK AND FILE

Hewett-Thayer, Harvey W. "Ferdinand Lassalle in the
Novels of Spielhagen and Meredith. " GR 19:186-196. October
1944.

Liptzin, Sol. Historical Survey of German Literature. New
York: Prentice-Hall, 1936. pp. 150-151.

Robertson, John G. History of German Literature. New
York: Putnam, 1902. p. 578.

Spitteler, Carl

CONRAD THE LIEUTENANT

Boyd, Ernest. Studies from Ten Literatures. New York:
Charles Scribner's Sons, 1925. pp. 206-209.

McHaffie, M. A. and J. M. Ritchie. "Narrative Technique
in Spitteler's CONRAD DER LEUTNANT. " GL&L 14:45-51.
October 1960 - January 1961.

PROMETHEUS UND EPIMETHEUS
> Boyd, Ernest. Studies from Ten Literatures. New York:
> Charles Scribner's Sons, 1925. pp. 200-204.

Stehr, Hermann
THE BURIED GOD
> Reichart, Walter A. "Hermann Stehr and His Work." PQ
> 10:53-55. January 1931.

DAMIAN
> Boeschenstein, H. The German Novel, 1939-1944. Univer-
> sity of Toronto Press, 1949. pp. 154-155.

> Weimar, Karl S. "DAMIAN, Posthumous Novel of Hermann
> Stehr." Monatshefte 38:479-491. December 1946.

HEILIGENHOF FARM
> Reichart, Walter A. "Hermann Stehr and His Work." PQ
> 10:57-60. January 1931.

THREE NIGHTS
> Reichart, Walter A. "Hermann Stehr and His Work." PQ
> 10:55-56. January 1931.

Stifter, Adalbert
ABDIAS
> Blackall, Eric A. Adalbert Stifter: A Critical Study. Cam-
> bridge: University Press, 1948. Chapter 12.

> Silz, Walter. Realism and Reality. Chapel Hill: University
> of North Carolina Press, 1954. pp. 52-66.

> Stern, J. P. Re-Interpretations. London: Thames and Hud-
> son, 1964. pp. 273-278.

> Urzidil, John. "Adalbert Stifter and Judaism." MJ 36:327-
> 338. Autumn 1948.

THE ANCIENT SEAL
> Blackall, Eric. A. Adalbert Stifter: A Critical Study. Cam-
> bridge: University Press, 1948. Chapter 12.

> Stern, J. P. Re-Interpretations. London: Thames and Hud-
> son, 1964. pp. 262-273.

ARGENTINE MICA
> Wohlfarth, Paul. "A Gypsy Story by Adalbert Stifter (1805-
> 1868)." JGLS 40:74-75. January - April 1961.

BRIGITTA
> Blackall, Eric A. Adalbert Stifter: A Critical Study. Cam-
> bridge: University Press, 1948. Chapter 12.

THE FORESTER
> Stern, J. P. Re-Interpretations. London: Thames and Hud-
> son, 1964. pp. 280-285.

DER HAGESTOLZ
> Gelley, Alex. "Stifter's DER HAGESTOLZ: An Interpreta-
> tion." Monatshefte 53:59-72. February 1961.

INDIAN SUMMER
    Blackall, Eric A. Adalbert Stifter: A Critical Study. Cambridge: University Press, 1948. pp. 331-340.

    Fuerst, Norbert. "Three German Novels of Education." Monatshefte 38:413-425. November 1946.

    Gillespie, Gerald. "Ritualism and Motivic Development in Adalbert Stifter's NACHSOMMER." Neophil 48:312-321. October 1964.

    Gillespie, Gerald. "Space and Time Seen Through Stifter's Telescope." GQ 37:121-127. March 1964.

    Pascal, Roy. The German Novel. Manchester: Manchester University Press, 1956. pp. 52-75.

    Sjogren, Christine Oertel. "Mathilde and the Roses in Stifter's NACHSOMMER." PMLA 81:400-408. October 1966.

    Stern, J. P. Re-Interpretations. London: Thames and Hudson, 1964. pp. 255-256; 285-300.

    Tucker, Harry, Jr. "Joseph, the Musician in Stifter's NACHSOMMER." Monatshefte 50:1-8. January 1958.
DIE MAPPE MEINES URGROSSVATERS
    Blackall, Eric A. Adalbert Stifter: A Critical Study. Cambridge: University Press, 1948. Chapter 11.
DIE NARRENBURG
    Blackall, Eric A. Adalbert Stifter: A Critical Study. Cambridge: University Press, 1948. Chapter 10.
PROKOPUS
    Blackall, Eric A. Adalbert Stifter: A Critical Study. Cambridge: University Press, 1948. Chapter 10.
THE ROCK CRYSTAL
    Struc, Roman S. "The Threat of Chaos: Stifter's BERGKRISTALL and Thomas Mann's 'Schnee.' " MLQ 24:323-332. December 1963.
THE TALL FOREST
    Blackall, Eric A. Adalbert Stifter: A Critical Study. Cambridge: University Press, 1948. Chapter 9.

    Gillespie, Gerald. "Space and Time Seen Through Stifter's Telescope." GQ 37:128-130. March 1964.
WIEN UND DIE WIENER
    Blackall, Eric A. Adalbert Stifter: A Critical Study. Cambridge: University Press, 1948. Chapter 10.
WITIKO
    Blackall, Eric A. Adalbert Stifter: A Critical Study. Cambridge: University Press, 1948. pp. 341-342.

    Schoolfield, George C. "The Churchmen in Stifter's WITIKO." Monatshefte 43:285-293. October 1951.

Stern, J. P. Re-Interpretations. London: Thames and Hudson, 1964. pp. 279-280.

Storm, Theodor
AM KAMIN
McCormick, E. Allen. Theodor Storm's Novellen: Essays on Literary Technique. Chapel Hill: University of North Carolina Press, 1964. pp. 41-51.

Rysan, Josef. "Theodor Storm and Psychic Phenomena." MP 53:43-45. August 1955.
AQUIS SUBMERSUS
Bernd, Clifford A. Theodor Storm's Craft of Fiction: The Torment of a Narrator. Chapel Hill: University of North Carolina Press, 1963. pp. 11-53.

McCormick, E. Allen. Theodor Storm's Novellen: Essays on Literary Technique. Chapel Hill: University of North Carolina Press, 1964. pp. 98-129.

Menhennet, A. "The Time-Element in Storm's Later Novellen." GL&L 20:46-48. October 1966.
EIN DOPPELGANGER
Braun, Frank X. "Theodor Storm's DOPPELGANGER." GR 32:267-272. December 1957.
FROM BEYOND THE SEAS
Coenen, Frederic E. "Foreign Elements in Theodor Storm's Novellen." SP 47:536-539. 1950.

Krumpelmann, John T. "Some Observations on Storm's VON JENSEIT DES MEERES." GR 15:46-49. February 1940.

Shears, L. A. "Storm and Sealsfield." GR 8:178-182. July 1933.

Willey, Norman L. "Exotic Elements in Storm and Sealsfield." GR 14:28-31. February 1939.
EINE HALLIGFAHRT
Menhennet, A. "The Time-Element in Storm's Later Novellen." GL&L 20:44-45. October 1966.
HINZELMEIER
McCormick, E. Allen. Theodor Storm's Novellen: Essays on Literary Technique. Chapel Hill: University of North Carolina Press, 1964. pp. 133-164.
IM NACHBARHAUSE LINKS
Stinchcombe, J. "Theodor Storm's IM NACHBARHAUSE LINKS: An Appreciation." GL&L 16:49-57. October 1962.
IMMENSEE
Andrews, John S. "IMMENSEE and Victorian England." MLR 54:406-410. July 1959.

McCormick, E. Allen. Theodor Storm's Novellen: Essays on Literary Technique. Chapel Hill: University of North

Carolina Press, 1964. pp. 1-37.

McHaffie, M. A. and J. M. Ritchie. "Bee's Lake, or the Curse of Silence: A Study of Theodor Storm's IMMENSEE." GL&L 16:36-48. October 1962.

Porterfield, Allen W. "WILHELM MEISTERS LEHRJAHRE and IMMENSEE. " MLN 41:513-516. December 1926.

Salinger, Herman. "The 'Gartensaal' in Storm's IM- MENSEE: An Interpretation. " GQ 13:149-150. May 1940.

Wooley, E. O. "Two Literary Sources of IMMENSEE. " Monatshefte 42:265-272. October 1950.

IN ST. JURGEN
Bernd, Clifford A. "The Pattern of Reminiscence in Storm's IN ST. JURGEN. " GR 36:137-147. May 1961.

Bernd, Clifford. Theodor Storm's Craft of Fiction: The Torment of a Narrator. Chapel Hill: University of North Carolina Press, 1963. pp. 57-78.

ON THE STAATSHOF
McCormick, E. Allen. Theodor Storm's Novellen: Essays on Literary Technique. Chapel Hill: University of North Carolina Press, 1964. pp. 38-41; 51-77.

PSYCHE
Rose, Ernst. "Psychological Problems in Theodor Storm's PSYCHE. " GQ 16:146-152. May 1943.

THE RIDER OF THE WHITE HORSE
Blankenagel, John C. "Tragic Guilt in Storm's SCHIMMEL- REITER. " GQ 25:170-181. May 1952.

Silz, Walter. Realism and Reality. Chapel Hill: University of North Carolina Press, 1954. pp. 117-136.

Silz, Walter. "Theodor Storm's SCHIMMELREITER. " PMLA 61:762-783. September 1946.

VERONIKA
Mainland, William F. "Theodor Storm. " German Men of Letters. Vol. I. (ed.) Alex Natan. London: Oswald Wolff, 1961. pp. 156-157.

Strittmatter, Erwin
TINKO
Andrews, R. C. "Re-education Through Literature: Erwin Strittmatter's TINKO. " GL&L 14:204-209. April 1961.

Sudermann, Hermann
DAME CARE
Feise, Ernst von. "Stilverwirrung in Sudermann's FRAU SORGE. " GR 5:225-237. July 1930.

Heller, Otto. Studies in Modern German Literature. Boston:

Ginn and Company, 1905. pp. 14-16.

Koch, Ernst. "The Key to Sudermann." PMLA 51:851-862.
September 1936.

Phelps, William L. Essays on Modern Novelists. New York:
The Macmillan Company, 1910. pp. 142-146.

Warner Library. (ed.) John W. Cunliffe and Ashby H.
Thorndike. New York: Knickerbocker Press, 1917. pp.
14, 164-14, 165.

Whitaker, Paul K. "The Inferiority Complex of Hermann
Sudermann's Life and Works." Monatshefte 40:73-76. Feb-
ruary 1948.
REGINA
Phelps, William L. Essays on Modern Novelists. New York:
The Macmillan Company, 1910. pp. 146-149.
SONG OF SONGS
Phelps, William L. Essays on Modern Novelists. New York:
The Macmillan Company, 1910. pp. 152-158.
THE UNDYING PAST
Phelps, William L. Essays on Modern Novelists. New York:
The Macmillan Company, 1910. pp. 150-152.

Tieck, Ludwig
ABDALLAH
Trainer, James. Ludwig Tieck. London: Mouton and Com-
pany, 1964. pp. 74-98.
DER BLONDE ECKBERT
Northcott, Kenneth J. "A Note on the Levels of Reality in
Tieck's DER BLONDE ECKBERT." GL&L 6:292-294. July
1953.
FRANZ STERNBALD'S WANDERINGS
Hoermann, Roland. "Historicity and Art in Tieck's STERN-
BALD." Monatshefte 47:209-220. April - May 1955.

Sammons, Jeffrey L. "Tieck's FRANZ STERNBALD: The
Loss of Thematic Control." SIR 5:30-43. Autumn 1965.

Trainer, James. Ludwig Tieck. London: Mouton and Company, 1964. pp. 99-109.

Trainer, James. "Ludwig Tieck." German Men of Letters.
(ed.) Alex Natan. London: Oswald Wolff, 1961. pp. 48-51.
LIFE'S OVERFLOW
Trainer, James. "Ludwig Tieck." German Men of Letters.
(ed.) Alex Natan. London: Oswald Wolff, 1961. pp. 54-55.
THE LOVE-CHARM
Galinsky, Hans K. "Is Thomas de Quincey the Author of
THE LOVE-CHARM?" MLN 52:389-394. June 1937.
THE MYSTERIOUS CUP
Barto, P. S. "Sources of Heine's 'Seegespenet.'" MLN

32:482-485. 1917.
PHANTASUS
   Robertson, John G. History of German Literature. New York:
   Putnam, 1902. p. 425.
THE REBELLION IN THE CEVENNES
   Porterfield, Allen W. "Tieck's AUFRUHR IN DEN CEVEN-
   NEN. " GQ 7:58-69. March 1934.
EINE SOMMERREISE
   Matenko, Percy. "Tieck's Diary Fragment of 1803 and His
   Novelle EINE SOMMERREISE. " JEGP 36:83-102. January
   1937.

Traven, B.
   DEATH SHIP
      Jannach, Hubert. "B. Traven-An American or German
      Author?" GQ 36:459-468. November 1963.
   TREASURE OF THE SIERRA MADRE
      Jannach, Hubert. "B. Traven--An American or German
      Author?" GQ 36:459-468. November 1963.

      Kirby, Thomas A. "The PARDONER'S TALE and THE
      TREASURE OF THE SIERRA MADRE. " MLN 66:269-270.
      April 1951.

Unruh, Fritz von
   THE END IS NOT YET
      Gode-von Aesch, A. "Readings and Misreadings of Fritz
      von Unruh's THE END IS NOT YET. " MLF 34:24-30. March-
      June 1949.
   THE WAY OF SACRIFICE
      Pfeiler, William K. War and the German Mind. New York:
      Columbia University Press, 1941. pp. 90-97.

      Rose, William. Men, Myths and Movements in German Lit-
      erature. London: Allen and Unwin, Ltd. , 1931. pp. 215-216.

Walser, Robert
   DER GEHULFE
      Waidson, H. M. "Robert Walser. " German Men of Letters.
      Vol. 2. (ed.) Alex Natan. London: Oswald Wolff, 1963. pp.
      184-187.
   DIE GESCHWISTER TANNER
      Waidson, H. M. "Robert Walser. " German Men of Letters.
      Vol. 2. (ed.) Alex Natan. London: Oswald Wolff, 1963. pp.
      181-184.
   JAKOB VON GUNTEN
      Waidson, H. M. "Robert Walser. " German Men of Letters.
      Vol. 2. (ed.) Alex Natan. London: Oswald Wolff, 1963. pp.
      187-190.
   DER SPAZIERGANG
      Waidson, H. M. "Robert Walser. " German Men of Letters.
      Vol. 2. (ed.) Alex Natan. London: Oswald Wolff, 1963. pp.
      178-181.

Wassermann, Jakob
  ALEXANDER IN BABYLON
    Blankenagel, John C. The Writings of Jakob Wassermann.
    Boston: Christopher Publishing House, 1942. pp. 67-77.
  THE AMULET
    Blankenagel, John C. The Writings of Jakob Wassermann.
    Boston: Christopher Publishing House, 1942. pp. 262-264.
  CASPAR HAUSER
    Blankenagel, John C. The Writings of Jakob Wassermann.
    Boston: Christopher Publishing House, 1942. pp. 84-103.
  CLARISSA MIRABEL
    Blankenagel, John C. "Human Fears in Jakob Wassermann's
    Writings." JEGP 50:311-312. July 1951.
  DIARY IN A NOOK
    Blankenagel, John C. The Writings of Jakob Wassermann.
    Boston: Christopher Publishing House, 1942. pp. 323-328.
  DOCTOR KERKHOVEN
    Blankenagel, John C. "Human Fears in Jakob Wassermann's
    Writings. " JEGP 50:315-316. July 1951.

    Blankenagel, John C. The Writings of Jakob Wassermann.
    Boston: Christopher Publishing House, 1942. pp. 287-305.
  ERWIN REINER
    Blankenagel, John C. The Writings of Jakob Wassermann.
    Boston: Christopher Publishing House, 1942. pp. 104-114.
  FABER, OR THE LOST YEARS
    Blankenagel, John C. "Human Fears in Jakob Wassermann's
    Writings. " JEGP 50:312-313. July 1951.

    Blankenagel, John C. The Writings of Jakob Wassermann.
    Boston: Christopher Publishing House, 1942. pp. 216-230.
  GOLD
    Blankenagel, John C. The Writings of Jakob Wassermann.
    Boston: Christopher Publishing House, 1942. pp. 201-215.
  THE GOLDEN MIRROR
    Blankenagel, John C. The Writings of Jakob Wassermann.
    Boston: Christopher Publishing House, 1942. pp. 115-121.
  THE GOOSE MAN
    Blankenagel, John C. The Writings of Jakob Wassermann.
    Boston: Christopher Publishing House, 1942. pp. 133-149.

    Liptzin, Sol. Historical Survey of German Literature. New
    York: Prentice-Hall, 1936. pp. 226-227.
  THE HOUSEKEEPER
    Blankenagel, John C. The Writings of Jakob Wassermann.
    Boston: Christopher Publishing House, 1942. pp. 40-42.
  THE JEWS OF ZIRNDORF
    Blankenagel, John C. The Writings of Jakob Wassermann.
    Boston: Christopher Publishing House, 1942. pp. 30-39.

    Liptzin, Sol. Historical Survey of German Literature. New
    York: Prentice-Hall, 1936. pp. 225-226.

JOSEPH KERKHOVENS DRITTE EXISTENZ
Blankenagel, John C. "Human Fears in Jakob Wassermann's
Writings. " JEGP 50:316-319. July 1951.

Blankenagel, John C. "Jakob Wassermann's Conception and
Treatment of Character. " MLQ 7:6-13. March 1946.

Blankenagel, John C. "More Unacknowledged Borrowing by
Jakob Wassermann. " GR 40:555-557. October 1941.

Blankenagel, John C. The Writings of Jakob Wassermann.
Boston: Christopher Publishing House, 1942. pp. 306-322.
LUKARDIS
Blankenagel, John C. "Jakob Wassermann's LUKARDIS. "
MLN 56:47-53. January 1941.
THE MAN OF FORTY
Blankenagel, John C. The Writings of Jakob Wassermann.
Boston: Christopher Publishing House, 1942. pp. 122-132.
THE MAURIZIUS CASE
Blankenagel, John C. "Human Fears in Jakob Wassermann's
Writings. " JEGP 50:314-315. July 1951.

Blankenagel, John C. "Jakob Wassermann's Views on America. " GQ 25:51-57. January 1954.

Blankenagel, John C. The Writings of Jakob Wassermann.
Boston: Christopher Publishing House, 1942. pp. 265-286.

Schneider, Franz. "Browning's THE RING AND THE BOOK
and Wassermann's DER FALL MAURIZIUS. " MLN 48:16-17.
January 1933.
MELUSINE
Blankenagel, John C. The Writings of Jakob Wassermann.
Boston: Christopher Publishing House, 1942. pp. 25-29.
THE MOLOCH
Blankenagel, John C. The Writings of Jakob Wassermann.
Boston: Christopher Publishing House, 1942. pp. 58-66.
OBERLIN'S THREE STAGES
Blankenagel, John C. The Writings of Jakob Wassermann.
Boston: Christopher Publishing House, 1942. pp. 189-196.
OLIVIA
Blankenagel, John C. The Writings of Jakob Wassermann.
Boston: Christopher Publishing House, 1942. pp. 150-156.
THE REBELLION FOR YOUNG SQUIRE ERNST
Blankenagel, John C. "Human Fears in Jakob Wassermann's
Writings. " JEGP 50:313-314. July 1951.

Blankenagel, John C. "Jakob Wassermann's Views on Amer-
ica. " GQ 25:51-53. January 1954.
THE SISTERS
Blankenagel, John C. The Writings of Jakob Wassermann.
Boston: Christopher Publishing House, 1942. pp. 78-83.

THE SPIRIT OF THE PILGRIM
Blankenagel, John C. The Writings of Jakob Wassermann.
Boston: Christopher Publishing House, 1942. pp. 231-236.
THE STORY OF YOUNG RENATE FUCHS
Blankenagel, John C. The Writings of Jakob Wassermann.
Boston: Christopher Publishing House, 1942. pp. 46-57.
STURREGANZ
Blankenagel, John C. The Writings of Jakob Wassermann.
Boston: Christopher Publishing House, 1942. pp. 197-200.
THE TRIUMPH OF YOUTH
Blankenagel, John C. The Writings of Jakob Wassermann.
Boston: Christopher Publishing House, 1942. pp. 252-261.
UNKISSED LIPS
Blankenagel, John C. The Writings of Jakob Wassermann.
Boston: Christopher Publishing House, 1942. pp. 43-45.
WEDLOCK
Blankenagel, John C. The Writings of Jakob Wassermann.
Boston: Christopher Publishing House, 1942. pp. 237-251.
WORLD'S END
Blankenagel, John C. The Writings of Jakob Wassermann.
Boston: Christopher Publishing House, 1942. pp. 177-188.
THE WORLD'S ILLUSION
Blankenagel, John C. The Writings of Jakob Wassermann.
Boston: Christopher Publishing House, 1942. pp. 157-176.

Liptzin, Sol. Historical Survey of German Literature. New
York: Prentice-Hall, 1936. pp. 227-229.

Werfel, Franz
THE CLASS REUNION
Kohn-Bramstedt, Ernst. "Franz Werfel as a Novelist."
ConRev 146:69-71. July 1934.
EMBEZZLED HEAVEN
Slochower, Harry. No Voice Is Wholly Lost. New York:
Creative Age Press, 1945. pp. 231-234.
THE FORTY DAYS OF MUSA DAGH
Liptzin, Sol. Historical Survey of German Literature. New
York: Prentice-Hall, 1936. pp. 247-248.

Pfeiler, William K. War and the German Mind. New York:
Columbia University Press, 1941. pp. 182-189.

Schulz-Behrend, George. "Sources and Background of Wer-
fel's Novel DIE VIERZIG TAGE DES MUSA DAGH." GR
26:111-123. April 1951.
NOT THE MURDERER BUT THE MURDERED MAN IS GUILTY
Fox, W. H. "The Problem of Guilt in Werfel's NIGHT DER
MORDER." GL&L 11:25-33. October 1957.
THE PURE IN HEART
Klarmann, Adolf D. "Franz Werfel's Eschatology and Cos-
mogony." MLQ 7:390. December 1946.

Kohn-Bramstedt, Ernst. "Franz Werfel as a Novelist."

ConRev 146:66-69. July 1934.

Slochower, Harry. "Franz Werfel and Alfred Doblin: The
Problem of Individualism Versus Collectivism in BARBARA
and in BERLIN ALEXANDERPLATZ. " JEGP 33:104-107.
January 1934.

Stamm, Israel S. "Religious Experience in Werfel's BAR-
BARA. " PMLA 54:332-347. March 1939.
THE SONG OF BERNADETTE
Frederick, John T. "Franz Werfel and THE SONG OF
BERNADETTE. " CE 4:335-441. March 1943.

Klarmann, Adolf D. "Franz Werfel's Eschatology and Cos-
mogony. " MLQ 7:389-390. December 1946.

McCrossen, Vincent A. "Zola, Werfel, and The Song of
Bernadette. " Renascence 14:38-40. Autumn 1961.

Slochower, Harry. "Franz Werfel and Sholom Asch: The
Yearning for Status. " Accent 5:77-78. Winter 1945.

Slochower, Harry. No Voice Is Wholly Lost. New York:
Creative Age Press, 1945. pp. 235-237.
STAR OF THE UNBORN
Arlt, Gustave O. "Franz Werfel and America. " MLF 36:4-
7. March - June 1951.

Klarmann, Adolf D. "Franz Werfel's Eschatology and Cos-
mogony. " MLQ 7:385-410. December 1946.
VERDI: A NOVEL OF THE OPERA
Kohn-Bramstedt, Ernst. "Werfel as a Novelist. " ConRev
146:71-72. July 1934.

Werner, Bruno E.
THE SLAVESHIP
Wunderlich, Eva C. "Saint Joseph in the Slaveship. " Monat-
shefte 46:278-280. October 1954.

Wiechert, Ernst
ALTI DER BESTMANN
Chick, Edson M. "Ernst Wiechert and the Conservative
Revolution. " Monatshefte 49:97-107. March 1957.
ANDREAS NYLAND
Frey, John R. "The 'Grim Reaper' in the Works of Ernst
Wiechert. " Monatshefte 42:209-210. May 1950.

Hollmann, Werner. "Ethical Responsibility and Personal
Freedom in the Works of Ernst Wiechert. " GR 25:40-42.
February 1950.

Workman, J. D. "Ernst Wiechert's Escapism. " Monatshefte 35:27-28. January 1943.

THE BARONESS

    Meyer, Selina. "The Plow and the Soil in Ernst Wiechert's
    Works." Monatshefte 30:318. October 1938.

DIE BLAUEN SCHWINGEN

    Baer, Lydia. "Ernst Wiechert's DIE BLAUEN SCHWINGEN."
    MLQ 10:198-219. June 1949.

DIE FLUCHT INS EWIGE

    Chick, Edson M. "Ernst Wiechert's Flight to the Circle of
    Eternity." GR 30:285-289. December 1955.

    Meyer, Selina. "The Plow and the Soil in Ernst Wiechert's
    Works." Monatshefte 30:315. October 1938.

    Workman, J. D. "Ernst Wiechert's Escapism." Monatshefte
    35:23-33. January 1943.

GESICHTER DES TODES

    Baer, Lydia. "Raabe's and Wiechert's Novel Trilogies."
    Monatshefte 46:14-16. January 1954.

HIRTENNOVELLE

    Hollmann, Werner. "Ethical Responsibility and Personal
    Freedom in the Works of Ernst Wiechert." GR 25:45-46.
    February 1950.

JEDERMANN

    Pfeiler, William K. War and the German Mind. New York:
    Columbia University Press, 1941. pp. 147-150.

THE JEROMINS

    Frey, John R. "The 'Grim Reaper' in the Works of Ernst
    Wiechert." Monatshefte 42:206-207. May 1950.

    Hollmann, Werner. "Ethical Responsibility and Personal
    Freedom in the Works of Ernst Wiechert." GR 25:38-40;
    46-49. February 1950.

DIE MAGD DES JURGEN DOSKOCIL

    Chick, Edson. "Ernst Wiechert and the Problem of Evil."
    Monatshefte 46:186-188. April - May 1954.

TOBIAS

    Chick, Edson M. "Ernst Wiechert and the Conservative
    Revolution." Monatshefte 49:97-107. March 1957.

TOTENWOLF

    Frey, John R. "The 'Grim Reaper' in the Works of Ernst
    Wiechert." Monatshefte 42:207. May 1950.

DER WALD

    Frey, John R. "The 'Grim Reaper' in the Works of Ernst
    Wiechert." Monatshefte 42:207-209. May 1950.

    Workman, J. D. "Ernst Wiechert's Escapism." Monatshefte
    35:26-27. January 1943.

Wieland, Christoph

    THE ABDERITES

        Francke, Kuno. Social Forces in German Literature. New
        York: Henry Holt and Company, 1901. pp. 261-262.

Robertson, John G. History of German Literature. New York: Putnam, 1902. pp. 286-287.

Rose, Ernst. History of German Literature. New York: New York University Press, 1960. p. 153.

Van Abbe, Derek Maurice. Christoph Martin Wieland. London: George G. Harrap, 1961. pp. 112-126.

Yuill, W. E. "Abderitis and Abderitism. " Essays in German Literature. Vol. I. (ed.) F. Norman. London: University of London, Institute of German Studies, 1965. pp. 72-91.

AGATHODAMON
Kistler, Mark O. "Dionysian Elements in Wieland. " GR 35:86-88. April 1960.

AGATHON
Francke, Kuno. Social Forces in German Literature. New York: Henry Holt and Company, 1901. pp. 252-261.

McNeely, James A. "Historical Relativism in Wieland's Concept of the Ideal State." MLQ 22:275-282. January 1961.

Reichert, H. W. "The Philosophy of Archytas in Wieland's AGATHON. " GR 24:8-17. February 1949.

Robertson, John G. History of German Literature. New York: Putnam, 1902. pp. 285-286.

Rose, Ernst. History of German Literature. New York: New York University Press, 1960. pp. 151-152.

Van Abbe, Derek Maurice. Christoph Martin Wieland. London: George G. Harrap, 1961. pp. 97-105.

Van Abbe, Derek. "Unfair to Wieland?" PEGS 32:14-15. 1961-1962.

ARISTIPP
Dufner, Max. "The Tragedy of Lais in C. M. Wieland's ARISTIPP. " Monatshefte 52:63-70. February 1960.

Kistler, Mark O. "Dionysian Elements in Wieland. " GR 35:91-92. April 1960.

Winter, John F. "A Forerunner of Moliere's MISAN-THROPE. " MLN 74:507-513. June 1959.

DON SYLVIO OF ROSALVA
Kurrelmeyer, W. "GIL BLAS and DON SYLVIO. " MLN 34: 78-81. January 1919.

Kurrelmeyer, W. "The Sources of Wieland's DON SYLVIO." MP 16:637-648. April 1919.

Stern, Guy. "Saint or Hypocrite: A Study of Wieland's 'Jacinte Episode.' " GR 29:96-101. April 1954.

Van Abbe, Derek Maurice. Christoph Martin Wieland. London: George G. Harrap, 1961. pp. 91-96.
THE GOLDEN MIRROR
McNeely, James A. "Historical Relativism in Wieland's Concept of the Ideal State. " MLQ 22:277. September 1961.

Van Abbe, Derek Maurice. Christoph Martin Wieland. London: George G. Harrap, 1961. pp. 109-112.
PEREGRINUS PROTEUS
Kistler, Mark O. "Dionysian Elements in Wieland. " GR 35:85-86. April 1960.

Zschokke, Heinrich
PRINZESSIN VON WOLFENBUTTEL
Clark, Robert T. , Jr. "The Fusion of Legends in Zschokke's PRINZESSIN VON WOLFENBUTTEL. " JEGP 42:185-196. April 1943.

Zweig, Arnold
THE CASE OF SERGEANT GRISCHA
Bennett, E. K. History of the German Novelle. Cambridge: University Press, 1961. p. 260.

Fishman, Solomon. "The War Novels of Arnold Zweig. " SR 49:433-451. October - December 1941.

Pfeiler, William K. War and the German Mind. New York: Columbia University Press, 1941. pp. 131-135.
THE CROWNING OF A KING
Fishman, Solomon. "The War Novels of Arnold Zweig. " SR 49:433-451. October - December 1941.
EDUCATION BEFORE VERDUN
Fishman, Solomon. "The War Novels of Arnold Zweig. " SR 49:433-451. October - December 1941.
YOUNG WOMAN OF 1914
Fishman, Solomon. "The War Novels of Arnold Zweig." SR 49:433-451. October - December 1941.

Zweig, Stefan
THE BURIED CANDELABRUM
Liptzin, Solomon. Germany's Stepchildren. Philadelphia: The Jewish Publication Society of America, 1944. pp. 218-223.
THE EYES OF THE UNDYING BROTHER
Teller, Gertrude. "Virata or THE EYES OF THE UNDYING BROTHER and Stefan Zweig's Thought. " GR 27:31-40. February 1952.
FANTASTIC NIGHT
Bennett, E. K. History of the German Novelle. Cambridge: University Press, 1961. pp. 271-272.

Andersen, Knud
THE BRAND OF THE SEA
Clausen, Julius. "Intellectual Currents in Denmark. " ASR
17:618-619. October 1929.

Andersson, Dan
DAVID RAMM'S INHERITANCE
Mortensen, Johan. "The Year's Books in Sweden. " ASR 8:
842-843. November 1920.
THREE HOMELESS ONES
Mortensen, Johan. "The Year's Books in Sweden. " ASR 8:
842. November 1920.

Bang, Herman
HAABLOSE SLAEGTER
Gustafson, Alrik. "Degenerate Heredity and Family Tradition in Herman Bang's HAABLOSE SLAEGTER. " JEGP 40:
366-390. July 1941.

Berger, Henning
WHO KNOWS
Mortensen, Johan. "Books of the Year in Sweden. " ASR
10:670-672. November 1922.

Bjornson, Bjornstjerne
THE FISHER MAIDEN
Sturtevant, Albert Morey. "The Cultural Elements in
Bjornson's FISKERJAENTEN with Special Reference to
Goethe's WILHELM MEISTER. " SS 7:257-264. November
1923.
FLAGS ARE FLYING IN TOWN AND HARBOUR
Phelps, William L. Essays on Modern Novelists. New York:
The Macmillan Company, 1940. pp. 90-93.
IN GOD'S WAY
Phelps, William L. Essays on Modern Novelists. New York:
The Macmillan Company, 1940. pp. 93-96.
MOTHER'S HANDS
Sturtevant, Albert Morey. "Bjornson's MORS HAENDER. "
SS 8:249-257. November 1925.

Blixen, Karen (Isak Dinesen)
THE ANGELIC AVENGERS
Lewis, Janet. "Isak Dinesen: An Appreciation. " SoR n. s. 2:
312-313. April 1966.
EHRENGARD
Langbaum, Robert. "EHRENGARD and Isak Dinesen. " ASch

32:639-656. Autumn 1963.

Bojer, Johan
    THE FACE OF THE WORLD
        Cabell, James Branch. "THE FACE OF THE WORLD. "
        Johan Bojer. (ed.) Carl Gad. New York: Moffat, Yard and
        Company, 1920. pp. 247-255.
    THE GREAT HUNGER
        Galsworthy, John. "THE GREAT HUNGER. " Johan Bojer.
        (ed.) Carl Gad. New York: Moffat, Yard and Company, 1920.
        pp. 229-236.

        Hergesheimer, Joseph. "THE GREAT HUNGER. " Johan
        Bojer. (ed.) Carl Gad. New York: Moffat, Yard and Com-
        pany, 1920. pp. 237-246.
    THE HOUSE AND THE SEA
        Larsen, Hanna Astrup. "New Books in Norway. " ASR 22:
        155-157. June 1934.
    THE LAST VIKING
        Larsen, Hanna Astrup. "Some Recent Norwegian Books. "
        ASR 10:659-661. November 1922.
    LIFE
        Boyd, Ernest. Studies from Ten Literatures. New York:
        Charles Scribner's Sons, 1925. pp. 264-266.

        Porterfield, Allen Wilson. "America Reads Johan Bojer. "
        ASR 9:478-479. July 1921.
    THE POWER OF A LIE
        Lodrup, Hans P. "Johan Bojer. " ASR 14:212. April 1926.
    THE PRISONER WHO SANG
        Lodrup, Hans P. "Johan Bojer. " ASR 14:212-214. April
        1926.
    TREACHEROUS GROUND
        Roberts, Cecil. "TREACHEROUS GROUND. " Johan Bojer.
        (ed.) Carl Gad. New York: Moffat, Yard and Company, 1920.
        pp. 256-260.

Bramson, Karen
    A NIGHT
        Clausen, Julius. "Truth and Fiction in Recent Danish Lit-
        erature. " ASR 21:361-362. June - July 1933.

Branner, H. C.
    ANGUISH
        Madsen, Borge Gedso. "H. C. Branner: A Modern Human-
        ist. " ASR 47:43-44. March 1959.
    THE CHILD PLAYS ON THE BEACH
        Madsen, Borge Gedso. "H. C. Branner: A Modern Human-
        ist. " ASR 47:42-43. March 1959.
    DREAM ABOUT A WOMAN
        Madsen, Borge Gedso. "H. C. Branner: A Modern Human-
        ist. " ASR 47:43. March 1959.

THE MOUNTAINS
    Madsen, Borge Gedso. "H. C. Branner: A Modern Human-
    ist. " ASR 47:43-44. March 1959.
THE RIDING MASTER
    Madsen, Borge Gedso. "H. C. Branner: A Modern Human-
    ist. " ASR 47:44-45. March 1959.

Bregendahl, Marie
    HIGHWAYS AND WAYSIDE INNS
        Toksvig, Signe. "Some Recent Danish Books. " ASR 11:668-
        669. November 1923.

Bremer, Fredrika
    GRANNARNE
        Gustafson, Alrik T. "English Influences in Fredrika Bremer.
        II. " JEGP 31:105-111. January 1932.
    NINA
        Gustafson, Alrik T. "English Influences in Fredrika Brem-
        er. II. " JEGP 31:99-105. January 1932.

Carlberg, Gosta
    BEAR YE ONE ANOTHER'S BURDENS
        Tegen, Gunhild. "Gosta Carlberg, Young Swedish Novelist. "
        BA 16:124-125. April 1942.

Christiansen, Sigurd
    DREAM AND LIFE
        Kielland, Eugenia. "Three Years in the World of Books in
        Norway. " ASR 25:241-242. September 1937.
    THE MAN WITH THE PETROL STATION
        Kielland, Eugenia. "Norwegian War Fiction. " ASR 34:55.
        March 1946.
    TWO LIVING AND ONE DEAD
        Thesen, Rolv. "Some Norwegian Prize Novels. " ASR 20:39.
        January 1932.

Collett, Camilla
    THE GOVERNOR'S DAUGHTERS
        Jorgenson, Theodore. History of Norwegian Literature.
        New York: Macmillan, 1933. pp. 297-298.

        Larsen, Hanna Astrup. "Four Scandinavian Feminists. "
        YR 5:349-350. January 1916.

Dunn, Olav
    IN MAKE-BELIEVE LAND
        Larsen, Hanna Astrup. "Some Recent Norwegian Books. "
        ASR 10:663-664. November 1922.
    OUR OWN AGE
        Kielland, Eugenia. "Three Years in the World of Books in
        Norway. " ASR 25:242-243. September 1937.

Egge, Peter
    BY THE DEEP FJORDS

Larsen, Hanna Astrup. "Recent Fiction in Norway." ASR 9:744-745. November 1921.
GUESTS
Thesen, Rolv. "Some Norwegian Prize Novels." ASR 20:40. January 1932.

Falkberget, Johan
THE BREAD OF NIGHT
Kielland, Eugenia. "Norwegian War Fiction." ASR 34:53-54. March 1946.
CHRISTIANUS SEXTUS
Beck, Richard. "Johan Falkberget." SS 16:312-316. November 1941.

Beck, Richard. "Johan Falkberget: A Great Social Novelist." ASR 38:249-250. September 1950.

Kielland, Eugenia. "Three Years in the World of Books in Norway." ASR 25:238-239. September 1937.
THE FOURTH NIGHT WATCH
Beck, Richard. "Johan Falkberget." SS 16:311-312. November 1941.
LISBETH OF JARNFIELD
Beck, Richard. "Johan Falkberget." SS 16:311. November 1941.

Fangen, Ronald
AN ANGEL OF LIGHT
Govig, Stewart D. "Ronald Fangen, a Christian Humanist." ASR 49:158. June 1961.
DUEL
Govig, Stewart D. "Ronald Fangen, a Christian Humanist." ASR 49:155-156. June 1961.
ERIK
Govig, Stewart D. "Ronald Fangen, a Christian Humanist." ASR 49:154-155. June 1961.
THE WAY OF A WOMAN
Larsen, Hanna Astrup. "New Books in Norway." ASR 22: 157. June 1934.

Garborg, Arne
A FREE THINKER
Lillehei, Ingebrigt. "The Language and Main Ideas of Arne Garborg's Works." SS 3:160-163. July 1916.

Wiehr, Josef. "Arne Garborg." SS 5:275-278. November 1919.
THE LOST FATHER
Lillehei, Ingebrigt. "The Language and Main Ideas of Arne Garborg's Works." SS 3:179-181. July 1916.
MENFOLK
Lillehei, Ingebrigt. "The Language and Main Ideas of Arne Garborg's Works." SS 3:166-170. July 1916.

PEACE
  Beyer, Harald. A History of Norwegian Literature. New
  York: New York University Press, 1956. p. 247.

  Larsen, Hanna Astrup. "Arne Garborg. " ASR 12:281-282.
  May 1924.

  Lillehei, Ingebrigt. "The Language and Main Ideas of Arne
  Garborg's Works. " SS 3:176-178. July 1916.
PEASANT STUDENTS
  Beyer, Harald. A History of Norwegian Literature. New
  York: New York University Press, 1956. p. 244.

  Lillehei, Ingebrigt. "The Language and Main Ideas of Arne
  Garborg's Works. " SS 3:163-166. July 1916.
SHE WHO STAYED WITH MOTHER
  Lillehei, Ingebrigt. "The Language and Main Ideas of Arne
  Garborg's Works. " SS 3:170-171. July 1916.
THE SON CAME HOME
  Lillehei, Ingebrigt. "The Language and Main Ideas of Arne
  Garborg's Works. " SS 3:181-183. July 1916.
WEARY MEN
  Beyer, Harald. A History of Norwegian Literature. New
  York: New York University Press, 1956. p. 246.

  Larsen, Hanna Astrup. "Arne Garborg. " ASR 12:280-281.
  May 1924.

  Lillehei, Ingebrigt. "The Language and Main Ideas of Arne
  Garborg's Works. " SS 3:171-176. July 1916.

Geijerstam, Gustaf
 BOKEN OM LILLE BROR
  Rapp, Esther H. "Gustaf af Geijerstam in the Field of the
  Psychological Novel. " SS 8:244-245. November 1925.
 KVINNOMAKT
  Rapp, Esther H. "Gustaf af Geijerstam in the Field of the
  Psychological Novel. " SS 8:245-248. November 1925.

Gunnarsson, Gunnar
 BLESSED ARE THE POOR IN SPIRIT
  Rimestad, Christian. "Danish Literature. " ASR 9:731-732.
  November 1921.

Hamsun, Knut
 CHAPTER THE LAST
  Gustafson, Alrik. Six Scandinavian Novelists. New York:
  Princeton University Press, 1940. pp. 265-268.
 CHILDREN OF THE TIMES
  Larsen, Hanna Astrup. "Knut Hamsun. " ASR 9:454-455.
  July 1921.
 EDITOR LYNGE
  Beyer, Harald. A History of Norwegian Literature. New

York: New York University Press, 1956. pp. 273-274.
GROWTH OF THE SOIL
  Gustafson, Alrik. "Hamsun's GROWTH OF THE SOIL."
  ASR 27:199-214. September 1939.

  Gustafson, Alrik. Six Scandinavian Novelists. New York:
  Princeton University Press, 1940. pp. 243-263.

  Larsen, Hanna Astrup. "Knut Hamsun." ASR 9:455-456.
  July 1921.

  Naess, Harald S. "The Three Hamsuns: The Changing Atti-
  tude in Recent Criticism." SS 32:134-136. August 1960.
HUNGER
  Beyer, Harald. A History of Norwegian Literature. New
  York: New York University Press, 1956. pp. 272-273.

  Gustafson, Alrik. Six Scandinavian Novelists. New York:
  Princeton University Press, 1940. pp. 236-237.

  Larsen, Hanna. Knut Hamsun. New York: Knopf, 1922. pp.
  32-41.

  McFarlane, J. W. "The Whisper of the Blood: A Study of
  Knut Hamsun's Early Novels." PMLA 71:569-578. Septem-
  ber 1956.
MYSTERIES
  McFarlane, J. W. "The Whisper of the Blood: A Study of
  Knut Hamsun's Early Novels." PMLA 71:578-585. Septem-
  ber 1956.

  Naess, Harald S. "A Strange Meeting and Hamsun's MYS-
  TERIER." SS 36:48-58. February 1964.

  Popperwell, Ronald G. "Interrelatedness in Hamsun's
  MYSTERIER." SS 38:295-301. November 1966.
NEW SOIL
  Beyer, Harald. A History of Norwegian Literature. New
  York: New York University Press, 1956. pp. 273-274.

  Ruud, M. B. "Knut Hamsun." SS 3:246-247. November
  1916.
PAN
  Larsen, Hanna Astrup. "Knut Hamsun." ASR 9:451-452.
  July 1921.

  McFarlane, J. W. "The Whisper of the Blood: A Study of
  Knut Hamsun's Early Novels." PMLA 71:585-590. Septem-
  ber 1956.
THE RING IS CLOSED
  Gustafson, Alrik. Six Scandinavian Novelists. New York:
  Princeton University Press, 1940. pp. 281-283.

THE ROAD LEADS ON
>Gustafson, Alrik. Six Scandinavian Novelists. New York:
>Princeton University Press, 1940. pp. 269-273.

>Larsen, Hanna Astrup. "New Books in Norway. " ASR 22:
>155. June 1934.

SEGELFOSS TOWN
>Gustafson, Alrik. Six Scandinavian Novelists. New York:
>Princeton University Press, 1940. pp. 239-243.

>Larsen, Hanna Astrup. "Knut Hamsun. " ASR 9:454-455.
>July 1921.

VICTORIA
>McFarlane, J. W. "The Whisper of the Blood: A Study of
>Knut Hamsun's Early Novels. " PMLA 71:590-591. Septem-
>ber 1956.

THE WOMEN AT THE PUMP
>Gustafson, Alrik. Six Scandinavian Novelists. New York:
>Princeton University Press, 1940. pp. 263-265.

Hansen, Martin A.
>JONATHAN'S JOURNEY
>>Vowles, Richard B. "Martin A. Hansen and the Uses of the
>>Past. " ASR 46:34-35. March 1958.

>THE LIAR
>>Printz-Pahlson, Goran. "THE LIAR: The Paradox of Fic-
>>tional Communication in Martin A. Hansen. " SS 36:263-
>>280. November 1964.

>>Vowles, Richard B. "Martin A. Hansen and the Uses of the
>>Past. " ASR 46:37-39. March 1958.

Heidenstam, Verner von
>SAINT BRIDGET'S PILGRIMAGE
>>Gustafson, Alrik. Six Scandinavian Novelists. New York:
>>Princeton University Press, 1940. pp. 139-140.

>THE TREE OF THE FOLKUNGS
>>Gustafson, Alrik. Six Scandinavian Novelists. New York:
>>Princeton University Press, 1940. pp. 140-169.

Heinesen, William
>THE BLACK POT
>>Stangerup, Hakon. "Recent Danish Literature. " ASR 39:
>>298. December 1951.

Hoel, Sigurd
>A DAY IN OCTOBER
>>Thesen, Rolv. "Some Norwegian Prize Novels. " ASR 20:39-
>>40. January 1932.

>A FORTNIGHT BEFORE FROST COMES
>>Kielland, Eugenia. "Three Years in the World of Books in
>>Norway. " ASR 25:244-245. September 1937.

I HAVE FALLEN IN LOVE WITH ANOTHER
    Grunt, Olav Paus. "Sigurd Hoel. " ASR 41:35-36. March
    1953.
THE ROAD TO THE END OF THE WORLD
    Grunt, Olav Paus. "Sigurd Hoel. " ASR 41:37-38. March
    1953.
SINNERS IN SUMMERTIME
    Grunt, Olav Paus. "Sigurd Hoel. " ASR 41:34-35. March
    1953.

Jacobsen, J. P.
    MARIE GRUBBE
        Gustafson, Alrik. Six Scandinavian Novelists. New York:
        Princeton University Press, 1940. pp. 86-89.

        Madsen, Borge Gedso. "J. P. Jacobsen Reconsidered. "
        ASR 50:274-278. September 1962.
    MOGENS
        Knudsen, Dagmar. "J. P. Jacobsen. " ASR 5:266-267. Sep-
        tember - October 1917.
    NIELS LYHNE
        Gustafson, Alrik. Six Scandinavian Novelists. New York:
        Princeton University Press, 1940. pp. 89-116.

        Knudsen, Dagmar. "J. P. Jacobsen. " ASR 5:268. Septem-
        ber - October 1917.

        Madsen, Borge Gedso. "Georg Brandes' Criticism of NIELS
        LYHNE. " SS 38:124-130. May 1966.

        Madsen, Borge Gedso. "J. P. Jacobsen Reconsidered. "
        ASR 50:274-278. September 1962.

Jaeger, Hans
    FROM THE CHRISTIANIA BOHEME
        Beyer, Harald. A History of Norwegian Literature. New
        York: New York University Press, 1956. pp. 201-202.

Jensen, Johannes V.
    THE LONG JOURNEY
        Knaplund, Paul. "Johannes V. Jensen. " SR 33:331-334.
        July 1925.

        Marcus, Aage. "Johannes V. Jensen. " ASR 20:344-347.
        June - July 1932.
    THE TREK OF THE CIMBRI
        Toksvig, Signe. "Some Recent Danish Books. " ASR 11:666-
        667. November 1923.

Jensen, Thit
    STYGGE KRUMPEN
        Clausen, Julius. "Current Books in Denmark. " ASR 26:67.
        March 1938.

Johnson, Eyvind
   THE CLOUDS OVER METAPONTION
      Orton, Gavin. "Eyvind Johnson--An Introduction. " Scan
      5:120-121. November 1966.
   DREAMS OF ROSES AND FIRE
      Orton, Gavin. "Eyvind Johnson--An Introduction. " Scan
      5:119. November 1966.
   HIS GRACE'S DAYS
      Orton, Gavin. "Eyvind Johnson--An Introduction. " Scan
      5:121-122. November 1966.
   KRILON
      Orton, Gavin. "Eyvind Johnson--An Introduction. " Scan
      5:116-117. November 1966.
   LIFE'S LONG DAY
      Orton, Gavin. "Eyvind Johnson--An Introduction. " Scan
      5:122-123. November 1966.
   THE NOVEL ABOUT OLOF
      Orton, Gavin. "Eyvind Johnson--An Introduction. " Scan
      5:114-115. November 1966.
   STRANDERNAS SVALL
      Stanford, W. B. The Ulysses Theme. Oxford: Basil Black-
      well, 1963. pp. 200-201.

Jorgensen, Johannes
   FORAARSSAGN
      Jones, W. Glyn. "The Early Novels of Jorgensen. " SS 36:
      104-106. May 1964.
   EN FREMMED
      Jones, W. Glyn. "The Early Novels of Jorgensen." SS 36:
      106-109. May 1964.
   HJEMVEE
      Jones, W. Glyn. "The Early Novels of Jorgensen." SS 36:
      115-116. May 1964.
   LIVETS TRAE
      Jones, W. Glyn. "The Early Novels of Jorgensen. " SS 36:
      113-115. May 1964.
   SOMMER
      Jones, W. Glyn. "The Early Novels of Jorgensen. " SS 36:
      109-112. May 1964.

Kamban, Gudmundur
   RAGNAR FINNSSON
      Worster, W. W. "Four Icelandic Writers. " Edinburgh Re-
      view 238:317-319. October 1923.
   THIRTIETH GENERATION
      Clausen, Julius. "Novels and Memoirs in Denmark. " ASR
      22:59-60. March 1934.

Kielland, Alexander
   GARMAN AND WORSE
      Beyer, Harald. A History of Norwegian Literature. New
      York: New York University Press, 1956. p. 235.

Sturtevant, Albert Morey. "Regarding the Chronology of
Events in Kielland's Novels. " SS 12:102-109. August 1933.
SKIPPER WORSE
Sturtevant, Albert Morey. "Regarding the Chronology of
Events in Kielland's Novels. " SS 12:102-109. August 1933.

Kierkegaard, S.
JOURNAL OF A SEDUCER
Fenger, Henning. "Kierkegaard--A Literary Approach. "
Scan 3:14-15. May 1964.

Kirk, Hans
THE SLAVE
Stangerup, Hakon. "Recent Danish Literature. " ASR 39:
297-298. December 1951.

Kivi, Aleksis
SEVEN BROTHERS
Laitinen, Kai. "Aleksis Kivi: The Man and His Work. " ASR
50:376-377. Winter 1962-63.

Knudsen, Jakob
FREMSKRIDT
Jones, W. Glyn. "DET FORJAETTEDE LAND and FREM-
SKRIDT as Social Novels: A Comparison. " SS 37:80-90.
February 1965.

Krusenstjerna, Agnes von
FROKNAMA VON PAHLEN
"Current Swedish Books. " ASR 24:256-257. September
1936.

Lagerkvist, Par
BARABBAS
Braybrooke, Neville. "Lagerkvist and His BARABBAS. "
QQ 59:369-372. Autumn 1952.

Gustafson, Walter W. "The Patterns of the Work of Par
Lagerkvist. " SS 26:14-16. February 1954.

Johannesson, Eric O. "Par Lagerkvist and the Art of Rebellion. " SS 30:26-29. February 1958.

Scobbie, Irene. "Contrasting Characters in BARABBAS. "
SS 32:212-220. November 1960.

Spector, Robert Donald. "Lagerkvist and Existentialism. "
SS 32:208-209. November 1960.

Spector, Robert Donald. "Lagerkvist's Uses of Deformity. "
SS 33:212-214. November 1961.

Swanson, Roy Arthur. "Evil and Love in Lagerkvist's

Crucifixion Cycle. " SS 38:302-306. November 1966.
THE DEATH OF AHASUERŪS
Ohmann, Richard M. "Apostle of Uncertainty. " Common-
weal 76:170-171. May 11, 1962.
DET HĒLĪGA LANDET
Swanson, Roy Arthur. "Evil and Love in Lagerkvist's
Crucifixion Cycle. " SS 38:312-315. November 1966.
THE DWARF
Ohmann, Richard M. "Apostle of Uncertainty. " Common-
weal 76:171-172. May 11, 1962.

Spector, Robert Donald. "THE DWARF: A Note on Lagerkvist's Use of Human Deformity. " MLN 70:432-433. June
1955.

Spector, Robert Donald. "Lagerkvist's Uses of Deformity. "
SS 33:214-217. November 1961.
THE ĒTERNAL SMILE
Linner, Sven. "Par Lagerkvist's THE ETERNAL SMILE
and THE SIBYL. " SS 37:160-167. May 1965.

Spector, Robert D. "The Structure and Meaning of THE
ETERNAL SMILE. " MLN 71:206-207. March 1956.

Vowles, Richard B. "The Fiction of Par Lagerkvist. "
WHR 8:116. Spring 1954.
THE HĀNGMAN
Vowles, Richard B. "The Fiction of Par Lagerkvist. "
WHR 8:116-117. Spring 1954.
THE SĪBȲL
Gustafson, Walter W. "SIBYLLAN and the Patterns of
Lagerkvist's Works. " SS 30:131-136. August 1958.

Hjorth, Daniel. "Swedish Letters in Recent Years. " ILA 2:
173-174. 1959.

Linner, Sven. "Par Lagerkvist's THE ETERNAL SMILE
and THE SIBYL. " SS 37:160-167. May 1965.

Spector, Robert Donald. "Lagerkvist and Existentialism. "
SS 32:209-210. November 1960.

Swanson, Roy Arthur. "Evil and Love in Lagerkvist's
Crucifixion Cycle. " SS 38:304-306. November 1966.

Lagerlof, Selma
ANNA SVARD
Larsen, Hanna Astrup. "Selma Lagerlof. " ASR 23:221-222.
September 1935.
CHARLOTTE LOWENSKOLD
Larsen, Hanna Astrup. "Selma Lagerlof. " ASR 23:221-222.
September 1935.

THE EMPEROR OF PORTUGALLIA
Larsen, Hanna Astrup. Selma Lagerlof. Garden City: Doubleday, 1936. pp. 79-81.

Maule, Harry E. Selma Lagerlof: The Woman, Her Work,
Her Message. Garden City: Doubleday, Doran and Company,
1928. pp. 56-60.
THE GIRL FROM MARSH CROFT
Larsen, Hanna Astrup. Selma Lagerlof. Garden City: Double-
day, 1936. pp. 76-78.

Larsen, Hanna Astrup. "Selma Lagerlof. " ASR 23:217-218.
September 1935.
GOSTA BERLING'S SAGA
Afzelius, Nils. "The Scandalous Selma Lagerlof. " Scan 5:
92-99. November 1966.

Berendsohn. Walter. Selma Lagerlof: Her Life and Work.
Garden City: Doubleday, 1932. pp. 37-41.

Fleisher, Frederic. "Selma Lagerlof: A Centennial Tribute."
ASR 46:244-245. September 1958.

Gustafson, Alrik. Six Scandinavian Novelists. New York:
Princeton University Press, 1940. pp. 177-178; 185-216.

Lagerroth, Erland. "The Narrative Art of Selma Lagerlof:
Two Problems. " SS 33:11-16. February 1961.

Lagerroth, Erland. "Selma Lagerlof Research 1900-1964:
A Survey and an Orientation. " SS 37:14-19. February 1965.

Larsen, Hanna Astrup. Selma Lagerlof. Garden City: Doubleday, 1936. pp. 32-48.

[Larsen, Hanna Astrup.] "Selma Lagerlof. " ASR 23:117-
125. June 1935.

Maule, Harry E. Selma Lagerlof: The Woman, Her Work,
Her Message. Garden City: Doubleday, Doran and Company,
1928. pp. 35-39.
JERUSALEM
Berendsohn, Walter. Selma Lagerlof: Her Life and Work.
Garden City: Doubleday, 1932. pp. 51-56.

Gustafson, Alrik. Six Scandinavian Novelists. New York:
Princeton University Press, 1940. pp. 216-220.

Larsen, Hanna Astrup. Selma Lagerlof. Garden City: Doubleday, 1936. pp. 58-69.

Larsen, Hanna Astrup. "Selma Lagerlof. " ASR 23:210-216.
September 1935.

Maule, Harry E. Selma Lagerlof: The Woman, Her Work,
Her Message. Garden City: Doubleday, Doran and Company,
1928. pp. 44-52.

Monroe, N. Elizabeth. The Novel and Society. Chapel Hill:
University of North Carolina Press, 1941. pp. 94-97.

Monroe, Elizabeth. "Selma Lagerlof's Art." ASR 28:144-
145. June 1940.
LILLIECRONA'S HOME
Larsen, Hanna Astrup. Selma Lagerlof. Garden City: Doubleday, 1936. pp. 75-76.

Monroe, N. Elizabeth. The Novel and Society. Chapel Hill:
University of North Carolina Press, 1941. pp. 100-101.
THE MIRACLES OF ANTICHRIST
Berendsohn, Walter. Selma Lagerlof: Her Life and Work.
Garden City: Doubleday, 1932. pp. 44-47.

Larsen, Hanna Astrup. Selma Lagerlof. Garden City: Doubleday, 1936. pp. 51-55.

[Larsen, Hanna Astrup.] "Selma Lagerlof." ASR 23:126-
128. June 1935.

Maule, Harry E. Selma Lagerlof: The Woman, Her Work,
Her Message. Garden City: Doubleday, Doran and Company,
1928. pp. 40-43.

Monroe, N. Elizabeth. The Novel and Society. Chapel Hill:
University of North Carolina Press, 1941. pp. 106-107.
THE OUTCAST
Lagerroth, Erland. "Selma Lagerlof Research 1900-1964:
A Survey and an Orientation." SS 37:23-24. February 1965.

Larsen, Hanna Astrup. "Selma Lagerlof." ASR 23:318-319.
December 1935.

Maule, Harry E. Selma Lagerlof: The Woman, Her Work,
Her Message. Garden City: Doubleday, Doran and Company,
1928. pp. 60-63.

Monroe, N. Elizabeth. The Novel and Society. Chapel Hill:
University of North Carolina Press, 1941. pp. 107-108.
OUTLAWED
Mortensen, Johan. "Books of a Year in Sweden." ASR 8:
24-25. January 1920.
THE RING OF THE LOWENSKOLDS
Monroe, N. Elizabeth. The Novel and Society. Chapel Hill:
University of North Carolina Press, 1941. p. 103.
THE TALE OF A MANOR
Berendsohn, Walter. Selma Lagerlof: Her Life and Work.
Garden City: Doubleday, 1932. pp. 50-51.

THY SOUL SHALL BEAR WITNESS
    Lagerroth, Erland. "Selma Lagerlof Research 1900-1964:
    A Survey and an Orientation. " SS 37:22-23. February 1965.

    Larsen, Hanna Astrup. Selma Lagerlof. Garden City: Double-
    day, 1936. pp. 78-79.
THE TREASURE
    Larsen, Hanna Astrup. "Selma Lagerlof. " ASR 23:216-217.
    September 1935.

    Monroe, N. Elizabeth. The Novel and Society. Chapel Hill:
    University of North Carolina Press, 1941. pp. 103-104.
THE WONDERFUL ADVENTURES OF NILS
    Berendsohn, Walter. Selma Lagerlof: Her Life and Work.
    Garden City: Doubleday, 1932. pp. 62-67.

    Larsen, Hanna Astrup. Selma Lagerlof. Garden City: Double-
    day, 1936. pp. 69-73.

    Monroe, N. Elizabeth. The Novel and Society. Chapel Hill:
    University of North Carolina Press, 1941. pp. 102-103.

    Terras, Victor. "Two Bronze Monarchs. " SS 33:150-154.
    August 1961.

Larsen, J. Anker
    THE PHILOSOPHER'S STONE
        Boyd, Ernest. Studies from Ten Literatures. New York:
        Charles Scribner's Sons, 1925. pp. 274-278.

        Toksvig, Signe. "Literary Tides in Denmark. " ASR 12:
        298-299. May 1924.

Larsen, Karl
    SPRING
        Rimestad, Christian. "Danish Literature. " ASR 9:730-731.
        November 1921.

Laxness, Halldor
THE ATOM-STATION
    Magnusson, Sigurdur A. "Halldor Kiljan Laxness: Iceland's
    First Nobel Prize Winner. " ASR 44:16-17. March 1956.
THE BELL OF ICELAND
    Beck, Richard. "The Literary Scene in Iceland. " ASR 34:
    56-57. March 1946.

    Magnusson, Sigurdur A. "Halldor Kiljan Laxness: Iceland's
    First Nobel Prize Winner. " ASR 44:15-16. March 1956.
INDEPENDENT PEOPLE
    Magnusson, Sigurdur A. "Halldor Kiljan Laxness: Iceland's
    First Nobel Prize Winner. " ASR 44:15. March 1956.
OLAF THE POET
    Magnusson, Sigurdur A. "Halldor Kiljan Laxness: Iceland's

First Nobel Prize Winner. " ASR 44:15. March 1956.
SALKA VALKA
    Magnusson, Sigurdur A. "Halldor Kiljan Laxness: Iceland's
    First Nobel Prize Winner. " ASR 44:14-15. March 1956.

Lidman, Sven
    AS THROUGH FIRE
        Mortensen, Johan. "Books of the Year in Sweden. " ASR
        9:737-738. November 1921.

Lie, Jonas
    ADAM SCHRADER
        Wiehr, Josef. "The Women Characters of Jonas Lie. "
        JEGP 28:48-49. January 1929.
    THE DAUGHTERS OF THE PORT COMMANDER
        Wiehr, Josef. "The Women Characters of Jonas Lie. "
        JEGP 28:60-61. January 1929.
    DYRE REIN
        Wiehr, Joseph. "The Women Characters of Jonas Lie. "
        JEGP 28:245-251. April 1929.
    EAST OF THE SUN, WEST OF THE MOON, AND BEHIND THE
    TOWER OF BABEL
        Wiehr, Joseph. "The Women Characters of Jonas Lie. "
        JEGP 28:259-260. April 1929.
    ET SAMLIO
        Wiehr, Josef. "The Women Characters of Jonas Lie. "
        JEGP 28:61-63. January 1929.
    THE FAMILY AT GILJE
        Gustafson, Alrik. Six Scandinavian Novelists. New York:
        Princeton University Press, 1940. pp. 40-64.

        Wiehr, Josef. "The Women Characters of Jonas Lie. "
        JEGP 28:53-58. January 1929.
    FASTE FORLAND
        Wiehr, Joseph. "The Women Characters of Jonas Lie. "
        JEGP 28:251-253. April 1929.
    FINNEBLOD
        Vowles, Guy R. "Gerstaecker's GERMELSHAUSEN and
        Lie's FINNEBLOD. " Monatshefte 41:293-294. October 1949.
    FORCES OF EVIL
        Wiehr, Josef. "The Women Characters of Jonas Lie. "
        JEGP 28:65-67. January 1929.
    GO ONWARD
        Wiehr, Josef. "The Women Characters of Jonas Lie. "
        JEGP 28:50-52. January 1929.
    LIVSSLAVEN
        Wiehr, Josef. "The Women Characters of Jonas Lie. "
        JEGP 28:52-53. January 1929.
    MAISA JONS
        Wiehr, Josef. "The Women Characters of Jonas Lie. "
        JEGP 28:63-65. January 1929.
    THE MAN OF SECOND SIGHT
        Wiehr, Josef. "The Women Characters of Jonas Lie. "

JEGP 28:42-43. January 1929.
NIOBE
Wiehr, Josef. "The Women Characters of Jonas Lie."
JEGP 28:67-71. January 1929.
OLD RUTLAND
Wiehr, Josef. "The Women Characters of Jonas Lie."
JEGP 28:49-50. January 1929.
THE PILOT AND HIS WIFE
Gustafson, Alrik. Six Scandinavian Novelists. New York:
Princeton University Press, 1940. pp. 38-39.

Wiehr, Josef. "The Women Characters of Jonas Lie."
JEGP 28:45-46. January 1929.
THOMAS ROSS
Wiehr, Josef. "The Women Characters of Jonas Lie."
JEGP 28:47-48. January 1929.
ULFVUNGERNE
Wiehr, Joseph. "The Women Characters of Jonas Lie."
JEGP 28:255-259. April 1929.
THE VISIONARY
Gustafson, Alrik. Six Scandinavian Novelists. New York:
Princeton University Press, 1940. pp. 37-38.

Jorgenson, Theodore. History of Norwegian Literature.
New York: Macmillan, 1933. pp. 301-302.
A VORTEX
Wiehr, Josef. "The Women Characters of Jonas Lie."
JEGP 28:58-60. January 1929.
WHEN THE SUN SETS
Wiehr, Joseph. "The Women Characters of Jonas Lie."
JEGP 28:244-245. April 1929.

Linna, Vaino
TAALLA POHJANTAHDEN ALLA
Stormbom, N. B. "Vaino Linna and His Tales of Toil and
War." ASR 51:248-250. Autumn 1963.
THE UNKNOWN SOLDIER
Stormbom, N. B. "Vaino Linna and His Tales of Toil and
War." ASR 51:245-248. Autumn 1963.

Martinson, Harry
THE NETTLES BLOOM
"Current Swedish Books." ASR 24:254-255. September 1936.

Moberg, Vilhelm
BAD CONDUCT MARK
"Current Swedish Books." ASR 24:253-254. September 1936.
THE EMIGRANTS
Alexis, Gerhard T. "Sweden to Minnesota: Vilhelm Mo-
berg's Fictional Reconstruction." AQ 18:81-94. Spring
1966.

Johnson, Walter. "Moberg's Emigrants and the Naturalistic

Tradition. " SS 25:134-146. November 1953.

Winther, Sophus Keith. "Moberg and a New Genre for the
Emigrant Novel. " SS 34:174-177. August 1962.
THE LAST LETTER HOME
    Alexis, Gerhard T. "Moberg's Immigrant Trilogy: A Dubious
    Conclusion. " SS 38:20-25. February 1966.

    Alexis, Gerhard T. "Sweden to Minnesota: Vilhelm Moberg's
    Fictional Reconstruction. " AQ 18:81-94. Spring 1966.

    Winther, Sophus Keith. "Moberg and a New Genre for the
    Emigrant Novel. " SS 34:179-182. August 1962.
UNTO A GOOD LAND
    Alexis, Gerhard T. "Sweden to Minnesota: Vilhelm Moberg's
    Fictional Reconstruction. " AQ 18:81-94. Spring 1966.

    Winther, Sophus Keith. "Moberg and a New Genre for the
    Emigrant Novel. " SS 34:177-179. August 1962.

Nexo, Martin A.
    PELLE, THE CONQUEROR
        Johanson, Joel M. "PELLE, THE CONQUEROR: An Epic of
        Labor. " SR 27:218-226. April 1919.

        Slochower, Harry. Three Ways of Modern Man. New York:
        International Publishers, 1937. pp. 105-144.

Paludan, Jacob
    JORGEN STEIN
        Clausen, Julius. "Novels and Memoirs in Denmark. " ASR
        22:60-61. March 1934.

        Heltberg, Niels. "Jacob Paludan. " ASR 40:144-145. June
        1952.

Petersen, Nis
    SPILLED MILK
        Clausen, Julius. "Truth and Fiction in Current Danish
        Books. " ASR 23:259-260. September 1935.

Pontoppidan, Henrik
    THE KINGDOM OF THE DEAD
        Ekman, Ernst. "Henrik Pontoppidan as a Critic of Modern
        Danish Society. " SS 29:171-183. November 1957.

        Jones, W. Glyn. "Henrik Pontoppidan (1857-1943). " MLR
        52:382. July 1957.

        Jones, W. Glyn. "Henrik Pontoppidan, the Church and
        Christianity After 1900. " SS 30:192-197. November 1958.

        Larsen, Hanna Astrup. "Pontoppidan of Denmark. " ASR 31:

236-237. September 1943.

Robertson, J. G. Essays and Addresses on Literature.
London: Geo. Routledge and Sons, 1935. pp. 252-254.
LUCKY PETER
Ekman, Ernst. "Henrik Pontoppidan as a Critic of Modern
Danish Society. " SS 29:171-183. November 1957.

Jones, W. Glyn. "Henrik Pontoppidan (1857-1943). " MLR
52:380-382. July 1957.

Larsen, Hanna Astrup. "Pontoppidan of Denmark. " ASR
31:235-236. September 1943.

Robertson, J. G. Essays and Addresses on Literature.
London: Geo. Routledge and Sons, 1935. pp. 249-253.
MAN'S HEAVEN
Larsen, Hanna Astrup. "Pontoppidan of Denmark. " ASR 31:
238-239. September 1943.
THE PROMISED LAND
Jones, W. Glyn. "DET FORJAETTEDE LAND and FREM-
SKRIDT as Social Novels: A Comparison. " SS 37:80-90.
February 1965.

Jones, W. Glyn. "Henrik Pontoppidan (1857-1943). " MLR
52:378-380. July 1957.

Larsen, Hanna Astrup. "Pontoppidan of Denmark. " ASR 31:
233-235. September 1943.

Rosenkrantz, Palle
THE HERMIT
Clausen, Julius. "New Danish Books. " ASR 25:62-63. March
1937.

Rung, Otto
THE BIRD OF PARADISE
Rimestad, Chr. "The Latest Danish Books. " ASR 8:833-834.
November 1920.
A GIRL IN TWO MIRRORS
Clausen, Julius. "Current Books in Denmark. " ASR 26:69-
70. March 1938.

Schack, Hans
PHANTASTERNE
Jorgensen, Aage. "On PHANTASTERNE, the Novel by Hans
Egede Schack. " Scan 5:50-52. May 1966.

Madsen, Borge Gedso. "Hans Egede Schack's PHANTAS-
TERNE. " SS 35:51-58. February 1963.

Seppanen, Unto
SUN AND STORM

Rothery, Agnes. "Three Novels from Finland." VQR 16: 298-299. Spring 1940.

Sillanpaa, Frans
 THE MAID SILJA
   Beck, Richard. "Sillanpaa--Finland's Winner of the Nobel Prize." Poet Lore 46:361-362. Winter 1940.

   Rothery, Agnes. "Three Novels from Finland." VQR 16:297. Spring 1940.

Siwertz, Sigfrid
 THE FLAME
   Hertzman-Ericson, Gurli. "Poetry and Prose in New Swedish Literature." ASR 22:257-258. September 1934.
 THE SELAMBS
   Mortensen, Johan. "Books of the Year in Sweden." ASR 9:734-736. November 1921.

Stolpe, Sven
 NIGHT MUSIC
   Rooney, F. Charles. "Sven Stolpe: The Human Way." Renascence 15:41-45. Fall 1962.
 SOUND OF A DISTANT HORN
   Rooney, F. Charles. "Sven Stolpe: The Human Way." Renascence 15:41-45. Fall 1962.

Strindberg, August
 BLACK BANNERS
   Johannesson, Eric O. "The Problem of Identity in Strindberg's Novels." SS 34:30-31. February 1962.

   Mortensen, Brita M. E. Strindberg: An Introduction to His Life and Work. Cambridge: Cambridge University Press, 1949. pp. 170-173.

   Sprigge, Elizabeth. The Strange Life of August Strindberg. London: Hamish Hamilton, 1949. pp. 207-209.
 THE CONFESSION OF A FOOL
   Johannesson, Eric O. "The Problem of Identity in Strindberg's Novels." SS 34:16-18. February 1962.
 THE DWELLERS OF HEMSO
   Borland, Harold H. "The Dramatic Quality of Strindberg's Novels." MD 5:301-303. December 1962.

   Johannesson, Eric O. "The Problem of Identity in Strindberg's Novels." SS 34:13-14. February 1962.
 ENSAM
   Berendsohn, Walter A. "Strindberg's ENSAM: A Study in Structure and Style." SS 31:168-179. November 1959.

   Johannesson, Eric O. "The Problem of Identity in Strindberg's Novels." SS 34:27-29. February 1962.

THE GOTHIC ROOMS
>Johannesson, Eric O. "The Problem of Identity in Strind-
berg's Novels. " SS 34:29-30. February 1962.

>Mortensen, Brita M. E. Strindberg: An Introduction to His
Life and Work. Cambridge: Cambridge University Press,
1949. pp. 170-173.

IN THE OUTER SKERRIES
>Borland, Harold H. "The Dramatic Quality of Strindberg's
Novels. " MD 5:303. December 1962.

>Johannesson, Eric O. "The Problem of Identity in Strind-
berg's Novels. " SS 34:22-24. February 1962.

>Lind-af-Hageby, L. August Strindberg: The Spirit of Re-
volt. New York: Appleton and Company, 1913. pp. 230-231.

>Mortensen, Brita M. E. Strindberg: An Introduction to His
Life and Work. Cambridge: Cambridge University Press,
1949. pp. 166-170.

INFERNO
>Johannesson, Eric O. "The Problem of Identity in Strind-
berg's Novels. " SS 34:24-27. February 1962.

THE ISLAND OF PARADISE
>Benson, Adolph B. "Humor and Satire in Strindberg's THE
ISLAND OF PARADISE. " SS 26:17-24. February 1954.

LEGENDER
>Johannesson, Eric O. "The Problem of Identity in Strind-
berg's Novels. " SS 34:24-27. February 1962.

THE PEOPLE OF HEMSÖ
>Mortensen, Brita M. E. Strindberg: An Introduction to His
Life and Work. Cambridge: Cambridge University Press,
1949. pp. 161-166.

THE RED ROOM
>Borland, Harold H. "The Dramatic Quality of Strind-
berg's Novels. " MD 5:300-301. December 1962.

>Campbell, G. A. Strindberg. New York: Macmillan, 1933.
pp. 51-52.

>Johannesson, Eric O. "The Problem of Identity in Strind-
berg's Novels. " SS 34:7-9. February 1962.

>Lind-af-Hageby, L. August Strindberg: The Spirit of Revolt.
New York: Appleton and Company, 1913. pp. 110-113; 137-
143.

>Mortensen, Brita M. E. Strindberg: An Introduction to His
Life and Work. Cambridge: Cambridge University Press,
1949. pp. 151-161.

>Sprigge, Elizabeth. The Strange Life of August Strindberg.
London: Hamish Hamilton, 1949. pp. 85-87.

Winther, S. K. "Strindberg and O'Neill: A Study of Influence." SS 31:116-118. August 1959.

THE ROMANTIC SEXTON OF RANO

Johannesson, Eric O. "The Problem of Identity in Strindberg's Novels." SS 34:18-19. February 1962.

THE ROOF-RAISING FEAST

Johannesson, Eric O. "The Problem of Identity in Strindberg's Novels." SS 34:32-33. February 1962.

Johannesson, Eric O. "Strindberg's TAKLAGSOL: An Early Experiment in the Psychological Novel." SS 35:223-238. August 1963.

THE SCAPEGOAT

Johannesson, Eric O. "The Problem of Identity in Strindberg's Novels." SS 34:33-34. February 1962.

Johannesson, Eric O. "SYNDABOCKEN: Strindberg's Last Novel." SS 35:1-28. February 1963.

TJANSTEKVINNANS SON

Johannesson, Eric O. "The Problem of Identity in Strindberg's Novels." SS 34:9-13. February 1962.

TSCHANDALA

Johannesson, Eric O. "The Problem of Identity in Strindberg's Novels." SS 34:20-22. February 1962.

Undset, Sigrid

THE BURNING BUSH (See also THE MASTER OF HESTVIKEN)

Monroe, N. Elizabeth. The Novel and Society. Chapel Hill: University of North Carolina Press, 1941. pp. 58-59; 71-72.

THE FAITHFUL WIFE

Monroe, N. Elizabeth. The Novel and Society. Chapel Hill: University of North Carolina Press, 1941. pp. 59-60.

FRU HJELDE

Larsen, Hanna Astrup. "Sigrid Undset: I. Modern Works." ASR 17:350-351. June 1929.

Vinde, Victor. Sigrid Undset: A Nordic Moralist. Seattle: University of Washington Book Store, 1930. pp. 18-21.

FRU MARTHA OULIE

Gustafson, Alrik. Six Scandinavian Novelists. New York: Princeton University Press, 1940. pp. 300-303.

FRU WAAGE

Larsen, Hanna Astrup. "Sigrid Undset: I. Modern Works." ASR 17:351-352. June 1929.

Vinde, Victor. Sigrid Undset: A Nordic Moralist. Seattle: University of Washington Book Store, 1930. pp. 21-22.

JENNY

Gustafson, Alrik. Six Scandinavian Novelists. New York: Princeton University Press, 1940. pp. 305-309.

Larsen, Hanna Astrup. "Sigrid Undset: I. Modern Works."

ASR 17:348-349. June 1929.

Monroe, N. Elizabeth. The Novel and Society. Chapel Hill:
University of North Carolina Press, 1941. pp. 52-53.

Vinde, Victor. Sigrid Undset: A Nordic Moralist. Seattle:
University of Washington Book Store, 1930. pp. 14-15.
KRISTIN LAVRANSDATTER
Beck, Richard. "Sigrid Undset and Her Novels on Medieval
Life." ASR 40:36-37. March 1952.

Gustafson, Alrik. Six Scandinavian Novelists. New York:
Princeton University Press, 1940. pp. 311-346.

Larsen, Hanna Astrup. "Recent Fiction in Norway." ASR
9:741-742. November 1921.

Larsen, Hanna Astrup. "Sigrid Undset: II. Medieval Works."
ASR 17:408-410. July 1929.

Larsen, Hanna Astrup. "Some Recent Norwegian Books."
ASR 10:661-663. November 1922.

Monroe, N. Elizabeth. The Novel and Society. Chapel Hill:
University of North Carolina Press, 1941. pp. 64-65.

Rogers, B. J. "The Divine Disappointment of KRISTIN
LAVRANSDATTER." Cithara 2:44-48. November 1962.

Slochower, Harry. Three Ways of Modern Man. New York:
International Publishers, 1937. pp. 25-49.
THE LONGEST YEARS
Monroe, N. Elizabeth. The Novel and Society. Chapel Hill:
University of North Carolina Press, 1941. pp. 49-50.
MADAME DOROTHEA
Monroe, N. Elizabeth. The Novel and Society. Chapel Hill:
University of North Carolina Press, 1941. p. 72.
THE MASTER OF HESTVIKEN
Dunn, Margaret Mary. "THE MASTER OF HESTVIKEN: A
New Reading." SS 38:281-294. November 1966.

Gustafson, Alrik. Six Scandinavian Novelists. New York:
Princeton University Press, 1940. pp. 346-354.

Larsen, Hanna Astrup. "Sigrid Undset: II. Medieval Works."
ASR 17:410-414. July 1929.

Monroe, N. Elizabeth. The Novel and Society. Chapel Hill:
University of North Carolina Press, 1941. pp. 64-69.
SPRING
Larsen, Hanna Astrup. "Sigrid Undset: I. Modern Works."
ASR 17:349-350. June 1929.

Vinde, Victor. Sigrid Undset: A Nordic Moralist. Seattle: University of Washington Book Store, 1930. pp. 22-23.

THE WILD ORCHID
Gustafson, Alrik. Six Scandinavian Novelists. New York: Princeton University Press, 1940. pp. 355-356.

Monroe, N. Elizabeth. The Novel and Society. Chapel Hill: University of North Carolina Press, 1941. pp. 58-59; 71-72.

Vesaas, Tarjei
THE BLEACHING PLACE
Dale, Johannes A. "Tarjei Vesaas." ASR 54:373. December 1966.
THE HOUSE IN THE DARK
Dale, Johannes A. "Tarjei Vesaas." ASR 54:370. December 1966.
THE ICE PALACE
Dale, Johannes A. "Tarjei Vesaas." ASR 54:374. December 1966.
THE SEED
Dale, Johannes A. "Tarjei Vesaas." ASR 54:370-371. December 1966.

Wagner, Elin
LIBERATED LOVE
Mortensen, Johan. "The Year's Books in Sweden." ASR 8:844-845. November 1920.

The Russian and East European Novel

Aksakov, Sergey
    FAMILY CHRONICLES
        Olgin, Moissaye J. A Guide to Russian Literature (1820-
        1917). New York: Harcourt, Brace and Howe, 1920. pp. 50-
        51.

Aksyonov, V.
    A TICKET TO THE STARS
        Rudy, Peter. "The Soviet Russian Literary Scene in 1961:
        A Mild Permafrost Thaw. " MLJ 46:252-253. October 1962.

Aldanov, Mark A.
    DEVIL'S BRIDGE
        Twarog, Leon I. "Aldanov as an Historical Novelist. " RusR
        8:234-244. July 1949.
    THE NINTH OF THERMIDOR
        Twarog, Leon I. "Aldanov as an Historical Novelist. " RusR
        8:234-244. July 1949.
    ST. HELENA
        Twarog, Leon I. "Aldanov as an Historical Novelist. " RusR
        8:234-244. July 1949.

Ambrus, Zoltan
    KING MIDAS
        Remenyi, Joseph. "A Hungarian Exponent of French Real-
        ism: Zoltan Ambrus, 1861-1933. " Symposium 2:270-271.
        November 1948.

        Remenyi, Joseph. Hungarian Writers and Literature. New
        Brunswick: Rutgers University Press, 1964. pp. 275-276.
    YOU WILL BE ALONE
        Remenyi, Joseph. Hungarian Writers and Literature. New
        Brunswick: Rutgers University Press, 1964. p. 276.

Andreyev, Leonid
    THE CURSE OF THE BEAST
        Woodward, J. B. "Leonid Andreyev's 'Divine Comedy. ' "
        CSP 6:71-73. 1964.
    JUDAS ISCARIOT AND THE OTHERS
        Kaun, Alexander. Leonid Andreyev. New York: Huebsch,
        1924. pp. 268-271.

        Wolfe, Archibald J. "Aspects of Recent Russian Liter-
        ature. " SR 16:136-147. April 1908.
    THE RED LAUGH
        Kaun, Alexander. Leonid Andreyev. New York: Huebsch,

369

1924. pp. 215-218.

MacAdam, George. "THE RED LAUGH." Methodist Review 108:875-889. November 1925.
SHASHKA ZHEGULEV
    Kaun, Alexander. Leonid Andreyev. New York: Huebsch, 1924. pp. 245-249.
THE STORY OF SEVEN WHO WERE HANGED
    Woodward, J. B. "Leonid Andreyev's 'Divine Comedy.' " CSP 6:73-78. 1964.
WAR'S BURDEN
    Kaun, Alexander. Leonid Andreyev. New York: Huebsch, 1924. pp. 134-135.

Andric, Ivo
    THE BRIDGE ON THE DRINA
        della Fazia, Alba. "Nobel Prize, 1962, and THE BRIDGE ON THE DRINA Revisited." BA 37:24-26. Winter 1963.
    CHRONICLE OF TRAVNIK
        Kadic, Ante. "The French in THE CHRONICLE OF TRAVNIK." CalSS 1:134-169. 1960.

Artsybashev, Mikhail
    AT THE BRINK
        Pachmuss, Temira. "Mikhail Artsybashev in the Criticism of Zinaida Gippius." SEER 44:81-85. January 1966.
    SANIN
        Olgin, Moissaye J. A Guide to Russian Literature (1820-1917). New York: Harcourt, Brace and Howe, 1920. pp. 268-269.

        Pachmuss, Temira. "Mikhail Artsybashev in the Criticism of Zinaida Gippius." SEER 44:77-83. January 1966.

        Phelps, William L. Essays on Russian Novelists. New York: Macmillan Company, 1917. pp. 251-261.
    THE WOMAN THAT STOOD BETWEEN
        Olgin, Moissaye J. A Guide to Russian Literature (1820-1917). New York: Harcourt, Brace and Howe, 1920. p. 269.

Asanov, N.
    THE SECRETARY OF THE PARTY BUREAU
        Eng-Liedmeier, A. M. Van der. Soviet Literary Characters. 'S Gravenhage: Mouton and Company, 1959. pp. 131-132; 141-142.

Aslanian, Mugerditch
    ASHKHEN SATYAN
        Alexander, Edward. "The Ferment in Soviet Armenian Literature." ASEER 17:499-503. December 1958.

Babayevski, S.
    CAVALIER OF THE GOLDEN STAR
        Alexandrova, Vera. "Soviet Literature Since Stalin." PoC

3:13-14. July - August 1954.
LIGHT OVER THE LAND
>Eng-Liedmeier, A. M. Van der. Soviet Literary Characters. 'S Gravenhage: Mouton and Company, 1959. pp. 130-131.

Baklanov, Gregorii
AN INCH OF GROUND
>Lochtin, S. "The War in the Soviet Novel from Heroic to Prosaic. " Survey 33:64-65. July - September 1960.

Bek, Alexander
THE LIFE OF BEREZHKOV
>Gibian, George. Interval of Freedom: Soviet Literature During the Thaw 1954-1957. Minneapolis: University of Minnesota Press, 1960. pp. 35-40.

Bely, Andrey
PETERSBURG
>Maslenikov, Oleg A. "Russian Symbolists: The Mirror Theme and Allied Motifs. " RusR 16:42-43. January 1957.

>von Mohrenschildt, D. S. "The Russian Symbolist Movement. " PMLA 53:1205. December 1938.

>Monas, Sidney. "Unreal City. " ChiR 13:107-112. Autumn 1959.

>Olgin, Moissaye J. A Guide to Russian Literature (1820-1917). New York: Harcourt, Brace and Howe, 1920. p. 204.

>Reeve, F. D. "A Geometry of Prose. " KR 25:9-25. Winter 1963.

>Reeve, F. D. The Russian Novel. New York: McGraw-Hill Book Company, 1966. pp. 325-345.
THE SECOND SYMPHONY
>Maslenikov, Oleg A. "Russian Symbolists: The Mirror Theme and Allied Motifs. " RusR 16:43-44. January 1957.
THE SILVER DOVE
>Olgin, Moissaye J. A Guide to Russian Literature (1820-1917). New York: Harcourt, Brace and Howe, 1920. pp. 203-204.
THIRD SYMPHONY: THE RETURN
>Maslenikov, Oleg A. "Russian Symbolists: The Mirror Theme and Allied Motifs. " RusR 16:44-46. January 1957.

Belyayev, Alexander
THE LEAP INTO NOTHING
>Yershov, Peter. Science Fiction and Utopian Fantasy in Soviet Literature. New York: Research Program on the USSR, Mimeographed Series No. 62, 1954. pp. 46-47.

Benesova, Bozena
    THE BLOW
        Hostovsky, Egon. "The Czech Novel Between the Two World
        Wars. " SEER 21:81-82. November 1943.
    SUBTERRANEAN FIRES
        Hostovsky, Egon. "The Czech Novel Between the Two World
        Wars. " SEER 21:81-82. November 1943.
    THE TRAGIC RAINBOW
        Hostovsky, Egon. "The Czech Novel Between the Two World
        Wars. " SEER 21:81-82. November 1943.

Berezko, Georgi
    GREATER THAN THE ATOM
        Lochtin, S. "The War in the Soviet Novel from Heroic to
        Prosaic. " Survey 33:67-68. July - September 1960.

Bernaskova, Alena
    THE ROAD IS OPEN
        Souckova, Milada. A Literature in Crisis: Czech Literature
        1938-1950. New York: Mid-European Studies Center, 1954.
        pp. 131-135.

Biadula, Zmitrok
    NIGHTINGALE
        Adamovich, Anthony. Opposition to Sovietization in Belo-
        russian Literature (1917-1957). Published by The Institute
        for the Study of the USSR, Munich, Germany, for Scare-
        crow Press, Inc. , New York, 1958. pp. 89-90.

Bobruk, A.
    MOTHER AND SON
        Gasiorowska, Xenia. "The Postwar Polish Historical Novel."
        CL 9:26-27. Winter 1957.

Brzozowski, Stanislaw
    ALONE AMONG MEN
        Milosz, Czeslaw. "A Controversial Polish Writer: Stanis-
        law Brzozowski. " CalSS 2:59-65. 1963.

Budantsev, Sergei
    REBELLION
        Zavalishin, Vyacheslav. Early Soviet Writers. New York:
        Frederick A. Praeger, 1958. pp. 206-207.

Bulgakov, Mikhail
    THE FATAL EGGS
        Yershov, Peter. Science Fiction and Utopian Fantasy in
        Soviet Literature. New York: Research Program on the
        USSR, Mimeographed Series No. 62, 1954. pp. 32-33.

Bunin, Ivan A.
    DRY VALLEY
        Poggioli, Renato. "The Art of Ivan Bunin. " HSS 1:270-277.

1953.

Struve, Gleb. "The Art of Ivan Bunin. " SEER 11:427. January 1933.
THE GENTLEMAN FROM SAN FRANCISCO
Gross, Seymour L. "Nature, Man, and God in Bunin's THE GENTLEMAN FROM SAN FRANCISCO. " MFS 6:153-163. Summer 1960.

Poggioli, Renato. "The Art of Ivan Bunin. " HSS 1:257-258. 1953.

Wasiolek, Edward. "A Classic Maimed: A Translation of Bunin's THE GENTLEMAN FROM SAN FRANCISCO Examined. " CE 20:25-28. October 1958.

West, Ray B., Jr. and Robert Wooster Stallman. The Art of Modern Fiction. New York: Holt, Rinehart and Winston, 1960. pp. 117-120.
THE LIFE OF ARSEN'EV
Bedford, C. H. "The Fulfilment of Ivan Bunin. " CSP 1: 31-44. 1956.

Pachmuss, Temira. "Ivan Bunin through the Eyes of Zinaida Gippius. " SEER 44:347. July 1966.
MITYA'S LOVE
Struve, Gleb. "The Art of Ivan Bunin. " SEER 11:428. January 1933.
THE VILLAGE
Mirsky, D. S. Contemporary Movements in European Literature. (ed.) William Rose and J. Isaacs. London: George Routledge and Sons, 1928. pp. 153-154.

Pachmuss, Temira. "Ivan Bunin through the Eyes of Zinaida Gippius. " SEER 44:338-340. July 1966.

Poggioli, Renato. "The Art of Ivan Bunin. " HSS 1:264-270. 1953.

Poggioli, Renato. The Phoenix and the Spider. Cambridge: Harvard University Press, 1957. pp. 144-156.

Struve, Gleb. "The Art of Ivan Bunin. " SEER 11:426-427. January 1933.

Cajanov
PUTESESTVIE
Shaw, Nonna D. "The Only Soviet Literary Peasant Utopia." SEEJ n. s. 7:279-283. Fall 1963.

Capek, Karel
FACTORY OF THE ABSOLUTE
Harkins, William E. Karel Capek. New York: Columbia

University Press, 1962. pp. 100-103.

Hostovsky, Egon. "The Czech Novel Between the Two
World Wars. " SEER 21:90-91. November 1943.

HORDUBAL

Harkins, William E. "Form and Thematic Unity in Karel
Capek's Trilogy. " SEEJ 15:92-99. Summer 1957.

Harkins, William E. "Imagery in Karel Capek's HORDU-
BAL. " PMLA 75:616-620. December 1960.

Harkins, William E. Karel Capek. New York: Columbia University Press, 1962. pp. 129-136; 142-144.

Harkins, William E. "The Real Legacy of Karel Capek. "
The Czechoslovak Contribution to World Culture. (ed.)
Miloslav Rechcigl, Jr. The Hague: Mouton and Company,
1964. pp. 65-66.

Wellek, Rene. "Karel Capek. " SEER 15:203-204. July 1936.
Reprinted in Rene Wellek, Essays on Czech Literature. The
Hague: Mouton and Company, 1963. pp. 58-59.

KRAKATIT

Harkins, William E. Karel Capek. New York: Columbia University Press, 1962. pp. 103-109.

Wellek, Rene. "Karel Capek. " SEER 15:197-198. July 1936.
Reprinted in Rene Wellek, Essays on Czech Literature. The
Hague: Mouton and Company, 1963. pp. 52-53.

THE METEOR

Elton, Oliver. Essays and Addresses. New York: Longmans, Green and Company, 1939. pp. 172-175.

Harkins, William E. "Form and Thematic Unity in Karel
Capek's Trilogy. " SEEJ 15:93-99. Summer 1957.

Harkins, William E. Karel Capek. New York: Columbia University Press, 1962. pp. 137-140; 142-144.

Harkins, William E. "The Real Legacy of Karel Capek. "
The Czechoslovak Contribution to World Culture. (ed.)
Miloslav Rechcigl, Jr. The Hague: Mouton and Company,
1964. pp. 65-66.

Wellek, Rene. "Karel Capek. " SEER 15:204-205. July 1936.
Reprinted in Rene Wellek, Essays on Czech Literature. The
Hague: Mouton and Company, 1963. pp. 59-60.

AN ORDINARY LIFE

Elton, Oliver. Essays and Addresses. New York: Longmans,
Green and Company, 1939. pp. 175-179.

Elton, Oliver. "Karel Capek's Stories. " Life and Letters
To-Day 21:40-42. June 1939.

Harkins, William E. "Form and Thematic Unity in Karel
Capek's Trilogy. " SEEJ 15:94-99. Summer 1957.

Harkins, William E. Karel Capek. New York: Columbia
University Press, 1962. pp. 140-144.

Harkins, William E. "Karel Capek and the 'Ordinary Life.' "
BA 36:273-276. Summer 1962.

Harkins, William E. "The Real Legacy of Karel Capek. "
The Czechoslovak Contribution to World Culture. (ed.)
Miloslav Rechcigl, Jr. The Hague: Mouton and Company,
1964. pp. 65-66.

Wellek, Rene. "Karel Capek. " SEER 15:205-206. July 1936.
Reprinted in Rene Wellek, Essays on Czech Literature. The
Hague: Mouton and Company, 1963. pp. 60-61.
WAR WITH THE NEWTS
Elton, Oliver. Essays and Addresses. New York: Longmans,
Green and Company, 1939. pp. 179-182.

Wellek, Rene. "Karel Capek. " SEER 15:206. July 1936.
Reprinted in Rene Wellek, Essays on Czech Literature. The
Hague: Mouton and Company, 1963. p. 61.

Chakovski
THE ROADS WE CHOOSE
Bode, Barbara. "1960: The Literary Harvest. " Survey 36:
41. April - June 1961.

Chekhov, Anton
THE BLACK MONK
Winner, Thomas G. "Cechov and Scientism; Observations
on the Searching Stories. " Anton Cechov: Some Essays.
(ed.) T. Eekman. Leiden: E. J. Brill, 1960. pp. 331-335.

Yermilov, Vladimir. Anton Pavlovich Chekhov. Moscow:
Foreign Languages Publishing House. pp. 281-287.
A DREARY STORY
Matlaw, Ralph E. "Cechov and Scientism; Observations on
the Searching Stories. " Anton Cechov: Some Essays. (ed.)
T. Eekman. Leiden: E. J. Brill, 1960. pp. 327-330.

Simmons, Ernest J. Chekhov: A Biography. Boston: Little,
Brown and Company, 1962. pp. 191-195.

Yermilov, Vladimir. Anton Pavlovich Chekhov. Moscow:
Foreign Languages Publishing House. pp. 215-219.
THE DUEL
Matlaw, Ralph E. "Cechov and the Novel. " Anton Cechov:
Some Essays. (ed.) T. Eekman. Leiden: E. J. Brill, 1960.
pp. 160-166.

O'Connor, Frank. The Mirror in the Roadway: A Study of the Modern Novel. New York: Alfred A. Knopf, 1956. pp. 259-262.

THE FIT
Yermilov, Vladimir. Anton Pavlovich Chekhov. Moscow: Foreign Languages Publishing House. pp. 96-102.

GOOD PEOPLE
Yermilov, Vladimir. Anton Pavlovich Chekhov. Moscow: Foreign Languages Publishing House. pp. 265-271.

THE HOUSE WITH THE MANSARD
Yermilov, Vladimir. Anton Pavlovich Chekhov. Moscow: Foreign Languages Publishing House. pp. 251-264.

IN THE RAVINE
Harrison, John Wm. "Symbolic Action in Chekhov's PEA-SANTS and IN THE RAVINE. " MFS 7:369-371. Winter 1961-62.

MY LIFE
Mann, Thomas. "Anton Chekhov. " Mainstream 12:11-13. March 1959.

Pritchett, V. S. "Books in General. " New S&N 25:209. March 27, 1943.

PEASANTS
Harrison, John Wm. "Symbolic Action in Chekhov's PEA-SANTS and IN THE RAVINE. " MFS 7:371-372. Winter 1961-62.

THE SHOOTING PARTY
Hagan, John. "THE SHOOTING PARTY, Cexov's Early Novel: Its Place in His Development. " SEEJ n. s. 9:123-139. Summer 1965.

THE STEPPE
Simmons, Ernest J. Chekhov: A Biography. Boston: Little, Brown and Company, 1962. pp. 144-146.

STORY OF AN UNKNOWN MAN
Yermilov, Vladimir. Anton Pavlovich Chekhov. Moscow: Foreign Languages Publishing House. pp. 271-281.

THREE YEARS
Reeve, F. D. The Russian Novel. New York: McGraw-Hill Book Company, 1966. pp. 274-301.

WARD NO. 6
Yermilov, Vladimir. Anton Pavlovich Chekhov. Moscow: Foreign Languages Publishing House. pp. 238-246.

Chernyshevsky, Nikolai
WHAT IS TO BE DONE?
Mathewson, Rufus W. , Jr. The Positive Hero in Russian Literature. New York: Columbia University Press, 1958. pp. 95-107; 104-106; 221-222.

Moser, Charles A. Antinihilism in the Russian Novel of the 1860's. The Hague: Mouton and Company, 1964. pp. 39-43.

Olgin, Moissaye J. A Guide to Russian Literature (1820-

1917). New York: Harcourt, Brace and Howe, 1920. pp. 58-
60.

Yershov, Peter. Science Fiction and Utopian Fantasy in
Soviet Literature. New York: Research Program on the
USSR, Mimeographed Series No. 62, 1954. pp. 9-10.

Zekulin, G. "Forerunner of Socialist Realism: The Novel
WHAT TO DO? by N. G. Chernyshevsky." SEER 41:467-
483. June 1963.

Chumandrin, Mikhail
  RABLE'S FACTORY
       Simmons, Ernest J. Through the Glass of Soviet Literature.
       New York: Columbia University Press, 1953. pp. 120-121.

Corny, Kuzma
  SISTER
       Adamovich, Anthony. Opposition to Sovietization in Belo-
       russian Literature (1917-1957). Published by the Institute
       for the Study of the USSR, Munich, Germany, for Scare-
       crow Press, Inc., New York, 1958. pp. 90-91.

Dabrowska, Marja
  NIGHTS AND DAYS
       Borowy, W. "Fifteen Years of Polish Literature." SEER
       12:688-689. April 1934.

       Folejewski, Z. "Maria Dabrowska's Place in European Lit-
       erature." BA 38:12-13. Winter 1964.

Daryan, Zarzant
  MAY
       Alexander, Edward. "The Ferment in Soviet Armenian Lit-
       erature." ASEER 17:499-503. December 1958.

Dery, Tibor
  MR. G. A. IN X
       Foldes, Anna. "Tibor Dery's MR. G. A. IN X." NHQ 6:164-
       168. Spring 1965.

Desnica, Vladan
  SUMMER HOLIDAYS IN WINTER
       Goy, E. D. "The Serbian and Croatian Novel Since 1948."
       SEER 40:68. December 1961.

Dostoevsky, Feodor
  THE BROTHERS KARAMAZOV
       Amend, Victor E. "Theme and Form in THE BROTHERS
       KARAMAZOV." MFS 4:240-252. Autumn 1958.

       Baring, Maurice. Landmarks in Russian Literature. London:
       Methuen and Company, 1910. pp. 240-250.

Baring, Maurice. An Outline of Russian Literature. New York: Holt and Company, 1915. pp. 220-221.

Carr, Edward Hallett. Dostoevsky: A New Biography. New York: Houghton Mifflin Company, 1931. pp. 281-301.

Cook, Albert. The Meaning of Fiction. Detroit: Wayne State University Press, 1960. pp. 168-171; 223-228.

Fayer, Mischa Harry. Gide, Freedom and Dostoevsky. Burlington, Vt.: The Lane Press, 1946. pp. 104-105.

Freud, Sigmund. "Modern Evidence: Dostoevski and Parricide." PR 12:539-541. Fall 1945.

Friedman, Maurice. "Martin Buber's FOR THE SAKE OF HEAVEN and F. M. Dostoevsky's THE BROTHERS KARAMAZOV." CLS 3:161-165. No. 2, 1966.

Gifford, Henry. The Novel in Russia: From Pushkin to Pasternak. New York: Harper and Row, 1964. pp. 106-117.

Glicksberg, Charles I. "Dostoevski and the Problem of Religion." BuR 8:212-215. May 1959.

Guardini, Romano. "The Legend of the Grand Inquisitor." CC 3:58-85. Fall 1952.

Hacker, Andrew. "Dostoevsky's Disciples: Man and Sheep in Political Theory." Journal of Politics 17:597-599. November 1955.

Hall, Vernon. "Dostoevsky's Use of French as a Symbolic Device in THE BROTHERS KARAMAZOV." CLS 2:171-174. No. 2, 1965.

Hamilton, William. " 'Banished from the Land of Unity': A Study of Dostoevski's Religious Vision Through the Eyes of Ivan and Alyosha Karamazov." JR 39:245-261. October 1959.

Hare, Richard. Portraits of Russian Personalities Between Reform and Revolution. London: Oxford University Press, 1959. pp. 142-145.

Harper, Ralph. The Seventh Solitude: Man's Isolation in Kierkegaard, Dostoevsky, and Nietzsche. Baltimore: Johns Hopkins Press, 1965. pp. 70-75.

Hesse, Hermann. "The Downfall of Europe: THE BROTHERS KARAMAZOFF." ER 35:108-120. August 1922.

Hingley, Ronald. The Undiscovered Dostoyevsky. London:

Hamish Hamilton, 1962. pp. 195-228.

Iswolsky, Helene. "Dostoyevsky: THE BROTHERS KARA-MAZOV. " The Great Books: A Christian Appraisal. Vol. 4. (ed.) Harold C. Gardiner. New York: The Devin-Adair Company, 1953. pp. 170-177.

Jackson, Robert L. "Dmitrij Karamazov and the 'Legend.' " SEEJ n. s. 9:257-266. Fall 1965.

Kunkel, Francis L. "Dostoevsky's 'Inquisitor': An Emblem of Paradox. " Renascence 16:208-213. Summer 1964.

Lavrin, Janko. Dostoevsky: A Study. New York: Macmillan Company, 1947. pp. 119-146.

Lavrin, Janko. An Introduction to the Russian Novel. New York: McGraw-Hill Book Company, Inc. , 1947. pp. 114-118.

Lavrin, Janko. Russian Writers: Their Lives and Literature. New York: D. Van Nostrand Company, Inc. , 1954. pp. 189-195.

Lednicki, Waclaw. "Mickiewicz, Dostoevsky and Blok. " Slavic Studies. (ed.) Alexander Kaun and Ernest J. Simmons. Ithaca: Cornell University Press, 1943. pp. 75-81.

Lord, R. "Dostoevsky and Vladimir Solovyov. " SEER 42: 415-426. June 1964.

Magarshack, David. Dostoevsky. New York: Harcourt, Brace and World, Inc. , 1961. pp. 363-366; 379-387.

Mathewson, Rufus W. , Jr. The Positive Hero in Russian Literature. New York: Columbia University Press, 1958. pp. 21-22.

Mathewson, Rufus W. , Jr. "The Soviet Hero and the Literary Heritage. " ASEER 12:513. December 1953.

Matlaw, Ralph E. "Recurrent Imagery in Dostoevskij. " HSS 3:221-225. 1957.

Maugham, W. Somerset. Great Novelists and Their Novels. Philadelphia: Winston Company, 1948. pp. 185-208.

Maurina, Zenta. A Prophet of the Soul: Fyodor Dostoievsky. James Clarke and Company. pp. 147-153.

Maximoff, Nicholas. "The Future of Russia: Marx, Tolstoi, or Dostoievsky?" Religion in Life 24:51-52. Winter 1954-1955.

Muchnic, Helen. An Introduction to Russian Literature. New York: Doubleday, 1947. pp. 165-172.

Muchnic, Helen. "The Leap and the Vision: A Note on the Pattern of Dostoevskij's Novels. " SEEJ n. s. 8:386-388. Winter 1964.

Murry, J. Middleton. Fyodor Dostoevsky: A Critical Study. New York: Dodd, Mead and Company, 1916. pp. 203-259.

Olgin, Moissaye J. A Guide to Russian Literature (1820- 1917). New York: Harcourt, Brace and Howe, 1920. pp. 108-109.

Pachmuss, Temira. F. M. Dostoevsky: Dualism and Synthesis of the Human Soul. Carbondale: Southern Illinois University Press, 1963. pp. 9-16; 47-58; 93-111; 121-124; 128- 132; 134-147; 151-154; 161-182.

Pachmuss, Temira. "The Theme of Vanity in Dostoevskij's Works. " SEEJ n. s. 7:158-159. Summer 1963.

Passage, Charles E. Dostoevski the Adapter: A Study in Dostoevski's Use of the Tales of Hoffmann. Chapel Hill: University of North Carolina Press, 1954. pp. 162-174.

Payne, Robert. Dostoyevsky: A Human Portrait. New York: Alfred Knopf, 1961. pp. 334-363.

Phelps, William L. Essays on Russian Novelists. New York: Macmillan Company, 1917. pp. 163-166.

Rader, Melvin M. "Dostoevsky and the Demiurge. " SR 39: 289-291. 1931.

Rahv, Philip. "The Legend of the Grand Inquisitor. " PR 21: 249-271. May - June 1954.

Ramsey, Paul. "God's Grace and Man's Guilt. " JR 31:25- 28. January 1951.

Ramsey, Paul. "No Morality Without Immortality: Dostoevski and the Meaning of Atheism. " JR 36:106-108. April 1956.

Riemer, Neal. "Some Reflections on the Grand Inquisitor and Modern Democratic Theory. " Ethics 67:249-256. July 1957.

Sajkovic, Miriam Taylor. "Dostoevskij's Redeeming Image of Man. " SEEJ n. s. 6:214-226. Fall 1962.

Sandoz, Ellis. "Philosophical Anthropology and Dostoevsky's

'Legend of the Grand Inquisitor. ' " RPol 26:353-377. July
1964.

Scott, Nathan A., Jr. "Dostoevski--Tragedian of the Modern Excursion into Unbelief. " The Tragic Vision and the
Christian Faith. (ed.) Nathan A. Scott, Jr. New York: Association Press, 1957. pp. 204-209.

Sewall, Richard B. "The Tragic World of the Karamazovs. "
Tragic Themes in Western Literature. (ed.) Cleanth Brooks.
New Haven: Yale University Press, 1955. pp. 107-127.

Silbajoris, Rimvydas. "The Children in THE BROTHERS
KARAMAZOV. " SEEJ n. s. 7:26-37. Spring 1963.

Simmons, Ernest J. Dostoevsky: The Making of a Novelist.
New York: Vintage Books, 1940. pp. 324-370.

Slochower, Harry. "Incest in THE BROTHERS KARA-
MAZOV. " AI 16:127-145. Summer 1959.

Spector, Ivar. The Golden Age of Russian Literature. Caldwell: The Caxton Printers, Ltd. , 1945. pp. 116-118; 134-
136.

Spilka, Mark. "Human Worth in THE BROTHERS KARA-
MAZOV. " MinnR 5:38-49. January - April 1965.

Squires, Paul C. "Dostoevsky's Doctrine of Criminal Re
sponsibility. " Journal of Criminal Law 27:823-824. March -
April 1937.

Steiner, George. Tolstoy or Dostoevsky. New York: Alfred
Knopf, 1959. pp. 327-343.

Strakosch, H. E. "Dostoevsky and the Man-God. " DubR
229:152-153. Second Quarter 1955.

Strem, George G. "The Moral World of Dostoevsky. " RusR
16:24-25. July 1957.

Thurneysen, Eduard. Dostoevsky. Richmond: John Knox
Press, 1963. pp. 51-67.

Troyat, Henry. Firebrand: The Life of Dostoevsky. New
York: Roy Publisher, 1946. pp. 395-416.

Vivas, Eliseo. Creation and Discovery. New York: The
Noonday Press, 1955. pp. 47-70.

Vivas, Eliseo. "The Two Dimensions of Reality in THE
BROTHERS KARAMAZOV. " Dostoevsky: A Collection of
Critical Essays. (ed.) Rene Wellek. Englewood Cliffs:

Prentice-Hall, 1962. pp. 71-89.

Vivas, Eliseo. "The Two Dimensions of Reality in THE
BROTHERS KARAMAZOV. " SR 59:28-49. Winter 1951.

Wasiolek, Edward. " 'Aut Caesar, Aut Nihil': A Study of
Dostoevsky's Moral Dialectic. " PMLA 78:89-94. March
1963.

Wasiolek, Edward. Dostoevsky: The Major Fiction. Cambridge: MIT Press, 1964. pp. 149-187.

Wasiolek, Edward. "Dostoevsky: A Revolutionary Conservative. " ModA 9:66-67. Winter 1964-1965.

Wasiolek, Edward. "Dostoevsky and SANCTUARY. " MLN
74:115-116. February 1959.

Wasiolek, Edward. "Dostoevsky's THE BROTHERS KARA-
MAZOV. " Expl 16: Item 7, October 1957.

Weinreich, Marcel I. "Ideological Antecedents of THE
BROTHERS KARAMAZOV. " MLN 64:400-406. June 1949.

Wernham, James C. S. "Guardini, Berdyaev and the Legend
of the Grand Inquisitor. " HJ 53:157-164. 1954-1955.

Yarmolinsky, Avrahm. Dostoevsky: His Life and Art. New
York: Criterion Books, 1957. pp. 355-361; 372-390; 405-
406.

Yarmolinsky, Avrahm. Dostoevsky: A Life. New York: Harcourt, Brace and Company, 1934. pp. 358-362; 366-368;
371-392.

Yarmolinsky, Avrahm. Russian Literature. Chicago: American Library Association, 1931. pp. 38-42.

Yermilov, V. Fyodor Dostoyevsky. Moscow: Foreign Languages Publishing House. pp. 250-294.
CRIME AND PUNISHMENT
Astrov, Vladimir. "Hawthorne and Dostoevski as Explorers
of the Human Conscience. " NEQ 15:310-313. June 1942.

Baring, Maurice. Landmarks in Russian Literature. London:
Methuen and Company, 1910. pp. 191-201.

Baring, Maurice. An Outline of Russian Literature. New
York: Holt and Company, 1915. pp. 214-216.

Beardsley, Monroe C. "Dostoyevsky's Metaphor of the
'Underground. ' " JHI 3:271-272. June 1942.

Beebe, Maurice. "The Three Motives of Raskolnikov: A Re-interpretation of CRIME AND PUNISHMENT. " CE 17:151-158. December 1955.

Blackmur, R. P. "CRIME AND PUNISHMENT: A Study of Dostoevsky's Novel. " Chimera 1:7-29. Winter 1943.

Brasol, Boris. The Mighty Three. New York: William Farquhar Payson, 1934. pp. 235-259.

Carr, Edward Hallett. Dostoevsky: A New Biography. New York: Houghton Mifflin Company, 1931. pp. 188-202.

Clive, Geoffrey. " 'The Teleological Suspension of the Ethical' in Nineteenth-Century Literature. " JR 34:84-87. April 1954.

Cook, Albert. The Meaning of Fiction. Detroit: Wayne State University Press, 1960. pp. 210-213.

Dauner, Louise. "Raskolnikov in Search of a Soul. " MFS 4: 199-210. Autumn 1958.

Eastman, Richard M. "Idea and Method in a Scene by Dostoevsky. " CE 17:143-150. December 1955.

Fagin, N. Bryllion. "CRIME AND PUNISHMENT. " Literary Masterpieces of the Western World. (ed.) Frances H. Horn. Baltimore: Johns Hopkins Press, 1953. pp. 208-222.

Fanger, Donald. Dostoevsky and Romantic Realism. Cambridge: Harvard University Press, 1965. pp. 184-213.

Fuelop-Miller, Rene. Fyodor Dostoevsky. New York: Scribner's Sons, 1950. Chapter 6.

Futrell, Michael H. "Dostoyevsky and Dickens. " EM 7:61-67. 1956.

Gibian, George. "Dostoevskij's Use of Russian Folklore. " JAF 69:242. July - September 1956.

Gibian, George. "The Grotesque in Dostoevsky. " MFS 4: 266-267. Autumn 1958.

Gibian, George. "Traditional Symbolism in CRIME AND PUNISHMENT. " PMLA 70:979-996. December 1955.

Glicksberg, Charles I. "Dostoevski and the Problem of Religion. " BuR 8:207-209. May 1959.

Haig, Stirling. "The Epilogue of CRIME AND PUNISHMENT and Camus' La 'Femme Adultere. ' " CLS 3:445-448. No. 4,

1966.

Harper, Ralph. The Seventh Solitude: Man's Isolation in Kierkegaard, Dostoevsky, and Nietzsche. Baltimore: Johns Hopkins Press, 1965. pp. 47-48.

Hemmings. F. W. J. The Russian Novel in France 1884-1914. London: Oxford University Press, 1950. pp. 25-26; 36-37; 127-128; 228-230.

Hingley, Ronald. The Undiscovered Dostoyevsky. London: Hamish Hamilton, 1962. pp. 86-104.

Hoffman, Frederick J. "The Scene of Violence: Dostoevsky and Dreiser. " MFS 6:96-100. Summer 1960.

Hooker, Kenneth Ward. "Dostoyevsky and Gide. " BUS 3:172-175. 1952.

Hunt, Joel. "Balzac and Dostoevskij: Ethics and Eschatology. " SEEJ 16:307-323. Winter 1958.

Kehler, Harold. "Dostoevsky's CRIME AND PUNISHMENT." Expl 24: Item 22, November 1965.

Lavrin, Janko. Dostoevsky: A Study. New York: Macmillan Company, 1947. pp. 75-86.

Lavrin, Janko. An Introduction to the Russian Novel. New York: McGraw-Hill, 1947. pp. 109-111.

Lavrin, Janko. Russian Writers: Their Lives and Literature. New York: D. Van Nostrand Company, Inc. , 1954. pp. 184-186.

Madeleine, Sister M. "Mauriac and Dostoevsky: Psychollogists of the Unconscious. " Renascence 5:10-11. Autumn 1952.

Magarshack, David. Dostoevsky. New York: Harcourt, Brace and World, Inc. , 1961. pp. 248-257.

Marx, Paul. "A Defense of the Epilogue to CRIME AND PUNISHMENT. " BuR 10:57-74. May 1961.

Mathewson, Rufus W. , Jr. The Positive Hero in Russian Literature. New York: Columbia University Press, 1958. pp. 20-21.

Matlaw, Ralph E. "Recurrent Imagery in Dostoevskij. " HSS 3:209-212. 1957.

Maurina, Zenta. A Prophet of the Soul: Fyodor Dostoievsky.

James Clarke and Company. pp. 124-132.

Meijer, J. M. "Situation Rhyme in a Novel of Dostoevskij. "
Dutch Contributions to the Fourth International Congress of
Slavicists. The Hague: Mouton and Company, 1958. pp. 115-
128.

Mirsky, D. S. A History of Russian Literature. New York:
Knopf, 1949. Chapter 8.

Moravia, Alberto. "The Marx-Dostoevsky Duel. " Encounter
7: 4-6. November 1956.

Mortimer, Ruth. "Dostoevski and the Dream. " MP 54:108-
114. November 1956.

Moseley, Edwin M. Pseudonyms of Christ in the Modern
Novel. Pittsburgh: University of Pittsburgh Press, 1962.
pp. 37-47.

Muchnic, Helen. An Introduction to Russian Literature. New
York: Doubleday, 1947. pp. 160-161.

Muchnic, Helen. "The Leap and the Vision: A Note on the
Pattern of Dostoevskij's Novels. " SEEJ n. s. 8:385-387.
Winter 1964.

Murry, J. Middleton. Fyodor Dostoevsky: A Critical Study.
New York: Dodd, Mead and Company, 1916. pp. 102-128.

Murry, J. Middleton. Selected Criticism 1916-1957. London:
Oxford University Press, 1960. pp. 31-40.

Niemeyer, Carl. "Raskolnikov and Lafcadio. " MFS 4:253-
261. Autumn 1958.

Niemi, Pearl C. "The Art of CRIME AND PUNISHMENT. "
MFS 9:291-313. Winter 1963-1964.

O'Connor, Frank. The Mirror in the Roadway: A Study of
the Modern Novel. New York: Alfred A. Knopf, 1956. pp.
210-217.

Olgin, Moissaye J. A Guide to Russian Literature (1820-
1917). New York: Harcourt, Brace and Howe, 1920. pp. 105-
106.

Pachmuss, Temira. F. M. Dostoevsky: Dualism and Synthesis of the Human Soul. Carbondale: Southern Illinois University Press, 1963. pp. 32-41; 72-76; 100-103; 115-116;
140-144; 150-154.

Pachmuss, Temira. "The Technique of Dream-Logic in the

Works of Dostoevskij. " SEEJ n. s. 4:231-233. Fall 1960.

Pachmuss, Temira. "The Theme of Vanity in Dostoevskij's Works. " SEEJ n. s. 7:146-148. Summer 1963.

Param, Charles. "Machado de Assis and Dostoyevsky. " Hispania 49:81-86. March 1966.

Passage, Charles E. Dostoevski the Adapter: A Study in Dostoevski's Use of the Tales of Hoffmann. Chapel Hill: University of North Carolina Press, 1954. pp. 142-145.

Payne, Robert. Dostoyevsky: A Human Portrait. New York: Alfred Knopf, 1961. pp. 195-216.

Phelps, William L. Essays on Russian Novelists. New York: Macmillan Company, 1917. pp. 151-156.

Powys, John Cowper. Dostoievsky. London: John Lane the Bodley Head, 1946. pp. 88-94.

Rader, Melvin M. "Dostoevsky and the Demiurge. " SR 39: 285-287. 1931.

Rahv, Philip. "Dostoevsky in CRIME AND PUNISHMENT. " Dostoevsky: Collected Essays. (ed.) Rene Wellek. Englewood Cliffs: Prentice-Hall, 1962. pp. 16-38.

Rahv, Philip. "Dostoevsky in CRIME AND PUNISHMENT. " PR 27:393-425. Summer 1960.

Rahv, Philip. "Dostoevsky in CRIME AND PUNISHMENT. " Varieties in Literary Experience: Eighteen Essays in World Literature. (ed.) Stanley Burnshaw. New York: New York University Press, 1962. pp. 353-385.

Ramsey, Paul. "God's Grace and Man's Guilt. " JR 31:30. January 1951.

Ramsey, Paul. "No Morality Without Immortality: Dostoevski and the Meaning of Atheism. " JR 36:91-92. April 1956.

Reck, Rima Drell. "A Crime: Dostoyevsky and Bernanos. " ForumH 4:10-13. Spring - Summer 1964.

Reeve, F. D. "In the Stinking City: Dostoevskij's CRIME AND PUNISHMENT. " SEEJ n. s. 4:127-135. Summer 1960.

Reeve, F. D. The Russian Novel. New York: McGraw-Hill Book Company, 1966. pp. 159-204.

Seduro, Vladimir. Dostoyevski in Russian Literary Criticism 1846-1956. New York: Columbia University Press,

1957. pp. 21-28.

Seeley, Frank Friedeberg. "Dostoyevsky's Women. " SEER
39:308-312. June 1961.

Simmons, Ernest J. Dostoevsky: The Making of a Novelist.
New York: Vintage Books, 1940. pp. 141-171.

Slonim, Marc. The Epic of Russian Literature. Oxford: University Press, 1950. Chapter 14.

Smith, Raymond. "A Note on Dostoyevsky's Dr. Zossimov."
CLAJ 10:162-164. December 1966.

Snodgrass, W. D. "Crime for Punishment: The Tenor of
Part One. " HudR 13:202-253. Summer 1960.

Spector, Ivar. The Golden Age of Russian Literature. Caldwell: The Caxton Printers, Ltd. , 1945. pp. 112-113; 125-129.

Squires, Paul C. "Dostoevsky's Doctrine of Criminal Responsibility. " Journal of Criminal Law 27:820-822. March -
April 1937.

Squires, Paul Chatham. "Dostoevsky's 'Raskolnikov': The
Criminalistic Protest. " Journal of Criminal Law 28:478-
494. November - December 1937.

Steiner, George. Tolstoy or Dostoevsky. New York: Alfred
Knopf, 1959. pp. 56-57; 201-202; 208-210.

Strakosch, H. E. "Dostoevsky and the Man-God. " DubR 229:
147-149. Second Quarter 1955.

Strem, George G. "The Moral World of Dostoevsky. " RusR
16:20-22. July 1957.

Wasiolek, Edward. Dostoevsky: The Major Fiction. Cambridge: MIT Press, 1964. pp. 60-84.

Wasiolek, Edward. "Dostoevsky and SANCTUARY. " MLN
74:114-115. February 1959.

Wasiolek, Edward. "On the Structure of CRIME AND PUN-
ISHMENT. " PMLA 74:131-136. March 1959.

Yarmolinsky, Avrahm. Dostoevsky: His Life and Art. New
York: Criterion Books, 1957. pp. 205-217.

Yarmolinsky, Avrahm. Dostoevsky: A Life. New York:
Harcourt, Brace and Company, 1934. pp. 210-222.

Yermilov, V. Fyodor Dostoyevsky. Moscow: Foreign Lan-

guages Publishing House. pp. 161-191.
THE DOUBLE
Chizhevsky, Dmitri. "The Theme of the Double in Dostoev-
sky. " Dostoevsky: A Collection of Critical Essays. (ed.)
Rene Wellek. Englewood Cliffs: Prentice Hall, 1962. pp.
112-116.

Fanger, Donald. Dostoevsky and Romantic Realism. Cambridge: Harvard University Press, 1965. pp. 159-162.

Harper, Ralph. The Seventh Solitude: Man's Isolation in
Kierkegaard, Dostoevsky, and Nietzsche. Baltimore: Johns
Hopkins Press, 1965. pp. 40-41.

Hingley, Ronald. The Undiscovered Dostoyevsky. London:
Hamish Hamilton, 1962. pp. 8-17.

Krag, Erik. "The Riddle of the Other Goljadkin: Some Observations on Dostoevskij's DOUBLE. " For Roman Jakobson. The Hague: Mouton and Company, 1956. pp. 265-272.

Louria, Yvette. " 'Dedoublement' in Dostoevsky and Camus."
MLR 56:82-83. January 1961.

Magarshack, David. Dostoevsky. New York: Harcourt,
Brace and World, Inc. , 1961. pp. 177-178.

Manning, Clarence A. "The Double of Dostoyevsky. " MLN
59:317-321. May 1944.

Mossman, Elliott D. "Dostoevskij's Early Works: The More
than Rational Distortion. " SEEJ 10:270-272. Fall 1966.

Muchnic, Helen. An Introduction to Russian Literature. New
York: Doubleday, 1947. pp. 152-155.

Pachmuss, Temira. F. M. Dostoevsky: Dualism and Synthesis of the Human Soul. Carbondale: Southern Illinois University Press, 1963. pp. 21-32; 63-76.

Pachmuss, Temira. "The Technique of Dream-Logic in the
Works of Dostoevskij. " SEEJ n. s. 4:221-230. Fall 1960.

Pachmuss, Temira. "The Theme of Vanity in Dostoevskij's
Works. " SEEJ n. s. 7:143-144. Summer 1963.

Passage, Charles E. Dostoevski the Adapter: A Study of
Dostoevski's Use of the Tales of Hoffmann. Chapel Hill: University of North Carolina Press, 1954. pp. 14-37.

Trubeckoj, Nikolaj S. "The Style of POOR FOLK and THE
DOUBLE. " ASEER 7:150-170. April 1948.

Yarmolinsky, Avrahm. Dostoevsky: His Life and Art. New

York: Criterion Books, 1957. pp. 92-93.

Yarmolinsky, Avrahm. Dostoevsky: A Life. New York: Har-
court, Brace and Company, 1934. pp. 93-94.
THE ETERNAL HUSBAND
Hingley, Ronald. The Undiscovered Dostoyevsky. London:
Hamish Hamilton, 1962. pp. 129-132.

Muchnic, Helen. An Introduction to Russian Literature. New
York: Doubleday, 1947. pp. 172-175.

Pachmuss, Temira. F. M. Dostoevsky: Dualism and Synthesis of the Human Soul. Carbondale: Southern Illinois University Press, 1963. pp. 37-38; 82-84.

Pachmuss, Temira. "The Technique of Dream-Logic in the
Works of Dostoevskij. " SEEJ n. s. 4:235-236. Fall 1960.

Passage, Charles E. Dostoevski the Adapter: A Study in
Dostoevski's Use of the Tales of Hoffmann. Chapel Hill:
University of North Carolina Press, 1954. pp. 145-149.

Pritchett, V. S. The Living Novel and Later Appreciations.
New York: Random House, 1964. pp. 410-412.

Yarmolinsky, Avrahm. Dostoevsky: A Life. New York: Har-
court, Brace and Company, 1934. pp. 271-273.
THE FRIEND OF THE FAMILY (See THE VILLAGE OF STEPAN-
CHIKOVO)
THE GAMBLER
Hingley, Ronald. The Undiscovered Dostoyevsky. London:
Hamish Hamilton, 1962. pp. 79-85.

Magarshack, David. Dostoevsky. New York: Harcourt,
Brace and World, Inc. , 1961. pp. 202-203; 220-222.

Payne, Robert. Dostoyevsky: A Human Portrait. New York:
Alfred Knopf, 1961. pp. 217-235.

Savage, D. S. "Dostoevski: The Idea of THE GAMBLER. "
SR 58:281-298. Spring 1950.

Simmons, Ernest J. Dostoevsky: The Making of a Novelist.
New York: Vintage Books, 1940. pp. 172-184.

Troyat, Henry. Firebrand: A Life of Dostoevsky. New York:
Roy Publisher, 1946. pp. 291-331.

Yarmolinsky, Avrahm. Dostoevsky: His Life and Art. New
York: Criterion Books, 1957. pp. 217-220.

Yarmolinsky, Avrahm. Dostoevsky: A Life. New York: Harcourt, Brace and Company, 1934. pp. 222-224.

THE IDIOT

Baring, Maurice. Landmarks in Russian Literature. London: Methuen and Company, 1910. pp. 201-215.

Baring, Maurice. An Outline of Russian Literature. New York: Holt and Company, 1915. pp. 216-217.

Beardsley, Monroe C. "Dostoyevsky's Metaphor of the 'Underground.' " JHI 3:274-275. June 1942.

Blanchard, Margaret. "Dostoyevsky's THE IDIOT." Expl 21: Item 41, January 1963.

Carr, Edward Hallett. Dostoevsky: A New Biography. New York: Houghton Mifflin Company, 1931. pp. 203-217.

Cook, Albert. The Meaning of Fiction. Detroit: Wayne State University Press, 1960. pp. 213-218.

Futrell, Michael H. "Dostoyevsky and Dickens." EM 7:67-70. 1956.

Gibian, George. "Dostoevskij's Use of Russian Folklore." JAF 69:241-242. July - September 1956.

Glicksberg, Charles I. "Dostoevski and the Problem of Religion." BuR 8:204-207. May 1959.

Hare, Richard. Portraits of Russian Personalities Between Reform and Revolution. London: Oxford University Press, 1959. pp. 126-129.

Hemmings, F. W. J. The Russian Novel in France 1884-1914. London: Oxford University Press, 1950. pp. 37-40; 105-107; 152-153.

Hesse, Hermann. "Thoughts on Dostoevsky's IDIOT." ER 35:190-196. September 1922.

Hingley, Ronald. The Undiscovered Dostoyevsky. London: Hamish Hamilton, 1962. pp. 110-129.

Krieger, Murray. "Dostoevsky's IDIOT: The Curse of Saintliness." Dostoevsky: A Collection of Critical Essays. (ed.) Rene Wellek. Englewood Cliffs: Prentice Hall, 1962. pp. 39-52.

Krieger, Murray. The Tragic Vision. New York: Holt, Rinehart, and Winston, 1960. pp. 209-227.

Lavrin, Janko. Dostoevsky: A Study. New York: Macmillan Company, 1947. pp. 87-94.

Lavrin, Janko. An Introduction to the Russian Novel. New

York: McGraw-Hill, 1947. pp. 111-112.

Lavrin, Janko. Russian Writers: Their Lives and Literature. New York: D. Van Nostrand Company, Inc., 1954. pp. 186-187.

Lesser, Simon O. "Saint and Sinner--Dostoevsky's IDIOT." MFS 4:211-224. Autumn 1958.

Magarshack, David. Dostoevsky. New York: Harcourt, Brace and World, Inc., 1961. pp. 296-302; 307-309; 327-328.

Malenko, Zinaida and James J. Gebhard. "The Artistic Use of Portraits in Dostoevskij's IDIOT." SEEJ n. s. 5:243-254. Fall 1961.

Manning, Clarence A. "Alyosha Valkovsky and Prince Myshkin." MLN 57:182-185. March 1942.

Matlaw, Ralph E. "Recurrent Imagery in Dostoevskij." HSS 3:212-216. 1957.

Maurina, Zenta. A Prophet of the Soul: Fyodor Dostoievsky. James Clarke and Company. pp. 132-135; 142-147.

Muchnic, Helen. An Introduction to Russian Literature. New York: Doubleday,1947. pp. 161-163.

Muchnic, Helen. "The Leap and the Vision: A Note on the Pattern of Dostoevskij's Novels." SEEJ n. s. 8:379-384. Winter 1964.

Murry, J. Middleton. Fyodor Dostoevsky: A Critical Study. New York: Dodd, Mead and Company, 1916. pp. 129-156.

Olgin, Moissaye J. A Guide to Russian Literature (1820-1917). New York: Harcourt, Brace and Howe, 1920. pp. 106-108.

Pachmuss, Temira. F. M. Dostoevsky: Dualism and Synthesis of the Human Soul. Carbondale: Southern Illinois University Press, 1963. pp. 13-15; 34-37; 75-84; 142-150.

Pachmuss, Temira. "The Technique of Dream-Logic in the Works of Dostoevskij." SEEJ n. s. 4:233-235. Fall 1960.

Pachmuss, Temira. "The Theme of Vanity in Dostoevskij's Works." SEEJ n. s. 7:148-151. Summer 1963.

Phelps, William L. Essays on Russian Novelists. New York: Macmillan Company, 1917. pp. 157-162.

Portnoff, George. "Cervantes and Dostoyevsky." MLF 19:

81-86. May 1934.

Seeley, Frank Friedeberg. "Dostoyevsky's Women. " SEER
39:305-308. June 1961.

Simmons, Ernest J. Dostoevsky: The Making of a Novelist.
New York: Vintage Books, 1940. pp. 183-218.

Spector, Ivar. The Golden Age of Russian Literature. Caldwell: The Caxton Printers, Ltd., 1945. pp. 113-114; 129-
130.

Steiner, George. Tolstoy or Dostoevsky. New York: Alfred
Knopf, 1959. pp. 151-169; 171-182.

Tate, Allen. "Dostoevsky's Hovering Fly: A Causerie on the
Imagination and the Actual World. " SR 51:353-369. 1943.

Wasiolek, Edward. Dostoevsky: The Major Fiction. Cambridge: MIT Press, 1964. pp. 85-109.

Yarmolinsky, Avrahm. Dostoevsky: His Life and Art. New
York: Criterion, 1957. pp. 85-87; 242-243; 246-261.

Yarmolinsky, Avrahm. Dostoevsky: A Life. New York: Harcourt, Brace and Company, 1934. pp. 259-267.

Yermilov, V. Fyodor Dostoyevsky. Moscow: Foreign Languages Publishing House. pp. 192-222.

THE INSULTED AND INJURED

Fanger, Donald. Dostoevsky and Romantic Realism. Cambridge: Harvard University Press, 1965. pp. 171-177.

Gibian, George. "C. G. Carus' PSYCHE and Dostoevsky. "
ASEER 14:379-382. October 1955.

Hingley, Ronald. The Undiscovered Dostoyevsky. London:
Hamish Hamilton, 1962. pp. 41-50.

Magarshack, David. Dostoevsky. New York: Harcourt,
Brace and World, Inc., 1961. pp. 196-197.

Manning, Clarence A. "Alyosha Valkovsky and Prince Myshkin. " MLN 57:182-185. March 1942.

Simmons, Ernest J. Dostoevsky: The Making of a Novelist.
New York: Vintage Books, 1940. pp. 94-108.

Wasiolek, Edward. Dostoevsky: The Major Fiction. Cambridge: MIT Press, 1964. pp. 27-38.

Yarmolinsky, Avrahm. Dostoevsky: His Life and Art. New
York: Criterion Books, 1957. pp. 160-161.

Yarmolinsky, Avrahm. Dostoevsky: A Life. New York: Harcourt, Brace and Company, 1934. pp. 162-163.

Yermilov, V. Fyodor Dostoyevsky. Moscow: Foreign Languages Publishing House. pp. 103-114.

THE LANDLADY

Gibian, George. "Dostoevskij's Use of Russian Folklore. " JAF 69:245-248. July-September 1956.

LETTERS FROM THE HOUSE OF THE DEAD

Baring, Maurice. Landmarks in Russian Literature. London: Methuen and Company, 1910. pp. 165-191.

Carr, Edward Hallett. Dostoevsky: A New Biography. New York: Houghton Mifflin Company, 1931. pp. 59-71.

Frank, Joseph. "Dostoevsky: THE HOUSE OF THE DEAD." SR 74:779-803. Autumn 1966.

Hingley, Ronald. The Undiscovered Dostoyevsky. London: Hamish Hamilton, 1962. pp. 50-59.

Jackson, Robert L. "The Narrator in Dostoevsky's NOTES FROM THE HOUSE OF THE DEAD. " Studies in Russian and Polish Literature. (ed.) Zbigniew Folejewski. 'S Gravenhage: Mouton and Company, 1962. pp. 192-216.

Magarshack, David. Dostoevsky. New York: Harcourt, Brace and World, Inc., 1961. pp. 22-23; 138-142; 196-198.

Muchnic, Helen. An Introduction to Russian Literature. New York: Doubleday, 1947. pp. 155-158.

Pachmuss, Temira. F. M. Dostoevsky: Dualism and Synthesis of the Human Soul. Carbondale: Southern Illinois University Press, 1963. pp. 49-51.

Payne, Robert. Dostoyevsky: A Human Portrait. New York: Alfred Knopf, 1961. pp. 101-120.

Phelps, William L. Essays on Russian Novelists. New York: Macmillan Company, 1917. pp. 147-150.

Simmons, Ernest J. Dostoevsky: The Making of a Novelist. New York: Vintage Books, 1940. pp. 89-93.

Squires, Paul C. "Dostoevsky's Doctrine of Criminal Responsibility. " Journal of Criminal Law 27:818-820. March - April 1937.

Troyat, Henry. Firebrand: A Life of Dostoevsky. New York: Roy Publishers, 1946. pp. 217-247.

Wasiolek, Edward. Dostoevsky: The Major Fiction. Cambridge: MIT Press, 1964. pp. 17-26.

Yarmolinsky, Avrahm. Dostoevsky: His Life and Art. New
York: Criterion Books, 1957. pp. 162-164.

Yarmolinsky, Avrahm. Dostoevsky: A Life. New York: Harcourt, Brace and Company, 1934. pp. 163-165.

Yermilov, V. Fyodor Dostoyevsky. Moscow: Foreign Languages Publishing House. pp. 91-103.

MISTER PROXARCIN

Mossman, Elliott D. "Dostoevskij's Early Works: The More
than Rational Distortion. " SEEJ 10:273-274. Fall 1966.

NETOCHKA NEZVANOVA

Hingley, Ronald. The Undiscovered Dostoyevsky. London:
Hamish Hamilton, 1962. pp. 18-20.

Magarshack, David. Dostoevsky. New York: Harcourt,
Brace and World, Inc., 1961. pp. 167-168.

Passage, Charles E. Dostoevski the Adapter: A Study of
Dostoevski's Use of the Tales of Hoffmann. Chapel Hill:
University of North Carolina Press, 1954. pp. 82-105.

Yarmolinsky, Avrahm. Dostoevsky: A Life. New York:
Harcourt, Brace and Company, 1934. pp. 97-99.

NOTES FROM UNDERGROUND

Beardsley, Monroe C. "Dostoyevsky's Metaphor of the 'Underground.' " JHI 3:266-269. June 1942.

Bercovitch, Sacvan. "Dramatic Irony in NOTES FROM UN-
DERGROUND. " SEEJ n. s. 8:284-289. Fall 1964.

Carrier, Warren. "Artistic Form and Unity in NOTES
FROM UNDERGROUND. " Renascence 16:142-145. Spring
1964.

Clive, Geoffrey. "The Sickness Unto Death in the Under-
world: A Study of Nihilism. " HTR 51:135-167. July 1958.

Fagin, N. Bryllion. "Dostoevsky's Underground Man Takes
Over. " AR 13:25-32. March 1953.

Fanger, Donald. Dostoevsky and Romantic Realism. Cambridge: Harvard University Press, 1965. pp. 177-183.

Fayer, Mischa Harry. Gide, Freedom and Dostoevsky.
Burlington, Vt.: The Lane Press, 1946. pp. 60-61.

Frank, Joseph. "Nihilism and NOTES FROM UNDER-
GROUND. " SR 69:1-33. Winter 1961.

Harper, Ralph. The Seventh Solitude: Man's Isolation in

Kierkegaard, Dostoevsky, and Nietzsche. Baltimore: Johns Hopkins Press, 1965. pp. 41-46.

Hingley, Ronald. The Undiscovered Dostoyevsky. London: Hamish Hamilton, 1962. pp. 69-79.

Lethcoe, James. "Self-Deception in Dostoevskij's NOTES FROM THE UNDERGROUND. " SEEJ 10:9-21. Spring 1966.

Magarshack, David. Dostoevsky. New York: Harcourt, Brace and World, Inc., 1961. pp. 233-235.

Matlaw, Ralph E. "Structure and Integration in NOTES FROM THE UNDERGROUND. " PMLA 73:101-109. March 1958.

Muchnic, Helen. An Introduction to Russian Literature. New York: Doubleday, 1947. pp. 158-160.

Pachmuss, Temira. F. M. Dostoevsky: Dualism and Synthesis of the Human Soul. Carbondale: Southern Illinois University Press, 1963. pp. 5-7; 69-72; 99-102; 134-136.

Pachmuss, Temira. "The Theme of Vanity in Dostoevskij's Works. " SEEJ n. s. 7:145-146. Summer 1963.

Pfleger, Karl. Wrestlers with Christ. London: Sheed and Ward, 1936. pp. 191-202.

Powys, John Cowper. Dostoievsky. London: John Lane the Bodley Head, 1946. pp. 82-87.

Pritchett, V. S. Books in General. London: Chatto and Windus, 1953. pp. 142-145.

Scott, Nathan A. , Jr. "Dostoevski--Tragedian of the Modern Excursion into Unbelief. " The Tragic Vision and the Christian Faith. (ed.) Nathan A. Scott, Jr. New York: Association Press, 1957. pp. 194-197.

Simmons, Ernest J. Dostoevsky: The Making of a Novelist. New York: Vintage Books, 1940. pp. 109-126.

Spilka, Mark. "Playing Crazy in the Underground. " MinnR 6:233-243. No. 3, 1966.

Squires, Paul C. "Dostoevsky's Doctrine of Criminal Responsibility. " Journal of Criminal Law 27:817-818. March - April 1937.

Steiner, George. Tolstoy or Dostoevsky. New York: Alfred Knopf, 1959. pp. 220-230.

Traschen, I. "Dostoyevsky's NOTES FROM UNDERGROUND."
Accent 16:255-264. Autumn 1956.

Troyat, Henry. Firebrand: A Life of Dostoevsky. New York:
Roy Publishers, 1946. pp. 248-290.

Walker, Herbert. "Observations on Fyodor Dostoevsky's
NOTES FROM THE UNDERGROUND. " AI 19:195-210. Summer 1962.

Wasiolek, Edward. " 'Aut Caesar, Aut Nihil': A Study of
Dostoevsky's Moral Dialectic. " PMLA 78:94-97. March
1963.

Wasiolek, Edward. Dostoevsky: The Major Fiction. Cambridge: MIT Press, 1964. pp. 39-59.

Yarmolinsky, Avrahm. Dostoevsky: His Life and Art. New
York: Criterion Books, 1957. pp. 177-178; 187-192.

Yarmolinsky, Avrahm. Dostoevsky: A Life. New York: Harcourt, Brace and Company, 1934. pp. 187-193.

Yermilov, V. Fyodor Dostoyevsky. Moscow: Foreign Languages Publishing House. pp. 143-160.

Zerner, Marianne. "Thomas Mann's DER BAJAZZO, a
Parody of Dostoevski's NOTES FROM UNDERGROUND. "
Monatshefte 56:286-290. November 1964.
POLZUNKOV
Mossman, Elliott D. "Dostoevskij's Early Works: The More
than Rational Distortion. " SEEJ 10:274-275. Fall 1966.
POOR FOLK
Baring, Maurice. Landmarks in Russian Literature. London:
Methuen and Company, 1910. pp. 165-191.

Fanger, Donald. Dostoevsky and Romantic Realism. Cambridge: Harvard University Press, 1965. pp. 153-159.

Hingley, Ronald. The Undiscovered Dostoyevsky. London:
Hamish Hamilton, 1962. pp. 3-8.

Jackson, Robert Louis. Dostoevsky's Quest for Form: A
Study of His Philosophy of Art. New Haven: Yale University
Press, 1966. pp. 18-26.

Magarshack, David. Dostoevsky. New York: Harcourt,
Brace and World, Inc., 1961. pp. 24-25; 78-85; 94-98.

Mossman, Elliott D. "Dostoevskij's Early Works: The More
than Rational Distortion. " SEEJ 10:269-270. Fall 1966.

Muchnic, Helen. An Introduction to Russian Literature.

New York: Doubleday, 1947. pp. 150-152.

Payne, Robert. Dostoyevsky: A Human Portrait. New York: Alfred Knopf, 1961. pp. 38-55.

Phelps, William L. Essays on Russian Novelists. New York: Macmillan Company, 1917. pp. 139-142.

Simmons, Ernest J. Dostoevsky: The Making of a Novelist. New York: Vintage Books, 1940. pp. 12-24.

Spector, Ivar. The Golden Age of Russian Literature. Caldwell: The Caxton Printers, Ltd., 1945. pp. 124-125.

Trubeckoj, Nikolaj S. "The Style of POOR FOLK and THE DOUBLE." ASEER 7:150-170. April 1948.

Yarmolinsky, Avrahm. Dostoevsky: His Life and Art. New York: Criterion Books, 1957. pp. 39-41; 91-92.

Yarmolinsky, Avrahm. Dostoevsky: A Life. New York: Harcourt, Brace and Company, 1934. pp. 40-42.

Yermilov, V. Fyodor Dostoyevsky. Moscow: Foreign Languages Publishing House. pp. 114-118.

THE POSSESSED

Baring, Maurice. Landmarks in Russian Literature. London: Methuen and Company, 1910. pp. 215-240.

Baring, Maurice. An Outline of Russian Literature. New York: Holt and Company, 1915. pp. 217-220.

Beardsley, Monroe C. "Dostoyevsky's Metaphor of the 'Underground.' " JHI 3:272-273. June 1942.

Carr, Edward Hallett. Dostoevsky: A New Biography. New York: Houghton Mifflin Company, 1931. pp. 218-232.

Cook, Albert. The Meaning of Fiction. Detroit: Wayne State University Press, 1960. pp. 218-223.

Futrell, Michael H. "Dostoyevsky and Dickens." EM 7:71-78. 1956.

Gibian, George. "The Grotesque in Dostoevsky." MFS 4:263-264. Autumn 1958.

Glicksberg, Charles I. "Dostoevski and the Problem of Religion." BuR 8:209-211. May 1959.

Glicksberg, Charles I. "To be or not to be: The Literature of Suicide." QQ 67:386-390. Autumn 1960.

Gomperts, H. A. "Contemporary Significance of Dostoevsky's Novel THE POSSESSED. " LitR 5:173-180. Winter 1961-1962.

Hare, Richard. Portraits of Russian Personalities Between Reform and Revolution. London: Oxford University Press, 1959. pp. 130-134.

Harper, Ralph. The Seventh Solitude: Man's Isolation in Kierkegaard, Dostoevsky, and Nietzsche. Baltimore: Johns Hopkins Press, 1965. pp. 52-54; 65-70.

Hemmings, F. W. J. The Russian Novel in France 1884-1914. London: Oxford University Press, 1950. pp. 37-38; 164-165; 175-176; 233-234.

Hingley, Ronald. The Undiscovered Dostoyevsky. London: Hamish Hamilton, 1962. pp. 133-161.

Howe, Irving. "Dostoevsky: The Politics of Salvation. " Dostoevsky: A Collection of Critical Essays. (ed.) Rene Wellek. Englewood Cliffs: Prentice-Hall, 1962. pp. 58-70.

Howe, Irving. "Dostoevsky: The Politics of Salvation. " KR 17:46-68. Winter 1955.

Howe, Irving. Politics and the Novel. New York: Meridan Books, 1957. pp. 57-75.

Kohn, Hans. "Dostoevsky's Nationalism. " JHI 6:401-403. October 1945.

Lavrin, Janko. Dostoevsky: A Study. New York: Macmillan Company, 1947. pp. 94-109.

Lavrin, Janko. An Introduction to the Russian Novel. New York: McGraw Hill, 1947. pp. 112-114.

Lavrin, Janko. Russian Writers: Their Lives and Literature. New York: D. Van Nostrand Company, Inc. , 1954. pp. 187-189.

Leer, Norman. "Stavrogin and Prince Hal: The Hero in Two Worlds. " SEEJ n. s. 6:99-115. Summer 1962.

McDowall, Arthur. "THE POSSESSED and Bolshevism. " LMerc 17:52-61. November 1927.

Magarshack, David. Dostoevsky. New York: Harcourt, Brace and World, Inc. , 1961. pp. 314-315; 319-322; 338-343.

Manning, Clarence Augustus. "Dostoyevsky and Modern

Russian Literature. " SR 30:290-292. July 1922.

Mathewson, Rufus W. , Jr. The Positive Hero in Russian Literature. New York: Columbia University Press, 1958. pp. 15-16.

Matlaw, Ralph E. "Recurrent Imagery in Dostoevskij. " HSS 3:216-220. 1957.

Matlaw, Ralph E. "Thanatos and Eros: Approaches to Dostoevsky's Universe. " SEEJ n. s. 4:18-19. Spring 1960.

Maurina, Zenta. A Prophet of the Soul: Fyodor Dostoievsky. James Clarke and Company. pp. 135-141.

Maximoff, Nicholas. "The Future of Russia: Marx, Tolstoi, or Dostoievsky?" Religion in Life 24:50-51. Winter 1954-1955.

Moser, Charles A. Antinihilism in the Russian Novel of the 1860's. The Hague: Mouton and Company, 1964. pp. 77-80.

Muchnic, Helen. An Introduction to Russian Literature. New York: Doubleday, 1947. pp. 163-165.

Murry, J. Middleton. Fyodor Dostoevsky: A Critical Study. New York: Dodd, Mead and Company, 1916. pp. 157-202.

Pachmuss, Temira. F. M. Dostoevsky: Dualism and Synthesis of the Human Soul. Carbondale: Southern Illinois University Press, 1963. pp. 8-14; 39-41; 49-55; 90-92; 116-119; 152-154.

Pachmuss, Temira. "The Technique of Dream-Logic in the Works of Dostoevskij. " SEEJ n. s. 4:236-238. Fall 1960.

Panichas, George A. "Dostoevski and Satanism. " JR 45:12-28. January 1965.

Pritchett, V. S. "Books in General. " New S&N 21:389-390. April 12, 1941.

Rahv, Phillip. Image and Idea. Norfolk: Laughlin, 1949. pp. 86-110.

Ramsey, Paul. "God's Grace and Man's Guilt. " JR 31:30-34. January 1951.

Ramsey, Paul. "No Morality Without Immortality: Dostoevski and the Meaning of Atheism. " JR 36:92-93. April 1956.

Ramsey, Warren. "Albert Camus on Capital Punishment: His Adaptation of THE POSSESSED. " YR 48:634-640. Summer 1959.

Samchuk, Ulace. "Dostoyevsky on Leninism. " UQ 6:301-
303. Autumn 1950.

Seduro, Vladimir. "The Fate of Stavrogin's Confession. "
RusR 25:397-404. October 1966.

Simmons, Ernest J. Dostoevsky: The Making of a Novelist.
New York: Vintage Books, 1940. pp. 232-283.

Spector, Ivar. The Golden Age of Russian Literature. Caldwell: The Caxton Printers, Ltd. , 1945. pp. 131-133.

Steiner, George. Tolstoy or Dostoevsky. New York: Alfred
Knopf, 1959. pp. 182-190; 211-213; 308-319.

Stenbock-Fermor, Elisabeth. "Lermontov and Dostoevskij's
Novel THE DEVILS. " SEEJ 17:215-227. Fall 1959.

Strem, George G. "The Moral World of Dostoevsky. " RusR
16:22-23. July 1957.

Strem, George G. "The Theme of Rebellion in the Works of
Camus and Dostoievsky. " RLC 40:249-250. April - June
1966.

Wasiolek, Edward. Dostoevsky: The Major Fiction. Cambridge: MIT Press, 1964. pp. 110-136.

Wasiolek, Edward. "Dostoevsky: A Revolutionary Conservative. " ModA 9:65-66. Winter 1964-1965.

Woodhouse, C. M. "The Two Russians. " EDH 29:18-36.
1958.

Yarmolinsky, Avrahm. Dostoevsky: His Life and Art. New
York: Criterion Books, 1957. pp. 371-372; 285-298; 304-
307.

Yarmolinsky, Avrahm. Dostoevsky: A Life. New York: Harcourt, Brace and Company, 1934. pp. 290-308.

Yermilov, V. Fyodor Dostoevsky. Moscow: Foreign Languages Publishing House. pp. 223-231.

A RAW YOUTH

Beardsley, Monroe C. "Dostoyevsky's Metaphor of the 'Underground. ' " JHI 3:270-271. June 1942.

Carr, Edward Hallett. Dostoevsky: A New Biography. New
York: Houghton Mifflin Company, 1931. pp. 251-265.

Futrell, Michael H. "Dostoyevsky and Dickens. " EM 7:80-

84. 1956.

Harper, Ralph. The Seventh Solitude: Man's Isolation in Kierkegaard, Dostoevsky, and Nietzsche. Baltimore: Johns Hopkins Press, 1965. pp. 54-56.

Hingley, Ronald. The Undiscovered Dostoyevsky. London: Hamish Hamilton, 1962. pp. 162-174.

Jackson, Robert Louis. Dostoevsky's Quest for Form: A Study of His Philosophy of Art. New Haven: Yale University Press, 1966. pp. 112-118.

Matlaw, Ralph E. "Recurrent Imagery in Dostoevskij. " HSS 3:220. 1957.

Pachmuss, Temira. F. M. Dostoevsky: Dualism and Synthesis of the Human Soul. Carbondale: Southern Illinois University Press, 1963. pp. 56-59; 149-150; 154-162.

Rosen, Nathan. "Breaking Out of the Underground: The 'Failure' of A RAW YOUTH. " MFS 4:225-239. Autumn 1958.

Yarmolinsky, Avrahm. Dostoevsky: His Life and Art. New York: Criterion Books, 1957. pp. 315-333.

Yarmolinsky, Avrahm. Dostoevsky: A Life. New York: Harcourt, Brace and Company, 1934. pp. 321-334.

UNCLE'S DREAM
Hingley, Ronald. The Undiscovered Dostoyevsky. London: Hamish Hamilton, 1962. pp. 27-29.

Lo Gatto, Ettore. "Genesis of Dostoevsky's UNCLE'S DREAM. " SEER 26:452-466. April 1948.

Phelps, William L. Essays on Russian Novelists. New York: Macmillan Company, 1917. pp. 143-144.

Simmons, Ernest J. Dostoevsky: The Making of a Novelist. New York: Vintage Books, 1940. Chapter 5.

Yarmolinsky, Avrahm. Dostoevsky: His Life and Art. New York: Criterion Books, 1957. pp. 143-144.

Yarmolinsky, Avrahm. Dostoevsky: A Life. New York: Harcourt, Brace and Company, 1934. pp. 145-146.

THE VILLAGE OF STEPANCHIKOVO
Hingley, Ronald. The Undiscovered Dostoyevsky. London: Hamish Hamilton, 1962. pp. 29-38.

Pachmuss, Temira. F. M. Dostoevsky: Dualism and Synthesis of the Human Soul. Carbondale: Southern Illinois University Press, 1963. pp. 65-76.

Phelps, William L. Essays on Russian Novelists. New York: Macmillan Company, 1917. pp. 144-145.

Simmons, Ernest J. Dostoevsky: The Making of a Novelist. New York: Vintage Books, 1940. Chapter 5.

Dudintsev, Vladimir
NOT BY BREAD ALONE
Folejewski, Zbigniew. "Notes on the Problem of Individual Versus Collective in Russian and Polish Literature, 1954-57." ISS 3:30-32. 1963.

Gayn, Mark. "A Party at the Kremlin: Soviet Literary Rebels." QQ 65:553-557. Winter 1959.

Gibian, George. Interval of Freedom: Soviet Literature During the Thaw 1954-1957. Minneapolis: University of Minnesota Press, 1960. pp. 54-59.

Harari, Manya. "NOT BY BREAD ALONE." Listener 57: 339-340. February 28, 1957.

Monas, Sidney. "The Private Muse: Some Notes on Recent Russian Literature." HudR 11:104-107. Spring 1958.

Pritchett, V. S. "Dudintsev." NewS 54:435-436. October 5, 1957.

Sklanczenko, Tatiana. "NE XLEBOM EDINYM: Revised Edition." SEEJ 16:27-31. Spring 1958.

West, Anthony. "The Party Wall." Spec 199:442-443. October 4, 1957.

Ehrenburg, Ilya
THE EXTRAORDINARY ADVENTURES OF JULIO JURENITO AND HIS DISCIPLES
Thomas, Martin. "The Adventures of Ilya Ehrenburg: Portrait of an Artist as a Soviet Journalist." Commentary 4:131. August 1947.
THE FALL OF PARIS
Struve, Gleb. Soviet Russian Literature 1917-1950. Norman: University of Oklahoma Press, 1951. pp. 302-303.
IN THE PROTOCHNY LANE
Eng-Liedmeier, A. M. Van der. Soviet Literary Characters. 'S Gravenhage: Mouton and Company, 1959. pp. 37-38.
THE NINTH WAVE
Yarmolinsky, Avrahm. Literature Under Communism. Russian and East European Series, Russian and East European Institute, Indiana University. Vol. 20. 1957. pp. 96-97.
OUT OF CHAOS
Mathewson, Rufus W., Jr. The Positive Hero in Russian Literature. New York: Columbia University Press, 1958.

pp. 280-281.

Simmons, Ernest J. Through the Glass of Soviet Literature.
New York: Columbia University Press, 1953. pp. 75-80.
THE SECOND DAY
Eng-Liedmeier, A. M. Van der. Soviet Literary Characters.
'S Gravenhage: Mouton and Company, 1959. pp. 97-99.
THE STORM
Struve, Gleb. Soviet Russian Literature 1917-1950. Norman:
University of Oklahoma Press, 1951. pp. 361-362.
THE THAW
E. H. "Towards a Soviet Bourgeoisie? Implications of THE
THAW and THE SEASONS. " World Today 11:300-308. July
1955.

Folejewski, Zbigniew. "Notes on the Problem of Individual
Versus Collective in Russian and Polish Literature, 1954-
57. " ISS 3:26-28. 1963.

Kirk, Russell. "The Death of Art: Ehrenburg's THAW. "
DubR 229:249-256. Third Quarter 1955.

Laber, Jeri. "The Soviet Writer's Search for New Values. "
PoC 5:14-20. January - February 1956.

Vickery, Walter N. The Cult of Optimism: Political and
Ideological Problems of Recent Soviet Literature. Bloom-
ington: Indiana University Press, 1963. (Indiana University
Humanities Series, No. 52) pp. 41-43.

Werth, Alexander. "Ehrenburg in Trouble. " New S&N 48:
288. September 11, 1954.
THE UNCOMMON LIFE OF LASIK ROITSCHWANTZ
Thomas, Martin. "The Adventures of Ilya Ehrenburg: Por-
trait of an Artist as a Soviet Journalist. " Commentary 4:133.
August 1947.

Eotvos, Jozsef
THE CARTHUSIAN
Remenyi, Joseph. Hungarian Writers and Literature. New
Brunswick: Rutgers University Press, 1964. pp. 122-124.

Remenyi, Joseph. "Two 19th Century Hungarian Men of Letters. " Symposium 6:174-175. May 1952.
HUNGARY IN 1514
Jones, D. Mervyn. Five Hungarian Writers. Oxford: Clarendon Press, 1966. pp. 186-198.

Remenyi, Joseph. Hungarian Writers and Literature. New
Brunswick: Rutgers University Press, 1964. pp. 124-125.

Riedl, Frederick. A History of Hungarian Literature. New
York: D. Appleton and Company, 1906. pp. 176-178.

THE SISTERS
    Jones, D. Mervyn. Five Hungarian Writers. Oxford: Claren-
    don Press, 1966. pp. 205-214.

    Remenyi, Joseph. Hungarian Writers and Literature. New
    Brunswick: Rutgers University Press, 1964. p. 125.
THE VILLAGE NOTARY
    Jones, D. Mervyn. Five Hungarian Writers. Oxford: Claren-
    don Press, 1966. pp. 175-186.

    Remenyi, Joseph. Hungarian Writers and Literature. New
    Brunswick: Rutgers University Press, 1964. p. 124.

    Remenyi, Joseph. "Two 19th Century Hungarian Men of
    Letters." Symposium 6:175-176. May 1952.

    Riedl, Frederick. A History of Hungarian Literature. New
    York: D. Appleton and Company, 1906. pp. 175-176.

Fadeyev, Alexander
    THE ROUT
    Struve, Gleb. Soviet Russian Literature 1917-1950. Norman:
    University of Oklahoma Press, 1951. pp. 128-129.
    THE YOUNG GUARD
    Yarmolinsky, Avrahm. Literature Under Communism. Rus-
    sian and East European Series, Russian and East European
    Institute, Indiana University. Vol. 20. 1957. pp. 65-70.

Fedin, Konstantin
    ARCTUR SANATORIUM
    Simmons, Ernest J. Russian Fiction and Soviet Ideology.
    New York: Columbia University Press, 1958. pp. 53-58.
    THE BROTHERS
    Simmons, Ernest J. Russian Fiction and Soviet Ideology.
    New York: Columbia University Press, 1958. pp. 31-41.

    Struve, Gleb. "Constantine Fedin." SEER 13:181-182. July
    1934.
    CITIES AND YEARS
    Eng-Liedmeier, A. M. Van der. Soviet Literary Characters.
    'S Gravenhage: Mouton and Company, 1959. pp. 52-54.

    Mathewson, Rufus W., Jr. The Positive Hero in Russian
    Literature. New York: Columbia University Press, 1958.
    pp. 254-255.

    Mirsky, D. S. "Russia." Contemporary Movements in
    European Literature. (ed.) William Rose and J. Isaacs.
    London: George Routledge and Sons, Ltd., 1928. pp. 173-
    175.

    Simmons, Ernest J. Russian Fiction and Soviet Ideology.
    New York: Columbia University Press, 1958. pp. 17-29.

Struve, Gleb. "Constantine Fedin." SEER 13:179-181. July 1934.

Struve, Gleb. Soviet Russian Literature 1917-1950. Norman: University of Oklahoma Press, 1951. pp. 89-90.
EARLY JOYS
Simmons, Ernest J. Russian Fiction and Soviet Ideology. New York: Columbia University Press, 1958. pp. 61-68.
NO ORDINARY SUMMER
Simmons, Ernest J. Russian Fiction and Soviet Ideology. New York: Columbia University Press, 1958. pp. 68-83.
THE RAPE OF EUROPE
Simmons, Ernest J. Russian Fiction and Soviet Ideology. New York: Columbia University Press, 1958. pp. 42-53.

Struve, Gleb. "New Novels of Fedin and Leonov." SEER 15: 692-695. April 1937.

Struve, Gleb. Soviet Russian Literature 1917-1950. Norman: University of Oklahoma Press, 1951. pp. 273-274.

Franko, Ivan
ZAKHAR
Manning, Clarence A. "The Literary Work of Ivan Franko." UQ 12:121. June 1956.

Furmanov, Dmitri
CAPAEV
Eng-Liedmeier, A. M. Van der. Soviet Literary Characters. 'S Gravenhage: Mouton and Company, 1959. pp. 61-62.

Mathewson, Rufus W., Jr. The Positive Hero in Russian Literature. New York: Columbia University Press, 1958. pp. 231-242.

Gardonyi, Geza
THE INVISIBLE MAN
Remenyi, Joseph. Hungarian Writers and Literature. New Brunswick: Rutgers University Press, 1964. pp. 149-150.

Gladkov, Feodor
CEMENT
Eng-Liedmeier, A. M. Van der. Soviet Literary Characters. 'S Gravenhage: Mouton and Company, 1959. pp. 33-34; 45- 46; 57-58.

Gasiorowska, Xenia. "Dasa Cumalova and Her Successors." SEEJ 15:260-269. Winter 1957.

Mathewson, Rufus W., Jr. The Positive Hero in Russian Literature. New York: Columbia University Press, 1958. pp. 260-267.

Simmons, Ernest J. Through the Glass of Soviet Literature. New York: Columbia University Press, 1953. pp. 38-39.

Struve, Gleb. Soviet Russian Literature 1917-1950. Norman: University of Oklahoma Press, 1951. pp. 126-127.

ENERGY
Eng-Liedmeier, A. M. Van der. Soviet Literary Characters. 'S Gravenhage: Mouton and Company, 1959. pp. 80-83.

Gogol, Nikolay
DEAD SOULS
Baring, Maurice. Landmarks in Russian Literature. London: Methuen and Company, 1910. pp. 66-73.

Brasol, Boris. The Mighty Three. New York: William Farquhar Payson, 1934. pp. 151-159.

Cook, Albert. The Meaning of Fiction. Detroit: Wayne State University Press, 1960. pp. 31-34.

Cook, Albert. "Reflexive Attitudes: Sterne, Gogol, Gide." Criticism 2:164-174. Spring 1960.

Florovsky, Georges. "Three Masters: The Quest for Religion in Nineteenth-Century Russian Literature." CLS 3:125. No. 2, 1966.

Futrell, Michael. "Gogol and Dickens." SEER 34:443-459. June 1956.

Gifford, Henry. The Novel in Russia: From Pushkin to Pasternak. New York: Harper and Row, 1964. pp. 40-50.

Kropotkin, O. Ideals and Realities in Russian Literature. New York: Knopf, 1919. pp. 79-81.

Lavrin, Janko. Gogol. London: George Routledge and Sons, Ltd., 1925. pp. 158-191.

Lavrin, Janko. An Introduction to the Russian Novel. New York: McGraw-Hill, 1947. pp. 33-39.

Lavrin, Janko. Nikolai Gogol: A Centenary Study. London: Sylvan Press, 1951. pp. 95-119.

Lavrin, Janko. Russian Writers: Their Lives and Literature. New York: D. Van Nostrand Company, Inc., 1954. pp. 72-77.

Lefevre, Carl. "Gogol and Anglo--Russian Literary Relations During the Crimean War." ASEER 8:106-125. April 1949.

Manning, Clarence A. "Nicholas Gogol." SEER 4:580-584. March 1926.

Masson, Edmond. "Russia's Gogol: A Centenary." PacSpec 7:324-326. Summer 1953.

Mathewson, Rufus W., Jr. The Positive Hero in Russian Literature. New York: Columbia University Press, 1958. pp. 18-19; 32-33.

Mathewson, Rufus W., Jr. "The Soviet Hero and the Literary Heritage." ASEER 12:511. December 1953.

Muchnic, Helen. An Introduction to Russian Literature. New York: Doubleday, 1947. pp. 113-119.

O'Connor, Frank. The Mirror in the Roadway: A Study of the Modern Novel. New York: Alfred A. Knopf, 1956. pp. 101-110.

Olgin, Moissaye J. A Guide to Russian Literature (1820-1917). New York: Harcourt, Brace and Howe, 1920. pp. 47-48.

Phelps, William L. Essays on Russian Novelists. New York: Macmillan Company, 1917. pp. 51-59.

Pritchett, V. S. "Books in General." New S&N 22:62. July 19, 1941.

Reeve, F. D. The Russian Novel. New York: McGraw-Hill Book Company, 1966. pp. 64-102.

Reeve, F. D. "Through Hell on a Hobby-Horse: Notes on Gogol and Sterne." Symposium 13:75-86. Spring 1959.

Selig, Karl Ludwig. "Concerning Gogol's DEAD SOULS and LAZARILLO DE TORMES." Symposium 8:138-139. Summer 1954.

Setschkareff, Vsevolod. Gogol: His Life and Works. New York: New York University Press, 1965. pp. 182-215; 247-256.

Spector, Ivar. The Golden Age of Russian Literature. Caldwell: The Caxton Printers, Ltd., 1945. pp. 57-60; 64-66.

Weathers, Winston. "Gogol's DEAD SOULS: The Degrees of Reality." CE 17:159-164. December 1955.

Yarmolinsky, Avrahm. Russian Literature. Chicago: American Library Association, 1931. pp. 21-24.

DIARY OF A MADMAN
    Gustafson, Richard F. "The Suffering Usurper: Gogol's
    DIARY OF A MADMAN. " SEEJ n. s. 9:268-280. Fall 1965.
THE FAIR AT SOROCHINSK
    Muchnic, Helen. An Introduction to Russian Literature.
    New York: Doubleday, 1947. pp. 99-103.
OLD-WORLD LANDOWNERS
    McLean, Hugh. "Gogol's Retreat from Love: Toward an In-
    terpretation of MIRGOROD. " American Contributions to the
    Fourth International Congress of Slavicists. The Hague: Mou-
    ton and Company, 1958. pp. 237-239.
THE OVERCOAT
    Baumgarten, Murray. "Gogol's THE OVERCOAT as a Picar-
    esque Epic. " DR 46:186-199. Summer 1966.

    Driessen, F. C. Gogol as a Short-Story Writer: A Study of
    His Technique of Composition. The Hague: Mouton and Com-
    pany, 1965. pp. 182-214.

    Eichenbaum, Boris. "The Structure of Gogol's THE OVER-
    COAT. " RusR 22:377-399. October 1963.

    Landry, Hilton. "Gogol's THE OVERCOAT. " Expl 19: Item
    54, May 1961.

    Setschkareff, Vsevolod. Gogol: His Life and Works. New
    York: New York University Press, 1965. pp. 216-226.

    Stilman, Leon. "Gogol's OVERCOAT--Thematic Pattern
    and Origins. " ASEER 11:138-148. April 1952.
TARAS BULBA
    Baumgarten, Murray. "Gogol's THE OVERCOAT as a
    Picaresque Epic. " DR 46:188-192. Summer 1966.

    Kropotkin, O. Ideals and Realities in Russian Literature.
    New York: Knopf, 1919. pp. 70-72.

    Lavrin, Janko. Nikolai Gogol: A Centenary Study. London:
    Sylvan Press, 1951. pp. 48-51.

    McLean, Hugh. "Gogol's Retreat from Love: Toward an In-
    terpretation of MIRGOROD. " American Contributions to the
    Fourth International Congress of Slavicists. The Hague: Mou-
    ton and Company, 1958. pp. 232-235.

    Manning, Clarence A. "Nicholas Gogol. " SEER 4:576. March
    1926.

    Proffer, Carl R. "Gogol's TARAS BULBA and the ILIAD. "
    CL 17:142-150. Spring 1965.

    Strakhovsky, Leonid I. "The Historianism of Gogol. " ASEER
    12:366-370. October 1953.

Vii

McLean, Hugh. "Gogol's Retreat from Love: Toward an Interpretation of MIRGOROD. " American Contributions to the
Fourth International Congress of Slavicists. The Hague: Mouton and Company, 1958. pp. 235-236.

Golovanov, Yaroslav
  FORGE OF THUNDER
    Steininger, Alexander. "Scientists in Soviet Literature. "
    Survey 52:162. July 1964.

Goncharov, Ivan A.
  OBLOMOV
    Gifford, Henry. The Novel in Russia: From Pushkin to
    Pasternak. New York: Harper and Row, 1964. pp. 55-63.

    Kropotkin, O. Ideals and Realities in Russian Literature.
    New York: Knopf, 1919. pp. 152-161.

    Lavrin, Janko. Goncharov. New Haven: Yale University
    Press, 1954. pp. 27-37.

    Lavrin, Janko. An Introduction to the Russian Novel. New
    York: McGraw-Hill, 1947. pp. 73-78.

    Lavrin, Janko. Russian Writers: Their Lives and Literature.
    New York: D. Van Nostrand Company, Inc. , 1954. pp. 155-
    159.

    Macauley, Robie. "The Superfluous Man." PR 19:170-182.
    March - April 1952.

    Manning, Clarence A. "Ivan Aleksandrovich Goncharov. "
    SAQ 26:69-72. January 1927.

    Mathewson, Rufus W. , Jr. The Positive Hero in Russian
    Literature. New York: Columbia University Press, 1958.
    pp. 62-63; 68-69; 72-73.

    Olgin, Moissaye J. A Guide to Russian Literature (1820-
    1917). New York: Harcourt, Brace and Howe, 1920. pp. 73-
    74.

    Poggioli, Renato. The Phoenix and the Spider. Cambridge:
    Harvard University Press, 1957. pp. 33-48.

    Pritchett, V. S. "Books in General. " New S&N 26:287-288.
    October 30, 1943.

    Pritchett, V. S. "Books in General. " New S&N 48:661-662.
    November 20, 1954.

    Pritchett, V. S. The Living Novel and Later Appreciations.

New York: Random House, 1964. pp. 397-404.

Rapp, Helen. "The Art of Ivan Goncharov. " SEER 36:376-395. June 1958.

Reeve, F. D. "Oblomovism Revisited." ASEER 15:112-118. February 1956.

Reeve, F. D. The Russian Novel. New York: McGraw-Hill Book Company, 1966. pp. 103-118.

Spector, Ivar. The Golden Age of Russian Literature. Caldwell: The Caxton Printers, Ltd. , 1945. pp. 74-78.

Stilman, Leon. "Oblomovka Revisited." ASEER 7:45-77. February 1948.

Woodhouse, C. M. "The Two Russians. " EDH 29:18-36. 1958.

Yarmolinsky, Avrahm. Russian Literature. Chicago: American Library Association, 1931. pp. 24-28.
AN ORDINARY STORY
Lavrin, Janko. Goncharov. New Haven: Yale University Press, 1954. pp. 18-25.

Manning, Clarence A. "Ivan Aleksandrovich Goncharov. " SAQ 26:67-69. January 1927.

Manning, Clarence A. "The Neglect of Time in the Russian Novel. " Slavic Studies. (ed.) Alexander Kaun and Ernest J. Simmons. Ithaca: Cornell University Press, 1943. pp. 109-111.

Pritchett, V. S. "Books in General. " New S&N 48:661. November 20, 1954.

Wilson, Colin. "Existential Criticism. " ChiR 13:177-180. Summer 1959.
THE PRECIPICE
Lavrin, Janko. An Introduction to the Russian Novel. New York: McGraw-Hill, 1947. pp. 79-81.

Manning, Clarence A. "Ivan Aleksandrovich Goncharov. " SAQ 26:72-75. January 1927.

Manning, Clarence A. "The Neglect of Time in the Russian Novel. " Slavic Studies. (ed.) Alexander Kaun and Ernest J. Simmons. Ithaca: Cornell University Press, 1943. pp. 112-113.

Olgin, Moissaye J. A Guide to Russian Literature (1820-1917. New York: Harcourt, Brace and Howe, 1920. p. 75.

Rapp, Helen. "The Art of Ivan Goncharov. " SEER 36:376-
395. June 1958.
THE RAVINE
Lavrin, Janko. Goncharov. New Haven: Yale University
Press, 1954. pp. 37-47.

Lavrin, Janko. Russian Writers: Their Lives and Literature.
New York: D. Van Nostrand Company, Inc. , 1954. pp. 159-
162.

Gorky, Maxim
THE ARTAMONOV BUSINESS
Levin, Dan. Stormy Petrel: The Life and Work of Maxim
Gorky. New York: Appleton-Century, 1965. pp. 259-262.
THE CONFESSION
Levin, Dan. Stormy Petrel: The Life and Work of Maxim
Gorky. New York: Appleton-Century, 1965. pp. 145-150.
FOMA GORDEYEV
Eoff, Sherman H. The Modern Spanish Novel. New York:
New York University Press, 1961. pp. 155-164.

Holtzman, Filia. The Young Maxim Gorky 1868-1902. New
York: Columbia University Press, 1948. pp. 162-164.

Levin, Dan. Stormy Petrel: The Life and Work of Maxim
Gorky. New York: Appleton-Century, 1965. pp. 67-71.

Phelps, William L. Essays on Russian Novelists. New York:
Macmillan Company, 1917. pp. 221-223.
THE LIFE OF KLIM SAMGIN
Levin, Dan. Stormy Petrel: The Life and Work of Maxim
Gorky. New York: Appleton-Century, 1965. pp. 264-266.
THE MOTHER
Levin, Dan. Stormy Petrel: The Life and Work of Maxim
Gorky. New York: Appleton-Century, 1965. pp. 135-138.

Mathewson, Rufus W. , Jr. The Positive Hero in Russian
Literature. New York: Columbia University Press, 1958.
pp. 212-221.

Olgin, Moissaye J. A Guide to Russian Literature (1820-
1917). New York: Harcourt, Brace and Howe, 1920. pp. 227-
228.

Phelps, William L. Essays on Russian Novelists. New York:
Macmillan Company, 1917. pp. 224-225.

Spector, Ivar. The Golden Age of Russian Literature. Cald-
well: The Caxton Printers, Ltd. , 1945. pp. 246-247.
ORPHAN PAUL
Holtzman, Filia. The Young Maxim Gorky 1868-1902. New
York: Columbia University Press, 1948. pp. 160-161.

THE SPY
> Phelps, William L. Essays on Russian Novelists. New York:
> Macmillan Company, 1917. pp. 225-226.

THE THREE
> Holtzman, Filia. The Young Maxim Gorky 1868-1902. New
> York: Columbia University Press, 1948. pp. 161-162.

> Levin, Dan. Stormy Petrel: The Life and Work of Maxim
> Gorky. New York: Appleton-Century, 1965. pp. 71-72.

VARENKA OLESSOVA
> Phelps, William L. Essays on Russian Novelists. New York:
> Macmillan Company, 1917. pp. 223-224.

Granin, Daniel
> IDU NA GROZU
>> Steininger, Alexander. "Scientists in Soviet Literature."
>> Survey 52:163-165. July 1964.
> THOSE WHO SEEK
>> Gibian, George. Interval of Freedom: Soviet Literature During the Thaw 1954-1957. Minneapolis: University of Minnesota Press, 1960. pp. 44-47.

>> Steininger, Alexander. "Scientists in Soviet Literature."
>> Survey 52:163. July 1964.

Green, A. (Alexander Grinevski)
> CRIMSON SAILS
>> Yershov, Peter. Science Fiction and Utopian Fantasy in Soviet Literature. New York: Research Program on the USSR, Mimeographed Series No. 62. 1954. pp. 24-27.

Grekova, I.
> BEHIND THE CONTROL ROOM
>> Steininger, Alexander. "Scientists in Soviet Literature."
>> Survey 52:160-162. July 1964.

Harecki, Maksim
> TWO SOULS
>> Adamovich, Anthony. Opposition to Sovietization in Belorussian Literature (1917-1957). Published by the Institute for the Study of the USSR, Munich, Germany, for Scarecrow Press, Inc., New York, 1958. pp. 35-37.

Hasek, J.
> GOOD SOLDIER SCHWEIK
>> Stern, J. P. "On the Integrity of the Good Soldier Schweik."
>> FMLS 2:14-24. January 1966.

>> Vlach, Robert. "Gogol and Hasek--Two Masters of 'Poshlost.' " ESl 7:240-242. Autumn - Winter 1962.

Herman, Yury
> OUR ACQUAINTANCES

Struve, Gleb. "Some Recent Novels. " SEER 16:689-691.
April 1938.

Ilf and Petrov
DIAMONDS TO SIT ON
Posin, J. A. "Soviet Satire. " RusR 9:299-301. October
1950.
THE LITTLE GOLDEN CALF
Posin, J. A. "Soviet Satire. " RusR 9:301-302. October
1950.

Irzykowski
PATUBA
Pietrkiewicz, Jerzy. "A Polish Psychoanalytical Novel of
1902. " SEER 30:63-86. December 1951.

Josika, Miklos
THE CZECHS IN HUNGARY
Remenyi, Joseph. Hungarian Writers and Literature. New
Brunswick: Rutgers University Press, 1964. pp. 68-69.
THE RECKLESS
Remenyi, Joseph. Hungarian Writers and Literature. New
Brunswick: Rutgers University Press, 1964. p. 69.

Kaffka, Margit
COLORS AND YEARS
Remenyi, Joseph. Hungarian Writers and Literature. New
Brunswick: Rutgers University Press, 1964. pp. 286-287;
290-291.

Katayev, Valentin
THE EMBEZZLERS
Posin, J. A. "Soviet Satire. " RusR 9:299. October 1950.
FOR THE POWER OF THE SOVIETS
Yarmolinsky, Avrahm. Literature Under Communism. Rus-
sian and East European Series, Russian and East European
Institute, Indiana University. Vol. 20. 1957. pp. 71-73.
FORWARD, OH TIME
Struve, Gleb. Soviet Russian Literature 1917-1950. Norman:
University of Oklahoma Press, 1951. pp. 232-233.
LONELY WHITE SAIL
Struve, Gleb. "Some Recent Novels. " SEER 16:687-688.
April 1938.

Struve, Gleb. Soviet Russian Literature 1917-1950. Norman:
University of Oklahoma Press, 1951. pp. 276-277.

Kaverin, V.
ARTIST UNKNOWN
Eng-Liedmeier, A. M. Van der. Soviet Literary Characters.
'S Gravenhage: Mouton and Company, 1959. pp. 96-97.

Oulanoff, Hongor. "Kaverin's XUDOZNIK NEIZVESTEN:

Structure and Motivation. '' SEEJ 10:389-399. Winter 1966.
A PIECE OF GLASS
   Steininger, Alexander. ''Scientists in Soviet Literature. ''
   Survey 52:157-159. July 1964.
SEARCHES AND HOPES
   Gibian, George. Interval of Freedom: Soviet Literature Dur-
   ing the Thaw 1954-1957. Minneapolis: University of Minne-
   sota Press, 1960. pp. 48-52; 115-119.

   Steininger, Alexander. ''Scientists in Soviet Literature. ''
   Survey 52:159-160. July 1964.

Kemeny, Sigismund
   THE ENTHUSIASTS
      Remenyi, Joseph. Hungarian Writers and Literature. New
      Brunswick: Rutgers University Press, 1964. p. 56.

      Riedl, Frederick. A History of Hungarian Literature. New
      York: D. Appleton and Company, 1906. pp. 181-183.
   GYULAI PAL
      Riedl, Frederick. A History of Hungarian Literature. New
      York: D. Appleton and Company, 1906. p. 183.
   STORMY TIMES
      Remenyi, Joseph. Hungarian Writers and Literature. New
      Brunswick: Rutgers University Press, 1964. pp. 55-56.

Khvylovy
   WOODCOCKS
      Boyko, Yuri. ''The Struggle of Ukrainian Literature Under
      the Soviets Against Russian Spiritual Enslavement. '' UQ 13:
      51-53. March - December 1957.

      Manning, Clarence A. ''Pasternak and Khvylovy. '' UQ 14:
      354-355. December 1958.

Kochetov, V.
   THE BROTHERS YERSHOV
      Alexandrova, Vera. ''Soviet Literature in 1958. '' RusR 18:
      126-127. April 1959.

      ''The Anti-Dudintsev. '' Survey 27:6-8. January - March
      1959.

      Dressler, Alfred. ''Party and Writers: 1956-58. '' Soviet
      Studies 10:420-427. April 1959.

      Katkov, George. ''THE BROTHERS YERSHOV: An Exercise
      in the New Orthodoxy. '' Survey 27:15-19. January - March
      1959.
   THE ZHURBINS
      Dressler, Alfred. ''Party and Writers: 1956-58. '' Soviet
      Studies 10:425-426. April 1959.

Kodolanyi, Janos
WATERSHED
Juhasz, William. "The Writer and Society. " EE 12:13-14.
January 1963.

Konovalov, Grigory
THE UNIVERSITY
Struve, Gleb. "Anti-Westernism in Recent Soviet Liter-
ature." YR 39:221-222. Winter 1950.

Konstantinovic, Radomir
GIVE US TODAY
Goy, E. D. "The Serbian and Croatian Novel Since 1948. "
SEER 40:67-68. December 1961.
THE PURE AND THE DEFILED
Goy, E. D. "The Serbian and Croatian Novel Since 1948. "
SEER 40:67-68. December 1961.

Konwicki, Tadeusz
A CONTEMPORARY DREAMBOOK
Milosz, Czeslaw. "The Novel in Poland. " Daedalus 95:1015.
Fall 1966.

Kopta, Josef
THE THIRD COMPANY
Hostovsky, Egon. "The Czech Novel Between the Two World
Wars. " SEER 21:80-81. November 1943.

Kostylev, Valentin
IVAN THE TERRIBLE
Twarog, Leon I. "A Novel in Flux: Valentin Kostylev's
IVAN GROZNYJ. " ASEER 14:359-370. October 1955.

Kosztolanyi, Dezso
ANNA EDES
Remenyi, Joseph. Hungarian Writers and Literature. New
Brunswick: Rutgers University Press, 1964. pp. 263-264.
THE BLOODY POET
Remenyi, Joseph. Hungarian Writers and Literature. New
Brunswick: Rutgers University Press, 1964. pp. 262-263.

Kratt, Ivan
BARANOV'S ISLAND
Twarog, Leon I. "Soviet Historical Novelists Look at Amer-
ica. " ASEER 19:564-569. December 1960.
ROSS COLONY
Twarog, Leon I. "Soviet Historical Novelists Look at Amer-
ica. " ASEER 19:565-569. December 1960.

Krestovskij, V.
PANURGE'S HERD
Moser, Charles A. Antinihilism in the Russian Novel of the
1860's. The Hague: Mouton and Company, 1964. pp. 167-168.

Krudy, Gyula
  AUTUMN RACES
      Remenyi, Joseph. Hungarian Writers and Literature. New
      Brunswick: Rutgers University Press, 1964. p. 236.
  THE RED MAILCOACH
      Remenyi, Joseph. Hungarian Writers and Literature. New
      Brunswick: Rutgers University Press, 1964. pp. 235-236.

Kuncz, Aladar
  BLACK MONASTERY
      Remenyi, Joseph. "Aladar Kuncz, Hungarian-Transylvanian
      Writer (1886-1931). " CE 10:136-137. December 1948.
  CLOUDS OVER A CITY
      Remenyi, Joseph. "Aladar Kuncz, Hungarian-Transylvanian
      Writer (1886-1931). " CE 10:135-136. December 1948.

Kuprin, Alexander I.
  IN HONOUR'S NAME
      Phelps, William L. Essays on Russian Novelists. New York:
      Macmillan Company, 1917. pp. 278-284.
  LIQUID SUN
      Yershov, Peter. Science Fiction and Utopian Fantasy in
      Soviet Literature. New York: Research Program on the USSR,
      Mimeographed Series No. 62, 1954. pp. 15-16.

Kuzmin, Mikhail
  THE QUIET GUARD
      Field, Andrew. "Mikhail Kuzmin: Notes on a Decadent's
      Prose. " RusR 22:298-300. July 1963.
  TRAVELLERS ON LAND AND SEA
      Field, Andrew. "Mikhail Kuzmin: Notes on a Decadent's
      Prose. " RusR 22:295-296. July 1963.
  WINGS
      Field, Andrew. "Mikhail Kuzmin: Notes on a Decadent's
      Prose. " RusR 22:297-298. July 1963.

Lazecnikov, I. I.
  ICE PALACE
      Twarog, Leon I. "The Soviet Revival of a Nineteenth-Cen-
      tury Historical Novelist: I. I. Lazecnikov. " HSS 4:108-126.
      1957.
  THE INFIDEL
      Twarog, Leon I. "The Soviet Revival of a Nineteenth-Cen-
      tury Historical Novelist: I. I. Lazecnikov. " HSS 4:110-117.
      1957.
  THE LAST PAGE
      Twarog, Leon I. "The Soviet Revival of a Nineteenth-Cen-
      tury Historical Novelist: I. I. Lazecnikov. " HSS 4:113-119.
      1957.

Lengyel, Joszef
  AN ANGRY OLD MAN
      Juhasz, William. "Writers and Politics. " EE 12:11-13.

July 1963.

Leonov, Leonid
THE BADGERS
Muchnic, Helen. "Leonid Leonov." RusR 18:38-39. January
1959.

Simmons, Ernest J. Russian Fiction and Soviet Ideology.
New York: Columbia University Press, 1958. pp. 92-95.

Struve, Gleb. Soviet Russian Literature 1917-1950. Norman:
University of Oklahoma Press, 1951. pp. 93-94.
LOCUSTS
Muchnic, Helen. "Leonid Leonov." RusR 18:45-47. January
1959.
THE ROAD TO THE OCEAN
Eng-Liedmeier, A. M. Van der. Soviet Literary Characters.
'S Gravenhage: Mouton and Company, 1959. pp. 111-113.

Mathewson, Rufus W., Jr. The Positive Hero in Russian
Literature. New York: Columbia University Press, 1958.
pp. 227-228; 301-310.

Simmons, Ernest J. "Leonov and ROAD TO THE OCEAN."
For Roman Jakobson. The Hague: Mouton and Company,
1956. pp. 467-474.

Simmons, Ernest J. Russian Fiction and Soviet Ideology.
New York: Columbia University Press, 1958. pp. 124-139.

Struve, Gleb. "New Novels of Fedin and Leonov." SEER 15:
695-697. April 1937.

Struve, Gleb. Soviet Russian Literature 1917-1950. Norman:
University of Oklahoma Press, 1951. pp. 272-273.

Thomson, R. D. B. "Leonid Leonov." FMLS 2:267-268.
July 1966.
RUSSIAN FOREST
Christesen, Nina. "Notes on Three Soviet Novels." Meanjin
17:88-89. April 1958.

Gibian, George. Interval of Freedom: Soviet Literature During the Thaw 1954-1957. Minneapolis: University of Minnesota Press, 1960. pp. 40-44; 110-115.

Simmons, Ernest J. Russian Fiction and Soviet Ideology.
New York: Columbia University Press, 1958. pp. 142-158.

Terras, Victor. "L. M. Leonov's Novel THE RUSSIAN
FOREST." SEEJ n. s. 8:123-135. Summer 1964.

Thomson, R. D. B. "Leonid Leonov." FMLS 2:270-271.

July 1966.
SKUTAREVSKY
Simmons, Ernest J. Russian Fiction and Soviet Ideology.
New York: Columbia University Press, 1958. pp. 111-124.

Struve, Gleb. "Leonid Leonov and His SKUTAREVSKY."
SEER 12:194-195. July 1933.
SOVIET RIVER
Eng-Liedmeier, A. M. Van der. Soviet Literary Characters.
'S Gravenhage: Mouton and Company, 1959. pp. 82-83.

Futrell, M. H. "A Central Soviet Novel: Leonov's SOT."
RMS 3:111-130.

Muchnic, Helen. "Leonid Leonov." RusR 18:43-44. January
1959.

Simmons, Ernest J. Russian Fiction and Soviet Ideology.
New York: Columbia University Press, 1958. pp. 104-111.

Simmons, Ernest J. Through the Glass of Soviet Literature.
New York: Columbia University Press, 1953. pp. 55-57.

Struve, Gleb. "Leonid Leonov and His SKUTAREVSKY."
SEER 12:193-194. July 1933.
THE TAKING OF VELIKOSHUMSK
Muchnic, Helen. "Leonid Leonov." RusR 18:48-49. January
1959.

Simmons, Ernest J. Russian Fiction and Soviet Ideology.
New York: Columbia University Press, 1958. pp. 140-142.
THE THIEF
Muchnic, Helen. "Leonid Leonov." RusR 18:39-43. January
1959.

Simmons, Ernest J. Russian Fiction and Soviet Ideology.
New York: Columbia University Press, 1958. pp. 96-102.

Struve, Gleb. "Leonid Leonov and His SKUTAREVSKY."
SEER 12:191-193. July 1933.

Struve, Gleb. Soviet Russian Literature 1917-1950. Norman:
University of Oklahoma Press, 1951. pp. 95-96.

Thomson, R. D. B. "Leonid Leonov." FMLS 2:264-266.
July 1966.

Leont'ev, Konstantin
IN MY OWN LAND
Ivask, George. "Konstantin Leont'ev's Fiction." ASEER 20:
625. December 1961.

Lermontov, Mikhail
> BELA
>> Lavrin, Janko. Lermontov. London: Bowes and Bowes, 1959.
>> pp. 81-85.

> A HERO OF OUR TIME
>> Baring, Maurice. An Outline of Russian Literature. New
>> York: Holt and Company, 1915. pp. 103-106.

>> Cross, Samuel H. "Mikhail Yurevich Lermontov." Amer-
>> ican Review on the Soviet Union 4:44-46. October - November
>> 1941.

>> Entwistle, W. J. "The Byronism of Lermontov's A HERO
>> OF OUR TIME. " CL 1:140-146. Spring 1949.

>> Gifford, Henry. The Novel in Russia: From Pushkin to
>> Pasternak. New York: Harper and Row, 1964. pp. 28-39.

>> Gronicka, Andre von. "Lermontov's Debt to Goethe: A Re-
>> appraisal. " RLC 40:579-584. October - December 1966.

>> Lavrin, Janko. An Introduction to the Russian Novel. New
>> York: McGraw-Hill, 1947. pp. 23-24.

>> Lavrin, Janko. Lermontov. London: Bowes and Bowes, 1959.
>> pp. 78-81; 90-91.

>> Manning, Clarence A. "Mikhail Yurevich Lermontov. " SAQ
>> 24:53-55. January 1925.

>> Mersereau, John, Jr. " 'The Fatalist' as a Keystone of A
>> HERO OF OUR TIMES. " SEEJ n. s. 4:137-145. Summer 1960.

>> Mersereau, John, Jr. Mikhail Lermontov. Carbondale:
>> Southern Illinois University Press, 1962. pp. 75-158.

>> Reeve, F. D. The Russian Novel. New York: McGraw-Hill
>> Book Company, 1966. pp. 45-63.

>> Stenbock-Fermor, Elisabeth. "Lermontov and Dostoevskij's
>> Novel THE DEVILS. " SEEJ 17:215-227. Fall 1959.

>> Yalom, Marilyn Koenick. "LA CHUTE and A HERO OF OUR
>> TIME. " FR 36:138-145. December 1962.

> SHTOSS
>> Mersereau, John, Jr. "Lermontov's SHTOSS: Hoax or Liter-
>> ary Credo?" ASEER 21:280-295. June 1962.

Leskov, N. S.
> AT KNIVES POINT
>> Olgin, Moissaye J. A Guide to Russian Literature (1820-
>> 1917). New York: Harcourt, Brace and Howe, 1920. p. 124.

THE BULLSHEEP
    Olgin, Moissaye J. A Guide to Russian Literature (1820-
    1917). New York: Harcourt, Brace and Howe, 1920. p. 123.
THE CATHEDRAL FOLK
    Eekman, Thomas A. "The Genesis of Leskov's SOBORJANE."
    CalSS 2:121-140. 1963.

    Lavrin, Janko. Russian Writers: Their Lives and Literature.
    New York: D. Van Nostrand Company, Inc., 1954. pp. 208-
    209.

    Reeve, F. D. The Russian Novel. New York: McGraw-Hill
    Book Company, 1966. pp. 205-235.
AN ENIGMATIC MAN
    McLean, Hugh. "Leskov and His Enigmatic Man." HSS 4:
    203-224. 1957.
LADY MACBETH OF MTSENSK
    Pritchett, V. S. "Leskov and Russian Life." NewS 60:126.
    July 23, 1960.
NIGHT OWLS
    McLean, Hugh. "Leskov and Ioann of Kronstadt: On the
    Origins of POLUNOSCNIKI." ASEER 12:97-108. February
    1953.

    McLean, Hugh. "On the Style of a Leskovian 'Skaz.' " HSS
    2:297-322. 1954.
NO WAY OUT
    Moser, Charles A. Antinihilism in the Russian Novel of the
    1860's. The Hague: Mouton and Company, 1964. pp. 102-104.
NOWHERE
    Olgin, Moissaye J. A Guide to Russian Literature (1820-
    1917). New York: Harcourt, Brace and Howe, 1920. p. 123.
THE SEALED ANGEL
    Lavrin, Janko. Russian Writers: Their Lives and Literature.
    New York: D. Van Nostrand Company, Inc., 1954. pp. 209-
    210.
ZAKHUDALYI ROD
    McLean, Hugh. "A Contribution to the Revival of Leskov."
    ASEER 22:748-750. December 1963.

Libedinskii, Yuri
    THE BIRTH OF A HERO
        Brown, Edward J. The Proletarian Episode in Russian Lit-
        erature 1928-1932. New York: Columbia University Press,
        1953. pp. 123-129.

        Cross, S. H. "Notes on Soviet Literary Criticism." SEER
        20:318. 1941.

        Eng-Liedmeier, A. M. Van der. Soviet Literary Characters.
        'S Gravenhage: Mouton and Company, 1959. pp. 29-30; 42-
        43.

THE WEEK
Eng-Liedmeier, A. M. Van der. Soviet Literary Characters. 'S Gravenhage: Mouton and Company, 1959. pp. 44-45; 54-55.

Lidin, V.
SHIPS ARE SAILING
Eng-Liedmeier, A. M. Van der. Soviet Literary Characters. 'S Gravenhage: Mouton and Company, 1959. pp. 31-32.

Loginov, Victor
OTHERWISE IT WOULDN'T BE LOVE
Anninsky, Lev. "Men and Morals. " SovR 3:35-41. May 1962.

Lukin, Nikolai
THE FATE OF THE DISCOVERY
Yershov, Peter. Science Fiction and Utopian Fantasy in Soviet Literature. New York: Research Program on the USSR, Mimeographed Series No. 62, 1954. pp. 52-53.

Lvov, S.
SAVE OUR SOULS
Bode, Barbara. "1960: The Literary Harvest. " Survey 36: 38. April - June 1961.

Lyashko, N.
THE BLAST FURNACE
Zavalishin, Vyacheslav. Early Soviet Writers. New York: Frederick A. Praeger, 1958. p. 176.
THE BREATH OF A DOVE
Zavalishin, Vyacheslav. Early Soviet Writers. New York: Frederick A. Praeger, 1958. pp. 175-176.

Macha, Karel H.
GYPSIES
Souckova, Milada. The Czech Romantics. The Hague: Mouton and Company, 1958. pp. 64-68.

Wellek, Rene. Essays on Czech Literature. The Hague: Mouton and Company, 1963. pp. 158-167.
THE HANGMAN
Souckova, Milada. The Czech Romantics. The Hague: Mouton and Company, 1958. pp. 50-52.
PICTURES FROM MY LIFE
Souckova, Milada. The Czech Romantics. The Hague: Mouton and Company, 1958. pp. 54-63.

Malyskin, A.
PEOPLE FROM THE BACKWOODS
Eng-Liedmeier, A. M. Van der. Soviet Literary Characters. 'S Gravenhage: Mouton and Company, 1959. pp. 123-124.

Mamin-Sibiryak, D. N.
THREE ENDS
Olgin, Moissaye J. A Guide to Russian Literature (1820-
1917). New York: Harcourt, Brace and Howe, 1920. p. 139.

Marai, S.
DIVORCE IN BUDA
Remenyi, Joseph. Hungarian Writers and Literature. New
Brunswick: Rutgers University Press, 1964. p. 412.
GUEST PERFORMANCE IN BOLZANO
Remenyi, Joseph. Hungarian Writers and Literature. New
Brunswick: Rutgers University Press, 1964. pp. 410-413.

Medek, Rudolf
ANABASIS
Hostovsky, Egon. "The Czech Novel Between the Two World
Wars. " SEER 21:79-80. November 1943.
THE FIERY DRAGON
Hostovsky, Egon. "The Czech Novel Between the Two World
Wars." SEER 21:79-80. November 1943.
GREAT DAYS
Hostovsky, Egon. "The Czech Novel Between the Two World
Wars. " SEER 21:79-80. November 1943.
THE ISLAND IN THE STORM
Hostovsky, Egon. "The Czech Novel Between the Two World
Wars. " SEER 21:79-80. November 1943.
THE MIGHTY DREAM
Hostovsky, Egon. "The Czech Novel Between the Two World
Wars. " SEER 21:79-80. November 1943.

Merezhkovsky, K. D.
JULIAN THE APOSTATE
Olgin, Moissaye J. A Guide to Russian Literature (1820-
1917). New York: Harcourt, Brace and Howe, 1920. pp. 182-
184.

Padelford, Frederick Morgan. "Merejkowski, a Prophet of
the New Russia. " SR 26:392-395. October 1918.
THE ROMANCE OF LEONARDO DA VINCI
Olgin, Moissaye J. A Guide to Russian Literature (1820-
1917). New York: Harcourt, Brace and Howe, 1920. pp. 182-
184.

Padelford, Frederick Morgan. "Merejkowski, a Prophet of
the New Russia. " SR 26:395-400. October 1918.

Mikszath, Kalman
ST. PETER'S UMBRELLA
Remenyi, Joseph. "Kalman Mikszath. " ASEER 8:221-222.
October 1949.
THE SIEGE OF BESZTERCE
Remenyi, Joseph. Hungarian Writers and Literature. New
Brunswick: Rutgers University Press, 1964. pp. 161-162.

Mora, Ferenc
GOLDEN COFFIN
Remenyi, Joseph. "Ferenc Mora, Hungarian Regionalist
(1879-1934)." SAQ 55:354-355. July 1956.

Remenyi, Joseph. Hungarian Writers and Literature. New
Brunswick: Rutgers University Press, 1964. pp. 248-249.
SONG OF THE WHEATFIELDS
Remenyi, Joseph. "Ferenc Mora, Hungarian Regionalist
(1879-1934)." SAQ 55:352-354. July 1956.

Remenyi, Joseph. Hungarian Writers and Literature. New
Brunswick: Rutgers University Press, 1964. pp. 247-248.

Moricz, Zsigmond
BE GOOD TILL YOU DIE
Remenyi, Joseph. Hungarian Writers and Literature. New
Brunswick: Rutgers University Press, 1964. pp. 334-335.
GOLDEN MUD
Remenyi, Joseph. Hungarian Writers and Literature. New
Brunswick: Rutgers University Press, 1964. pp. 331-333.

Remenyi, Joseph. "Zsigmond Moricz, Hungarian Realist."
ASEER 4:171-172. August 1945.
TRANSYLVANIA
Remenyi, Joseph. Hungarian Writers and Literature. New
Brunswick: Rutgers University Press, 1964. pp. 335-336.

Remenyi, Joseph. "Zsigmond Moricz, Hungarian Realist."
ASEER 4:175-176. August 1945.

Mucha, Jiri
THE PROBLEMS OF LIEUTENANT KNAP
Souckova, Milada. A Literature in Crisis: Czech Literature
1938-1950. New York: Mid-European Studies Center, 1954.
pp. 97-99.

Mujzhel, V.
A YEAR
Olgin, Moissaye J. A Guide to Russian Literature (1820-
1917). New York: Harcourt, Brace and Howe, 1920. pp. 289-
290.

Nabokov, Vladimir (See also V. Sirin)
BEND SINISTER
Stegner, Page. Escape into Aesthetics: The Art of Vladimir
Nabokov. New York: The Dial Press, 1966. pp. 76-89.
THE GIFT
Karlinsky, Simon. "Vladimir Nabokov's Novel DAR as a
Work of Literary Criticism: A Structural Analysis." SEEJ
n. s. 7:284-289. Fall 1963.
LOLITA
Amis, Kingsley. "She Was a Child and I Was a Child." Spec

203:635-636. November 6, 1959.

Green, Martin. "The Morality of LOLITA. " KR 28:352-377.
June 1966.

Ivask, George. "The World of Vladimir Nabokov. " RusR 20:
137-138. April 1961.

Jones, David L. " 'Dolores Disparue. ' " Symposium 20:
135-140. Summer 1966.

Levin, Bernard. "Why All the Fuss?" Spec 202:32-33. January 9, 1959.

Phillips, Elizabeth. "The Hocus-Pocus of LOLITA. " L&P
10:97-101. Summer 1960.

Pritchett, V. S. "LOLITA. " NewS 57:38. January 10, 1959.

Rubinstein, E. "Approaching LOLITA. " MinnR 6:361-367.
No. 4, 1966.

Scott, W. J. "The Lolita Case. " Landfall 15:134-138. June
1961.

Slonim, Marc. "DOCTOR ZHIVAGO and LOLITA. " ILA 2:
221-225. 1959.

Stegner, Page. Escape into Aesthetics: The Art of Vladimir
Nabokov. New York: The Dial Press, 1966. pp. 102-115.

Trilling, Lionel. "The Last Lover. " Encounter 11:9-19.
October 1958.

Williams, Carol T. " 'Web of Sense': PALE FIRE in the
Nabokov Canon. " Crit 6:31-33. Winter 1963.
PALE FIRE
     Kermode, Frank. "Zemblances. " NewS 64:671-672. Novem-
ber 9, 1962.

Stegner, Page. Escape into Aesthetics: The Art of Vladimir
Nabokov. New York: The Dial Press, 1966. pp. 116-132.

Williams, Carol T. " 'Web of Sense': PALE FIRE in the
Nabokov Canon. " Crit 6:33-44. Winter 1963.
PNIN
     Stegner, Page. Escape into Aesthetics: The Art of Vladimir
Nabokov. New York: The Dial Press, 1966. pp. 90-101.
THE REAL LIFE OF SEBASTIAN KNIGHT
     Stegner, Page. Escape into Aesthetics: The Art of Vladimir
Nabokov. New York: The Dial Press, 1966. pp. 63-75.

Stegner, S. Page. "The Immortality of Art: Vladimir Nabo-

kov's THE REAL LIFE OF SEBASTIAN KNIGHT. " SoR n. s.
2:286-296. April 1966.

Nekrasov, Viktor
  HOME TOWN
      Gibian, George. Interval of Freedom: Soviet Literature Dur-
      ing the Thaw 1954-1957. Minneapolis: University of Minne-
      sota Press, 1960. pp. 82-86.

      Lindsay, Richard. "Writers and Their Public. " Survey 37:
      57-58. July - September 1961.
  KIRA GEORGIEVNA
      Carmel, Herman. "Viktor Nekrasov: Pioneer of Renais-
      sance in Post-Stalin Russian Prose. " BA 40:383. Autumn
      1966.

Nemcova, B.
  BABICKA
      Souckova, Milada. The Czech Romantics. The Hague: Mou-
      ton and Company, 1958. pp. 150-160.
  KARLA
      Souckova, Milada. The Czech Romantics. The Hague: Mou-
      ton and Company, 1958. pp. 142-143.

Nemes, Gyorgy
  ONE BRIEF MOMENT
      Farago, Vilmos. "A Novel About the Psychology of a Revo-
      lution. " NHQ 7:76-77. Autumn 1966.

Nemtsov, Vladimir
  THE GOLDEN BOTTOM
      Yershov, Peter. Science Fiction and Utopian Fantasy in
      Soviet Literature. New York: Research Program on the
      USSR, Mimeographed Series No. 62, 1954. pp. 53-55.

Neuls, Jan
  THE STRUGGLE FOR COAL
      Souckova, Milada. A Literature in Crisis: Czech Literature
      1938-1950. New York: Mid-European Studies Center, 1954.
      pp. 128-131.

Niholic-Micki, D.
  JUDAS DID NOT BETRAY GOD
      Goy, E. D. "The Serbian and Croatian Novel Since 1948. "
      SEER 40:66-67. December 1961.

Nikolaeva, Galina
  A BATTLE ON THE WAY
      Gibian, George. "The Factory Manager in Soviet Fiction. "
      PoC 8:45-50. March - April 1959.

      Gibian, George. Interval of Freedom: Soviet Literature Dur-
      ing the Thaw 1954-1957. Minneapolis: University of Minne-

426 The Russian and East European Novel

sota Press, 1960. pp. 91-100.

Olesha, Yuri
ENVY
Alexandrova, Vera. " 'In every herd there is some restive
steer': An Enduring Theme. " Survey 24:75-76. April - June
1958.

Harkins, William E. "The Theme of Sterility in Olesha's
ENVY. " SlavR 25:443-457. September 1966.

Mathewson, Rufus W. , Jr. The Positive Hero in Russian
Literature. New York: Columbia University Press, 1958. pp.
265-267.

Reeve, F. D. The Russian Novel. New York: McGraw-Hill
Book Company, 1966. pp. 346-359.

Struve, Gleb. Soviet Russian Literature 1917-1950. Norman:
University of Oklahoma Press, 1951. pp. 98-105.

Struve, Gleb. "Yury Olesha. " SEER 13:644-648. April 1935.
THREE FAT MEN
Struve, Gleb. Soviet Russian Literature 1917-1950. Norman:
University of Oklahoma Press, 1951. pp. 105-106.

Orzeszkowa, Eliza
BENE NATI
Kridl, Manfred. A Survey of Polish Literature and Culture.
New York: Columbia University Press, 1956. pp. 376-377.
THE BOOR
Welsh, David J. "Two Talkative Authors: Orzeszkowa and
George Eliot. " PolR 10:57-58. Winter 1945.
MEIR EZOFOWICZ
Kridl, Manfred. A Survey of Polish Literature and Culture.
New York: Columbia University Press, 1956. pp. 377-378.
ON THE BANKS OF THE NIEMAN
Kridl, Manfred. A Survey of Polish Literature and Culture.
New York: Columbia University Press, 1956. pp. 378-379.

Welsh, David J. "Two Talkative Authors: Orzeszkowa and
George Eliot. " PolR 10:58-60. Winter 1945.

Ostrovsky, Alexander
STORM
Mathewson, Rufus W. , Jr. The Positive Hero in Russian
Literature. New York: Columbia University Press, 1958.
pp. 72-75.

Spector, Ivar. The Golden Age of Russian Literature. Caldwell: The Caxton Printers, Ltd. , 1945. pp. 195-196.

Ostrovskij, N.
   THAT'S HOW STEEL WAS TEMPERED
      Eng-Liedmeier, A. M. Van der. Soviet Literary Characters.
      'S Gravenhage: Mouton and Company, 1959. pp. 113-116.

Ottlik, Geza
   SCHOOL AT THE BORDER
      Juhasz, William. "The Writer and Society." EE 12:14. Jan-
      uary 1963.

Ovechkin, Valentin
   GREETINGS FROM THE FRONT
      Alexandrova, Vera. " 'In every herd there is some restive
      steer': An Enduring Theme." Survey 24:77. April - June
      1958.

      Alexandrova, Vera. "Postwar Literary Patterns of Soviet
      Russia." RusR 8:222. July 1949.

Panferov, F. I.
   BRUSKI
      Eng-Liedmeier, A. M. Van der. Soviet Literary Characters.
      'S Gravenhage: Mouton and Company, 1959. pp. 90-91; 118-
      120.
   IN THE NAME OF THE YOUNG
      Bode, Barbara. "1960: The Literary Harvest." Survey 36:
      42. April - June 1961.

Panova, Vera
   THE BRIGHT SHORE
      Eng-Liedmeier, A. M. Van der. Soviet Literary Characters.
      'S Gravenhage: Mouton and Company, 1959. pp. 140; 149-
      150.
   KRUZHILIKHA
      Alexandrova, Vera. "Postwar Literary Patterns of Soviet
      Russia." RusR 8:226-228. July 1949.

      Eng-Liedmeier, A. M. Van der. Soviet Literary Characters.
      'S Gravenhage: Mouton and Company, 1959. pp. 151-152.

      Gibian, George. Interval of Freedom: Soviet Literature Dur-
      ing the Thaw 1954-1957. Minneapolis: University of Minne-
      sota Press, 1960. pp. 101-104.
   SEASONS OF THE YEAR
      E. H. "Towards a Soviet Bourgeoisie? Implications of THE
      THAW and THE SEASONS." World Today 11:300-308. July
      1955.

      Laber, Jeri. "The Soviet Writer's Search for New Values."
      PoC 5:16-19. January - February 1956.

      Vickery, Walter N. The Cult of Optimism: Political and
      Ideological Problems of Recent Soviet Literature. Blooming-

ton: Indiana University Press, 1963. (Indiana University Humanities Series, No. 52.) pp. 43-44.

Pasternak, Boris
    DOCTOR ZHIVAGO
        Avegno, Hamilton P. "Some Notes on Pasternak's DR. ZHIVAGO and Bernanos' JOY. " XUS 1:26-33. April 1961.

        Baird, Sister Mary Julian. "Pasternak's Vision of the Fair Rowan Tree. " CathW 189:427-431. September 1959.

        Baird, Sister M. Julian. "Pasternak's Zhivago--Hamlet--Christ. " Renascence 14:179-184. Summer 1962.

        Bayley, John and Donald Davie. "Argument: I. Dr. Zhivago's Poems. " EIC 16:212-219. April 1966.

        Bowman, Herbert E. "Postscript on Pasternak. " Survey 36: 106-110. April - June 1961.

        Chiaromonte, Nicola. "Pasternak's Message. " PR 25:127-134. Winter 1958.

        Conquest, Robert. The Pasternak Affair: Courage of Genius. Philadelphia: J. B. Lippincott Company, 1962. 192 pp.

        Davie, Donald. The Poems of Doctor Zhivago. New York: Barnes and Noble, 1965. 204 pp.

        Deutsch, Babette. " 'Talent for Life' in a New Russian Novel. " Harper's 217:72-76. September 1958.

        Deutscher, Isaac. "Pasternak and the Calendar of the Revolution. " PR 26:248-265. Spring 1959.

        Dyck, J. W. "DOKTOR ZIVAGO: A Quest for Self-Realization. " SEEJ n. s. 6:117-123. Summer 1962.

        Erlick, Victor. "A Testimony and a Challenge--Pasternak's DOCTOR ZHIVAGO. " PoC 7:46-49. November - December 1958.

        Fitch, Robert E. "The Sickness of an Affluent Society. " Religion in Life 29:609-611. Autumn 1960.

        Folejewski, Zbigniew. "Notes on the Problem of Individual Versus Collective in Russian and Polish Literature, 1954-57. " ISS 3:32-33. 1963.

        Frank, Victor S. "A Russian Hamlet: Boris Pasternak's Novel. " DubR 232:212-220. Autumn 1958.

        Gerschenkron, Alexander. "Notes on DOCTOR ZHIVAGO. "

MP 58:194-200. February 1961.

Gibian, George. Interval of Freedom: Soviet Literature During the Thaw 1954-1957. Minneapolis: University of Minnesota Press, 1960. pp. 145-158.

Gifford, Henry. "DR. ZHIVAGO: The Last Russian Classic." EIC 9:159-170. April 1959.

Gifford, Henry. The Novel in Russia: From Pushkin to Pasternak. New York: Harper and Row, 1964. pp. 183-192.

Grigorieff, Dmitry Felix. "Pasternak and Dostoevskij." SEEJ n. s. 3:335-341. Winter 1959.

Hampshire, Stuart. "DOCTOR ZHIVAGO." Encounter 11: 3-5. November 1958.

Harari, Manya. "On Translating ZHIVAGO." Encounter 12: 51-53. May 1959.

Harari, Manya. "Pasternak." TC 164:525-526. December 1958.

Hayward, Max. "DOCTOR ZHIVAGO and the Soviet Intelligentsia." Survey 24:65-69. April - June 1958.

Hayward, Max. "Pasternak's DR. ZHIVAGO." Encounter 10:38-48. May 1958.

Howe, Irving. "Freedom and the Ashcan of History." PR 26:266-275. Spring 1959.

Iswolsky, Helene. "The Voice of Boris Pasternak." Commonweal 69:168-170. November 14, 1958.

Ivask, George. "A Note on the Real Zhivagos." RusR 25: 405-408. October 1966.

Jackson, Robert L. "DOKTOR ZIVAGO and the Living Tradition." SEEJ n. s. 4:103-118. Summer 1960.

Jackson, Robert L. "The Symbol of the Wild Duck in DR. ZHIVAGO." CL 15:39-45. Winter 1963.

Lamont, Rosette C. " 'As a Gift...' Zhivago, the Poet." PMLA 75:621-633. December 1960.

Lehrman, Edgar H. "A Minority Opinion on DOCTOR ZHIVAGO." EUQ 16:77-84. Summer 1960.

Livingstone, Angela. "Pasternak's Early Prose." AUMLA 22:249-252. November 1964.

Loose, Gerhard. "Pasternak's DOCTOR ZHIVAGO." ColQ 7:263-270. Winter 1959.

Macintyre, Alasdair. "Dr. Marx and Dr. Zhivago." Listener 61:61-62. January 8, 1959.

Manning, Clarence A. "Pasternak and Khvylovy." UQ 14: 348-352. December 1958.

Markov, Vladimir. "Notes on Pasternak's DOCTOR ZHI-VAGO." RusR 18:14-22. January 1959.

Matlaw, Ralph E. "A Visit with Pasternak." Nation 189: 134-135. September 12, 1959.

Merton, Thomas. "The Pasternak Affair in Perspective." Thought 34:485-517. Winter 1959-1960.

Monas, Sidney. "A Miracle is a Miracle." HudR 11:612-619. Winter 1958-1959.

Mottley, Robert C., Jr. "Boris Pasternak: The Late Phase." Shenandoah 13:45-47. Autumn 1961.

Nilsson, Nils Ake. "Pasternak: 'We Are the Guests of Existence.' " Reporter 19:34-35. November 27, 1958.

"Pasternak." Survey 27:2-3. January - March 1959.

Payne, Robert. "Boris Pasternak." LitR 2:328-333. Spring 1959.

Payne, Robert. The Three Worlds of Boris Pasternak. New York: Coward-McCann, Inc., 1961. pp. 168-186.

Poggioli, Renato. "Boris Pasternak." PR 25:548-554. Fall 1958.

Powers, Richard Howard. "Ideology and DOCTOR ZHIVAGO." AR 19:224-236. Summer 1959.

Pritchett, V. S. "In the Great Tradition." NewS 56:354-355. September 13, 1958.

Reeve, F. D. "DOCTOR ZHIVAGO: From Prose to Verse." KR 22:123-136. Winter 1960.

Reeve, F. D. The Russian Novel. New York: McGraw-Hill Book Company, 1966. pp. 360-378.

Rowland, Mary and Paul. "DOCTOR ZHIVAGO: A Russian Apocalypse." Religion in Life 30:118-130. Winter 1960-1961.

Rowland, Mary and Paul. "Larisa Feodorovna: From Another World. " KR 22:493-501. Summer 1960.

Rowland, Mary and Paul. "The Mission of Yury and Evgraf Zhivago. " TSLL 5:199-218. Summer 1963.

Ruge, Gerd. "A Visit to Pasternak. " Encounter 10:23-24. March 1958.

Sajkovic, Miriam Taylor. "Notes on Boris Pasternak's DOKTOR ZIVAGO." SEEJ n. s. 4:319-328. Winter 1960.

Slonim, Marc. "DOCTOR ZHIVAGO and LOLITA. " ILA 2: 213-221. 1959.

Stern, Richard D. "DOCTOR ZHIVAGO as a Novel. " KR 21: 154-160. Winter 1959.

Steussy, R. E. "The Myth Behind DR. ZHIVAGO. " RusR 18:184-198. July 1959.

Struve, Gleb. " Sense and Nonsense in DOCTOR ZHIVAGO." Studies in Russian and Polish Literature. (ed.) Zhigniew Folejewski. 'S Gravenhage: Mouton and Company, 1962. pp. 229-250.

Toynbee, Philip. "Book Reviews. " TC 164:404-406. October 1958.

Urbanski, Edmund Stephen. "Revolutionary Novels of Gironella and Pasternak. " Hispania 43:191-197. May 1960.

Vickery, Walter. "Symbolism Aside: DOKTOR ZIVAGO. " SEEJ n. s. 3:343-347. Winter 1959.

Wagner, Geoffrey. "Notes on DOCTOR ZHIVAGO. " CJF 17: 157-161. Spring 1959.

Wall, Bernard. "A Great New Russian Novel. " Listener 60:387-388. September 11, 1958.

Wasiolek, Edward. "Courage but not Excellence. " ChiR 13: 77-83. Winter- Spring 1959.

Wilson, Edmund. "Legend and Symbol in DOCTOR ZHIVAGO." Nation 188:363-373. April 25, 1959. (Reprinted in Encounter 12:5-16. June 1959.)

"Zhivago's Defence. " TLS 3289:186. March 11, 1965.

Pavlenko, P.
    HAPPINESS
        Eng-Liedmeier, A. M. Van der. Soviet Literary Characters.

'S Gravenhage: Mouton and Company, 1959. pp. 137-139.
IN THE EAST
    Struve, Gleb. "Anti-Westernism in Recent Soviet Literature."
    YR 39:215-221. Winter 1950.

    Struve, Gleb. "Some Recent Novels. " SEER 16:691-693.
    April 1938.

Pilnyak, Boris
  MACHINES AND WOLVES
    Zavalishin, Vyacheslav. Early Soviet Writers. New York:
    Frederick A. Praeger, 1958. pp. 198-199.
  MAHOGANY
    Eng-Liedmeier, A. M. Van der. Soviet Literary Characters.
    'S Gravenhage: Mouton and Company, 1959. pp. 47-49.

    Struve, Gleb. Soviet Russian Literature 1917-1950. Norman:
    University of Oklahoma Press, 1951. pp. 210-211.

    Wilson, Peter. "Boris Pilnyak. " Survey 46:139-141. Jan-
    uary 1963.
  THE NAKED YEAR
    Wilson, Peter. "Boris Pilnyak. " Survey 46:134-136. Jan-
    uary 1963.

    Zavalishin, Vyacheslav. Early Soviet Writers. New York:
    Frederick A. Praeger, 1958. pp. 196-198.
  THE RIPENING OF THE FRUIT
    Zavalishin, Vyacheslav. Early Soviet Writers. New York:
    Frederick A. Praeger, 1958. pp. 201-202.
  THE VOLGA FLOWS INTO THE CASPIAN SEA
    Eng-Liedmeier, A. M. Van der. Soviet Literary Characters.
    'S Gravenhage: Mouton and Company, 1959. pp. 85-87; 91-
    92.

    Struve, Gleb. Soviet Russian Literature 1917-1950. Norman:
    University of Oklahoma Press, 1951. pp. 212-213.

Pogorel'skij
  THE DOUBLE
    Passage, Charles E. "Pogorel'skij, the First Russian Hoff-
    mannist. " ASEER 15:253-263. April 1956.
  THE POPPY SEED CAKE WOMAN
    Passage, Charles E. "Pogorel'skij, the First Russian Hoff-
    mannist. " ASEER 15:247-252. April 1956.

Prus, Boleslav
  THE DOLL
    Kridl, Manfred. A Survey of Polish Literature and Culture.
    New York: Columbia University Press, 1956. pp. 365-368.

    Krzyzanowski, J. "Boleslav Prus. " SEER 9:701-704. March
    1931.

Pietrkiewicz, Jerzy. "Justified Failure in the Novels of
Boleslaw Prus. " SEER 39:99-103. December 1960.

Welsh, David J. " 'Realism' in Prus' Novel LALKA (THE
DOLL). " PolR 8:33-38. Autumn 1963.
THE EMANCIPATIONISTS
    Kridl, Manfred. A Survey of Polish Literature and Culture.
New York: Columbia University Press, 1956. pp. 368-370.

Pietrkiewicz, Jerzy. "Justified Failure in the Novels of
Boleslaw Prus. " SEER 39:103-104. December 1960.
THE OUTPOST
    Kridl, Manfred. A Survey of Polish Literature and Culture.
New York: Columbia University Press, 1956. pp. 364-365.

Krzyzanowski, J. "Boleslav Prus. " SEER 9:699-701. March
1931.

Pietrkiewicz, Jerzy. "Justified Failure in the Novels of
Boleslaw Prus. " SEER 39:97-98. December 1960.
PHARAOH
    Kridl, Manfred. A Survey of Polish Literature and Culture.
New York: Columbia University Press, 1956. pp. 370-373.

Krzyzanowski, J. "Boleslav Prus. " SEER 9:705-706. March
1931.

Pietrkiewicz, Jerzy. "Justified Failure in the Novels of
Boleslaw Prus. " SEER 39:104-106. December 1960.

Pushkin, Alexander
    THE CAPTAIN'S DAUGHTER
        Greene, Militsa. "Pushkin and Sir Walter Scott. " FMLS 1:
212-215. July 1965.

        Lavrin, Janko. Pushkin and Russian Literature. New York:
Macmillan Company, 1948. pp. 190-193.

        Stenbock-Fermor, Elisabeth. "Some Neglected Features of
the Epigraphs in THE CAPTAIN'S DAUGHTER and Other
Stories of Puskin. " IJSLP 8:110-119. 1964.
    THE QUEEN OF SPADES
        Gregg, Richard A. "Balzac and Women in THE QUEEN OF
SPADES. " SEEJ 10:279-281. Fall 1966.

        Stenbock-Fermor, Elisabeth. "Some Neglected Features of
the Epigraphs in THE CAPTAIN'S DAUGHTER and Other
Stories of Puskin. " IJSLP 8:119-123. 1964.

Putinas, V.
    IN THE SHADOW OF ALTARS
        Sictynas, Andrius. "The Condition of a Free Prisoner:
Poetry and Prose of Vincas Mykolaitis-Putinas. " Lituanus

11:56-59. Spring 1965.
THE REBELS
        Sietynas, Andrius. "The Condition of a Free Prisoner: Poetry
        and Prose of Vincas Mykolaitis-Putinas. " Lituanus 11:61-
        62. Spring 1965.

Reymont, Ladislas
    THE DREAMER
        Boyd, Ernest. "Wladyslaw Reymont. " Saturday Review of
        Literature 1:318. November 29, 1924.
    THE PEASANTS
        Almedingen, Edith M. "Ladislas Reymont--Peasant and
        Writer. " ER 42:121-122. January 1926.

        Borowy, Waclaw. "Reymont. " SEER 16:445-448. January
        1938.

        Boyd, Ernest. Studies from Ten Literatures. New York:
        Charles Scribner's Sons, 1925. pp. 286-287.

        Boyd, Ernest. "Wladyslaw Reymont. " Saturday Review of
        Literature 1:318. November 29, 1924.

        Dyboski, R. "Zeromski and Reymont. " SEER 4:558-559.
        March 1926.

        Stender-Petersen, Ad. "Reymont, Winner of the Nobel
        Prize. " Living Age 324:168-169. January 17, 1925.

        Zielinski, T. "The Peasant in Polish Literature (II). " SEER
        2:85-100. June 1923.
    THE PROMISED LAND
        Boyd, Ernest. "Wladyslaw Reymont. " Saturday Review of
        Literature 1:318. November 29, 1924.

Romanov, P.
    THREE PAIRS OF SILK STOCKINGS
        Kain, Richard M. "The Plight of the Intelligentsia in the
        Soviet Novel. " RusR 2:73-74. Autumn 1942.

Ropshin, V.
    WHAT NEVER HAPPENED
        Olgin, Moissaye J. A Guide to Russian Literature (1820-
        1917). New York: Harcourt, Brace and Howe, 1920. pp. 278-
        280.

Rzhrevskaya, Elena
    MANY YEARS LATER
        Alexandrova, Vera. "Soviet Literature in 1958. " RusR 18:
        128-129. April 1959.

Saltykov, M. E.
    THE GOLOVLYOV FAMILY

Gifford, Henry. The Novel in Russia: From Pushkin to Pasternak. New York: Harper and Row, 1964. pp. 95-105.

Lavrin, Janko. An Introduction to the Russian Novel. New York: McGraw-Hill, 1947. pp. 88-92.

Olgin, Moissaye J. A Guide to Russian Literature (1820-1917). New York: Harcourt, Brace and Howe, 1920. pp. 127-128.

MONREPOS THE REFUGE

Olgin, Moissaye J. A Guide to Russian Literature (1820-1917). New York: Harcourt, Brace and Howe, 1920. p. 128.

Savel'ev, A.

SYN KREST'JANSKIJ

Twarog, Leon I. "Ivan Bolotnikov in Soviet Historical Fiction." SEEJ n. s. 3:236-239. Fall 1959.

Semenov, S.

NATAL'JA TARPOVA

Eng-Liedmeier, A. M. Van der. Soviet Literary Characters. 'S Gravenhage: Mouton and Company, 1959. pp. 40-42.

Senchenko, Ivan

HIS GENERATION

Romanenchuk, Bohdan. "Ten Years of Soviet Literature in Ukraine." UQ 6:251. Summer 1950.

Serge, V.

THE CASE OF COMRADE TULAYEV

Howe, Irving. Politics and the Novel. New York: Meridan Books, 1957. pp. 232-234.

Roland, Albert. "Christian Implications in Anti-Stalinist Novels." Religion in Life 22:402-404. Summer 1953.

Sergeyev-Tzensky, O. G.

THE OBLIQUE HELENA

Olgin, Moissaye J. A Guide to Russian Literature (1820-1917). New York: Harcourt, Brace and Howe, 1920. pp. 263-264.

THE SADNESS OF THE FIELDS

Olgin, Moissaye J. A Guide to Russian Literature (1820-1917). New York: Harcourt, Brace and Howe, 1920. pp. 262-263.

Sholokhov, M.

THE SILENT DON

Eng-Liedmeier, A. M. Van der. Soviet Literary Characters. 'S Gravenhage: Mouton and Company, 1959. pp. 30-31; 63-65.

Friedberg, Maurice. "Soviet Literature and Retroactive

Truth. " PoC 3:34-35. January - February 1954.

Gasiorowska, Xenia. "Akin'ia Astakhova of THE QUIET
DON. " Studies in Russian and Polish Literature. (ed.)
Zhigniew Folejewski. s' Gravenhage: Mouton and Company,
1962. pp. 217-228.

Kaun, Alexander. "A Note on Mikhail Sholokhov. " BA 15:
405-407. Autumn 1941.

Mathewson, Rufus W. , Jr. The Positive Hero in Russian
Literature. New York: Columbia University Press, 1958.
pp. 227-228; 255-256; 296-299.

Muchnic, Helen. "Sholokhov and Tolstoy. " RusR 16:25-34.
April 1957.

Schneider, Isidor. "The Quiet Don Flows Home. " Soviet
Russia Today 9:10-11; 32. April 1941.

Simmons, Ernest J. Russian Fiction and Soviet Ideology.
New York: Columbia University Press, 1958. pp. 170-220.

Simmons, Ernest J. Through the Glass of Soviet Literature.
New York: Columbia University Press, 1953. pp. 117-119.

Spector, Ivar. The Golden Age of Russian Literature. Caldwell: The Caxton Printers, Ltd. , 1945. pp. 257-260.

Stewart, David H. "Epic Design and Meaning in Michail
Sholokhov's SILENT DON. " QQ 67:415-430. Autumn 1960.

Stewart, David H. "THE SILENT DON in English. " ASEER
15:265-275. April 1956.

Stewart, David H. "The Textual Evolution of THE SILENT
DON. " ASEER 18:226-237. April 1959.
VIRGIN SOIL UPTURNED
Ermolaev, Herman. "Sholokhov Thirty Years After VIRGIN
SOIL UPTURNED. " Survey 36:20-26. April - June 1961.

Mathewson, Rufus W. , Jr. The Positive Hero in Russian
Literature. New York: Columbia University Press, 1958. pp.
282-287.

Simmons, Ernest J. Russian Fiction and Soviet Ideology. New
York: Columbia University Press, 1958. pp. 220-245.

Suhadolc, Joseph. "The Strain Within the Frame of Soloxov's
VIRGIN SOIL UPTURNED. " SEEJ n. s. 6:236-252. Fall 1962.

Shpanov, Nikolai
CONSPIRATORS

Yarmolinsky, Avrahm. Literature Under Communism. Russian and East European Series, Russian and East European Institute, Indiana University. Vol. 20. 1957. pp. 100-104.

INCENDIARIES

Yarmolinsky, Avrahm. Literature Under Communism. Russian and East European Series, Russian and East European Institute, Indiana University. Vol. 20. 1957. pp. 98-100.

Sienkiewicz, H.

CHILDREN OF THE SOIL

Gardner, Monica M. The Patriot Novelist of Poland: Henryk Sienkiewicz. London: Dent and Sons, Ltd., 1926. pp. 187-207.

Lednicki, Waclaw. Bits of Table Talk on Pushkin, Mickiewicz, Goethe, Turgenev, and Sienkiewicz. The Hague: Martinus Nijhoff, 1956. pp. 242-247.

Lednicki, Waclaw. Henryk Sienkiewicz. New York: Polish Institute of Arts and Sciences in America, 1948. Chapter 6.

Lockert, Lacy. "Henryk Sienkiewicz." SR 27:269-272. July 1919.

Phelps, William L. Essays on Modern Novelists. New York: The Macmillan Company, 1940. pp. 128-130.

THE DELUGE (See also TRILOGY)

Gardner, Monica M. The Patriot Novelist of Poland: Henryk Sienkiewicz. London: Dent and Sons, Ltd., 1926. pp. 84-115.

Lockert, Lacy. "Henryk Sienkiewicz." SR 27:263-264. July 1919.

Segel, H. B. "From Albertus to Zagloba: The Soldier-Braggart in Polish Literature." ISS 3:104-110. 1963.

Welsh, D. J. "Sienkiewicz as Narrator." SEER 43:375-382. June 1965.

HANIA

Gardner, Monica M. The Patriot Novelist of Poland: Henryk Sienkiewicz. London: Dent and Sons, Ltd., 1926. pp. 166-170.

THE LITTLE KNIGHT

Gardner, Monica M. The Patriot Novelist of Poland: Henryk Sienkiewicz. London: Dent and Sons, Ltd., 1926. pp. 116-164.

PAN MICHAEL (See also TRILOGY)

Segel, H. B. "From Albertus to Zagloba: The Soldier-Braggart in Polish Literature." ISS 3:104-110. 1963.

QUO VADIS

Coleman, Arthur Prudden and Marion Moore Coleman. Wanderers Twain. Cheshire: Cherry Hill Books, 1964. pp. 79-80.

Gardner, Monica M. The Patriot Novelist of Poland: Henryk
Sienkiewicz. London: Dent and Sons, Ltd., 1926. pp. 208-
236.

Kridl, Manfred. A Survey of Polish Literature and Culture.
New York: Columbia University Press, 1956. p. 385.

Lednicki, Waclaw. Bits of Table Talk on Pushkin, Mickiewicz, Goethe, Turgenev, and Sienkiewicz. The Hague: Martinus Nijhoff, 1956. pp. 249-250.

Lednicki, Waclaw. Henryk Sienkiewicz. New York: Polish
Institute of Arts and Sciences in America, 1948. Chapter 7.

Phelps, William L. Essays on Modern Novelists. New York:
The Macmillan Company, 1940. pp. 130-131.

Welsh, D. J. "Sienkiewicz as a Narrator." SEER 43:382-
383. June 1965.

THE TEUTONIC KNIGHTS
Gardner, Monica M. The Patriot Novelist of Poland: Henryk
Sienkiewicz. London: Dent and Sons, Ltd., 1926. pp. 237-
265.

Kridl, Manfred. A Survey of Polish Literature and Culture.
New York: Columbia University Press, 1956. pp. 385-386.

Lednicki, Waclaw. Bits of Table Talk on Pushkin, Mickiewicz, Goethe, Turgenev, and Sienkiewicz. The Hague: Martinus Nijhoff, 1956. pp. 249-250.

Lednicki, Waclaw. Henryk Sienkiewicz. New York: Polish
Institute of Arts and Sciences in America, 1948. Chapter 7.

TRILOGY
Gardner, Monica M. "Sienkiewicz." SEER 3:525-531. March
1925.

Kridl, Manfred. A Survey of Polish Literature and Culture.
New York: Columbia University Press, 1956. pp. 382-385.

Lednicki, Waclaw. Bits of Table Talk on Pushkin, Mickiewicz, Goethe, Turgenev, and Sienkiewicz. The Hague: Martinus Nijhoff, 1956. pp. 220-222.

Lednicki, Waclaw. Henryk Sienkiewicz. New York: Polish
Institute of Arts and Sciences in America, 1948. pp. 17-22.

WITH FIRE AND SWORD (See also TRILOGY)
Gardner, Monica M. The Patriot Novelist of Poland: Henryk
Sienkiewicz. London: Dent and Sons, Ltd., 1926. pp. 48-83.

Lockert, Lacy. "Henryk Sienkiewicz." SR 27:261-263. July
1919.

Segel, H. B. "From Albertus to Zagloba: The Soldier- Brag-
gart in Polish Literature. " ISS 3:104-110. 1963.

Welsh, D. J. "Sienkiewicz as a Narrator. " SEER 43:375-
382. June 1965.
WITHOUT DOGMA
Gardner, Monica M. The Patriot Novelist of Poland: Henryk
Sienkiewicz. London: Dent and Sons, Ltd., 1926. pp. 170-
187.

Lednicki, Waclaw. Bits of Table Talk on Pushkin, Mickiewicz, Goethe, Turgenev, and Sienkiewicz. The Hague: Martinus Nijhoff, 1956. pp. 242-248.

Lednicki, Waclaw. Henryk Sienkiewicz. New York: Polish
Institute of Arts and Sciences in America, 1948. Chapter 6.

Lockert, Lacy. "Henryk Sienkiewicz. " SR 27:267-269. July
1919.

Phelps, William L. Essays on Modern Novelists. New York:
The Macmillan Company, 1940. pp. 125-128.

Sieroszewski, Waclaw
THE DANCER COREENNE
Teslar, Joseph Andrew. "Waclaw Sieroszewski (1860-1960):
Some Reminiscences on the Literary Career of a Political
Convict. " PolR 6:17-18. Summer 1961.
THE FLIGHT
Teslar, Joseph Andrew. "Waclaw Sieroszewski (1860-1960):
Some Reminiscences on the Literary Career of a Political
Convict. " PolR 6:17. Summer 1961.

Simonov, K.
THE LIVING AND THE DEAD
Lochtin, S. "The War in the Soviet Novel from Heroic to
Prosaic. " Survey 33:65-67. July - September 1960.

Sirin, V. (V. Nabokov)
KING, QUEEN, KNAVE
Struve, Gleb. "Vladimir Sirin. " SEER 12:438-439. January
1934.
LUZHIN'S DEFENCE
Struve, Gleb. "Vladimir Sirin. " SEER 12:441-442. January
1934.
MASHENKA
Struve, Gleb. "Vladimir Sirin. " SEER 12:436-438. January
1934.

Sivachov, Mikhail
YELLOW DEVIL
Zavalishin, Vyacheslav. Early Soviet Writers. New York:
Frederick A. Praeger, 1958. p. 173.

Slonimskij, Mikhail
    FOMA KLESNEV
        Eng-Liedmeier, A. M. Van der. Soviet Literary Characters.
        s' Gravenhage: Mouton and Company, 1959. pp. 59-61.
    THE LAVROVS
        Eng-Liedmeier, A. M. Van der. Soviet Literary Characters.
        s' Gravenhage: Mouton and Company, 1959. pp. 59-60.

        Struve, Gleb. Soviet Russian Literature 1917-1950. Norman:
        University of Oklahoma Press, 1951. pp. 113-114.

Sologub, Fedor
    THE CREATED LEGEND
        Field, Andrew. "THE CREATED LEGEND: Sologub's Sym-
        bolic Universe." SEEJ n. s. 5:341-348. Winter 1961.
    THE PETTY DEMON
        Reeve, F. D. "Art as Solution: Sologub's Devil." MFS 3:
        110-118. Summer 1957.

        Reeve, F. D. The Russian Novel. New York: McGraw-Hill
        Book Company, 1966. pp. 302-324.

Solzhenitsyn, A.
    FOR THE GOOD OF THE CAUSE
        Zekulin, Gleb. "Solzhenitsyn's Four Stories." Soviet Stud-
        ies 16:56-60. July 1964.
    AN INCIDENT AT KRECHETOVKA STATION
        Zekulin, Gleb. "Solzhenitsyn's Four Stories." Soviet Stud-
        ies 16:53-56. July 1964.
    MATRYONA'S HOUSEHOLD
        Zekulin, Gleb. "Solzhenitsyn's Four Stories." Soviet Stud-
        ies 16:48-53. July 1964.
    ONE DAY IN THE LIFE OF IVAN DENISOVICH
        Monas, Sidney. "Ehrenburg's Life, Solzhenitsyn's Day."
        HudR 16:118-121. Spring 1963.

        "Moscow." NewS 64:729. November 23, 1962.

        Rubin, Burton. "The Shock of Recognition." Survey 47: 162-
        169. April 1963.

        Zekulin, Gleb. "Solzhenitsyn's Four Stories." Soviet Stud-
        ies 16:45-48. July 1964.

Storm, G.
    THE TALE OF BOLOTNIKOV
        Twarog, Leon I. "Ivan Bolotnikov in Soviet Historical Fic-
        tion." SEEJ n. s. 3:233-235. Fall 1959.

Szabo, Dezso
    THE LOST VILLAGE
        Remenyi, Joseph. "Dezso Szabo." SEER 24:108-109. Jan-
        uary 1946.

Remenyi, Joseph. Hungarian Writers and Literature. New
Brunswick: Rutgers University Press, 1964. pp. 345-346.

Tamasi, Aron
    ABEL
        Remenyi, Joseph. "Aron Tamasi, the Transylvanian Region-
        alist." ASEER 5:143-145. November 1946.

        Remenyi, Joseph. Hungarian Writers and Literature. New
        Brunswick: Rutgers University Press, 1964. pp. 432-433.
    MATTHIAS, THE ICE-BREAKER
        Nagy, Laszlo B. "The Last Magician: Aron Tamasi." NHQ
        7:73-74. Winter 1966.

        Remenyi, Joseph. Hungarian Writers and Literature. New
        Brunswick: Rutgers University Press, 1964. pp. 433-434.
    PRINCE OF THE VIRGIN MARY
        Remenyi, Joseph. "Aron Tamasi, the Transylvanian Region-
        alist." ASEER 5:145. November 1946.

        Remenyi, Joseph. Hungarian Writers and Literature. New
        Brunswick: Rutgers University Press, 1964. p. 433.
    A STAR IS SHINING
        Remenyi, Joseph. Hungarian Writers and Literature. New
        Brunswick: Rutgers University Press, 1964. p. 434.

Tammsaare, Anton H.
    TRUTH AND JUSTICE
        Judas, Elizabeth. Russian Influences on Estonian Literature:
        A Study of Jakob Tamm and Anton H. Tammsaare. Los
        Angeles: Wetzel Publishing Company, 1941. pp. 104-138.

Tarsis
    THE TALE OF THE BLUBOTTLE
        Struve, Gleb. "A Soviet Political Satire." New Republic
        149:19-22. September 28, 1963.

Tendriakov, Vladimir
    AN EXTRAORDINARY STORY
        Klimenko, Michael. "The Question of Religion in Modern
        Russian Literature." Religion in Life 35:608-616. Autumn
        1966.
    ON THE HEELS OF TIME
        Garrard, J. G. "Vladimir Tendrjakov." SEEJ n. s. 9:9-11.
        Spring 1965.
    THREE, SEVEN, ACE
        Garrard, J. G. "Vladimir Tendrjakov." SEEJ n. s. 9:12-16.
        Spring 1965.

        Meray, Tibor. "THREE, SEVEN, ACE." Survey 36:117-
        119. April - June 1961.

        Simmons, Ernest J. "Recent Trends in Soviet Literature."

ModA 7:399. Fall 1963.
THE TRIAL
    Garrard, J. G. "Vladimir Tendrjakov." SEEJ n. s. 9:11-12.
    Spring 1965.

Tersanszky, J.
    KAKUK MARCI
    Remenyi, Joseph. "J. Jeno Tersanszky: Writer of Picar-
    esque Stories. " SAQ 52:395-398. July 1953.

Tertz, A.
    THE TRIAL BEGINS
    Simmons, Ernest J. "Recent Trends in Soviet Literature. "
    ModA 7:397-398. Fall 1963.

Tolstoy, A.
    AELITA
    Yershov, Peter. Science Fiction and Utopian Fantasy in
    Soviet Literature. New York: Research Program on the USSR,
    Mimeographed Series No. 62, 1954. pp. 19-21.
    ENGINEER GARIN'S HYPERBOLOID
    Yershov, Peter. Science Fiction and Utopian Fantasy in
    Soviet Literature. New York: Research Program on the USSR,
    Mimeographed Series No. 62, 1954. pp. 22-23.
    PETER THE FIRST
    Kaun, Alexander. "Historical Sense in Soviet Fiction. "
    Slavonic Yearbook, SEER 19:56-58. 1939-1940.
    ROAD TO CALVARY
    Mathewson, Rufus W. , Jr. The Positive Hero in Russian
    Literature. New York: Columbia University Press, 1958.
    pp. 310-315.

Tolstoy, Leo
    ANNA KARENINA
    Baring, Maurice. Landmarks in Russian Literature. London:
    Methuen and Company, 1910. pp. 88-91.

    Baring, Maurice. An Outline of Russian Literature. New
    York: Holt and Company, 1915. pp. 205-206.

    Blackmur, R. P. "ANNA KARENINA: The Dialectic of In-
    carnation. " KR 12:433-456. Summer 1950.

    Clutton-Brock, A. More Essays on Books. London: Methuen
    Company, 1921. pp. 150-159.

    Cook, Albert. The Meaning of Fiction. Detroit: Wayne State
    University Press, 1960. pp. 195-201.

    Dole, Nathan Haskell. The Life of Count Lyof N. Tolstoi.
    New York: Crowell Company, 1911. pp. 240-247.

    Edel, Leon. The Modern Psychological Novel. New York:

Grosset and Dunlap, 1955. pp. 148-149.

Farrell, James T. Literature and Morality. New York: Vanguard Press, 1945. pp. 296-304.

Flint, Martha M. "The Epigraph of ANNA KARENINA."
PMLA 80: 461-462. September 1965.

Garnett, Edward. Tolstoy: His Life and Writings. London:
Constable and Company, 1914. pp. 47-53.

Geiger, Don. "Tolstoy as Defender of a 'Pure Art' That
Unwraps Something." JAAC 20:81-89. Fall 1961.

Gifford, Henry. "Anna, Lawrence and 'The Law.' " CritQ
1:203-206. Autumn 1959.

Gifford, Henry. "Further Notes on ANNA KARENINA."
CritQ 2:158-160. Summer 1960.

Gifford, Henry. The Novel in Russia: From Pushkin to
Pasternak. New York: Harper and Row, 1964. pp. 83-94.

Gorin, Bernard. "Feminine Types in Tolstoy's Works."
SR 16:444-450. October 1908.

Gorodetsky, Nadezhda. "Anna Karenina." SEER 24:121-126.
January 1946.

Greenwood, E. B. "The Unity of ANNA KARENINA." Landfall 15:124-134. June 1961.

Hare, Richard. Portraits of Russian Personalities Between
Reform and Revolution. London: Oxford University Press,
1959. pp. 199-208.

Hemmings, F. W. J. The Russian Novel in France 1884-
1914. London: Oxford University Press, 1950. pp. 44-51;
110-115; 177-179.

Hyman, Lawrence W. "Moral Values and the Literary Experience." JAAC 24:545-547. Summer 1966.

Jones, W. Gareth. "George Eliot's ADAM BEDE and Tolstoy's Conception of ANNA KARENINA." MLR 61:473-481.
July 1966.

Kenworthy, John C. Tolstoy: His Life and Works. London:
Walter Scott Publishing Company, 1902. pp. 185-188.

Lavrin, Janko. An Introduction to the Russian Novel. New
York: McGraw-Hill Book Company, Inc., 1947. pp. 130-
131.

Lavrin, Janko. Tolstoy: An Approach. New York: Macmillan
Company, 1946. pp. 30-34.

Mann, Thomas. Essays of Three Decades. New York: Alfred
A. Knopf, 1947. pp. 176-188.

Manning, Clarence Augustus. "Tolstoy and ANNA KARE-
NINA. " PMLA 42:505-521. June 1927.

Mathewson, Rufus W. , Jr. The Positive Hero in Russian
Literature. New York: Columbia University Press, 1958.
pp. 17-18.

Maude, Aylmer. The Life of Tolstoy: First Fifty Years.
New York: Dodd, Mead and Company, 1911. pp. 438-445.

Mayer, Frederick. "Tolstoy as World Citizen. " Person
28:362-364. Autumn 1947.

Muchnic, Helen. An Introduction to Russian Literature. New
York: Doubleday, 1947. pp. 203-206.

Nazarov, Alexander I. Tolstoy: The Inconstant Genius. New
York: Stokes and Company, 1924. pp. 191-198.

Noyes, George Rapall. Master Spirits of Literature: Tolstoy.
New York: Duffield and Company, 1918. pp. 189-204.

Olgin, Moissaye J. A Guide to Russian Literature (1820-
1917). New York: Harcourt, Brace and Howe, 1920. pp. 115-
116.

Phelps, William L. Essays on Russian Novelists. New York:
Macmillan Company, 1917. pp. 180-182; 198-206.

Portnoff, George. "The Influence of Tolstoy's ANA KARE-
NINA on Galdos' REALIDAD. " Hispania 15:208-214. May
1932.

Redpath, Theodore. Tolstoy. New York: Hillary House Publishers, Ltd. , 1960. pp. 65-74.

Reeve, F. D. The Russian Novel. New York: McGraw-Hill
Book Company, 1966. pp. 236-273.

Rolland, Romain. Tolstoy. New York: E. P. Dutton and
Company, 1911. pp. 117-130.

Simmons, Ernest J. Leo Tolstoy. Boston: Little, Brown
and Company, 1946. pp. 303-314.

Spector, Ivar. The Golden Age of Russian Literature.
Caldwell: The Caxton Printers, Ltd. , 1945. pp. 146-147;

168-169; 172-178.

Steiner, Edward A. Tolstoy: The Man and His Message. New York: Fleming H. Revell Company, 1908. pp. 187-197.

Steiner, George. Tolstoy or Dostoevsky. New York: Alfred Knopf, 1959. pp. 47-49; 54-71; 95-98; 102-105; 110-112; 282-283.

Stern, J. P. M. "EFFI BRIEST: MADAME BOVARY: ANNA KARENINA." MLR 52:363-375. July 1957.

Stewart, David H. "ANNA KARENINA: The Dialectic of Prophecy." PMLA 79:266-282. June 1964.

Trilling, Lionel. The Opposing Self: Nine Essays in Criticism. New York: Viking Press, 1955. pp. 66-75.

Williams, Raymond. "Tolstoy, Lawrence, and Tragedy." KR 25:637-644. Autumn 1963.

Yarmolinsky, Avrahm. Russian Literature. Chicago: American Library Association, 1931. pp. 35-38.
CHILDHOOD
Lavrin, Janko. An Introduction to the Russian Novel. New York: McGraw-Hill Book Company, Inc., 1947. pp. 124-126.

Muchnic, Helen. An Introduction to Russian Literature. New York: Doubleday, 1947. pp. 181-188.

Nazarov, Alexander I. Tolstoy: The Inconstant Genius. New York: Stokes Company, 1924. pp. 58-65.

Noyes, George Rapall. Master Spirits of Literature: Tolstoy. New York: Duffield and Company, 1918. pp. 24-37.

Phelps, William L. Essays on Russian Novelists. New York: Macmillan Company, 1917. pp. 173-174.

Redpath, Theodore. Tolstoy. New York: Hillary House Publishers, Ltd., 1960. pp. 47-50.

Rudy, Peter. "Leo Tolstoy's Enigmatic 'A History M. D.' " PQ 39:126-129. January 1960.

Simmons, Ernest J. "L. N. Tolstoi: A Cadet in the Caucasus." Slavonic Year Book, SEER 20:13-17. 1941.

Steiner, George. Tolstoy or Dostoevsky. New York: Alfred Knopf, 1959. pp. 71-73; 76-77; 84-85.

THE COSSACKS
Dole, Nathan Haskell. The Life of Count Lyof N. Tolstoi.
New York: Crowell Company, 1911. pp. 187-189.

Garnett, Edward. Tolstoy: His Life and Writings. London:
Constable and Company, 1914. pp. 30-32.

Maude, Aylmer. The Life of Tolstoy: First Fifty Years.
New York: Dodd, Mead and Company, 1911. pp. 78-80.

Nazarov, Alexander I. Tolstoy: The Inconstant Genius.
New York: Stokes Company, 1924. pp. 160-162.

Noyes, George Rapall. Master Spirits of Literature: Tolstoy. New York: Duffield and Company, 1918. pp. 49-53.

Redpath, Theodore. Tolstoy. New York: Hillary House
Publishers, Ltd., 1960. pp. 51-52.
THE DEATH OF IVAN ILYICH
Garnett, Edward. Tolstoy: His Life and Writings. London:
Constable and Company, 1914. pp. 72-74.

Halperin, Irving. "The Structural Integrity of THE DEATH
OF IVAN IL'IC. " SEEJ n. s. 5:334-339. Winter 1961.

Hemmings, F. W. J. The Russian Novel in France 1884-
1914. London: Oxford University Press, 1950. pp. 115-
116; 203-204.

Noyes, George Rapall. Master Spirits of Literature: Tolstoy. New York: Duffield and Company, 1918. pp. 307-
308.

Pachmuss, Temira. "The Theme of Love and Death in
Tolstoy's THE DEATH OF IVAN ILYICH. " ASEER 20:72-
83. February 1961.

Rahv, Philip. "THE DEATH OF IVAN ILYICH and Joseph
K. " SoR 5:174-185. Summer 1939.

Rahv, Philip. Image and Idea. Norfolk: Laughlin, 1949.
pp. 111-127.

Wasiolek, Edward. "Tolstoy's THE DEATH OF IVAN
ILYICH and Jamesian Fictional Imperatives. " MFS 6:314-
324. Winter 1960-1961.
FAMILY HAPPINESS
Pavlov, P. "Tolstoy's Novel FAMILY HAPPINESS. " SEER
7:492-510. January 1929.
KREUTZER SONATA
Dole, Nathan Haskell. The Life of Count Lyof N. Tolstoi.
New York: Crowell Company, 1911. pp. 329-331.

Ellis, Havelock. "The Supreme Russian." NewS 9:590-591. September 22, 1917.

Garnett, Edward. Tolstoy: His Life and Writings. London: Constable and Company, 1914. pp. 76-78.

Nazarov, Alexander I. Tolstoy: The Inconstant Genius. New York: Stokes Company, 1924. pp. 258-264.

Noyes, George Rapall. Master Spirits of Literature: Tolstoy. New York: Duffield and Company, 1918. pp. 311-317.

Redpath, Theodore. Tolstoy. New York: Hillary House Publishers, Ltd., 1960. pp. 76-79.
MASTER AND MAN
    Trahan, Elizabeth. "L. N. Tolstoj's MASTER AND MAN-- A Symbolic Narrative." SEEJ n. s. 7:258-267. Fall 1963.
RESURRECTION
    Garnett, Edward. Tolstoy: His Life and Writings. London: Constable and Company, 1914. pp. 89-92.

Gorin, Bernard. "Feminine Types in Tolstoy's Works." SR 16:445-447. October 1908.

Heier, Edmund. "A Note on the Pashkovites and L. N. Tolstoy." CSP 5:117-119. 1961.

Kenworthy, John C. Tolstoy: His Life and Works. London: Walter Scott Publishing Company, 1902. pp. 193-196.

Mayer, Frederick. "Tolstoy as World Citizen." Person 28:366-367. Autumn 1947.

Nazarov, Alexander I. Tolstoy: The Inconstant Genius. New York: Stokes Company, 1924. pp. 285-293.

Noyes, George Rapall. Master Spirits of Literature: Tolstoy. New York: Duffield and Company, 1918. pp. 319-323.

Olgin, Moissaye J. A Guide to Russian Literature (1820-1917). New York: Harcourt, Brace and Howe, 1920. pp. 118-119.

Pritchett, V. S. "Books in General." New S&N 36:96. July 31, 1948.

Redpath, Theodore. Tolstoy. New York: Hillary House Publishers, Ltd., 1960. pp. 79-83.

Rolland, Romain. Tolstoy. New York: E. P. Dutton and Company, 1911. pp. 237-248.

Simmons, Ernest J. Leo Tolstoy. Boston: Little, Brown

and Company, 1946. pp. 571-592.

Spector, Ivar. The Golden Age of Russian Literature.
Caldwell: The Caxton Printers, Ltd., 1945. pp. 170-172.

Steiner, George. Tolstoy or Dostoevsky. New York: Alfred
Knopf, 1959. pp. 92-93.
SEVASTOPOL IN DECEMBER
Muchnic, Helen. An Introduction to Russian Literature.
New York: Doubleday, 1947. pp. 189-190.
THREE ARSHINS OF LAND
West, Ray B., Jr. and Robert Wooster Stallman. The Art
of Modern Fiction. New York: Holt, Rinehart and Winston,
1960. pp. 131-133.
WAR AND PEACE
Baring, Maurice. Landmarks in Russian Literature. London:
Methuen and Company, 1910. pp. 87-88.

Baring, Maurice. An Outline of Russian Literature. New
York: Holt and Company, 1915. pp. 202-205.

Berlin, Isaiah. The Hedgehog and the Fox: An Essay on
Tolstoy's View of History. New York: Simon and Schuster,
1953. 86 pp.

Clifford, Emma. "WAR AND PEACE and THE DYNASTS."
MP 54:33-44. August 1956.

Clutton-Brock, A. More Essays on Books. London: Methuen
Company, 1921. pp. 150-159.

Cook, Albert. The Meaning of Fiction. Detroit: Wayne State
University Press, 1960. pp. 180-195.

Cook, Albert. "The Unity of WAR AND PEACE." Western
Rev 22:243-255. Summer 1958.

Dole, Nathan Haskell. The Life of Count Lyof N. Tolstoi.
New York: Crowell Company, 1911. pp. 215-222; 244-247.

Edel, Leon. The Modern Psychological Novel. New York:
Grosset and Dunlap, 1955. pp. 149-151.

Farrell, James T. Literature and Morality. New York: Vanguard Press, 1945. pp. 185-295.

Feuer, Kathryn. "The Book That Became WAR AND
PEACE." Reporter 20:33-36. May 14, 1959.

Garnett, Edward. Tolstoy: His Life and Writings. London:
Constable and Company, 1914. pp. 36-44.

Golding, William. "Tolstoy's Mountain." Spec 207:325-326.

September 8, 1961.

Gorin, Bernard. "Feminine Types in Tolstoy's Works."
SR 16:443-451. October 1908.

Hagan, John. "On the Craftsmanship of WAR AND PEACE."
EIC 13:17-49. January 1963.

Hare, Richard. Portraits of Russian Personalities Between
Reform and Revolution. London: Oxford University Press,
1959. pp. 183-195.

Hare, Richard. "Tolstoy's Motives for Writing WAR AND
PEACE." RusR 15:110-121. April 1956.

Hemmings, F. W. J. The Russian Novel in France 1884-
1914. London: Oxford University Press, 1950. pp. 12-13;
19-25; 43-44; 49-53; 177-180.

Lavrin, Janko. An Introduction to the Russian Novel. New
York: McGraw-Hill Book Company, Inc., 1947. pp. 127-
129.

Lavrin, Janko. Tolstoy: An Approach. New York: Macmillan Company, 1946. pp. 26-30.

Leon, Philip. "Who Makes History? A Study of Tolstoy's
Answer in WAR AND PEACE." HJ 42:254-258. April 1944.

Lytle, Andrew Nelson. "The Image as Guide to Meaning
in the Historical Novel." SR 61:414-426. Summer 1953.

Mathewson, Rufus W., Jr. The Positive Hero in Russian
Literature. New York: Columbia University Press, 1958.
pp. 17-18; 130-131.

Mathewson, Rufus W., Jr. "The Soviet Hero and the Literary
Heritage." ASEER 12:510. December 1953.

Maugham, W. Somerset. Great Novelists and Their Novels.
Philadelphia: Winston Company, 1948. pp. 17-39.

Muchnic, Helen. An Introduction to Russian Literature.
New York: Doubleday, 1947. pp. 190-203.

Muchnic, Helen. "Sholokhov and Tolstoy." RusR 16:25-34.
April 1957.

Noyes, George Rapall. Master Spirits of Literature: Tolstoy.
New York: Duffield and Company, 1918. pp. 158-189.

O'Connor, Frank. The Mirror in the Roadway: A Study of
the Modern Novel. New York: Alfred A. Knopf, 1956. pp.

153-164.

Olgin, Moissaye J. A Guide to Russian Literature (1820-
1917). New York: Harcourt, Brace and Howe, 1920. pp.
116-118.

Phelps, William L. Essays on Russian Novelists. New
York: Macmillan Company, 1917. pp. 178-179.

Redpath, Theodore. Tolstoy. New York: Hillary House
Publishers, Ltd., 1960. pp. 56-65.

Simmons, Ernest J. Leo Tolstoy. Boston: Little, Brown
and Company, 1946. pp. 270-302.

Simmons, Ernest J. "The Writing of WAR AND PEACE."
Slavic Studies. (ed.) Alexander Kaun and Ernest J. Simmons. Ithaca: Cornell University Press, 1943. pp. 180-
197.

Spector, Ivar. The Golden Age of Russian Literature.
Caldwell: The Caxton Printers, Ltd., 1945. pp. 166-170;
257-260.

Spence, G. W. "Tolstoy's Dualism." RusR 20:217-231. July
1961.

States, Bert O. "The Hero and the World: Our Sense of
Space in WAR AND PEACE." MFS 11:153-164. Summer
1965.

Steiner, Edward A. Tolstoy: The Man and His Message.
New York: Fleming H. Revell Company, 1908. pp. 172-186.

Steiner, George. Tolstoy or Dostoevsky. New York: Alfred
Knopf, 1959. pp. 85-87; 98-101; 105-115; 117-119; 268-275;
278-281.

Stonier, G. W. "Books in General." New S&N 23:27. January 10, 1942.

Thale, Jerome. "WAR AND PEACE: The Art of Incoherence."
EIC 16:398-414. October 1966.

Yarmolinsky, Avrahm. Russian Literature. Chicago: American Library Association, 1931. pp. 31-35.

Trifonov, I.
      STUDENTY
      Dunham, Vera S. "The Villain in Soviet Literature."
      AATSEEL 9:49-50. March 15, 1952.

Tuglas, Friedebert
    FELIX ORMUSSON
        Kallas, Aino. "An Estonian Novelist: Friedebert Tuglas."
        SEER 6:31-37. June 1927.

Turgenev, Ivan
    THE DIARY OF A SUPERFLUOUS MAN
        Howe, Irving. Politics and the Novel. New York: Meridan
        Books, 1957. pp. 123-124.
    FATHERS AND SONS
        Baring, Maurice. Landmarks in Russian Literature. London:
        Methuen and Company, 1910. pp. 105-106.

        Folejewski, Zbigniew. "The Recent Storm Around Turgenev
        as a Point in Soviet Aesthetics." SEEJ n. s. 6:21-26. Spring
        1962.

        Garnett, Edward. Turgenev. Port Washington: Kennikat
        Press, 1924. pp. 109-125.

        Gifford, Henry. The Novel in Russia: From Pushkin to
        Pasternak. New York: Harper and Row, 1964. pp. 63-72.

        Hershkowitz, Harry. Democratic Ideas in Turgenev's Works.
        New York: Columbia University Press, 1932. pp. 64-82.

        Hindus, Milton. "The Duels in Mann and Turgenev." CL 11:
        308-312. Fall 1959.

        Howe, Irving. Politics and the Novel. New York: Meridan
        Books, 1957. pp. 129-133.

        Howe, Irving. "Turgenev: the Virtues of Hesitation." HudR
        8:545-547. Winter 1956.

        Justus, James H. "FATHERS AND SONS: The Novel as
        Idyll." WHR 15:259-265. Summer 1961.

        Kochan, Lionel. "Russian History in Turgenev's Novels."
        History Today 14:30-32. January 1964.

        Lavrin, Janko. An Introduction to the Russian Novel. New
        York: McGraw Hill, 1947. pp. 65-67.

        Lavrin, Janko. Russian Writers: Their Lives and Literature.
        New York: D. Van Nostrand Company, Inc., 1954. pp. 124-
        126.

        Magarshack, David. Turgenev: A Life. London: Faber and
        Faber, 1954. pp. 215-220.

        Mandel, Oscar. "Moliere and Turgenev: The Literature of
        No-Judgment." CL 11:233-249. Summer 1959.

Manning, Clarence A. "Ivan Sergyeyevich Turgenev."
SAQ 30:375-377. October 1931.

Mathewson, Rufus W., Jr. The Positive Hero in Russian
Literature. New York: Columbia University Press, 1958.
pp. 115-116.

Moseley, Edwin M. Pseudonyms of Christ in the Modern
Novel. Pittsburgh: University of Pittsburgh Press, 1962.
pp. 49-66.

Moser, Charles A. Antinihilism in the Russian Novel of
the 1860's. The Hague: Mouton and Company, 1964. pp.
81-84.

Olgin, Moissaye J. A Guide to Russian Literature (1820-
1917). New York: Harcourt, Brace and Howe, 1920. pp.
79-80.

Phelps, William L. Essays on Russian Novelists. New York:
Macmillan Company, 1917. pp. 90-109.

Reeve, F. D. The Russian Novel. New York: McGraw-Hill
Book Company, 1966. pp. 119-158.

Spector, Ivar. The Golden Age of Russian Literature. Caldwell: The Caxton Printers, Ltd., 1945. pp. 89-91; 96-98;
103-105.

Turgenev, Ivan. "Apropos of FATHERS AND SONS." PR
25:265-273. Spring 1958.

Willcocks, M. P. "Turgenev." ER 33:180-185. September
1921.

Yarmolinsky, Avrahm. Russian Literature. Chicago: American Library Association, 1931. pp. 28-31.

Yarmolinsky, Avrahm. Turgenev: The Man--His Art--His
Age. New York: Century Company, 1926. pp. 190-198; 239-
240; 243-244.
FIRST LOVE
Morgan, Charles. "Turgenev's Treatment of a Love-Story."
EDH 25:107-119. 1950.
A HOUSE OF GENTLEFOLK
Garnett, Edward. Turgenev. Port Washington: Kennikat
Press, 1924. pp. 73-90.

Gettmann, Royal A. Turgenev in England and America. Ur-
bana: University of Illinois Press, 1941. pp. 33-35.

Hershkowitz, Harry. Democratic Ideas in Turgenev's Works.
New York: Columbia University Press, 1932. pp. 48-55.

Howe, Irving. Politics and the Novel. New York: Meridan Books, 1957. pp. 121-123; 125-127.

Howe, Irving. "Turgenev: the Virtues of Hesitation." HudR 8:541-542. Winter 1956.

Kochan, Lionel. "Russian History in Turgenev's Novels." History Today 14:28-29. January 1964.

Lavrin, Janko. An Introduction to the Russian Novel. New York: McGraw-Hill, 1947. pp. 64-65.

Lavrin, Janko. Russian Writers: Their Lives and Literature. New York: D. Van Nostrand Company, Inc., 1954. pp. 123-124.

Lednicki, Waclaw. Bits of Table Talk on Pushkin, Mickiewicz, Goethe, Turgenev, and Sienkiewicz. The Hague: Martinus Nijhoff, 1956. pp. 60-86.

Magarshack, David. Turgenev: A Life. London: Faber and Faber, 1954. pp. 190-192.

Manning, Clarence A. "Ivan Sergyeyevich Turgenev." SAQ 30:374. October 1931.

Phelps, William L. Essays on Russian Novelists. New York: Macmillan Company, 1917. pp. 82-86.

Pritchett, V. S. The Living Novel and Later Appreciations. New York: Random House, 1964. pp. 385-386.

Spector, Ivar. The Golden Age of Russian Literature. Caldwell: The Caxton Printers, Ltd., 1945. pp. 87-88.

Willcocks, M. P. "Turgenev." ER 33:186-187. September 1921.

Woodcock, George. "The Elusive Ideal: Notes on Turgenev." SR 69:38-39. Winter 1961.

Yarmolinsky, Avrahm. Turgenev: The Man--His Art--His Age. New York: Century Company, 1926. pp. 155-157.

ON THE EVE

Baring, Maurice. Landmarks in Russian Literature. London: Methuen and Company, 1910. pp. 107-108.

Garnett, Edward. Turgenev. Port Washington: Kennikat Press, 1924. pp. 91-105.

Hare, Richard. Portraits of Russian Personalities Between Reform and Revolution. London: Oxford University Press, 1959. pp. 78-82.

Hershkowitz, Harry. Democratic Ideas in Turgenev's Works. New York: Columbia University Press, 1932. pp. 55-63.

Howe, Irving. "Turgenev: the Virtues of Hesitation. " HudR 8:538-539. Winter 1956.

Kochan, Lionel. "Russian History in Turgenev's Novels. " History Today 14:29-30. January 1964.

Lavrin, Janko. Russian Writers: Their Lives and Literature. New York: D. Van Nostrand Company, Inc. , 1954. p. 124.

Magarshack, David. Turgenev: A Life. London: Faber and Faber, 1954. pp. 196-200.

Manning, Clarence A. "Ivan Sergyeyevich Turgenev. " SAQ 30:375. October 1931.

Mathewson, Rufus W. , Jr. The Positive Hero in Russian Literature. New York: Columbia University Press, 1958. pp. 69-73.

Phelps, William L. Essays on Russian Novelists. New York: Macmillan Company, 1917. pp. 86-89.

Spector, Ivar. The Golden Age of Russian Literature. Caldwell: The Caxton Printers, Ltd. , 1945. pp. 102-103.

Tucker, H. St. George. "A Russian Novelist's Estimate of the Russian Intellectual. " SR 24:67-68. January 1916.

Willcocks, M. P. "Turgenev. " ER 33:186-187. September 1921.

Yarmolinsky, Avrahm. Turgenev: The Man--His Art--His Age. New York: Century Company, 1926. pp. 42-43; 133-134; 161-168; 182-183.
RUDIN
Garnett, Edward. Turgenev. Port Washington: Kennikat Press, 1924. pp. 55-72.

Hershkowitz, Harry. Democratic Ideas in Turgenev's Works. New York: Columbia University Press, 1932. pp. 43-50.

Howe, Irving. Politics and the Novel. New York: Meridan Books, 1957. pp. 128-129.

Howe, Irving. "Turgenev: the Virtues of Hesitation. " HudR 8:543-545. Winter 1956.

Kochan, Lionel. "Russian History in Turgenev's Novels. " History Today 14:27-28. January 1964.

Lavrin, Janko. An Introduction to the Russian Novel. New York: McGraw-Hill, 1947. pp. 63-64.

Lavrin, Janko. Russian Writers: Their Lives and Literature. New York: D. Van Nostrand Company, Inc., 1954. pp. 122-123.

Manning, Clarence A. "Ivan Sergyeyevich Turgenev." SAQ 30:373-374. October 1931.

Manning, Clarence A. "The Neglect of Time in the Russian Novel." Slavic Studies. (ed.) Alexander Kaun and Ernest J. Simmons. Ithaca: Cornell University Press, 1943. pp. 103-108.

Phelps, William L. Essays on Russian Novelists. New York: Macmillan Company, 1917. pp. 75-82.

Pritchett, V. S. "A Hero of Our Time?" LMerc 36:359-364. August 1937.

Spector, Ivar. The Golden Age of Russian Literature. Caldwell: The Caxton Printers, Ltd., 1945. pp. 101-102.

Tucker, H. St. George. "A Russian Novelist's Estimate of the Russian Intellectual." SR 24:65-68. January 1916.

Woodcock, George. "The Elusive Ideal: Notes on Turgenev." SR 69:37-38. Winter 1961.

SMOKE
Chamberlin, William Henry. "Turgenev, the Eternal Romantic." RusR 5:13-14. Spring 1946.

Finch, Chauncey E. "Turgenev as a Student of the Classics." CJ 49:120-121. December 1953.

Garnett, Edward. Turgenev. Port Washington: Kennikat Press, 1924. pp. 129-136.

Hare, Richard. Portraits of Russian Personalities Between Reform and Revolution. London: Oxford University Press, 1959. pp. 86-89.

Hershkowitz, Harry. Democratic Ideas in Turgenev's Works. New York: Columbia University Press, 1932. pp. 84-91.

Kochan, Lionel. "Russian History in Turgenev's Novels." History Today 14:32. January 1964.

Lavrin, Janko. An Introduction to the Russian Novel. New York: McGraw Hill, 1947. pp. 67-68.

Lavrin, Janko. Russian Writers: Their Lives and Literature.

New York: D. Van Nostrand Company, Inc., 1954. pp. 127-128.

Magarshack, David. Turgenev: A Life. London: Faber and Faber, 1954. pp. 241-244; 248-250.

Manning, Clarence A. "Ivan Sergyeyevich Turgenev. " SAQ 30:377-378. October 1931.

Phelps, William L. Essays on Russian Novelists. New York: Macmillan Company, 1917. pp. 110-114.

Woodcock, George. "The Elusive Ideal: Notes on Turgenev." SR 69:39-41. Winter 1961.

Yarmolinsky, Avrahm. Turgenev: The Man--His Art--His Age. New York: Century Company, 1926. pp. 244-246; 265-267.

SPORTSMAN'S NOTEBOOK
Delaney, Sister Consolata. "Turgenev's Sportsman: Experiment in Unity. " SEEJ n. s. 8:17-24. Spring 1964.

Lainoff, Seymour. "The Country Doctors of Kafka and Turgenev. " Symposium 16:130-135. Summer 1962.

Manning, Clarence A. "Ivan Sergyeyevich Turgenev. " SAQ 30:368-371. October 1931.

Mortimer, Raymond. "Books in General. " New S&N 26:27. July 10, 1943.

Willcocks, M. P. "Turgenev. " ER 33:188-189. September 1921.

SPRING TORRENTS
Matlaw, Ralph. "Turgenev's Art in SPRING TORRENTS. " SEER 35:157-171. December 1956.

Phelps, William L. Essays on Russian Novelists. New York: Macmillan Company, 1917. pp. 114-118.

Woodcock, George. "The Elusive Ideal: Notes on Turgenev." SR 69:34-44. Winter 1961.

Yarmolinsky, Avrahm. Turgenev: The Man--His Art--His Age. New York: Century Company, 1926. pp. 294-296.

VIRGIN SOIL
Baring, Maurice. Landmarks in Russian Literature. London: Methuen and Company, 1910. pp. 106-107.

Cargill, Oscar. "The PRINCESS CASAMASSIMA: A Critical Reappraisal. " PMLA 71:97-117. March 1956.

Chamberlin, William Henry. "Turgenev: The Eternal Romantic. " RusR 5:15-16. Spring 1946.

Garnett, Edward. Turgenev. Port Washington: Kennikat
Press, 1924. pp. 139-160.

Gettmann, Royal A. Turgenev in England and America. Ur-
bana: University of Illinois Press, 1941. pp. 85-87; 100-103.

Hamilton, Eunice C. "Henry James's THE PRINCESS
CASAMASSIMA and Ivan Turgenev's VIRGIN SOIL. " SAQ 61:
354-364. Summer 1962.

Hershkowitz, Harry. Democratic Ideas in Turgenev's Works.
New York: Columbia University Press, 1932. pp. 91-104.

Howe, Irving. Politics and the Novel. New York: Meridan
Books, 1957. pp. 133-137.

Howe, Irving. "Turgenev: the Virtues of Hesitation. " HudR
8:547-550. Winter 1956.

Kochan, Lionel. "Russian History in Turgenev's Novels. "
History Today 14:32-33. January 1964.

Lavrin, Janko. An Introduction to the Russian Novel. New
York: McGraw-Hill, 1947. pp. 67-68.

Lavrin, Janko. Russian Writers: Their Lives and Literature.
New York: D. Van Nostrand Company, Inc. , 1954. pp. 128-
129.

Magarshack, David. Turgenev: A Life. London: Faber and
Faber, 1954. pp. 278-282.

Manning, Clarence A. "Ivan Sergyeyevich Turgenev. " SAQ
30:378-379. October 1931.

Olgin, Moissaye J. A Guide to Russian Literature (1820-
1917). New York: Harcourt, Brace and Howe, 1920. pp. 80-
81.

Phelps, William L. Essays on Russian Novelists. New York:
Macmillan Company, 1917. pp. 118-122.

Spector, Ivar. The Golden Age of Russian Literature. Caldwell: The Caxton Printers, Ltd. , 1945. pp. 106-107.

Yarmolinsky, Avrahm. Turgenev: The Man--His Art--His
Age. New York: Century Company, 1926. pp. 336-340.

Tynyanov, Yuri
      DEATH OF THE VAZIR-MUKHTAR
      Mirsky, D. S. "Centenary of the Death of Griboyedov. "

SEER 8:141-143. June 1929.

Vazoff, Ivan
  UNDER THE YOKE
    Tsanoff, Radoslav A. "Ivan Vazoff: Balkan Poet and Novel-
    ist. " Poet Lore 19:104-106. Spring 1908.

Veresaev, V.
  IN A BLIND ALLEY
    Eng-Liedmeier, A. M. Van der. Soviet Literary Characters.
    'S Gravenhage: Mouton and Company, 1959. pp. 55-57.
  THE SISTERS
    Eng-Liedmeier, A. M. Van der. Soviet Literary Characters.
    'S Gravenhage: Mouton and Company, 1959. pp. 94-95; 102-
    103.

    Simmons, Ernest J. Through the Glass of Soviet Literature.
    New York: Columbia University Press, 1953. pp. 58-62.

Voinova, A. I.
  SEMI-PRECIOUS STONES
    Kain, Richard M. "The Plight of the Intelligentsia in the
    Soviet Novel. " RusR 2:74-75. Autumn 1942.

    Simmons, Ernest J. Through the Glass of Soviet Literature.
    New York: Columbia University Press, 1953. pp. 65-66.

Vynnychenko, V. K.
  THE SUN MACHINE
    Yershov, Peter. Science Fiction and Utopian Fantasy in
    Soviet Literature. New York: Research Program on the USSR,
    Mimeographed Series No. 62, 1954. pp. 30-31.

Weil, Jiri
  LIFE WITH THE STAR
    Souckova, Milada. A Literature in Crisis: Czech Literature
    1938-1950. New York: Mid-European Studies Center, 1954.
    pp. 110-112.

Yakubovitch, P.
  IN THE WORLD OF CASTAWAYS
    Olgin, Moissaye J. A Guide to Russian Literature (1820-
    1917). New York: Harcourt, Brace and Howe, 1920. pp. 134-
    135.

Yanovsky, Yury
  LIVING WATER
    Romanenchuk, Bohdan. "Ten Years of Soviet Literature in
    Ukraine. " UQ 6:249-250. Summer 1950.

Yushkevitch, S.
  THE JEWS
    Olgin, Moissaye J. A Guide to Russian Literature (1820-

1917). New York: Harcourt, Brace and Howe, 1920. pp.
295-296.

Zaika, Nikolai
    MY LOVE
        Anninsky, Lev. "Men and Morals. " SovR 3:33-35. May 1962.

Zamyatin, E. I.
    WE
        Alexandrova, Vera. " 'In every herd there is some restive
        steer': An Enduring Theme. " Survey 24:74-75. April - June
        1958.

        Collins, Christopher. "Zamyatin, Wells and the Utopian
        Literary Tradition. " SEER 44:351-360. July 1966.

        Collins, Christopher. "Zamjatin's WE as Myth. " SEEJ 10:
        125-132. Summer 1966.

        Proffer, Carl R. "Notes on the Imagery in Zamjatin's WE. "
        SEEJ n. s. 7:269-278. Fall 1963.

        White, John J. "Mathematical Imagery In Musil's YOUNG
        TORLESS And Zamyatin's WE. " CL 18:71-78. Winter 1966.

        Woodcock, George. "Utopias in Negative. " SR 64:81-97.
        Winter 1956.

        Yershov, Peter. Science Fiction and Utopian Fantasy in
        Soviet Literature. New York: Research Program on the USSR,
        Mimeographed Series No. 62, 1954. pp. 33-35.

Zaytsev, Boris
    ANNA
        Struve, Gleb. "Boris Zaytsev. " SEER 17:447-449. January
        1939.
    GLEB'S JOURNEY
        Struve, Gleb. "Boris Zaytsev. " SEER 17:449-451. January
        1939.

Zeromski, Stefan
    ASHES
        Borowy, Waclaw. "Zeromski. " SEER 14:407-408. January
        1936.
    THE FAITHFUL RIVER
        Borowy, Waclaw. "Zeromski. " SEER 14:409. January 1936.
    THE HOMELESS
        Borowy, Waclaw. "Zeromski. " SEER 14:405-406. January
        1936.
    LABOURS OF SISYPHUS
        Borowy, Waclaw. "Zeromski. " SEER 14:406-407. January
        1936.

A STORY OF A SIN
  Borowy, Waclaw. "Zeromski." SEER 14:410-411. January
  1936.

Zilahy, L.
  THE ANGRY ANGEL
    Remenyi, Joseph. Hungarian Writers and Literature. New
    Brunswick: Rutgers University Press, 1964. pp. 422-423.
  THE DESERTER
    Remenyi, Joseph. Hungarian Writers and Literature. New
    Brunswick: Rutgers University Press, 1964. p. 418.
  THE DUKAYS
    Remenyi, Joseph. Hungarian Writers and Literature. New
    Brunswick: Rutgers University Press, 1964. pp. 418-422.
  TWO PRISONERS
    Remenyi, Joseph. Hungarian Writers and Literature. New
    Brunswick: Rutgers University Press, 1964. pp. 417-418.

Zoshchenko, Mikhail
  BEFORE SUNRISE
    McLean, Hugh. "Zoshchenko's Unfinished Novel: BEFORE
    SUNRISE." Survey 36:99-105. April - June 1961.
  YOUTH RESTORED
    Simmons, Ernest J. Through the Glass of Soviet Literature.
    New York: Columbia University Press, 1953. pp. 218-223.